the unbeatable Squirrel Girl

& the

GREAT LAKES AVENGERS

THE UNBEATABLE SQUIRREL GIRL & THE GREAT LAKES AVENGERS. Contains material originally published in magazine form as GLA #1-4, GLX-MAS SPECIAL, THING #8, CABLE & DEADPOOL #30, DEADPOOL/GLI SUMMER FUN SPECTACULAR, MARVEL SUPER-HEROES #8, I HEART MARVEL: MASKED INTENTIONS, AGE OF HEROES #3 and I AM AN AVENGER #1. First printing 2016. ISBN# 978-1-302-90066-3. Published by MARVEL WORLDWIDE, INC., a subsidiary of MARVEL ENTERTAINMENT, LLC. OFFICE OF PUBLICATION: 135 West 50th Street, New York, NY 10020. Copyright © 2016 MARVEL No similarity between any of the names, characters, persons, and/or institutions in this magazine with those of any living or dead person or institution is intended, and any such similarity which may exist is purely coincidental. **Printed in the U.S.A.** ALAN FINE, President, Marvel Entertainment; DAN BUCKLEY, President, TV, Publishing & Brand Management; JOE QUESADA, Chief Creative Officer; TOM BREVOORT, SVP of Publishing; DAVID BOGART, SVP of Business Affairs & Operations, Publishing & Partnership; C.B. CEBULSKI, VP of Brand Management & Development, Asia; DAVID GABRIEL, SVP of Sales & Marketing, Publishing; JEFF YOUNGQUIST, VP of Production & Special Projects; DAN CARR, Executive Director of Publishing Technology; ALEX MORALES, Director of Publishing Operations; SUSAN CRESPI, Production Manager; STAN LEE, Chairman Emeritus. For information regarding advertising in Marvel Comics or on Marvel.com, please contact Vit DeBellis, Integrated Sales Manager, at vdebellis@marvel.com. For Marvel subscription inquiries, please call 888-511-5480. Manufactured between 5/27/2016 and 7/4/2016 by R.R. DONNELLEY, INC., SALEM, VA, USA.

10 9 8 7 6 5 4 3 2 1

MARVEL SUPER-HEROES #8

writers Steve Ditko & Will Murray
artist Steve Ditko
colorist Christie Scheele
cover art Erik Larsen

GLX-MAS SPECIAL

writer Dan Slott
artists Matt Haley, Georges Jeanty &
Drew Geraci, Ty Templeton,
Paul Grist, Mike Kazaleh and
Mike Wieringo & Karl Kesel
colorists Matt Haley, Sotocolor's Larry Molinar,
Wil Quintana, Laura Allred & Bill Crabtree
cover art Paul Pelletier, Rick Magyar & Wil Quintana

THING #8

writer Dan Slott
artist Kieron Dwyer
colorist Laura Villari
cover art Andrea Di Vito & Laura Villari

DEADPOOL/GLI SUMMER FUN SPECTACULAR

writers Fabian Nicieza & Dan Slott
artists Kieron Dwyer, Nelson, Paul Pelletier
& Dave Meikis, and Clio Chiang
colorists Pete Pantazis, Giulia Brusco,
Wil Quintana & Clio Chiang
cover art Paul Pelletier, Dave Meikis & Wil Quintana
Special Thanks to Tom Brevoort

AGE OF HEROES #3

writer Dan Slott
artist Ty Templeton
colorist Jorge Maese
cover art Yanick Paquette, Michel Lacombe &
Nathan Fairbairn

GLA #1-4

writer Dan Slott
penciler Paul Pelletier
inker Rick Magyar
colorist Wil Quintana
cover art Paul Pelletier, Rick Magyar & Wil Quintana

I ♥ MARVEL: MASKED INTENTIONS

writer Fabian Nicieza
penciler Paco Medina
inker Juan Vlasco
colorist Sotocolor's Adam Street
cover art Gez Fry

CABLE & DEADPOOL #30

writer Fabian Nicieza
penciler Staz Johnson
inker Klaus Janson
colorist Gotham
cover art Amanda Conner & Paul Mounts
Special Thanks to Cliff Benston

CABLE & DEADPOOL #30

writer Fabian Nicieza
penciler Staz Johnson
inker Klaus Janson
colorist Gotham
cover art Amanda Conner & Paul Mounts
Special Thanks to Cliff Benston

I AM AN AVENGER #1

writer Alex Zalben
artist Tom Fowler
colorist Matt Wilson
cover art Leinil Francis Yu, Gerry Alanguilan &
Dave McCaig

---

letterers Brad K. Joyce, Dave Lanphear & Dave Sharpe
assistant editors Andy Schmidt, Stephanie Moore,
Molly Lazer & Aubrey Sitterson
editors Mike Rockwitz, Tom Brevoort, Nicole Boose &
Lauren Sankovitch with Aubrey Sitterson
executive editor Tom Brevoort (Age Of Heroes, I Am An Avenger)

front cover artists Gurihiru
back cover artists Paul Pelletier, Dave Meikis & Wil Quintana

collection editor Mark D. Beazley
associate editor Sarah Brunstad
associate manager, digital assets Joe Hochstein
associate managing editor Alex Starbuck
editor, special projects Jennifer Grünwald
vp, production & special projects Jeff Youngquist
research & layout Jeph York
book designer Adam Del Re
svp print, sales & marketing David Gabriel

editor in chief Axel Alonso
chief creative officer Joe Quesada
publisher Dan Buckley
executive producer Alan Fine

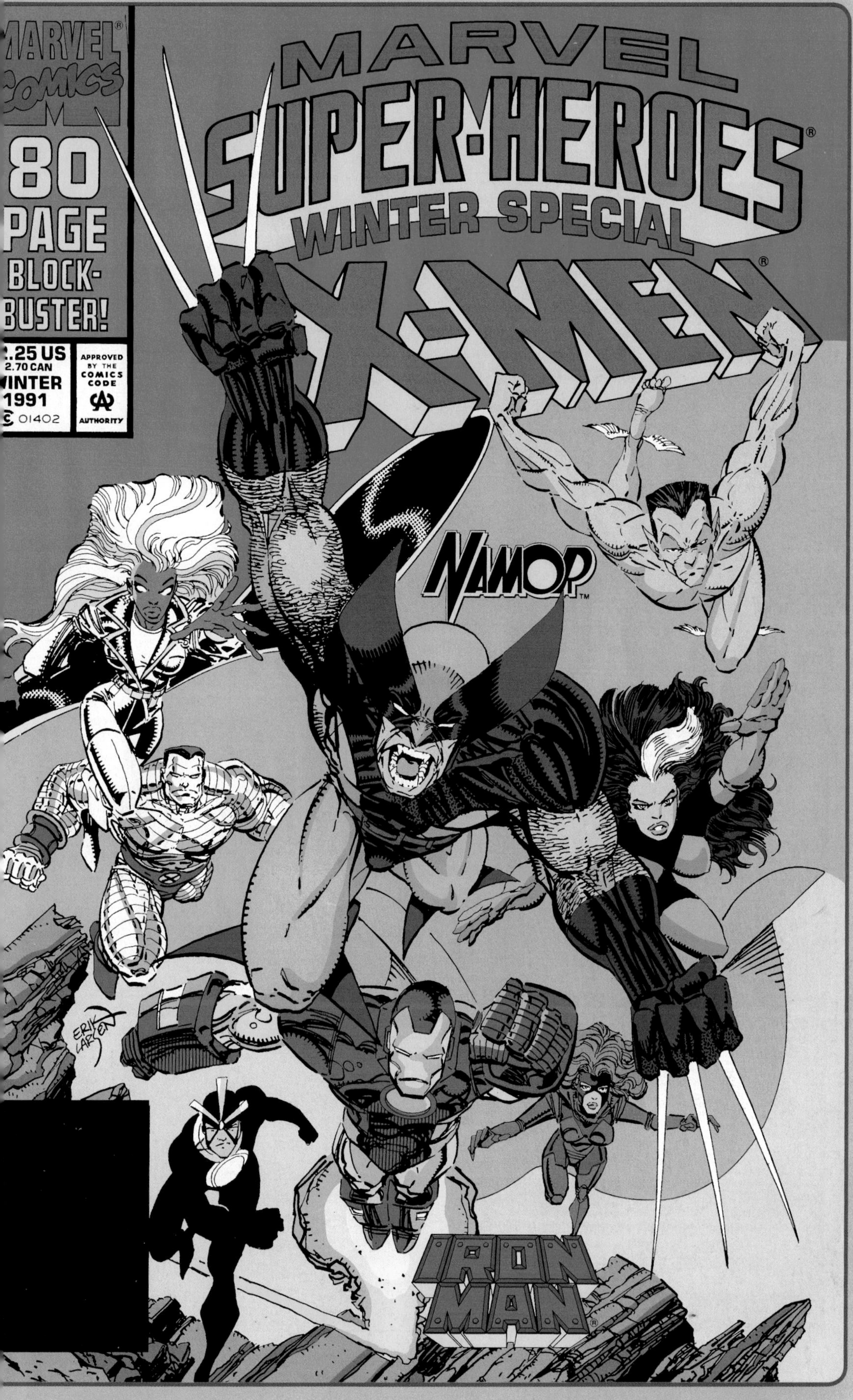

MARVEL COMICS
80 PAGE BLOCK-BUSTER!
.25 US
2.70 CAN
WINTER
1991
01402
APPROVED BY THE COMICS CODE AUTHORITY
MARVEL
SUPER-HEROES
WINTER SPECIAL
X-MEN
NAMOR
ERIK LARSEN
IRON MAN

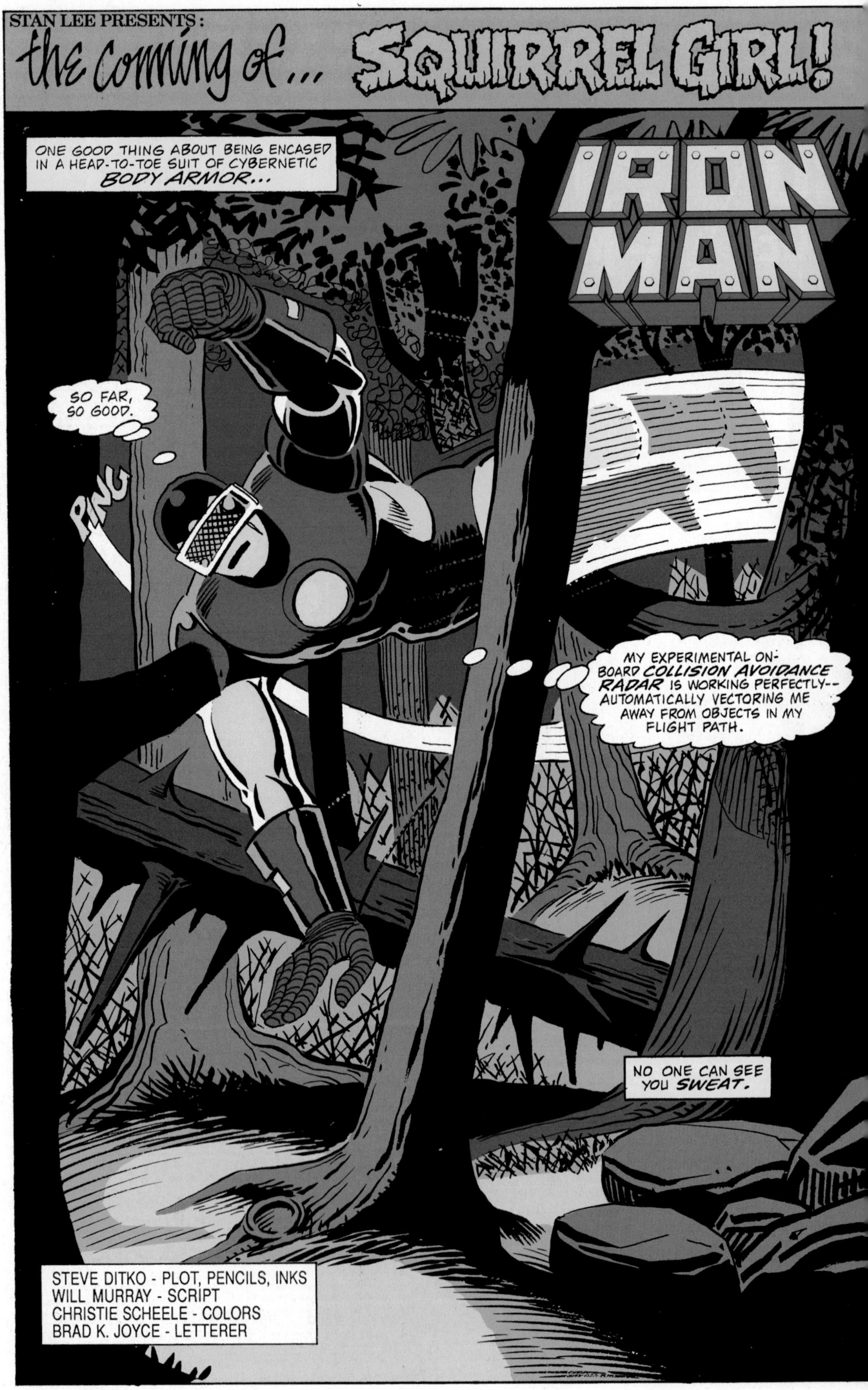
STAN LEE PRESENTS:
the coming of... SQUIRREL GIRL!
ONE GOOD THING ABOUT BEING ENCASED IN A HEAD-TO-TOE SUIT OF CYBERNETIC BODY ARMOR...
IRON MAN
SO FAR, SO GOOD.
PING
MY EXPERIMENTAL ON-BOARD COLLISION AVOIDANCE RADAR IS WORKING PERFECTLY--AUTOMATICALLY VECTORING ME AWAY FROM OBJECTS IN MY FLIGHT PATH.
NO ONE CAN SEE YOU SWEAT.
STEVE DITKO - PLOT, PENCILS, INKS
WILL MURRAY - SCRIPT
CHRISTIE SCHEELE - COLORS
BRAD K. JOYCE - LETTERER

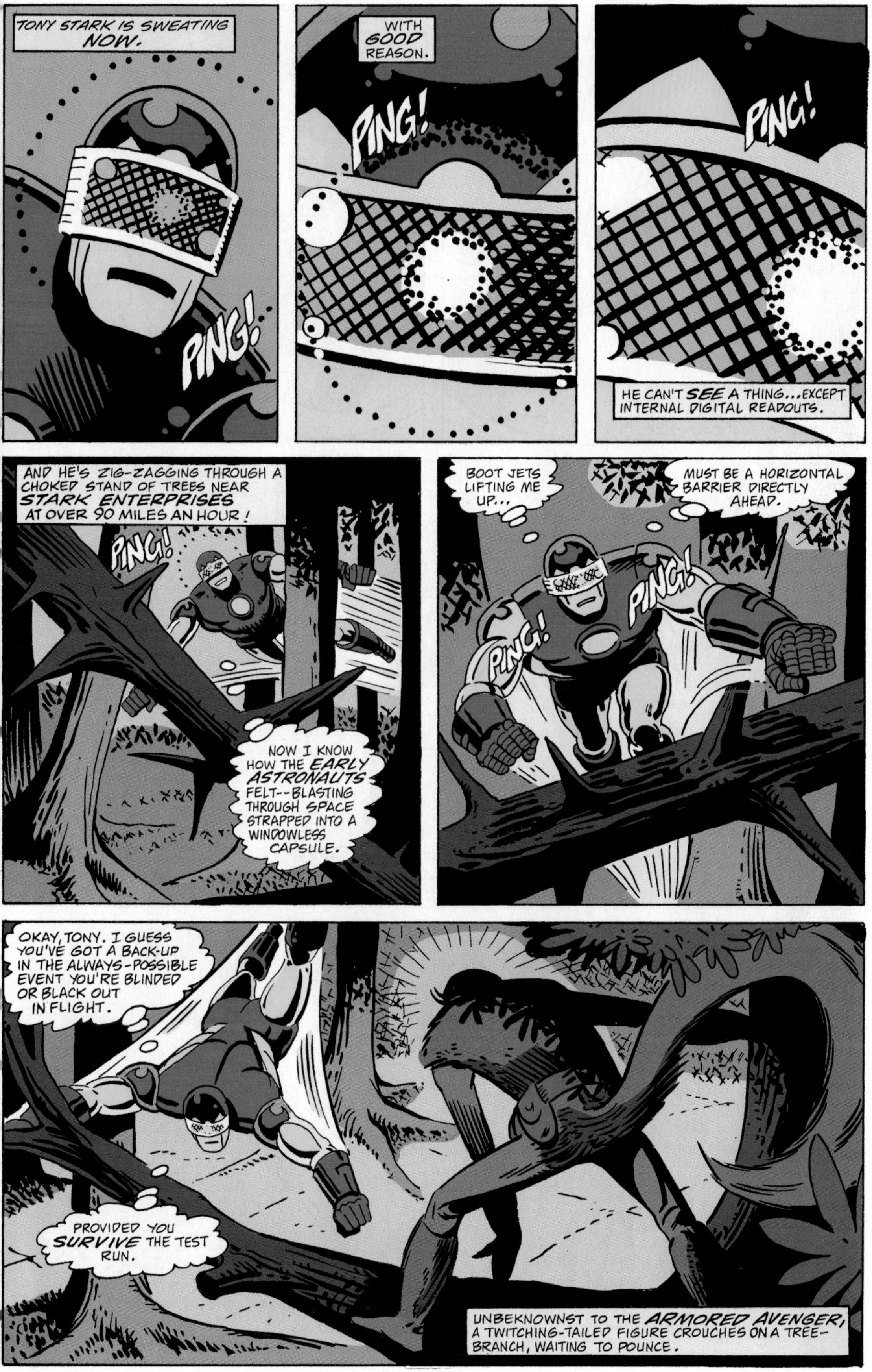
TONY STARK IS SWEATING NOW.
PING!
WITH GOOD REASON.
PING!
PING!
HE CAN'T SEE A THING...EXCEPT INTERNAL DIGITAL READOUTS.
AND HE'S ZIG-ZAGGING THROUGH A CHOKED STAND OF TREES NEAR STARK ENTERPRISES AT OVER 90 MILES AN HOUR!
PING!
NOW I KNOW HOW THE EARLY ASTRONAUTS FELT--BLASTING THROUGH SPACE STRAPPED INTO A WINDOWLESS CAPSULE.
BOOT JETS LIFTING ME UP...
MUST BE A HORIZONTAL BARRIER DIRECTLY AHEAD.
PING!
PING!
OKAY, TONY. I GUESS YOU'VE GOT A BACK-UP IN THE ALWAYS-POSSIBLE EVENT YOU'RE BLINDED OR BLACK OUT IN FLIGHT.
PROVIDED YOU SURVIVE THE TEST RUN.
UNBEKNOWNST TO THE ARMORED AVENGER, A TWITCHING-TAILED FIGURE CROUCHES ON A TREE-BRANCH, WAITING TO POUNCE.

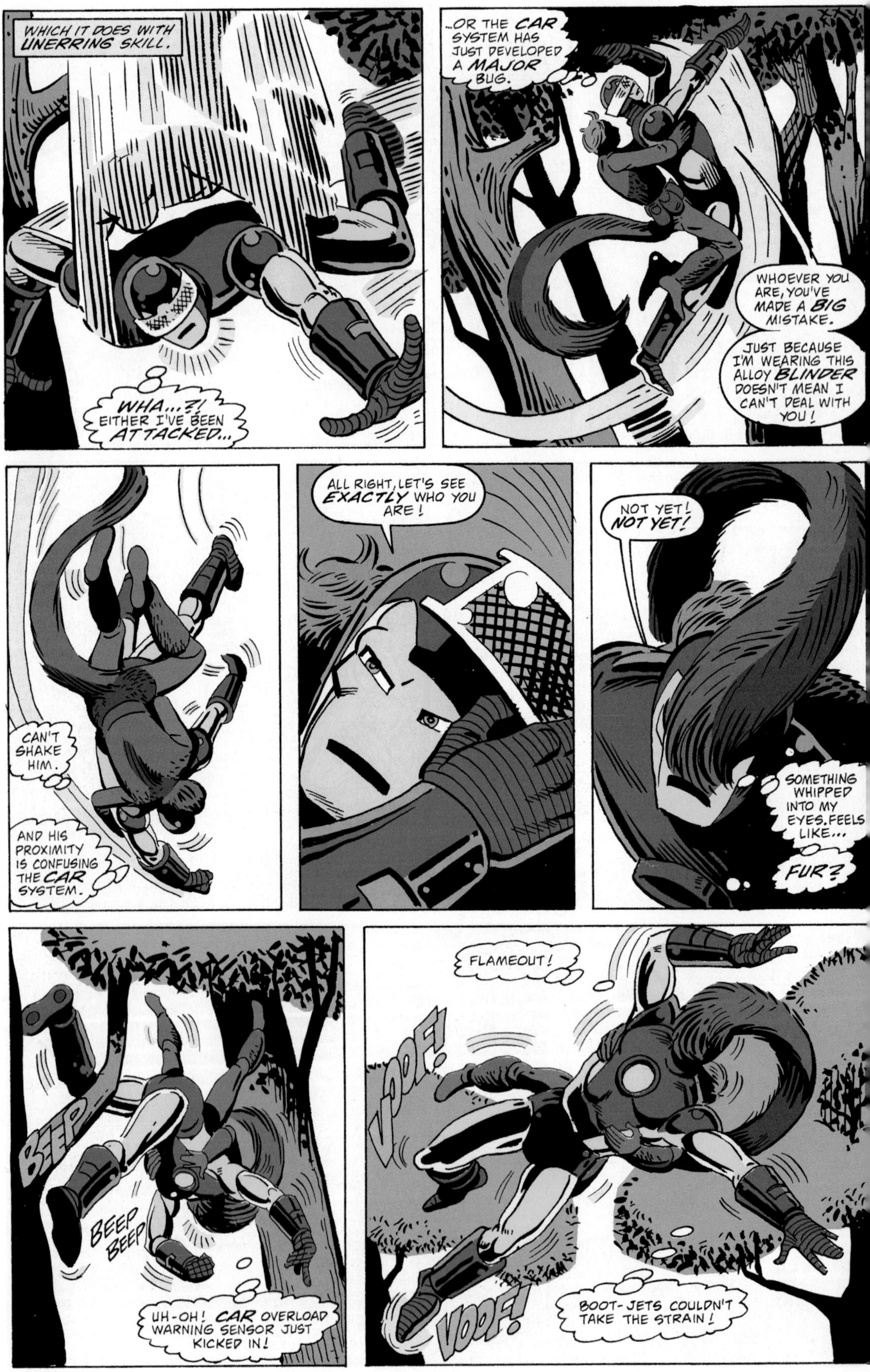
WHICH IT DOES WITH UNERRING SKILL.
WHA...?! EITHER I'VE BEEN ATTACKED...
...OR THE CAR SYSTEM HAS JUST DEVELOPED A MAJOR BUG.
WHOEVER YOU ARE, YOU'VE MADE A BIG MISTAKE.
JUST BECAUSE I'M WEARING THIS ALLOY BLINDER DOESN'T MEAN I CAN'T DEAL WITH YOU!
CAN'T SHAKE HIM.
AND HIS PROXIMITY IS CONFUSING THE CAR SYSTEM.
ALL RIGHT, LET'S SEE EXACTLY WHO YOU ARE!
NOT YET! NOT YET!
SOMETHING WHIPPED INTO MY EYES. FEELS LIKE...
FUR?
BEEP
BEEP BEEP
UH-OH! CAR OVERLOAD WARNING SENSOR JUST KICKED IN!
FLAMEOUT!
VOOF!
VOOF!
BOOT-JETS COULDN'T TAKE THE STRAIN!

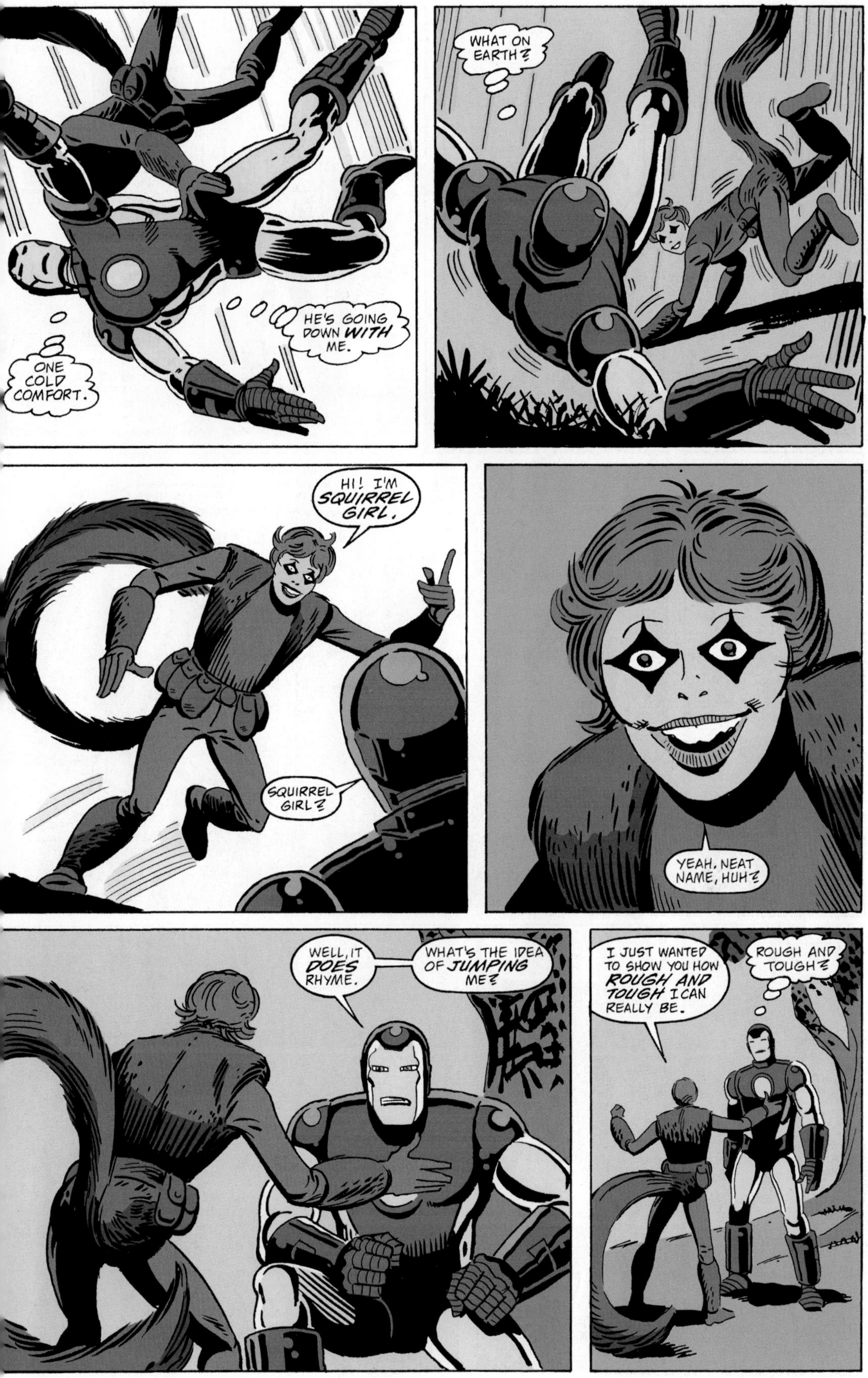
HE'S GOING DOWN WITH ME.
ONE COLD COMFORT.
WHAT ON EARTH?
HI! I'M SQUIRREL GIRL.
SQUIRREL GIRL?
YEAH, NEAT NAME, HUH?
WHAT'S THE IDEA OF JUMPING ME?
WELL, IT DOES RHYME.
I JUST WANTED TO SHOW YOU HOW ROUGH AND TOUGH I CAN REALLY BE.
ROUGH AND TOUGH?

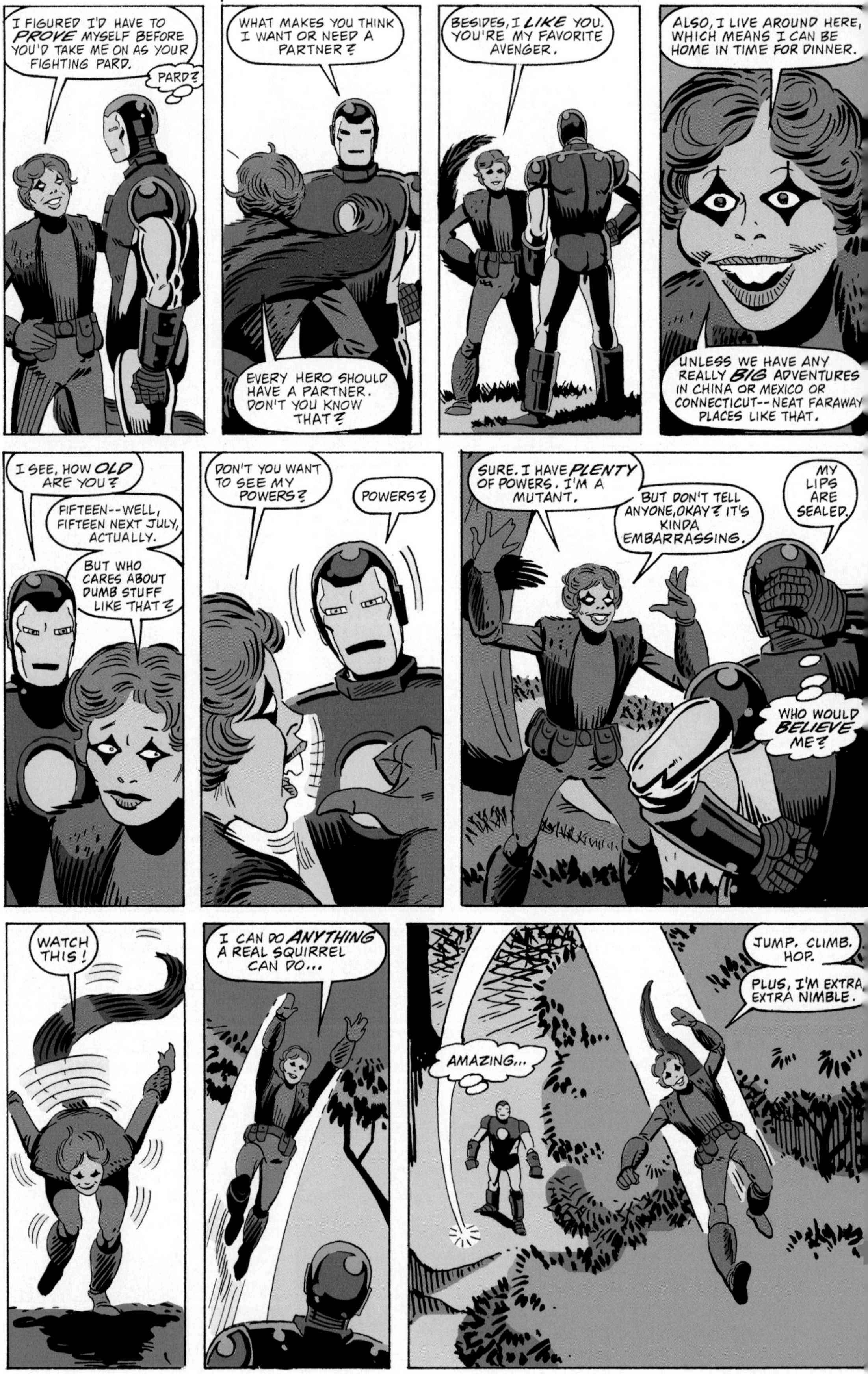
I FIGURED I'D HAVE TO PROVE MYSELF BEFORE YOU'D TAKE ME ON AS YOUR FIGHTING PARD.
PARD?
WHAT MAKES YOU THINK I WANT OR NEED A PARTNER?
EVERY HERO SHOULD HAVE A PARTNER. DON'T YOU KNOW THAT?
BESIDES, I LIKE YOU. YOU'RE MY FAVORITE AVENGER.
ALSO, I LIVE AROUND HERE, WHICH MEANS I CAN BE HOME IN TIME FOR DINNER.
UNLESS WE HAVE ANY REALLY BIG ADVENTURES IN CHINA OR MEXICO OR CONNECTICUT--NEAT FARAWAY PLACES LIKE THAT.
I SEE. HOW OLD ARE YOU?
FIFTEEN--WELL, FIFTEEN NEXT JULY, ACTUALLY.
BUT WHO CARES ABOUT DUMB STUFF LIKE THAT?
DON'T YOU WANT TO SEE MY POWERS?
POWERS?
SURE. I HAVE PLENTY OF POWERS. I'M A MUTANT.
BUT DON'T TELL ANYONE, OKAY? IT'S KINDA EMBARRASSING.
MY LIPS ARE SEALED.
WHO WOULD BELIEVE ME?
WATCH THIS!
I CAN DO ANYTHING A REAL SQUIRREL CAN DO...
JUMP. CLIMB. HOP.
PLUS, I'M EXTRA, EXTRA NIMBLE.
AMAZING...

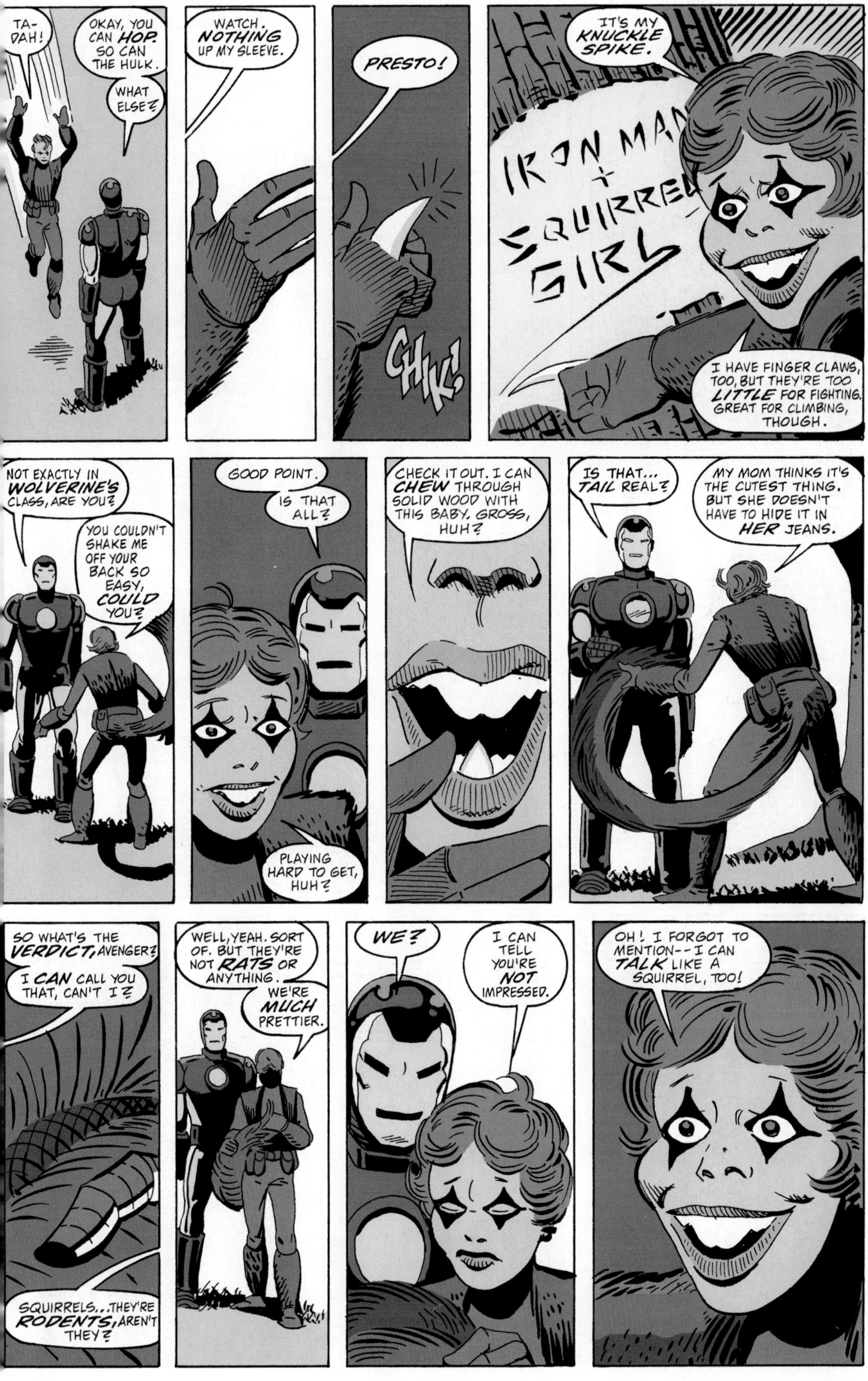
TA-DAH!
OKAY, YOU CAN HOP. SO CAN THE HULK.
WHAT ELSE?
WATCH. NOTHING UP MY SLEEVE.
PRESTO!
CHK!
IT'S MY KNUCKLE SPIKE.
IRON MAN + SQUIRREL GIRL
I HAVE FINGER CLAWS, TOO, BUT THEY'RE TOO LITTLE FOR FIGHTING. GREAT FOR CLIMBING, THOUGH.
NOT EXACTLY IN WOLVERINE'S CLASS, ARE YOU?
YOU COULDN'T SHAKE ME OFF YOUR BACK SO EASY, COULD YOU?
GOOD POINT.
IS THAT ALL?
PLAYING HARD TO GET, HUH?
CHECK IT OUT. I CAN CHEW THROUGH SOLID WOOD WITH THIS BABY. GROSS, HUH?
IS THAT... TAIL REAL?
MY MOM THINKS IT'S THE CUTEST THING. BUT SHE DOESN'T HAVE TO HIDE IT IN HER JEANS.
SO WHAT'S THE VERDICT, AVENGER?
I CAN CALL YOU THAT, CAN'T I?
SQUIRRELS... THEY'RE RODENTS, AREN'T THEY?
WELL, YEAH. SORT OF. BUT THEY'RE NOT RATS OR ANYTHING.
WE'RE MUCH PRETTIER.
WE?
I CAN TELL YOU'RE NOT IMPRESSED.
OH! I FORGOT TO MENTION--I CAN TALK LIKE A SQUIRREL, TOO!

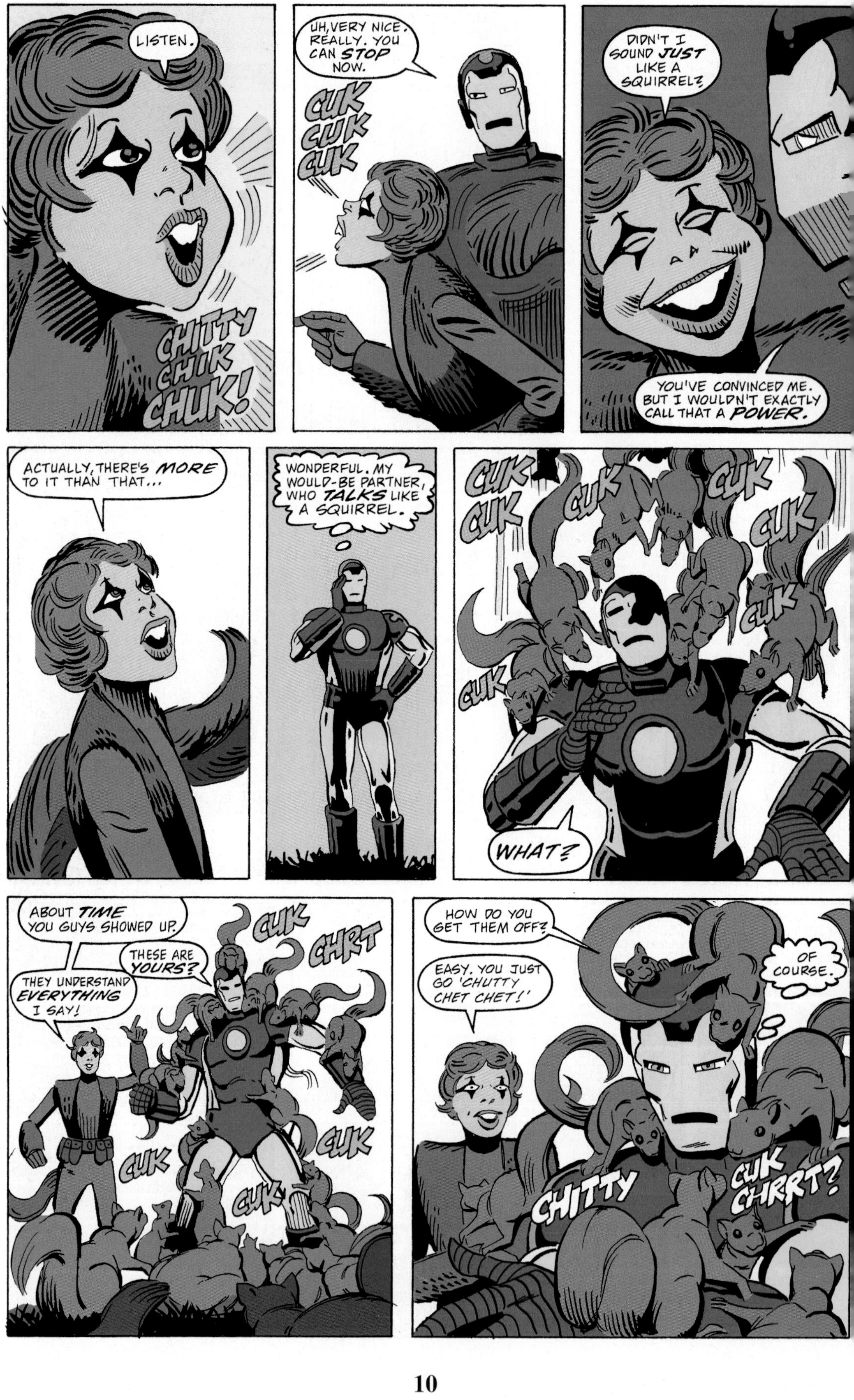
LISTEN.
CHITTY CHIK CHUK!
UH, VERY NICE. REALLY. YOU CAN STOP NOW.
CUK CUK CUK
DIDN'T I SOUND JUST LIKE A SQUIRREL?
YOU'VE CONVINCED ME. BUT I WOULDN'T EXACTLY CALL THAT A POWER.
ACTUALLY, THERE'S MORE TO IT THAN THAT...
WONDERFUL. MY WOULD-BE PARTNER, WHO TALKS LIKE A SQUIRREL.
CUK CUK
CUK
CUK
CUK
CUK
CUK
WHAT?
ABOUT TIME YOU GUYS SHOWED UP.
THESE ARE YOURS?
THEY UNDERSTAND EVERYTHING I SAY!
CUK
CHRT
CUK
CUK
CUK
HOW DO YOU GET THEM OFF?
EASY. YOU JUST GO 'CHUTTY CHET CHET!'
OF COURSE.
CHITTY
CUK CHRRT?

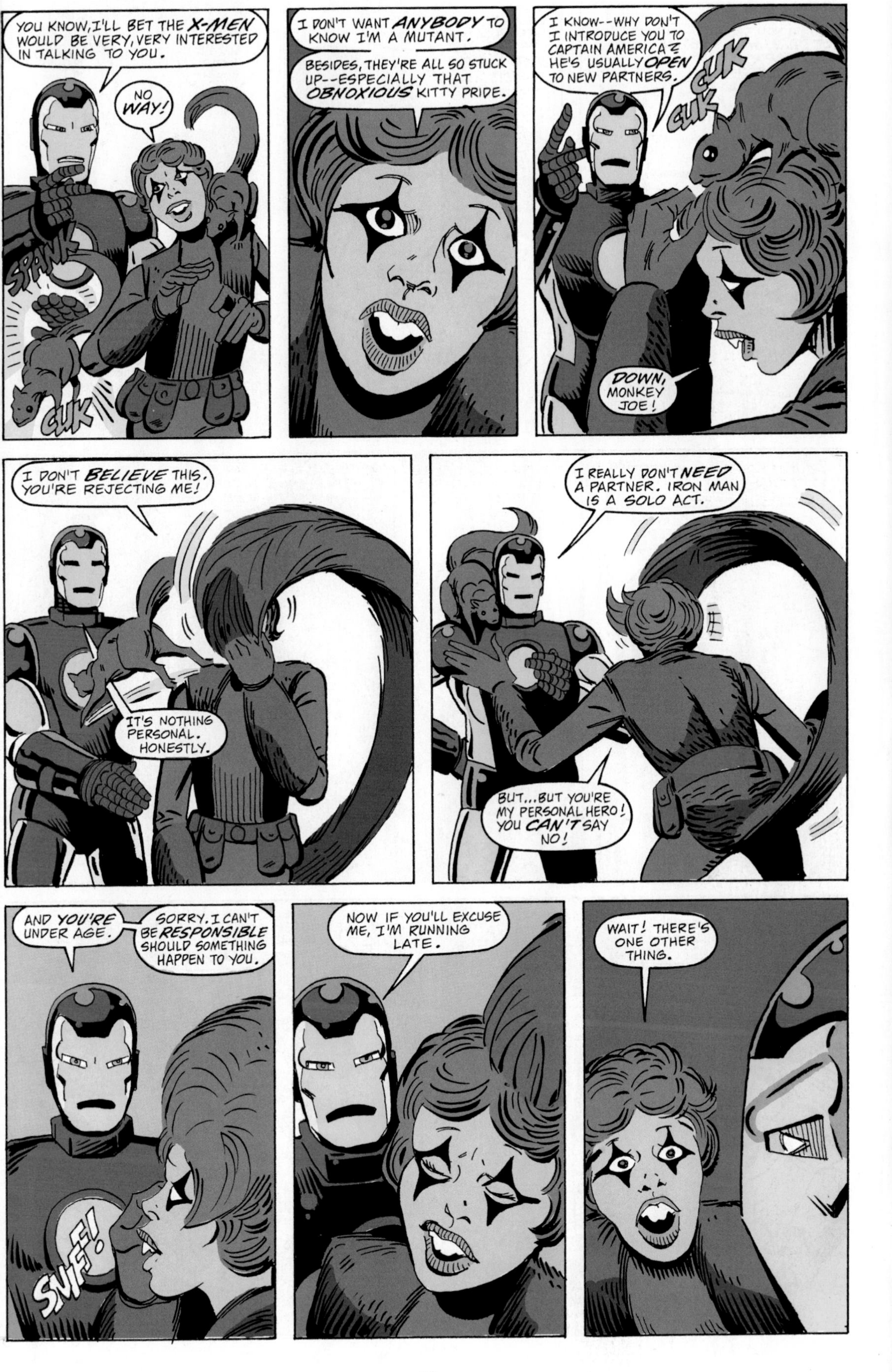
YOU KNOW, I'LL BET THE X-MEN WOULD BE VERY, VERY INTERESTED IN TALKING TO YOU.
NO WAY!
SPANK
CUK
I DON'T WANT ANYBODY TO KNOW I'M A MUTANT.
BESIDES, THEY'RE ALL SO STUCK UP--ESPECIALLY THAT OBNOXIOUS KITTY PRIDE.
I KNOW--WHY DON'T I INTRODUCE YOU TO CAPTAIN AMERICA? HE'S USUALLY OPEN TO NEW PARTNERS.
CUK CUK
DOWN, MONKEY JOE!
I DON'T BELIEVE THIS. YOU'RE REJECTING ME!
IT'S NOTHING PERSONAL. HONESTLY.
I REALLY DON'T NEED A PARTNER. IRON MAN IS A SOLO ACT.
BUT...BUT YOU'RE MY PERSONAL HERO! YOU CAN'T SAY NO!
AND YOU'RE UNDER AGE.
SORRY. I CAN'T BE RESPONSIBLE SHOULD SOMETHING HAPPEN TO YOU.
SNIFF!
NOW IF YOU'LL EXCUSE ME, I'M RUNNING LATE.
WAIT! THERE'S ONE OTHER THING.

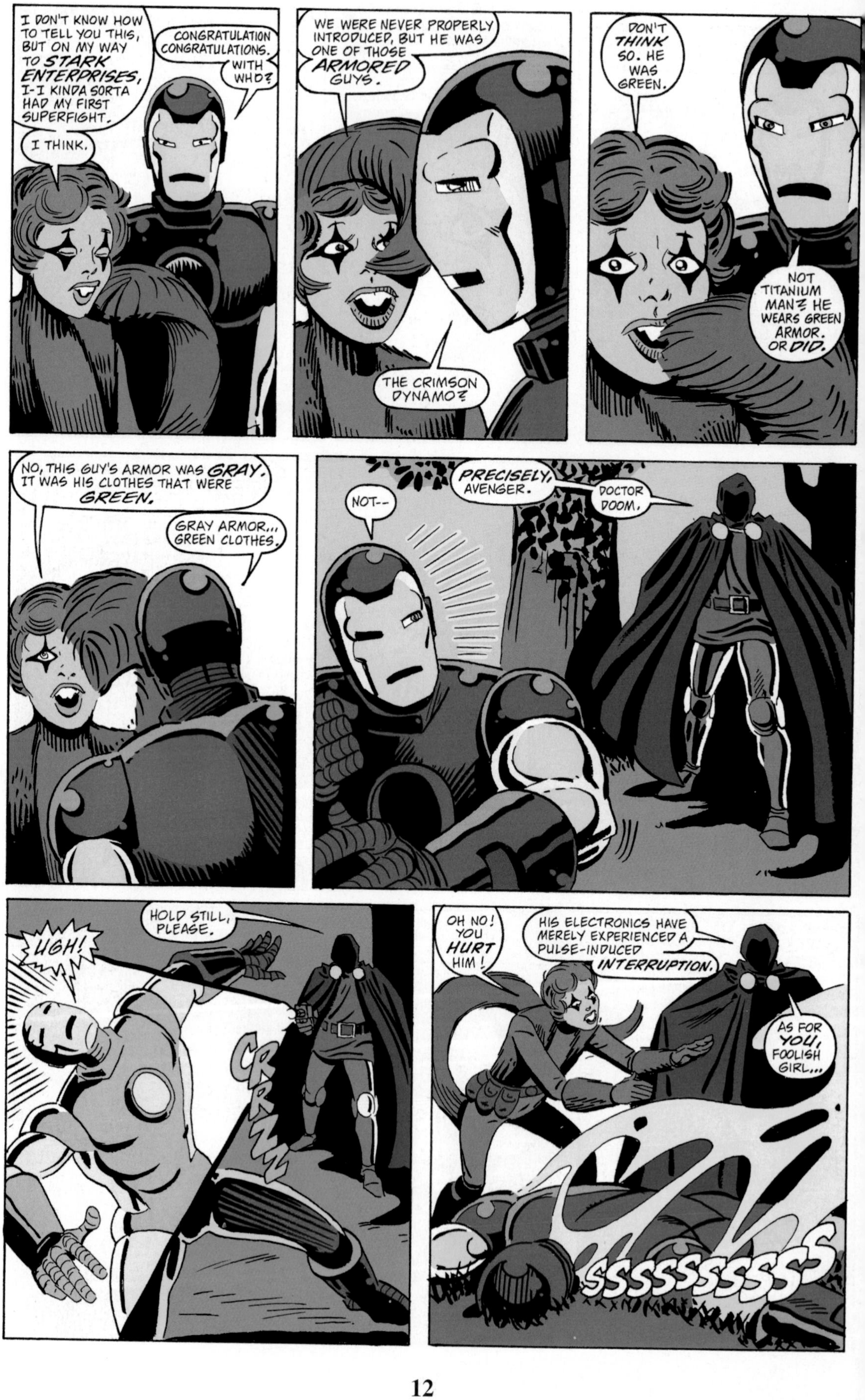
I DON'T KNOW HOW TO TELL YOU THIS, BUT ON MY WAY TO STARK ENTERPRISES, I-I KINDA SORTA HAD MY FIRST SUPERFIGHT.
I THINK.
CONGRATULATION CONGRATULATIONS.
WITH WHO?
WE WERE NEVER PROPERLY INTRODUCED, BUT HE WAS ONE OF THOSE ARMORED GUYS.
THE CRIMSON DYNAMO?
DON'T THINK SO. HE WAS GREEN.
NOT TITANIUM MAN? HE WEARS GREEN ARMOR. OR DID.
NO, THIS GUY'S ARMOR WAS GRAY. IT WAS HIS CLOTHES THAT WERE GREEN.
GRAY ARMOR... GREEN CLOTHES.
NOT--
PRECISELY, AVENGER.
DOCTOR DOOM.
UGH!
HOLD STILL, PLEASE.
CRRNN
OH NO! YOU HURT HIM!
HIS ELECTRONICS HAVE MERELY EXPERIENCED A PULSE-INDUCED INTERRUPTION.
AS FOR YOU, FOOLISH GIRL...
SSSSSSSSSS

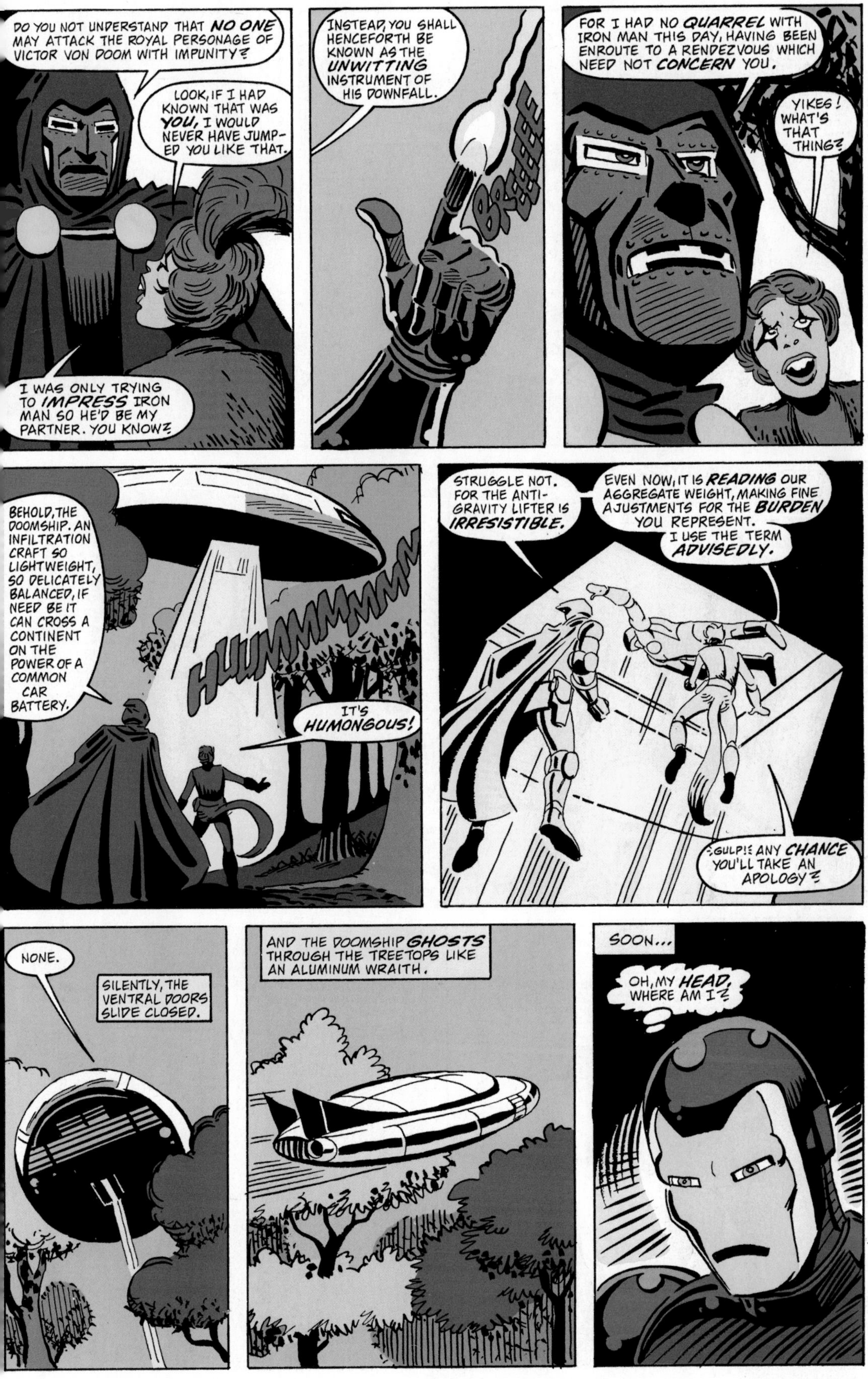

DO YOU NOT UNDERSTAND THAT NO ONE MAY ATTACK THE ROYAL PERSONAGE OF VICTOR VON DOOM WITH IMPUNITY?
LOOK, IF I HAD KNOWN THAT WAS YOU, I WOULD NEVER HAVE JUMPED YOU LIKE THAT.
I WAS ONLY TRYING TO IMPRESS IRON MAN SO HE'D BE MY PARTNER. YOU KNOW?
INSTEAD, YOU SHALL HENCEFORTH BE KNOWN AS THE UNWITTING INSTRUMENT OF HIS DOWNFALL.
BREEEE
FOR I HAD NO QUARREL WITH IRON MAN THIS DAY, HAVING BEEN ENROUTE TO A RENDEZVOUS WHICH NEED NOT CONCERN YOU.
YIKES! WHAT'S THAT THING?
BEHOLD, THE DOOMSHIP. AN INFILTRATION CRAFT SO LIGHTWEIGHT, SO DELICATELY BALANCED, IF NEED BE IT CAN CROSS A CONTINENT ON THE POWER OF A COMMON CAR BATTERY.
HUUMMMMMMMM
IT'S HUMONGOUS!
STRUGGLE NOT. FOR THE ANTI-GRAVITY LIFTER IS IRRESISTIBLE.
EVEN NOW, IT IS READING OUR AGGREGATE WEIGHT, MAKING FINE AJUSTMENTS FOR THE BURDEN YOU REPRESENT. I USE THE TERM ADVISEDLY.
GULP! ANY CHANCE YOU'LL TAKE AN APOLOGY?
NONE.
SILENTLY, THE VENTRAL DOORS SLIDE CLOSED.
AND THE DOOMSHIP GHOSTS THROUGH THE TREETOPS LIKE AN ALUMINUM WRAITH.
SOON...
OH, MY HEAD. WHERE AM I?

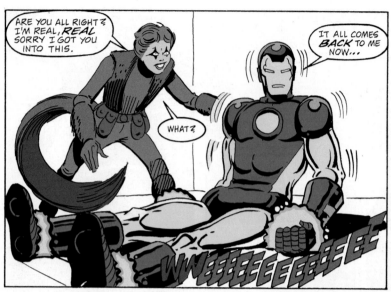

ARE YOU ALL RIGHT? I'M REAL, *REAL* SORRY I GOT YOU INTO THIS.

WHAT?

IT ALL COMES *BACK* TO ME NOW...

NEVER MIND.

SOME KIND OF MANACLE... SURROUNDED BY AN ENERGY FIELD.

WEEEEEEE

STAND BACK. I'M GOING TO... *UGH*... SHATTER THESE...BONDS.

PIECES MAY... *UUHHH*... FLY.

RRRREE-AAAARRRRRRR

NO GO. THE HARDER I TRY, THE *BRIGHTER* THEY GLOW. SOME KIND OF *ENERGY SINK*, ACCORDING TO MY ONBOARD POWER INDICATORS.

THEY'RE DRAINING... MY ARMOR. CAN'T... BREAK THEM.

BUT YOU *CAN'T* FAIL! YOU'RE MY HERO!

THERE'S ALWAYS A *FIRST* TIME.

DO YOU HAVE ANY *TOOLS* IN THOSE POUCHES?

NO. THIS IS MY *NUT STASH*. I EAT THEM FOR ENERGY.

TRY SOME *MACADAMIAS*. THEY'RE GREAT FOR *EXTRA* PEP.

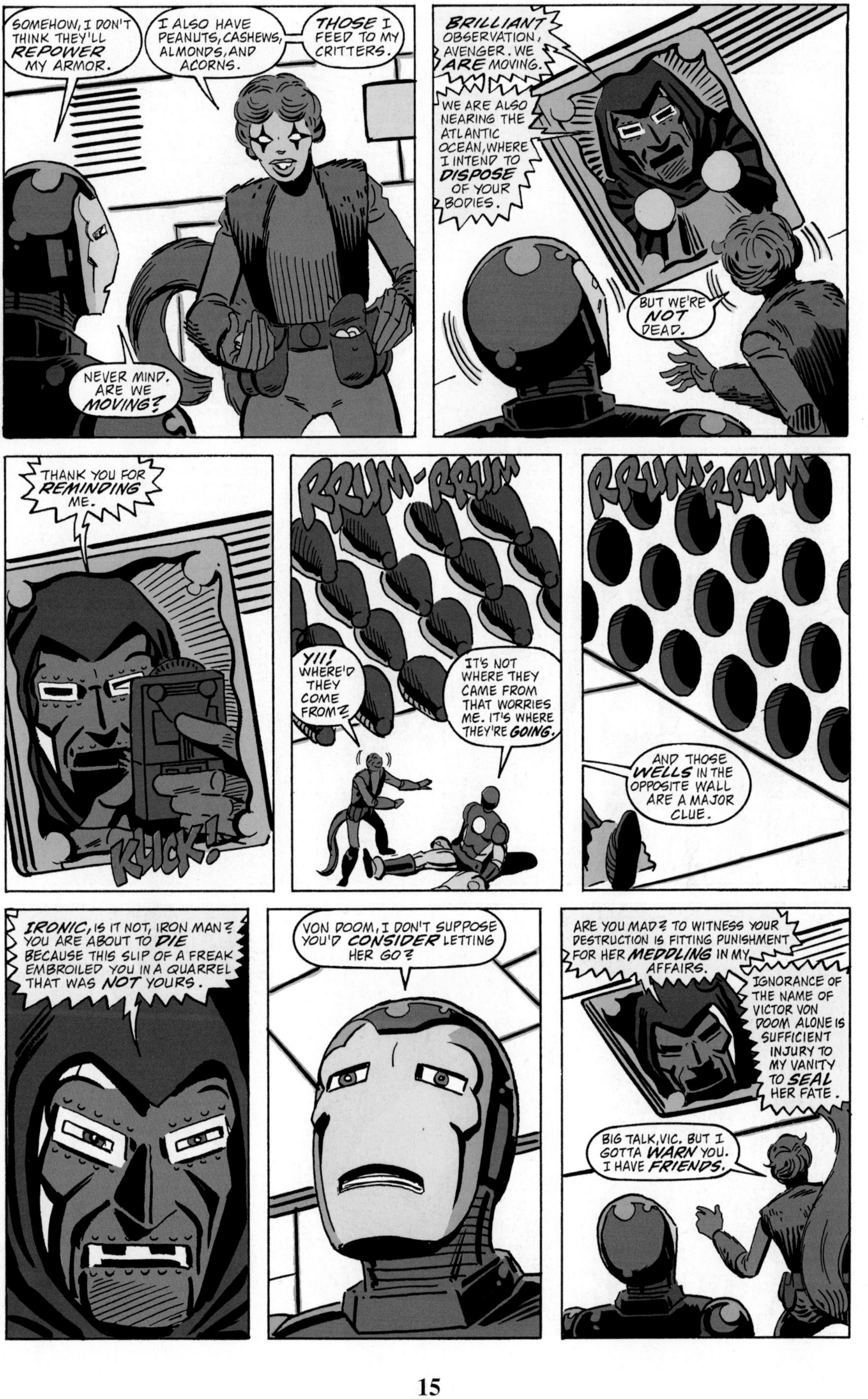

SOMEHOW, I DON'T THINK THEY'LL REPOWER MY ARMOR.
I ALSO HAVE PEANUTS, CASHEWS, ALMONDS, AND ACORNS.
THOSE I FEED TO MY CRITTERS.
NEVER MIND. ARE WE MOVING?
BRILLIANT OBSERVATION, AVENGER. WE ARE MOVING.
WE ARE ALSO NEARING THE ATLANTIC OCEAN, WHERE I INTEND TO DISPOSE OF YOUR BODIES.
BUT WE'RE NOT DEAD.
THANK YOU FOR REMINDING ME.
KLICK!
RRUM-RRUM
YII! WHERE'D THEY COME FROM?
IT'S NOT WHERE THEY CAME FROM THAT WORRIES ME. IT'S WHERE THEY'RE GOING.
RRUM-RRUM
AND THOSE WELLS IN THE OPPOSITE WALL ARE A MAJOR CLUE.
IRONIC, IS IT NOT, IRON MAN? YOU ARE ABOUT TO DIE BECAUSE THIS SLIP OF A FREAK EMBROILED YOU IN A QUARREL THAT WAS NOT YOURS.
VON DOOM, I DON'T SUPPOSE YOU'D CONSIDER LETTING HER GO?
ARE YOU MAD? TO WITNESS YOUR DESTRUCTION IS FITTING PUNISHMENT FOR HER MEDDLING IN MY AFFAIRS.
IGNORANCE OF THE NAME OF VICTOR VON DOOM ALONE IS SUFFICIENT INJURY TO MY VANITY TO SEAL HER FATE.
BIG TALK, VIC. BUT I GOTTA WARN YOU. I HAVE FRIENDS.

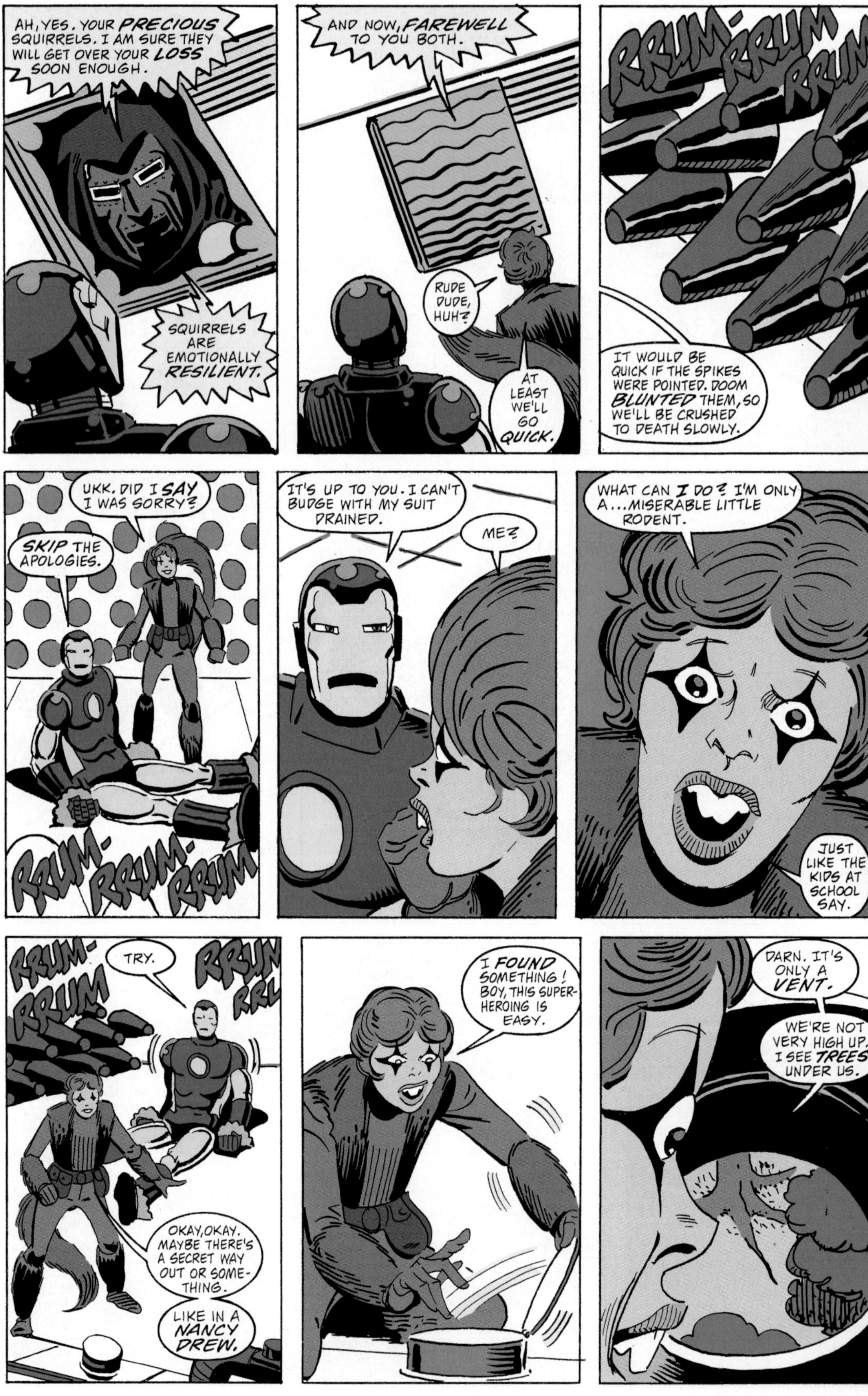
AH, YES. YOUR PRECIOUS SQUIRRELS. I AM SURE THEY WILL GET OVER YOUR LOSS SOON ENOUGH.
SQUIRRELS ARE EMOTIONALLY RESILIENT.
AND NOW, FAREWELL TO YOU BOTH.
RUDE DUDE, HUH?
AT LEAST WE'LL GO QUICK.
RRUM-RRUM-RRUM
IT WOULD BE QUICK IF THE SPIKES WERE POINTED. DOOM BLUNTED THEM, SO WE'LL BE CRUSHED TO DEATH SLOWLY.
UKK. DID I SAY I WAS SORRY?
SKIP THE APOLOGIES.
RRUM-RRUM-RRUM
IT'S UP TO YOU. I CAN'T BUDGE WITH MY SUIT DRAINED.
ME?
WHAT CAN I DO? I'M ONLY A...MISERABLE LITTLE RODENT.
JUST LIKE THE KIDS AT SCHOOL SAY.
RRUM-RRUM
TRY.
OKAY, OKAY. MAYBE THERE'S A SECRET WAY OUT OR SOMETHING.
LIKE IN A NANCY DREW.
I FOUND SOMETHING! BOY, THIS SUPER-HEROING IS EASY.
DARN. IT'S ONLY A VENT.
WE'RE NOT VERY HIGH UP. I SEE TREES UNDER US.

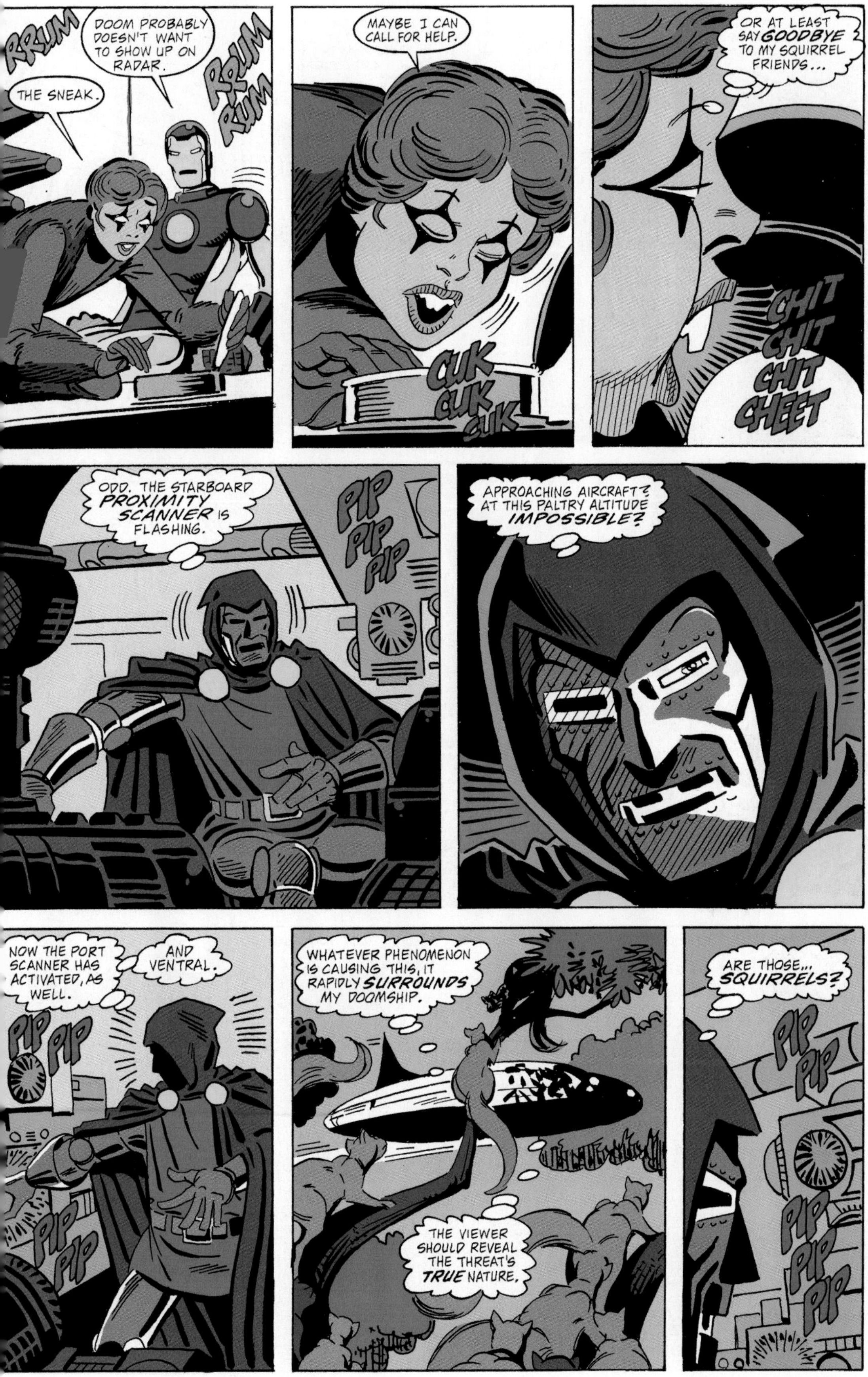
RRUM
DOOM PROBABLY DOESN'T WANT TO SHOW UP ON RADAR.
THE SNEAK.
RRUM RRUM
MAYBE I CAN CALL FOR HELP.
CLIK CLIK CLIK
OR AT LEAST SAY GOODBYE TO MY SQUIRREL FRIENDS...
CHIT CHIT CHIT CHEET
ODD. THE STARBOARD PROXIMITY SCANNER IS FLASHING.
PIP PIP PIP
APPROACHING AIRCRAFT? AT THIS PALTRY ALTITUDE IMPOSSIBLE?
NOW THE PORT SCANNER HAS ACTIVATED, AS WELL.
AND VENTRAL.
PIP PIP
PIP PIP
WHATEVER PHENOMENON IS CAUSING THIS, IT RAPIDLY SURROUNDS MY DOOMSHIP.
THE VIEWER SHOULD REVEAL THE THREAT'S TRUE NATURE.
ARE THOSE... SQUIRRELS?
PIP PIP
PIP PIP PIP

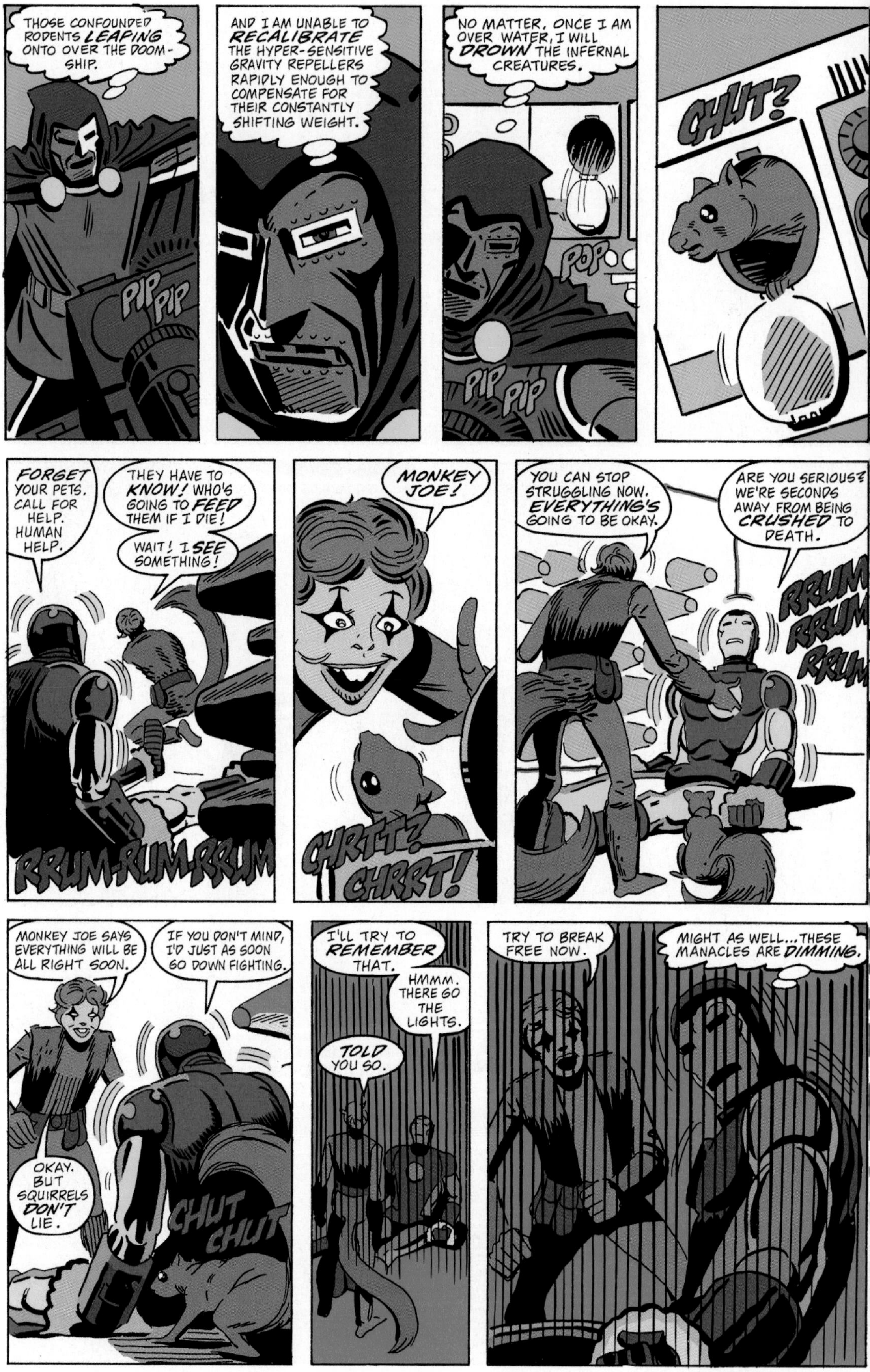
THOSE CONFOUNDED RODENTS LEAPING ONTO OVER THE DOOM-SHIP.
PIP PIP
AND I AM UNABLE TO RECALIBRATE THE HYPER-SENSITIVE GRAVITY REPELLERS RAPIDLY ENOUGH TO COMPENSATE FOR THEIR CONSTANTLY SHIFTING WEIGHT.
NO MATTER. ONCE I AM OVER WATER, I WILL DROWN THE INFERNAL CREATURES.
POP
PIP PIP
CHUT?
FORGET YOUR PETS. CALL FOR HELP. HUMAN HELP.
THEY HAVE TO KNOW! WHO'S GOING TO FEED THEM IF I DIE!
WAIT! I SEE SOMETHING!
RRUM-RUM-RRUM
MONKEY JOE!
CHRTT? CHRRT!
YOU CAN STOP STRUGGLING NOW. EVERYTHING'S GOING TO BE OKAY.
ARE YOU SERIOUS? WE'RE SECONDS AWAY FROM BEING CRUSHED TO DEATH.
RRUM RRUM RRUM
MONKEY JOE SAYS EVERYTHING WILL BE ALL RIGHT SOON.
IF YOU DON'T MIND, I'D JUST AS SOON GO DOWN FIGHTING.
OKAY. BUT SQUIRRELS DON'T LIE.
CHUT CHUT
I'LL TRY TO REMEMBER THAT.
HMMM. THERE GO THE LIGHTS.
TOLD YOU SO.
TRY TO BREAK FREE NOW.
MIGHT AS WELL... THESE MANACLES ARE DIMMING.

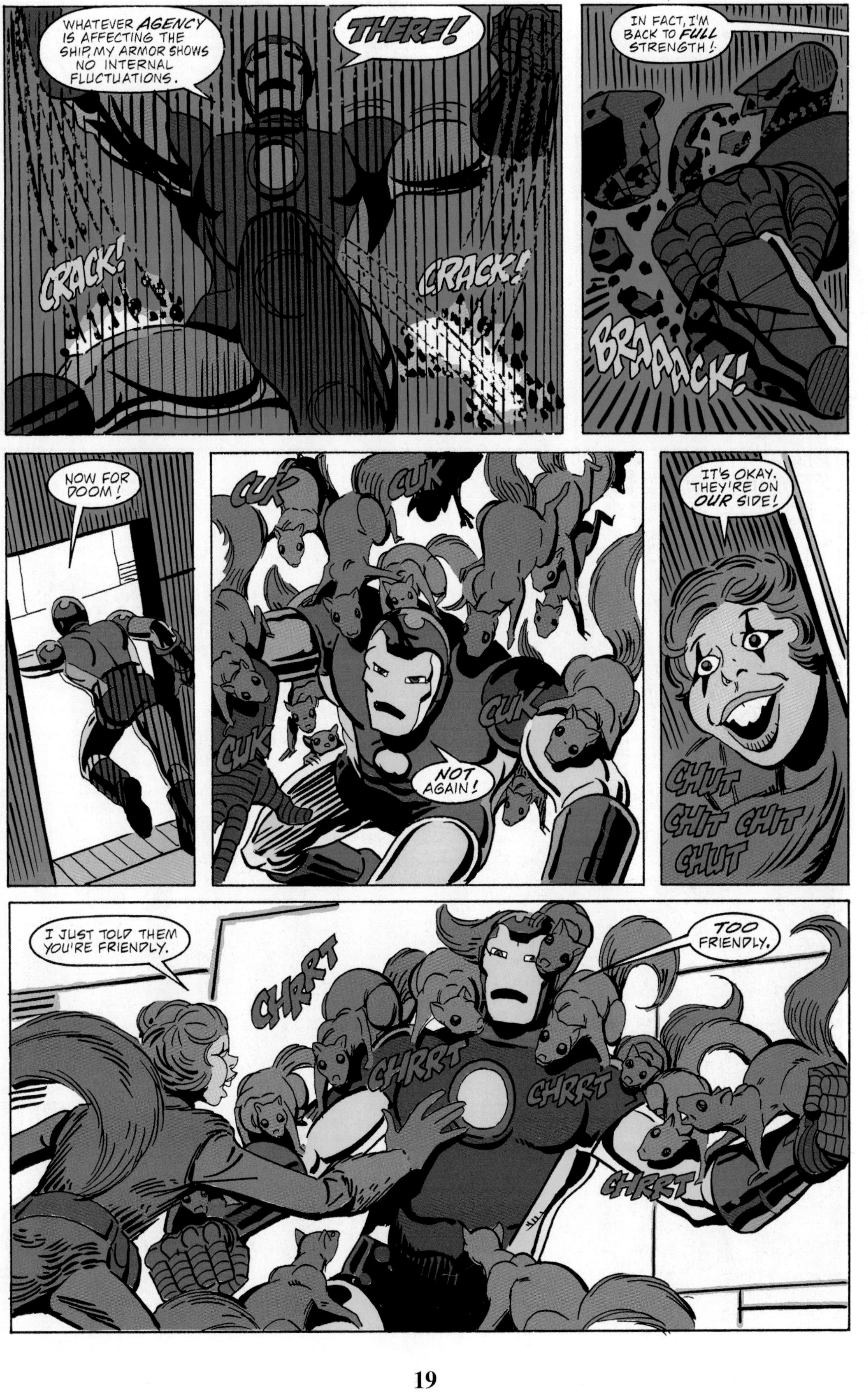
WHATEVER AGENCY IS AFFECTING THE SHIP, MY ARMOR SHOWS NO INTERNAL FLUCTUATIONS.
THERE!
CRACK!
CRACK!
IN FACT, I'M BACK TO FULL STRENGTH!
BRAAACK!
NOW FOR DOOM!
CUK
CUK
CUK
CUK
NOT AGAIN!
IT'S OKAY. THEY'RE ON OUR SIDE!
CHUT
CHIT CHIT
CHUT
I JUST TOLD THEM YOU'RE FRIENDLY.
TOO FRIENDLY.
CHRRT
CHRRT
CHRRT
CHRRT

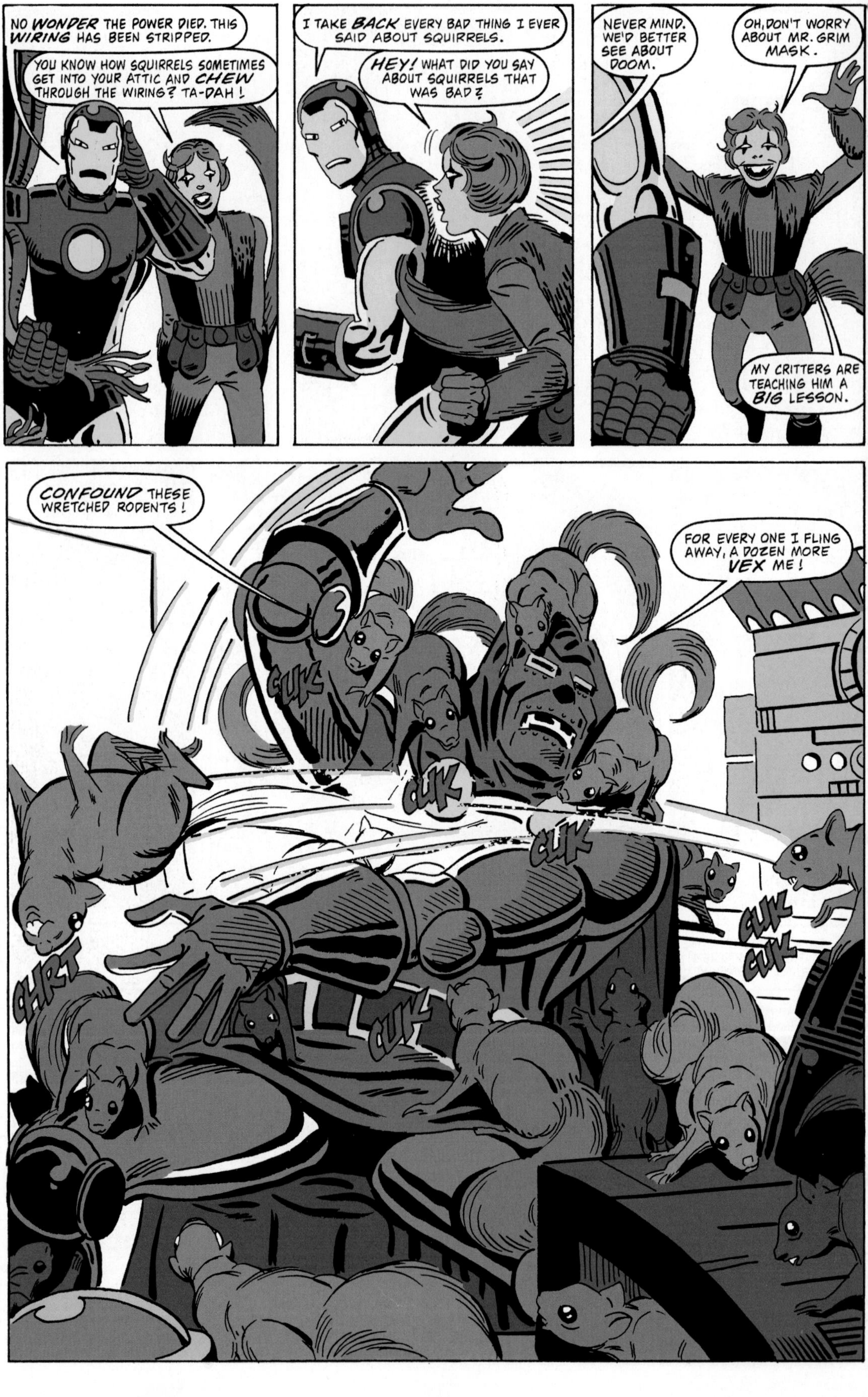
NO WONDER THE POWER DIED. THIS WIRING HAS BEEN STRIPPED.
YOU KNOW HOW SQUIRRELS SOMETIMES GET INTO YOUR ATTIC AND CHEW THROUGH THE WIRING? TA-DAH!
I TAKE BACK EVERY BAD THING I EVER SAID ABOUT SQUIRRELS.
HEY! WHAT DID YOU SAY ABOUT SQUIRRELS THAT WAS BAD?
NEVER MIND. WE'D BETTER SEE ABOUT DOOM.
OH, DON'T WORRY ABOUT MR. GRIM MASK.
MY CRITTERS ARE TEACHING HIM A BIG LESSON.
CONFOUND THESE WRETCHED RODENTS!
FOR EVERY ONE I FLING AWAY, A DOZEN MORE VEX ME!
CUK
CUK
CUK
CUK CUK
CHRT
CUK

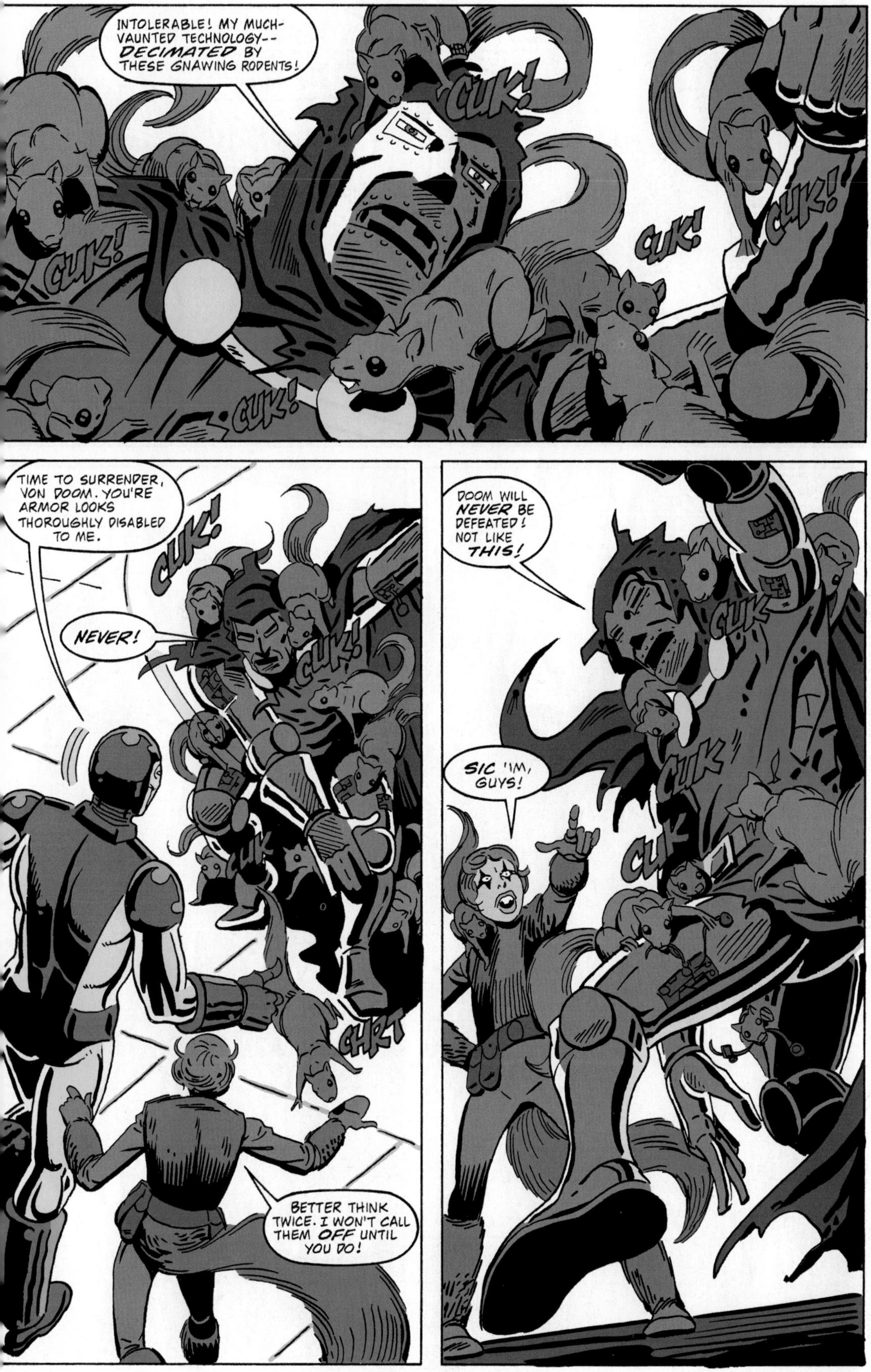
INTOLERABLE! MY MUCH-VAUNTED TECHNOLOGY-- DECIMATED BY THESE GNAWING RODENTS!
CUK!
CUK!
CUK!
CUK!
CUK!
TIME TO SURRENDER, VON DOOM. YOU'RE ARMOR LOOKS THOROUGHLY DISABLED TO ME.
NEVER!
CUK!
CUK!
CUK
CHRT
BETTER THINK TWICE. I WON'T CALL THEM OFF UNTIL YOU DO!
DOOM WILL NEVER BE DEFEATED! NOT LIKE THIS!
SIC 'IM, GUYS!
CUK
CUK
CUK

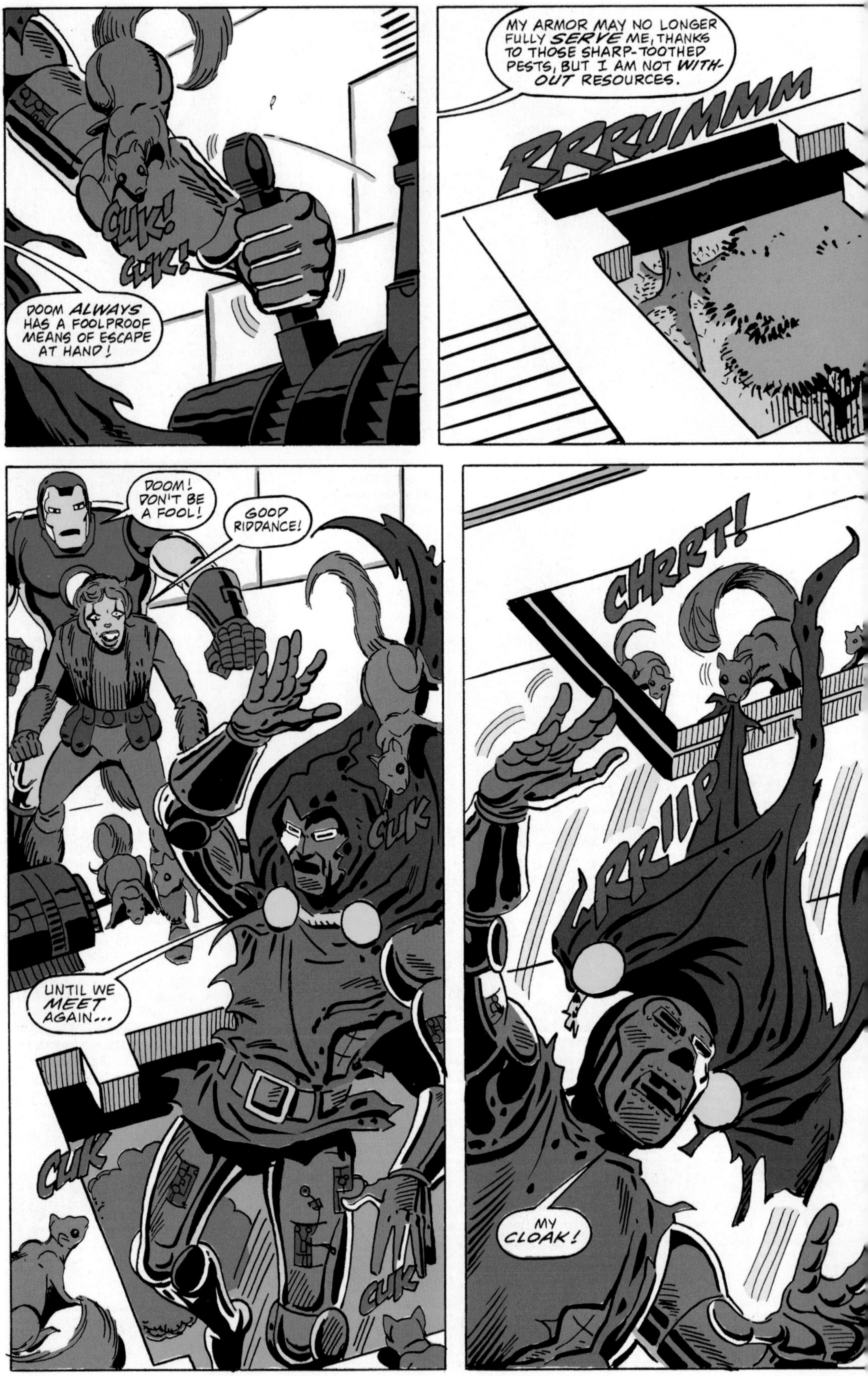
CUK!
CUK!
DOOM ALWAYS HAS A FOOLPROOF MEANS OF ESCAPE AT HAND!
MY ARMOR MAY NO LONGER FULLY SERVE ME, THANKS TO THOSE SHARP-TOOTHED PESTS, BUT I AM NOT WITHOUT RESOURCES.
RRRUMMMM
DOOM! DON'T BE A FOOL!
GOOD RIDDANCE!
CUK
UNTIL WE MEET AGAIN...
CUK
CUK
CHRRT!
RRIIP
MY CLOAK!

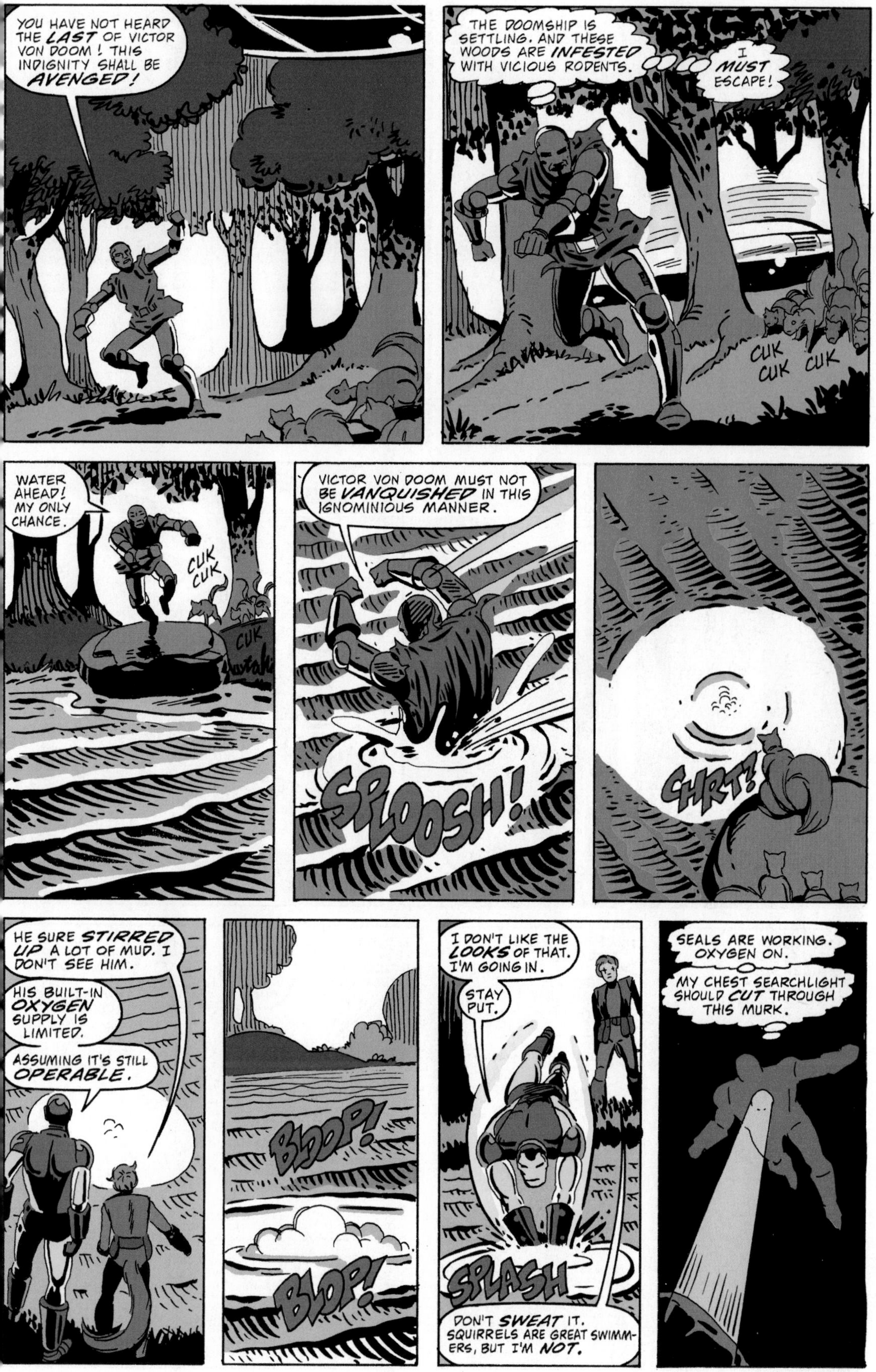
YOU HAVE NOT HEARD THE LAST OF VICTOR VON DOOM! THIS INDIGNITY SHALL BE AVENGED!
THE DOOMSHIP IS SETTLING. AND THESE WOODS ARE INFESTED WITH VICIOUS RODENTS.
I MUST ESCAPE!
CUK CUK CUK
WATER AHEAD! MY ONLY CHANCE.
CUK CUK
CUK
VICTOR VON DOOM MUST NOT BE VANQUISHED IN THIS IGNOMINIOUS MANNER.
SPLOOSH!
CHRT?
HE SURE STIRRED UP A LOT OF MUD. I DON'T SEE HIM.
HIS BUILT-IN OXYGEN SUPPLY IS LIMITED.
ASSUMING IT'S STILL OPERABLE.
BLOOP!
BLOP!
I DON'T LIKE THE LOOKS OF THAT. I'M GOING IN.
STAY PUT.
SPLASH
DON'T SWEAT IT. SQUIRRELS ARE GREAT SWIMMERS, BUT I'M NOT.
SEALS ARE WORKING. OXYGEN ON.
MY CHEST SEARCHLIGHT SHOULD CUT THROUGH THIS MURK.

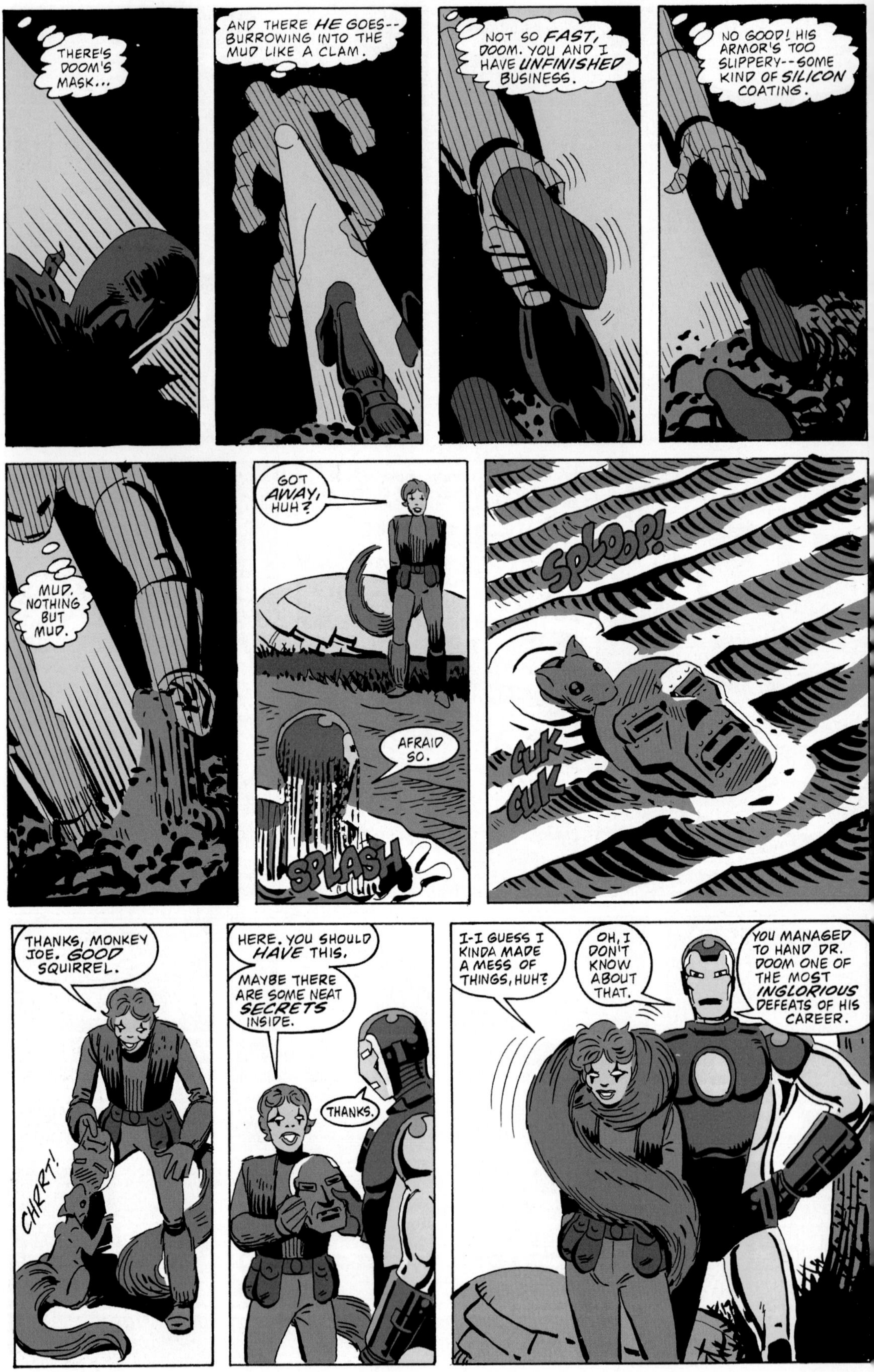

THERE'S DOOM'S MASK...
AND THERE HE GOES-- BURROWING INTO THE MUD LIKE A CLAM.
NOT SO FAST, DOOM. YOU AND I HAVE UNFINISHED BUSINESS.
NO GOOD! HIS ARMOR'S TOO SLIPPERY--SOME KIND OF SILICON COATING.
MUD. NOTHING BUT MUD.
GOT AWAY, HUH?
AFRAID SO.
SPLASH
SPLOOP!
CLIK CLIK
THANKS, MONKEY JOE. GOOD SQUIRREL.
CHRT!
HERE. YOU SHOULD HAVE THIS.
MAYBE THERE ARE SOME NEAT SECRETS INSIDE.
THANKS.
I-I GUESS I KINDA MADE A MESS OF THINGS, HUH?
OH, I DON'T KNOW ABOUT THAT.
YOU MANAGED TO HAND DR. DOOM ONE OF THE MOST INGLORIOUS DEFEATS OF HIS CAREER.

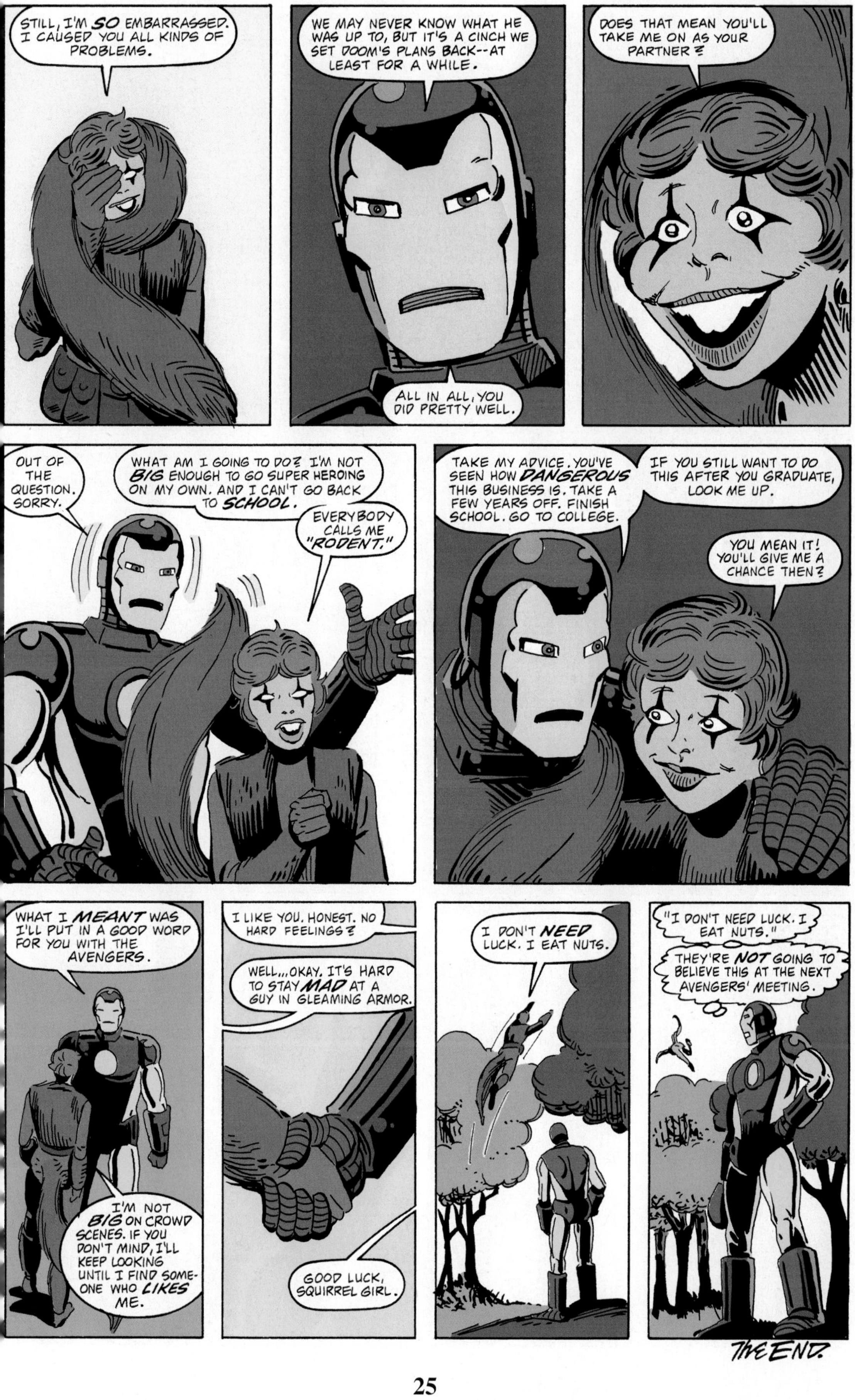
STILL, I'M SO EMBARRASSED. I CAUSED YOU ALL KINDS OF PROBLEMS.
WE MAY NEVER KNOW WHAT HE WAS UP TO, BUT IT'S A CINCH WE SET DOOM'S PLANS BACK--AT LEAST FOR A WHILE.
ALL IN ALL, YOU DID PRETTY WELL.
DOES THAT MEAN YOU'LL TAKE ME ON AS YOUR PARTNER?
OUT OF THE QUESTION. SORRY.
WHAT AM I GOING TO DO? I'M NOT BIG ENOUGH TO GO SUPER HEROING ON MY OWN. AND I CAN'T GO BACK TO SCHOOL.
EVERYBODY CALLS ME "RODENT."
TAKE MY ADVICE. YOU'VE SEEN HOW DANGEROUS THIS BUSINESS IS. TAKE A FEW YEARS OFF. FINISH SCHOOL. GO TO COLLEGE.
IF YOU STILL WANT TO DO THIS AFTER YOU GRADUATE, LOOK ME UP.
YOU MEAN IT! YOU'LL GIVE ME A CHANCE THEN?
WHAT I MEANT WAS I'LL PUT IN A GOOD WORD FOR YOU WITH THE AVENGERS.
I'M NOT BIG ON CROWD SCENES. IF YOU DON'T MIND, I'LL KEEP LOOKING UNTIL I FIND SOMEONE WHO LIKES ME.
I LIKE YOU. HONEST. NO HARD FEELINGS?
WELL... OKAY. IT'S HARD TO STAY MAD AT A GUY IN GLEAMING ARMOR.
GOOD LUCK, SQUIRREL GIRL.
I DON'T NEED LUCK. I EAT NUTS.
"I DON'T NEED LUCK. I EAT NUTS."
THEY'RE NOT GOING TO BELIEVE THIS AT THE NEXT AVENGERS' MEETING.
THE END.

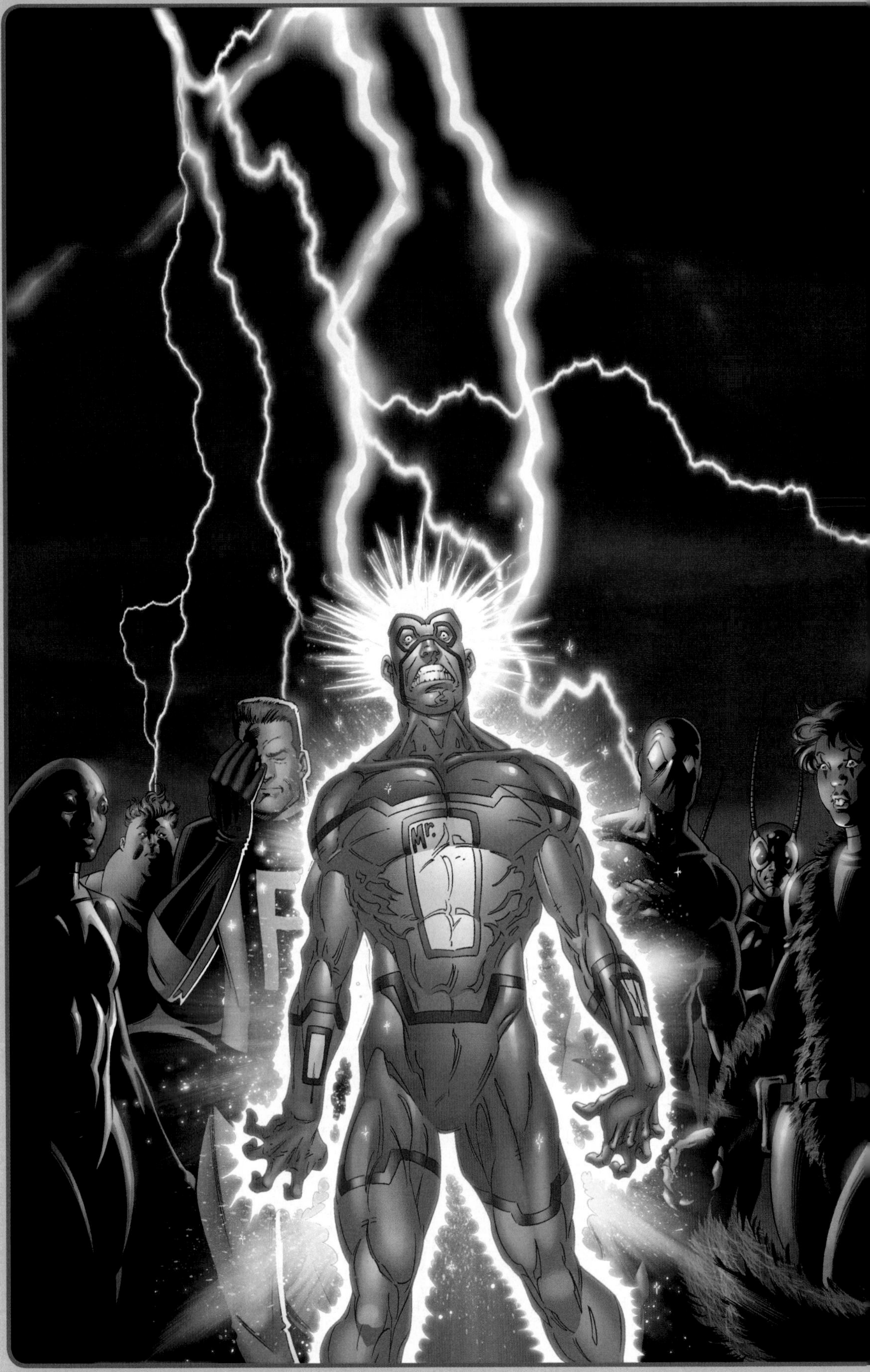
Mr.

GLA #1

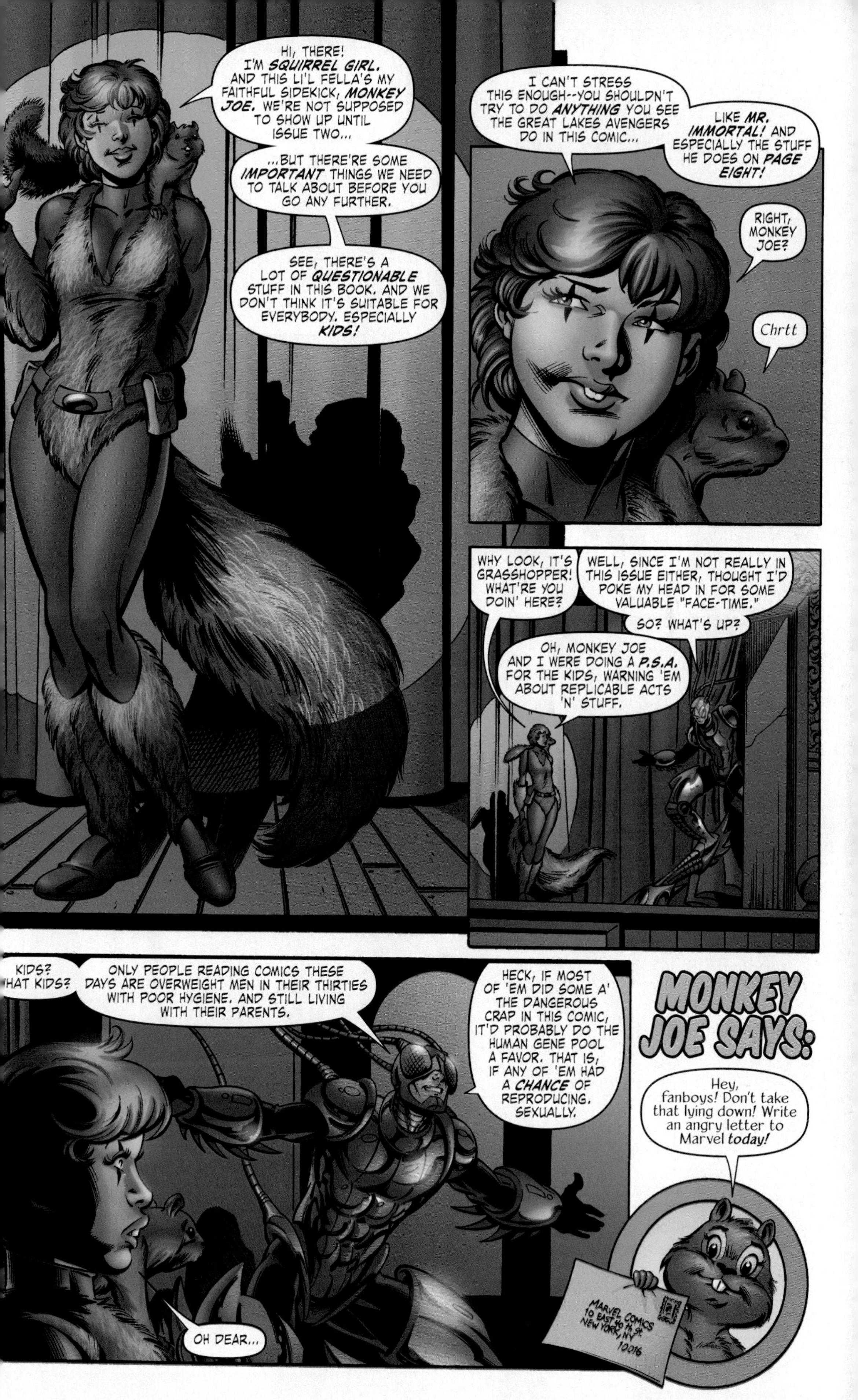
HI, THERE! I'M SQUIRREL GIRL. AND THIS LI'L FELLA'S MY FAITHFUL SIDEKICK, MONKEY JOE. WE'RE NOT SUPPOSED TO SHOW UP UNTIL ISSUE TWO...
...BUT THERE'RE SOME IMPORTANT THINGS WE NEED TO TALK ABOUT BEFORE YOU GO ANY FURTHER.
SEE, THERE'S A LOT OF QUESTIONABLE STUFF IN THIS BOOK. AND WE DON'T THINK IT'S SUITABLE FOR EVERYBODY. ESPECIALLY KIDS!
I CAN'T STRESS THIS ENOUGH--YOU SHOULDN'T TRY TO DO ANYTHING YOU SEE THE GREAT LAKES AVENGERS DO IN THIS COMIC...
LIKE MR. IMMORTAL! AND ESPECIALLY THE STUFF HE DOES ON PAGE EIGHT!
RIGHT, MONKEY JOE?
Chrtt
WHY LOOK, IT'S GRASSHOPPER! WHAT'RE YOU DOIN' HERE?
WELL, SINCE I'M NOT REALLY IN THIS ISSUE EITHER, THOUGHT I'D POKE MY HEAD IN FOR SOME VALUABLE "FACE-TIME."
SO? WHAT'S UP?
OH, MONKEY JOE AND I WERE DOING A P.S.A. FOR THE KIDS, WARNING 'EM ABOUT REPLICABLE ACTS 'N' STUFF.
KIDS? WHAT KIDS?
ONLY PEOPLE READING COMICS THESE DAYS ARE OVERWEIGHT MEN IN THEIR THIRTIES WITH POOR HYGIENE. AND STILL LIVING WITH THEIR PARENTS.
HECK, IF MOST OF 'EM DID SOME A' THE DANGEROUS CRAP IN THIS COMIC, IT'D PROBABLY DO THE HUMAN GENE POOL A FAVOR. THAT IS, IF ANY OF 'EM HAD A CHANCE OF REPRODUCING. SEXUALLY.
OH DEAR...
MONKEY JOE SAYS:
Hey, fanboys! Don't take that lying down! Write an angry letter to Marvel today!
MARVEL COMICS 10 EAST 40 th St. NEW YORK, NY 10016

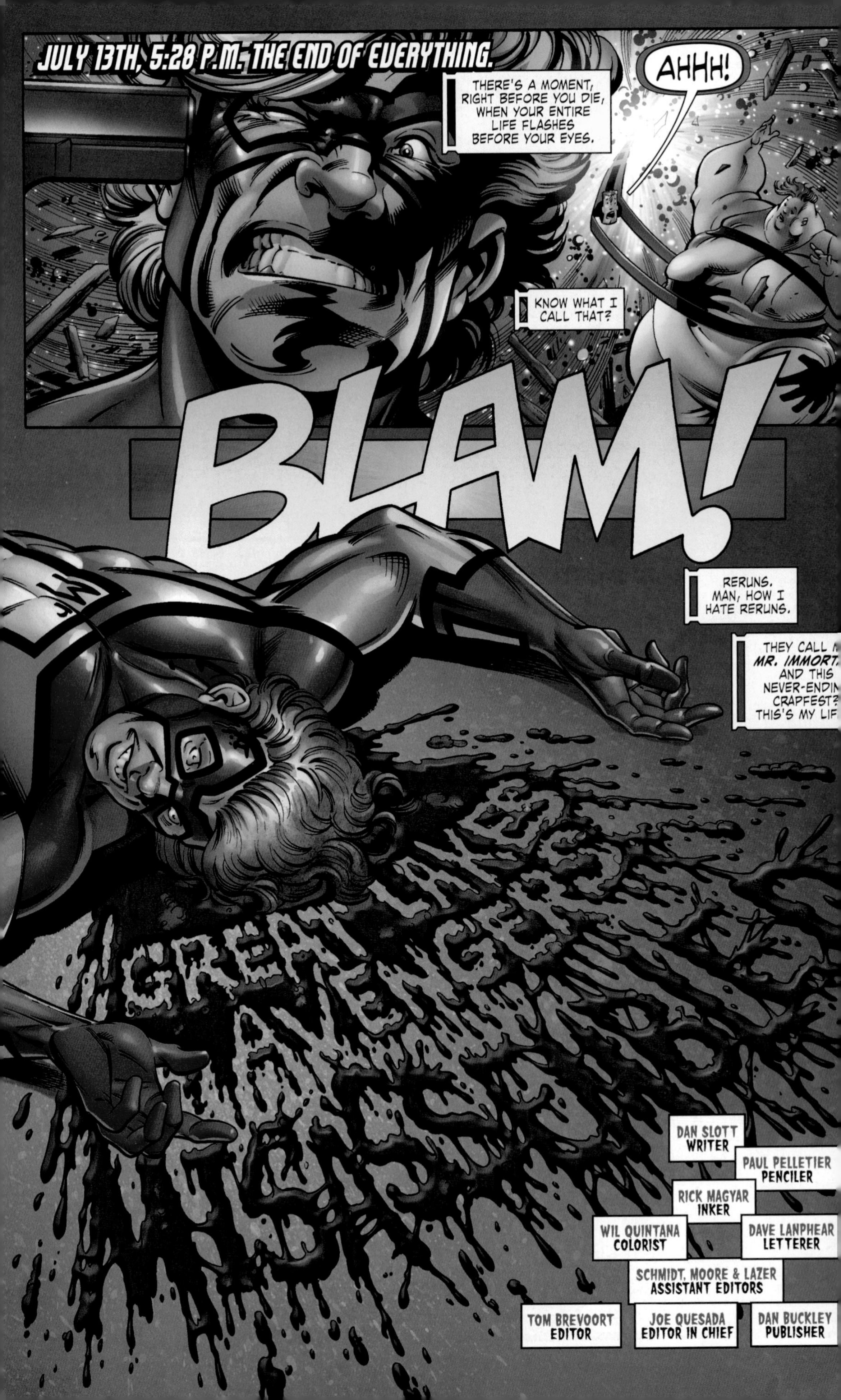
JULY 13TH, 5:28 P.M. THE END OF EVERYTHING.
THERE'S A MOMENT, RIGHT BEFORE YOU DIE, WHEN YOUR ENTIRE LIFE FLASHES BEFORE YOUR EYES.
AHHH!
KNOW WHAT I CALL THAT?
BLAM!
RERUNS. MAN, HOW I HATE RERUNS.
THEY CALL M
MR. IMMORT.
AND THIS
NEVER-ENDIN
CRAPFEST?
THIS'S MY LIF
DAN SLOTT WRITER
PAUL PELLETIER PENCILER
RICK MAGYAR INKER
WIL QUINTANA COLORIST
DAVE LANPHEAR LETTERER
SCHMIDT, MOORE & LAZER ASSISTANT EDITORS
TOM BREVOORT EDITOR
JOE QUESADA EDITOR IN CHIEF
DAN BUCKLEY PUBLISHER

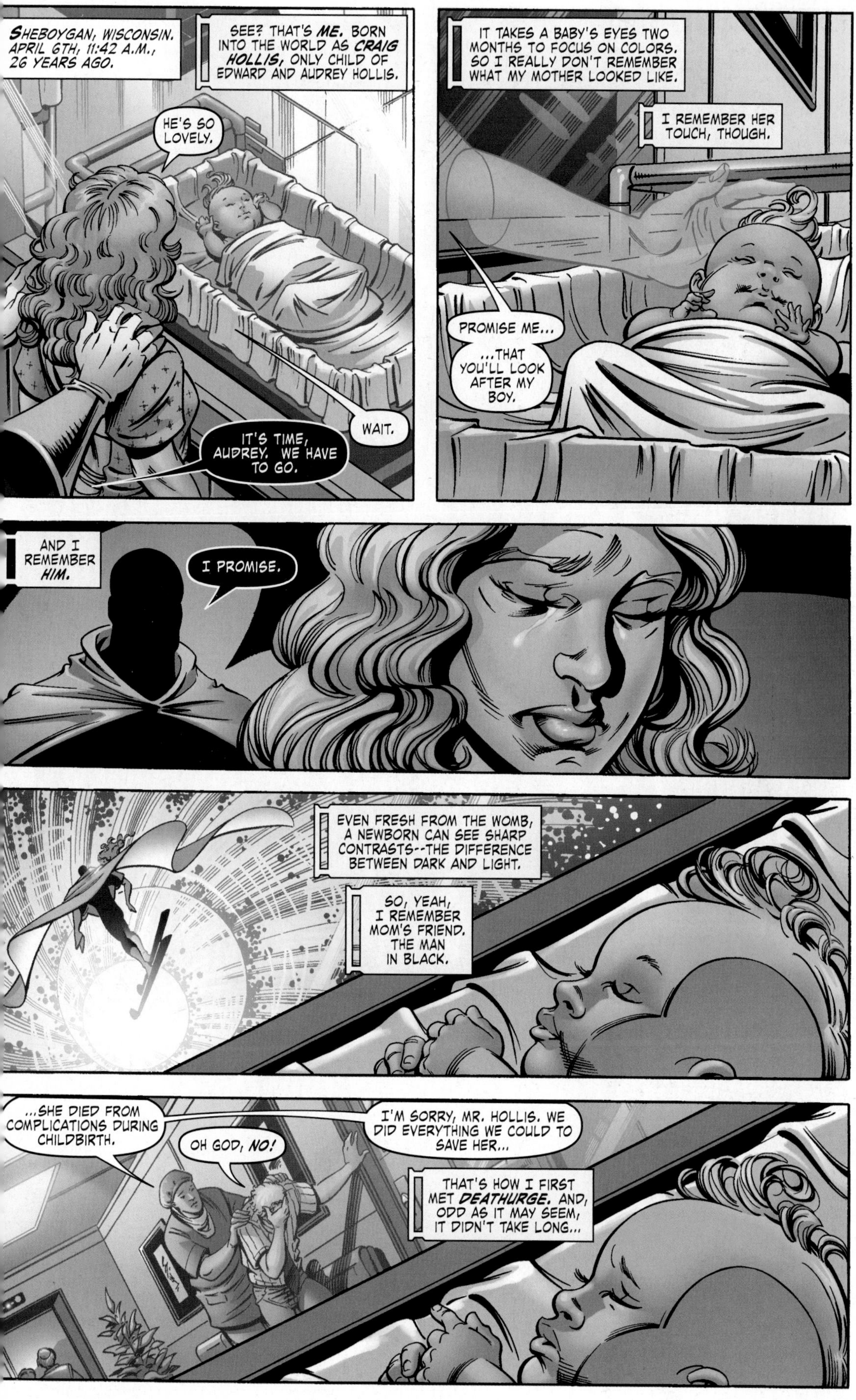

SHEBOYGAN, WISCONSIN. APRIL 6TH, 11:42 A.M., 26 YEARS AGO.
SEE? THAT'S ME. BORN INTO THE WORLD AS CRAIG HOLLIS, ONLY CHILD OF EDWARD AND AUDREY HOLLIS.
HE'S SO LOVELY.
WAIT.
IT'S TIME, AUDREY. WE HAVE TO GO.
IT TAKES A BABY'S EYES TWO MONTHS TO FOCUS ON COLORS. SO I REALLY DON'T REMEMBER WHAT MY MOTHER LOOKED LIKE.
I REMEMBER HER TOUCH, THOUGH.
PROMISE ME...
...THAT YOU'LL LOOK AFTER MY BOY.
AND I REMEMBER HIM.
I PROMISE.
EVEN FRESH FROM THE WOMB, A NEWBORN CAN SEE SHARP CONTRASTS--THE DIFFERENCE BETWEEN DARK AND LIGHT.
SO, YEAH, I REMEMBER MOM'S FRIEND. THE MAN IN BLACK.
I'M SORRY, MR. HOLLIS. WE DID EVERYTHING WE COULD TO SAVE HER...
...SHE DIED FROM COMPLICATIONS DURING CHILDBIRTH.
OH GOD, NO!
THAT'S HOW I FIRST MET DEATHURGE. AND, ODD AS IT MAY SEEM, IT DIDN'T TAKE LONG...

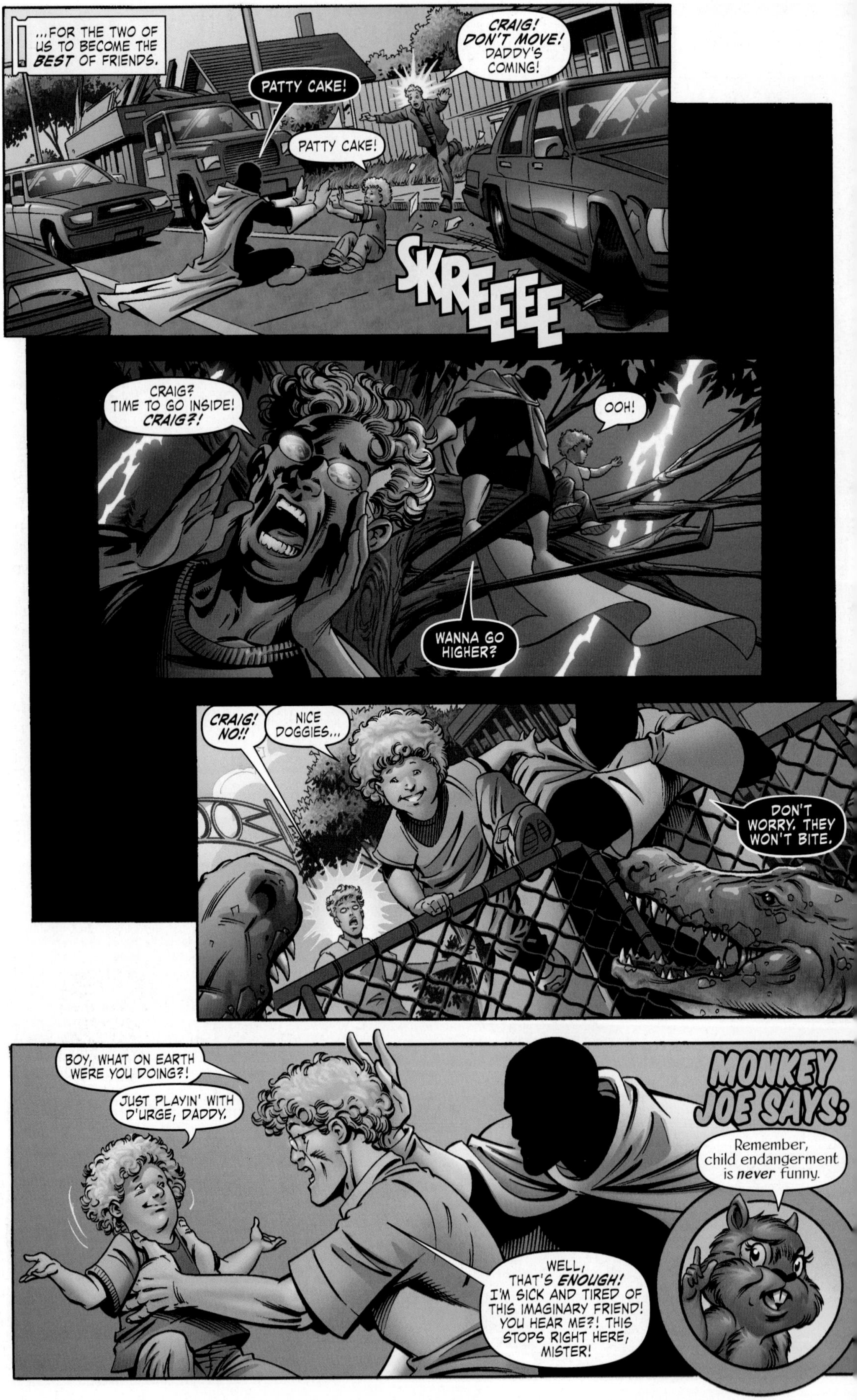
...FOR THE TWO OF US TO BECOME THE BEST OF FRIENDS.
CRAIG! DON'T MOVE! DADDY'S COMING!
PATTY CAKE!
PATTY CAKE!
SKREEEE
CRAIG? TIME TO GO INSIDE! CRAIG?!
OOH!
WANNA GO HIGHER?
CRAIG! NO!!
NICE DOGGIES...
DON'T WORRY. THEY WON'T BITE.
BOY, WHAT ON EARTH WERE YOU DOING?!
JUST PLAYIN' WITH D'URGE, DADDY.
MONKEY JOE SAYS:
Remember, child endangerment is never funny.
WELL, THAT'S ENOUGH! I'M SICK AND TIRED OF THIS IMAGINARY FRIEND! YOU HEAR ME?! THIS STOPS RIGHT HERE, MISTER!

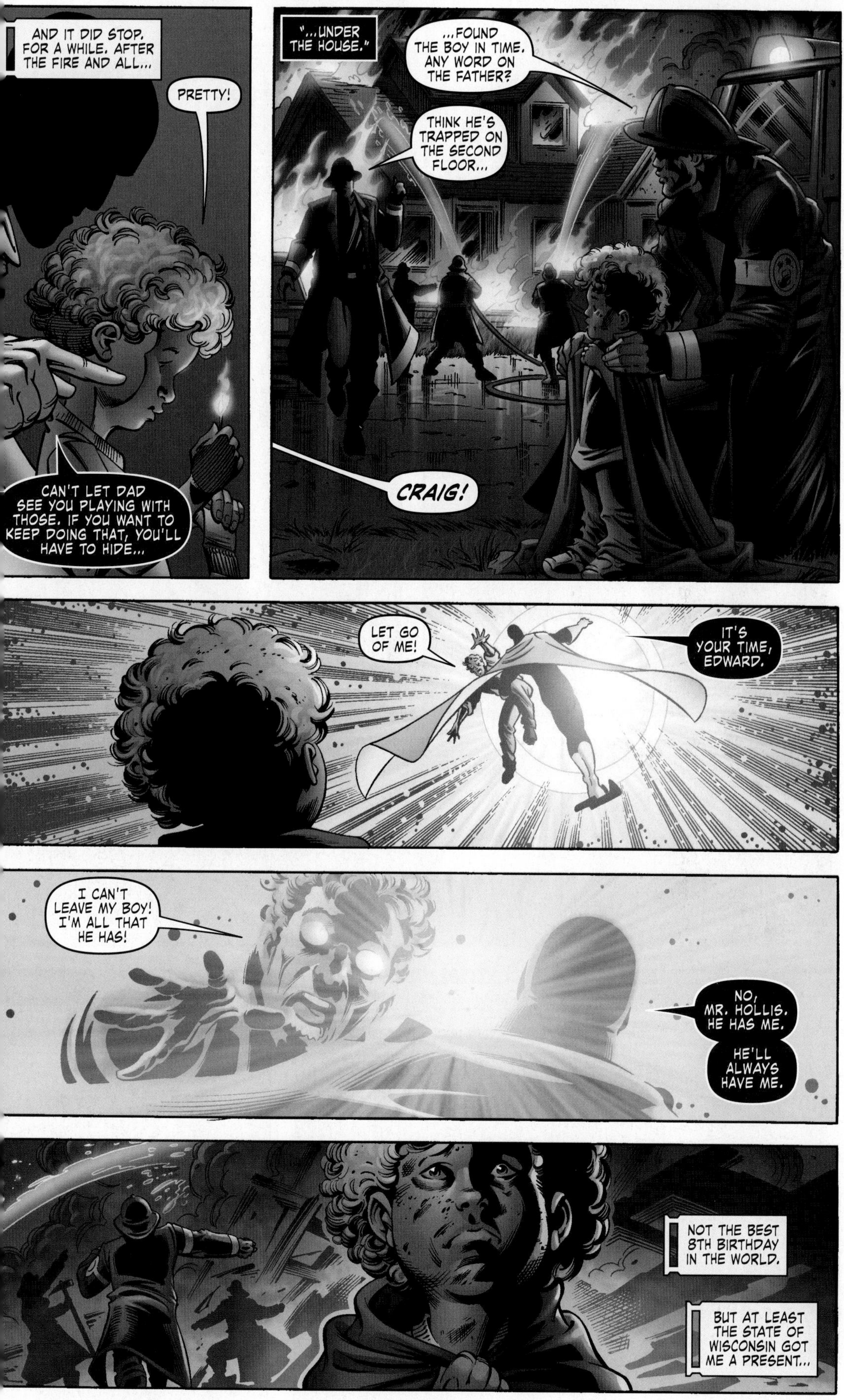
AND IT DID STOP. FOR A WHILE. AFTER THE FIRE AND ALL...
PRETTY!
CAN'T LET DAD SEE YOU PLAYING WITH THOSE. IF YOU WANT TO KEEP DOING THAT, YOU'LL HAVE TO HIDE...
"...UNDER THE HOUSE."
...FOUND THE BOY IN TIME. ANY WORD ON THE FATHER?
THINK HE'S TRAPPED ON THE SECOND FLOOR...
CRAIG!
LET GO OF ME!
IT'S YOUR TIME, EDWARD.
I CAN'T LEAVE MY BOY! I'M ALL THAT HE HAS!
NO, MR. HOLLIS. HE HAS ME.
HE'LL ALWAYS HAVE ME.
NOT THE BEST 8TH BIRTHDAY IN THE WORLD.
BUT AT LEAST THE STATE OF WISCONSIN GOT ME A PRESENT...

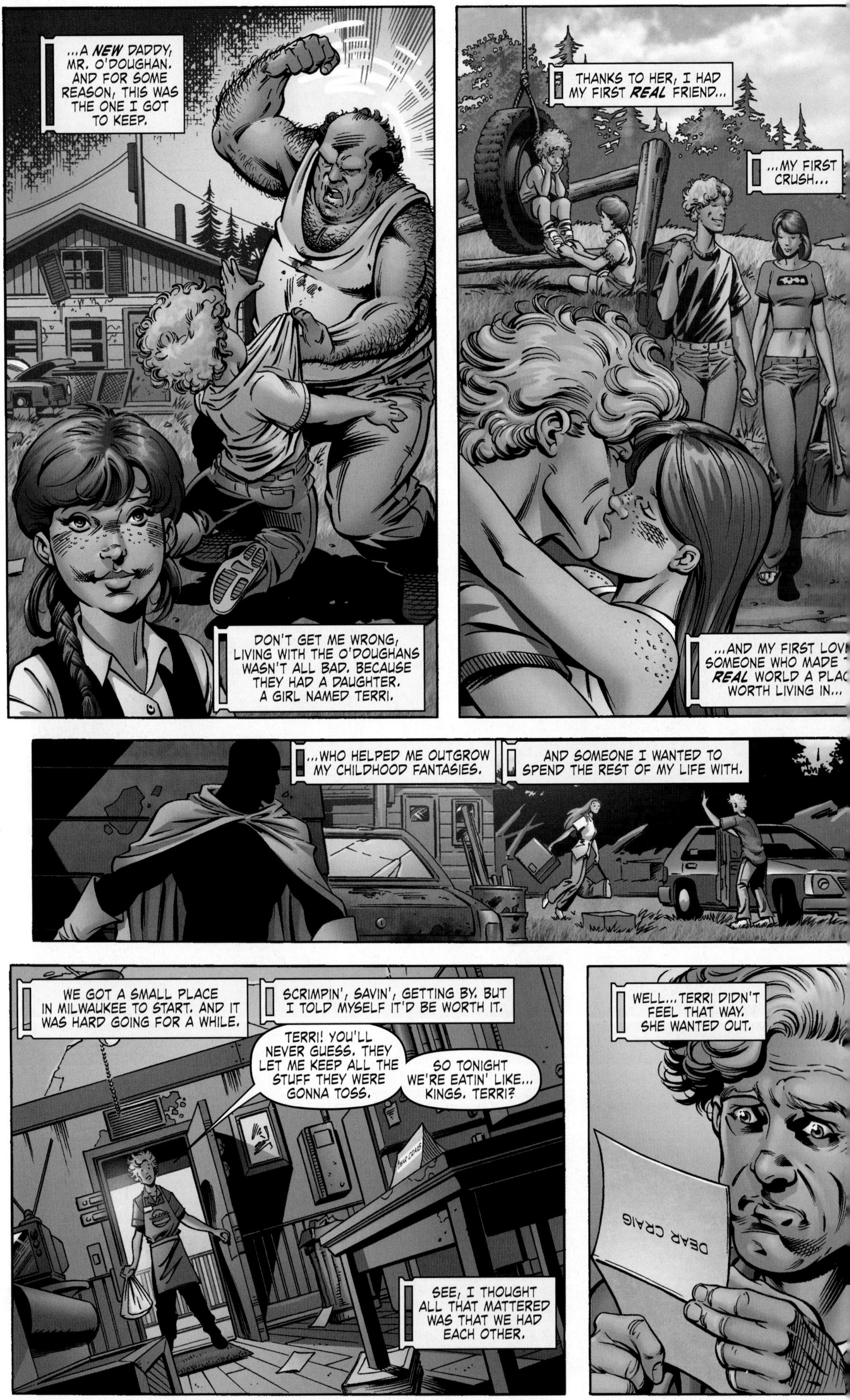
...A NEW DADDY, MR. O'DOUGHAN. AND FOR SOME REASON, THIS WAS THE ONE I GOT TO KEEP.
DON'T GET ME WRONG, LIVING WITH THE O'DOUGHANS WASN'T ALL BAD. BECAUSE THEY HAD A DAUGHTER. A GIRL NAMED TERRI.
THANKS TO HER, I HAD MY FIRST REAL FRIEND...
...MY FIRST CRUSH...
...AND MY FIRST LOV
SOMEONE WHO MADE
REAL WORLD A PLA
WORTH LIVING IN...
...WHO HELPED ME OUTGROW MY CHILDHOOD FANTASIES.
AND SOMEONE I WANTED TO SPEND THE REST OF MY LIFE WITH.
WE GOT A SMALL PLACE IN MILWAUKEE TO START. AND IT WAS HARD GOING FOR A WHILE.
SCRIMPIN', SAVIN', GETTING BY. BUT I TOLD MYSELF IT'D BE WORTH IT.
TERRI! YOU'LL NEVER GUESS. THEY LET ME KEEP ALL THE STUFF THEY WERE GONNA TOSS.
SO TONIGHT WE'RE EATIN' LIKE... KINGS. TERRI?
SEE, I THOUGHT ALL THAT MATTERED WAS THAT WE HAD EACH OTHER.
WELL...TERRI DIDN'T FEEL THAT WAY. SHE WANTED OUT.
DEAR CRAIG

AND I WANTED IT OVER.

ALL THE LOSS.

THE PAIN.

LOOK! UP THERE!

JUMP!

JUMP!

JUMP!

MONKEY JOE SAYS:

Killing yourself is stupid. When you die, that's it!

No more nuts for you! Be happy. Eat more nuts.

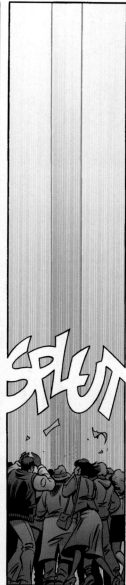

SPLUT

EEWWWW!

AAAAHHHH!

HEY! WHAT GIVES?!

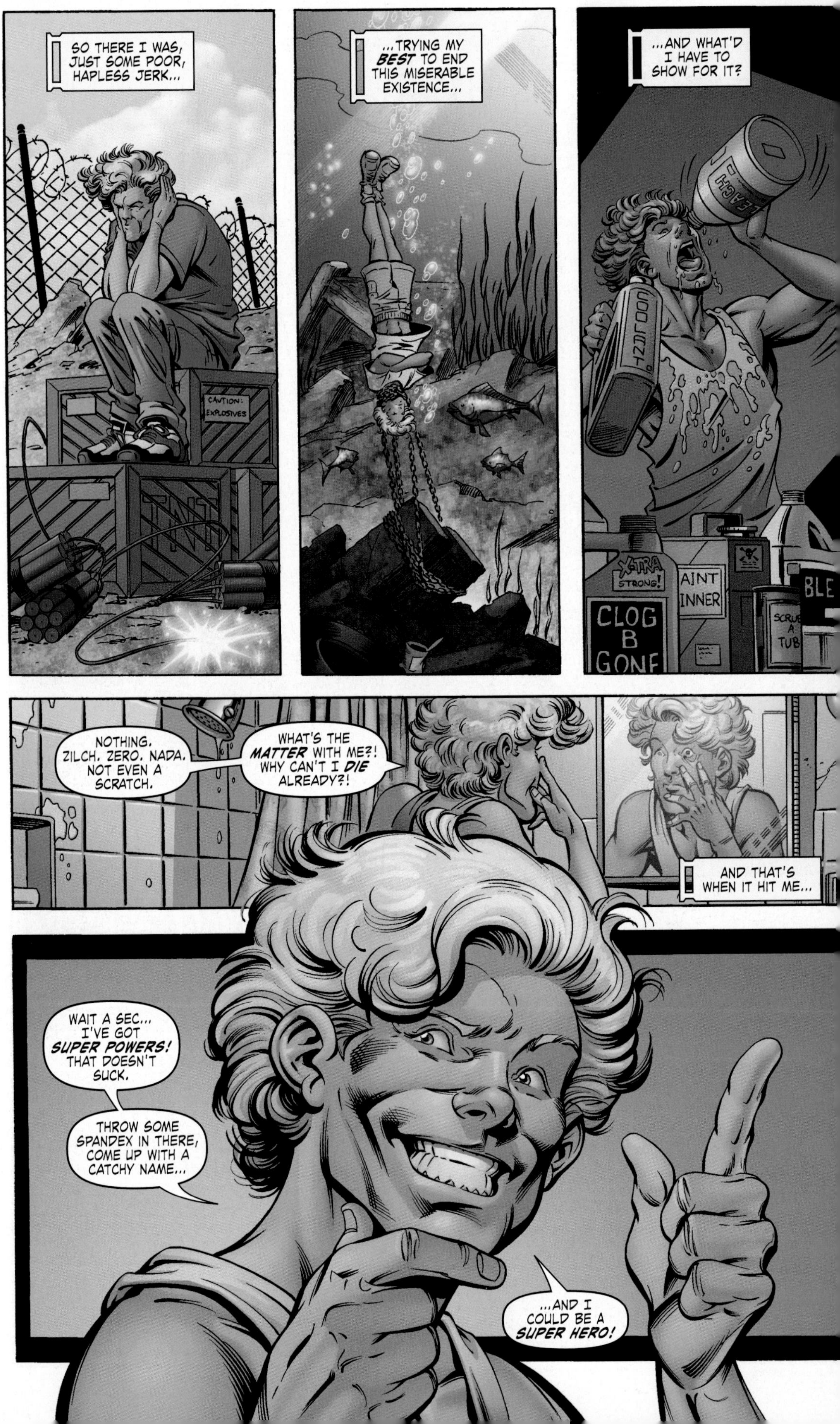
SO THERE I WAS, JUST SOME POOR, HAPLESS JERK...
CAUTION: EXPLOSIVES
TNT
...TRYING MY BEST TO END THIS MISERABLE EXISTENCE...
...AND WHAT'D I HAVE TO SHOW FOR IT?
COOLANT
X-TRA STRONG!
CLOG B GONE
AINT INNER
SCRUB A TUB
BLE
NOTHING. ZILCH. ZERO. NADA. NOT EVEN A SCRATCH.
WHAT'S THE MATTER WITH ME?! WHY CAN'T I DIE ALREADY?!
AND THAT'S WHEN IT HIT ME...
WAIT A SEC... I'VE GOT SUPER POWERS! THAT DOESN'T SUCK.
THROW SOME SPANDEX IN THERE, COME UP WITH A CATCHY NAME...
...AND I COULD BE A SUPER HERO!

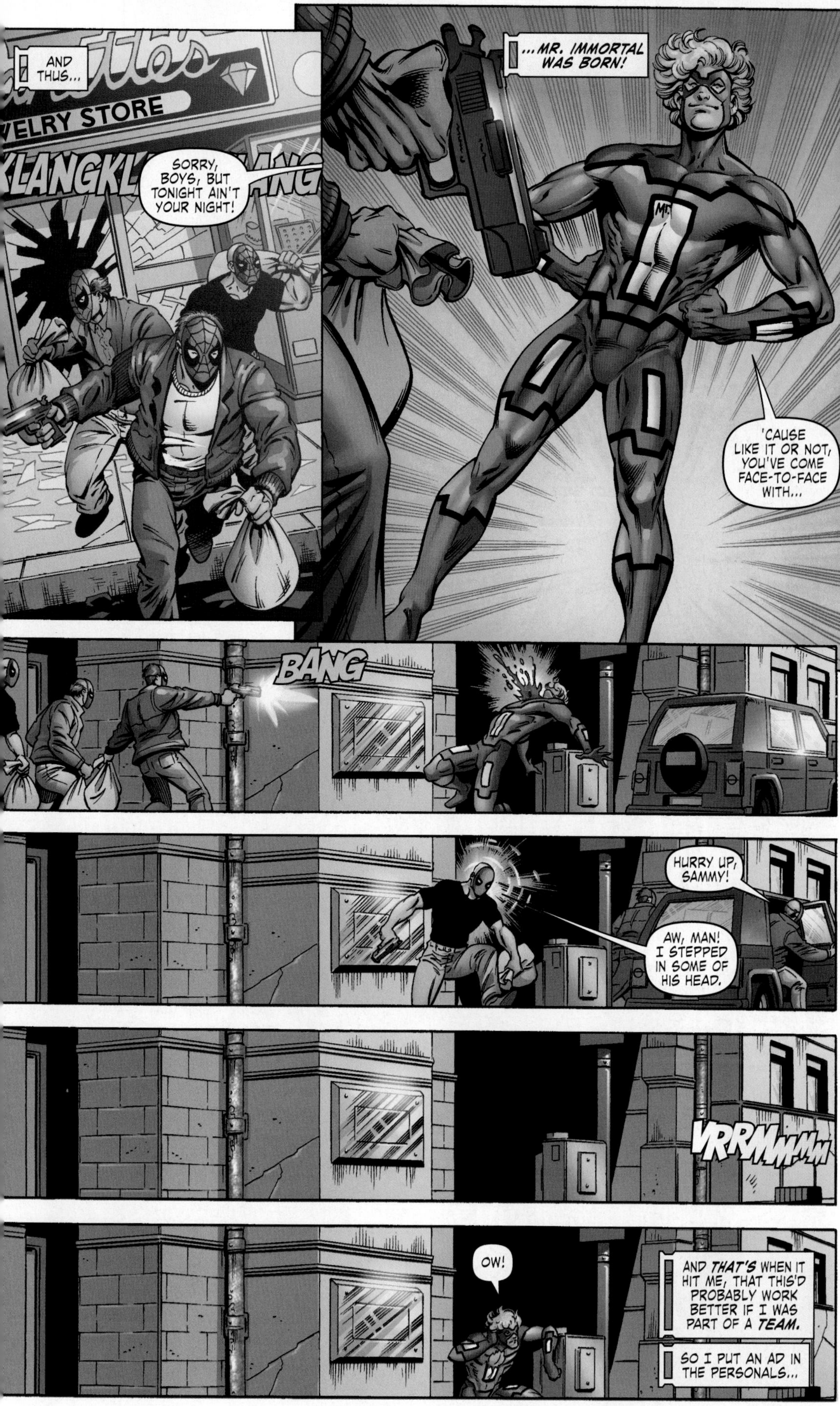

...ELRY STORE
AND THUS...
KLANGKL...ANG
SORRY, BOYS, BUT TONIGHT AIN'T YOUR NIGHT!
...MR. IMMORTAL WAS BORN!
'CAUSE LIKE IT OR NOT, YOU'VE COME FACE-TO-FACE WITH...
BANG
HURRY UP, SAMMY!
AW, MAN! I STEPPED IN SOME OF HIS HEAD.
VRRMMMMM
OW!
AND THAT'S WHEN IT HIT ME, THAT THIS'D PROBABLY WORK BETTER IF I WAS PART OF A TEAM.
SO I PUT AN AD IN THE PERSONALS...

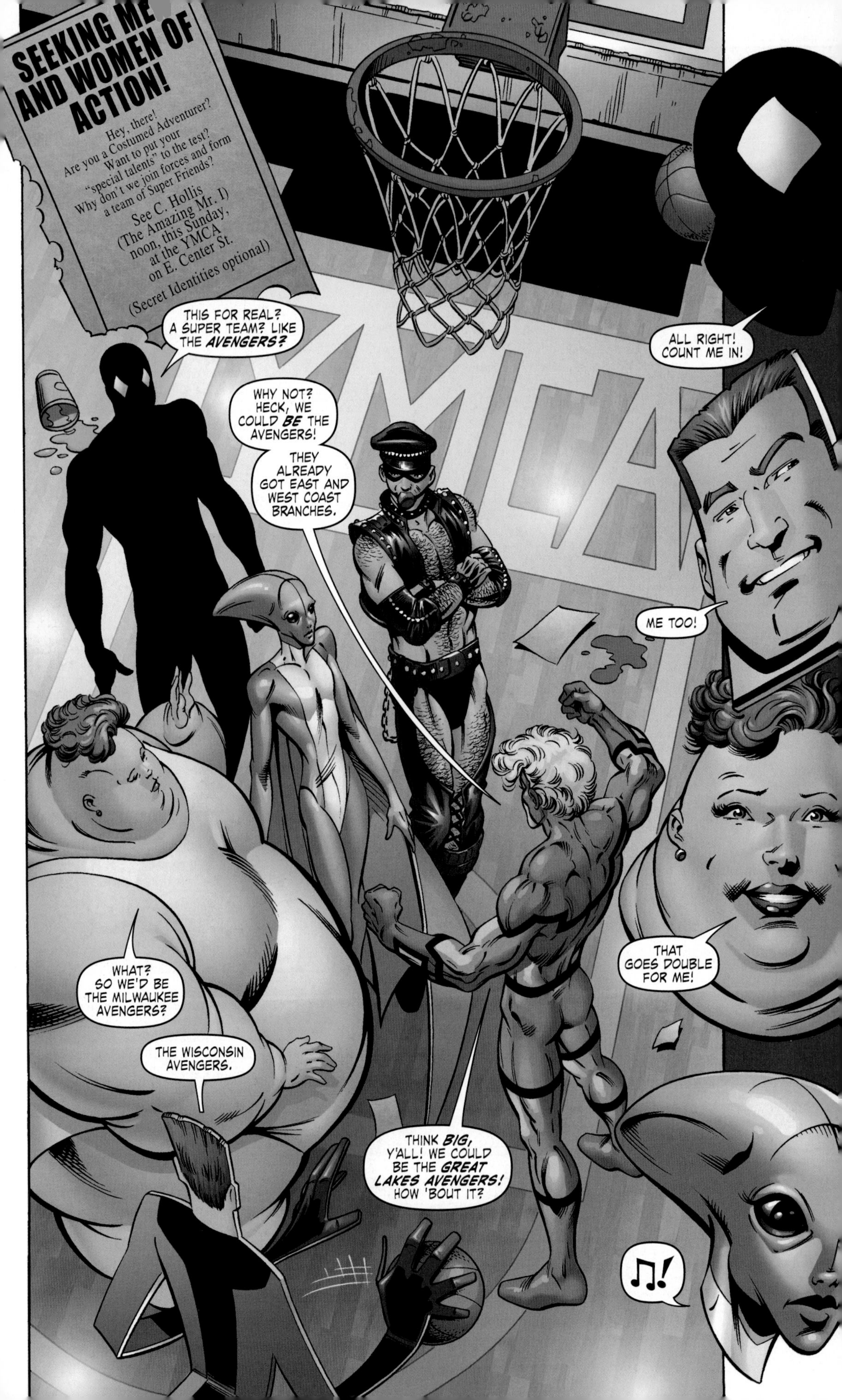
SEEKING ME AND WOMEN OF ACTION!
Hey, there! Are you a Costumed Adventurer? Want to put your "special talents" to the test? Why don't we join forces and form a team of Super Friends?
See C. Hollis (The Amazing Mr. I) noon, this Sunday, at the YMCA on E. Center St.
(Secret Identities optional)
THIS FOR REAL? A SUPER TEAM? LIKE THE AVENGERS?
WHY NOT? HECK, WE COULD BE THE AVENGERS!
THEY ALREADY GOT EAST AND WEST COAST BRANCHES.
ALL RIGHT! COUNT ME IN!
ME TOO!
THAT GOES DOUBLE FOR ME!
WHAT? SO WE'D BE THE MILWAUKEE AVENGERS?
THE WISCONSIN AVENGERS.
THINK BIG, Y'ALL! WE COULD BE THE GREAT LAKES AVENGERS! HOW 'BOUT IT?
♫!
YMCA

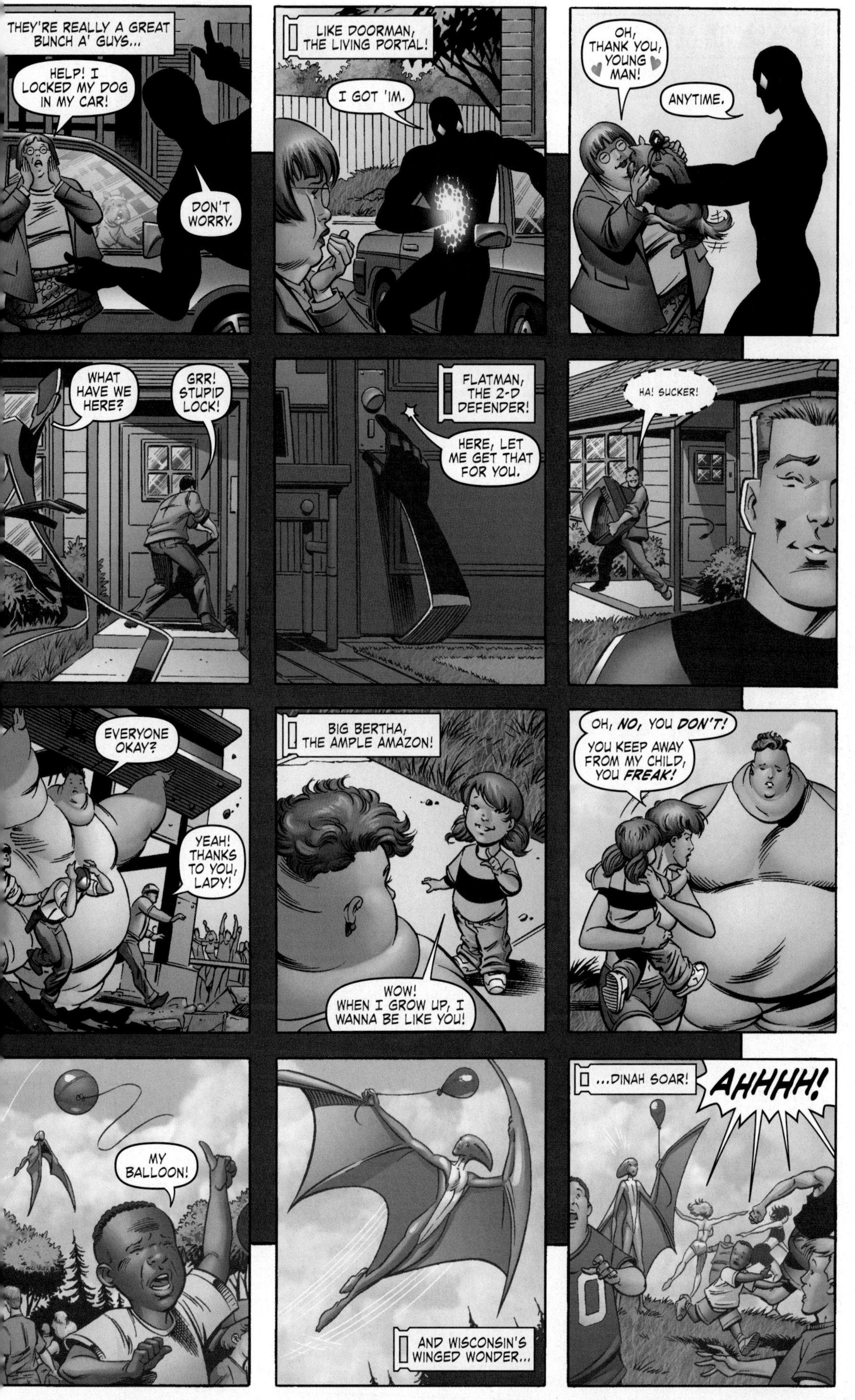
THEY'RE REALLY A GREAT BUNCH A' GUYS...
HELP! I LOCKED MY DOG IN MY CAR!
DON'T WORRY.
LIKE DOORMAN, THE LIVING PORTAL!
I GOT 'IM.
OH, THANK YOU, YOUNG MAN!
ANYTIME.
WHAT HAVE WE HERE?
GRR! STUPID LOCK!
FLATMAN, THE 2-D DEFENDER!
HERE, LET ME GET THAT FOR YOU.
HA! SUCKER!
EVERYONE OKAY?
YEAH! THANKS TO YOU, LADY!
BIG BERTHA, THE AMPLE AMAZON!
WOW! WHEN I GROW UP, I WANNA BE LIKE YOU!
OH, NO, YOU DON'T!
YOU KEEP AWAY FROM MY CHILD, YOU FREAK!
MY BALLOON!
AND WISCONSIN'S WINGED WONDER...
...DINAH SOAR!
AHHHH!

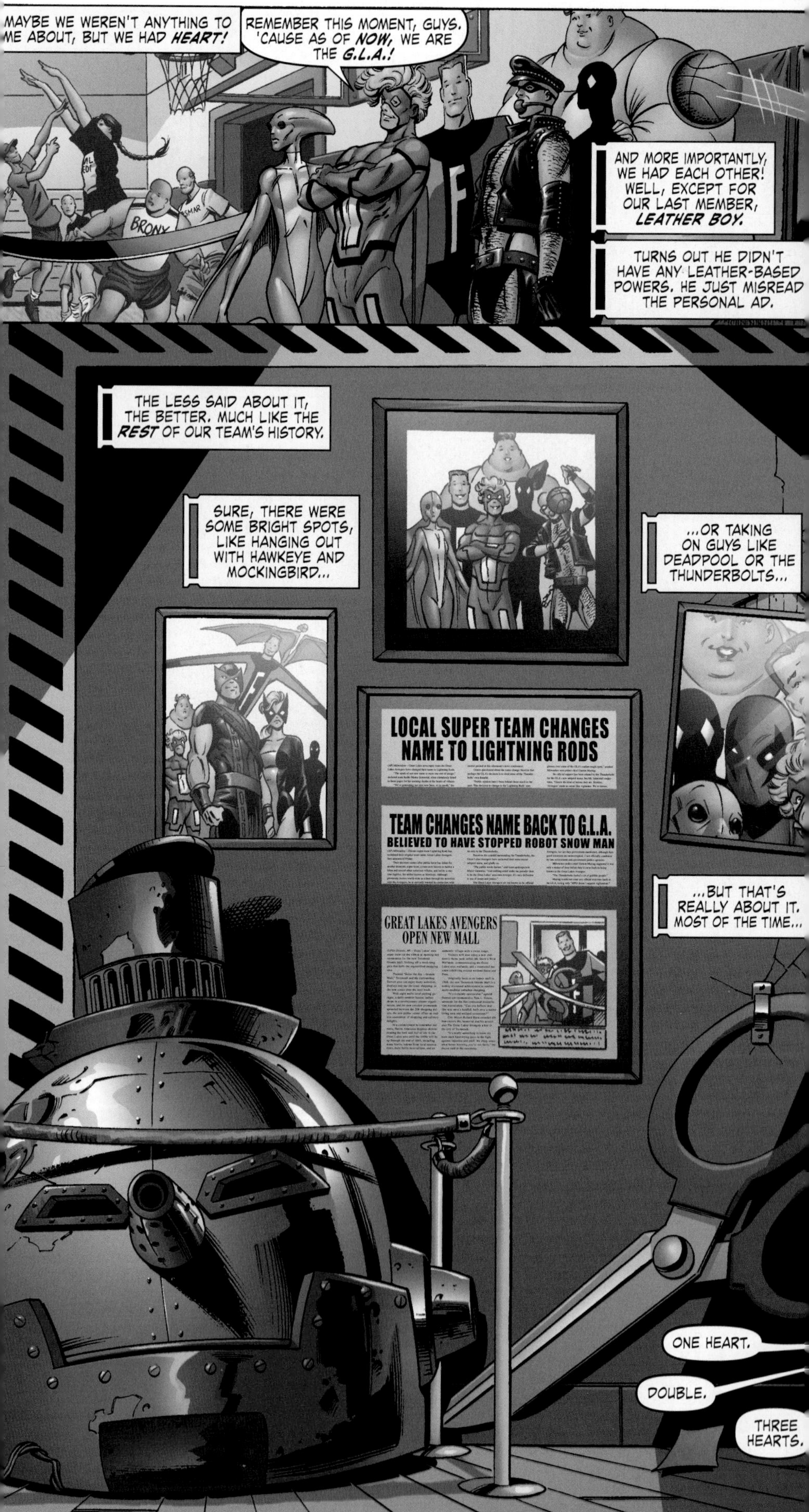
MAYBE WE WEREN'T ANYTHING TO ME ABOUT, BUT WE HAD HEART!
REMEMBER THIS MOMENT, GUYS. 'CAUSE AS OF NOW, WE ARE THE G.L.A.!
AND MORE IMPORTANTLY, WE HAD EACH OTHER! WELL, EXCEPT FOR OUR LAST MEMBER, LEATHER BOY.
TURNS OUT HE DIDN'T HAVE ANY LEATHER-BASED POWERS. HE JUST MISREAD THE PERSONAL AD.
THE LESS SAID ABOUT IT, THE BETTER. MUCH LIKE THE REST OF OUR TEAM'S HISTORY.
SURE, THERE WERE SOME BRIGHT SPOTS, LIKE HANGING OUT WITH HAWKEYE AND MOCKINGBIRD...
...OR TAKING ON GUYS LIKE DEADPOOL OR THE THUNDERBOLTS...
LOCAL SUPER TEAM CHANGES NAME TO LIGHTNING RODS
TEAM CHANGES NAME BACK TO G.L.A.
BELIEVED TO HAVE STOPPED ROBOT SNOW MAN
GREAT LAKES AVENGERS OPEN NEW MALL
...BUT THAT'S REALLY ABOUT IT. MOST OF THE TIME...
ONE HEART.
DOUBLE.
THREE HEARTS.

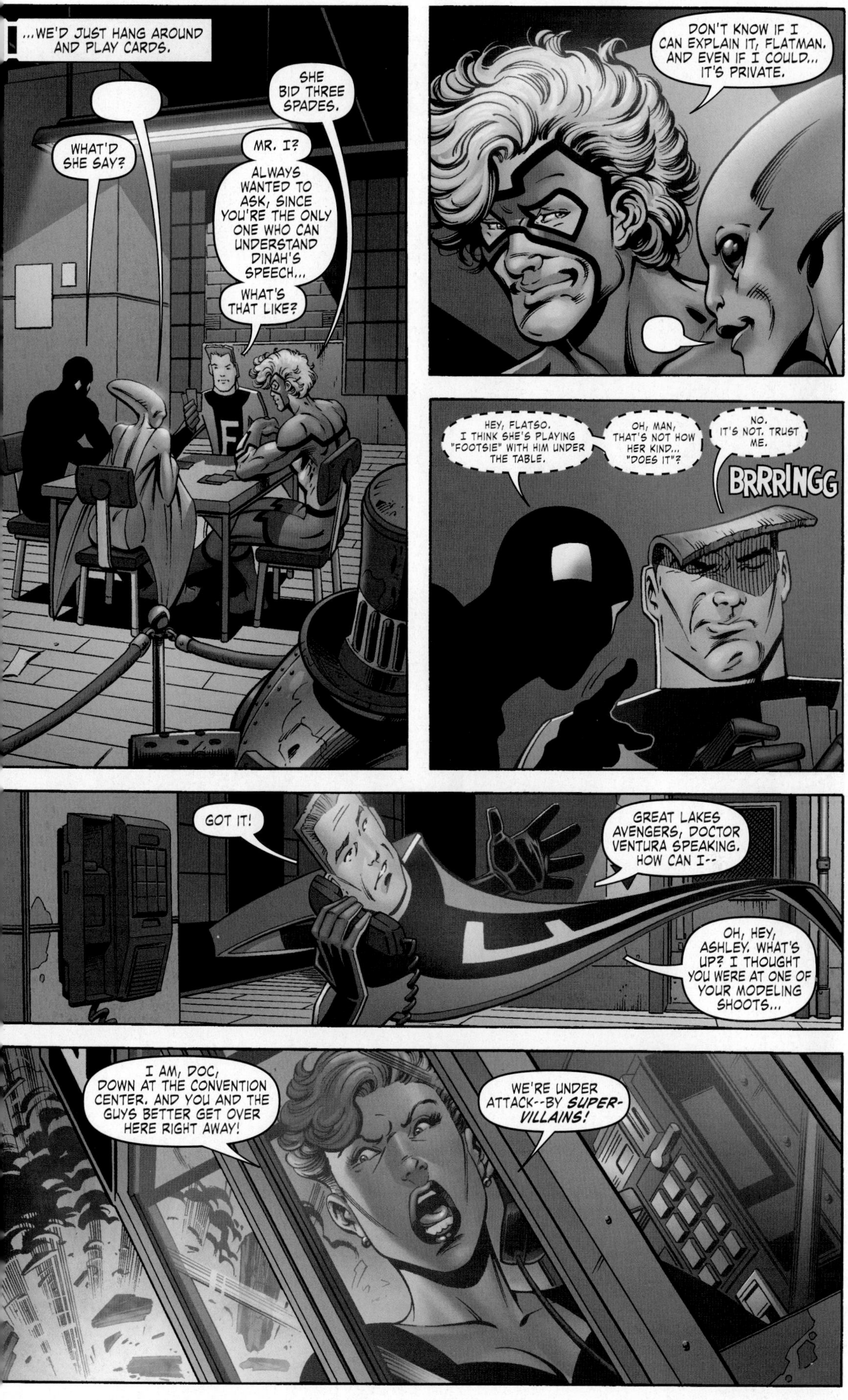
...WE'D JUST HANG AROUND AND PLAY CARDS.
WHAT'D SHE SAY?
SHE BID THREE SPADES.
MR. I? ALWAYS WANTED TO ASK, SINCE YOU'RE THE ONLY ONE WHO CAN UNDERSTAND DINAH'S SPEECH...
WHAT'S THAT LIKE?
DON'T KNOW IF I CAN EXPLAIN IT, FLATMAN. AND EVEN IF I COULD... IT'S PRIVATE.
HEY, FLATSO. I THINK SHE'S PLAYING "FOOTSIE" WITH HIM UNDER THE TABLE.
OH, MAN, THAT'S NOT HOW HER KIND... "DOES IT"?
NO. IT'S NOT. TRUST ME.
BRRRINGG
GOT IT!
GREAT LAKES AVENGERS, DOCTOR VENTURA SPEAKING. HOW CAN I--
OH, HEY, ASHLEY. WHAT'S UP? I THOUGHT YOU WERE AT ONE OF YOUR MODELING SHOOTS...
I AM, DOC, DOWN AT THE CONVENTION CENTER. AND YOU AND THE GUYS BETTER GET OVER HERE RIGHT AWAY!
WE'RE UNDER ATTACK--BY SUPER-VILLAINS!

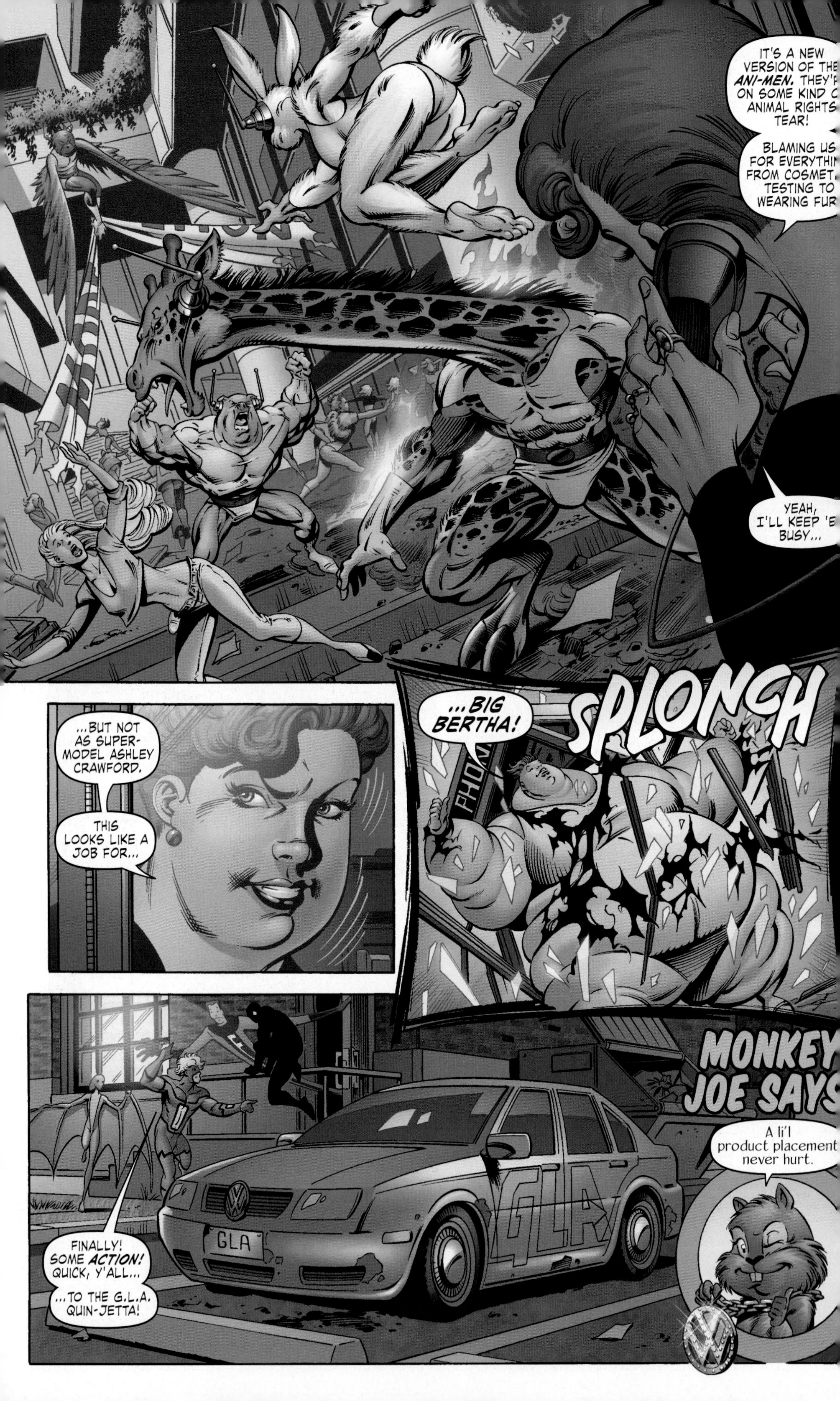
IT'S A NEW VERSION OF THE ANI-MEN. THEY'R ON SOME KIND O ANIMAL RIGHTS TEAR!
BLAMING US FOR EVERYTHIN FROM COSMET TESTING TO WEARING FUR
YEAH, I'LL KEEP 'E BUSY...
...BUT NOT AS SUPER-MODEL ASHLEY CRAWFORD.
THIS LOOKS LIKE A JOB FOR...
...BIG BERTHA!
SPLONCH
MONKEY JOE SAYS
A li'l product placement never hurt.
FINALLY! SOME ACTION! QUICK, Y'ALL...
...TO THE G.L.A. QUIN-JETTA!
GLA

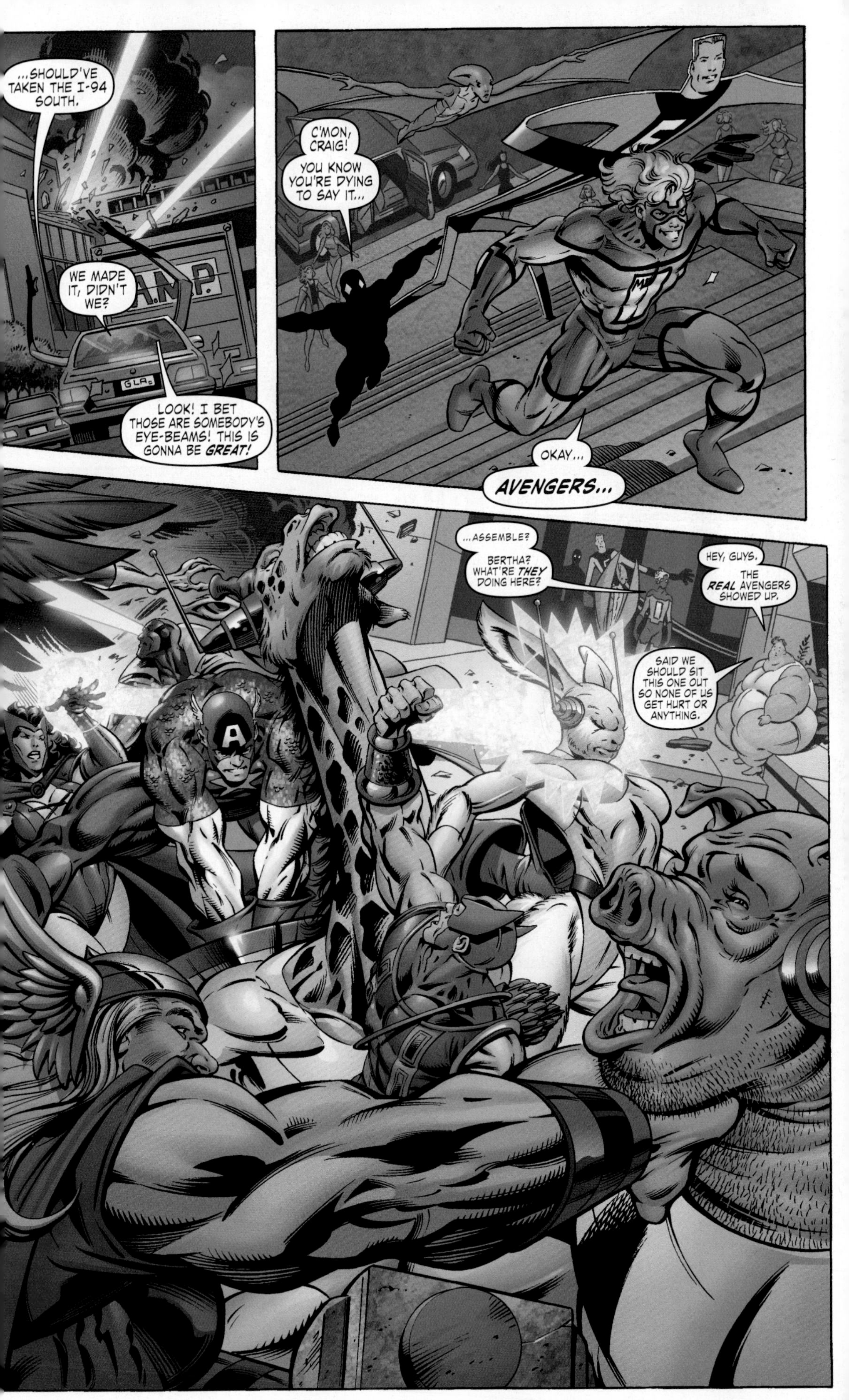

...SHOULD'VE TAKEN THE I-94 SOUTH.
WE MADE IT, DIDN'T WE?
LOOK! I BET THOSE ARE SOMEBODY'S EYE-BEAMS! THIS IS GONNA BE GREAT!
C'MON, CRAIG!
YOU KNOW YOU'RE DYING TO SAY IT...
OKAY...
AVENGERS...
...ASSEMBLE?
BERTHA? WHAT'RE THEY DOING HERE?
HEY, GUYS.
THE REAL AVENGERS SHOWED UP.
SAID WE SHOULD SIT THIS ONE OUT SO NONE OF US GET HURT OR ANYTHING.

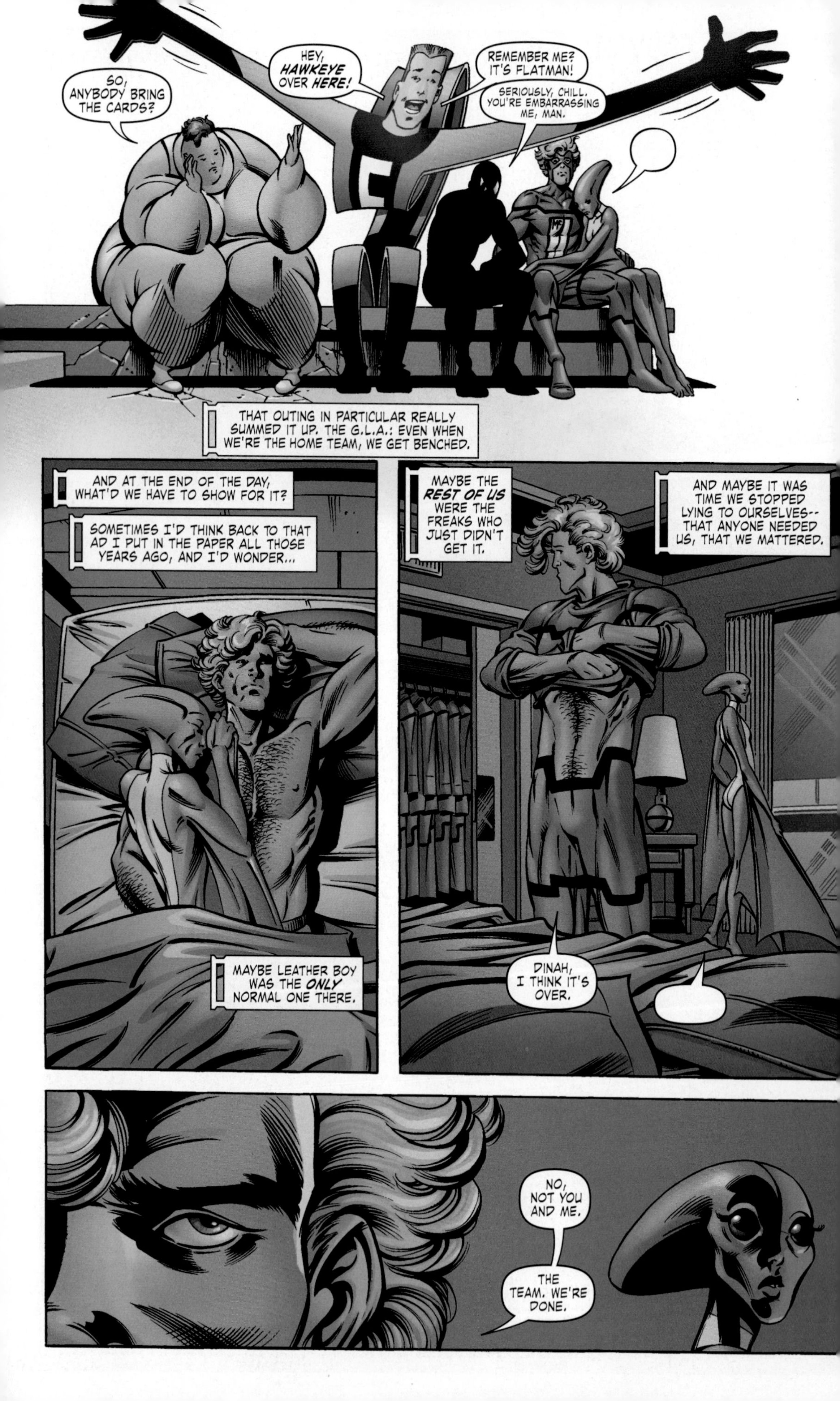
SO, ANYBODY BRING THE CARDS?
HEY, HAWKEYE OVER HERE!
REMEMBER ME? IT'S FLATMAN!
SERIOUSLY, CHILL. YOU'RE EMBARRASSING ME, MAN.
THAT OUTING IN PARTICULAR REALLY SUMMED IT UP. THE G.L.A.: EVEN WHEN WE'RE THE HOME TEAM, WE GET BENCHED.
AND AT THE END OF THE DAY, WHAT'D WE HAVE TO SHOW FOR IT?
SOMETIMES I'D THINK BACK TO THAT AD I PUT IN THE PAPER ALL THOSE YEARS AGO, AND I'D WONDER...
MAYBE LEATHER BOY WAS THE ONLY NORMAL ONE THERE.
MAYBE THE REST OF US WERE THE FREAKS WHO JUST DIDN'T GET IT.
AND MAYBE IT WAS TIME WE STOPPED LYING TO OURSELVES-- THAT ANYONE NEEDED US, THAT WE MATTERED.
DINAH, I THINK IT'S OVER.
NO, NOT YOU AND ME.
THE TEAM. WE'RE DONE.

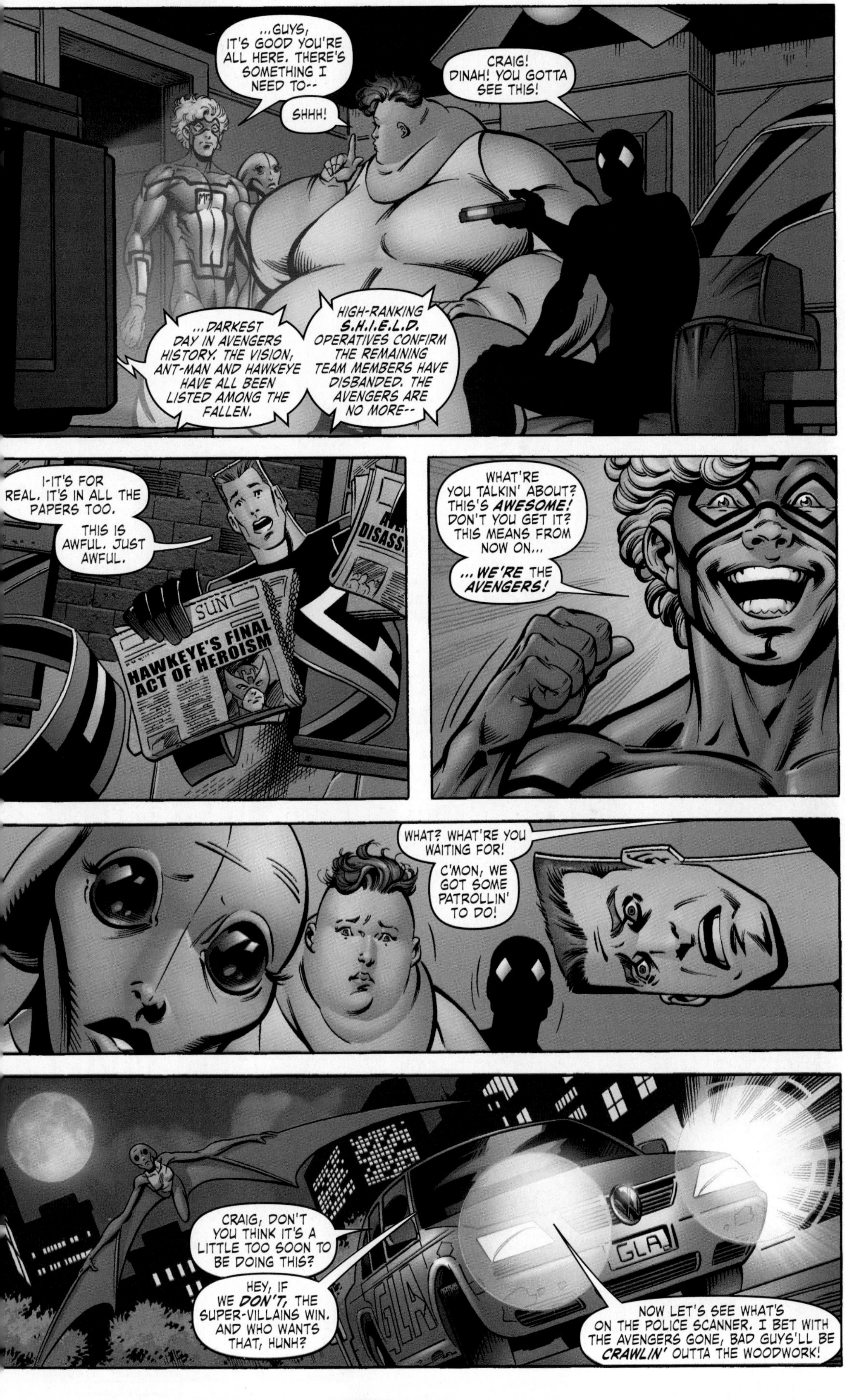
...GUYS, IT'S GOOD YOU'RE ALL HERE. THERE'S SOMETHING I NEED TO--
SHHH!
CRAIG! DINAH! YOU GOTTA SEE THIS!
...DARKEST DAY IN AVENGERS HISTORY. THE VISION, ANT-MAN AND HAWKEYE HAVE ALL BEEN LISTED AMONG THE FALLEN.
HIGH-RANKING S.H.I.E.L.D. OPERATIVES CONFIRM THE REMAINING TEAM MEMBERS HAVE DISBANDED. THE AVENGERS ARE NO MORE--
I-IT'S FOR REAL. IT'S IN ALL THE PAPERS TOO.
THIS IS AWFUL. JUST AWFUL.
SUN
HAWKEYE'S FINAL ACT OF HEROISM
WHAT'RE YOU TALKIN' ABOUT? THIS'S AWESOME! DON'T YOU GET IT? THIS MEANS FROM NOW ON...
...WE'RE THE AVENGERS!
WHAT? WHAT'RE YOU WAITING FOR!
C'MON, WE GOT SOME PATROLLIN' TO DO!
CRAIG, DON'T YOU THINK IT'S A LITTLE TOO SOON TO BE DOING THIS?
HEY, IF WE DON'T, THE SUPER-VILLAINS WIN. AND WHO WANTS THAT, HUNH?
NOW LET'S SEE WHAT'S ON THE POLICE SCANNER. I BET WITH THE AVENGERS GONE, BAD GUYS'LL BE CRAWLIN' OUTTA THE WOODWORK!
GLA

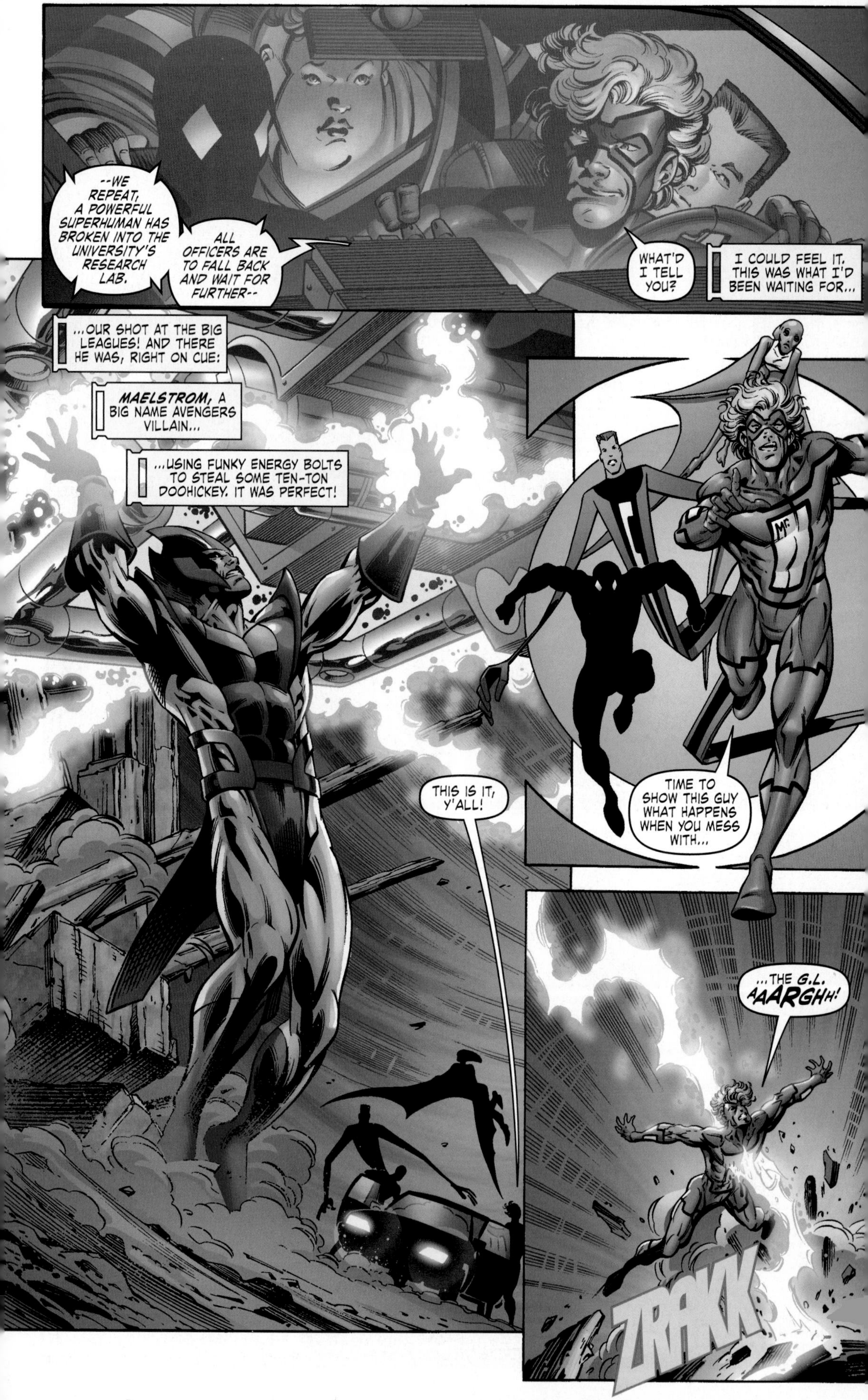
--WE REPEAT, A POWERFUL SUPERHUMAN HAS BROKEN INTO THE UNIVERSITY'S RESEARCH LAB.
ALL OFFICERS ARE TO FALL BACK AND WAIT FOR FURTHER--
WHAT'D I TELL YOU?
I COULD FEEL IT. THIS WAS WHAT I'D BEEN WAITING FOR...
...OUR SHOT AT THE BIG LEAGUES! AND THERE HE WAS, RIGHT ON CUE:
MAELSTROM, A BIG NAME AVENGERS VILLAIN...
...USING FUNKY ENERGY BOLTS TO STEAL SOME TEN-TON DOOHICKEY. IT WAS PERFECT!
THIS IS IT, Y'ALL!
TIME TO SHOW THIS GUY WHAT HAPPENS WHEN YOU MESS WITH...
...THE G.L. AAARGHH!
ZRAKK

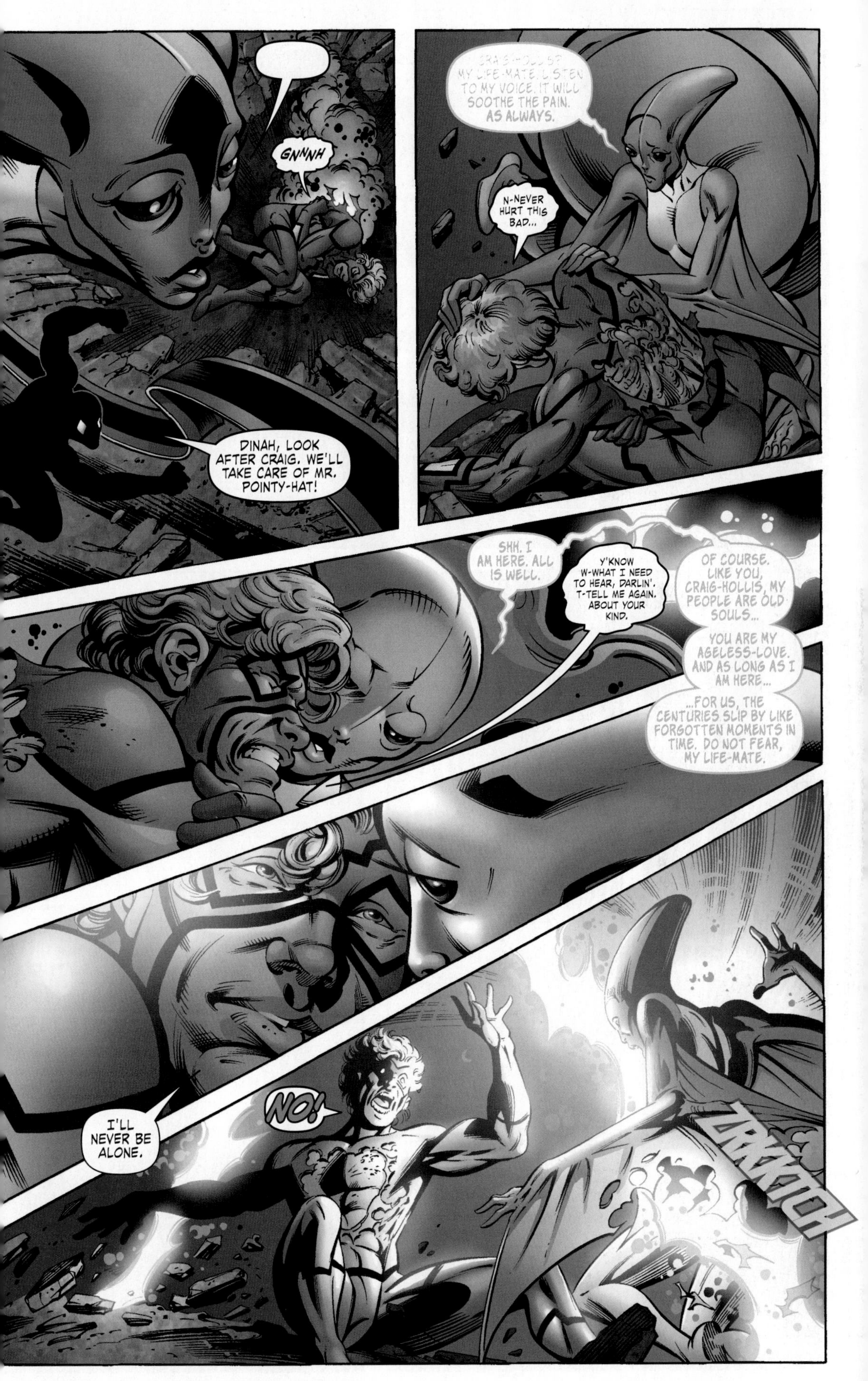
GNNNH
DINAH, LOOK AFTER CRAIG. WE'LL TAKE CARE OF MR. POINTY-HAT!
MY LIFE-MATE. LISTEN TO MY VOICE. IT WILL SOOTHE THE PAIN. AS ALWAYS.
N-NEVER HURT THIS BAD...
SHH. I AM HERE. ALL IS WELL.
Y'KNOW W-WHAT I NEED TO HEAR, DARLIN'. T-TELL ME AGAIN. ABOUT YOUR KIND.
OF COURSE. LIKE YOU, CRAIG-HOLLIS, MY PEOPLE ARE OLD SOULS...
YOU ARE MY AGELESS-LOVE. AND AS LONG AS I AM HERE...
...FOR US, THE CENTURIES SLIP BY LIKE FORGOTTEN MOMENTS IN TIME. DO NOT FEAR, MY LIFE-MATE.
I'LL NEVER BE ALONE.
NO!
ZRKKTCH!

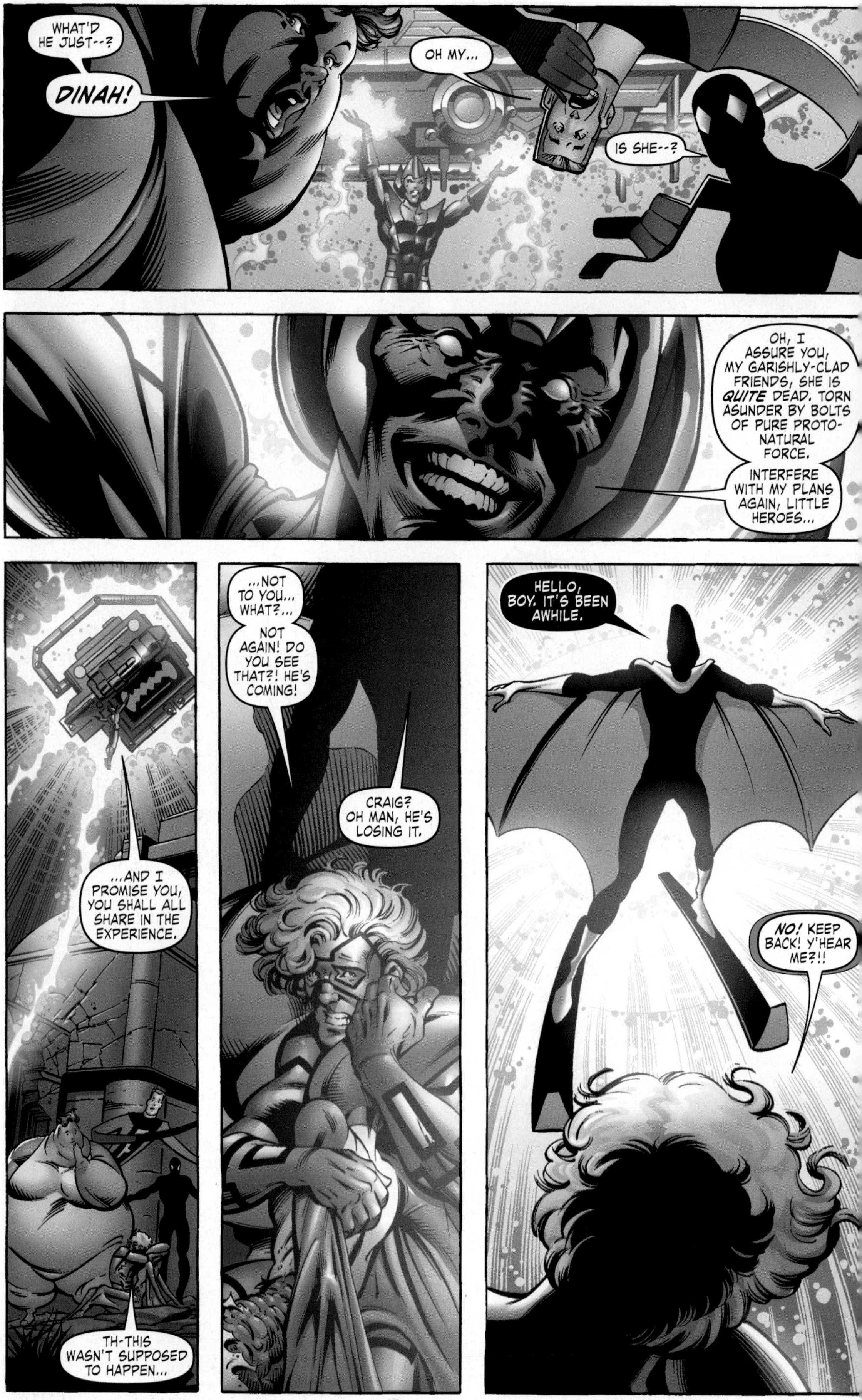

WHAT'D HE JUST--?
DINAH!
OH MY...
IS SHE--?
OH, I ASSURE YOU, MY GARISHLY-CLAD FRIENDS, SHE IS QUITE DEAD. TORN ASUNDER BY BOLTS OF PURE PROTO-NATURAL FORCE.
INTERFERE WITH MY PLANS AGAIN, LITTLE HEROES...
...AND I PROMISE YOU, YOU SHALL ALL SHARE IN THE EXPERIENCE.
TH-THIS WASN'T SUPPOSED TO HAPPEN...
...NOT TO YOU... WHAT?...
NOT AGAIN! DO YOU SEE THAT?! HE'S COMING!
CRAIG? OH MAN, HE'S LOSING IT.
HELLO, BOY. IT'S BEEN AWHILE.
NO! KEEP BACK! Y'HEAR ME?!!

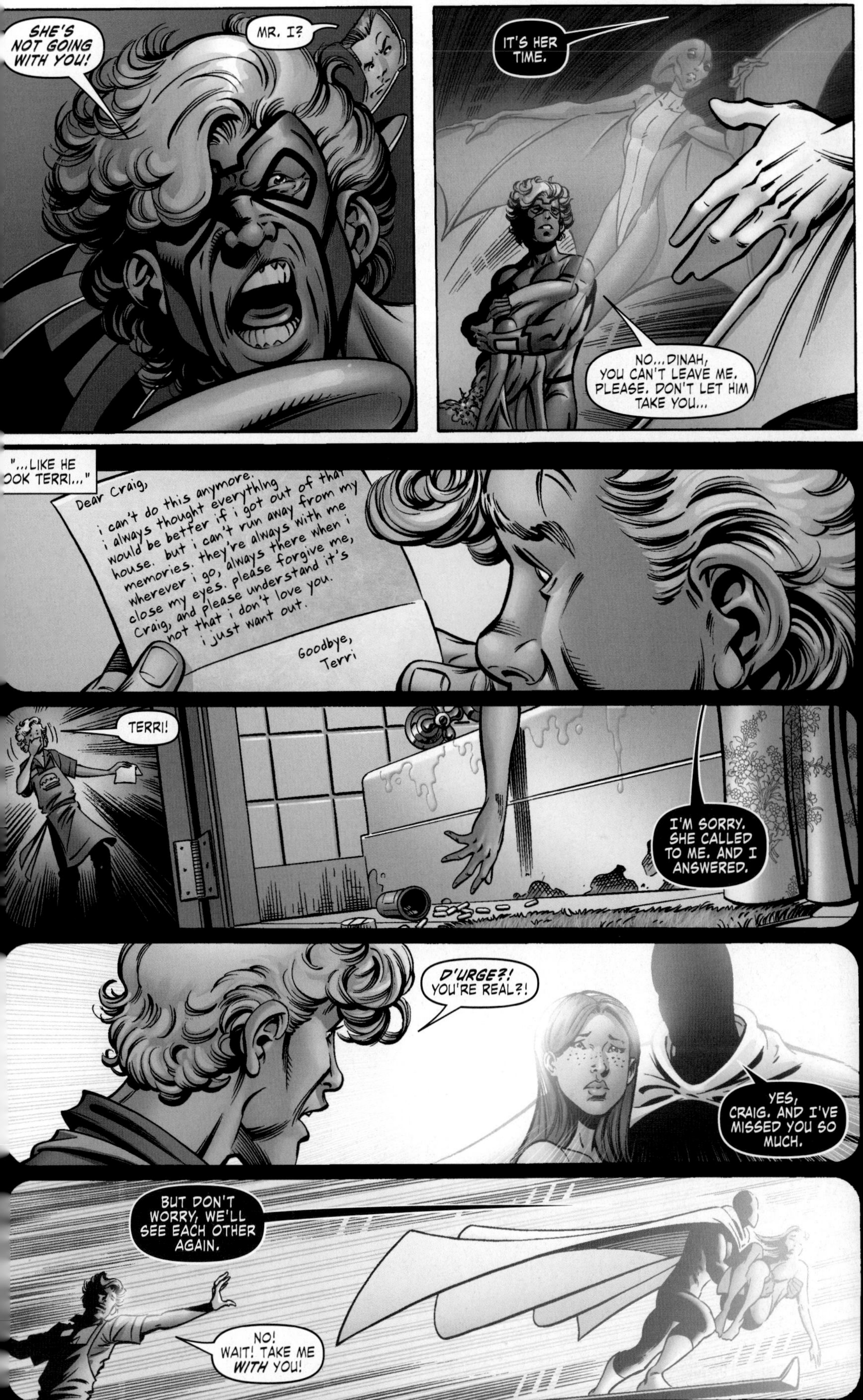

SHE'S NOT GOING WITH YOU!
MR. I?
IT'S HER TIME.
NO...DINAH, YOU CAN'T LEAVE ME. PLEASE. DON'T LET HIM TAKE YOU...
"...LIKE HE OOK TERRI..."
Dear Craig,
i can't do this anymore. i always thought everything would be better if i got out of that house. but i can't run away from my memories. they're always with me wherever i go, always there when i close my eyes. please forgive me, Craig, and please understand it's not that i don't love you. i just want out.
Goodbye, Terri
TERRI!
I'M SORRY. SHE CALLED TO ME. AND I ANSWERED.
D'URGE?! YOU'RE REAL?!
YES, CRAIG. AND I'VE MISSED YOU SO MUCH.
BUT DON'T WORRY, WE'LL SEE EACH OTHER AGAIN.
NO! WAIT! TAKE ME WITH YOU!

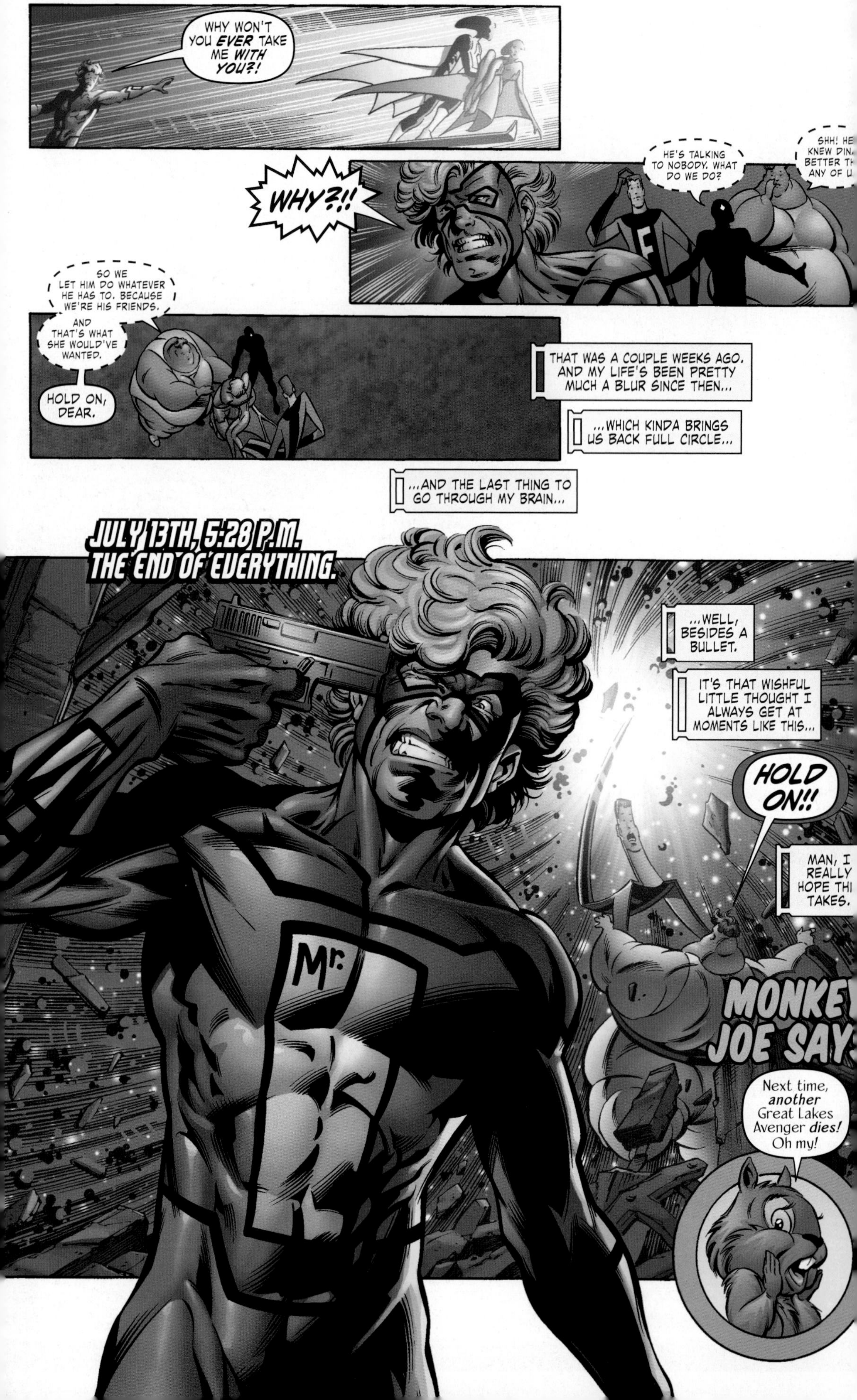

WHY WON'T YOU *EVER* TAKE ME *WITH YOU?!*
WHY?!!
HE'S TALKING TO NOBODY. WHAT DO WE DO?
SHH! HE KNEW DIN BETTER T ANY OF U
SO WE LET HIM DO WHATEVER HE HAS TO. BECAUSE WE'RE HIS FRIENDS.
AND THAT'S WHAT SHE WOULD'VE WANTED.
HOLD ON, DEAR.
THAT WAS A COUPLE WEEKS AGO. AND MY LIFE'S BEEN PRETTY MUCH A BLUR SINCE THEN...
...WHICH KINDA BRINGS US BACK FULL CIRCLE...
...AND THE LAST THING TO GO THROUGH MY BRAIN...
JULY 13TH, 5:28 P.M. THE END OF EVERYTHING.
...WELL, BESIDES A BULLET.
IT'S THAT WISHFUL LITTLE THOUGHT I ALWAYS GET AT MOMENTS LIKE THIS...
HOLD ON!!
MAN, I REALLY HOPE THI TAKES.
Mr.
MONKE JOE SAY
Next time, *another* Great Lakes Avenger *dies!* Oh my!

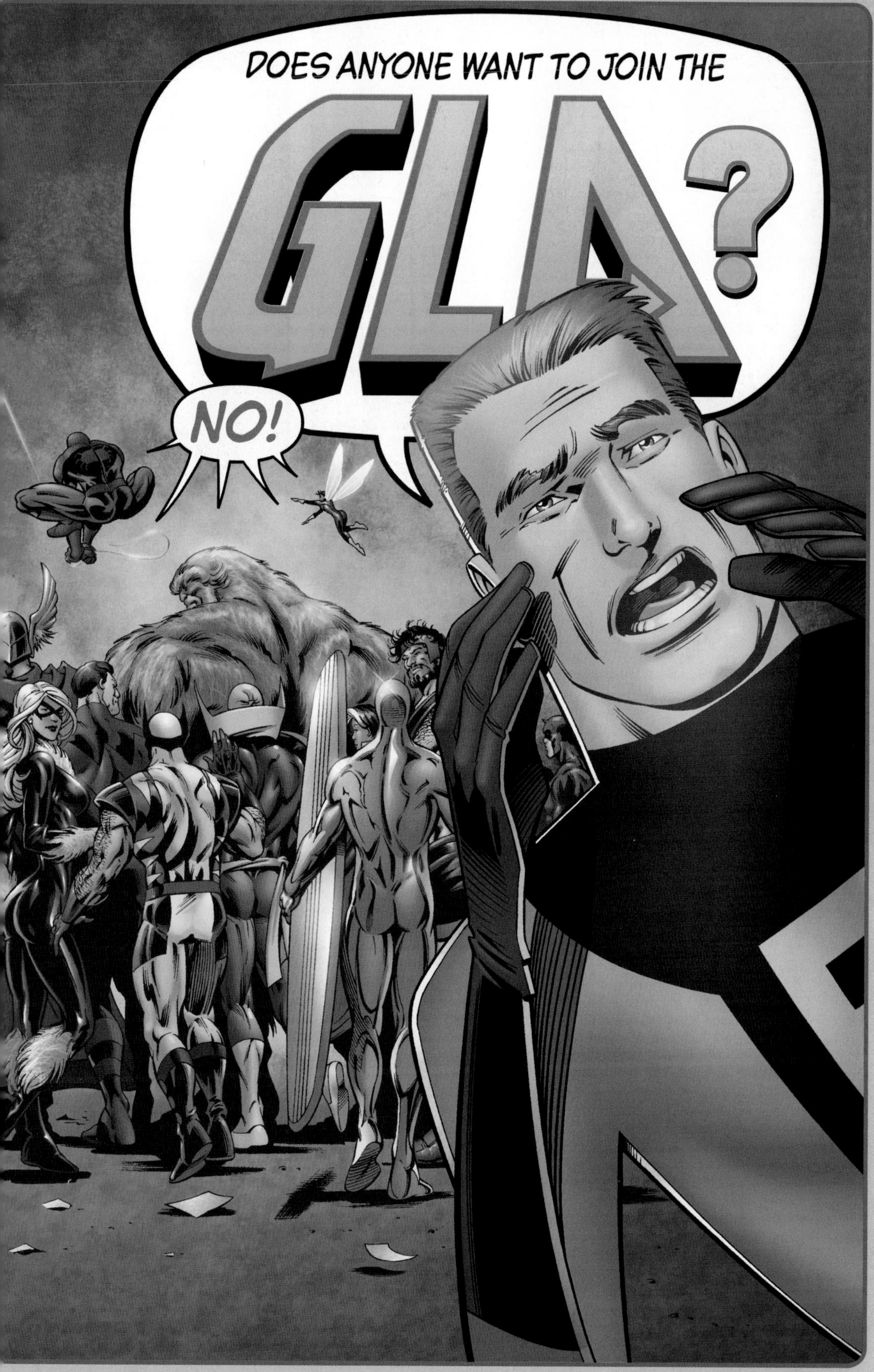
DOES ANYONE WANT TO JOIN THE
GLA?
NO!

GLA #2

OH? YOU'RE BACK? GOSH, DIDN'T SEE *THAT* COMING. MAYBE IT'S JUST ME...

...BUT I'M NOT CRAZY ABOUT SUPER HERO STORIES WHERE EVERYTHING'S ALL DARK AND MOODY.

PERSONALLY, I LIKE THE ONES WHERE GOOD GUYS FIGHT GIANT APES ON THE MOON AND STUFF. REMEMBER THOSE?

I DO. THAT WAS BACK WHEN COMIC BOOK WORLDS WERE PLACES YOU WANTED TO ESCAPE TO...

...NOT FROM.

ANYWAY, GUESS IT'S TIME AGAIN FOR ME TO WARN YOU...

PLEASE DON'T DO ANYTHING YOU SEE *MR. IMMORTAL* DO IN THIS ISSUE. ESPECIALLY ON *PAGE SEVEN*.

THAT'S WHERE HE DOWNLOADS STUFF OFF THE INTERNET FOR FREE.

MONKEY JOE SAYS

Downloading music, films or comics without paying for 'em is stealing. And stealing is bad.

See? This's the indicia. And it says that all of us are trademarks of Marvel Characters, Inc.

So if you upload or download our stories without Marvel's consent, they can sue you blind.

G.L.A. No. 2, July, 2005. Published Miniseries by MARVEL COMICS, a division of MARVEL ENTERTAINMENT GROUP, INC. OFFICE OF PUBLICATION: 417 5th Avenue, New York, NY 10016. © 2005 Marvel Characters, Inc. All rights reserved. All characters featured in this issue and the distinctive names and likenesses thereof, and all related indicia are trademarks of Marvel Characters, Inc. No similarity between any of the names, characters, persons, and/or institutions in this magazine with those of any living or dead person or institution is intended, and any such similarity which may exist is purely coincidental. $2.99 per copy in the U.S. and $4.25 in Canada (GST #R127032852) in the direct market and $2.99 per copy in the U.S. and $4.25 in Canada (GST #R127032852) through the newsstand; Canadian Agreement #40668537. **Printed in the USA.** AVI ARAD, Chief Creative Officer; ALAN FINE, President & CEO Of Toy Biz and Marvel Publishing; DAN CARR, Director of Production; ELAINE CALLENDER, Director of Manufacturing; DAVID BOGART, Managing Editor; STAN LEE, Chairman Emeritus. For information regarding advertising in Marvel Comics or on Marvel.com, please contact Joe Maimone, Advertising Director, at jmaimone@marvel.com or 212-576-8534. For Marvel subscription inquiries, please call 800-217-9158.

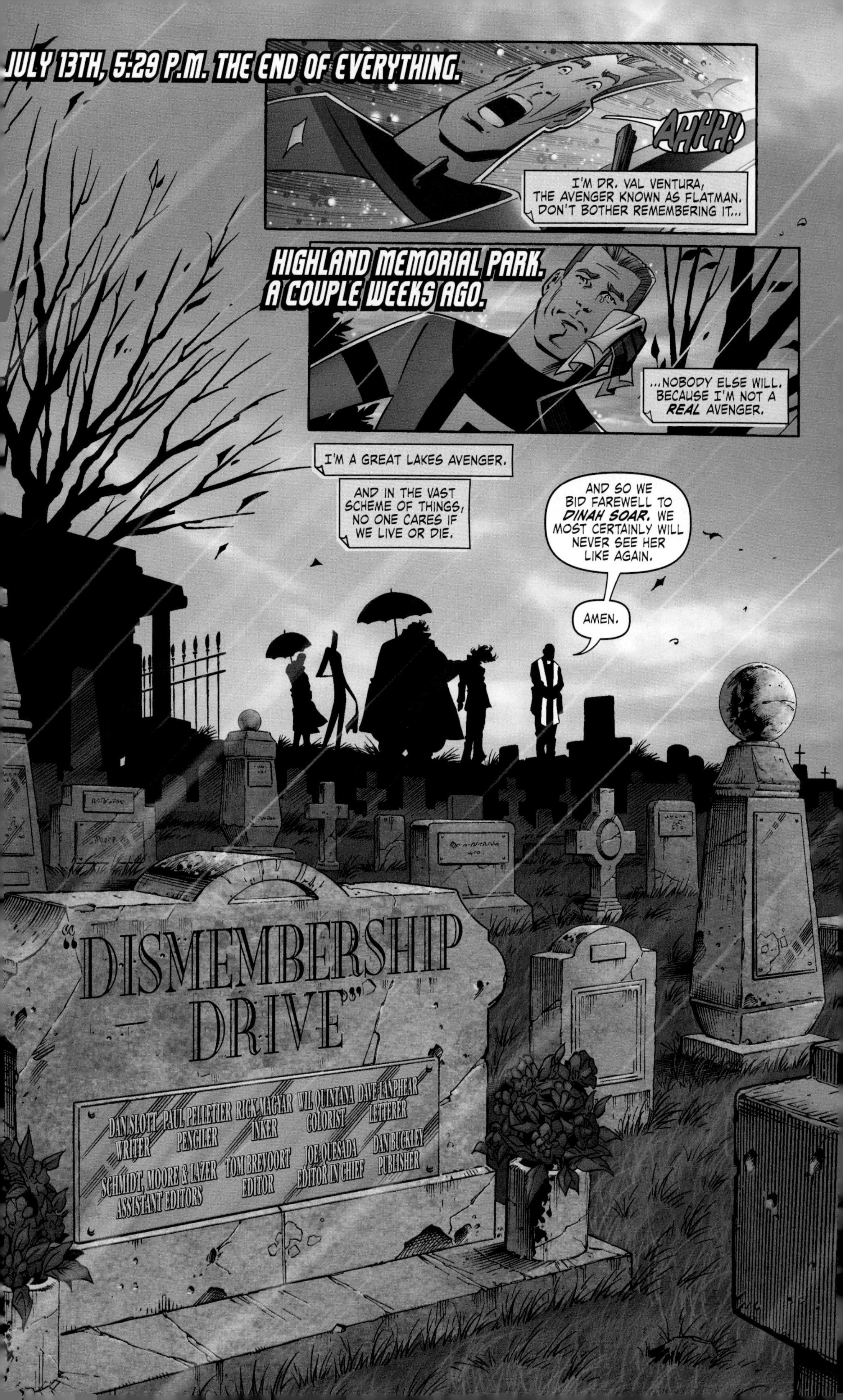

JULY 13TH, 5:29 P.M. THE END OF EVERYTHING.
AHHH!
I'M DR. VAL VENTURA, THE AVENGER KNOWN AS FLATMAN. DON'T BOTHER REMEMBERING IT...
HIGHLAND MEMORIAL PARK. A COUPLE WEEKS AGO.
...NOBODY ELSE WILL. BECAUSE I'M NOT A REAL AVENGER.
I'M A GREAT LAKES AVENGER.
AND IN THE VAST SCHEME OF THINGS, NO ONE CARES IF WE LIVE OR DIE.
AND SO WE BID FAREWELL TO DINAH SOAR. WE MOST CERTAINLY WILL NEVER SEE HER LIKE AGAIN.
AMEN.
"DISMEMBERSHIP DRIVE"
DAN SLOTT WRITER
PAUL PELLETIER PENCILER
RICK MAGYAR INKER
WIL QUINTANA COLORIST
DAVE LANPHEAR LETTERER
SCHMIDT, MOORE & LAZER ASSISTANT EDITORS
TOM BREVOORT EDITOR
JOE QUESADA EDITOR IN CHIEF
DAN BUCKLEY PUBLISHER

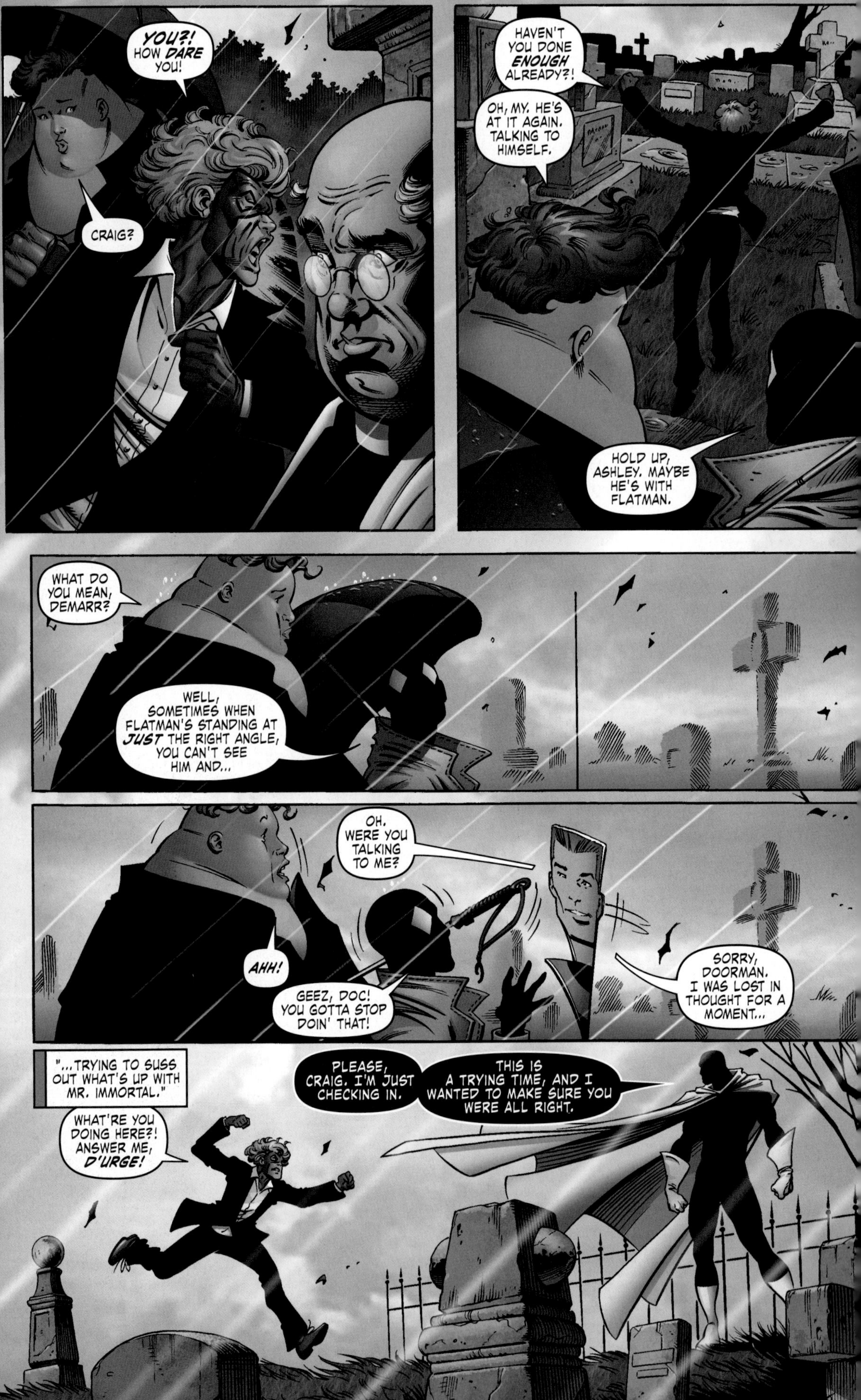

YOU?! HOW DARE YOU!
CRAIG?
HAVEN'T YOU DONE ENOUGH ALREADY?!
OH, MY. HE'S AT IT AGAIN. TALKING TO HIMSELF.
HOLD UP, ASHLEY. MAYBE HE'S WITH FLATMAN.
WHAT DO YOU MEAN, DEMARR?
WELL, SOMETIMES WHEN FLATMAN'S STANDING AT JUST THE RIGHT ANGLE, YOU CAN'T SEE HIM AND...
OH, WERE YOU TALKING TO ME?
AHH!
GEEZ, DOC! YOU GOTTA STOP DOIN' THAT!
SORRY, DOORMAN. I WAS LOST IN THOUGHT FOR A MOMENT...
"...TRYING TO SUSS OUT WHAT'S UP WITH MR. IMMORTAL."
WHAT'RE YOU DOING HERE?! ANSWER ME, D'URGE!
PLEASE, CRAIG. I'M JUST CHECKING IN.
THIS IS A TRYING TIME, AND I WANTED TO MAKE SURE YOU WERE ALL RIGHT.

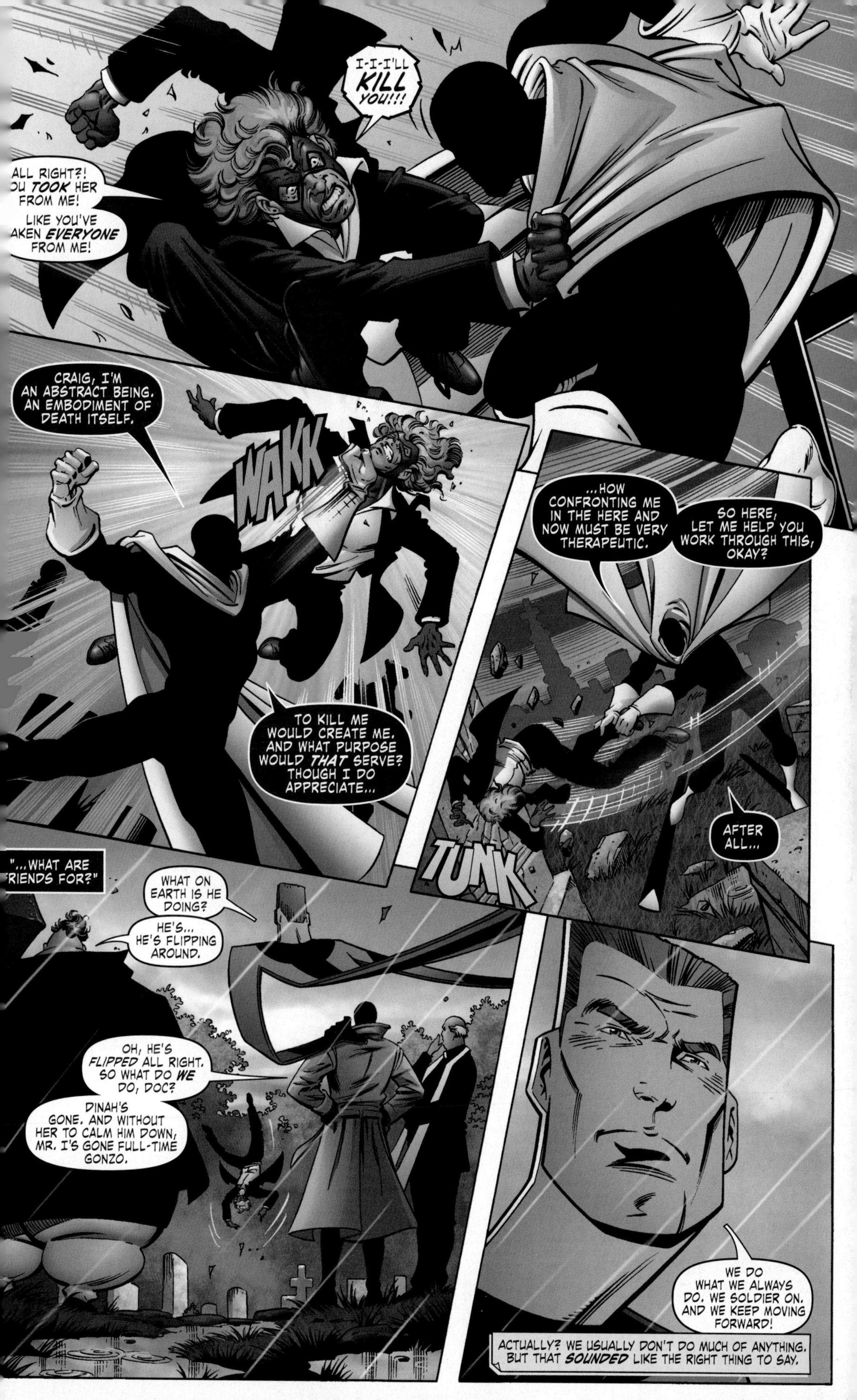
I-I-I'LL KILL YOU!!!
ALL RIGHT?! OU TOOK HER FROM ME!
LIKE YOU'VE AKEN EVERYONE FROM ME!
CRAIG, I'M AN ABSTRACT BEING. AN EMBODIMENT OF DEATH ITSELF.
WAKK
TO KILL ME WOULD CREATE ME. AND WHAT PURPOSE WOULD THAT SERVE? THOUGH I DO APPRECIATE...
...HOW CONFRONTING ME IN THE HERE AND NOW MUST BE VERY THERAPEUTIC.
SO HERE, LET ME HELP YOU WORK THROUGH THIS, OKAY?
AFTER ALL...
TUNK
"...WHAT ARE RIENDS FOR?"
WHAT ON EARTH IS HE DOING?
HE'S... HE'S FLIPPING AROUND.
OH, HE'S FLIPPED ALL RIGHT. SO WHAT DO WE DO, DOC?
DINAH'S GONE. AND WITHOUT HER TO CALM HIM DOWN, MR. I'S GONE FULL-TIME GONZO.
WE DO WHAT WE ALWAYS DO. WE SOLDIER ON. AND WE KEEP MOVING FORWARD!
ACTUALLY? WE USUALLY DON'T DO MUCH OF ANYTHING. BUT THAT SOUNDED LIKE THE RIGHT THING TO SAY.

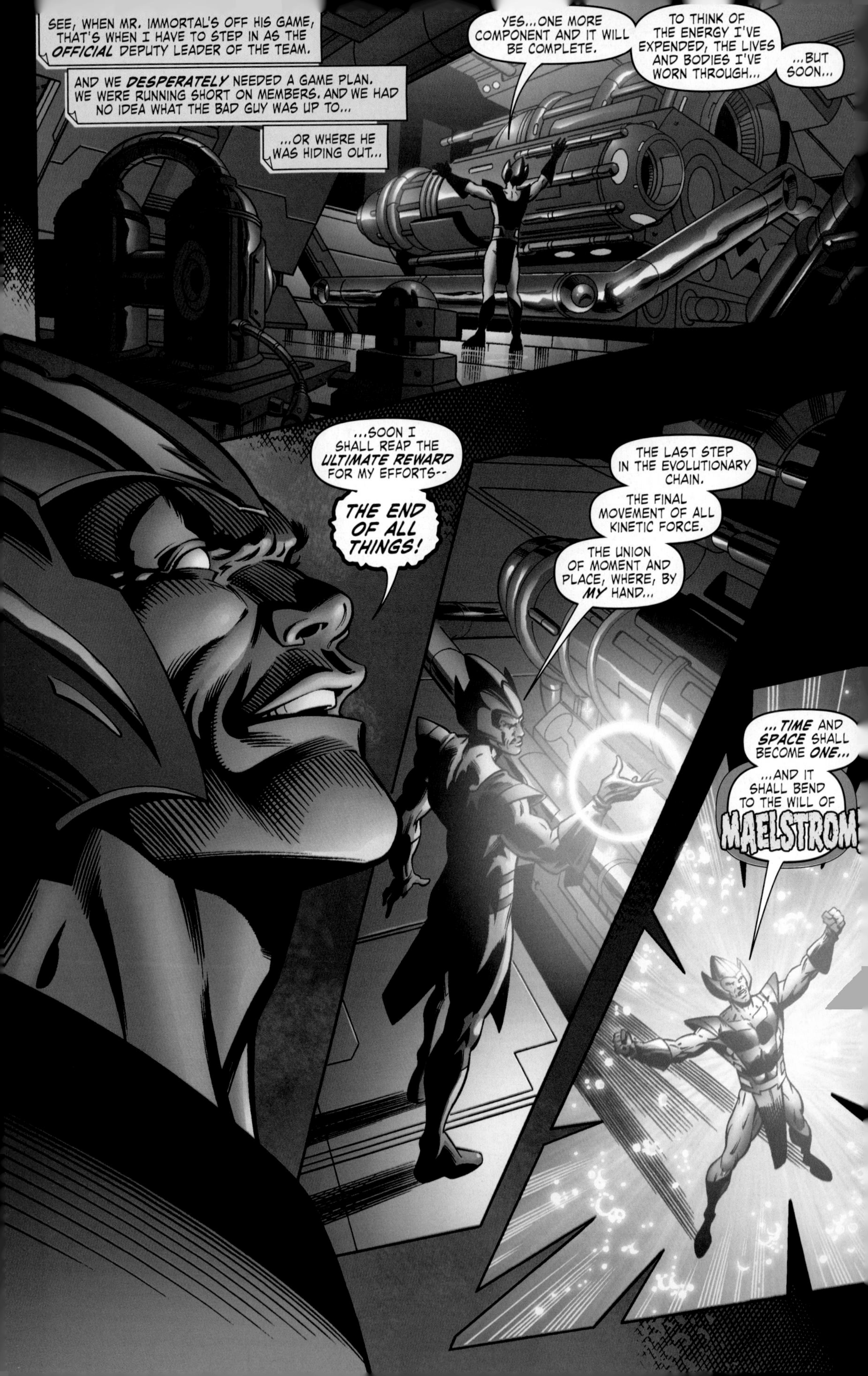

SEE, WHEN MR. IMMORTAL'S OFF HIS GAME, THAT'S WHEN I HAVE TO STEP IN AS THE OFFICIAL DEPUTY LEADER OF THE TEAM.
AND WE DESPERATELY NEEDED A GAME PLAN. WE WERE RUNNING SHORT ON MEMBERS. AND WE HAD NO IDEA WHAT THE BAD GUY WAS UP TO...
...OR WHERE HE WAS HIDING OUT...
YES...ONE MORE COMPONENT AND IT WILL BE COMPLETE.
TO THINK OF THE ENERGY I'VE EXPENDED, THE LIVES AND BODIES I'VE WORN THROUGH...
...BUT SOON...
...SOON I SHALL REAP THE ULTIMATE REWARD FOR MY EFFORTS--
THE END OF ALL THINGS!
THE LAST STEP IN THE EVOLUTIONARY CHAIN.
THE FINAL MOVEMENT OF ALL KINETIC FORCE.
THE UNION OF MOMENT AND PLACE, WHERE, BY MY HAND...
...TIME AND SPACE SHALL BECOME ONE...
...AND IT SHALL BEND TO THE WILL OF
MAELSTROM

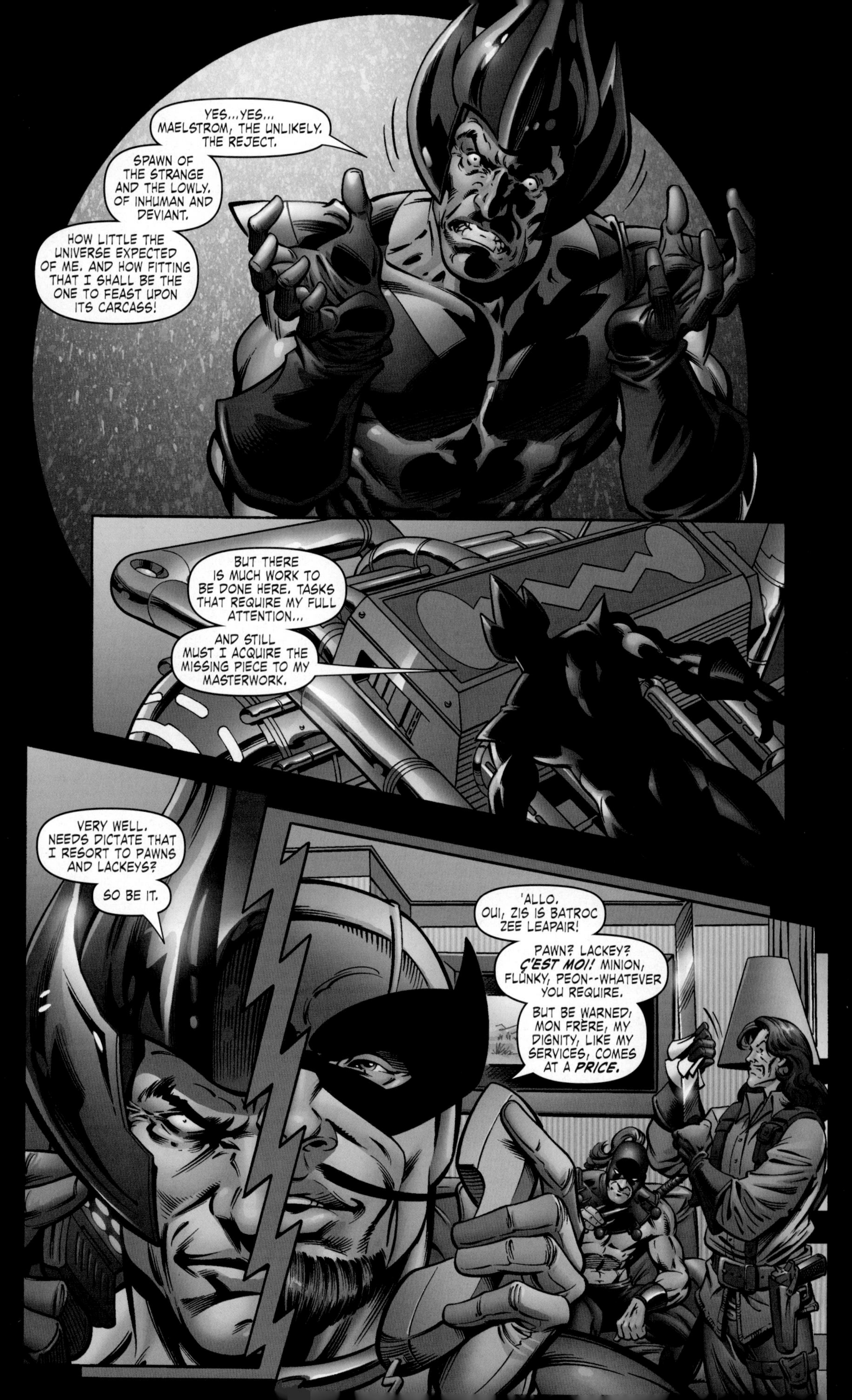
YES...YES... MAELSTROM, THE UNLIKELY. THE REJECT.
SPAWN OF THE STRANGE AND THE LOWLY. OF INHUMAN AND DEVIANT.
HOW LITTLE THE UNIVERSE EXPECTED OF ME. AND HOW FITTING THAT I SHALL BE THE ONE TO FEAST UPON ITS CARCASS!
BUT THERE IS MUCH WORK TO BE DONE HERE. TASKS THAT REQUIRE MY FULL ATTENTION...
AND STILL MUST I ACQUIRE THE MISSING PIECE TO MY MASTERWORK.
VERY WELL. NEEDS DICTATE THAT I RESORT TO PAWNS AND LACKEYS?
SO BE IT.
'ALLO. OUI, ZIS IS BATROC ZEE LEAPAIR!
PAWN? LACKEY? ÇEST MOI! MINION, FLUNKY, PEON--WHATEVER YOU REQUIRE.
BUT BE WARNED, MON FRÈRE, MY DIGNITY, LIKE MY SERVICES, COMES AT A PRICE.

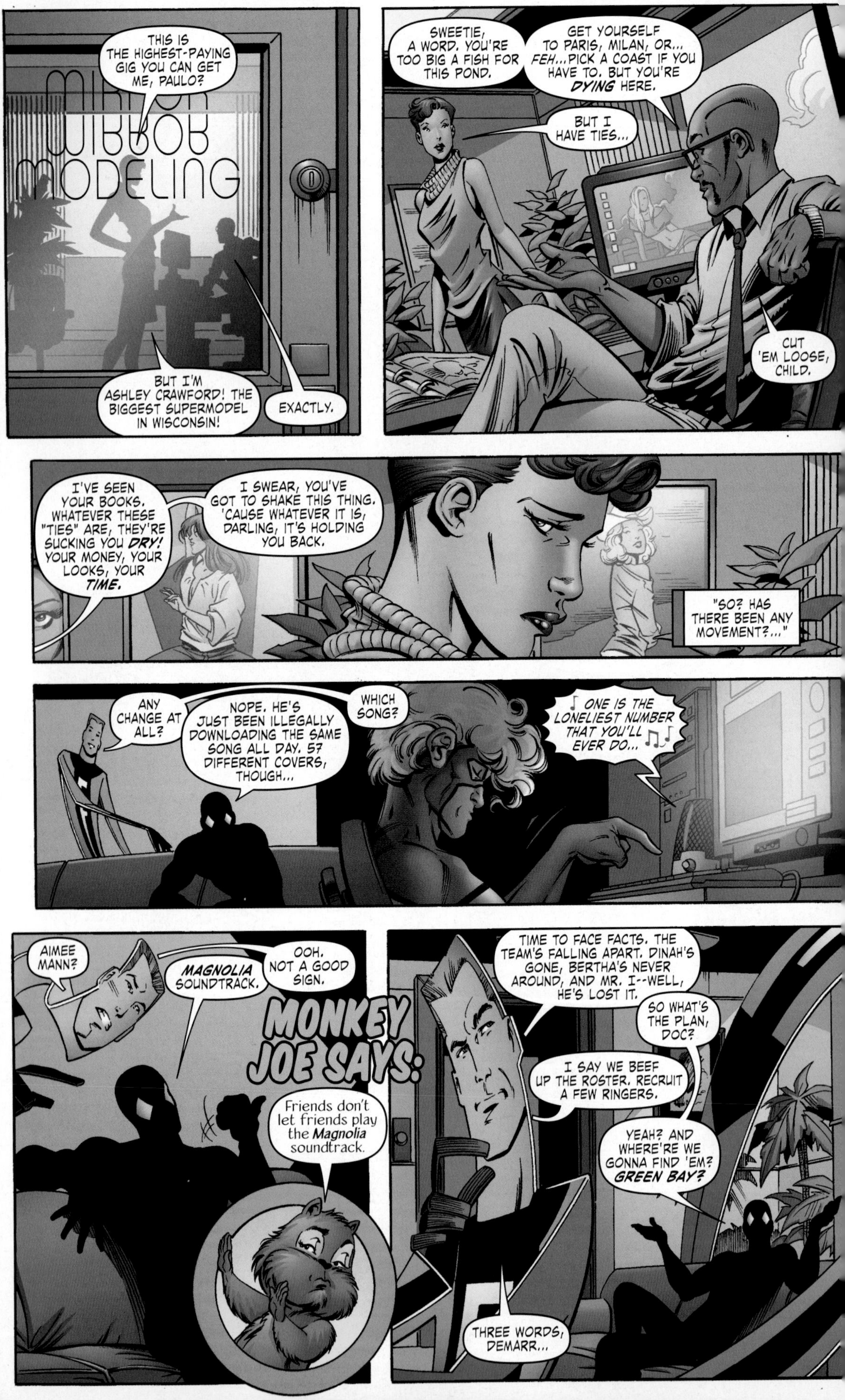
THIS IS THE HIGHEST-PAYING GIG YOU CAN GET ME, PAULO?
MIRROR MODELING
BUT I'M ASHLEY CRAWFORD! THE BIGGEST SUPERMODEL IN WISCONSIN!
EXACTLY.
SWEETIE, A WORD. YOU'RE TOO BIG A FISH FOR THIS POND.
GET YOURSELF TO PARIS, MILAN, OR... FEH...PICK A COAST IF YOU HAVE TO. BUT YOU'RE DYING HERE.
BUT I HAVE TIES...
CUT 'EM LOOSE, CHILD.
I'VE SEEN YOUR BOOKS. WHATEVER THESE "TIES" ARE, THEY'RE SUCKING YOU DRY! YOUR MONEY, YOUR LOOKS, YOUR TIME.
I SWEAR, YOU'VE GOT TO SHAKE THIS THING. 'CAUSE WHATEVER IT IS, DARLING, IT'S HOLDING YOU BACK.
"SO? HAS THERE BEEN ANY MOVEMENT?..."
ANY CHANGE AT ALL?
NOPE. HE'S JUST BEEN ILLEGALLY DOWNLOADING THE SAME SONG ALL DAY. 57 DIFFERENT COVERS, THOUGH...
WHICH SONG?
♩ ONE IS THE LONELIEST NUMBER THAT YOU'LL EVER DO... ♫♩
AIMEE MANN?
MAGNOLIA SOUNDTRACK.
OOH. NOT A GOOD SIGN.
MONKEY JOE SAYS:
Friends don't let friends play the Magnolia soundtrack.
TIME TO FACE FACTS. THE TEAM'S FALLING APART. DINAH'S GONE, BERTHA'S NEVER AROUND, AND MR. I--WELL, HE'S LOST IT.
SO WHAT'S THE PLAN, DOC?
I SAY WE BEEF UP THE ROSTER. RECRUIT A FEW RINGERS.
YEAH? AND WHERE'RE WE GONNA FIND 'EM? GREEN BAY?
THREE WORDS, DEMARR...

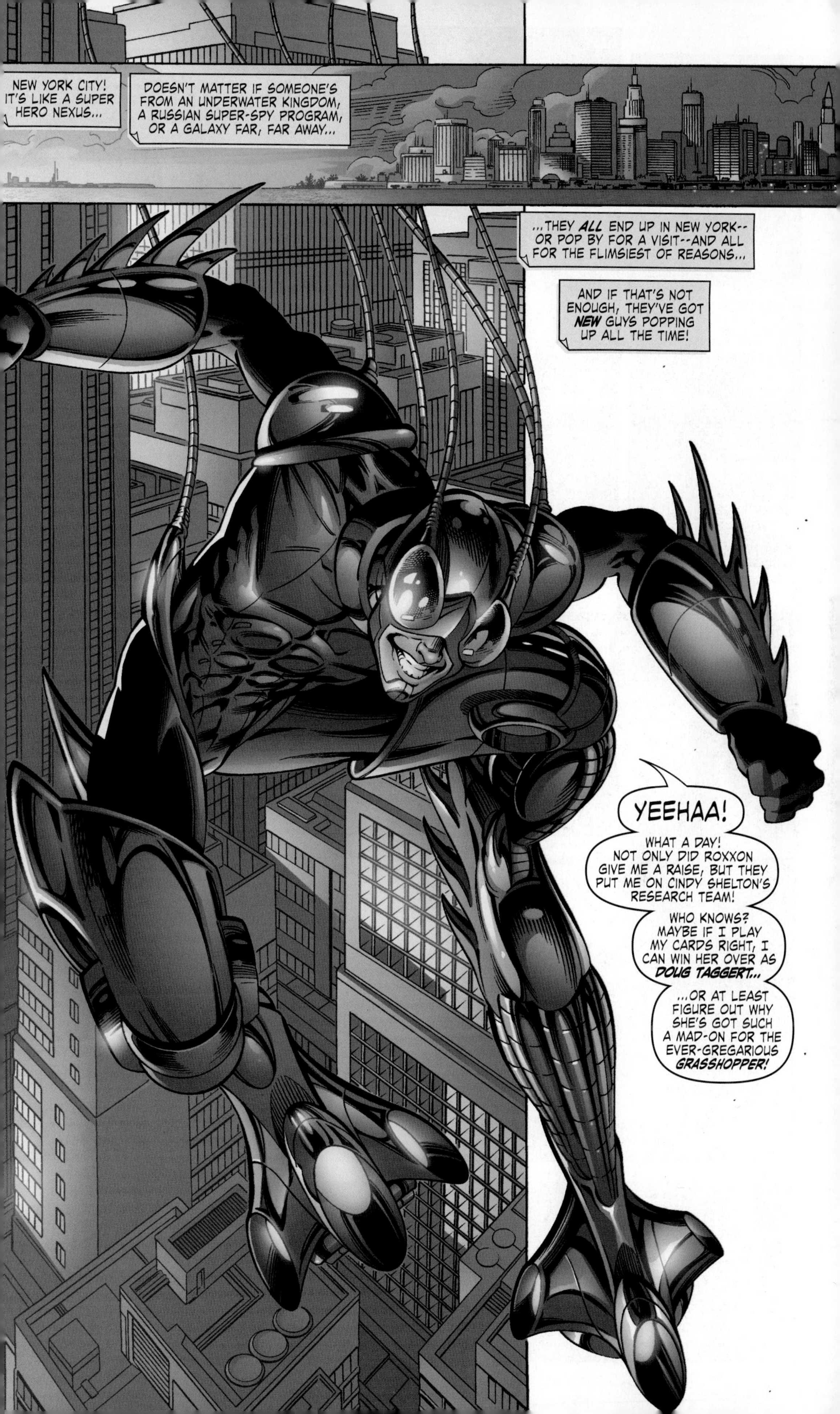
NEW YORK CITY! IT'S LIKE A SUPER HERO NEXUS...
DOESN'T MATTER IF SOMEONE'S FROM AN UNDERWATER KINGDOM, A RUSSIAN SUPER-SPY PROGRAM, OR A GALAXY FAR, FAR AWAY...
...THEY ALL END UP IN NEW YORK--OR POP BY FOR A VISIT--AND ALL FOR THE FLIMSIEST OF REASONS...
AND IF THAT'S NOT ENOUGH, THEY'VE GOT NEW GUYS POPPING UP ALL THE TIME!
YEEHAA!
WHAT A DAY! NOT ONLY DID ROXXON GIVE ME A RAISE, BUT THEY PUT ME ON CINDY SHELTON'S RESEARCH TEAM!
WHO KNOWS? MAYBE IF I PLAY MY CARDS RIGHT, I CAN WIN HER OVER AS DOUG TAGGERT...
...OR AT LEAST FIGURE OUT WHY SHE'S GOT SUCH A MAD-ON FOR THE EVER-GREGARIOUS GRASSHOPPER!

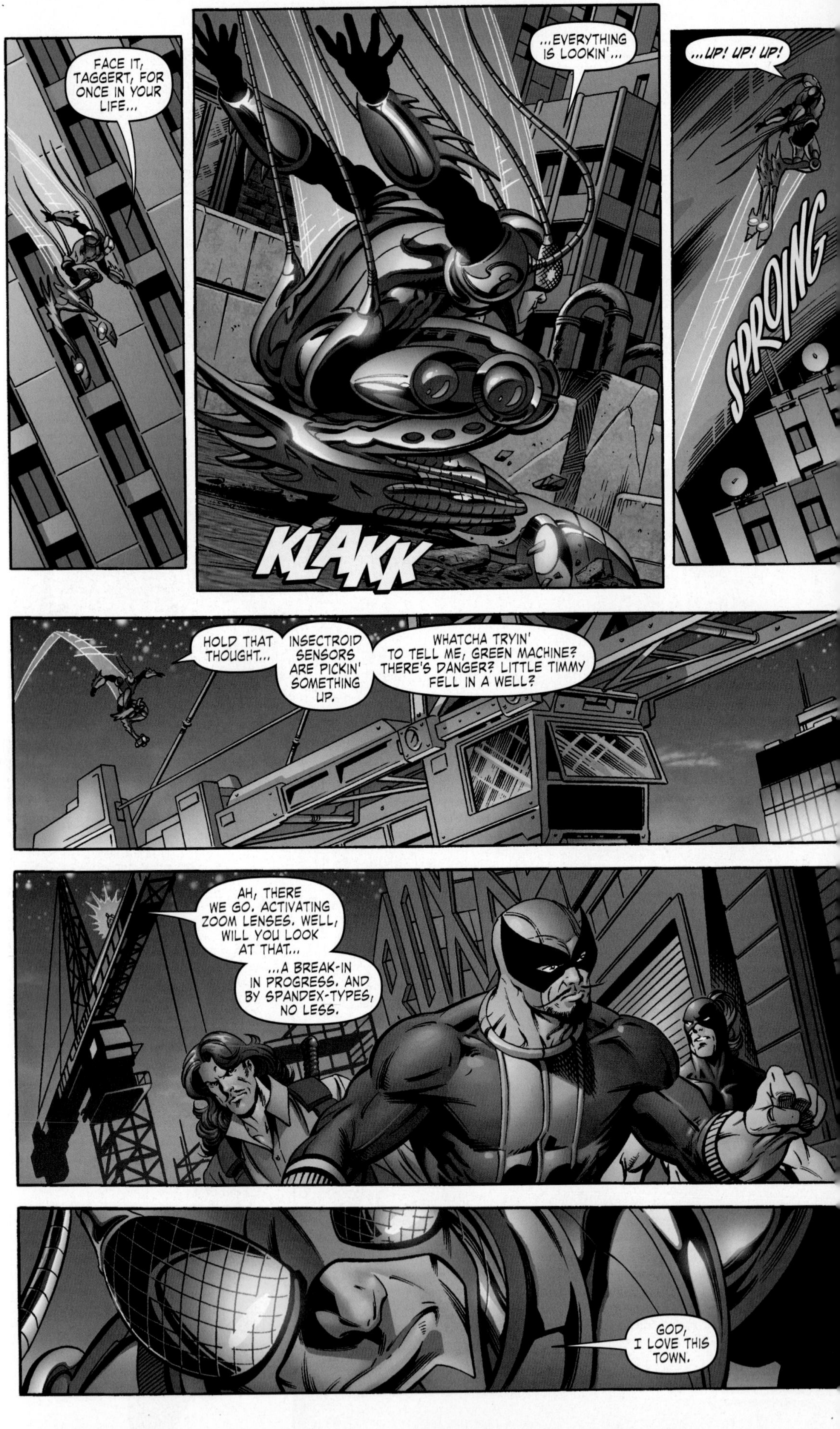
FACE IT, TAGGERT, FOR ONCE IN YOUR LIFE...
...EVERYTHING IS LOOKIN'...
KLAKK
...UP! UP! UP!
SPROING
HOLD THAT THOUGHT...
INSECTROID SENSORS ARE PICKIN' SOMETHING UP.
WHATCHA TRYIN' TO TELL ME, GREEN MACHINE? THERE'S DANGER? LITTLE TIMMY FELL IN A WELL?
AH, THERE WE GO. ACTIVATING ZOOM LENSES. WELL, WILL YOU LOOK AT THAT...
...A BREAK-IN IN PROGRESS. AND BY SPANDEX-TYPES, NO LESS.
GOD, I LOVE THIS TOWN.

...AND HERE WE ARE. NEW YORK, NEW YORK!

SO NICE, THEY NAMED IT TWICE. THE BIG APPLE. THE CITY THAT NEVER SLEEPS!

IT SMELLS LIKE PEE.

THAT'S JUST PENN STATION, DEMARR. COME ON...

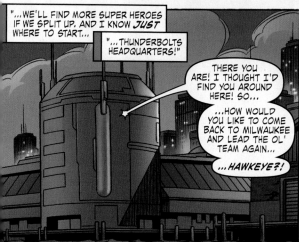

"...WE'LL FIND MORE SUPER HEROES IF WE SPLIT UP, AND I KNOW JUST WHERE TO START...

"...THUNDERBOLTS HEADQUARTERS!"

THERE YOU ARE! I THOUGHT I'D FIND YOU AROUND HERE! SO...

...HOW WOULD YOU LIKE TO COME BACK TO MILWAUKEE AND LEAD THE OL' TEAM AGAIN...

...HAWKEYE?!

YOU MUST HAVE ME MISTAKEN FOR SOMEONE ELSE. I'M THE SWORDSMAN.

YEAH, BUT THAT'S JUST A DISGUISE, RIGHT? UNDERNEATH THAT YOU'RE REALLY--

I AM NOT HAWKEYE!

BUT I READ ON THE INTERNET THAT--

LISTEN! I'M NOT CLINT BARTON! I'M NOT EVEN A SUPER HERO!

I'M A MIND-CONTROLLED KILLER WHO COULD GUT YOU AT ANY MOMENT!

WE'RE NOT PICKY.

GO AWAY!

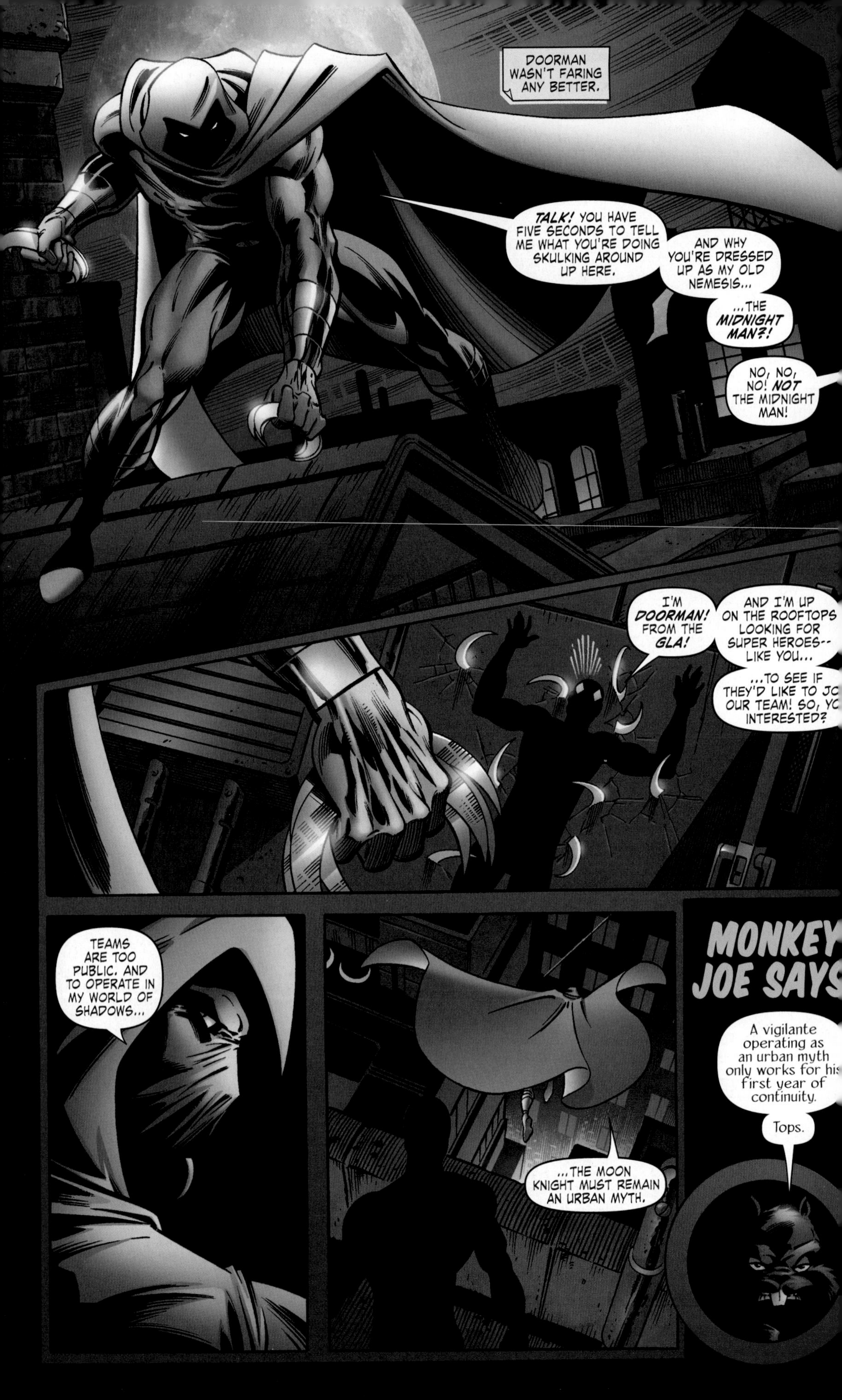
DOORMAN WASN'T FARING ANY BETTER.
TALK! YOU HAVE FIVE SECONDS TO TELL ME WHAT YOU'RE DOING SKULKING AROUND UP HERE.
AND WHY YOU'RE DRESSED UP AS MY OLD NEMESIS...
...THE MIDNIGHT MAN?!
NO, NO, NO! NOT THE MIDNIGHT MAN!
I'M DOORMAN! FROM THE GLA!
AND I'M UP ON THE ROOFTOPS LOOKING FOR SUPER HEROES-- LIKE YOU...
TEAMS ARE TOO PUBLIC. AND TO OPERATE IN MY WORLD OF SHADOWS...
...THE MOON KNIGHT MUST REMAIN AN URBAN MYTH.
A vigilante operating as an urban myth only works for his first year of continuity.
Tops.

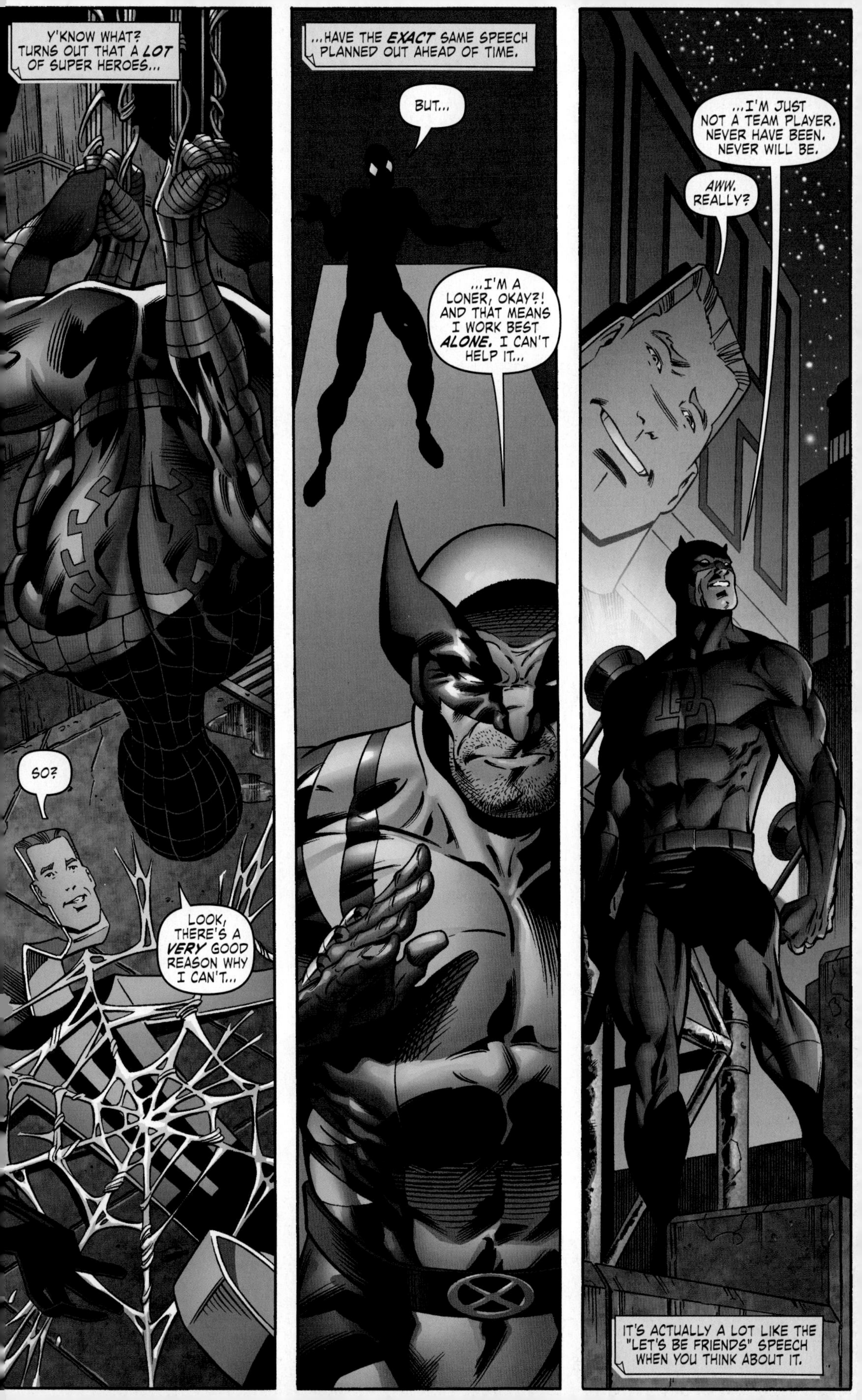
Y'KNOW WHAT? TURNS OUT THAT A LOT OF SUPER HEROES...
SO?
LOOK, THERE'S A VERY GOOD REASON WHY I CAN'T...
...HAVE THE EXACT SAME SPEECH PLANNED OUT AHEAD OF TIME.
BUT...
...I'M A LONER, OKAY?! AND THAT MEANS I WORK BEST ALONE. I CAN'T HELP IT...
...I'M JUST NOT A TEAM PLAYER. NEVER HAVE BEEN. NEVER WILL BE.
AWW. REALLY?
IT'S ACTUALLY A LOT LIKE THE "LET'S BE FRIENDS" SPEECH WHEN YOU THINK ABOUT IT.

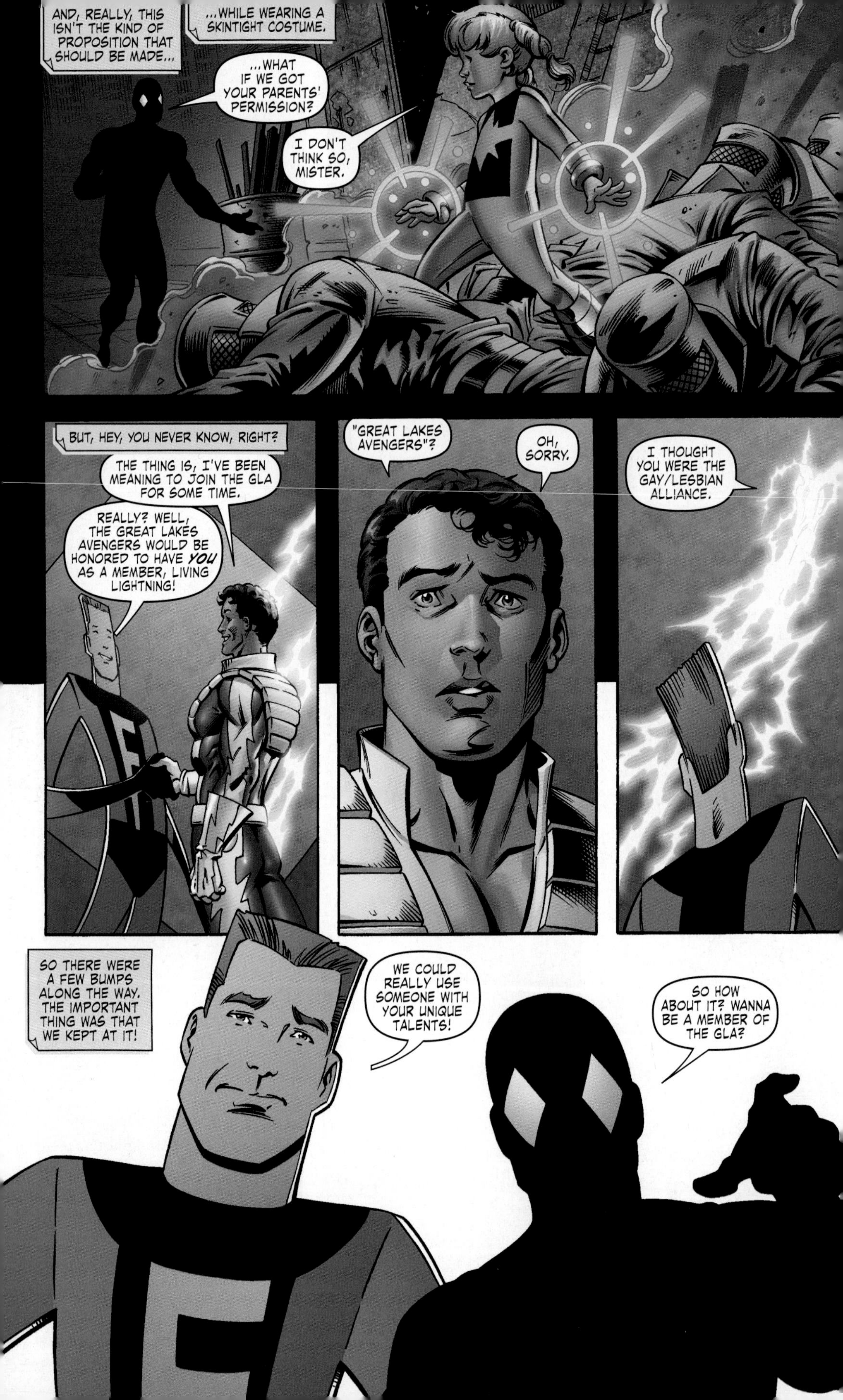

AND, REALLY, THIS ISN'T THE KIND OF PROPOSITION THAT SHOULD BE MADE...
...WHILE WEARING A SKINTIGHT COSTUME.
...WHAT IF WE GOT YOUR PARENTS' PERMISSION?
I DON'T THINK SO, MISTER.
BUT, HEY, YOU NEVER KNOW, RIGHT?
THE THING IS, I'VE BEEN MEANING TO JOIN THE GLA FOR SOME TIME.
REALLY? WELL, THE GREAT LAKES AVENGERS WOULD BE HONORED TO HAVE *YOU* AS A MEMBER, LIVING LIGHTNING!
"GREAT LAKES AVENGERS"?
OH, SORRY.
I THOUGHT YOU WERE THE GAY/LESBIAN ALLIANCE.
SO THERE WERE A FEW BUMPS ALONG THE WAY. THE IMPORTANT THING WAS THAT WE KEPT AT IT!
WE COULD REALLY USE SOMEONE WITH YOUR UNIQUE TALENTS!
SO HOW ABOUT IT? WANNA BE A MEMBER OF THE GLA?

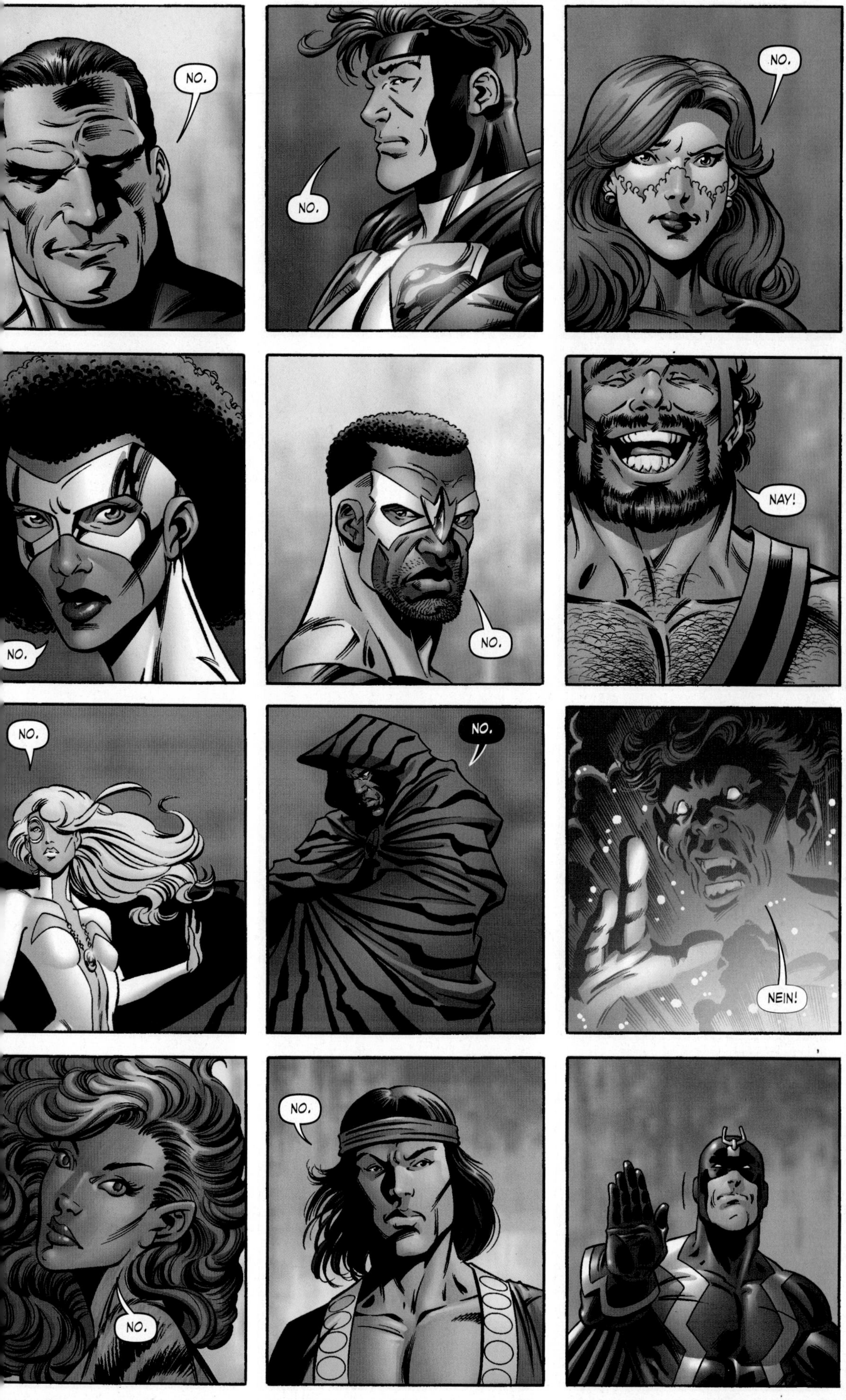
NO.
NO.
NO.
NO.
NO.
NAY!
NO.
NO.
NEIN!
NO.
NO.

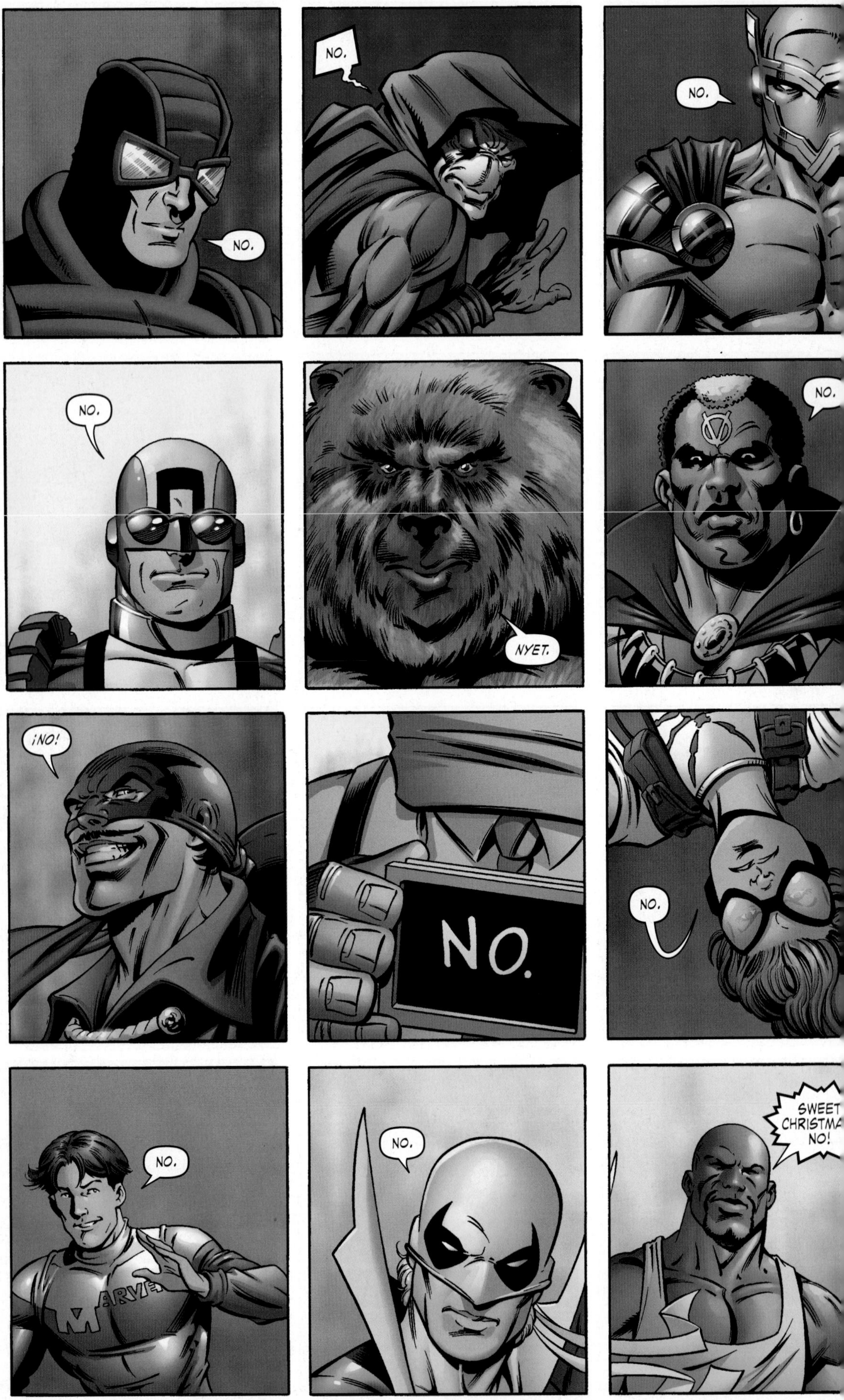
NO.
NO.
NO.
NO.
NYET.
NO.
¡NO!
NO.
NO.
NO.
NO.
SWEET
CHRISTMA
NO!

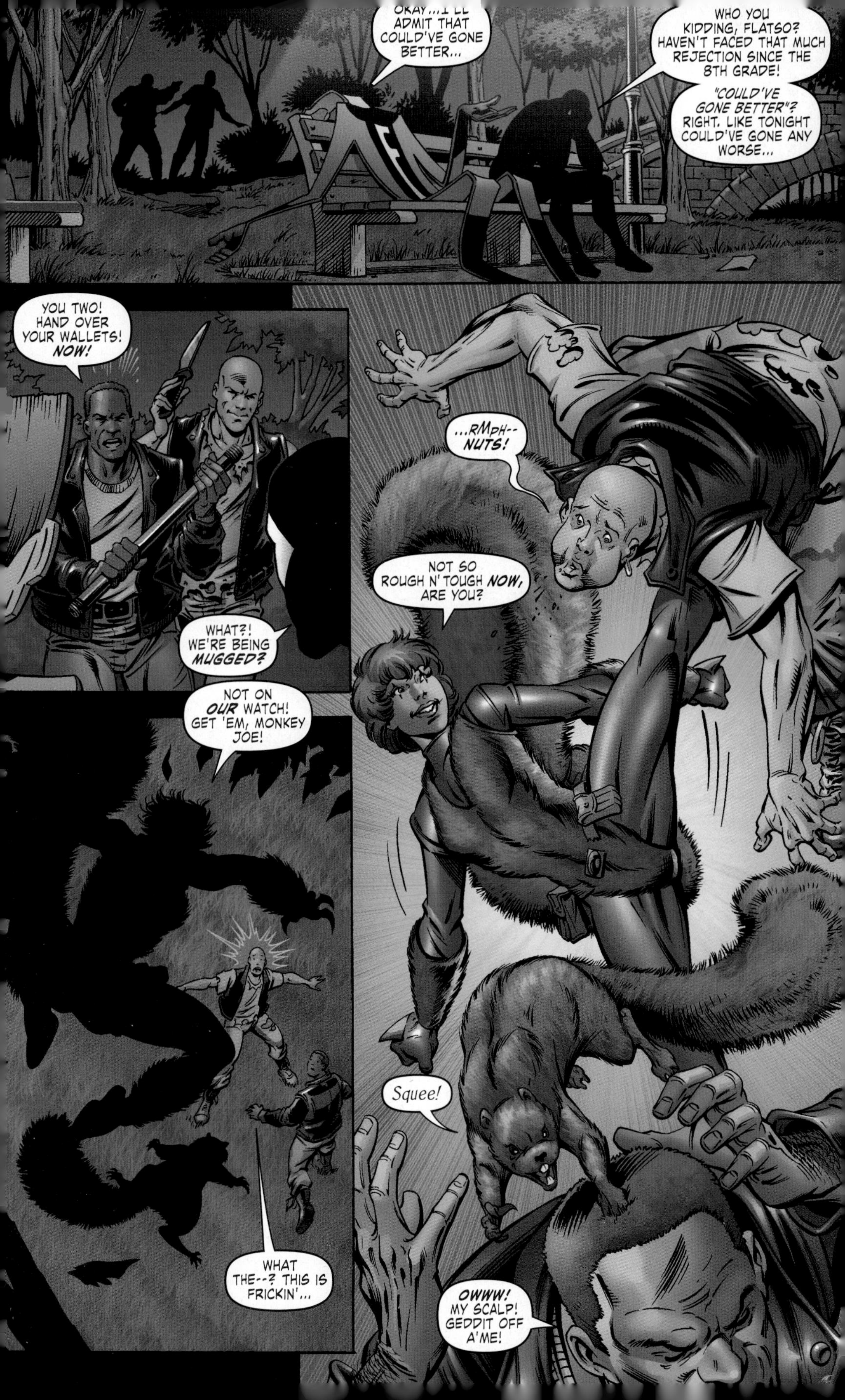
OKAY...I'LL ADMIT THAT COULD'VE GONE BETTER...
WHO YOU KIDDING, FLATSO? HAVEN'T FACED THAT MUCH REJECTION SINCE THE 8TH GRADE!
"COULD'VE GONE BETTER"? RIGHT. LIKE TONIGHT COULD'VE GONE ANY WORSE...
YOU TWO! HAND OVER YOUR WALLETS! NOW!
WHAT?! WE'RE BEING MUGGED?
NOT ON OUR WATCH! GET 'EM, MONKEY JOE!
WHAT THE--? THIS IS FRICKIN'...
...RMPH-- NUTS!
NOT SO ROUGH N' TOUGH NOW, ARE YOU?
Squee!
OWWW! MY SCALP! GEDDIT OFF A'ME!

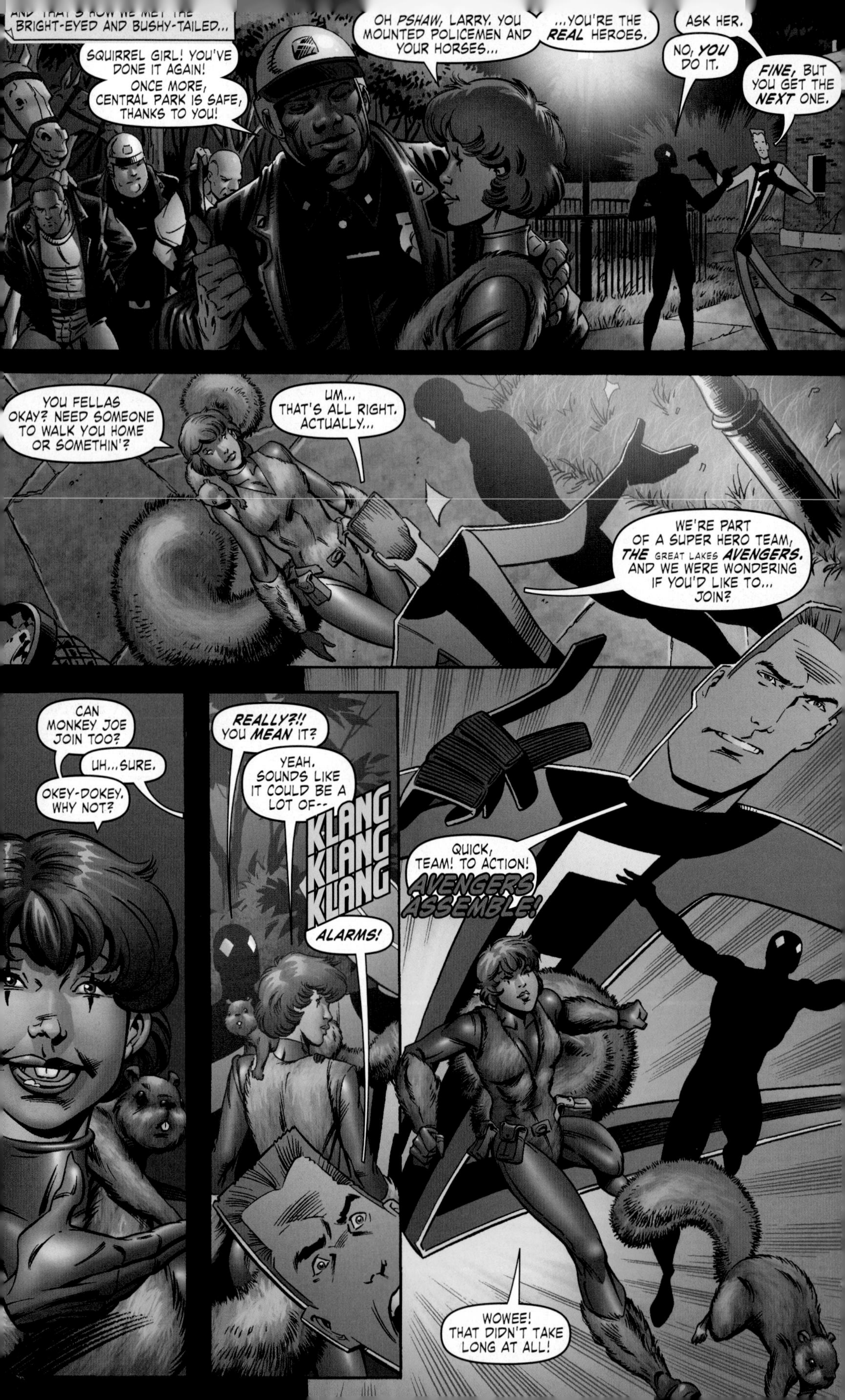
AND THAT'S HOW WE MET THE BRIGHT-EYED AND BUSHY-TAILED...
SQUIRREL GIRL! YOU'VE DONE IT AGAIN! ONCE MORE, CENTRAL PARK IS SAFE, THANKS TO YOU!
OH PSHAW, LARRY. YOU MOUNTED POLICEMEN AND YOUR HORSES...
...YOU'RE THE REAL HEROES.
ASK HER.
NO, YOU DO IT.
FINE, BUT YOU GET THE NEXT ONE.
YOU FELLAS OKAY? NEED SOMEONE TO WALK YOU HOME OR SOMETHIN'?
UM... THAT'S ALL RIGHT. ACTUALLY...
WE'RE PART OF A SUPER HERO TEAM, THE GREAT LAKES AVENGERS. AND WE WERE WONDERING IF YOU'D LIKE TO... JOIN?
CAN MONKEY JOE JOIN TOO?
UH...SURE.
OKEY-DOKEY. WHY NOT?
REALLY?!! YOU MEAN IT?
YEAH. SOUNDS LIKE IT COULD BE A LOT OF--
KLANG KLANG KLANG
ALARMS!
QUICK, TEAM! TO ACTION! AVENGERS ASSEMBLE!
WOWEE! THAT DIDN'T TAKE LONG AT ALL!

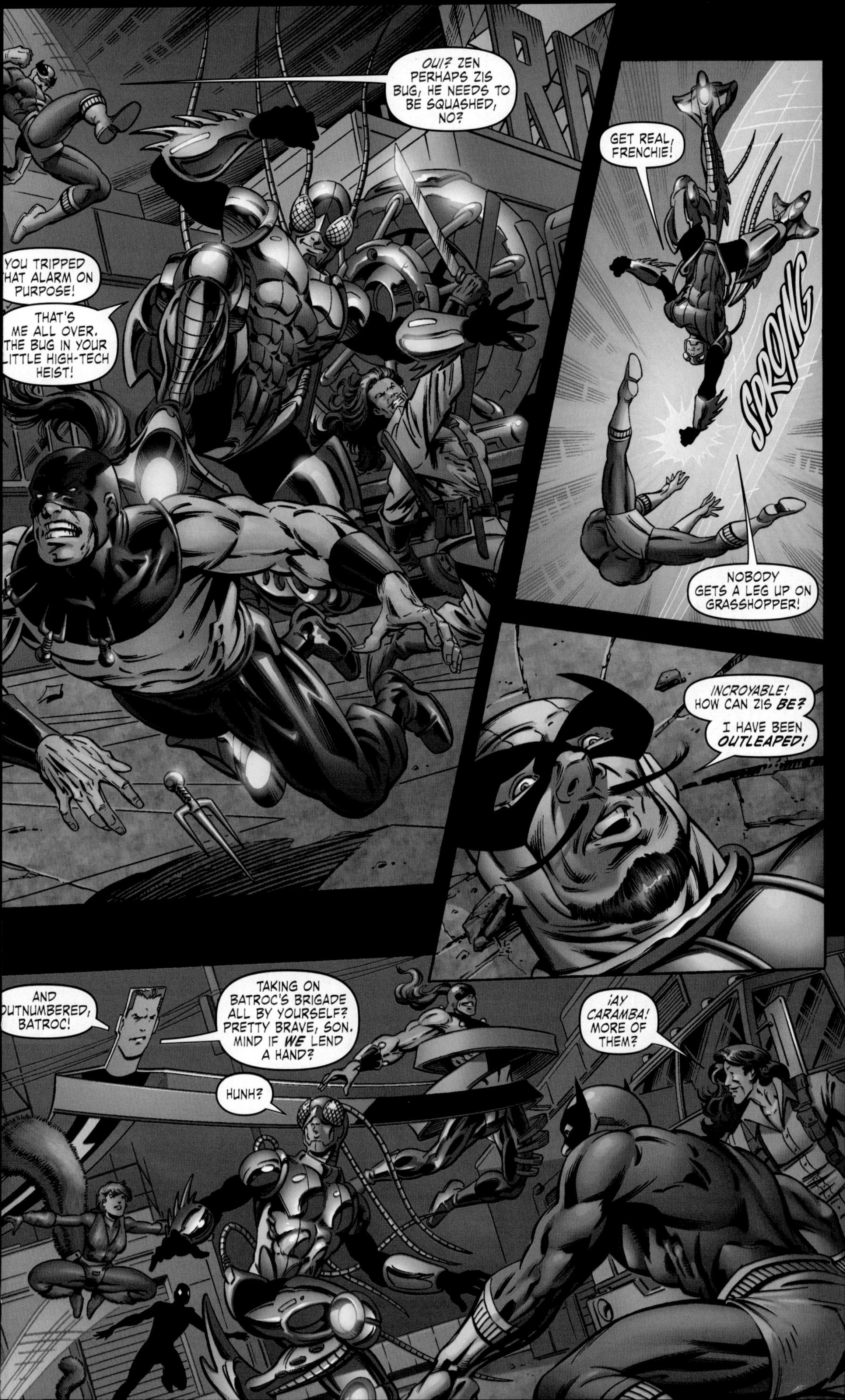
OUI? ZEN PERHAPS ZIS BUG, HE NEEDS TO BE SQUASHED, NO?
YOU TRIPPED THAT ALARM ON PURPOSE!
THAT'S ME ALL OVER. THE BUG IN YOUR LITTLE HIGH-TECH HEIST!
GET REAL, FRENCHIE!
SPROING
NOBODY GETS A LEG UP ON GRASSHOPPER!
INCROYABLE! HOW CAN ZIS BE?
I HAVE BEEN OUTLEAPED!
AND OUTNUMBERED, BATROC!
TAKING ON BATROC'S BRIGADE ALL BY YOURSELF? PRETTY BRAVE, SON. MIND IF WE LEND A HAND?
HUNH?
¡AY CARAMBA! MORE OF THEM?

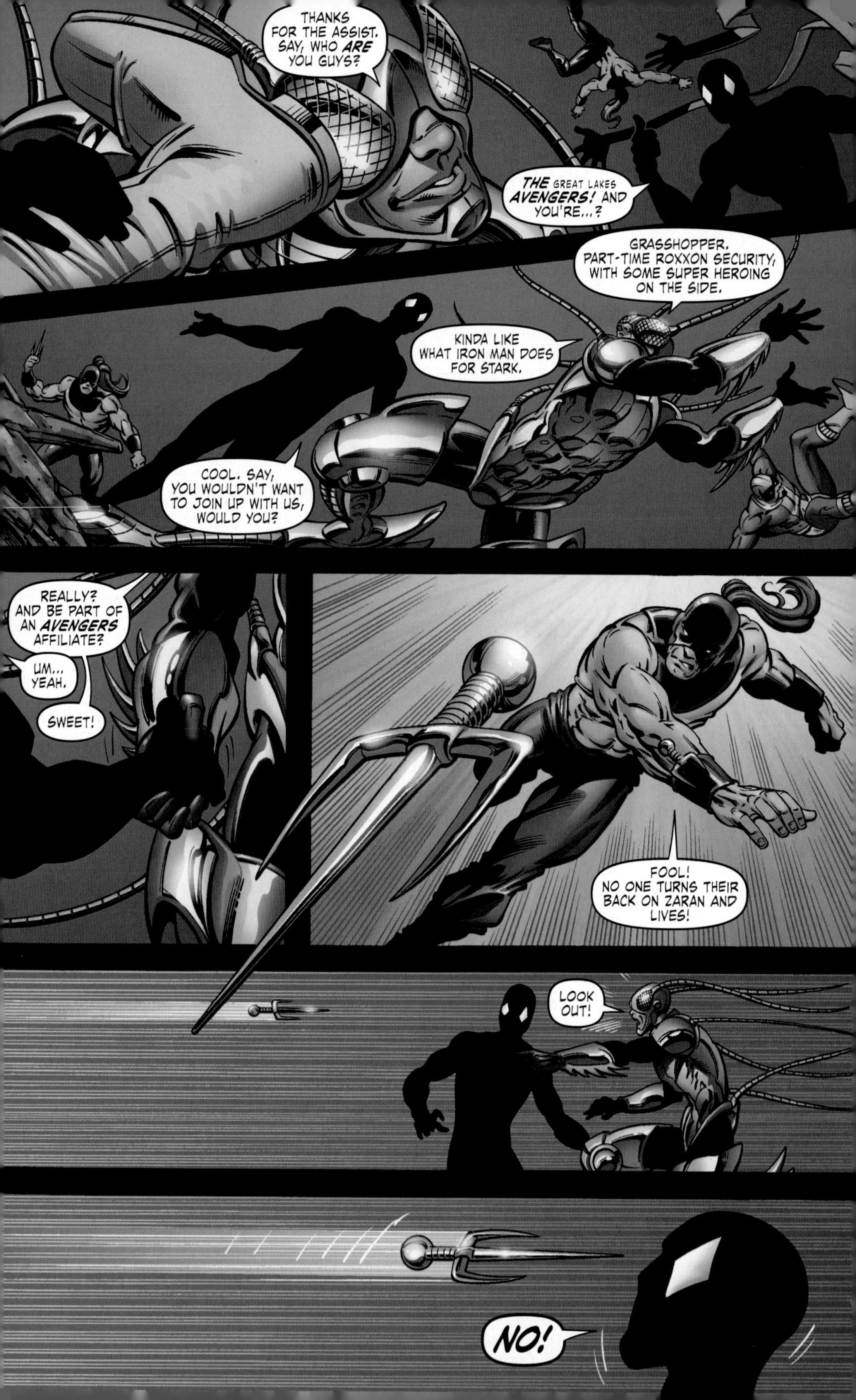
THANKS FOR THE ASSIST. SAY, WHO ARE YOU GUYS?
THE GREAT LAKES AVENGERS! AND YOU'RE...?
GRASSHOPPER. PART-TIME ROXXON SECURITY, WITH SOME SUPER HEROING ON THE SIDE.
KINDA LIKE WHAT IRON MAN DOES FOR STARK.
COOL. SAY, YOU WOULDN'T WANT TO JOIN UP WITH US, WOULD YOU?
REALLY? AND BE PART OF AN AVENGERS AFFILIATE?
UM... YEAH.
SWEET!
FOOL! NO ONE TURNS THEIR BACK ON ZARAN AND LIVES!
LOOK OUT!
NO!

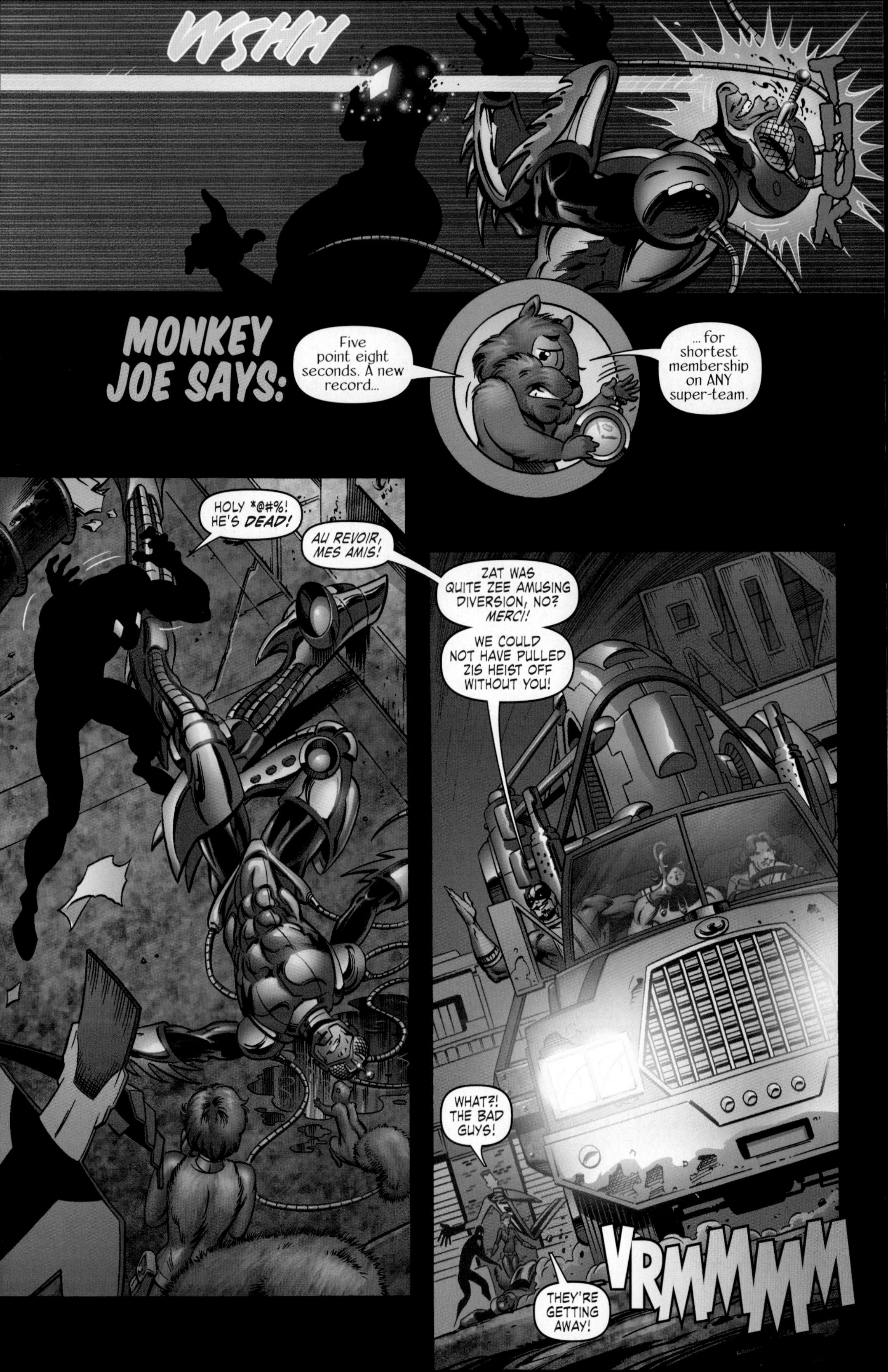
WSHH
THUK
MONKEY JOE SAYS:
Five point eight seconds. A new record...
...for shortest membership on ANY super-team.
HOLY *@#%! HE'S DEAD!
AU REVOIR, MES AMIS!
ZAT WAS QUITE ZEE AMUSING DIVERSION, NO? MERCI!
WE COULD NOT HAVE PULLED ZIS HEIST OFF WITHOUT YOU!
WHAT?! THE BAD GUYS!
VRMMMMM
THEY'RE GETTING AWAY!

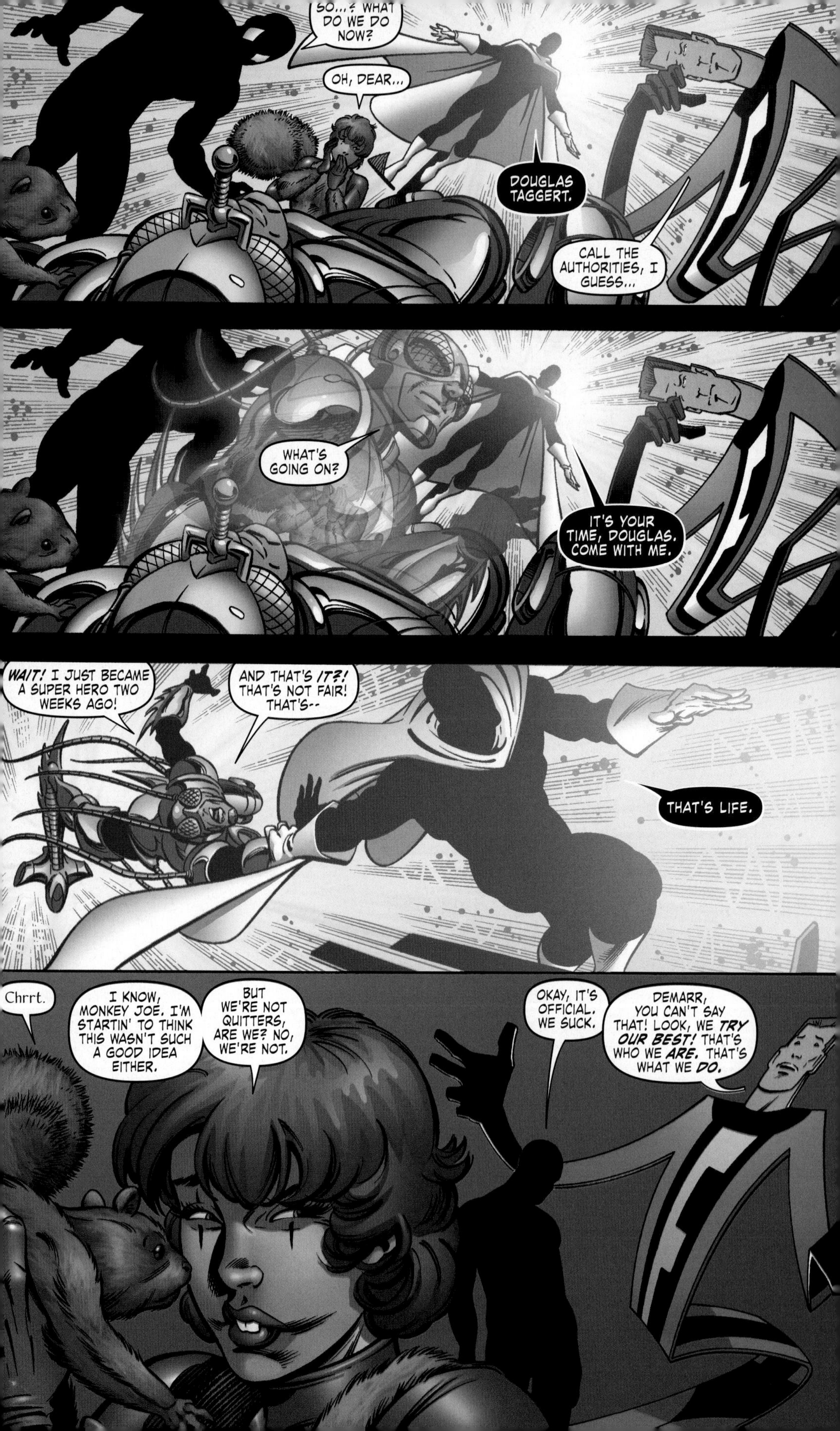

SO...? WHAT DO WE DO NOW?
OH, DEAR...
DOUGLAS TAGGERT.
CALL THE AUTHORITIES, I GUESS...
WHAT'S GOING ON?
IT'S YOUR TIME, DOUGLAS. COME WITH ME.
WAIT! I JUST BECAME A SUPER HERO TWO WEEKS AGO!
AND THAT'S IT?! THAT'S NOT FAIR! THAT'S--
THAT'S LIFE.
Chrrt.
I KNOW, MONKEY JOE. I'M STARTIN' TO THINK THIS WASN'T SUCH A GOOD IDEA EITHER.
BUT WE'RE NOT QUITTERS, ARE WE? NO, WE'RE NOT.
OKAY, IT'S OFFICIAL. WE SUCK.
DEMARR, YOU CAN'T SAY THAT! LOOK, WE TRY OUR BEST! THAT'S WHO WE ARE. THAT'S WHAT WE DO.

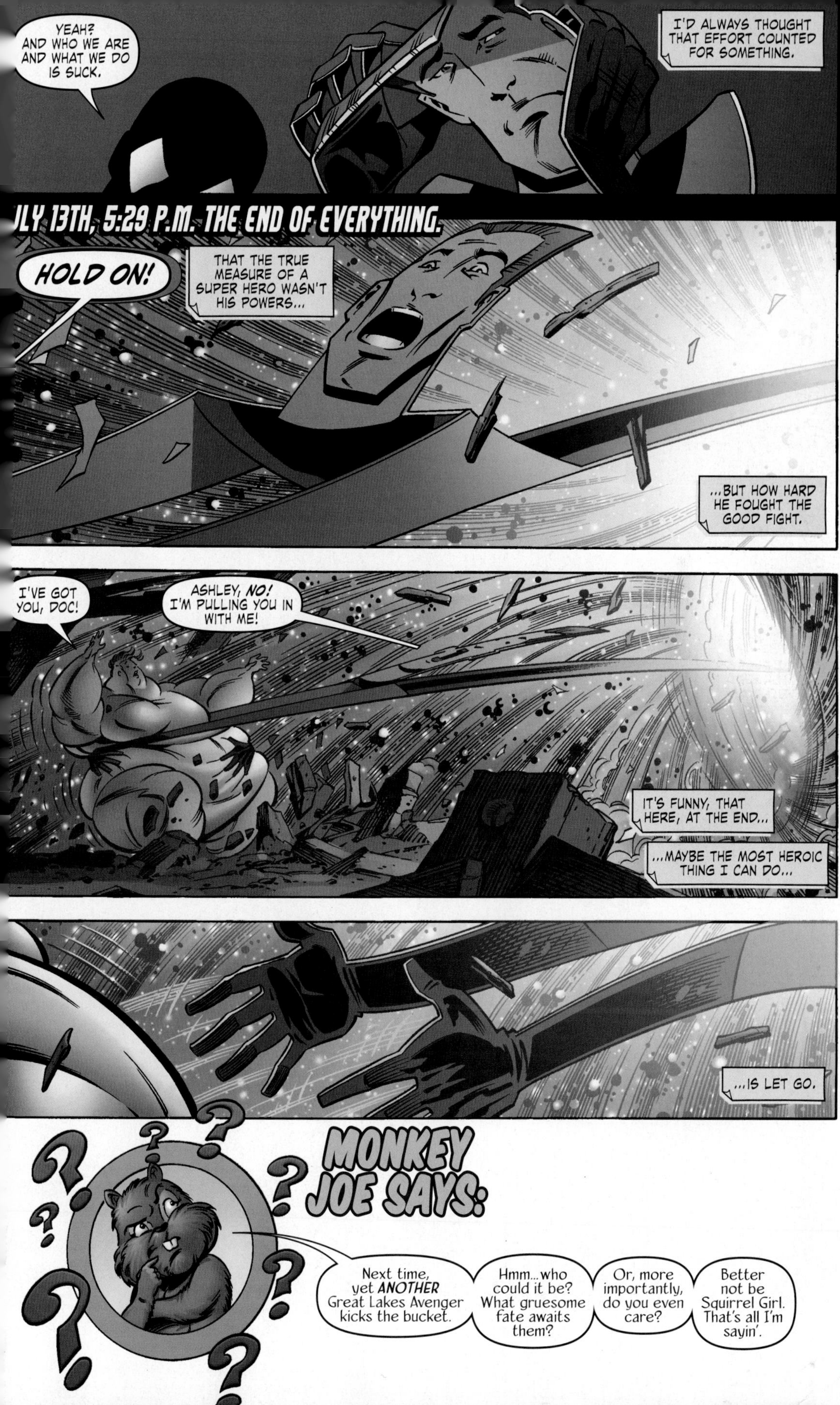
YEAH? AND WHO WE ARE AND WHAT WE DO IS SUCK.
I'D ALWAYS THOUGHT THAT EFFORT COUNTED FOR SOMETHING.
ULY 13TH, 5:29 P.M. THE END OF EVERYTHING.
HOLD ON!
THAT THE TRUE MEASURE OF A SUPER HERO WASN'T HIS POWERS...
...BUT HOW HARD HE FOUGHT THE GOOD FIGHT.
I'VE GOT YOU, DOC!
ASHLEY, NO! I'M PULLING YOU IN WITH ME!
IT'S FUNNY, THAT HERE, AT THE END...
...MAYBE THE MOST HEROIC THING I CAN DO...
...IS LET GO.
MONKEY JOE SAYS:
Next time, yet ANOTHER Great Lakes Avenger kicks the bucket.
Hmm...who could it be? What gruesome fate awaits them?
Or, more importantly, do you even care?
Better not be Squirrel Girl. That's all I'm sayin'.

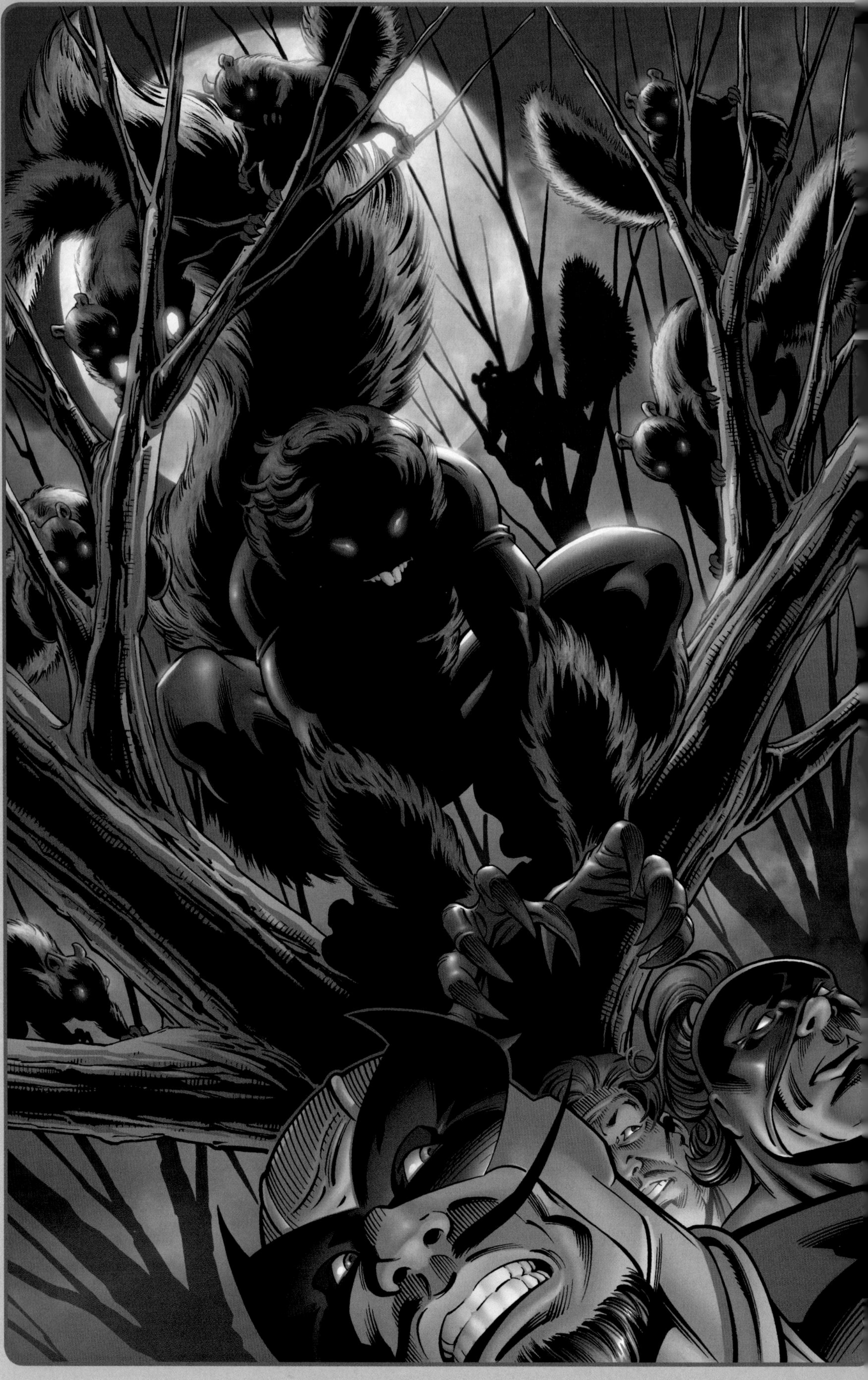

GLA #3

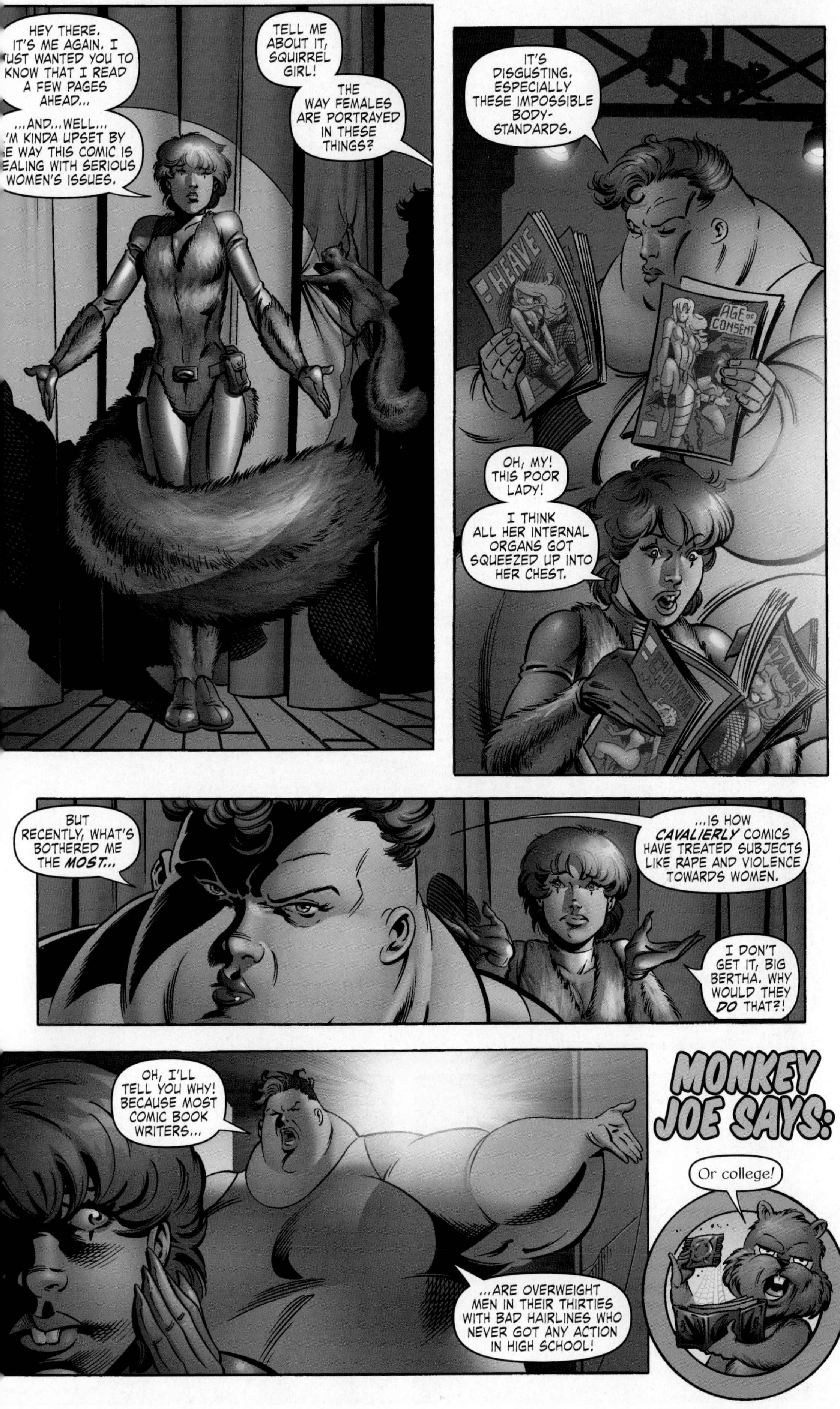
HEY THERE. IT'S ME AGAIN. I UST WANTED YOU TO KNOW THAT I READ A FEW PAGES AHEAD...
...AND...WELL... 'M KINDA UPSET BY E WAY THIS COMIC IS EALING WITH SERIOUS WOMEN'S ISSUES.
TELL ME ABOUT IT, SQUIRREL GIRL!
THE WAY FEMALES ARE PORTRAYED IN THESE THINGS?
IT'S DISGUSTING. ESPECIALLY THESE IMPOSSIBLE BODY-STANDARDS.
HEAVE
AGE OF CONSENT
OH, MY! THIS POOR LADY!
I THINK ALL HER INTERNAL ORGANS GOT SQUEEZED UP INTO HER CHEST.
BUT RECENTLY, WHAT'S BOTHERED ME THE MOST...
...IS HOW CAVALIERLY COMICS HAVE TREATED SUBJECTS LIKE RAPE AND VIOLENCE TOWARDS WOMEN.
I DON'T GET IT, BIG BERTHA. WHY WOULD THEY DO THAT?!
OH, I'LL TELL YOU WHY! BECAUSE MOST COMIC BOOK WRITERS...
...ARE OVERWEIGHT MEN IN THEIR THIRTIES WITH BAD HAIRLINES WHO NEVER GOT ANY ACTION IN HIGH SCHOOL!
MONKEY JOE SAYS:
Or college!

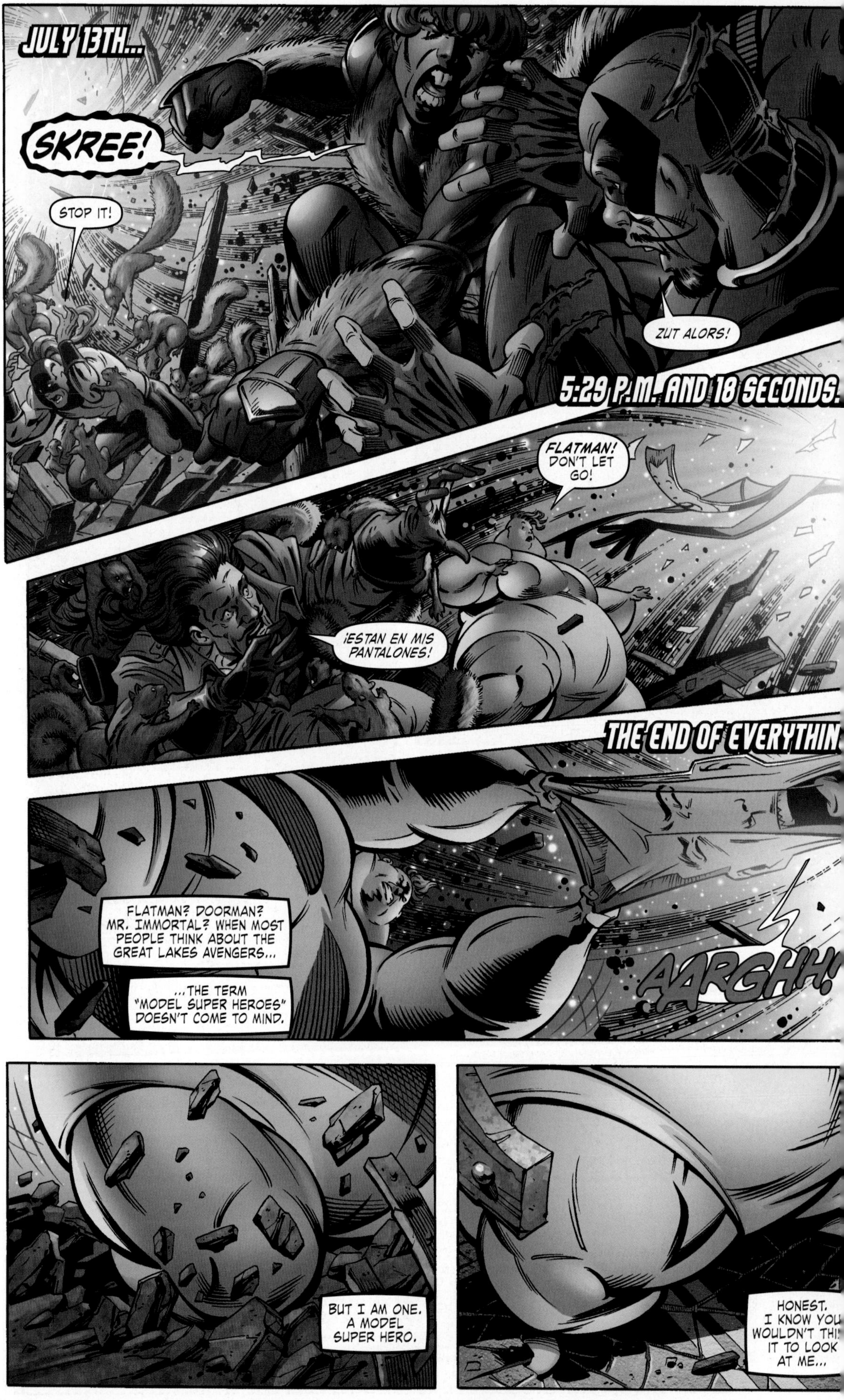
JULY 13TH...
SKREE!
STOP IT!
ZUT ALORS!
5:29 P.M. AND 18 SECONDS.
FLATMAN! DON'T LET GO!
¡ESTAN EN MIS PANTALONES!
THE END OF EVERYTHIN
FLATMAN? DOORMAN? MR. IMMORTAL? WHEN MOST PEOPLE THINK ABOUT THE GREAT LAKES AVENGERS...
...THE TERM "MODEL SUPER HEROES" DOESN'T COME TO MIND.
AARGHH!
BUT I AM ONE. A MODEL SUPER HERO.
HONEST. I KNOW YOU WOULDN'T THI IT TO LOOK AT ME...

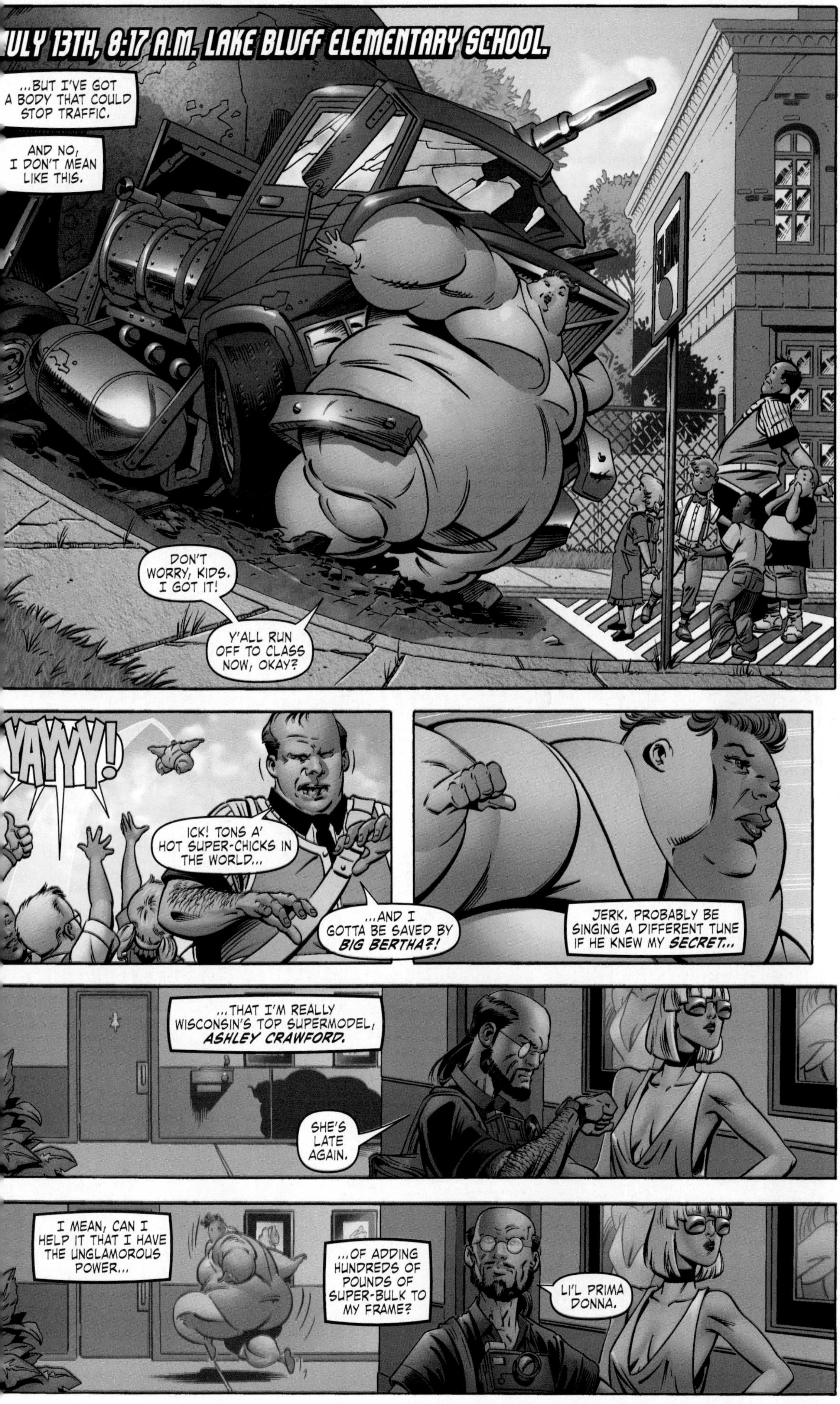

ULY 13TH, 8:17 A.M. LAKE BLUFF ELEMENTARY SCHOOL.
...BUT I'VE GOT A BODY THAT COULD STOP TRAFFIC.
AND NO, I DON'T MEAN LIKE THIS.
DON'T WORRY, KIDS. I GOT IT!
Y'ALL RUN OFF TO CLASS NOW, OKAY?
YAYYY!
ICK! TONS A' HOT SUPER-CHICKS IN THE WORLD...
...AND I GOTTA BE SAVED BY BIG BERTHA?!
JERK. PROBABLY BE SINGING A DIFFERENT TUNE IF HE KNEW MY SECRET...
...THAT I'M REALLY WISCONSIN'S TOP SUPERMODEL, ASHLEY CRAWFORD.
SHE'S LATE AGAIN.
I MEAN, CAN I HELP IT THAT I HAVE THE UNGLAMOROUS POWER...
...OF ADDING HUNDREDS OF POUNDS OF SUPER-BULK TO MY FRAME?
LI'L PRIMA DONNA.

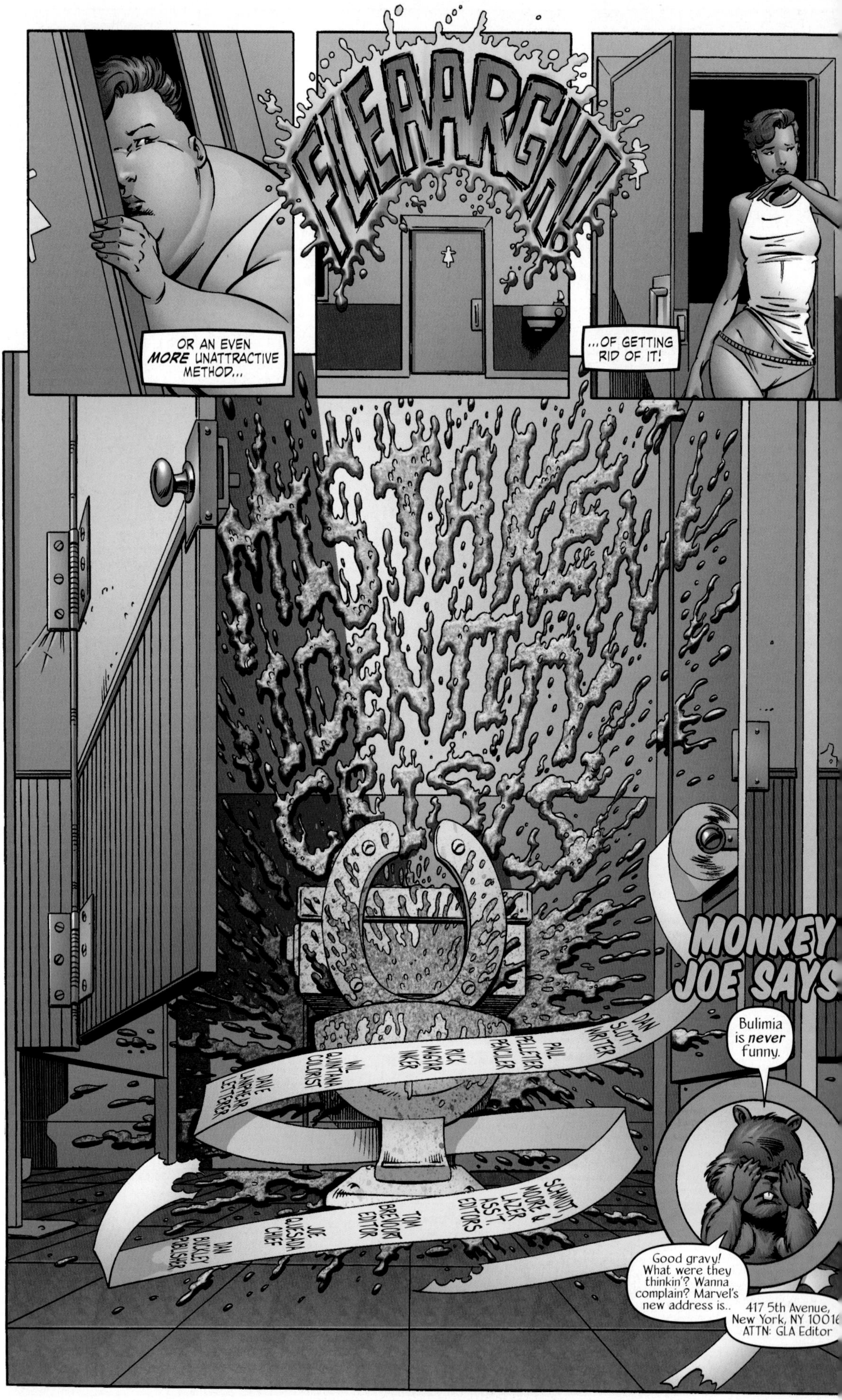
OR AN EVEN MORE UNATTRACTIVE METHOD...
FLEEARGH!!
...OF GETTING RID OF IT!
MISTAKEN IDENTITY CRISIS
DAN SLOTT WRITER
PAUL PELLETIER PENCILER
RICK MAGYAR INKER
WIL QUINTANA COLORIST
DAVE LANPHEAR LETTERER
SCHMIDT, MOORE & LAZER ASST. EDITORS
TOM BREVOORT EDITOR
JOE QUESADA CHIEF
DAN BUCKLEY PUBLISHER
MONKEY JOE SAYS
Bulimia is never funny.
Good gravy! What were they thinkin'? Wanna complain? Marvel's new address is..
417 5th Avenue, New York, NY 10016 ATTN: GLA Editor

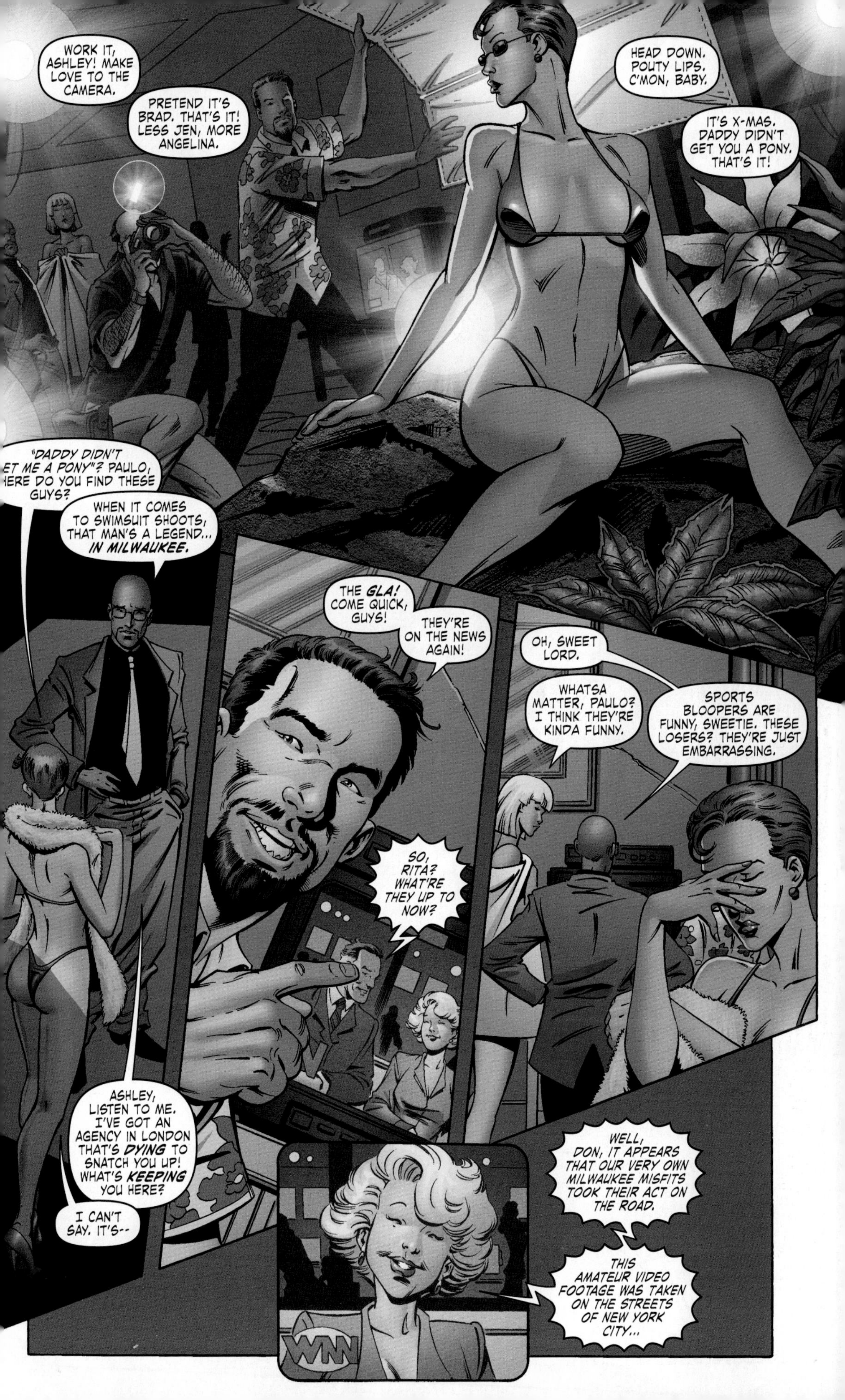

WORK IT, ASHLEY! MAKE LOVE TO THE CAMERA.
PRETEND IT'S BRAD. THAT'S IT! LESS JEN, MORE ANGELINA.
HEAD DOWN. POUTY LIPS. C'MON, BABY.
IT'S X-MAS. DADDY DIDN'T GET YOU A PONY. THAT'S IT!
"DADDY DIDN'T ET ME A PONY"? PAULO, HERE DO YOU FIND THESE GUYS?
WHEN IT COMES TO SWIMSUIT SHOOTS, THAT MAN'S A LEGEND... IN MILWAUKEE.
THE GLA! COME QUICK, GUYS!
THEY'RE ON THE NEWS AGAIN!
OH, SWEET LORD.
WHATSA MATTER, PAULO? I THINK THEY'RE KINDA FUNNY.
SPORTS BLOOPERS ARE FUNNY, SWEETIE. THESE LOSERS? THEY'RE JUST EMBARRASSING.
SO, RITA? WHAT'RE THEY UP TO NOW?
ASHLEY, LISTEN TO ME. I'VE GOT AN AGENCY IN LONDON THAT'S DYING TO SNATCH YOU UP! WHAT'S KEEPING YOU HERE?
I CAN'T SAY. IT'S--
WELL, DON, IT APPEARS THAT OUR VERY OWN MILWAUKEE MISFITS TOOK THEIR ACT ON THE ROAD.
THIS AMATEUR VIDEO FOOTAGE WAS TAKEN ON THE STREETS OF NEW YORK CITY...
WNN

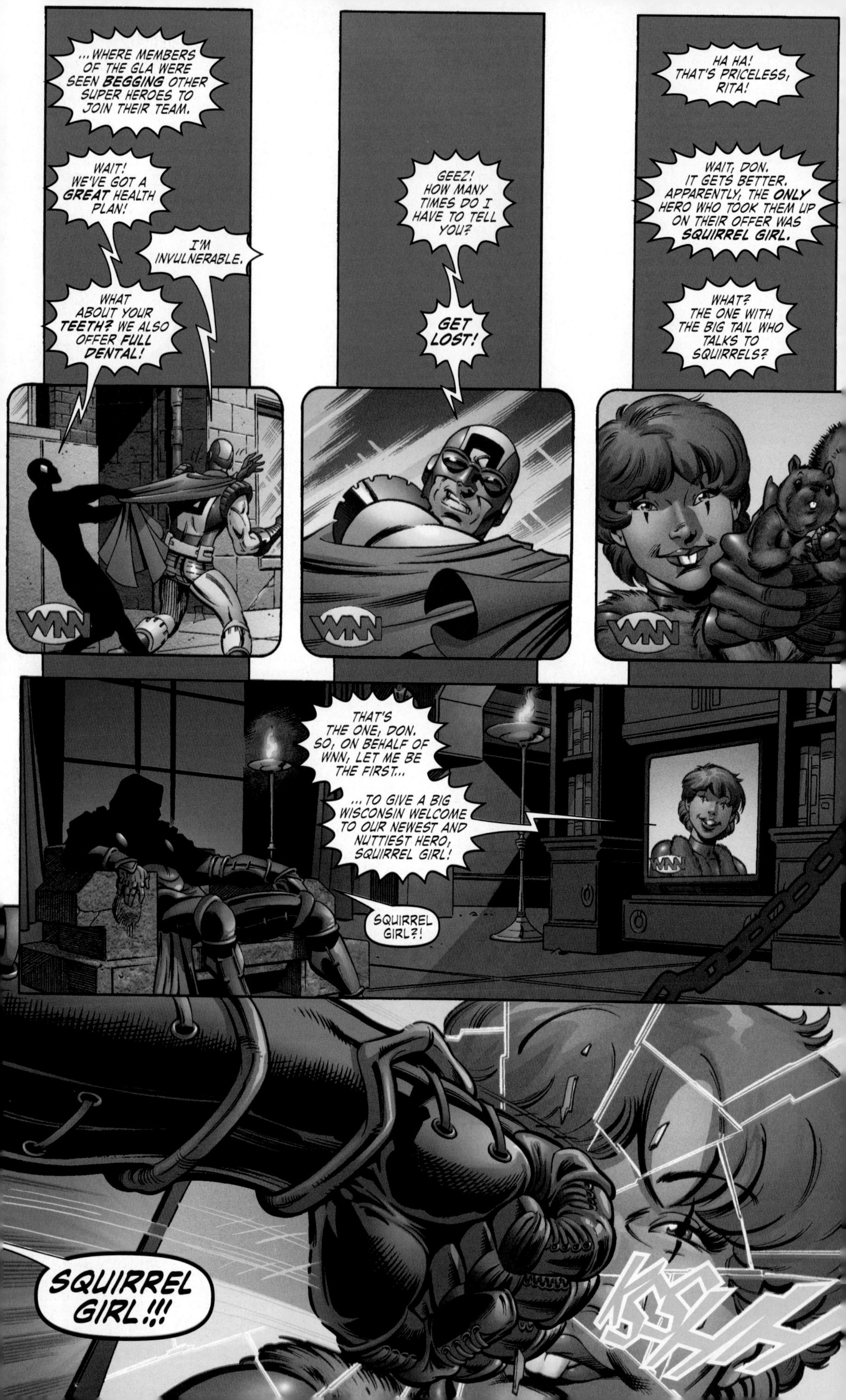
...WHERE MEMBERS OF THE GLA WERE SEEN BEGGING OTHER SUPER HEROES TO JOIN THEIR TEAM.
WAIT! WE'VE GOT A GREAT HEALTH PLAN!
I'M INVULNERABLE.
WHAT ABOUT YOUR TEETH? WE ALSO OFFER FULL DENTAL!
WNN
GEEZ! HOW MANY TIMES DO I HAVE TO TELL YOU?
GET LOST!
WNN
HA HA! THAT'S PRICELESS, RITA!
WAIT, DON. IT GETS BETTER. APPARENTLY, THE ONLY HERO WHO TOOK THEM UP ON THEIR OFFER WAS SQUIRREL GIRL.
WHAT? THE ONE WITH THE BIG TAIL WHO TALKS TO SQUIRRELS?
WNN
THAT'S THE ONE, DON. SO, ON BEHALF OF WNN, LET ME BE THE FIRST...
...TO GIVE A BIG WISCONSIN WELCOME TO OUR NEWEST AND NUTTIEST HERO, SQUIRREL GIRL!
WNN
SQUIRREL GIRL?!
SQUIRREL GIRL!!!
KSSH

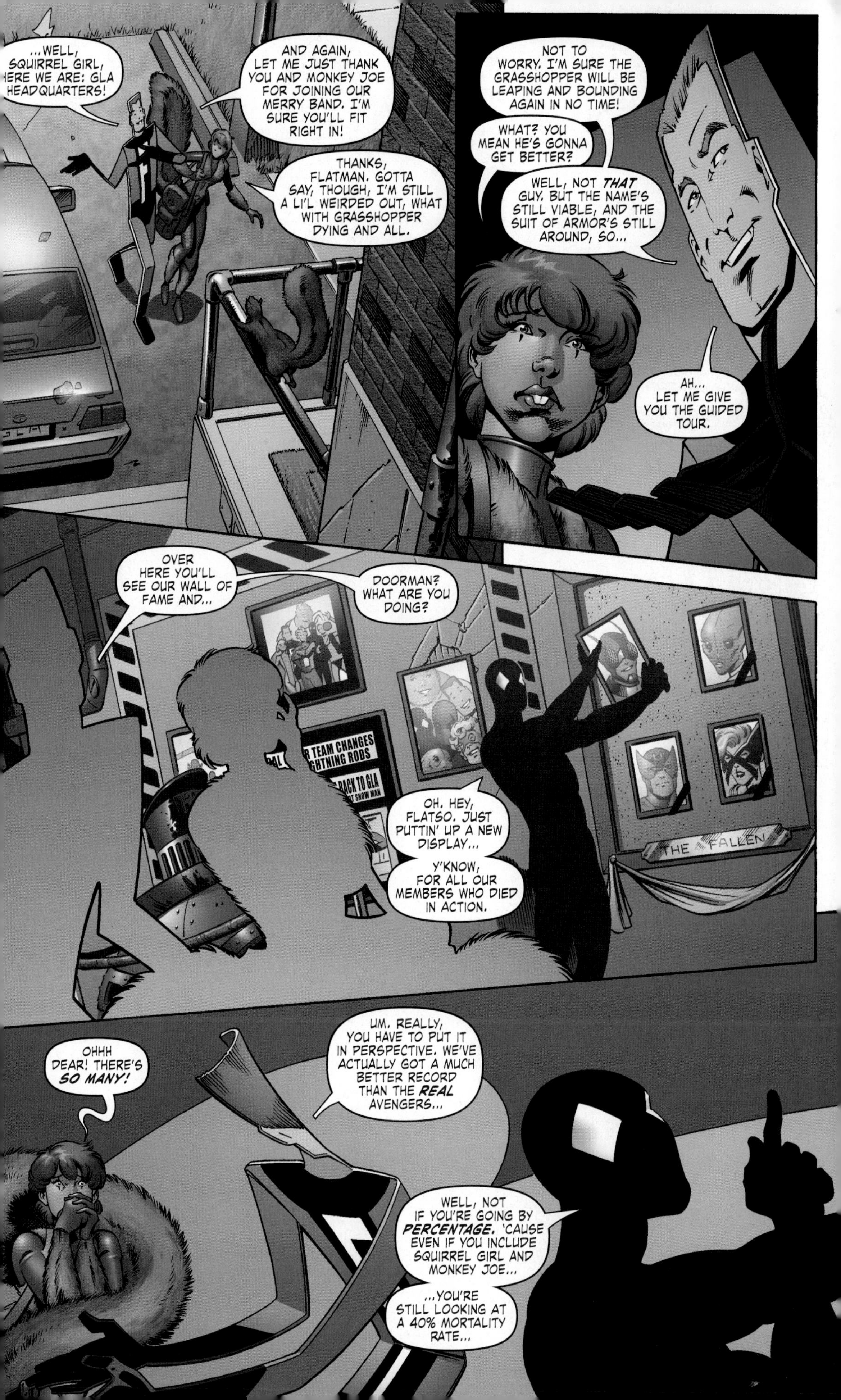

...WELL, SQUIRREL GIRL, HERE WE ARE: GLA HEADQUARTERS!
AND AGAIN, LET ME JUST THANK YOU AND MONKEY JOE FOR JOINING OUR MERRY BAND. I'M SURE YOU'LL FIT RIGHT IN!
THANKS, FLATMAN. GOTTA SAY, THOUGH, I'M STILL A LI'L WEIRDED OUT, WHAT WITH GRASSHOPPER DYING AND ALL.
NOT TO WORRY. I'M SURE THE GRASSHOPPER WILL BE LEAPING AND BOUNDING AGAIN IN NO TIME!
WHAT? YOU MEAN HE'S GONNA GET BETTER?
WELL, NOT *THAT* GUY. BUT THE NAME'S STILL VIABLE, AND THE SUIT OF ARMOR'S STILL AROUND, SO...
AH... LET ME GIVE YOU THE GUIDED TOUR.
OVER HERE YOU'LL SEE OUR WALL OF FAME AND...
DOORMAN? WHAT ARE YOU DOING?
OH. HEY, FLATSO. JUST PUTTIN' UP A NEW DISPLAY...
Y'KNOW, FOR ALL OUR MEMBERS WHO DIED IN ACTION.
THE FALLEN
OHHH DEAR! THERE'S ***SO MANY!***
UM. REALLY, YOU HAVE TO PUT IT IN PERSPECTIVE. WE'VE ACTUALLY GOT A MUCH BETTER RECORD THAN THE ***REAL*** AVENGERS...
WELL, NOT IF YOU'RE GOING BY ***PERCENTAGE.*** 'CAUSE EVEN IF YOU INCLUDE SQUIRREL GIRL AND MONKEY JOE...
...YOU'RE STILL LOOKING AT A 40% MORTALITY RATE...

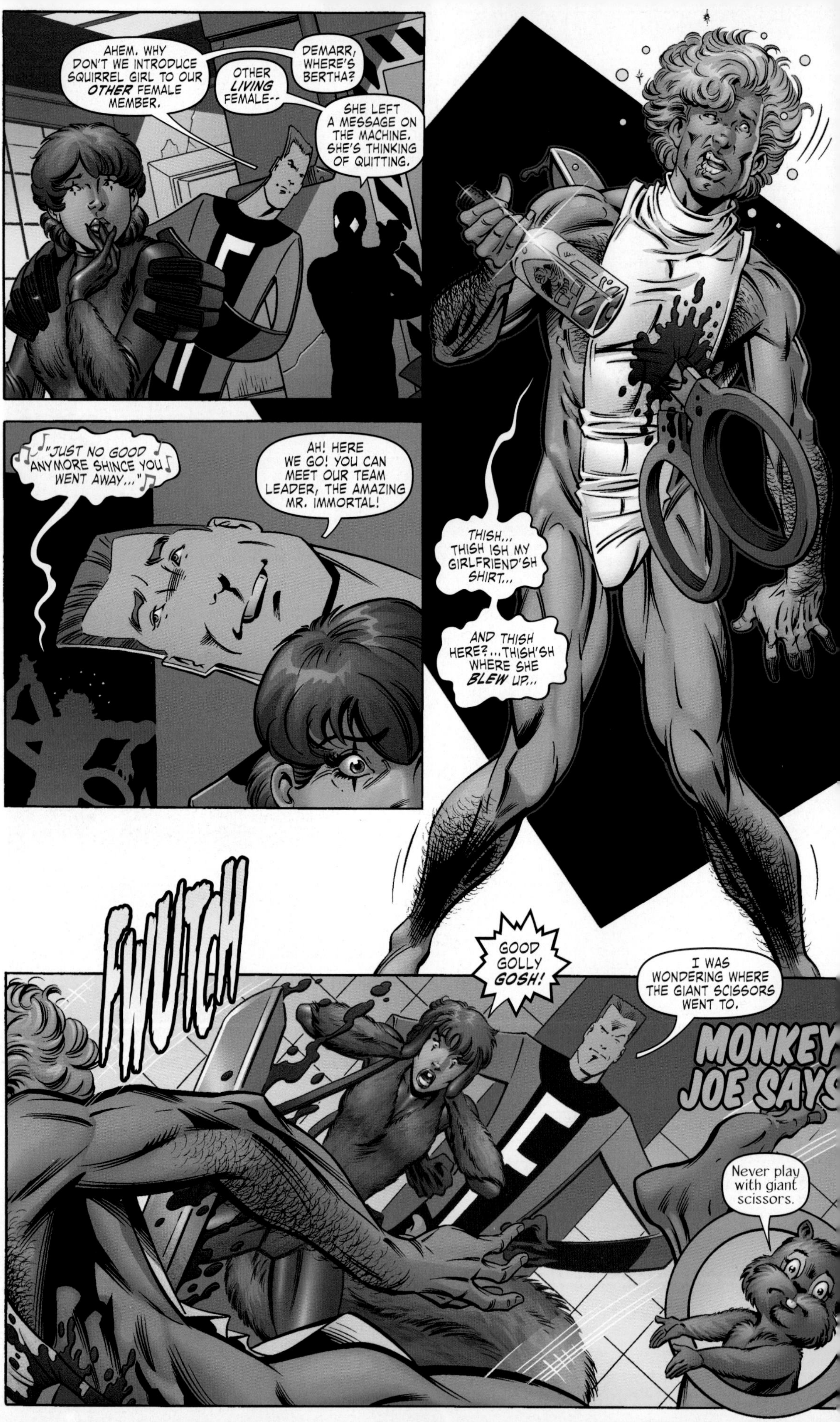
AHEM. WHY DON'T WE INTRODUCE SQUIRREL GIRL TO OUR OTHER FEMALE MEMBER.
OTHER LIVING FEMALE--
DEMARR, WHERE'S BERTHA?
SHE LEFT A MESSAGE ON THE MACHINE. SHE'S THINKING OF QUITTING.
"JUST NO GOOD ANYMORE SHINCE YOU WENT AWAY..."
AH! HERE WE GO! YOU CAN MEET OUR TEAM LEADER, THE AMAZING MR. IMMORTAL!
THISH... THISH ISH MY GIRLFRIEND'SH SHIRT...
AND THISH HERE?...THISH'SH WHERE SHE BLEW UP...
FWUTCH
GOOD GOLLY GOSH!
I WAS WONDERING WHERE THE GIANT SCISSORS WENT TO.
MONKEY JOE SAYS
Never play with giant scissors.

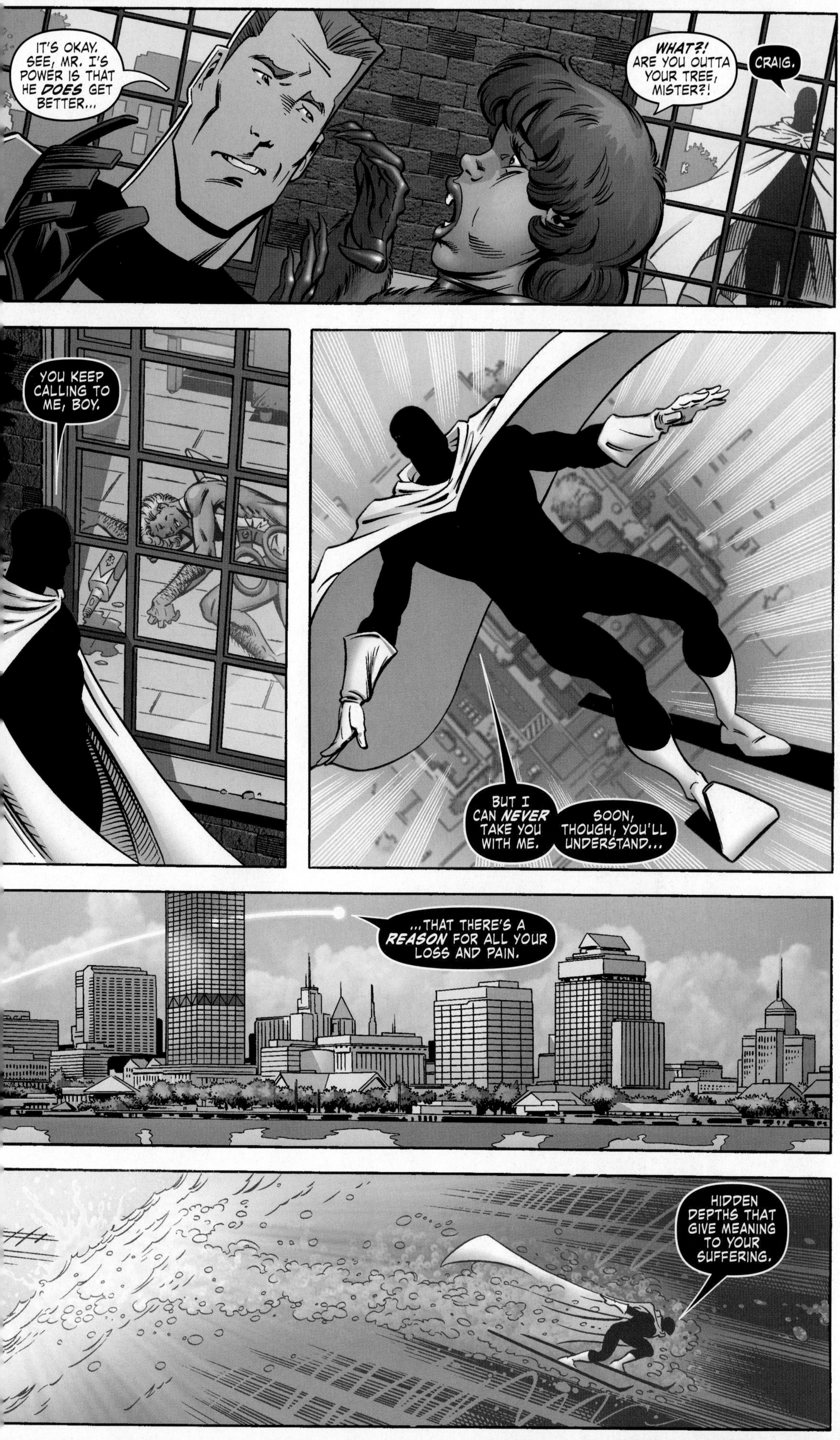
IT'S OKAY. SEE, MR. I'S POWER IS THAT HE DOES GET BETTER...
WHAT?! ARE YOU OUTTA YOUR TREE, MISTER?!
CRAIG.
YOU KEEP CALLING TO ME, BOY.
BUT I CAN NEVER TAKE YOU WITH ME.
SOON, THOUGH, YOU'LL UNDERSTAND...
...THAT THERE'S A REASON FOR ALL YOUR LOSS AND PAIN.
HIDDEN DEPTHS THAT GIVE MEANING TO YOUR SUFFERING.

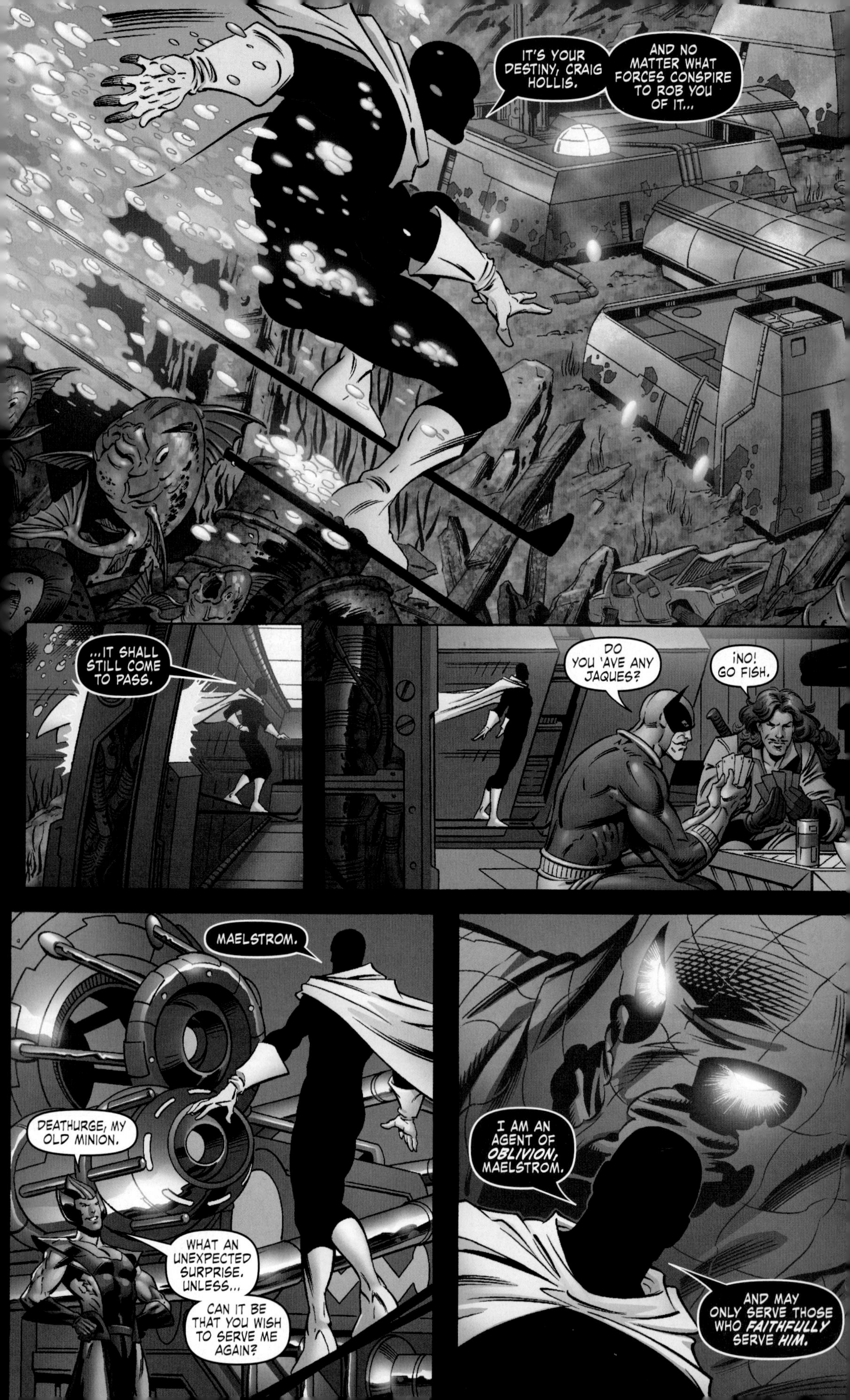
IT'S YOUR DESTINY, CRAIG HOLLIS.
AND NO MATTER WHAT FORCES CONSPIRE TO ROB YOU OF IT...
...IT SHALL STILL COME TO PASS.
DO YOU 'AVE ANY JAQUES?
¡NO! GO FISH.
MAELSTROM.
DEATHURGE, MY OLD MINION.
WHAT AN UNEXPECTED SURPRISE. UNLESS...
CAN IT BE THAT YOU WISH TO SERVE ME AGAIN?
I AM AN AGENT OF OBLIVION, MAELSTROM.
AND MAY ONLY SERVE THOSE WHO FAITHFULLY SERVE HIM.

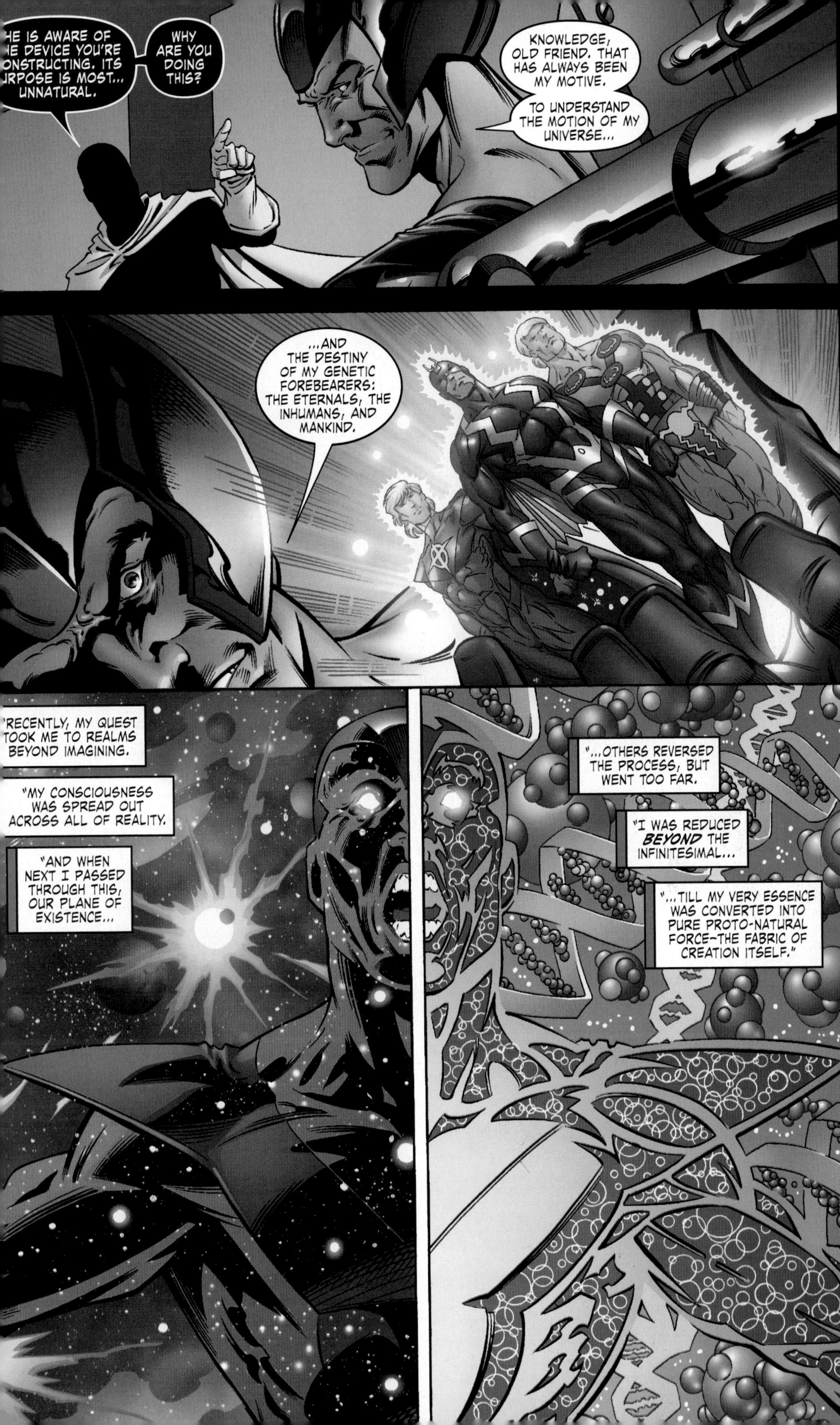
HE IS AWARE OF HE DEVICE YOU'RE ONSTRUCTING. ITS URPOSE IS MOST... UNNATURAL.
WHY ARE YOU DOING THIS?
KNOWLEDGE, OLD FRIEND. THAT HAS ALWAYS BEEN MY MOTIVE.
TO UNDERSTAND THE MOTION OF MY UNIVERSE...
...AND THE DESTINY OF MY GENETIC FOREBEARERS: THE ETERNALS, THE INHUMANS, AND MANKIND.
"RECENTLY, MY QUEST TOOK ME TO REALMS BEYOND IMAGINING.
"MY CONSCIOUSNESS WAS SPREAD OUT ACROSS ALL OF REALITY.
"AND WHEN NEXT I PASSED THROUGH THIS, OUR PLANE OF EXISTENCE...
"...OTHERS REVERSED THE PROCESS, BUT WENT TOO FAR.
"I WAS REDUCED *BEYOND* THE INFINITESIMAL...
"...TILL MY VERY ESSENCE WAS CONVERTED INTO PURE PROTO-NATURAL FORCE–THE FABRIC OF CREATION ITSELF."

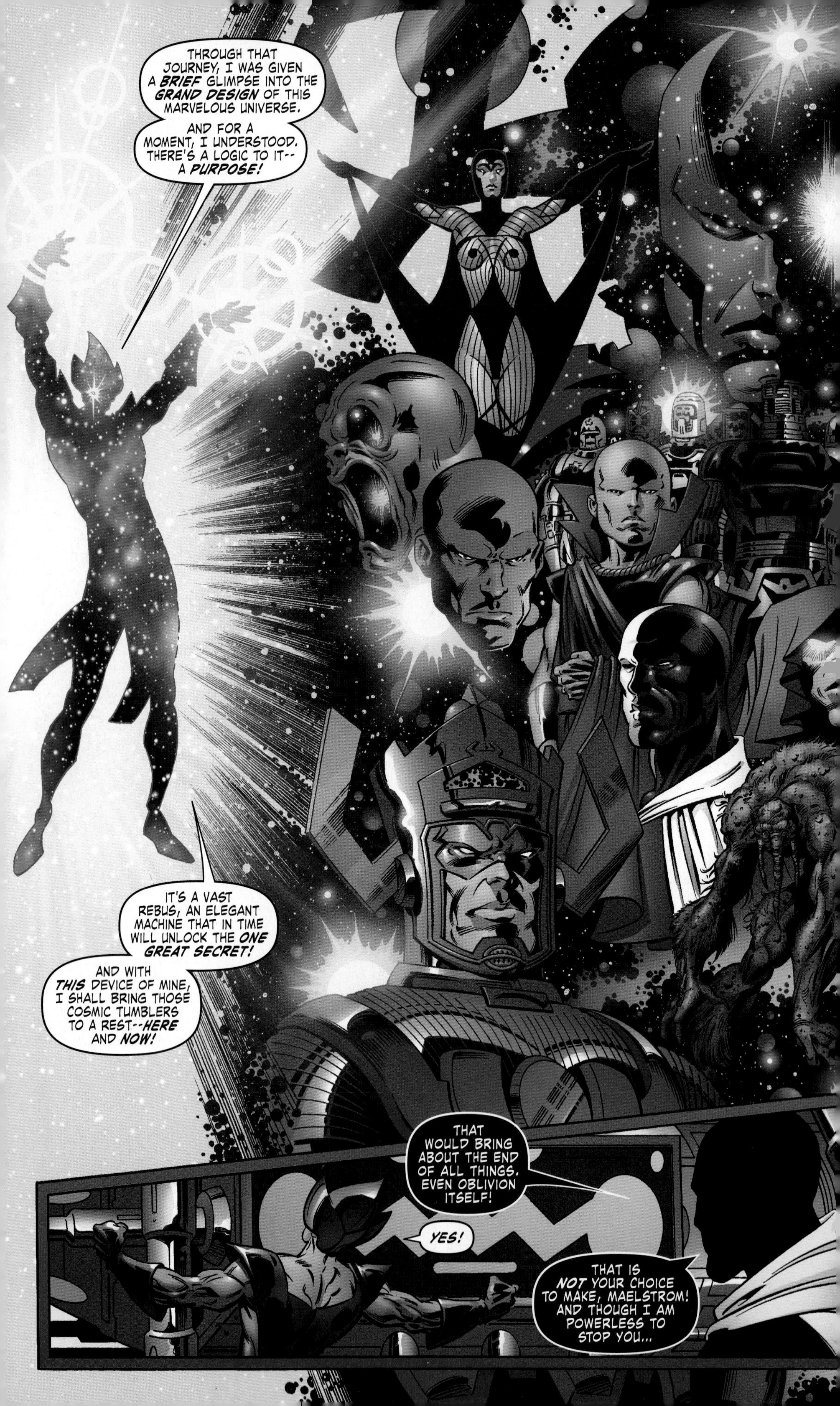

THROUGH THAT JOURNEY, I WAS GIVEN A BRIEF GLIMPSE INTO THE GRAND DESIGN OF THIS MARVELOUS UNIVERSE.
AND FOR A MOMENT, I UNDERSTOOD. THERE'S A LOGIC TO IT-- A PURPOSE!
IT'S A VAST REBUS, AN ELEGANT MACHINE THAT IN TIME WILL UNLOCK THE ONE GREAT SECRET!
AND WITH THIS DEVICE OF MINE, I SHALL BRING THOSE COSMIC TUMBLERS TO A REST--HERE AND NOW!
THAT WOULD BRING ABOUT THE END OF ALL THINGS. EVEN OBLIVION ITSELF!
YES!
THAT IS NOT YOUR CHOICE TO MAKE, MAELSTROM! AND THOUGH I AM POWERLESS TO STOP YOU...

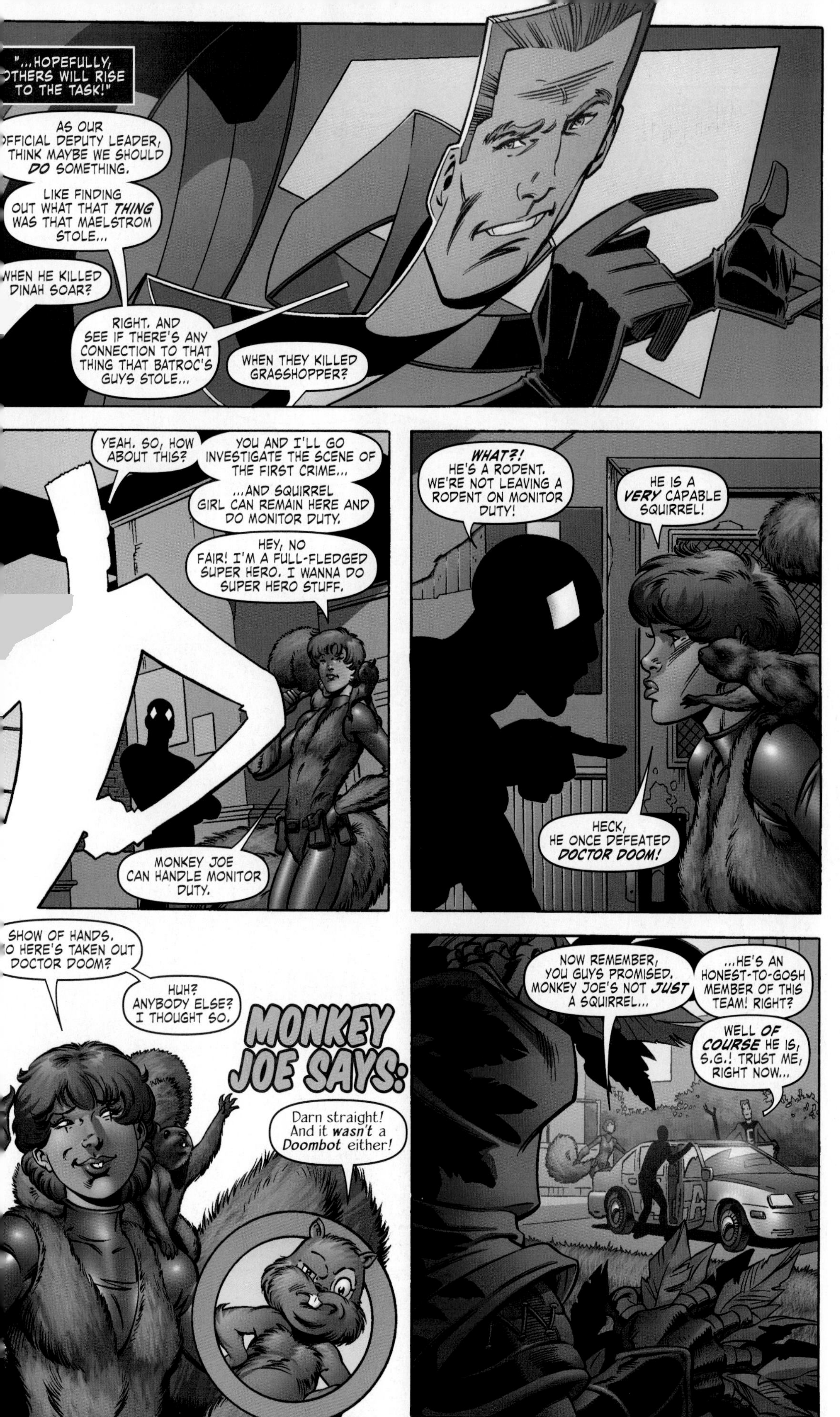
"...HOPEFULLY, OTHERS WILL RISE TO THE TASK!"
AS OUR OFFICIAL DEPUTY LEADER, THINK MAYBE WE SHOULD DO SOMETHING.
LIKE FINDING OUT WHAT THAT THING WAS THAT MAELSTROM STOLE...
WHEN HE KILLED DINAH SOAR?
RIGHT. AND SEE IF THERE'S ANY CONNECTION TO THAT THING THAT BATROC'S GUYS STOLE...
WHEN THEY KILLED GRASSHOPPER?
YEAH. SO, HOW ABOUT THIS?
YOU AND I'LL GO INVESTIGATE THE SCENE OF THE FIRST CRIME...
...AND SQUIRREL GIRL CAN REMAIN HERE AND DO MONITOR DUTY.
HEY, NO FAIR! I'M A FULL-FLEDGED SUPER HERO. I WANNA DO SUPER HERO STUFF.
MONKEY JOE CAN HANDLE MONITOR DUTY.
WHAT?! HE'S A RODENT. WE'RE NOT LEAVING A RODENT ON MONITOR DUTY!
HE IS A VERY CAPABLE SQUIRREL!
HECK, HE ONCE DEFEATED DOCTOR DOOM!
SHOW OF HANDS. WHO HERE'S TAKEN OUT DOCTOR DOOM?
HUH? ANYBODY ELSE? I THOUGHT SO.
MONKEY JOE SAYS:
Darn straight! And it wasn't a Doombot either!
NOW REMEMBER, YOU GUYS PROMISED. MONKEY JOE'S NOT JUST A SQUIRREL...
...HE'S AN HONEST-TO-GOSH MEMBER OF THIS TEAM! RIGHT?
WELL OF COURSE HE IS, S.G.! TRUST ME, RIGHT NOW...

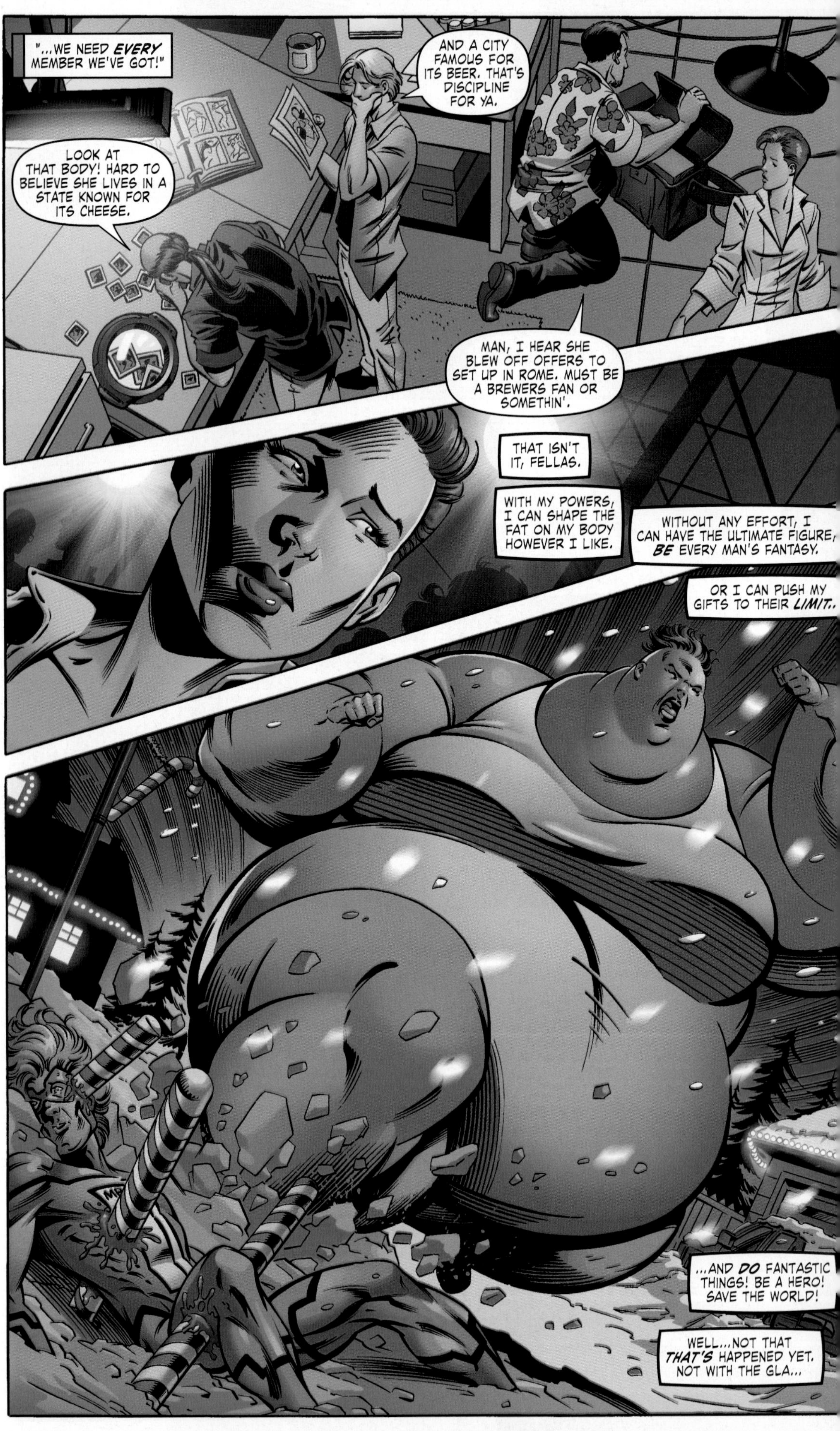
"...WE NEED EVERY MEMBER WE'VE GOT!"
LOOK AT THAT BODY! HARD TO BELIEVE SHE LIVES IN A STATE KNOWN FOR ITS CHEESE.
AND A CITY FAMOUS FOR ITS BEER. THAT'S DISCIPLINE FOR YA.
MAN, I HEAR SHE BLEW OFF OFFERS TO SET UP IN ROME. MUST BE A BREWERS FAN OR SOMETHIN'.
THAT ISN'T IT, FELLAS.
WITH MY POWERS, I CAN SHAPE THE FAT ON MY BODY HOWEVER I LIKE.
WITHOUT ANY EFFORT, I CAN HAVE THE ULTIMATE FIGURE, BE EVERY MAN'S FANTASY.
OR I CAN PUSH MY GIFTS TO THEIR LIMIT...
...AND DO FANTASTIC THINGS! BE A HERO! SAVE THE WORLD!
WELL...NOT THAT THAT'S HAPPENED YET. NOT WITH THE GLA...

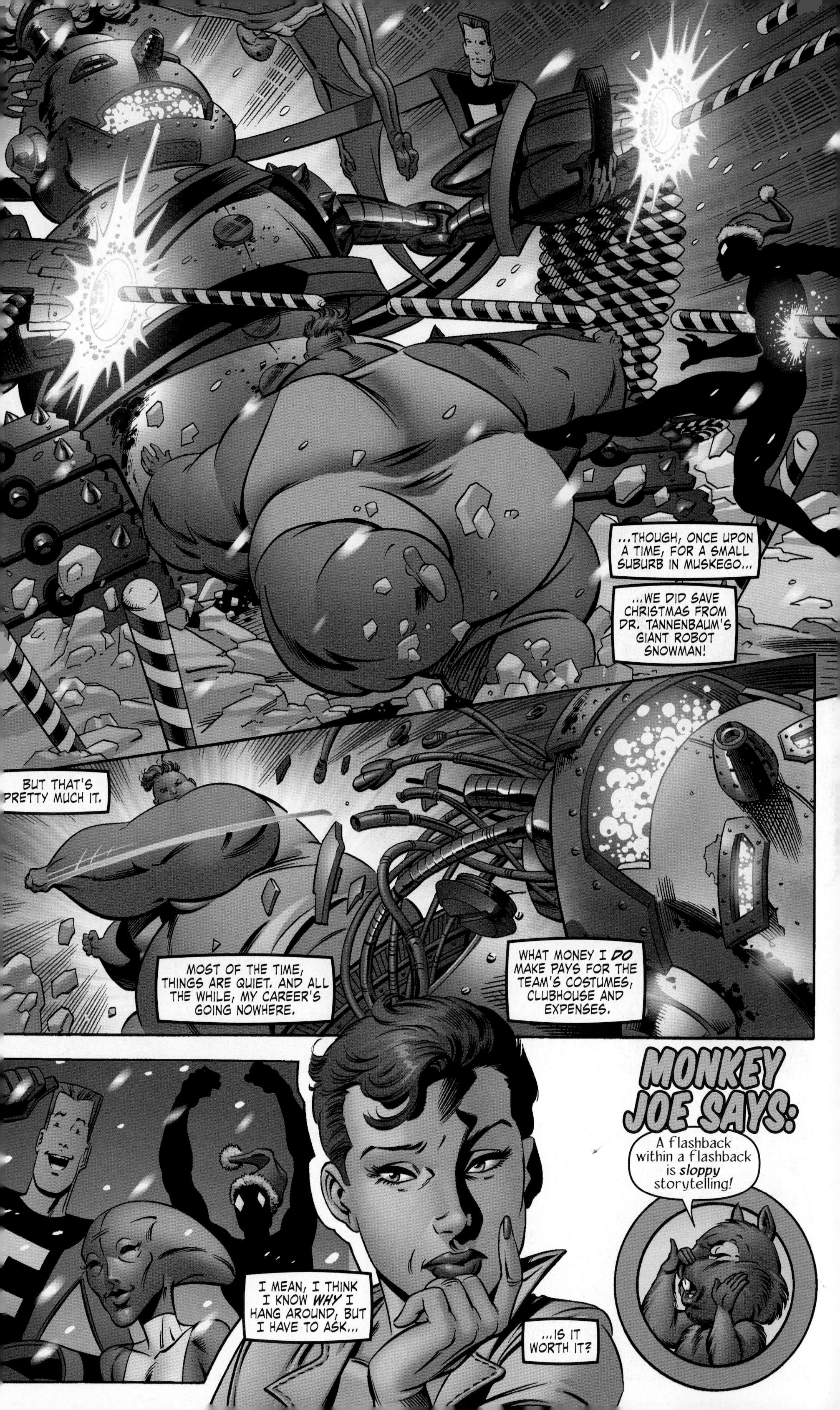
...THOUGH, ONCE UPON A TIME, FOR A SMALL SUBURB IN MUSKEGO...
...WE DID SAVE CHRISTMAS FROM DR. TANNENBAUM'S GIANT ROBOT SNOWMAN!
BUT THAT'S PRETTY MUCH IT.
MOST OF THE TIME, THINGS ARE QUIET. AND ALL THE WHILE, MY CAREER'S GOING NOWHERE.
WHAT MONEY I DO MAKE PAYS FOR THE TEAM'S COSTUMES, CLUBHOUSE AND EXPENSES.
I MEAN, I THINK I KNOW WHY I HANG AROUND, BUT I HAVE TO ASK...
...IS IT WORTH IT?
MONKEY JOE SAYS:
A flashback within a flashback is sloppy storytelling!

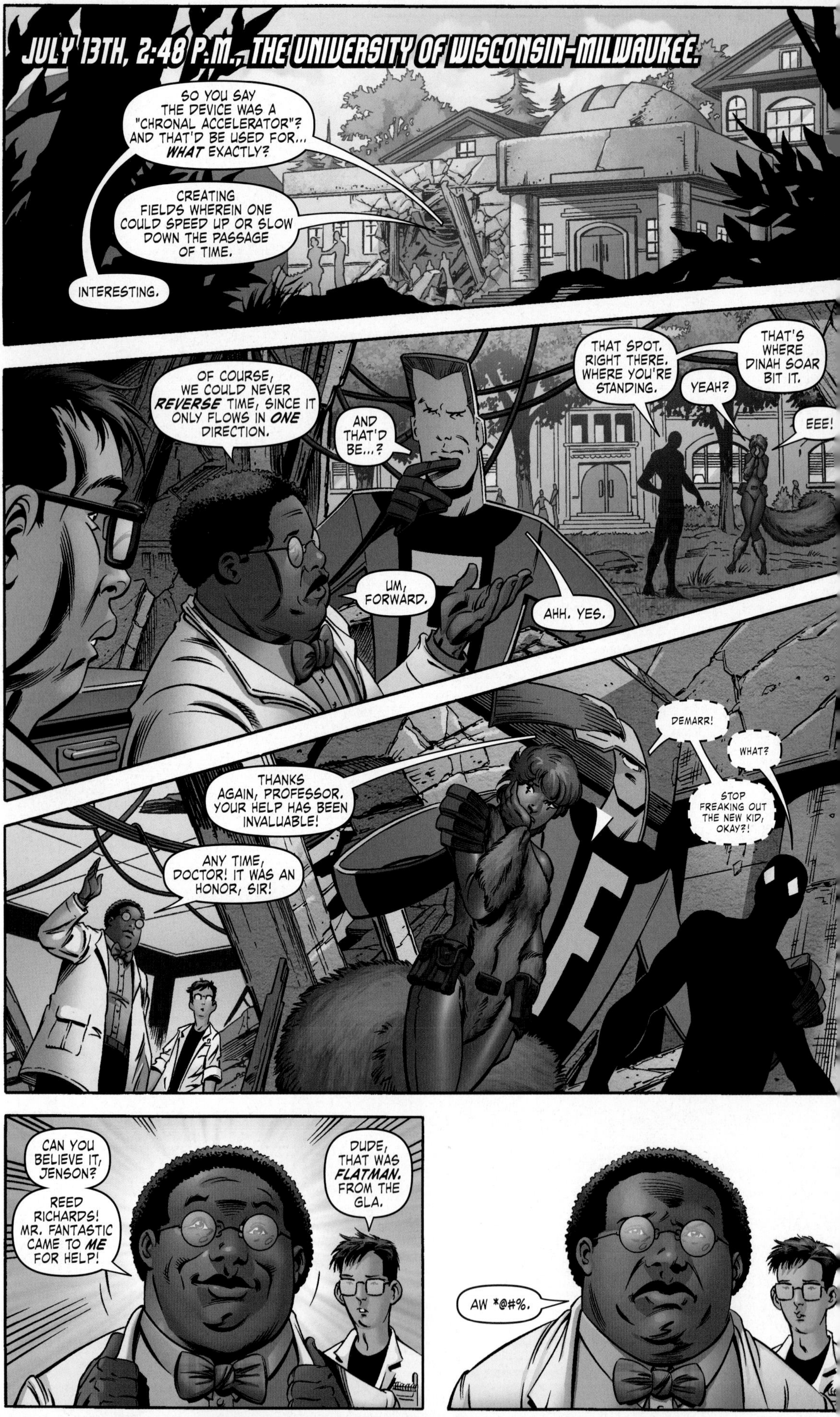
JULY 13TH, 2:48 P.M., THE UNIVERSITY OF WISCONSIN-MILWAUKEE.
SO YOU SAY THE DEVICE WAS A "CHRONAL ACCELERATOR"? AND THAT'D BE USED FOR... WHAT EXACTLY?
CREATING FIELDS WHEREIN ONE COULD SPEED UP OR SLOW DOWN THE PASSAGE OF TIME.
INTERESTING.
OF COURSE, WE COULD NEVER REVERSE TIME, SINCE IT ONLY FLOWS IN ONE DIRECTION.
AND THAT'D BE...?
UM, FORWARD.
AHH. YES.
THAT SPOT. RIGHT THERE. WHERE YOU'RE STANDING.
YEAH?
THAT'S WHERE DINAH SOAR BIT IT.
EEE!
THANKS AGAIN, PROFESSOR. YOUR HELP HAS BEEN INVALUABLE!
ANY TIME, DOCTOR! IT WAS AN HONOR, SIR!
DEMARR!
WHAT?
STOP FREAKING OUT THE NEW KID, OKAY?!
CAN YOU BELIEVE IT, JENSON?
REED RICHARDS! MR. FANTASTIC CAME TO ME FOR HELP!
DUDE, THAT WAS FLATMAN. FROM THE GLA.
AW *@#%.

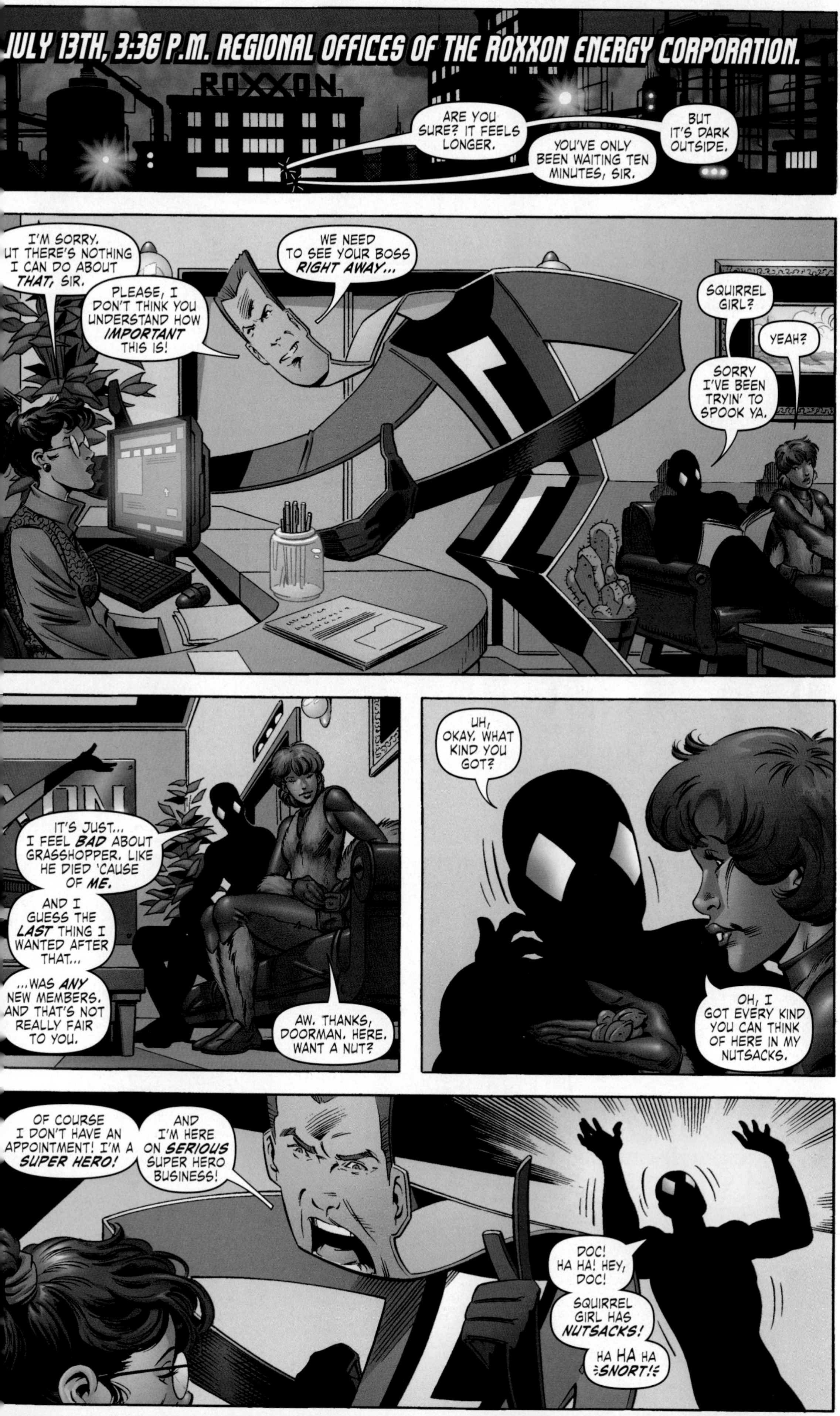

JULY 13TH, 3:36 P.M. REGIONAL OFFICES OF THE ROXXON ENERGY CORPORATION.
ROXXON
ARE YOU SURE? IT FEELS LONGER.
YOU'VE ONLY BEEN WAITING TEN MINUTES, SIR.
BUT IT'S DARK OUTSIDE.
I'M SORRY. UT THERE'S NOTHING I CAN DO ABOUT THAT, SIR.
WE NEED TO SEE YOUR BOSS RIGHT AWAY...
PLEASE, I DON'T THINK YOU UNDERSTAND HOW IMPORTANT THIS IS!
SQUIRREL GIRL?
YEAH?
SORRY I'VE BEEN TRYIN' TO SPOOK YA.
IT'S JUST... I FEEL BAD ABOUT GRASSHOPPER. LIKE HE DIED 'CAUSE OF ME.
AND I GUESS THE LAST THING I WANTED AFTER THAT...
...WAS ANY NEW MEMBERS. AND THAT'S NOT REALLY FAIR TO YOU.
AW. THANKS, DOORMAN. HERE. WANT A NUT?
UH, OKAY. WHAT KIND YOU GOT?
OH, I GOT EVERY KIND YOU CAN THINK OF HERE IN MY NUTSACKS.
OF COURSE I DON'T HAVE AN APPOINTMENT! I'M A SUPER HERO!
AND I'M HERE ON SERIOUS SUPER HERO BUSINESS!
DOC! HA HA! HEY, DOC!
SQUIRREL GIRL HAS NUTSACKS!
HA HA HA SNORT!

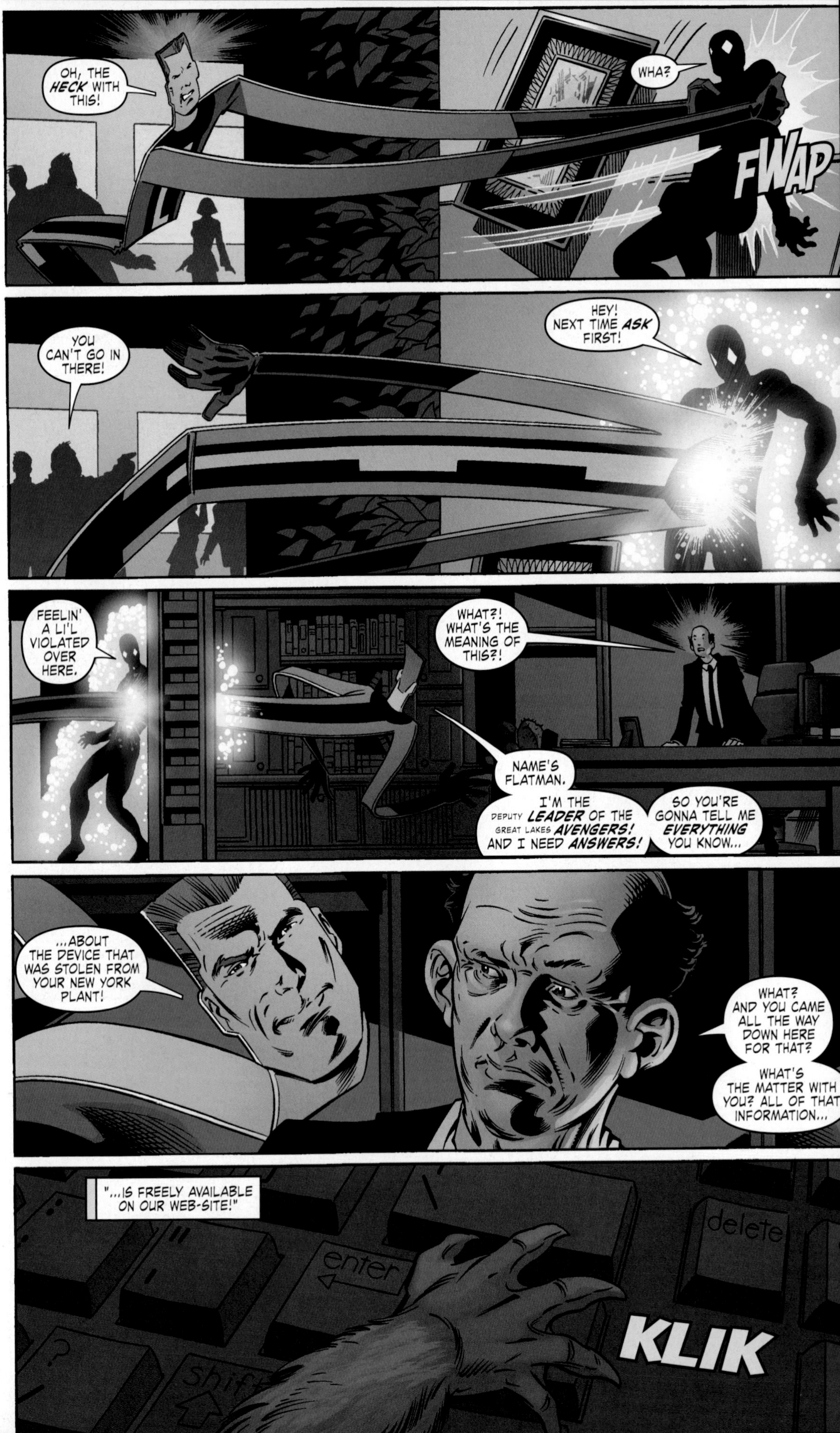
OH, THE HECK WITH THIS!
WHA?
FWAP
YOU CAN'T GO IN THERE!
HEY! NEXT TIME ASK FIRST!
FEELIN' A LI'L VIOLATED OVER HERE.
WHAT?! WHAT'S THE MEANING OF THIS?!
NAME'S FLATMAN.
I'M THE DEPUTY LEADER OF THE GREAT LAKES AVENGERS! AND I NEED ANSWERS!
SO YOU'RE GONNA TELL ME EVERYTHING YOU KNOW...
...ABOUT THE DEVICE THAT WAS STOLEN FROM YOUR NEW YORK PLANT!
WHAT? AND YOU CAME ALL THE WAY DOWN HERE FOR THAT?
WHAT'S THE MATTER WITH YOU? ALL OF THAT INFORMATION...
"...IS FREELY AVAILABLE ON OUR WEB-SITE!"
delete
enter
KLIK

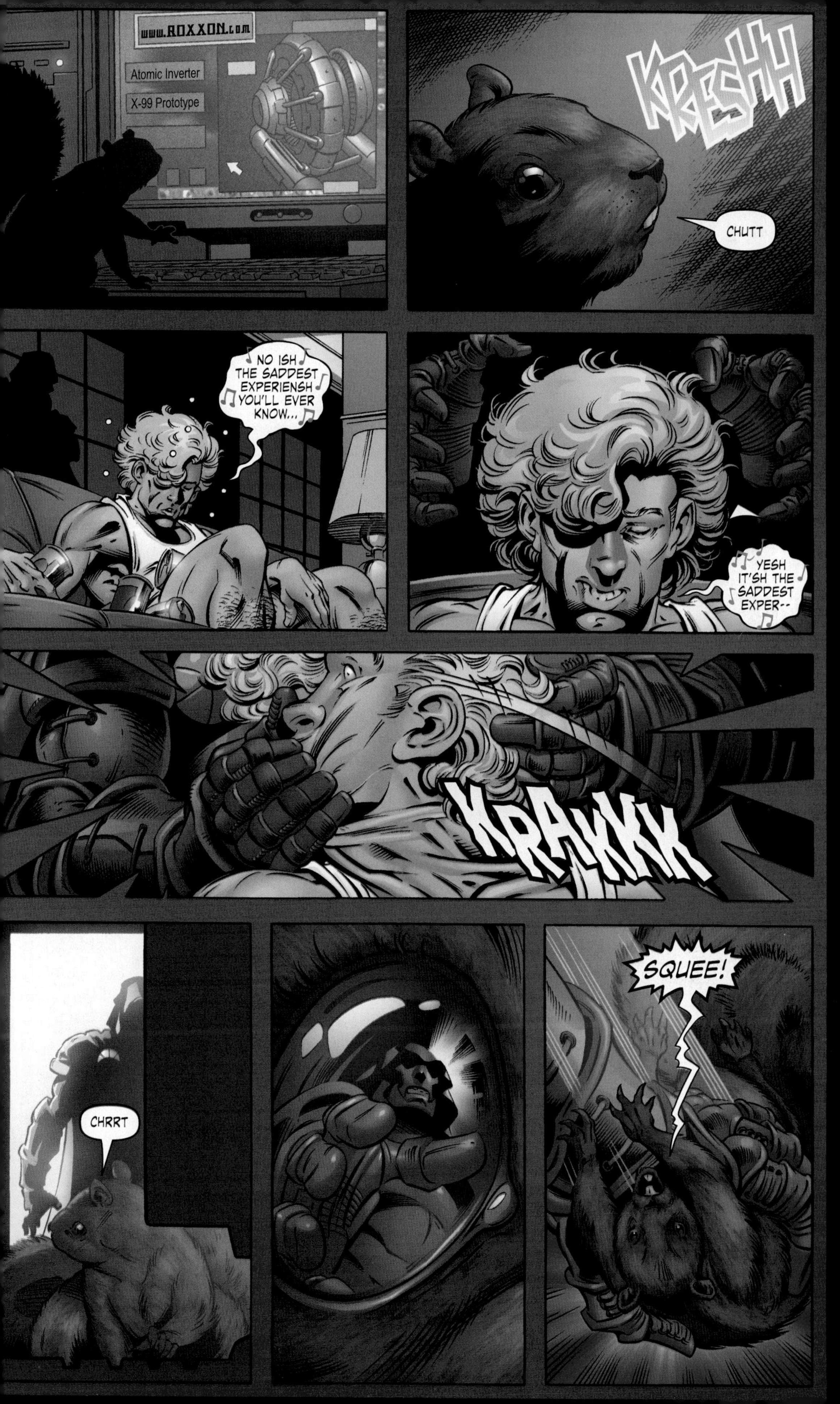

www.ROXXON.com
Atomic Inverter
X-99 Prototype
KRESHH
CHUTT
NO ISH THE SADDEST EXPERIENSH YOU'LL EVER KNOW...
YESH IT'SH THE SADDEST EXPER--
KRAKKK
CHRRT
SQUEE!

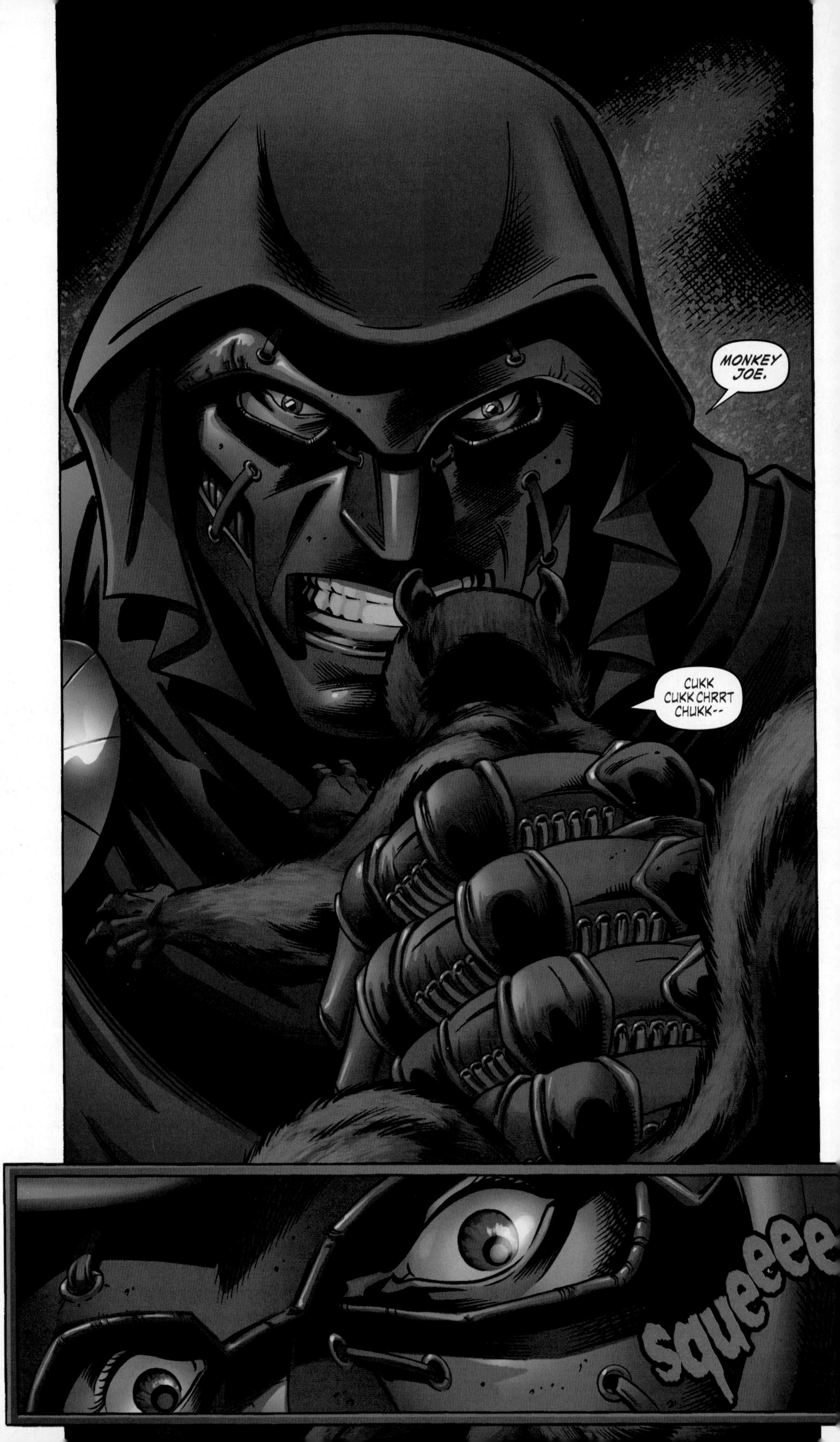
MONKEY JOE.
CUKK CUKK CHRRT CHUKK--
squeeee

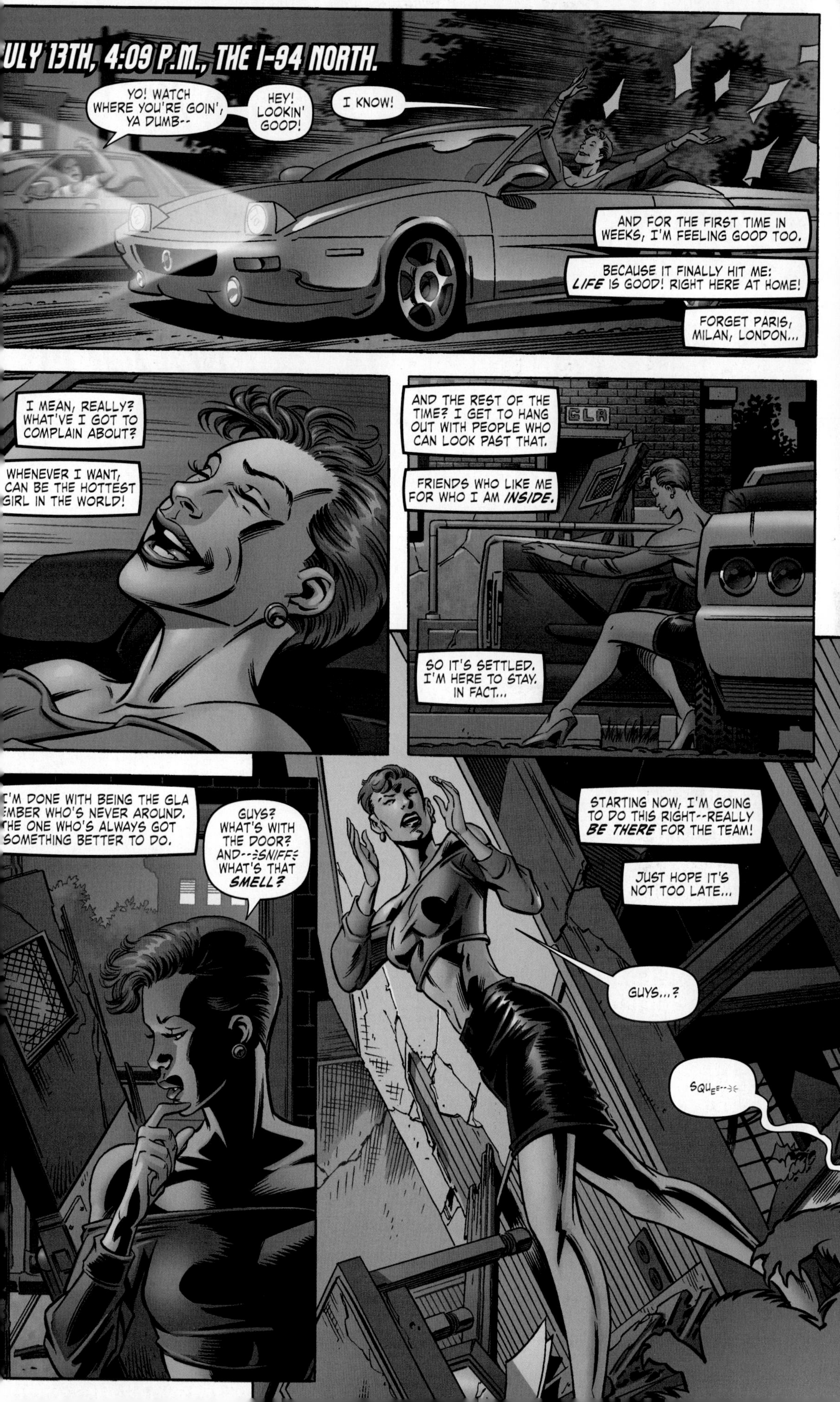
ULY 13TH, 4:09 P.M., THE I-94 NORTH.
YO! WATCH WHERE YOU'RE GOIN', YA DUMB--
HEY! LOOKIN' GOOD!
I KNOW!
AND FOR THE FIRST TIME IN WEEKS, I'M FEELING GOOD TOO.
BECAUSE IT FINALLY HIT ME: LIFE IS GOOD! RIGHT HERE AT HOME!
FORGET PARIS, MILAN, LONDON...
I MEAN, REALLY? WHAT'VE I GOT TO COMPLAIN ABOUT?
WHENEVER I WANT, CAN BE THE HOTTEST GIRL IN THE WORLD!
AND THE REST OF THE TIME? I GET TO HANG OUT WITH PEOPLE WHO CAN LOOK PAST THAT.
GLA
FRIENDS WHO LIKE ME FOR WHO I AM INSIDE.
SO IT'S SETTLED. I'M HERE TO STAY. IN FACT...
I'M DONE WITH BEING THE GLA EMBER WHO'S NEVER AROUND. THE ONE WHO'S ALWAYS GOT SOMETHING BETTER TO DO.
GUYS? WHAT'S WITH THE DOOR? AND--SNIFF= WHAT'S THAT SMELL?
STARTING NOW, I'M GOING TO DO THIS RIGHT--REALLY BE THERE FOR THE TEAM!
JUST HOPE IT'S NOT TOO LATE...
GUYS...?
SQUEE--

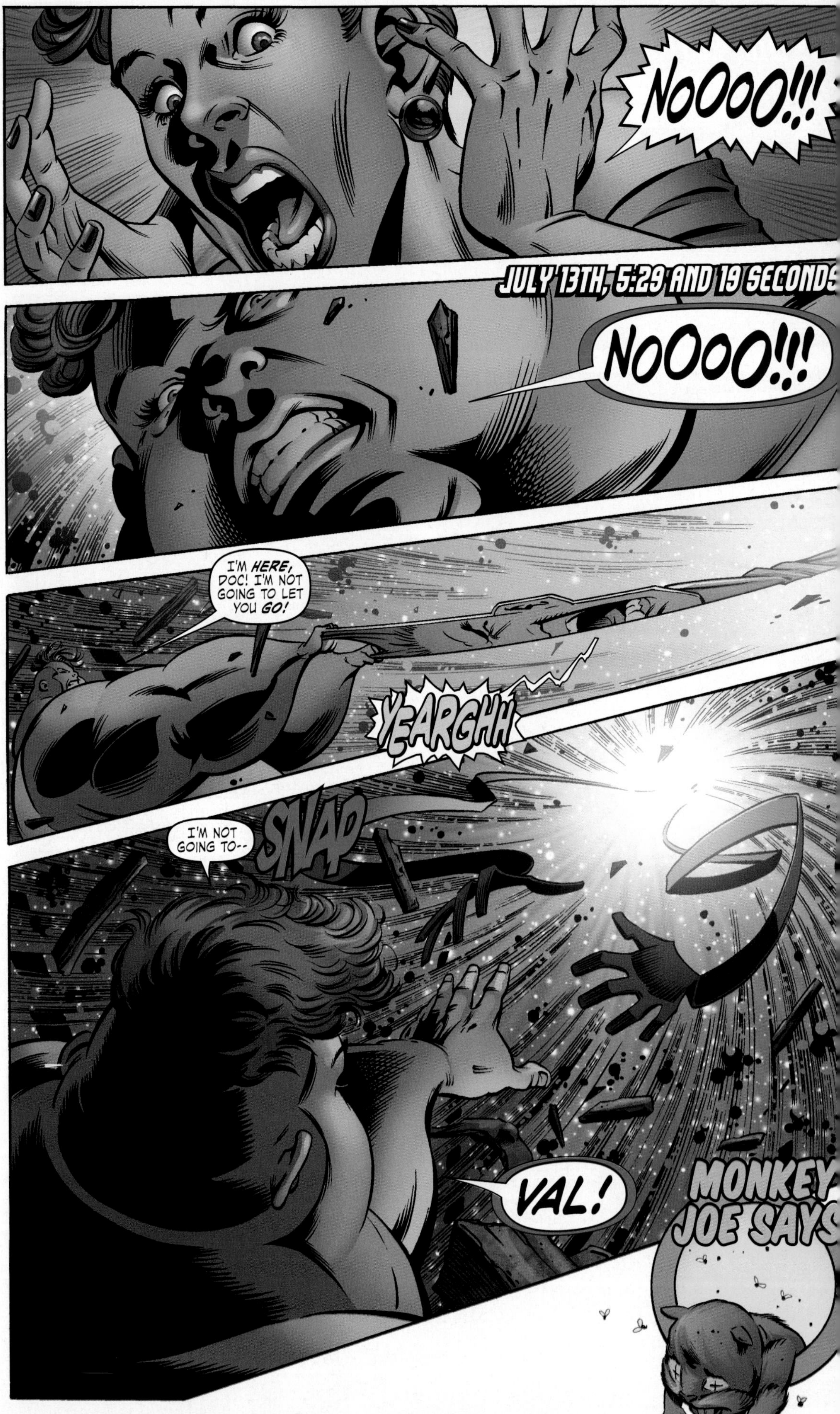

NOOOO!!!
JULY 13TH, 5:29 AND 19 SECONDS
NOOOO!!!
I'M HERE, DOC! I'M NOT GOING TO LET YOU GO!
YEARGHH
SNAP
I'M NOT GOING TO--
VAL!
MONKEY JOE SAYS

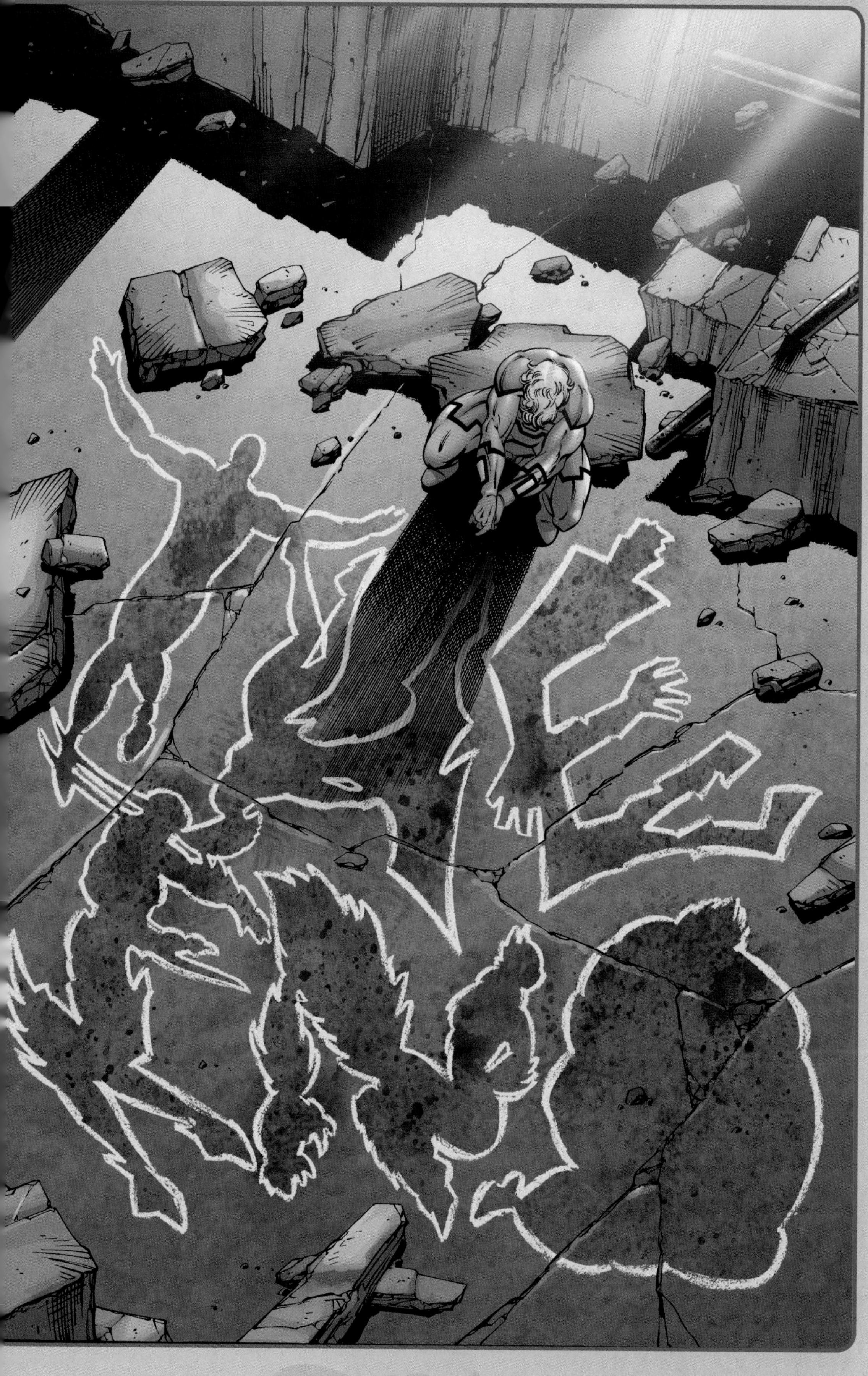

GLA #4

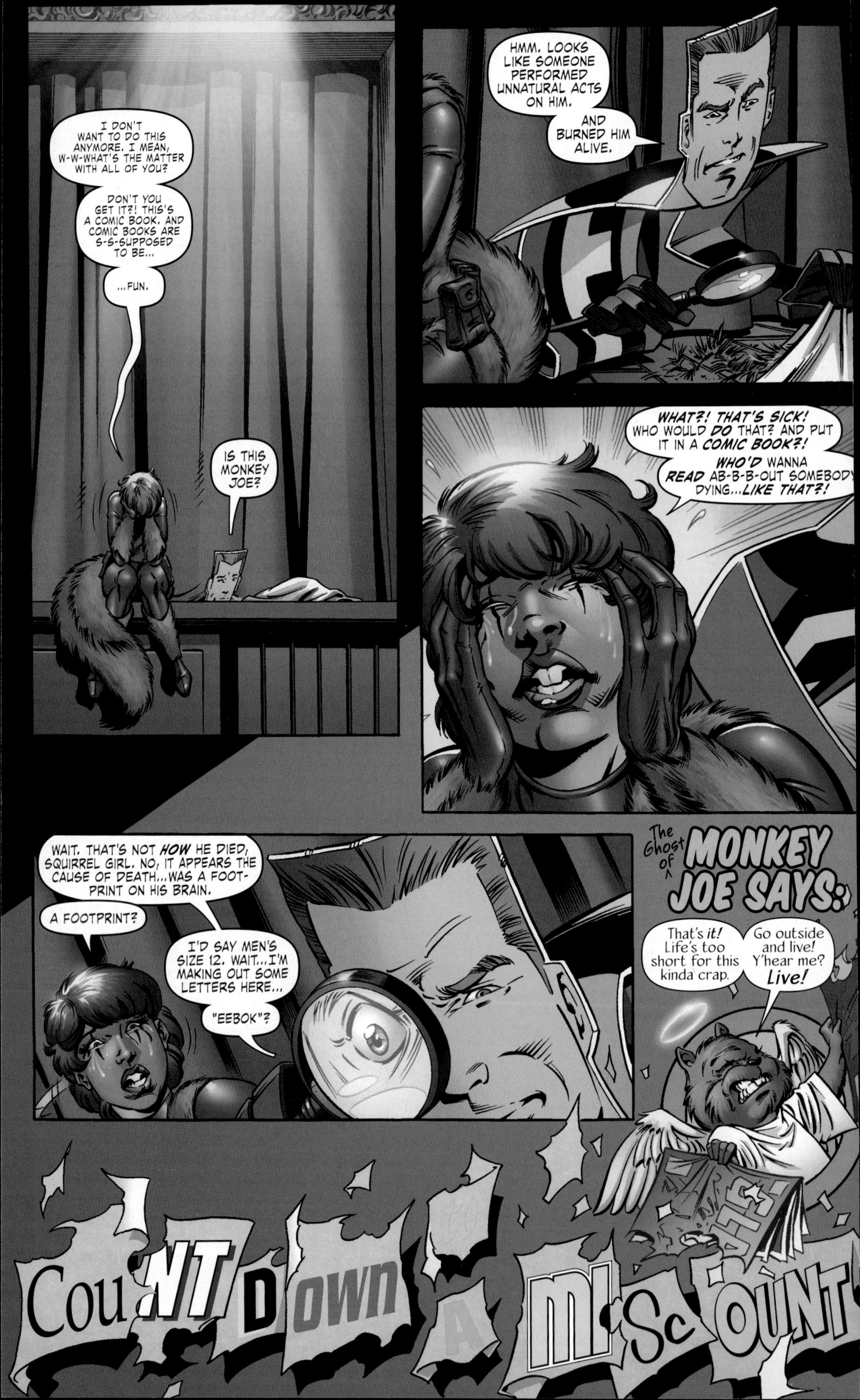

I DON'T WANT TO DO THIS ANYMORE. I MEAN, W-W-WHAT'S THE MATTER WITH ALL OF YOU?
DON'T YOU GET IT?! THIS'S A COMIC BOOK. AND COMIC BOOKS ARE S-S-SUPPOSED TO BE...
...FUN.
IS THIS MONKEY JOE?
HMM. LOOKS LIKE SOMEONE PERFORMED UNNATURAL ACTS ON HIM.
AND BURNED HIM ALIVE.
WHAT?! THAT'S SICK! WHO WOULD DO THAT? AND PUT IT IN A COMIC BOOK?!
WHO'D WANNA READ AB-B-B-OUT SOMEBODY DYING...LIKE THAT?!
WAIT. THAT'S NOT HOW HE DIED, SQUIRREL GIRL. NO, IT APPEARS THE CAUSE OF DEATH...WAS A FOOT-PRINT ON HIS BRAIN.
A FOOTPRINT?
I'D SAY MEN'S SIZE 12. WAIT...I'M MAKING OUT SOME LETTERS HERE...
"EEBOK"?
The Ghost of MONKEY JOE SAYS:
That's it! Life's too short for this kinda crap.
Go outside and live! Y'hear me? Live!
CouNT Down to A MISCOUNT

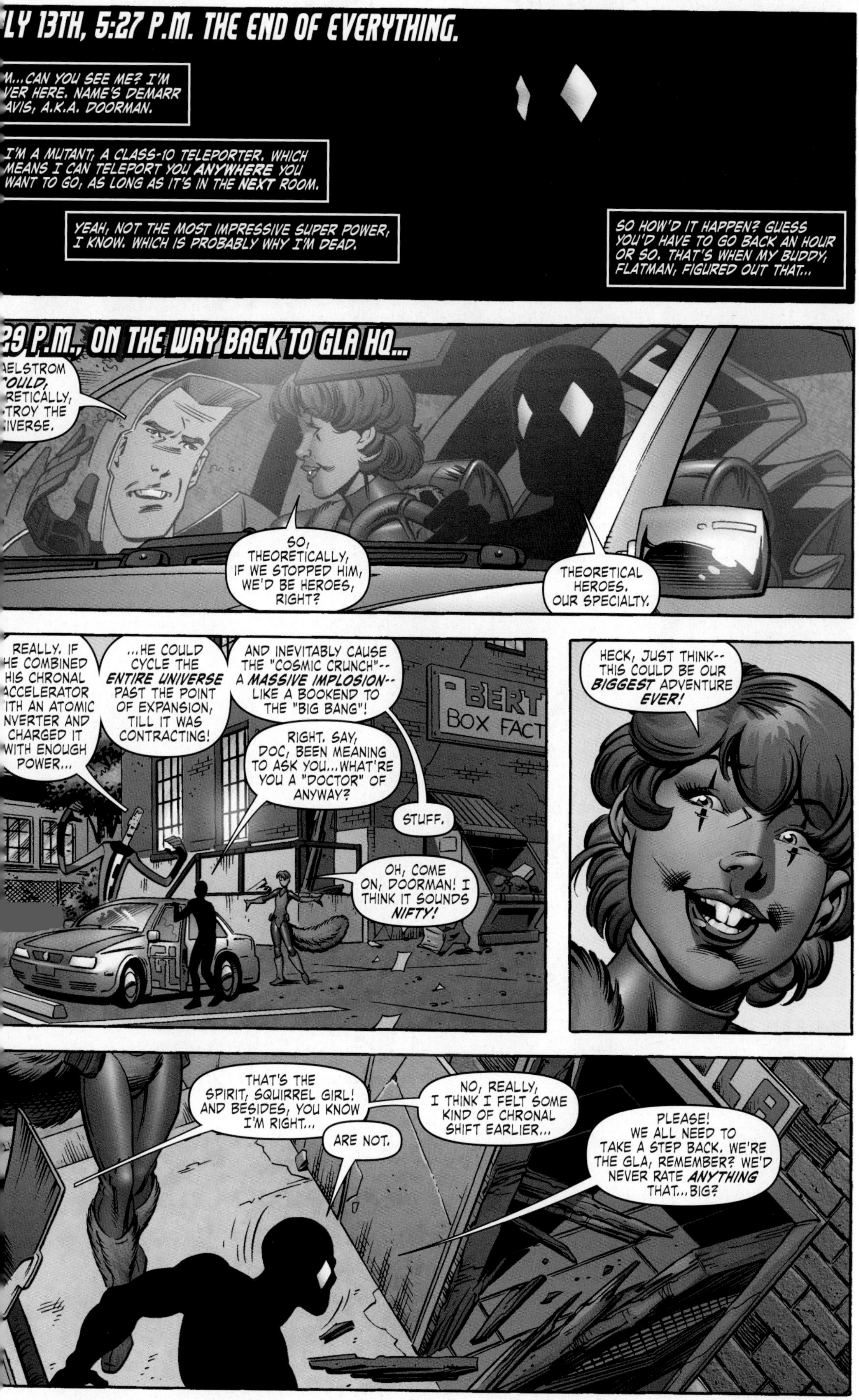

LY 13TH, 5:27 P.M. THE END OF EVERYTHING.
M...CAN YOU SEE ME? I'M VER HERE. NAME'S DEMARR AVIS, A.K.A. DOORMAN.
I'M A MUTANT, A CLASS-10 TELEPORTER. WHICH MEANS I CAN TELEPORT YOU ANYWHERE YOU WANT TO GO, AS LONG AS IT'S IN THE NEXT ROOM.
YEAH, NOT THE MOST IMPRESSIVE SUPER POWER, I KNOW. WHICH IS PROBABLY WHY I'M DEAD.
SO HOW'D IT HAPPEN? GUESS YOU'D HAVE TO GO BACK AN HOUR OR SO. THAT'S WHEN MY BUDDY, FLATMAN, FIGURED OUT THAT...
29 P.M., ON THE WAY BACK TO GLA HQ...
AELSTROM COULD, RETICALLY, TROY THE IVERSE.
SO, THEORETICALLY, IF WE STOPPED HIM, WE'D BE HEROES, RIGHT?
THEORETICAL HEROES. OUR SPECIALTY.
REALLY. IF HE COMBINED HIS CHRONAL ACCELERATOR ITH AN ATOMIC NVERTER AND CHARGED IT WITH ENOUGH POWER...
...HE COULD CYCLE THE ENTIRE UNIVERSE PAST THE POINT OF EXPANSION, TILL IT WAS CONTRACTING!
AND INEVITABLY CAUSE THE "COSMIC CRUNCH"--A MASSIVE IMPLOSION--LIKE A BOOKEND TO THE "BIG BANG"!
BERT BOX FACT
RIGHT. SAY, DOC, BEEN MEANING TO ASK YOU...WHAT'RE YOU A "DOCTOR" OF ANYWAY?
STUFF.
OH, COME ON, DOORMAN! I THINK IT SOUNDS NIFTY!
HECK, JUST THINK--THIS COULD BE OUR BIGGEST ADVENTURE EVER!
THAT'S THE SPIRIT, SQUIRREL GIRL! AND BESIDES, YOU KNOW I'M RIGHT...
ARE NOT.
NO, REALLY, I THINK I FELT SOME KIND OF CHRONAL SHIFT EARLIER...
PLEASE! WE ALL NEED TO TAKE A STEP BACK. WE'RE THE GLA, REMEMBER? WE'D NEVER RATE ANYTHING THAT...BIG?

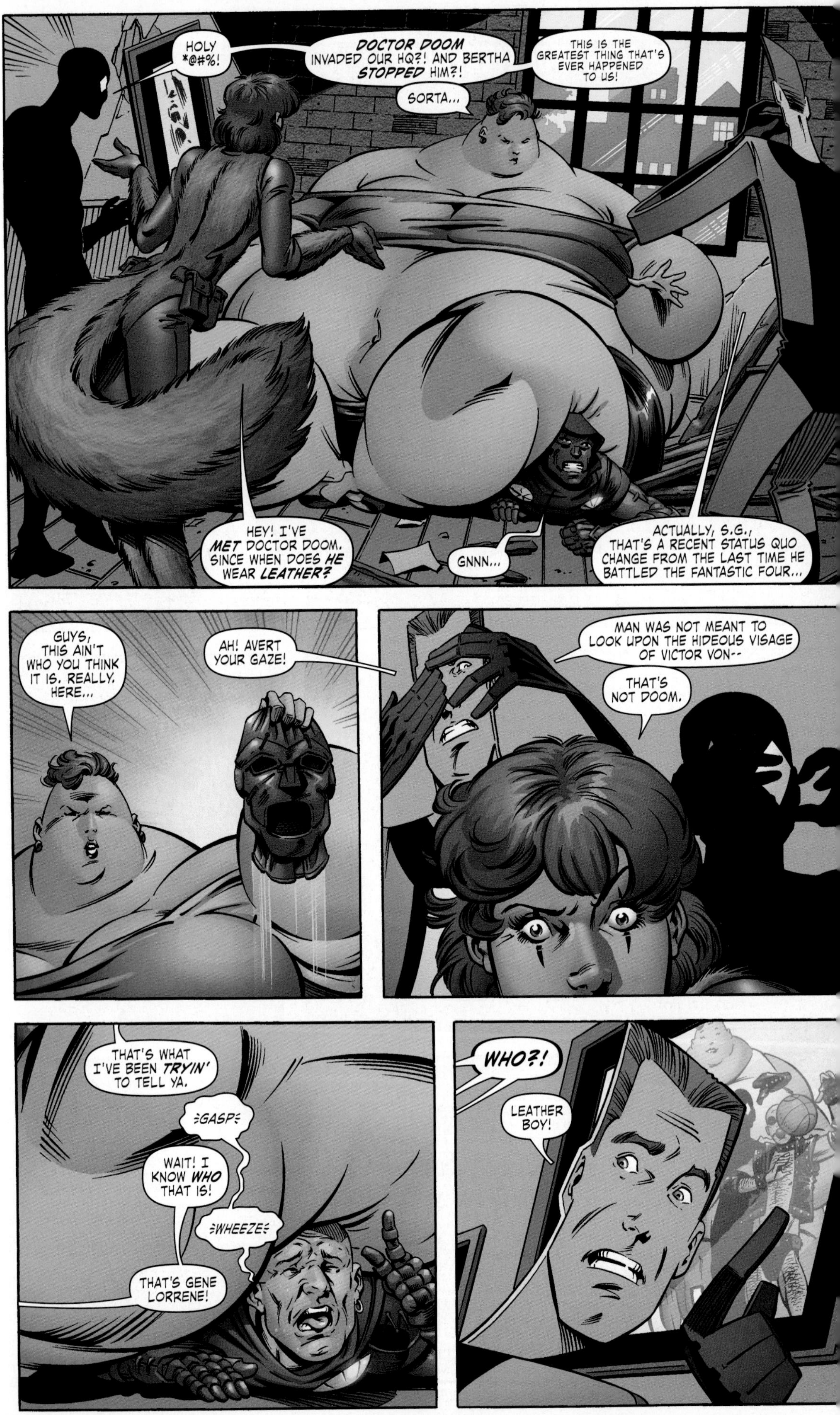
HOLY *@#%!
DOCTOR DOOM INVADED OUR HQ?! AND BERTHA STOPPED HIM?!
THIS IS THE GREATEST THING THAT'S EVER HAPPENED TO US!
SORTA...
HEY! I'VE MET DOCTOR DOOM. SINCE WHEN DOES HE WEAR LEATHER?
GNNN...
ACTUALLY, S.G., THAT'S A RECENT STATUS QUO CHANGE FROM THE LAST TIME HE BATTLED THE FANTASTIC FOUR...
GUYS, THIS AIN'T WHO YOU THINK IT IS. REALLY. HERE...
AH! AVERT YOUR GAZE!
MAN WAS NOT MEANT TO LOOK UPON THE HIDEOUS VISAGE OF VICTOR VON--
THAT'S NOT DOOM.
THAT'S WHAT I'VE BEEN TRYIN' TO TELL YA.
GASP
WAIT! I KNOW WHO THAT IS!
WHEEZE
THAT'S GENE LORRENE!
WHO?!
LEATHER BOY!

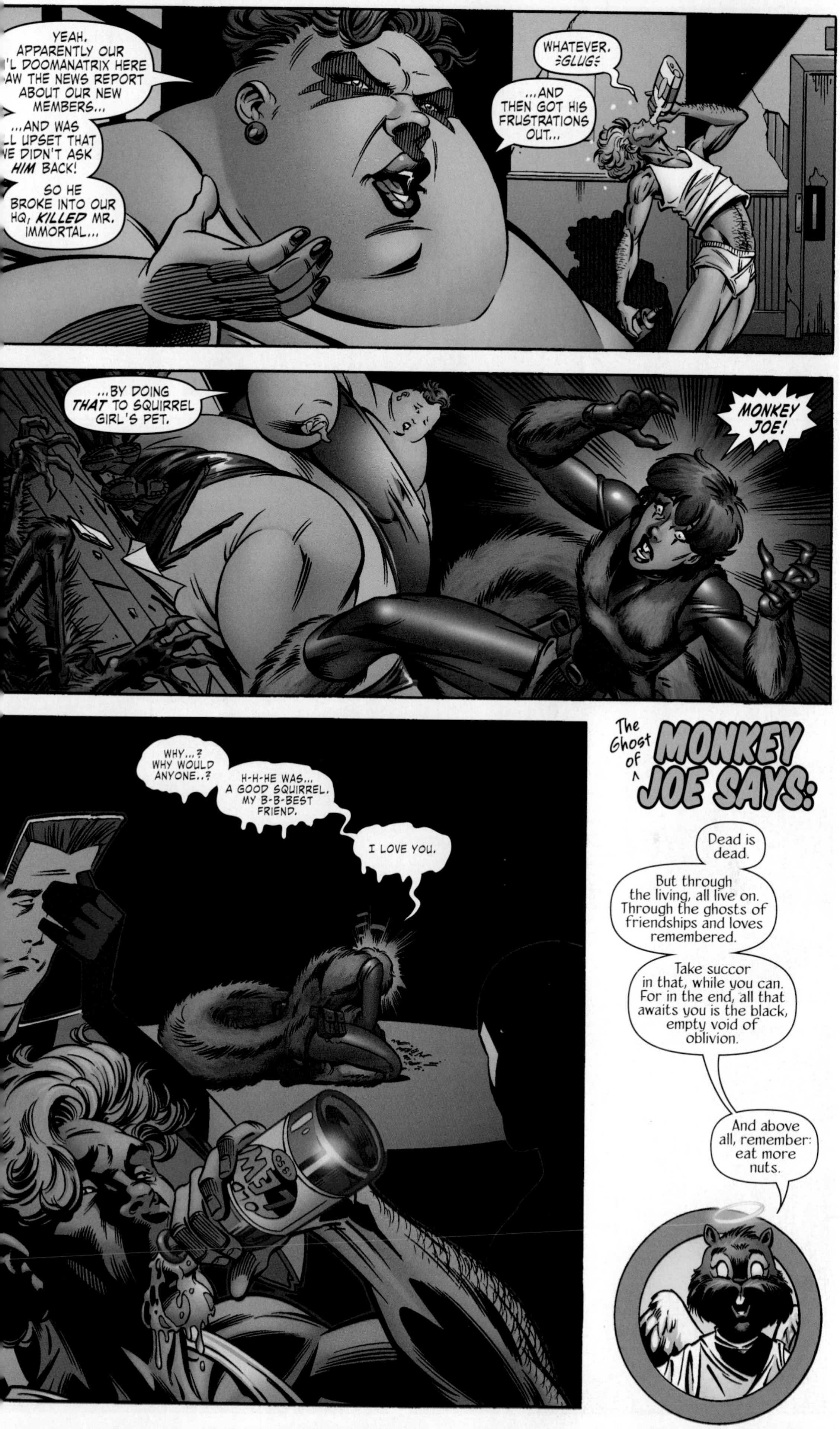

YEAH. APPARENTLY OUR 'L DOOMANATRIX HERE AW THE NEWS REPORT ABOUT OUR NEW MEMBERS...
...AND WAS LL UPSET THAT E DIDN'T ASK *HIM* BACK!
SO HE BROKE INTO OUR HQ, *KILLED* MR. IMMORTAL...
WHATEVER. *GLUG*
...AND THEN GOT HIS FRUSTRATIONS OUT...
...BY DOING *THAT* TO SQUIRREL GIRL'S PET.
MONKEY JOE!
WHY...? WHY WOULD ANYONE..?
H-H-HE WAS... A GOOD SQUIRREL. MY B-B-BEST FRIEND.
I LOVE YOU.
The Ghost of MONKEY JOE SAYS:
Dead is dead.
But through the living, all live on. Through the ghosts of friendships and loves remembered.
Take succor in that, while you can. For in the end, all that awaits you is the black, empty void of oblivion.
And above all, remember: eat more nuts.

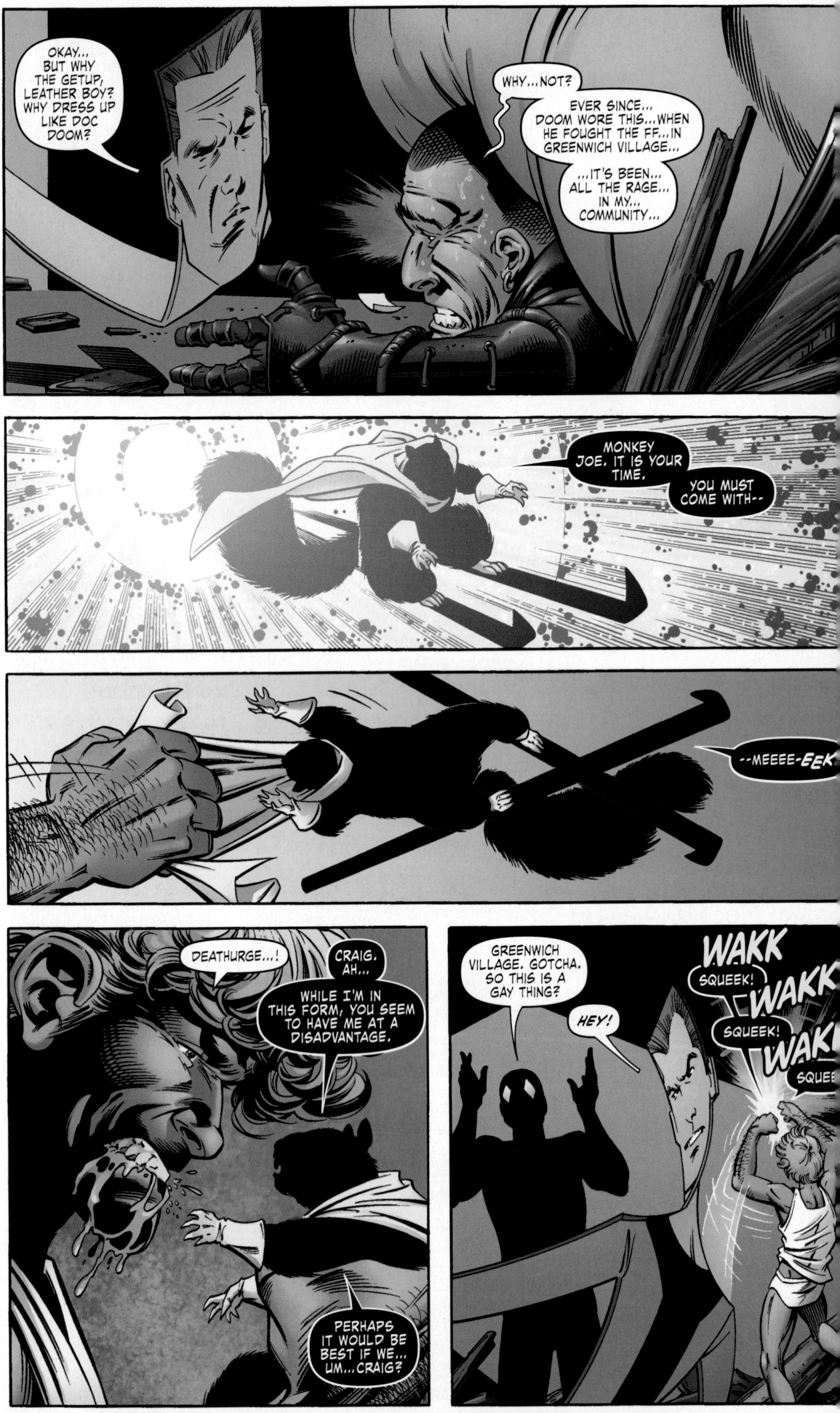
OKAY... BUT WHY THE GETUP, LEATHER BOY? WHY DRESS UP LIKE DOC DOOM?
WHY...NOT?
EVER SINCE... DOOM WORE THIS...WHEN HE FOUGHT THE FF...IN GREENWICH VILLAGE...
...IT'S BEEN... ALL THE RAGE... IN MY... COMMUNITY...
MONKEY JOE. IT IS YOUR TIME.
YOU MUST COME WITH--
--MEEEE-EEK
DEATHURGE...!
CRAIG. AH...
WHILE I'M IN THIS FORM, YOU SEEM TO HAVE ME AT A DISADVANTAGE.
PERHAPS IT WOULD BE BEST IF WE... UM...CRAIG?
GREENWICH VILLAGE. GOTCHA. SO THIS IS A GAY THING?
HEY!
WAKK
SQUEEK!
SQUEEK!

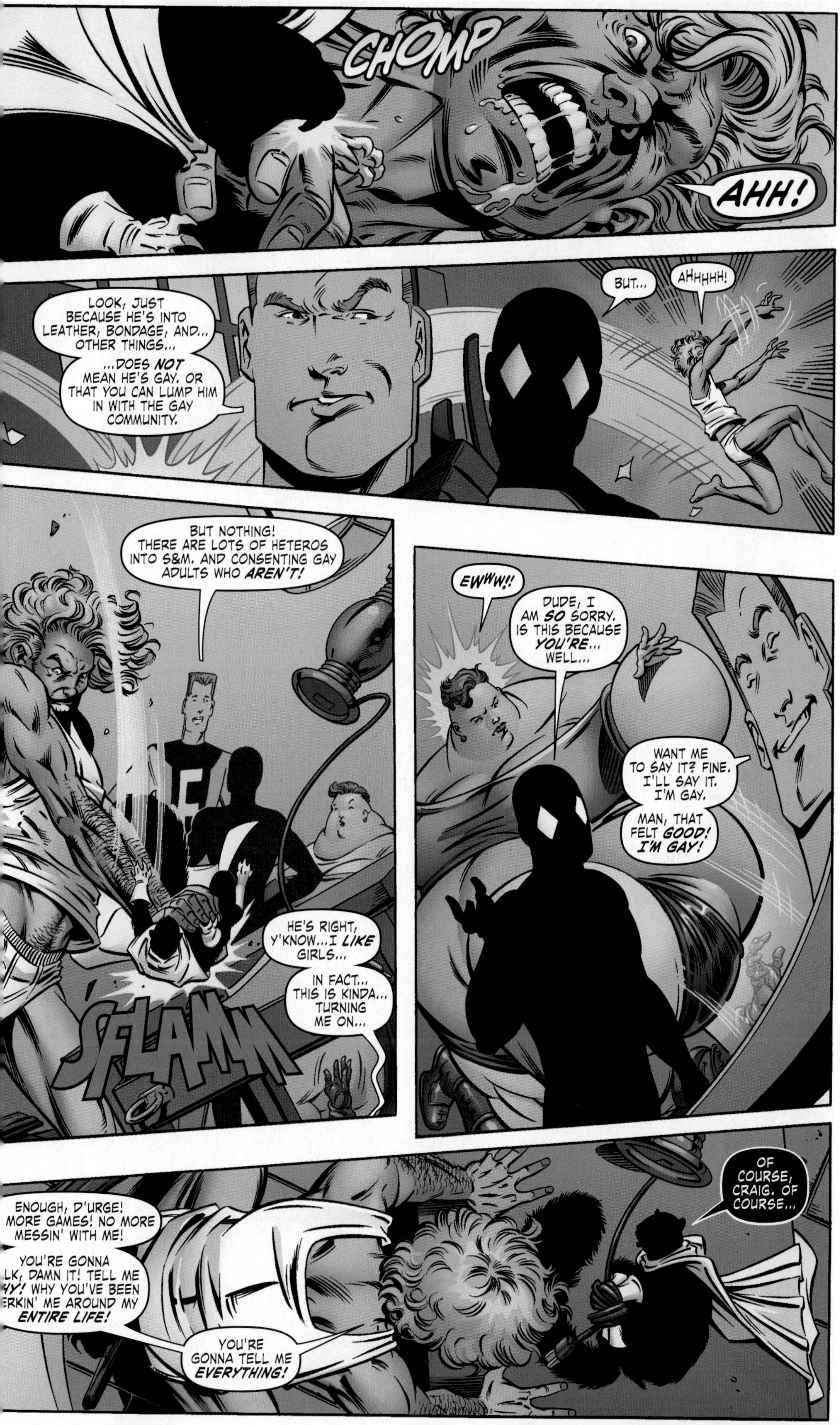
CHOMP
AHH!
LOOK, JUST BECAUSE HE'S INTO LEATHER, BONDAGE, AND... OTHER THINGS...
...DOES NOT MEAN HE'S GAY. OR THAT YOU CAN LUMP HIM IN WITH THE GAY COMMUNITY.
BUT...
AHHHHH!
BUT NOTHING! THERE ARE LOTS OF HETEROS INTO S&M. AND CONSENTING GAY ADULTS WHO AREN'T!
HE'S RIGHT, Y'KNOW...I LIKE GIRLS...
IN FACT... THIS IS KINDA... TURNING ME ON...
SFLAMM
EWWW!!
DUDE, I AM SO SORRY. IS THIS BECAUSE YOU'RE... WELL...
WANT ME TO SAY IT? FINE. I'LL SAY IT. I'M GAY.
MAN, THAT FELT GOOD! I'M GAY!
ENOUGH, D'URGE! MORE GAMES! NO MORE MESSIN' WITH ME!
YOU'RE GONNA LK, DAMN IT! TELL ME HY! WHY YOU'VE BEEN ERKIN' ME AROUND MY ENTIRE LIFE!
YOU'RE GONNA TELL ME EVERYTHING!
OF COURSE, CRAIG. OF COURSE...

YOU SEE, BOY, YOU HAVE A DESTINY. *YOU* ARE GOING TO LIVE *FOREVER*. THINK ABOUT THAT.

THERE ARE BEINGS THAT STRIDE THE COSMOS WITH *CLAIMS* OF IMMORTALITY, OF GODHOOD. BUT EVEN *THEY* CAN BE KILLED. EVEN THEIR LIFE FORCES CAN BE SNUFFED OUT.

BUT NOT YOURS, CRAIG HOLLIS.

"YOU SHALL OUTLIVE US ALL. ALL THAT YOU HOLD DEAR. EVERY-THING THAT YOU LOVE.

"MOTHER, FATHER, SOULMATE...

"...TRUE FRIENDS, ONE AND ALL...

"ANYTHING THAT WALKS, CRAWLS, OR BREATHES.

"IMAGINE IT, CRAIG. AS THE LAST STAR BURNS ITSELF OUT, YOU ALONE WILL HOLD VIGIL OVER THIS EXISTENCE.

"AND YOU *ALONE* WILL LEARN TH' *GRAND SECRET* THAT WILL REVEAL ITSELF AT THE END OF ALL THINGS."

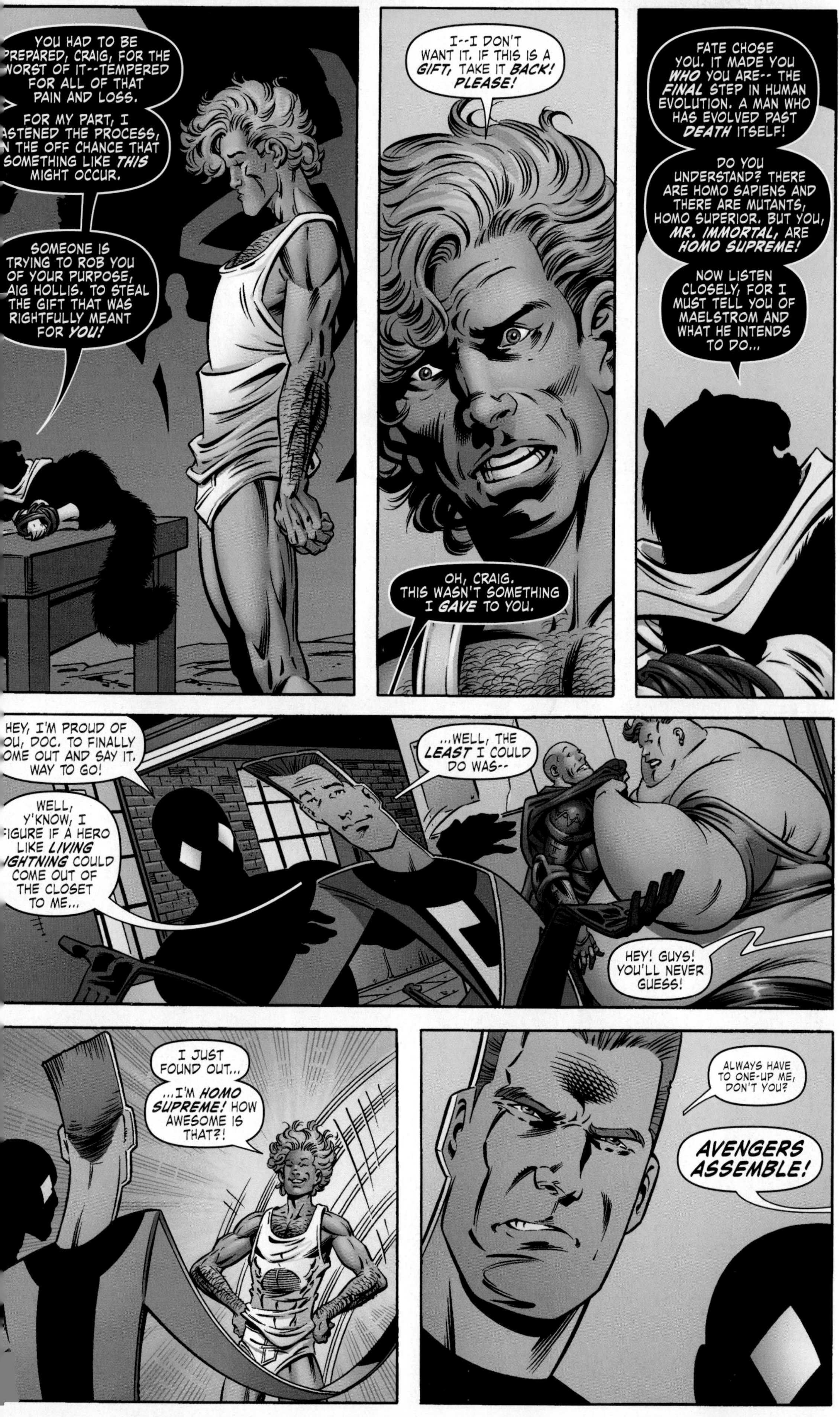
YOU HAD TO BE PREPARED, CRAIG, FOR THE WORST OF IT--TEMPERED FOR ALL OF THAT PAIN AND LOSS.
FOR MY PART, I ASTENED THE PROCESS, N THE OFF CHANCE THAT SOMETHING LIKE THIS MIGHT OCCUR.
SOMEONE IS TRYING TO ROB YOU OF YOUR PURPOSE, AIG HOLLIS. TO STEAL THE GIFT THAT WAS RIGHTFULLY MEANT FOR YOU!
I--I DON'T WANT IT. IF THIS IS A GIFT, TAKE IT BACK! PLEASE!
OH, CRAIG. THIS WASN'T SOMETHING I GAVE TO YOU.
FATE CHOSE YOU. IT MADE YOU WHO YOU ARE-- THE FINAL STEP IN HUMAN EVOLUTION. A MAN WHO HAS EVOLVED PAST DEATH ITSELF!
DO YOU UNDERSTAND? THERE ARE HOMO SAPIENS AND THERE ARE MUTANTS, HOMO SUPERIOR. BUT YOU, MR. IMMORTAL, ARE HOMO SUPREME!
NOW LISTEN CLOSELY, FOR I MUST TELL YOU OF MAELSTROM AND WHAT HE INTENDS TO DO...
HEY, I'M PROUD OF OU, DOC. TO FINALLY OME OUT AND SAY IT. WAY TO GO!
WELL, Y'KNOW, I FIGURE IF A HERO LIKE LIVING IGHTNING COULD COME OUT OF THE CLOSET TO ME...
...WELL, THE LEAST I COULD DO WAS--
HEY! GUYS! YOU'LL NEVER GUESS!
I JUST FOUND OUT...
...I'M HOMO SUPREME! HOW AWESOME IS THAT?!
ALWAYS HAVE TO ONE-UP ME, DON'T YOU?
AVENGERS ASSEMBLE!

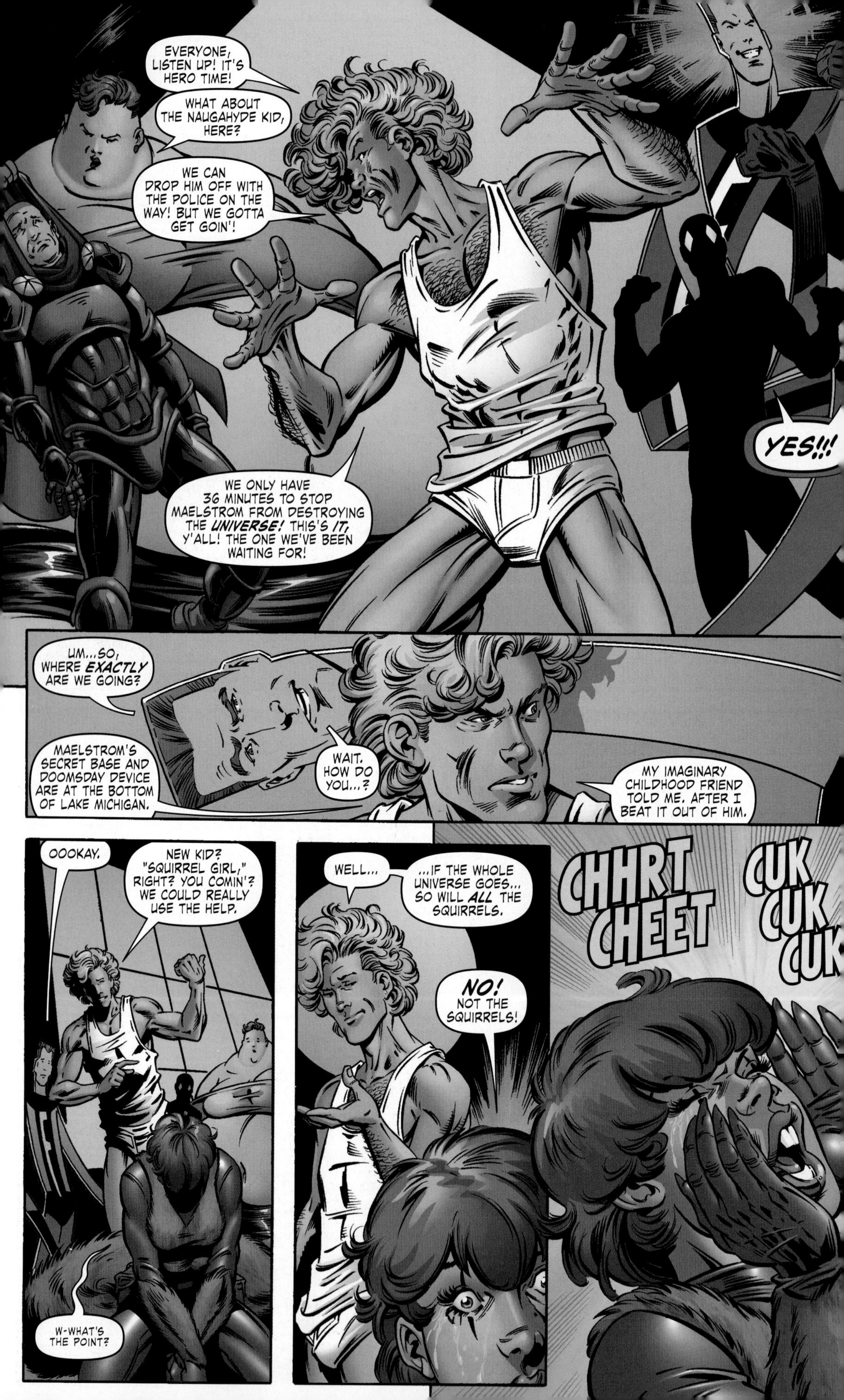
EVERYONE, LISTEN UP! IT'S HERO TIME!
WHAT ABOUT THE NAUGAHYDE KID, HERE?
WE CAN DROP HIM OFF WITH THE POLICE ON THE WAY! BUT WE GOTTA GET GOIN'!
YES!!!
WE ONLY HAVE 36 MINUTES TO STOP MAELSTROM FROM DESTROYING THE UNIVERSE! THIS'S IT, Y'ALL! THE ONE WE'VE BEEN WAITING FOR!
UM...SO, WHERE EXACTLY ARE WE GOING?
MAELSTROM'S SECRET BASE AND DOOMSDAY DEVICE ARE AT THE BOTTOM OF LAKE MICHIGAN.
WAIT. HOW DO YOU...?
MY IMAGINARY CHILDHOOD FRIEND TOLD ME. AFTER I BEAT IT OUT OF HIM.
OOOKAY.
NEW KID? "SQUIRREL GIRL," RIGHT? YOU COMIN'? WE COULD REALLY USE THE HELP.
W-WHAT'S THE POINT?
WELL...
...IF THE WHOLE UNIVERSE GOES... SO WILL ALL THE SQUIRRELS.
NO! NOT THE SQUIRRELS!
CHHRT CHEET
CUK CUK CUK

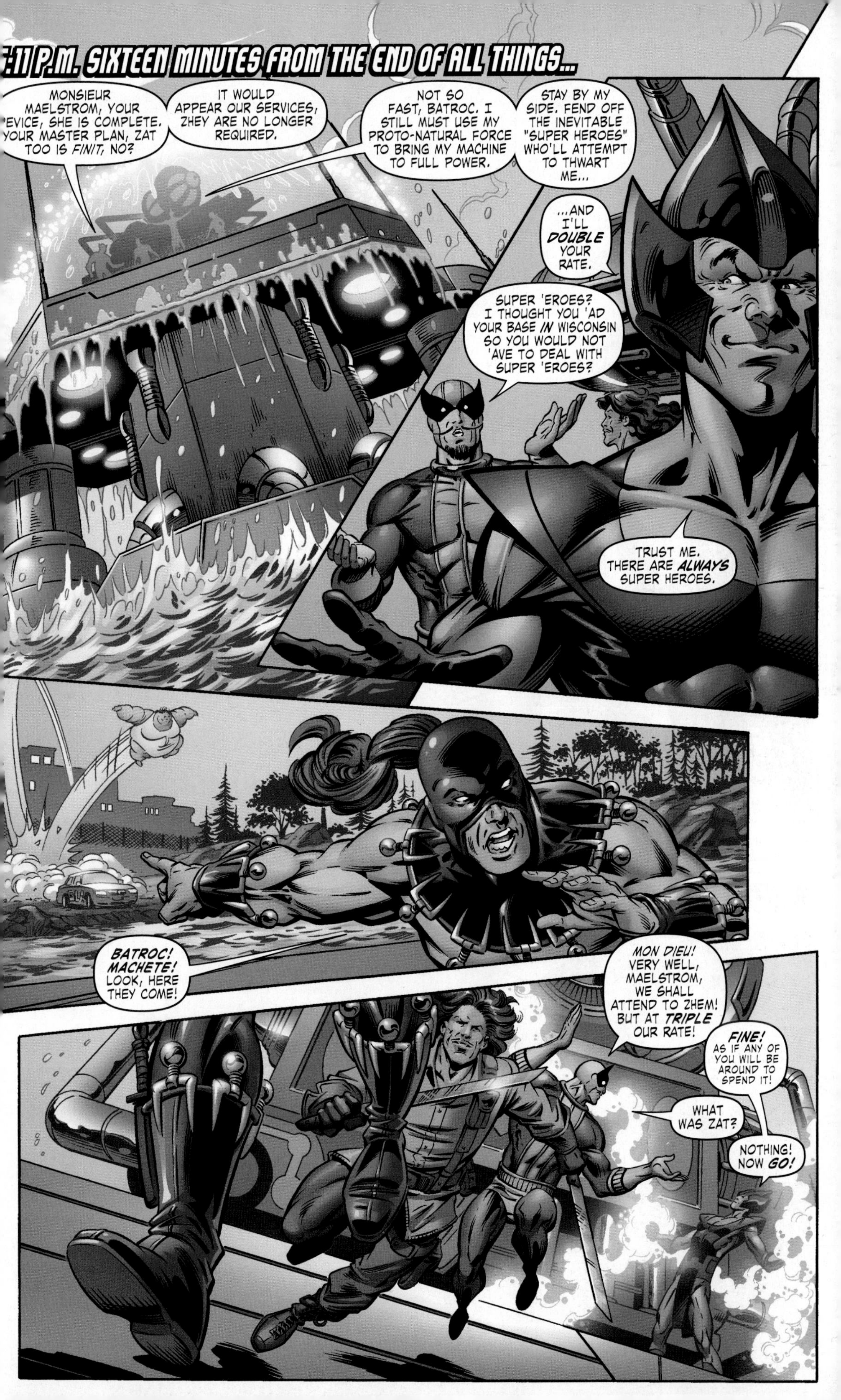
:11 P.M. SIXTEEN MINUTES FROM THE END OF ALL THINGS...
MONSIEUR MAELSTROM, YOUR 'EVICE, SHE IS COMPLETE. YOUR MASTER PLAN, ZAT TOO IS FINIT, NO?
IT WOULD APPEAR OUR SERVICES, ZHEY ARE NO LONGER REQUIRED.
NOT SO FAST, BATROC. I STILL MUST USE MY PROTO-NATURAL FORCE TO BRING MY MACHINE TO FULL POWER.
STAY BY MY SIDE. FEND OFF THE INEVITABLE "SUPER HEROES" WHO'LL ATTEMPT TO THWART ME...
...AND I'LL DOUBLE YOUR RATE.
SUPER 'EROES? I THOUGHT YOU 'AD YOUR BASE IN WISCONSIN SO YOU WOULD NOT 'AVE TO DEAL WITH SUPER 'EROES?
TRUST ME. THERE ARE ALWAYS SUPER HEROES.
BATROC! MACHETE! LOOK, HERE THEY COME!
MON DIEU! VERY WELL, MAELSTROM, WE SHALL ATTEND TO ZHEM! BUT AT TRIPLE OUR RATE!
FINE! AS IF ANY OF YOU WILL BE AROUND TO SPEND IT!
WHAT WAS ZAT?
NOTHING! NOW GO!

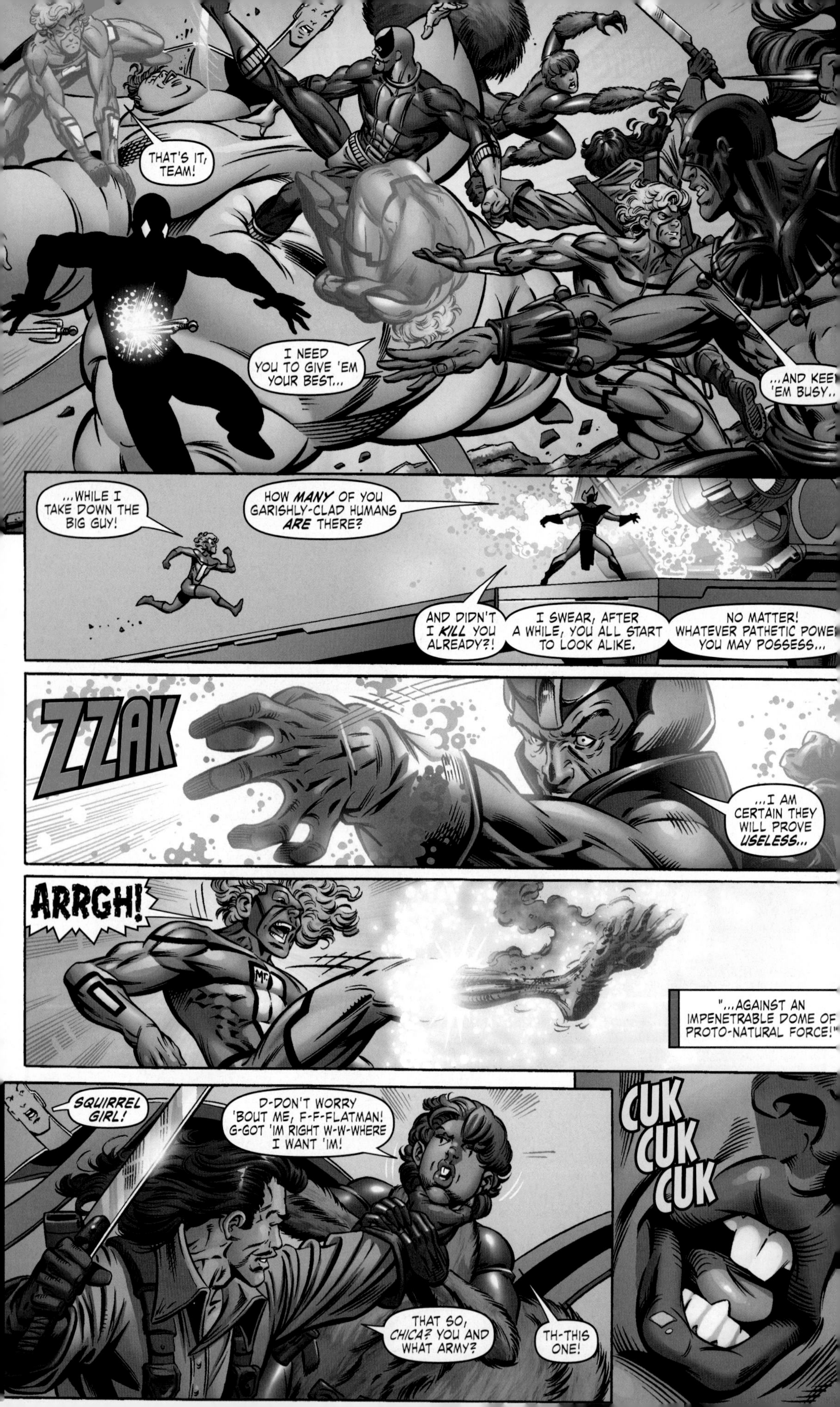
THAT'S IT, TEAM!
I NEED YOU TO GIVE 'EM YOUR BEST...
...AND KEE 'EM BUSY...
...WHILE I TAKE DOWN THE BIG GUY!
HOW MANY OF YOU GARISHLY-CLAD HUMANS ARE THERE?
AND DIDN'T I KILL YOU ALREADY?!
I SWEAR, AFTER A WHILE, YOU ALL START TO LOOK ALIKE.
NO MATTER! WHATEVER PATHETIC POWE YOU MAY POSSESS...
ZZAK
...I AM CERTAIN THEY WILL PROVE USELESS...
ARRGH!
"...AGAINST AN IMPENETRABLE DOME OF PROTO-NATURAL FORCE!"
SQUIRREL GIRL!
D-DON'T WORRY 'BOUT ME, F-F-FLATMAN! G-GOT 'IM RIGHT W-W-WHERE I WANT 'IM!
THAT SO, CHICA? YOU AND WHAT ARMY?
TH-THIS ONE!
CUK CUK CUK

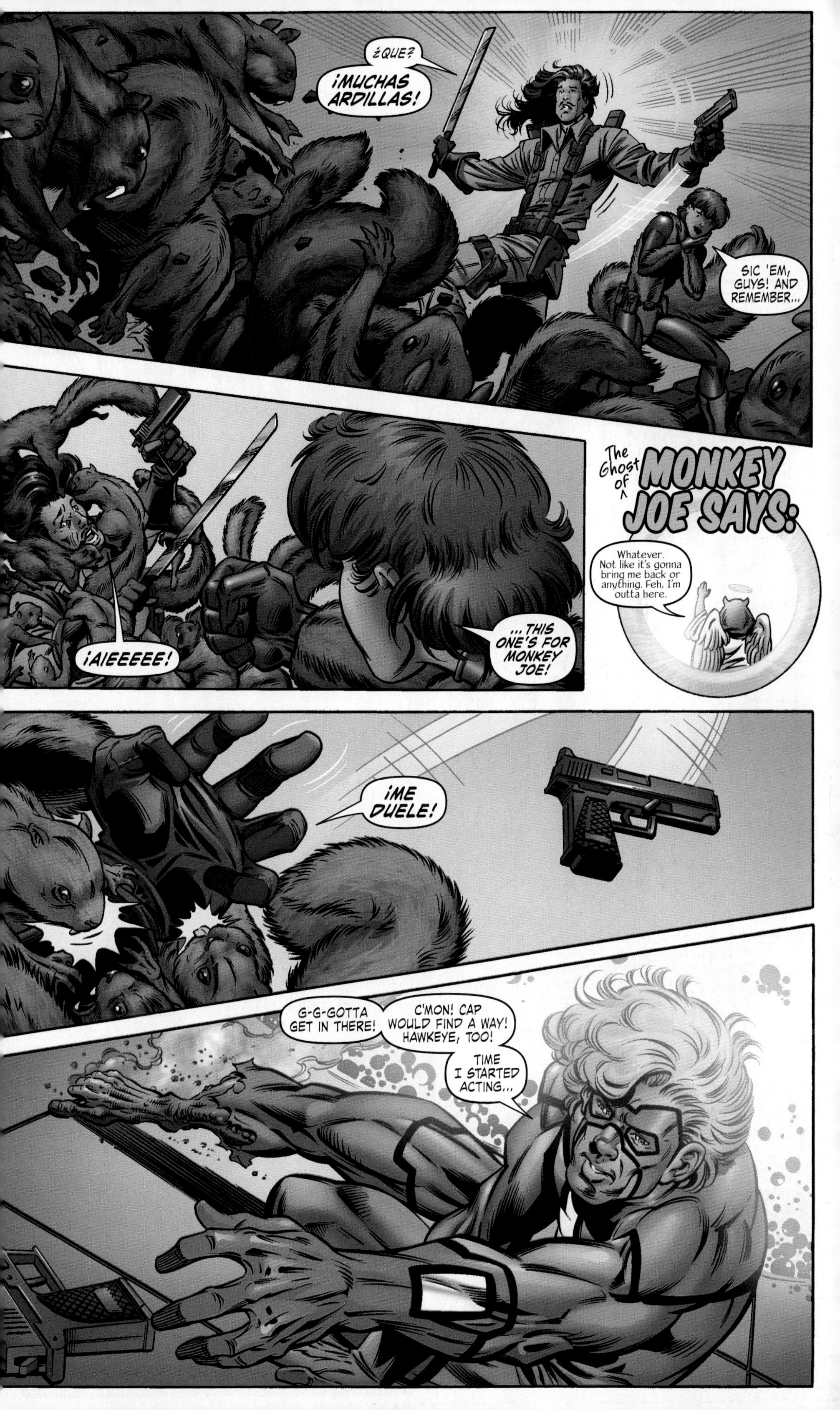

¿QUE? ¡MUCHAS ARDILLAS!
SIC 'EM, GUYS! AND REMEMBER...
¡AIEEEEE!
...THIS ONE'S FOR MONKEY JOE!
The Ghost of MONKEY JOE SAYS:
Whatever. Not like it's gonna bring me back or anything. Feh, I'm outta here.
¡ME DUELE!
G-G-GOTTA GET IN THERE!
C'MON! CAP WOULD FIND A WAY! HAWKEYE, TOO!
TIME I STARTED ACTING...

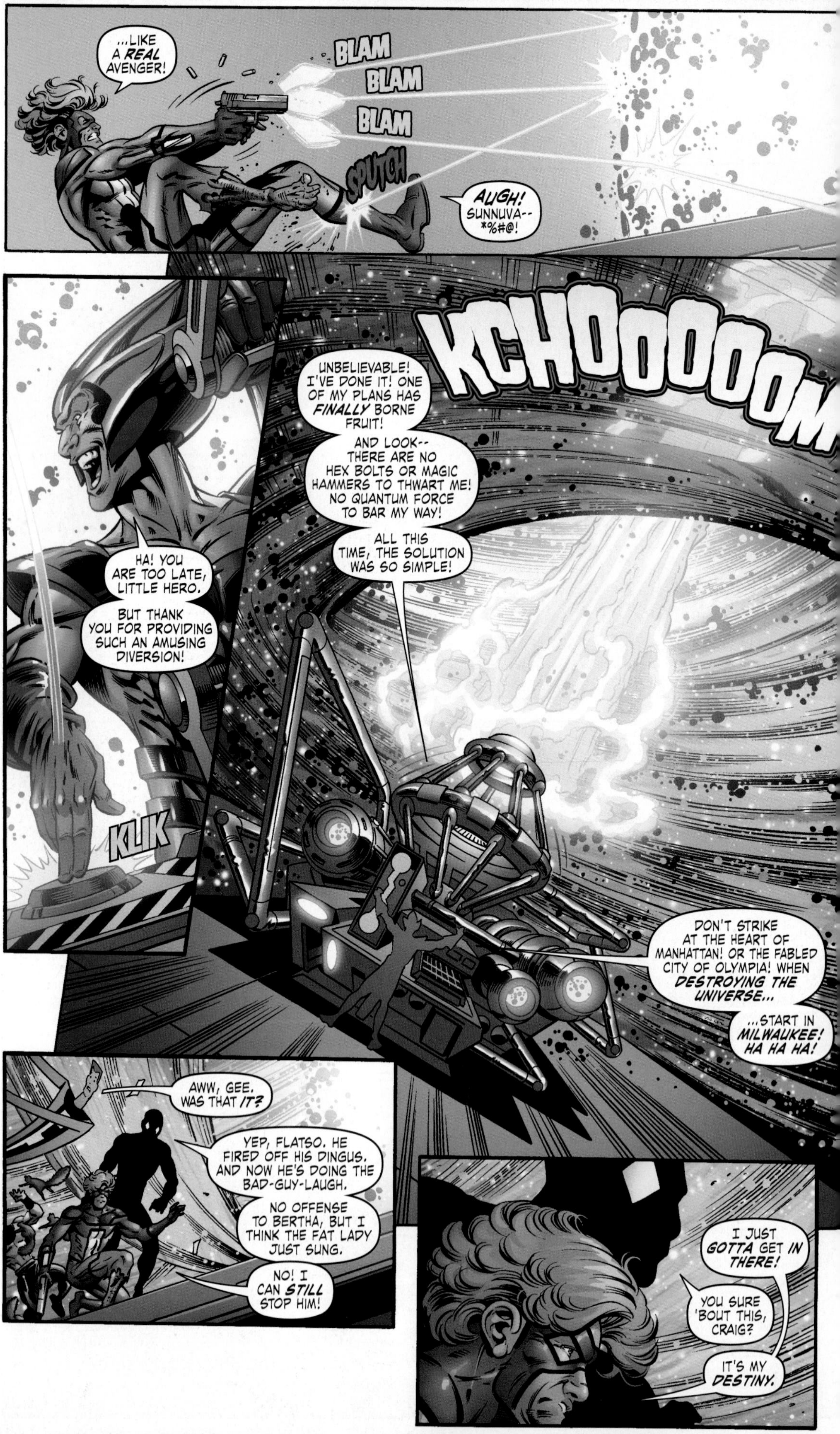

...LIKE A *REAL* AVENGER!
BLAM
BLAM
BLAM
SPUTCH
AUGH! SUNNUVA-- *%#@!
KCHOOOOOOM
UNBELIEVABLE! I'VE DONE IT! ONE OF MY PLANS HAS *FINALLY* BORNE FRUIT!
AND LOOK-- THERE ARE NO HEX BOLTS OR MAGIC HAMMERS TO THWART ME! NO QUANTUM FORCE TO BAR MY WAY!
ALL THIS TIME, THE SOLUTION WAS SO SIMPLE!
HA! YOU ARE TOO LATE, LITTLE HERO.
BUT THANK YOU FOR PROVIDING SUCH AN AMUSING DIVERSION!
KLIK
DON'T STRIKE AT THE HEART OF MANHATTAN! OR THE FABLED CITY OF OLYMPIA! WHEN *DESTROYING THE UNIVERSE...*
...START IN *MILWAUKEE! HA HA HA!*
AWW, GEE. WAS THAT *IT?*
YEP, FLATSO. HE FIRED OFF HIS DINGUS. AND NOW HE'S DOING THE BAD-GUY-LAUGH.
NO OFFENSE TO BERTHA, BUT I THINK THE FAT LADY JUST SUNG.
NO! I CAN *STILL* STOP HIM!
I JUST *GOTTA* GET *IN THERE!*
YOU SURE 'BOUT THIS, CRAIG?
IT'S MY *DESTINY.*

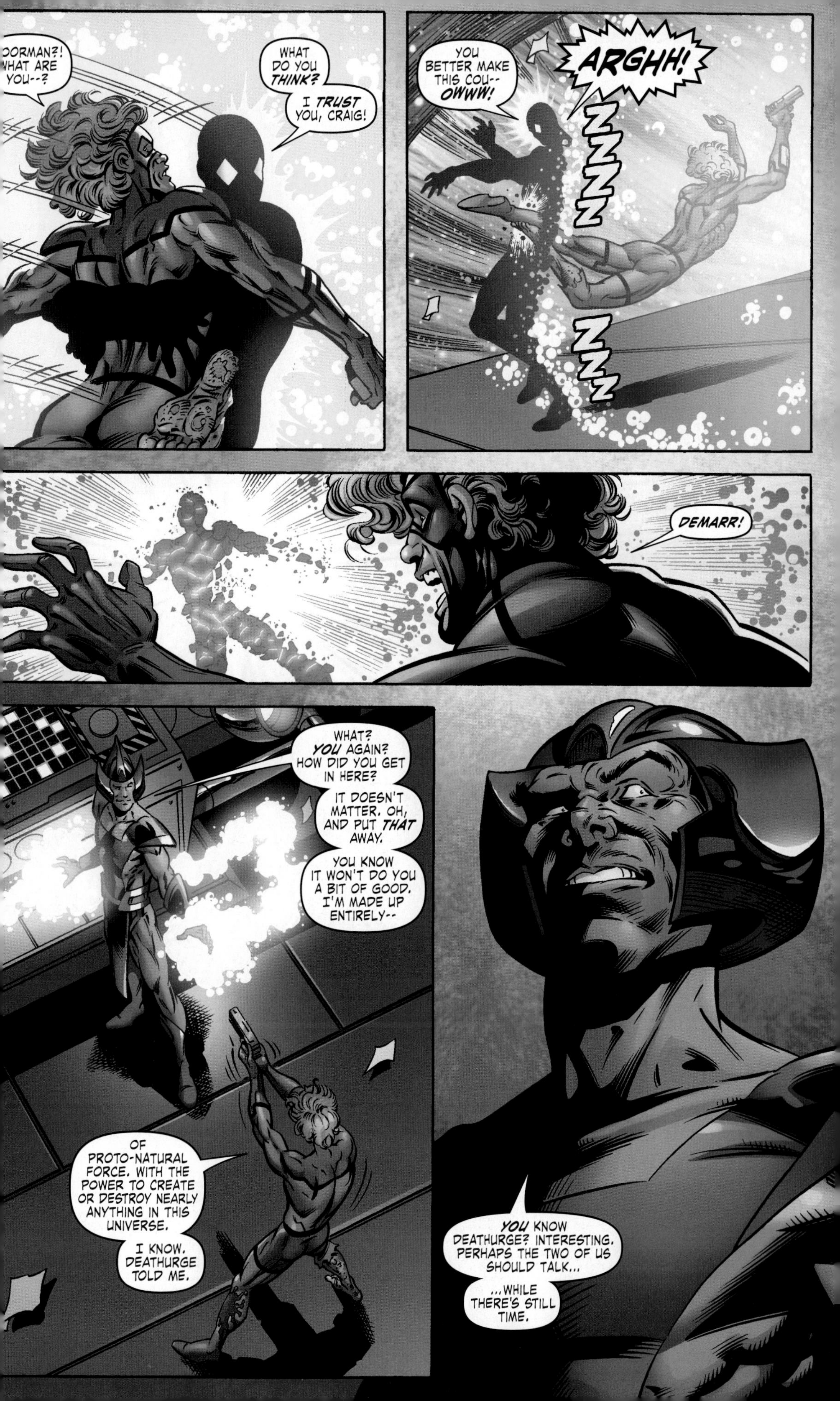

OORMAN?! WHAT ARE YOU--?
WHAT DO YOU THINK?
I TRUST YOU, CRAIG!
YOU BETTER MAKE THIS COU-- OWWW!
ARGHH!
ZZZZZ
ZZZ
DEMARR!
WHAT? YOU AGAIN? HOW DID YOU GET IN HERE?
IT DOESN'T MATTER. OH, AND PUT THAT AWAY.
YOU KNOW IT WON'T DO YOU A BIT OF GOOD. I'M MADE UP ENTIRELY--
OF PROTO-NATURAL FORCE. WITH THE POWER TO CREATE OR DESTROY NEARLY ANYTHING IN THIS UNIVERSE.
I KNOW. DEATHURGE TOLD ME.
YOU KNOW DEATHURGE? INTERESTING. PERHAPS THE TWO OF US SHOULD TALK...
...WHILE THERE'S STILL TIME.

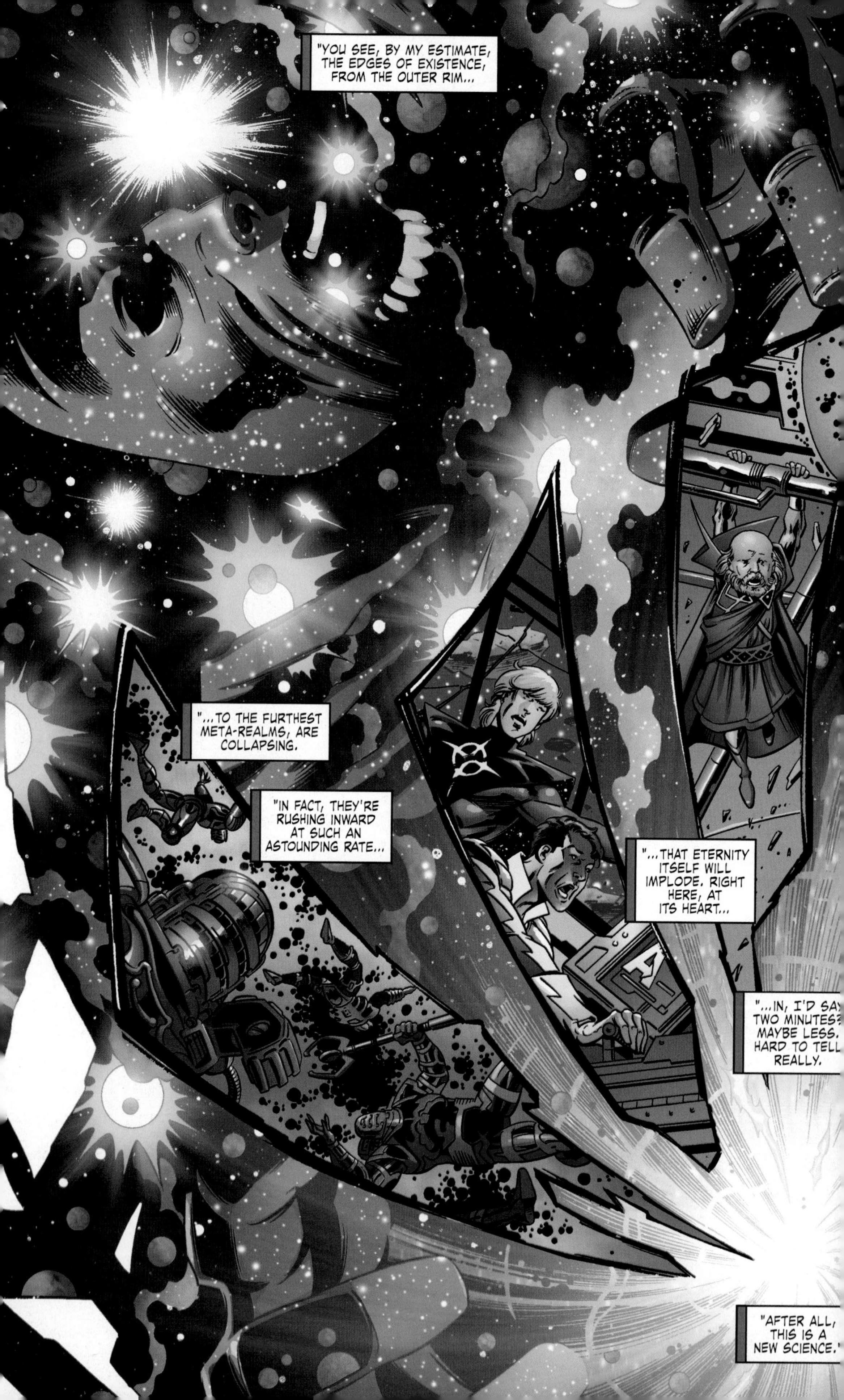
"YOU SEE, BY MY ESTIMATE, THE EDGES OF EXISTENCE, FROM THE OUTER RIM...
"...TO THE FURTHEST META-REALMS, ARE COLLAPSING.
"IN FACT, THEY'RE RUSHING INWARD AT SUCH AN ASTOUNDING RATE...
"...THAT ETERNITY ITSELF WILL IMPLODE. RIGHT HERE, AT ITS HEART...
"...IN, I'D SAY TWO MINUTES? MAYBE LESS. HARD TO TELL REALLY.
"AFTER ALL, THIS IS A NEW SCIENCE."

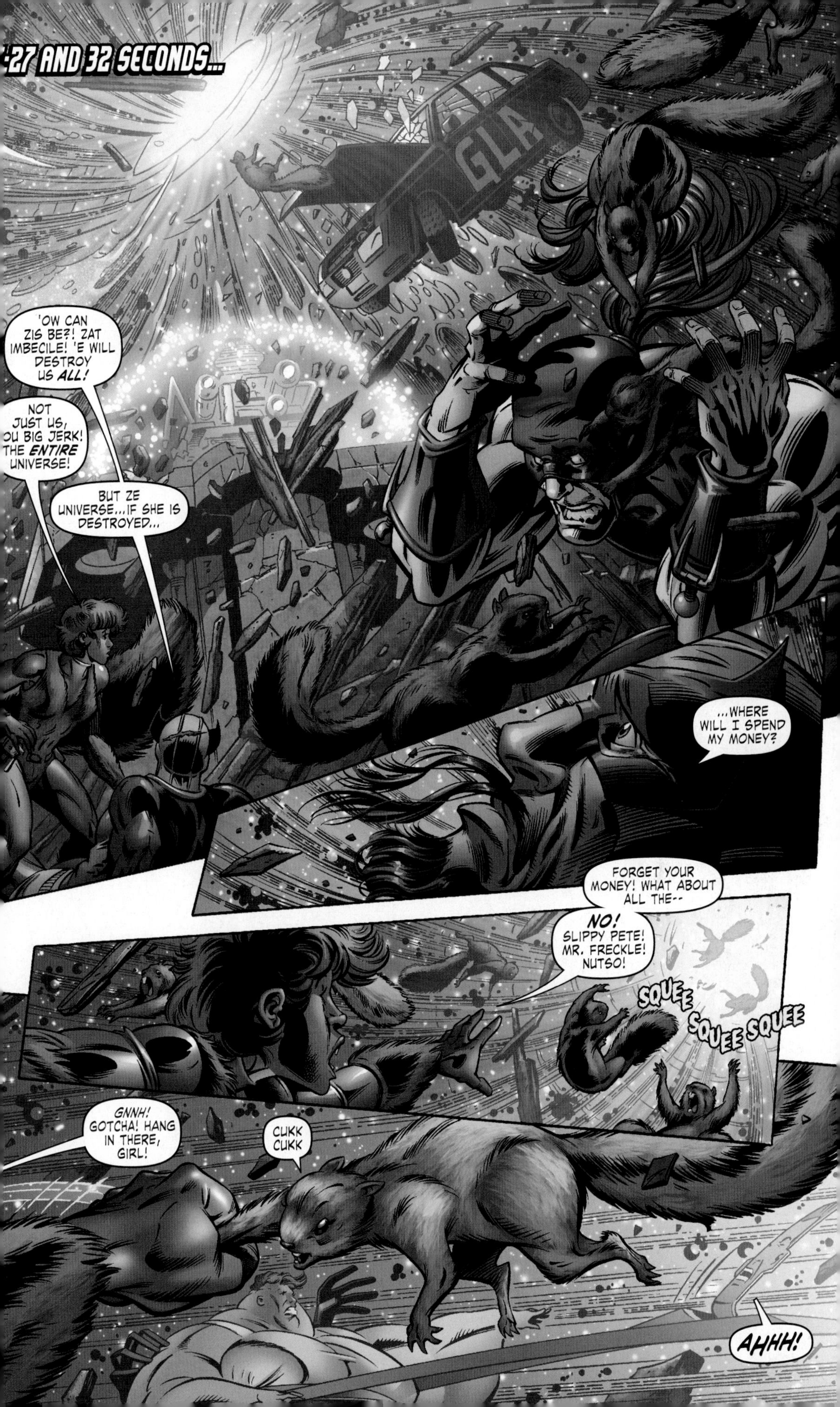
-27 AND 32 SECONDS...
'OW CAN ZIS BE?! ZAT IMBECILE! 'E WILL DESTROY US ALL!
NOT JUST US, YOU BIG JERK! THE ENTIRE UNIVERSE!
BUT ZE UNIVERSE...IF SHE IS DESTROYED...
...WHERE WILL I SPEND MY MONEY?
FORGET YOUR MONEY! WHAT ABOUT ALL THE--
NO! SLIPPY PETE! MR. FRECKLE! NUTSO!
SQUEE SQUEE SQUEE
GNNH! GOTCHA! HANG IN THERE, GIRL!
CUKK CUKK
AHHH!

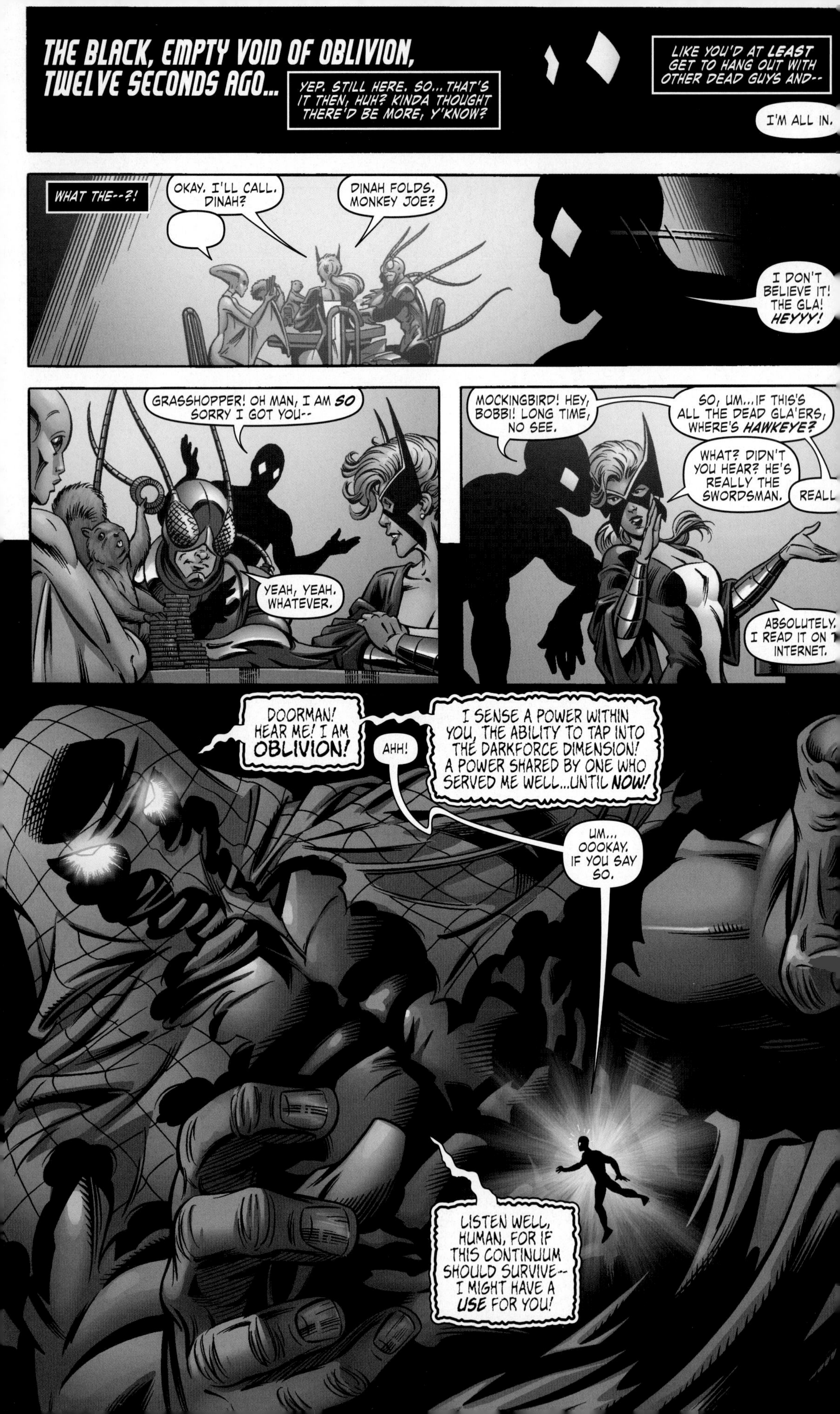
THE BLACK, EMPTY VOID OF OBLIVION, TWELVE SECONDS AGO...
YEP. STILL HERE. SO...THAT'S IT THEN, HUH? KINDA THOUGHT THERE'D BE MORE, Y'KNOW?
LIKE YOU'D AT LEAST GET TO HANG OUT WITH OTHER DEAD GUYS AND--
I'M ALL IN.
WHAT THE--?!
OKAY. I'LL CALL. DINAH?
DINAH FOLDS. MONKEY JOE?
I DON'T BELIEVE IT! THE GLA! HEYYY!
GRASSHOPPER! OH MAN, I AM SO SORRY I GOT YOU--
YEAH, YEAH. WHATEVER.
MOCKINGBIRD! HEY, BOBBI! LONG TIME, NO SEE.
SO, UM...IF THIS'S ALL THE DEAD GLA'ERS, WHERE'S HAWKEYE?
WHAT? DIDN'T YOU HEAR? HE'S REALLY THE SWORDSMAN.
REALL
ABSOLUTELY. I READ IT ON INTERNET.
DOORMAN! HEAR ME! I AM OBLIVION!
AHH!
I SENSE A POWER WITHIN YOU, THE ABILITY TO TAP INTO THE DARKFORCE DIMENSION! A POWER SHARED BY ONE WHO SERVED ME WELL...UNTIL NOW!
UM... OOOKAY. IF YOU SAY SO.
LISTEN WELL, HUMAN, FOR IF THIS CONTINUUM SHOULD SURVIVE-- I MIGHT HAVE A USE FOR YOU!

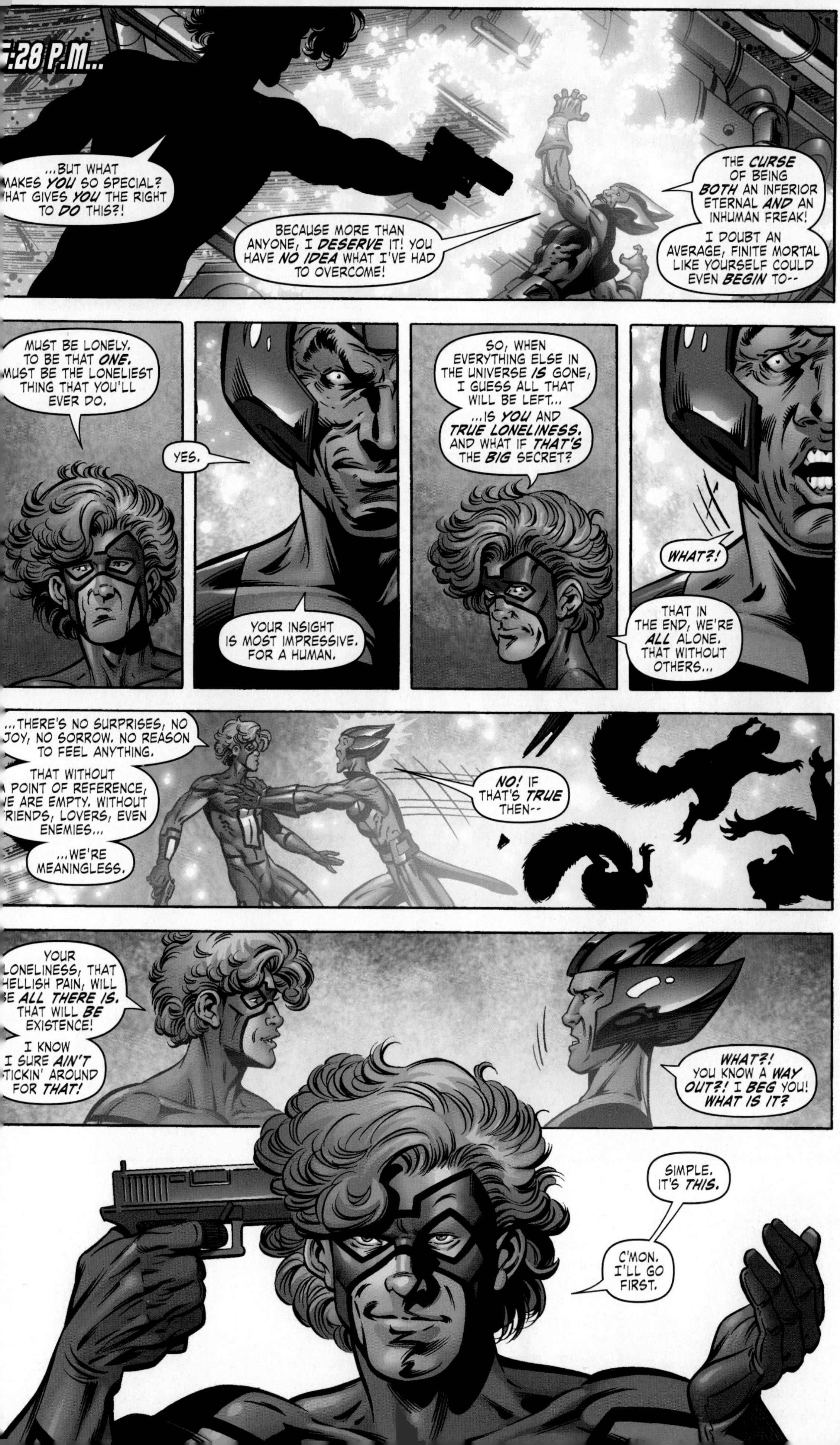

:28 P.M...
...BUT WHAT MAKES YOU SO SPECIAL? HAT GIVES YOU THE RIGHT TO DO THIS?!
BECAUSE MORE THAN ANYONE, I DESERVE IT! YOU HAVE NO IDEA WHAT I'VE HAD TO OVERCOME!
THE CURSE OF BEING BOTH AN INFERIOR ETERNAL AND AN INHUMAN FREAK!
I DOUBT AN AVERAGE, FINITE MORTAL LIKE YOURSELF COULD EVEN BEGIN TO--
MUST BE LONELY. TO BE THAT ONE. MUST BE THE LONELIEST THING THAT YOU'LL EVER DO.
YES.
YOUR INSIGHT IS MOST IMPRESSIVE. FOR A HUMAN.
SO, WHEN EVERYTHING ELSE IN THE UNIVERSE IS GONE, I GUESS ALL THAT WILL BE LEFT...
...IS YOU AND TRUE LONELINESS. AND WHAT IF THAT'S THE BIG SECRET?
WHAT?!
THAT IN THE END, WE'RE ALL ALONE. THAT WITHOUT OTHERS...
...THERE'S NO SURPRISES, NO JOY, NO SORROW. NO REASON TO FEEL ANYTHING.
THAT WITHOUT A POINT OF REFERENCE, WE ARE EMPTY. WITHOUT FRIENDS, LOVERS, EVEN ENEMIES...
...WE'RE MEANINGLESS.
NO! IF THAT'S TRUE THEN--
YOUR LONELINESS, THAT HELLISH PAIN, WILL BE ALL THERE IS. THAT WILL BE EXISTENCE!
I KNOW I SURE AIN'T STICKIN' AROUND FOR THAT!
WHAT?! YOU KNOW A WAY OUT?! I BEG YOU! WHAT IS IT?
SIMPLE. IT'S THIS.
C'MON. I'LL GO FIRST.

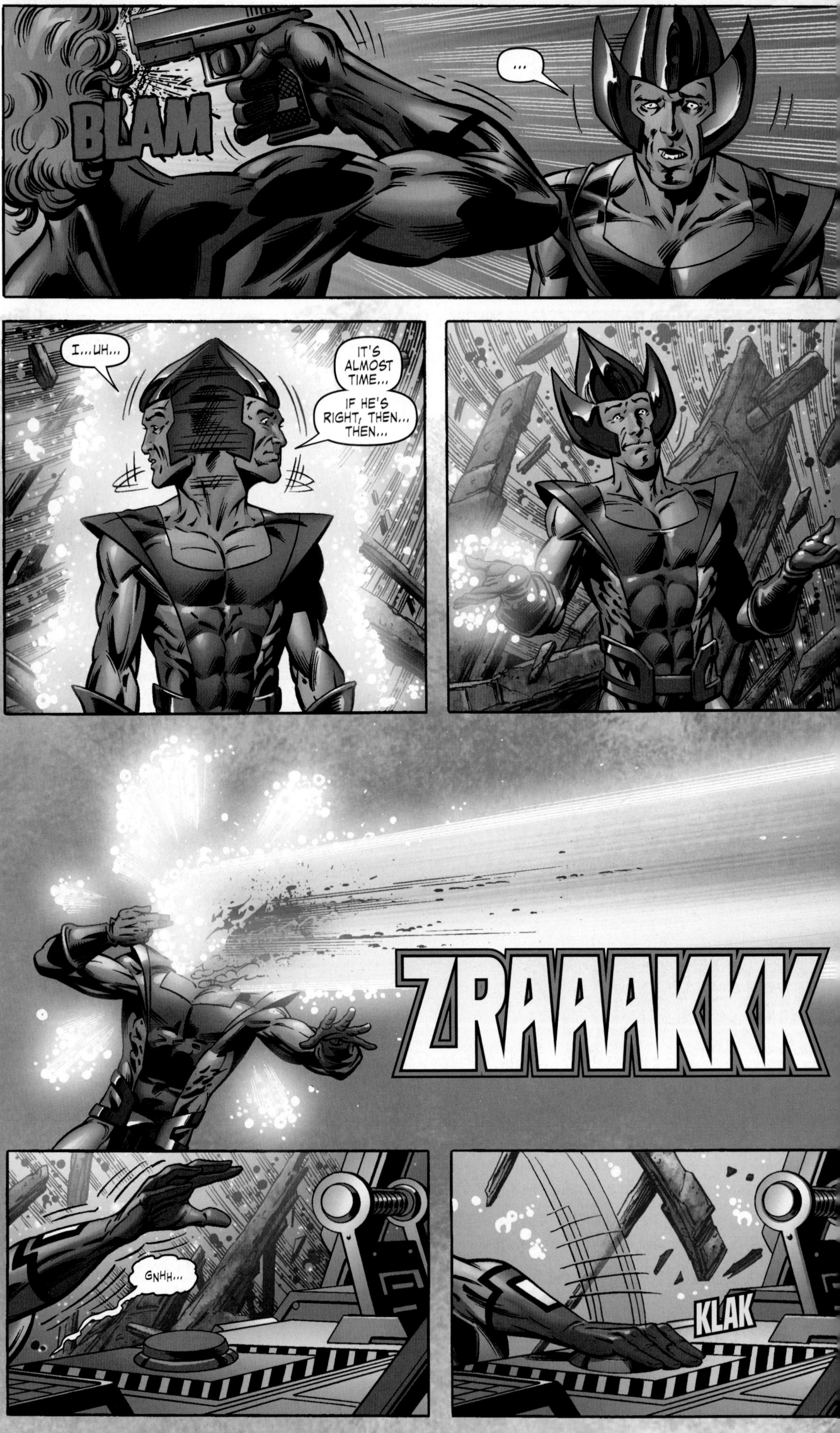

BLAM
...
I...UH...
IT'S ALMOST TIME...
IF HE'S RIGHT, THEN... THEN...
ZRAAAKKK
GNHH...
KLAK

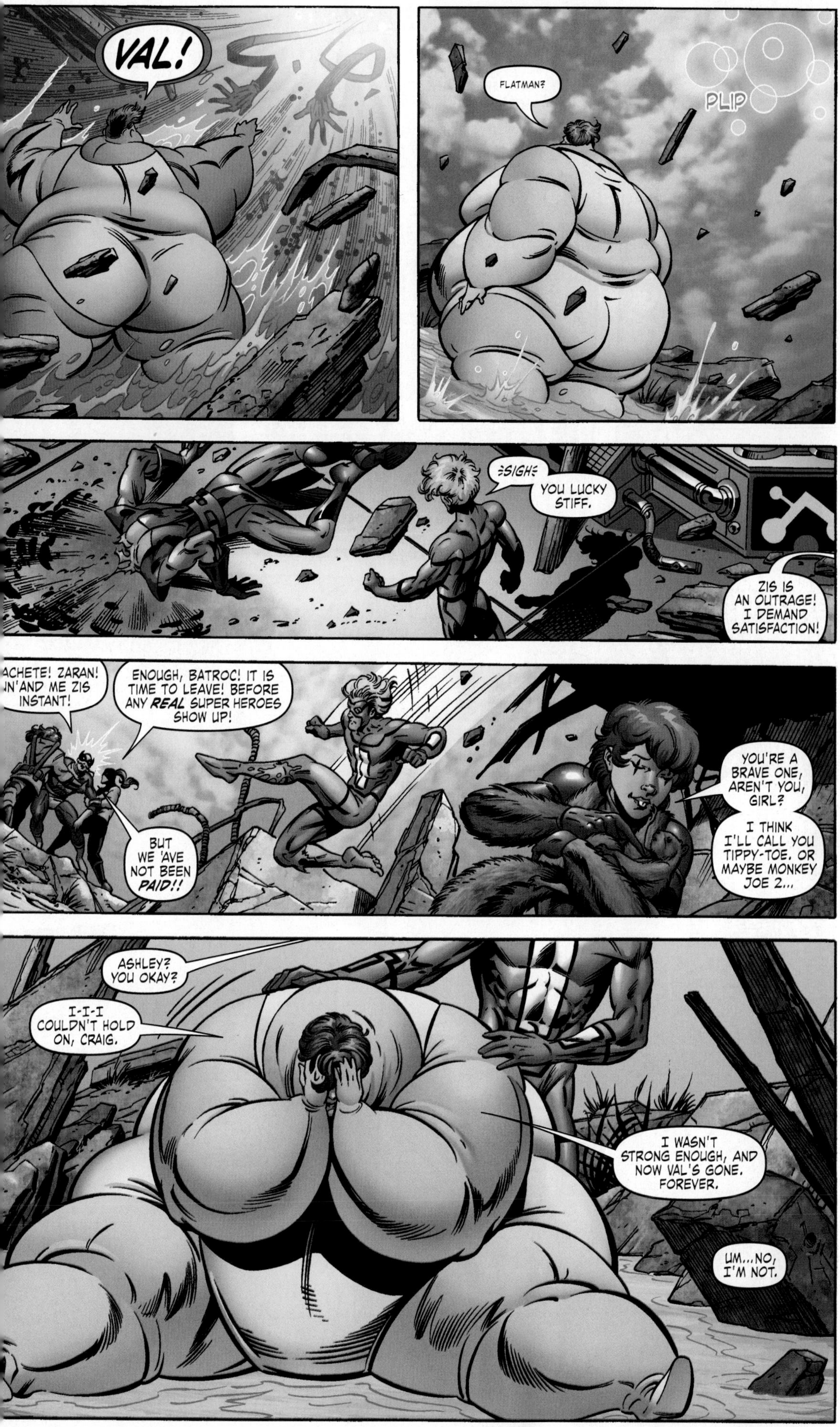
VAL!
FLATMAN?
PLIP
≈SIGH≈
YOU LUCKY STIFF.
ZIS IS AN OUTRAGE! I DEMAND SATISFACTION!
ACHETE! ZARAN! IN'AND ME ZIS INSTANT!
ENOUGH, BATROC! IT IS TIME TO LEAVE! BEFORE ANY REAL SUPER HEROES SHOW UP!
BUT WE 'AVE NOT BEEN PAID!!
YOU'RE A BRAVE ONE, AREN'T YOU, GIRL?
I THINK I'LL CALL YOU TIPPY-TOE. OR MAYBE MONKEY JOE 2...
ASHLEY? YOU OKAY?
I-I-I COULDN'T HOLD ON, CRAIG.
I WASN'T STRONG ENOUGH, AND NOW VAL'S GONE. FOREVER.
UM...NO, I'M NOT.

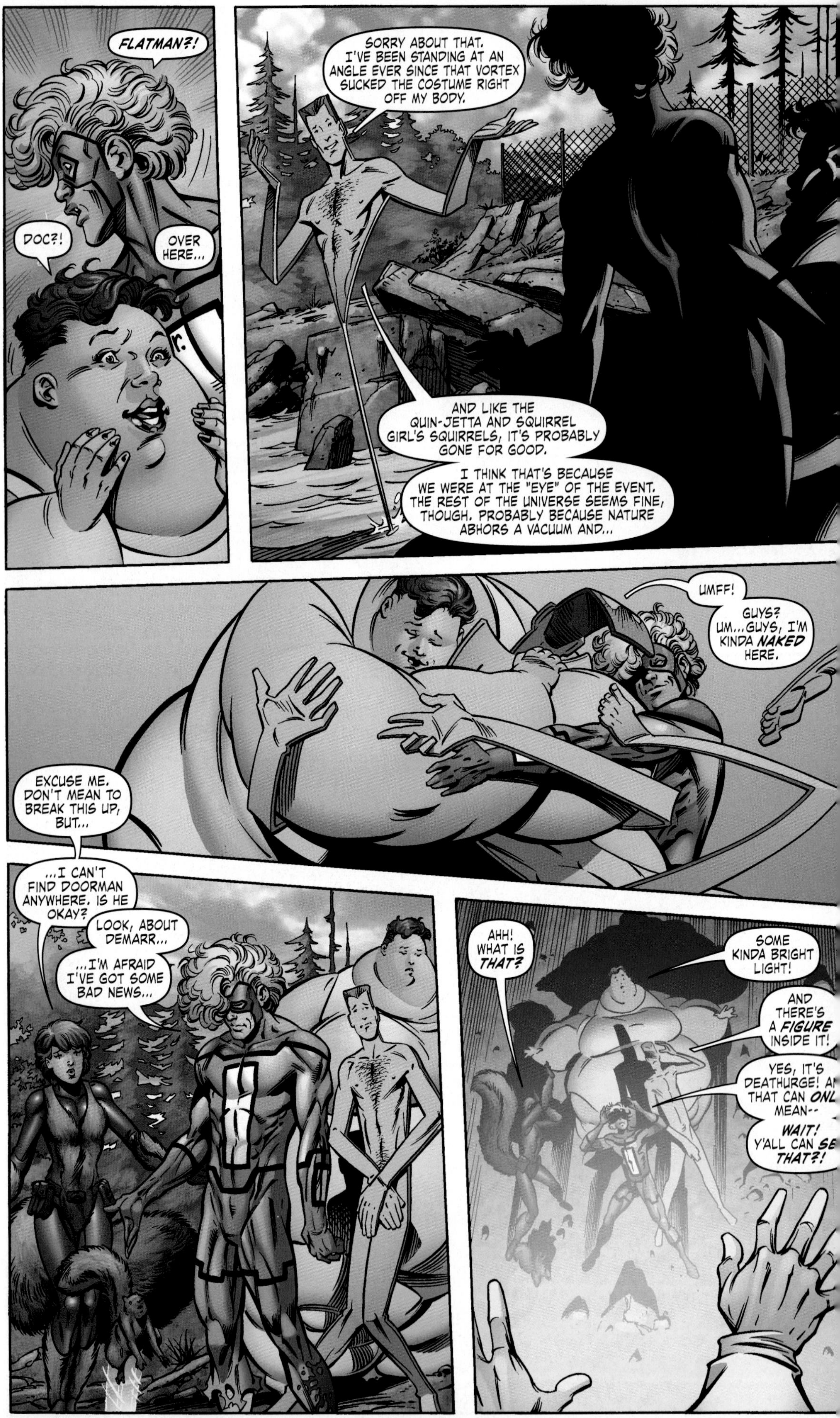

FLATMAN?!
DOC?!
OVER HERE...
SORRY ABOUT THAT. I'VE BEEN STANDING AT AN ANGLE EVER SINCE THAT VORTEX SUCKED THE COSTUME RIGHT OFF MY BODY.
AND LIKE THE QUIN-JETTA AND SQUIRREL GIRL'S SQUIRRELS, IT'S PROBABLY GONE FOR GOOD.
I THINK THAT'S BECAUSE WE WERE AT THE "EYE" OF THE EVENT. THE REST OF THE UNIVERSE SEEMS FINE, THOUGH. PROBABLY BECAUSE NATURE ABHORS A VACUUM AND...
UMFF!
GUYS? UM...GUYS, I'M KINDA NAKED HERE.
EXCUSE ME. DON'T MEAN TO BREAK THIS UP, BUT...
...I CAN'T FIND DOORMAN ANYWHERE. IS HE OKAY?
LOOK, ABOUT DEMARR...
...I'M AFRAID I'VE GOT SOME BAD NEWS...
AHH! WHAT IS THAT?
SOME KINDA BRIGHT LIGHT!
AND THERE'S A FIGURE INSIDE IT!
WAIT!

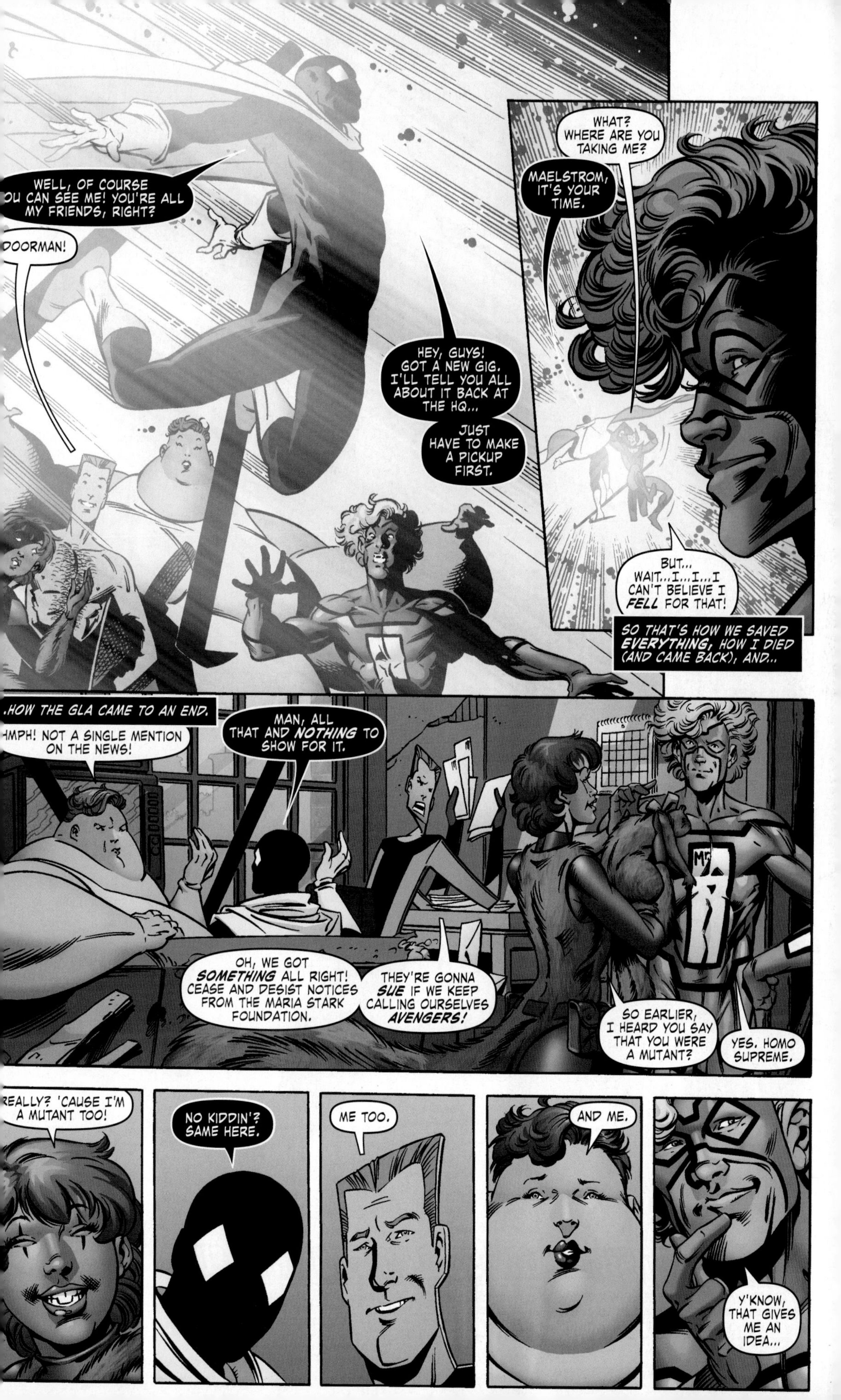
WELL, OF COURSE OU CAN SEE ME! YOU'RE ALL MY FRIENDS, RIGHT?
DOORMAN!
HEY, GUYS! GOT A NEW GIG. I'LL TELL YOU ALL ABOUT IT BACK AT THE HQ...
JUST HAVE TO MAKE A PICKUP FIRST.
WHAT? WHERE ARE YOU TAKING ME?
MAELSTROM, IT'S YOUR TIME.
BUT... WAIT...I...I...I CAN'T BELIEVE I FELL FOR THAT!
SO THAT'S HOW WE SAVED EVERYTHING, HOW I DIED (AND CAME BACK), AND...
.HOW THE GLA CAME TO AN END.
HMPH! NOT A SINGLE MENTION ON THE NEWS!
MAN, ALL THAT AND NOTHING TO SHOW FOR IT.
OH, WE GOT SOMETHING ALL RIGHT! CEASE AND DESIST NOTICES FROM THE MARIA STARK FOUNDATION.
THEY'RE GONNA SUE IF WE KEEP CALLING OURSELVES AVENGERS!
SO EARLIER, I HEARD YOU SAY THAT YOU WERE A MUTANT?
YES. HOMO SUPREME.
REALLY? 'CAUSE I'M A MUTANT TOO!
NO KIDDIN'? SAME HERE.
ME TOO.
AND ME.
Y'KNOW, THAT GIVES ME AN IDEA...

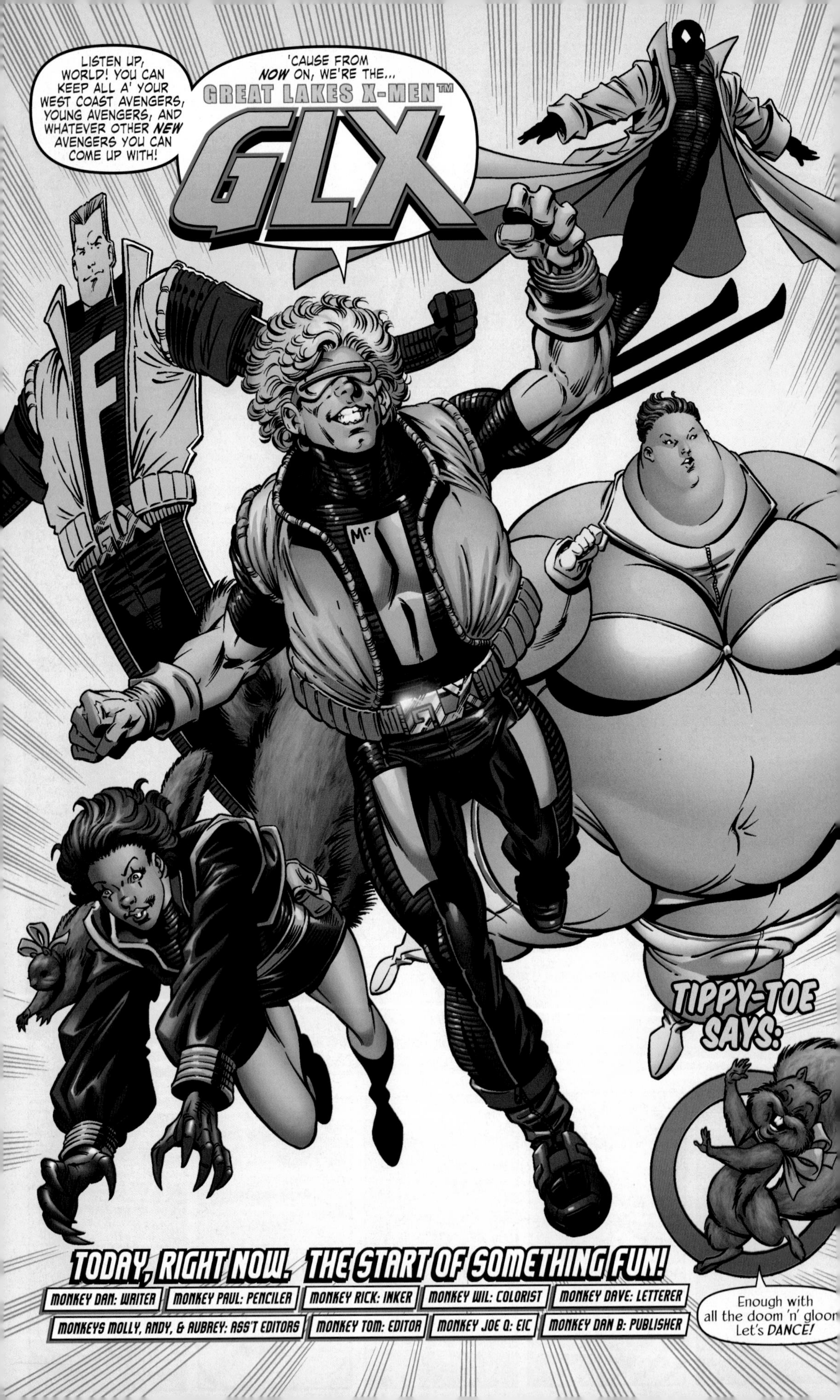

LISTEN UP, WORLD! YOU CAN KEEP ALL A' YOUR WEST COAST AVENGERS, YOUNG AVENGERS, AND WHATEVER OTHER NEW AVENGERS YOU CAN COME UP WITH!
'CAUSE FROM NOW ON, WE'RE THE...
GREAT LAKES X-MEN™
GLX
TIPPY-TOE SAYS:
Enough with all the doom 'n' gloom! Let's DANCE!
TODAY, RIGHT NOW. THE START OF SOMETHING FUN!
MONKEY DAN: WRITER
MONKEY PAUL: PENCILER
MONKEY RICK: INKER
MONKEY WIL: COLORIST
MONKEY DAVE: LETTERER
MONKEYS MOLLY, ANDY, & AUBREY: ASS'T EDITORS
MONKEY TOM: EDITOR
MONKEY JOE Q: EIC
MONKEY DAN B: PUBLISHER

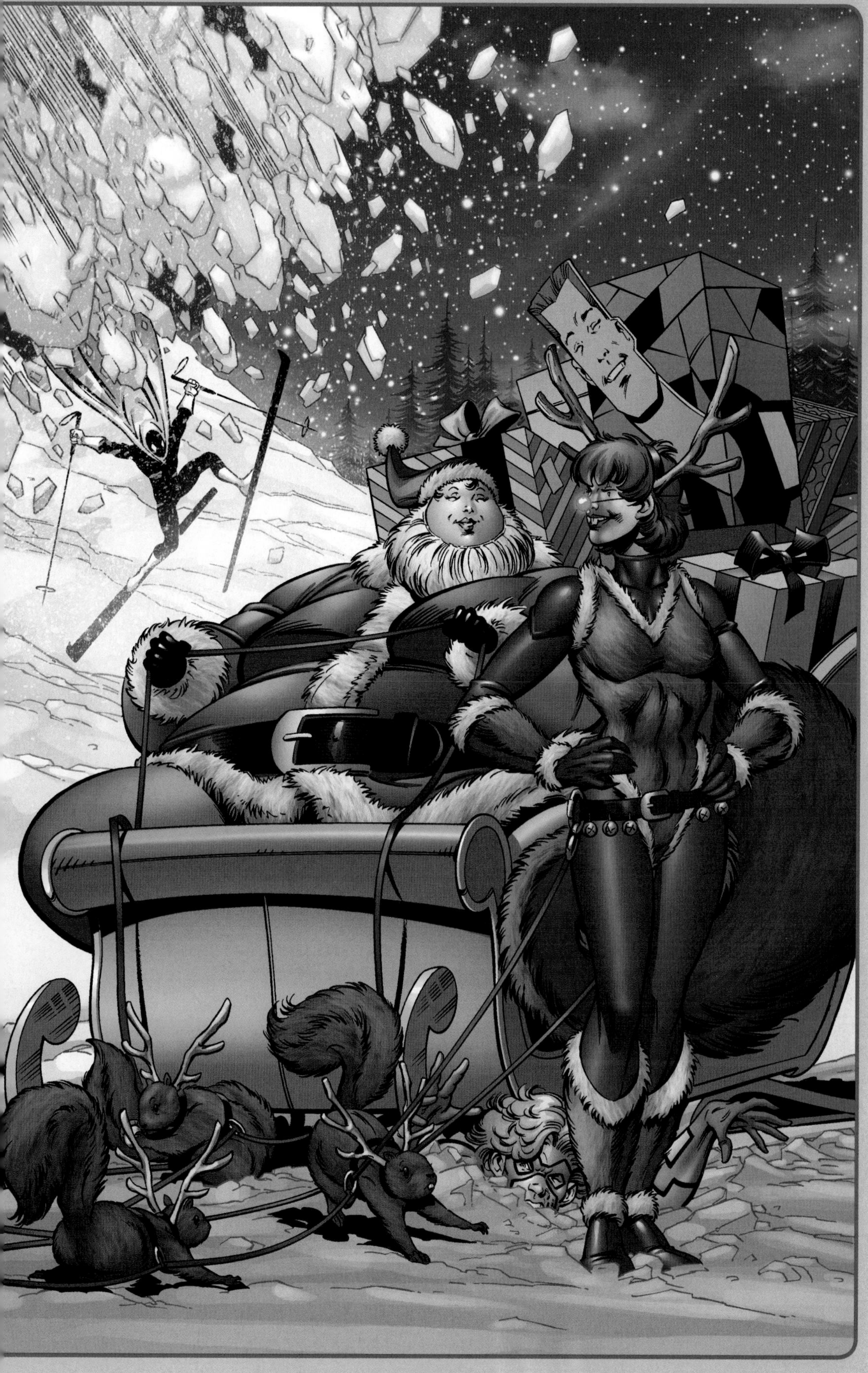

GLX-Mas Special

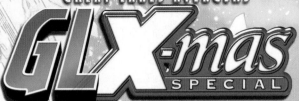

GREAT LAKES AVENGERS

GLX-mas SPECIAL

written by Dan Slott

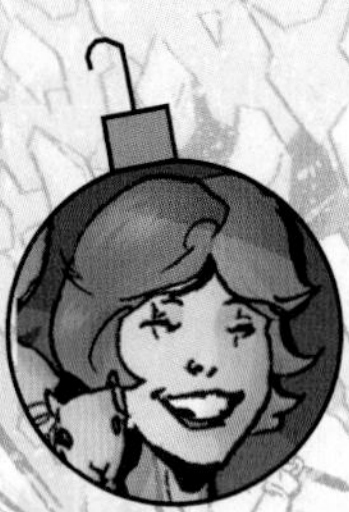

Squirrel Girl in
"Eggnog, Toilet Paper, and Peace on Earth"
Matt Haley -- Artist

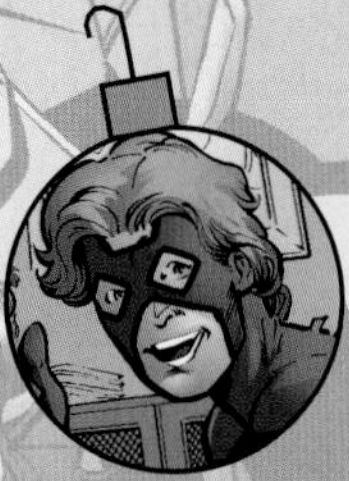

Mr. Immortal in
"Days of X-Mas Past"
Georges Jeanty -- Penciler
Drew Geraci -- Inker
SotoColor's L. Molinar -- Colorist

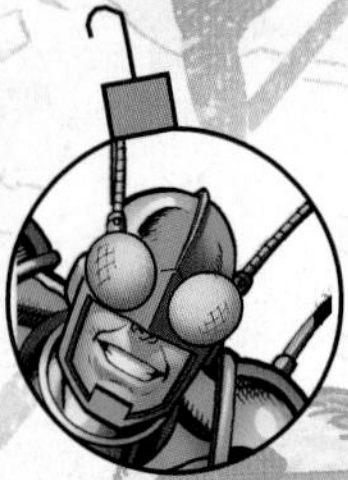

Grasshopper in
"Getting Off On The Right Foot"
Ty Templeton -- Artist
Wil Quintana -- Colorist

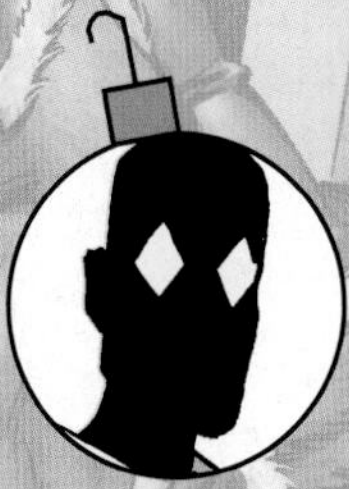

Doorman in
"Working Holiday"
Paul Grist -- Artist
Laura Allred -- Colorist

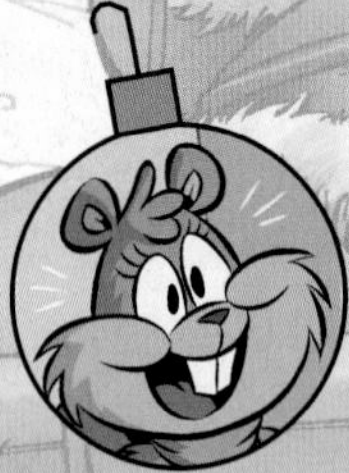

Tippy Toe in
"Squirrel on Squirrel Action"
Mike Kazaleh -- Artist
Bill Crabtree -- Colorist

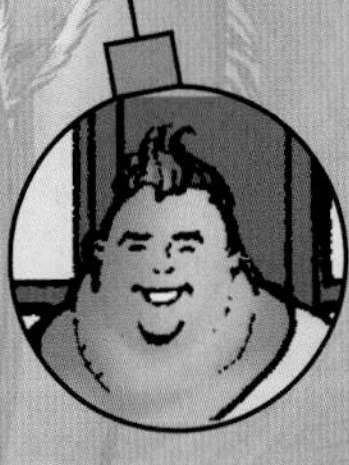

"Seasons Greetings from the GLX"
Ty Templeton -- Artist
Wil Quintana -- Colorist

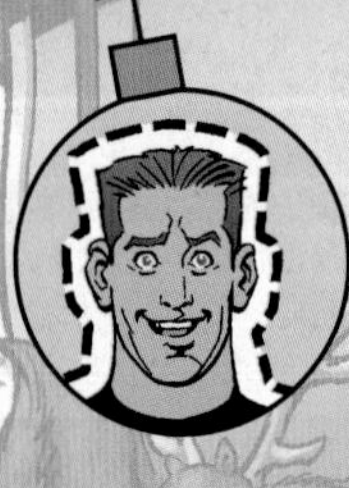

Flatman's Special Christmas Gift to You
Mike Wieringo -- Penciler
Karl Kesel -- Inker
Wil Quintana -- Colorist

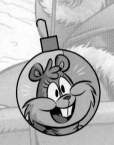

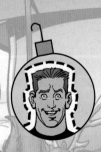

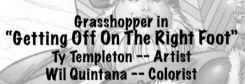

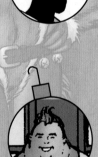

Dave Lanphear
LETTERER

Tom Valente
PRODUCTION

Schmidt, Lazer, & Sitterson
ASSISTANT EDITORS

Tom Brevoort
EDITOR

Joe Quesada
EDITOR IN CHIEF

Dan Buckley
PUBLISHER

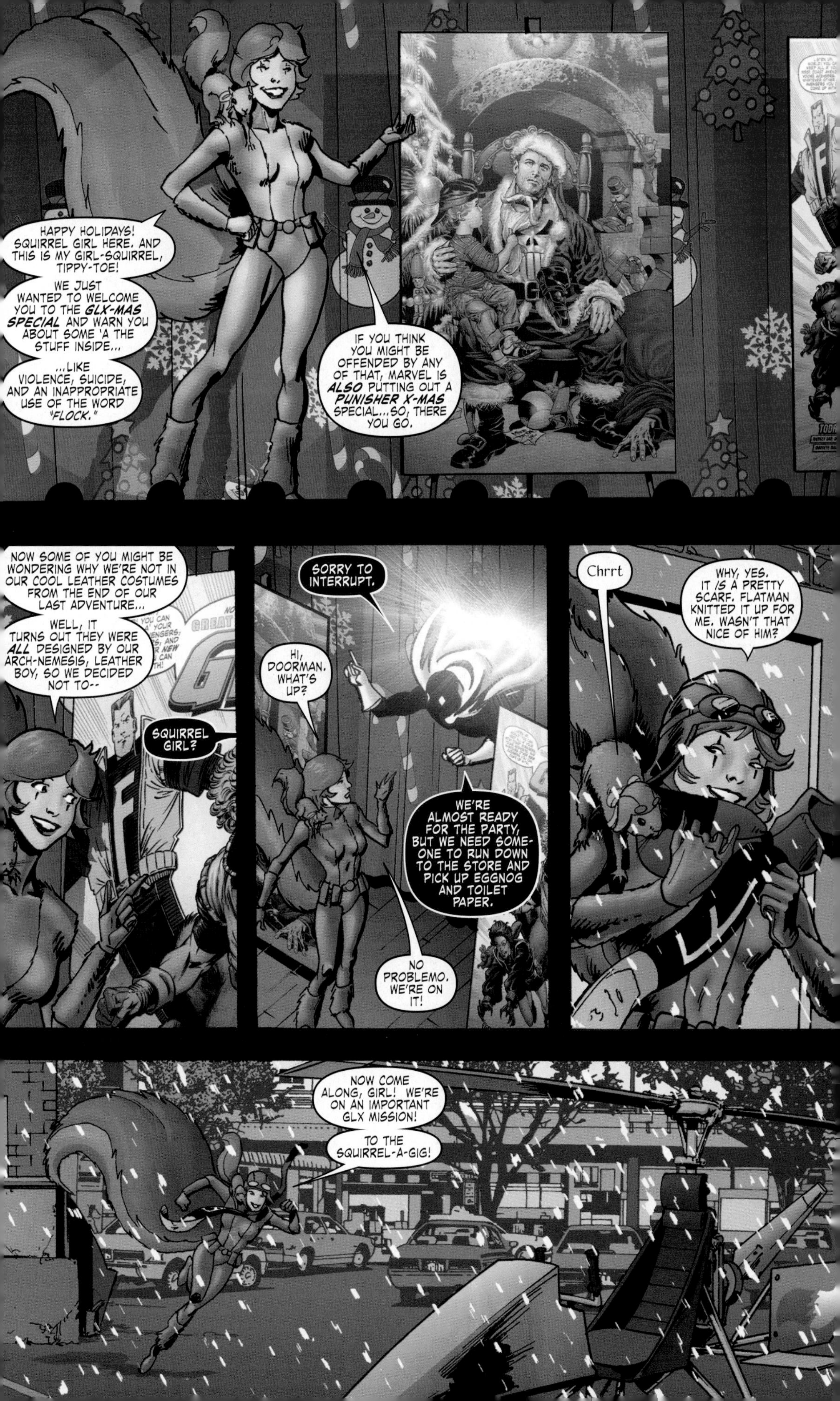

HAPPY HOLIDAYS! SQUIRREL GIRL HERE. AND THIS IS MY GIRL-SQUIRREL, TIPPY-TOE!
WE JUST WANTED TO WELCOME YOU TO THE GLX-MAS SPECIAL AND WARN YOU ABOUT SOME 'A THE STUFF INSIDE...
...LIKE VIOLENCE, SUICIDE, AND AN INAPPROPRIATE USE OF THE WORD "FLOCK."
IF YOU THINK YOU MIGHT BE OFFENDED BY ANY OF THAT, MARVEL IS ALSO PUTTING OUT A PUNISHER X-MAS SPECIAL...SO, THERE YOU GO.
NOW SOME OF YOU MIGHT BE WONDERING WHY WE'RE NOT IN OUR COOL LEATHER COSTUMES FROM THE END OF OUR LAST ADVENTURE...
WELL, IT TURNS OUT THEY WERE ALL DESIGNED BY OUR ARCH-NEMESIS, LEATHER BOY, SO WE DECIDED NOT TO--
SQUIRREL GIRL?
SORRY TO INTERRUPT.
HI, DOORMAN. WHAT'S UP?
WE'RE ALMOST READY FOR THE PARTY, BUT WE NEED SOME-ONE TO RUN DOWN TO THE STORE AND PICK UP EGGNOG AND TOILET PAPER.
NO PROBLEMO. WE'RE ON IT!
Chrrt
WHY, YES. IT IS A PRETTY SCARF. FLATMAN KNITTED IT UP FOR ME. WASN'T THAT NICE OF HIM?
NOW COME ALONG, GIRL! WE'RE ON AN IMPORTANT GLX MISSION!
TO THE SQUIRREL-A-GIG!

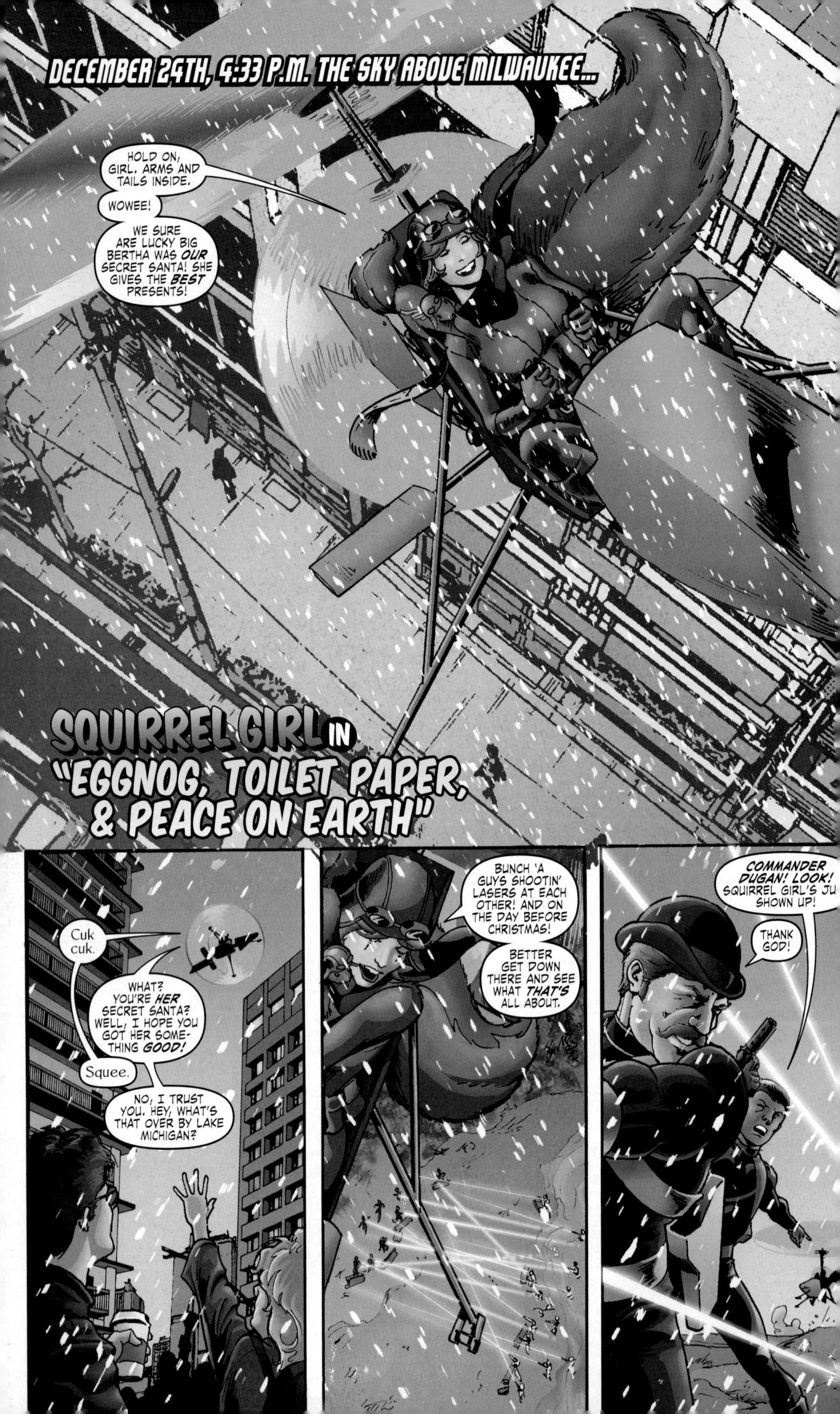
DECEMBER 24TH, 4:33 P.M. THE SKY ABOVE MILWAUKEE...
HOLD ON, GIRL. ARMS AND TAILS INSIDE.
WOWEE!
WE SURE ARE LUCKY BIG BERTHA WAS OUR SECRET SANTA! SHE GIVES THE BEST PRESENTS!
SQUIRREL GIRL IN
"EGGNOG, TOILET PAPER, & PEACE ON EARTH"
Cuk cuk.
WHAT? YOU'RE HER SECRET SANTA? WELL, I HOPE YOU GOT HER SOMETHING GOOD!
Squee.
NO, I TRUST YOU. HEY, WHAT'S THAT OVER BY LAKE MICHIGAN?
BUNCH 'A GUYS SHOOTIN' LASERS AT EACH OTHER! AND ON THE DAY BEFORE CHRISTMAS!
BETTER GET DOWN THERE AND SEE WHAT THAT'S ALL ABOUT.
COMMANDER DUGAN! LOOK! SQUIRREL GIRL'S JU SHOWN UP!
THANK GOD!

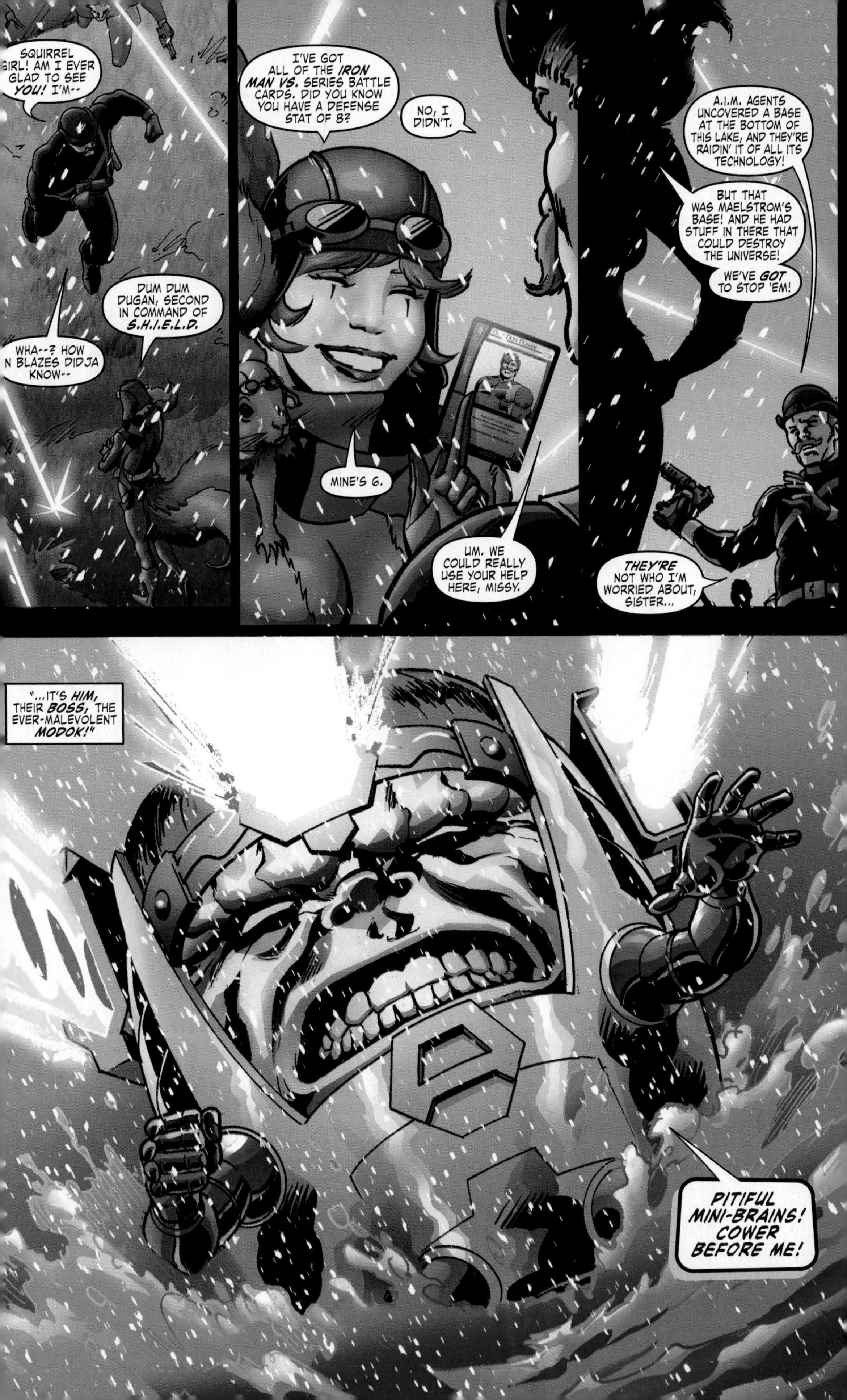
SQUIRREL GIRL! AM I EVER GLAD TO SEE YOU! I'M--
DUM DUM DUGAN, SECOND IN COMMAND OF S.H.I.E.L.D.
WHA--? HOW N BLAZES DIDJA KNOW--
I'VE GOT ALL OF THE IRON MAN VS. SERIES BATTLE CARDS. DID YOU KNOW YOU HAVE A DEFENSE STAT OF 8?
NO, I DIDN'T.
MINE'S 6.
UM. WE COULD REALLY USE YOUR HELP HERE, MISSY.
A.I.M. AGENTS UNCOVERED A BASE AT THE BOTTOM OF THIS LAKE, AND THEY'RE RAIDIN' IT OF ALL ITS TECHNOLOGY!
BUT THAT WAS MAELSTROM'S BASE! AND HE HAD STUFF IN THERE THAT COULD DESTROY THE UNIVERSE!
WE'VE GOT TO STOP 'EM!
THEY'RE NOT WHO I'M WORRIED ABOUT, SISTER...
"...IT'S HIM, THEIR BOSS, THE EVER-MALEVOLENT MODOK!"
PITIFUL MINI-BRAINS! COWER BEFORE ME!

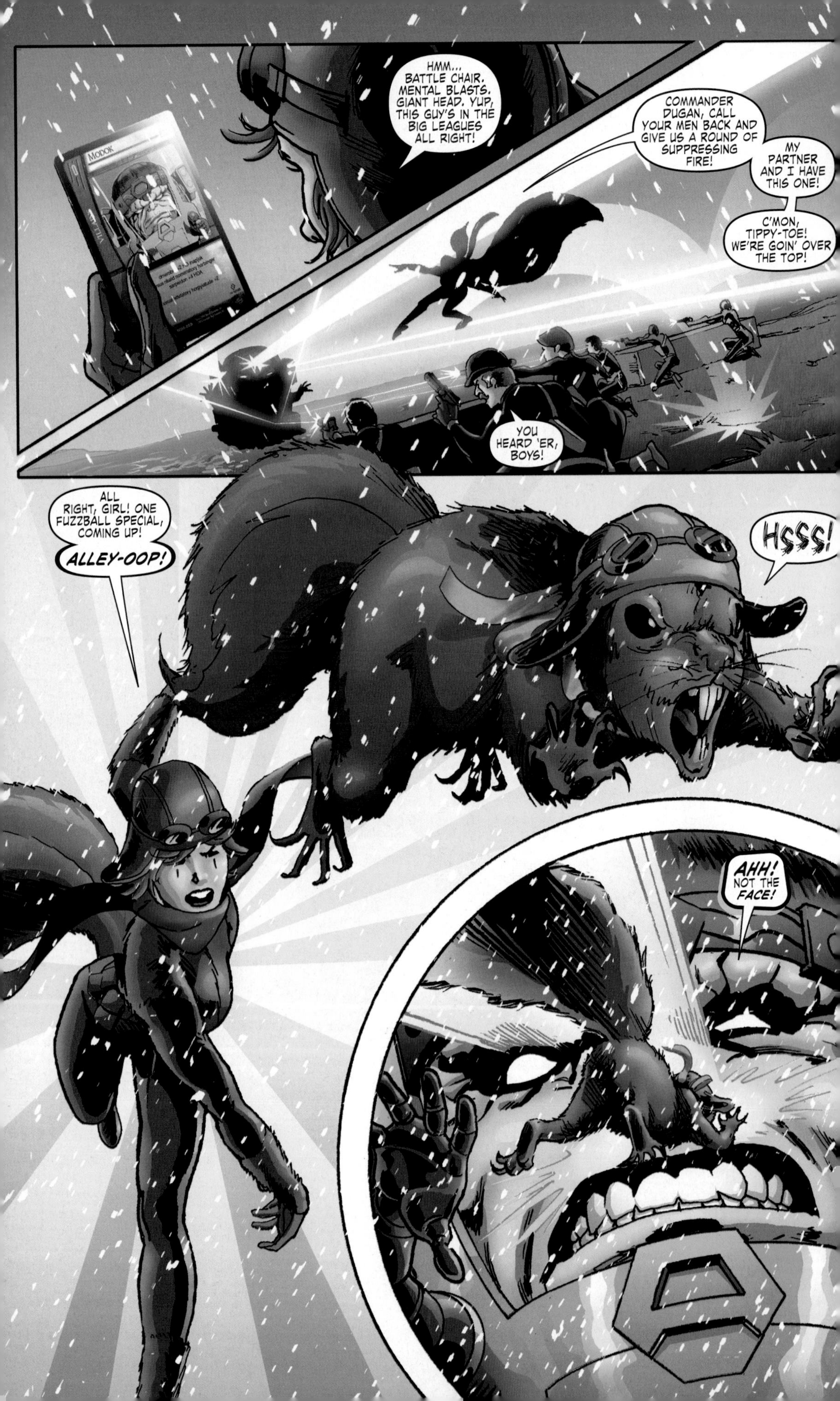
HMM... BATTLE CHAIR. MENTAL BLASTS. GIANT HEAD. YUP, THIS GUY'S IN THE BIG LEAGUES ALL RIGHT!
MODOK
COMMANDER DUGAN, CALL YOUR MEN BACK AND GIVE US A ROUND OF SUPPRESSING FIRE!
MY PARTNER AND I HAVE THIS ONE!
C'MON, TIPPY-TOE! WE'RE GOIN' OVER THE TOP!
YOU HEARD 'ER, BOYS!
ALL RIGHT, GIRL! ONE FUZZBALL SPECIAL, COMING UP!
ALLEY-OOP!
HSSS!
AHH! NOT THE FACE!

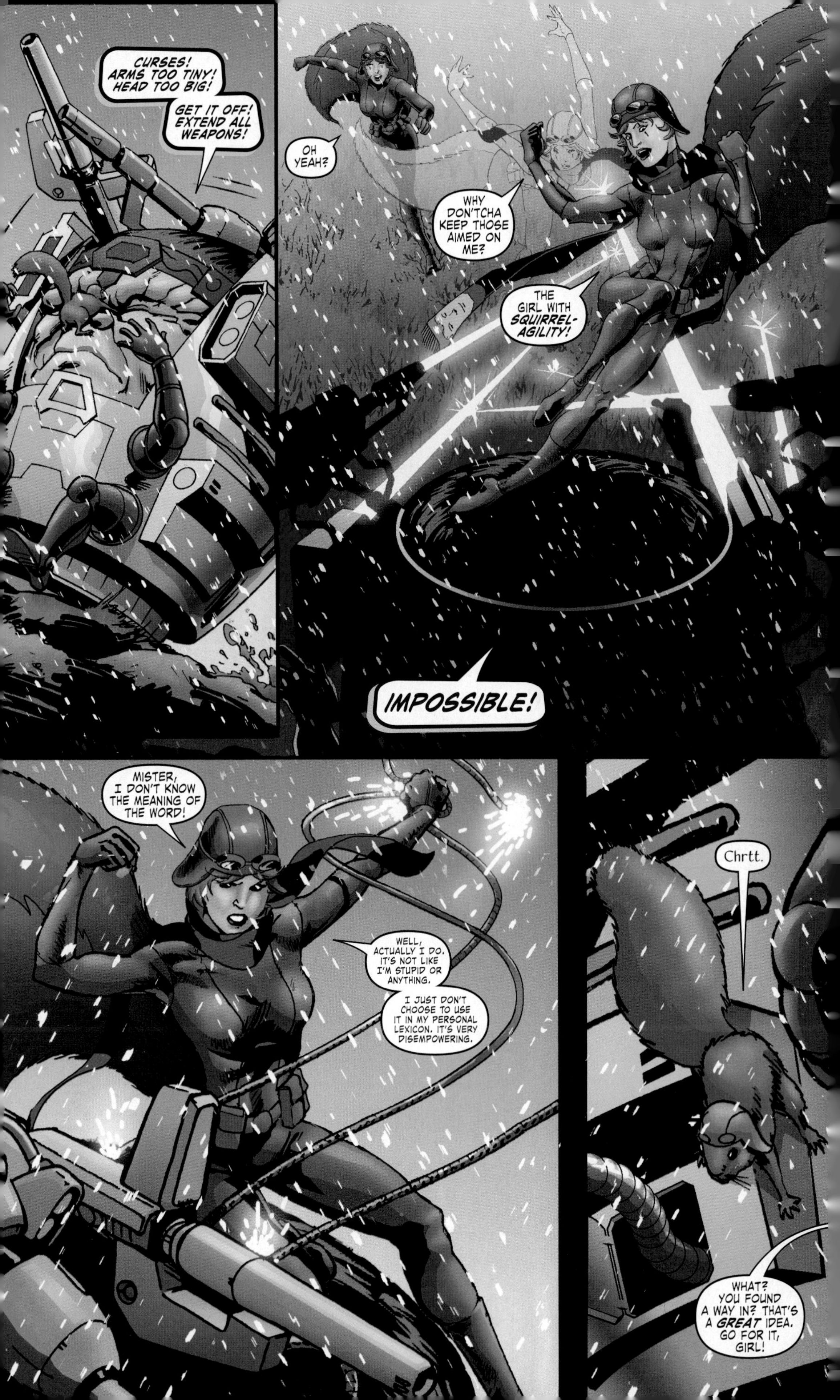
CURSES! ARMS TOO TINY! HEAD TOO BIG!
GET IT OFF! EXTEND ALL WEAPONS!
OH YEAH?
WHY DON'TCHA KEEP THOSE AIMED ON ME?
THE GIRL WITH SQUIRREL-AGILITY!
IMPOSSIBLE!
MISTER, I DON'T KNOW THE MEANING OF THE WORD!
WELL, ACTUALLY I DO. IT'S NOT LIKE I'M STUPID OR ANYTHING.
I JUST DON'T CHOOSE TO USE IT IN MY PERSONAL LEXICON. IT'S VERY DISEMPOWERING.
Chrtt.
WHAT? YOU FOUND A WAY IN? THAT'S A GREAT IDEA. GO FOR IT, GIRL!

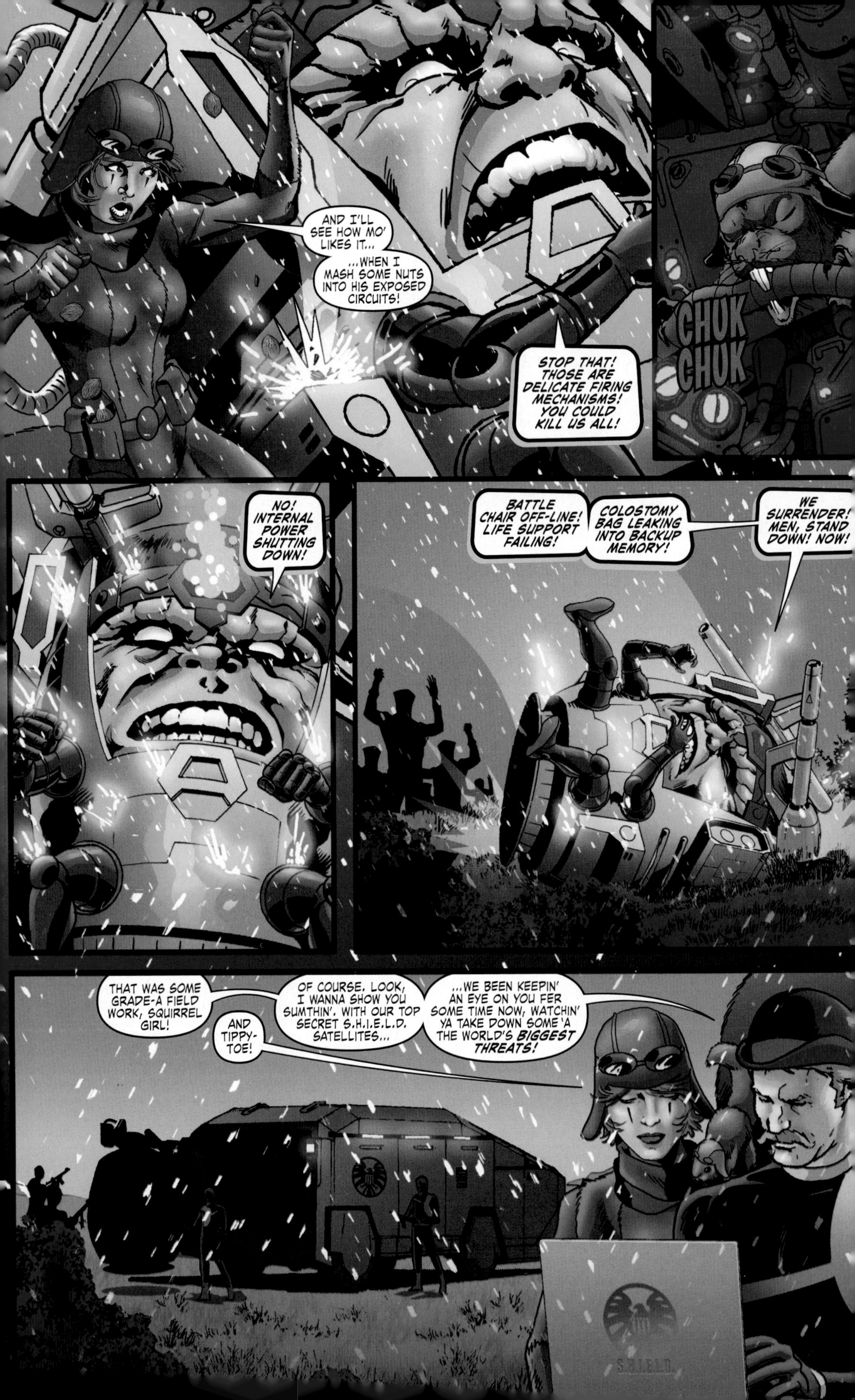
AND I'LL SEE HOW MO' LIKES IT...
...WHEN I MASH SOME NUTS INTO HIS EXPOSED CIRCUITS!
STOP THAT! THOSE ARE DELICATE FIRING MECHANISMS! YOU COULD KILL US ALL!
CHUK CHUK
NO! INTERNAL POWER SHUTTING DOWN!
BATTLE CHAIR OFF-LINE! LIFE SUPPORT FAILING!
COLOSTOMY BAG LEAKING INTO BACKUP MEMORY!
WE SURRENDER! MEN, STAND DOWN! NOW!
THAT WAS SOME GRADE-A FIELD WORK, SQUIRREL GIRL!
AND TIPPY-TOE!
OF COURSE. LOOK, I WANNA SHOW YOU SUMTHIN', WITH OUR TOP SECRET S.H.I.E.L.D. SATELLITES...
...WE BEEN KEEPIN' AN EYE ON YOU FER SOME TIME NOW, WATCHIN' YA TAKE DOWN SOME 'A THE WORLD'S BIGGEST THREATS!
S.H.I.E.L.D.

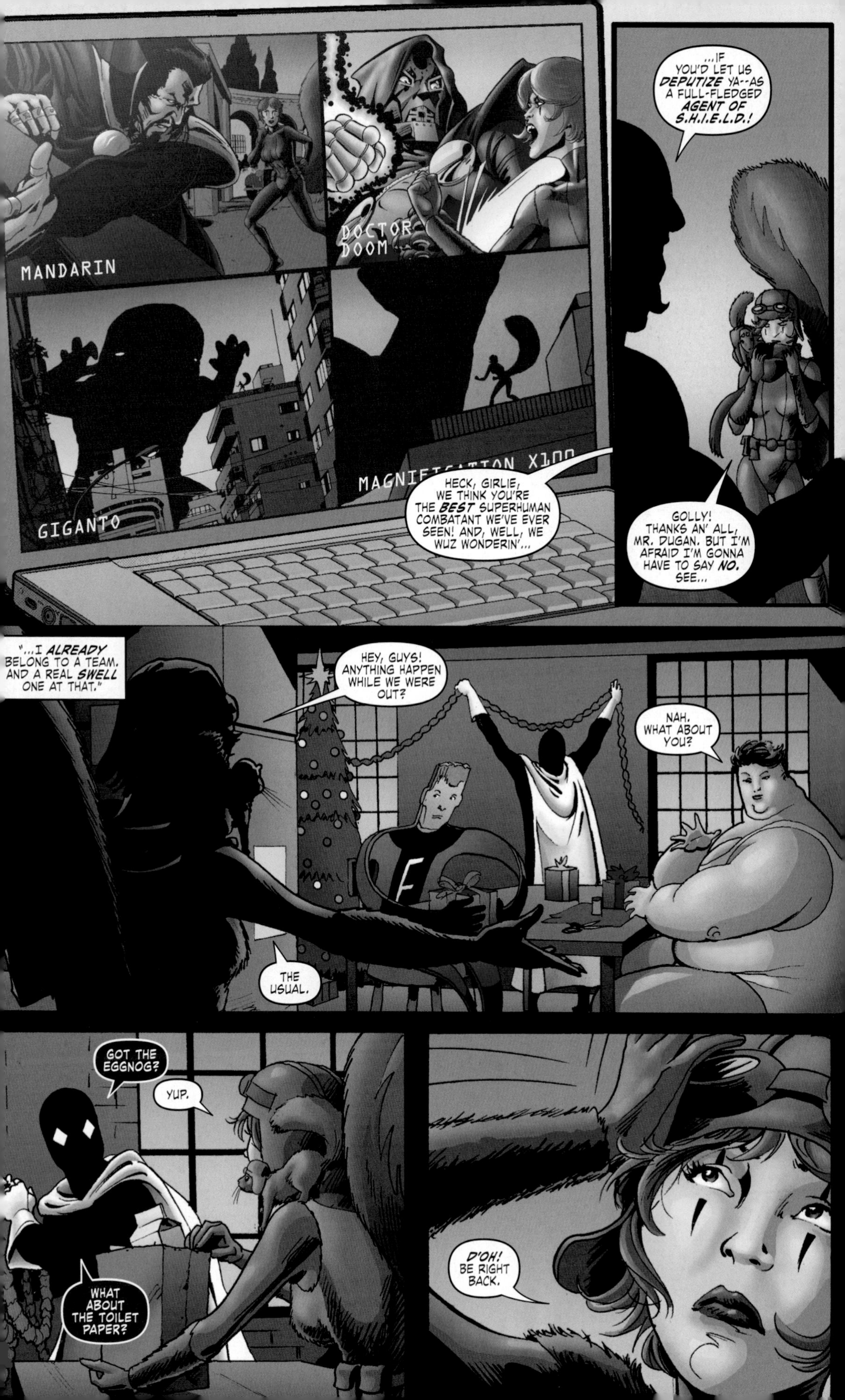
MANDARIN
DOCTOR DOOM
GIGANTO
MAGNIFICATION X100
...IF YOU'D LET US DEPUTIZE YA--AS A FULL-FLEDGED AGENT OF S.H.I.E.L.D.!
HECK, GIRLIE, WE THINK YOU'RE THE BEST SUPERHUMAN COMBATANT WE'VE EVER SEEN! AND, WELL, WE WUZ WONDERIN'...
GOLLY! THANKS AN' ALL, MR. DUGAN. BUT I'M AFRAID I'M GONNA HAVE TO SAY NO. SEE...
"...I ALREADY BELONG TO A TEAM. AND A REAL SWELL ONE AT THAT."
HEY, GUYS! ANYTHING HAPPEN WHILE WE WERE OUT?
NAH. WHAT ABOUT YOU?
THE USUAL.
GOT THE EGGNOG?
YUP.
WHAT ABOUT THE TOILET PAPER?
D'OH! BE RIGHT BACK.

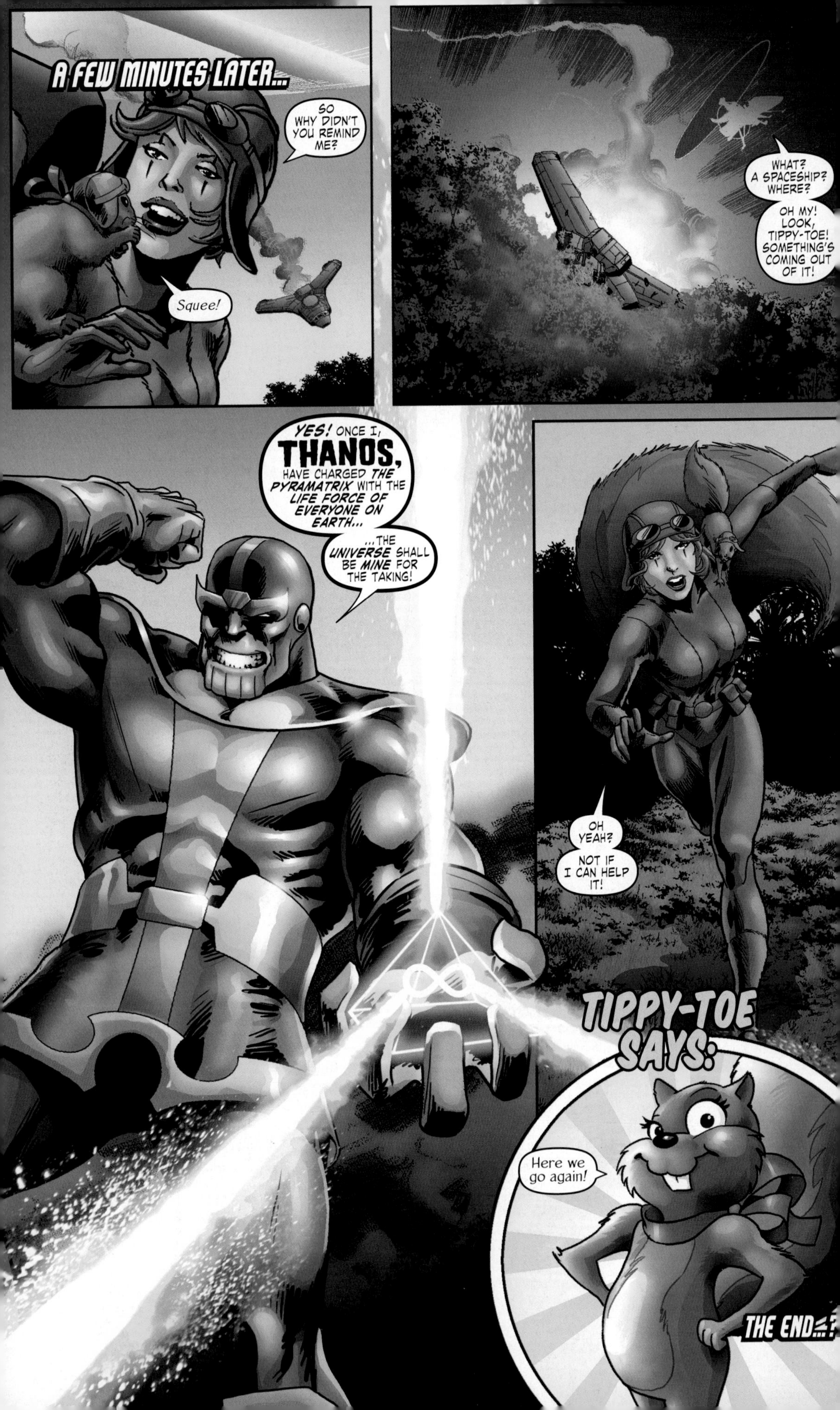
A FEW MINUTES LATER...
SO WHY DIDN'T YOU REMIND ME?
Squee!
WHAT? A SPACESHIP? WHERE?
OH MY! LOOK, TIPPY-TOE! SOMETHING'S COMING OUT OF IT!
YES! ONCE I, THANOS, HAVE CHARGED THE PYRAMATRIX WITH THE LIFE FORCE OF EVERYONE ON EARTH...
...THE UNIVERSE SHALL BE MINE FOR THE TAKING!
OH YEAH? NOT IF I CAN HELP IT!
TIPPY-TOE SAYS:
Here we go again!
THE END...?

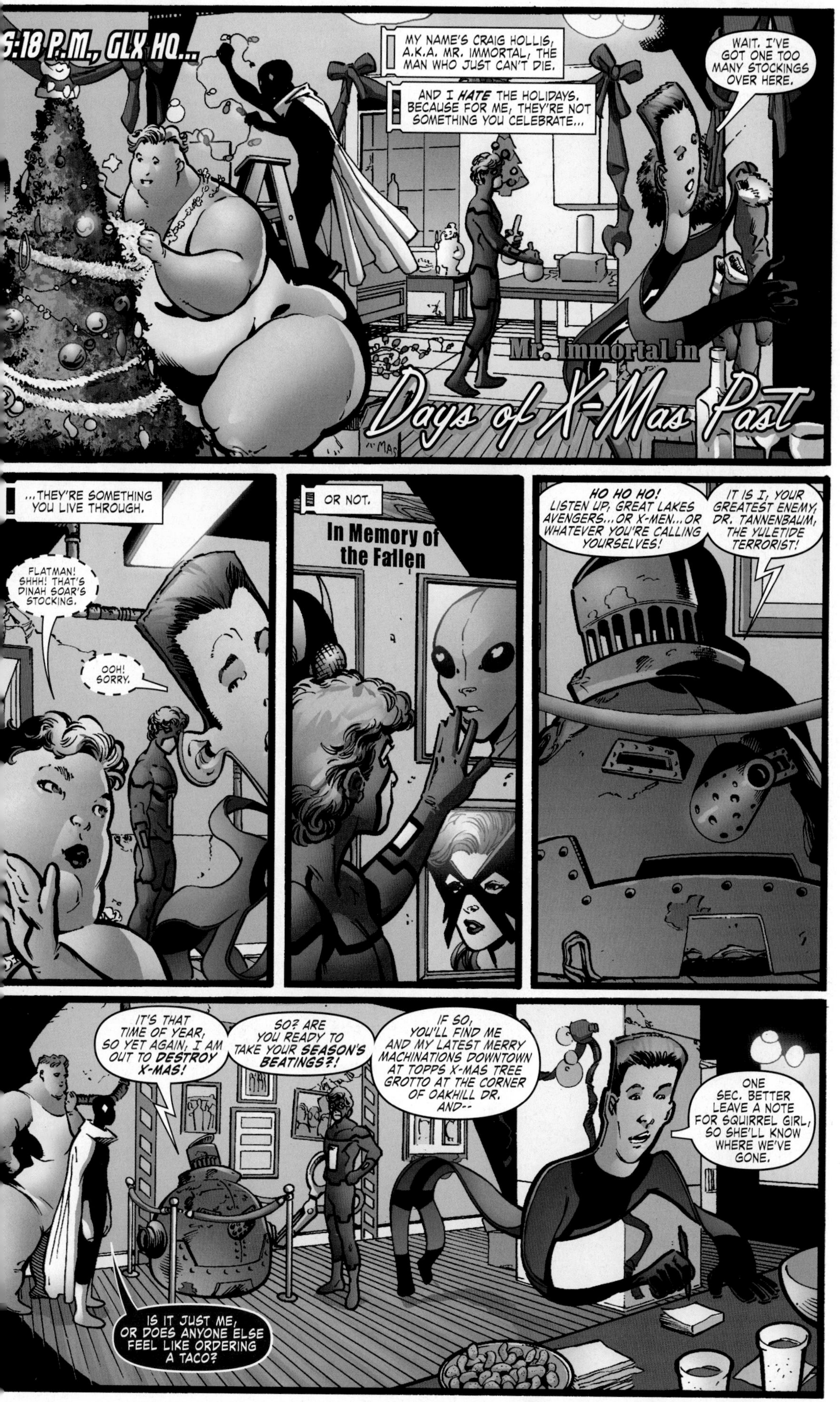
6:18 P.M., GLX HQ...
MY NAME'S CRAIG HOLLIS, A.K.A. MR. IMMORTAL, THE MAN WHO JUST CAN'T DIE.
AND I HATE THE HOLIDAYS. BECAUSE FOR ME, THEY'RE NOT SOMETHING YOU CELEBRATE...
WAIT. I'VE GOT ONE TOO MANY STOCKINGS OVER HERE.
Mr. Immortal in
Days of X-Mas Past
...THEY'RE SOMETHING YOU LIVE THROUGH.
FLATMAN! SHHH! THAT'S DINAH SOAR'S STOCKING.
OOH! SORRY.
OR NOT.
In Memory of the Fallen
HO HO HO! LISTEN UP, GREAT LAKES AVENGERS...OR X-MEN...OR WHATEVER YOU'RE CALLING YOURSELVES!
IT IS I, YOUR GREATEST ENEMY, DR. TANNENBAUM, THE YULETIDE TERRORIST!
IT'S THAT TIME OF YEAR, SO YET AGAIN, I AM OUT TO DESTROY X-MAS!
SO? ARE YOU READY TO TAKE YOUR SEASON'S BEATINGS?!
IF SO, YOU'LL FIND ME AND MY LATEST MERRY MACHINATIONS DOWNTOWN AT TOPPS X-MAS TREE GROTTO AT THE CORNER OF OAKHILL DR. AND--
ONE SEC. BETTER LEAVE A NOTE FOR SQUIRREL GIRL, SO SHE'LL KNOW WHERE WE'VE GONE.
IS IT JUST ME, OR DOES ANYONE ELSE FEEL LIKE ORDERING A TACO?

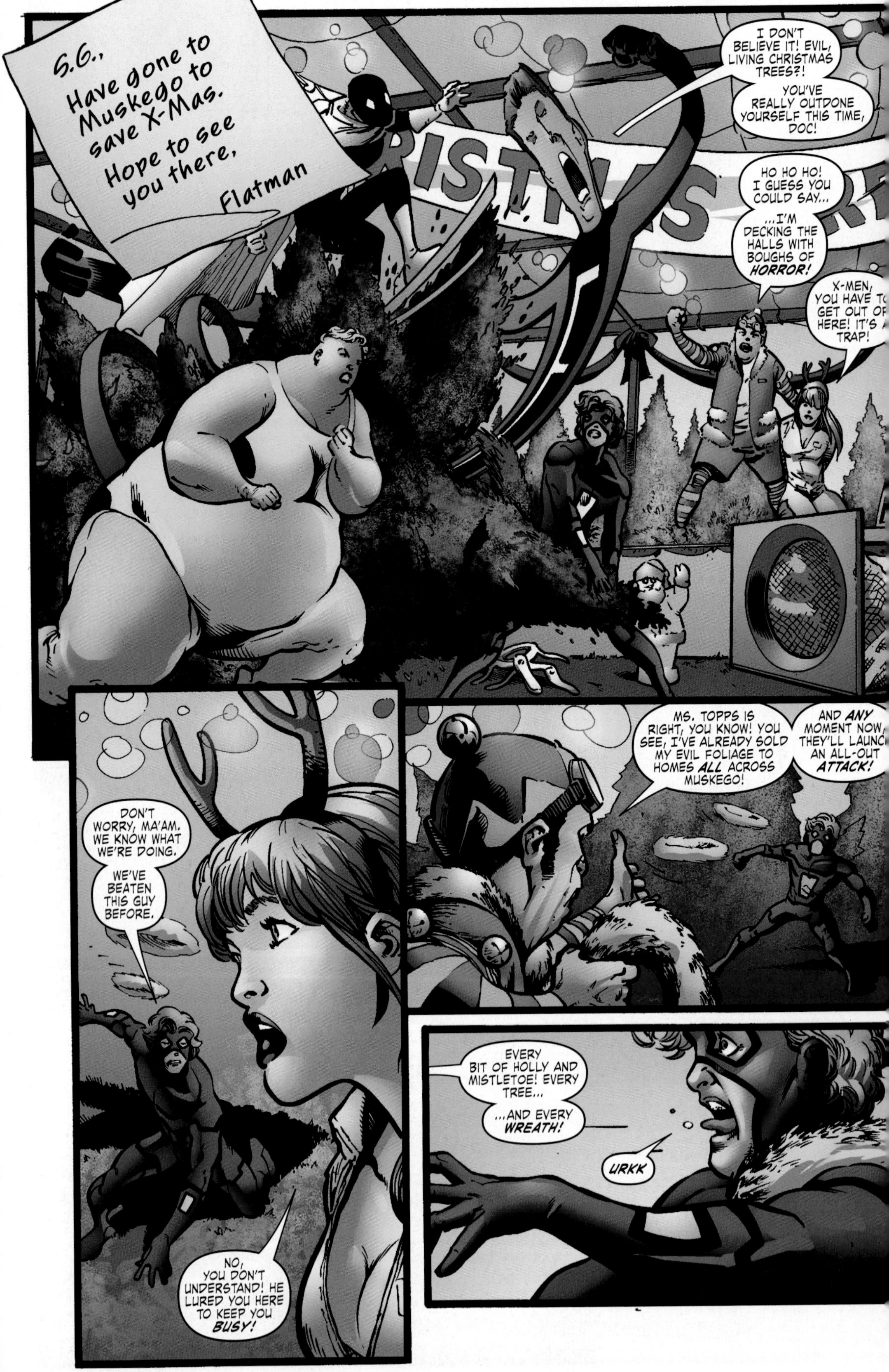
S.G.,
Have gone to Muskego to save X-Mas. Hope to see you there,
Flatman
I DON'T BELIEVE IT! EVIL, LIVING CHRISTMAS TREES?!
YOU'VE REALLY OUTDONE YOURSELF THIS TIME, DOC!
HO HO HO! I GUESS YOU COULD SAY...
...I'M DECKING THE HALLS WITH BOUGHS OF HORROR!
X-MEN, YOU HAVE T GET OUT OF HERE! IT'S TRAP!
DON'T WORRY, MA'AM. WE KNOW WHAT WE'RE DOING.
WE'VE BEATEN THIS GUY BEFORE.
NO, YOU DON'T UNDERSTAND! HE LURED YOU HERE TO KEEP YOU BUSY!
MS. TOPPS IS RIGHT, YOU KNOW! YOU SEE, I'VE ALREADY SOLD MY EVIL FOLIAGE TO HOMES ALL ACROSS MUSKEGO!
AND ANY MOMENT NOW, THEY'LL LAUNC AN ALL-OUT ATTACK!
EVERY BIT OF HOLLY AND MISTLETOE! EVERY TREE...
...AND EVERY WREATH!
URKK

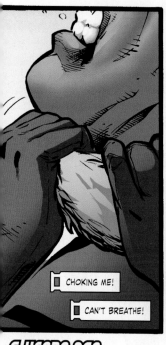

CHOKING ME!

CAN'T BREATHE!

MAN, I HATE X-MAS.

HI, TERRI.

IT'S OUR FIRST CHRISTMAS APART.

4 YEARS AGO...

AND I WANT TO BE WITH YOU, BABE. I DO.

YOU WOULDN'T BELIEVE THE NUMBER OF TIMES I'VE TRIED TO KILL MYSELF TODAY.

I KNOW IT'S NEVER WORKED BEFORE, WHAT WITH THESE POWERS OF MINE AND ALL.

BUT THIS'S THE "SEASON OF HOPE," RIGHT? THE TIME FOR MIRACLES...

KRIKK

WHAT?!

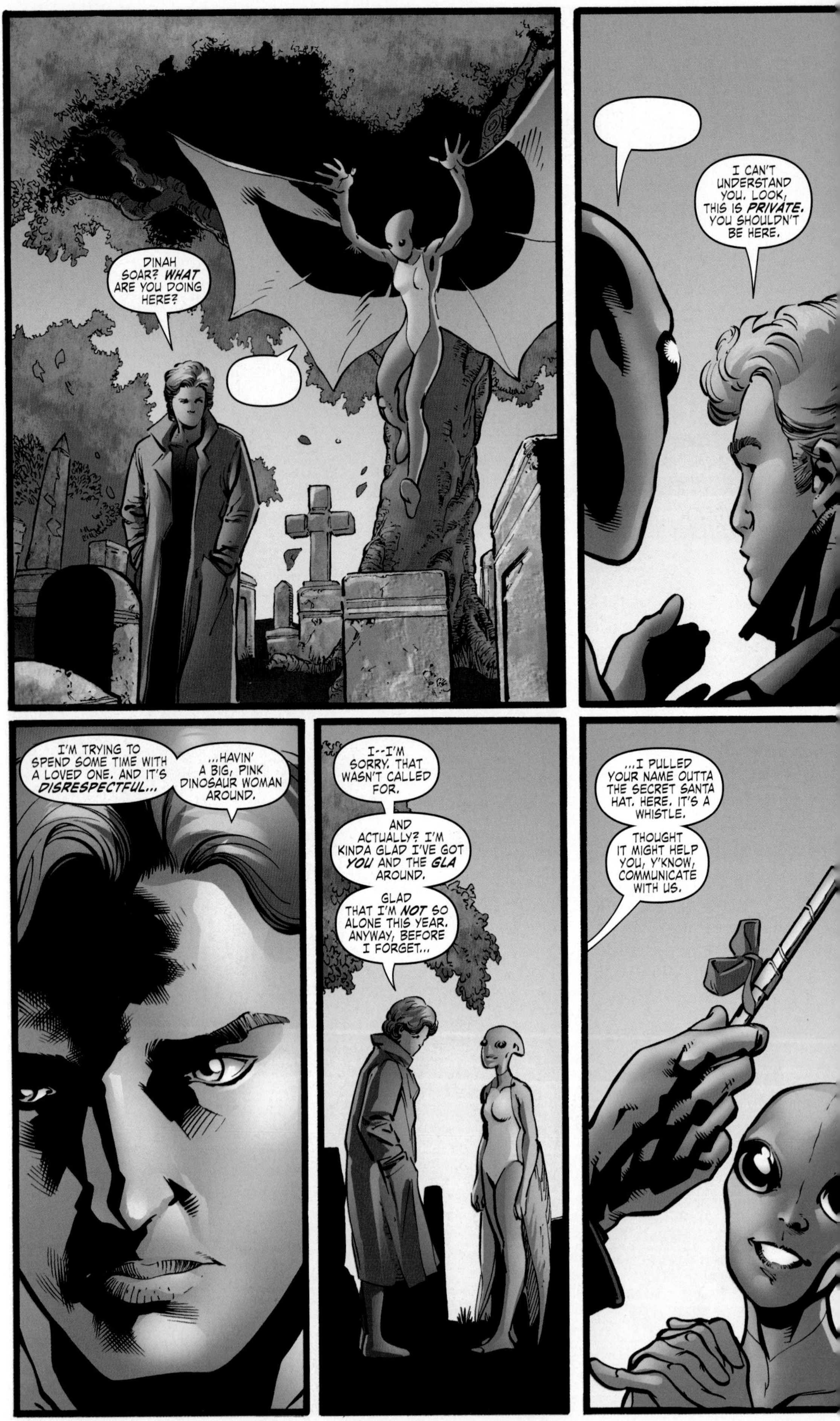
DINAH SOAR? *WHAT* ARE YOU DOING HERE?
I CAN'T UNDERSTAND YOU. LOOK, THIS IS *PRIVATE.* YOU SHOULDN'T BE HERE.
I'M TRYING TO SPEND SOME TIME WITH A LOVED ONE. AND IT'S *DISRESPECTFUL...*
...HAVIN' A BIG, PINK DINOSAUR WOMAN AROUND.
I--I'M SORRY. THAT WASN'T CALLED FOR.
AND ACTUALLY? I'M KINDA GLAD I'VE GOT *YOU* AND THE *GLA* AROUND.
GLAD THAT I'M *NOT* SO ALONE THIS YEAR. ANYWAY, BEFORE I FORGET...
...I PULLED YOUR NAME OUTTA THE SECRET SANTA HAT. HERE. IT'S A WHISTLE.
THOUGHT IT MIGHT HELP YOU, Y'KNOW, COMMUNICATE WITH US.

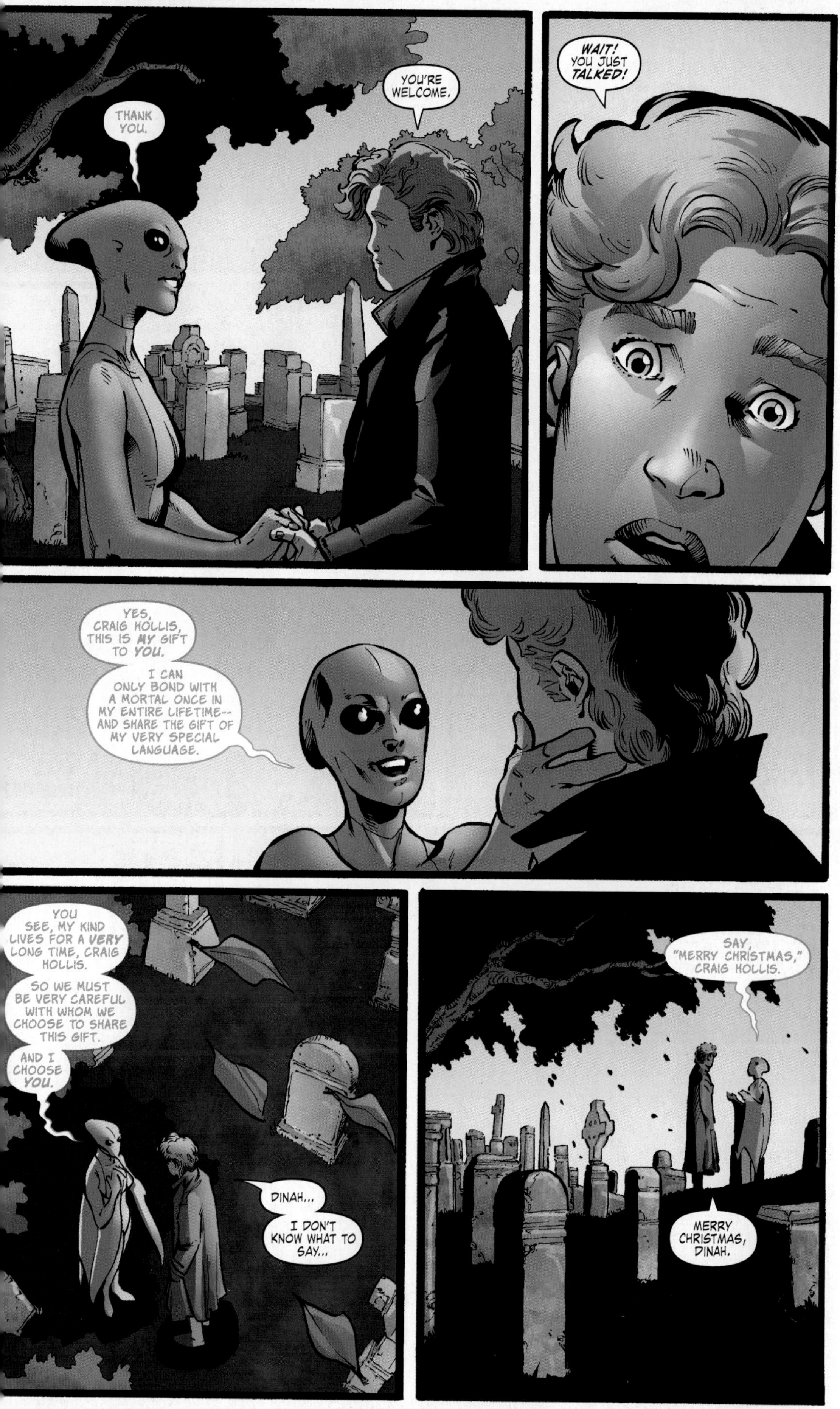
THANK YOU.
YOU'RE WELCOME.
WAIT! YOU JUST TALKED!
YES, CRAIG HOLLIS, THIS IS MY GIFT TO YOU.
I CAN ONLY BOND WITH A MORTAL ONCE IN MY ENTIRE LIFETIME-- AND SHARE THE GIFT OF MY VERY SPECIAL LANGUAGE.
YOU SEE, MY KIND LIVES FOR A VERY LONG TIME, CRAIG HOLLIS.
SO WE MUST BE VERY CAREFUL WITH WHOM WE CHOOSE TO SHARE THIS GIFT.
AND I CHOOSE YOU.
DINAH...
I DON'T KNOW WHAT TO SAY...
SAY, "MERRY CHRISTMAS," CRAIG HOLLIS.
MERRY CHRISTMAS, DINAH.

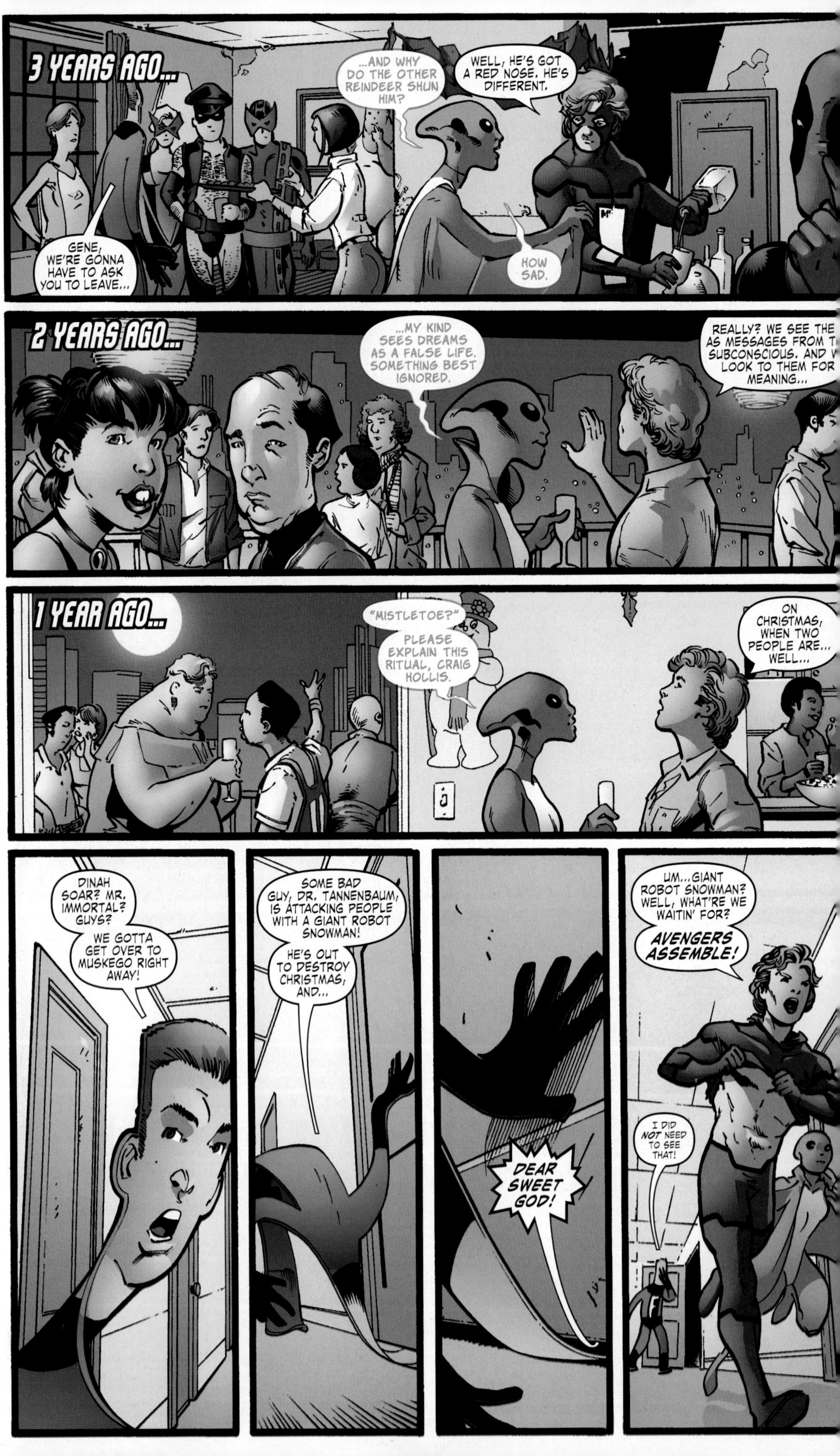
3 YEARS AGO...
...AND WHY DO THE OTHER REINDEER SHUN HIM?
WELL, HE'S GOT A RED NOSE. HE'S DIFFERENT.
GENE, WE'RE GONNA HAVE TO ASK YOU TO LEAVE...
HOW SAD.
2 YEARS AGO...
...MY KIND SEES DREAMS AS A FALSE LIFE. SOMETHING BEST IGNORED.
REALLY? WE SEE THE AS MESSAGES FROM T SUBCONSCIOUS. AND W LOOK TO THEM FOR MEANING...
1 YEAR AGO...
"MISTLETOE?"
PLEASE EXPLAIN THIS RITUAL, CRAIG HOLLIS.
ON CHRISTMAS, WHEN TWO PEOPLE ARE... WELL...
DINAH SOAR? MR. IMMORTAL? GUYS?
WE GOTTA GET OVER TO MUSKEGO RIGHT AWAY!
SOME BAD GUY, DR. TANNENBAUM, IS ATTACKING PEOPLE WITH A GIANT ROBOT SNOWMAN!
HE'S OUT TO DESTROY CHRISTMAS, AND...
DEAR SWEET GOD!
UM...GIANT ROBOT SNOWMAN? WELL, WHAT'RE WE WAITIN' FOR?
AVENGERS ASSEMBLE!
I DID NOT NEED TO SEE THAT!

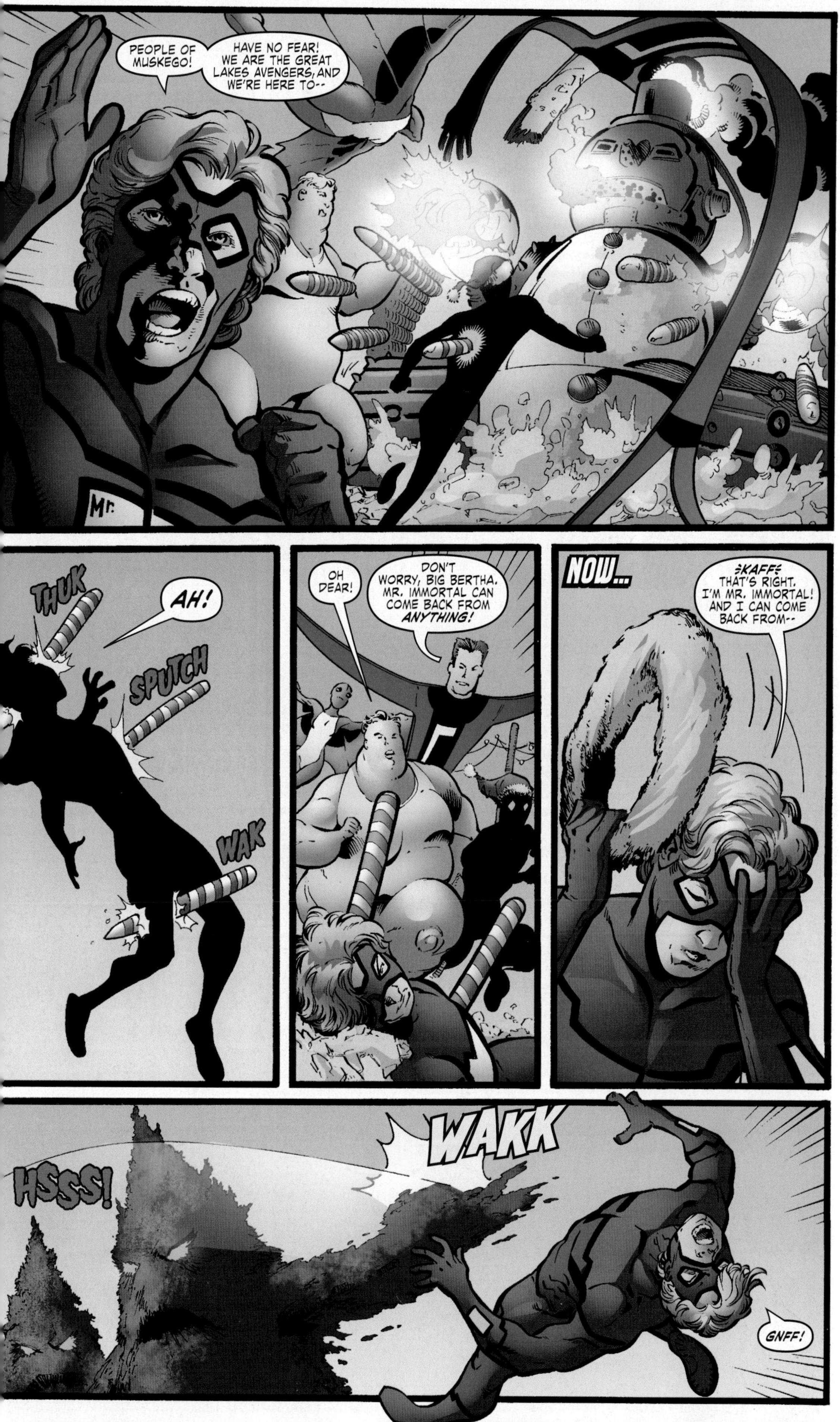
PEOPLE OF MUSKEGO!
HAVE NO FEAR! WE ARE THE GREAT LAKES AVENGERS, AND WE'RE HERE TO--
Mr.
THUK
AH!
SPUTCH
WAK
OH DEAR!
DON'T WORRY, BIG BERTHA. MR. IMMORTAL CAN COME BACK FROM ANYTHING!
NOW...
KAFF THAT'S RIGHT. I'M MR. IMMORTAL! AND I CAN COME BACK FROM--
WAKK
HSSS!
GNFF!

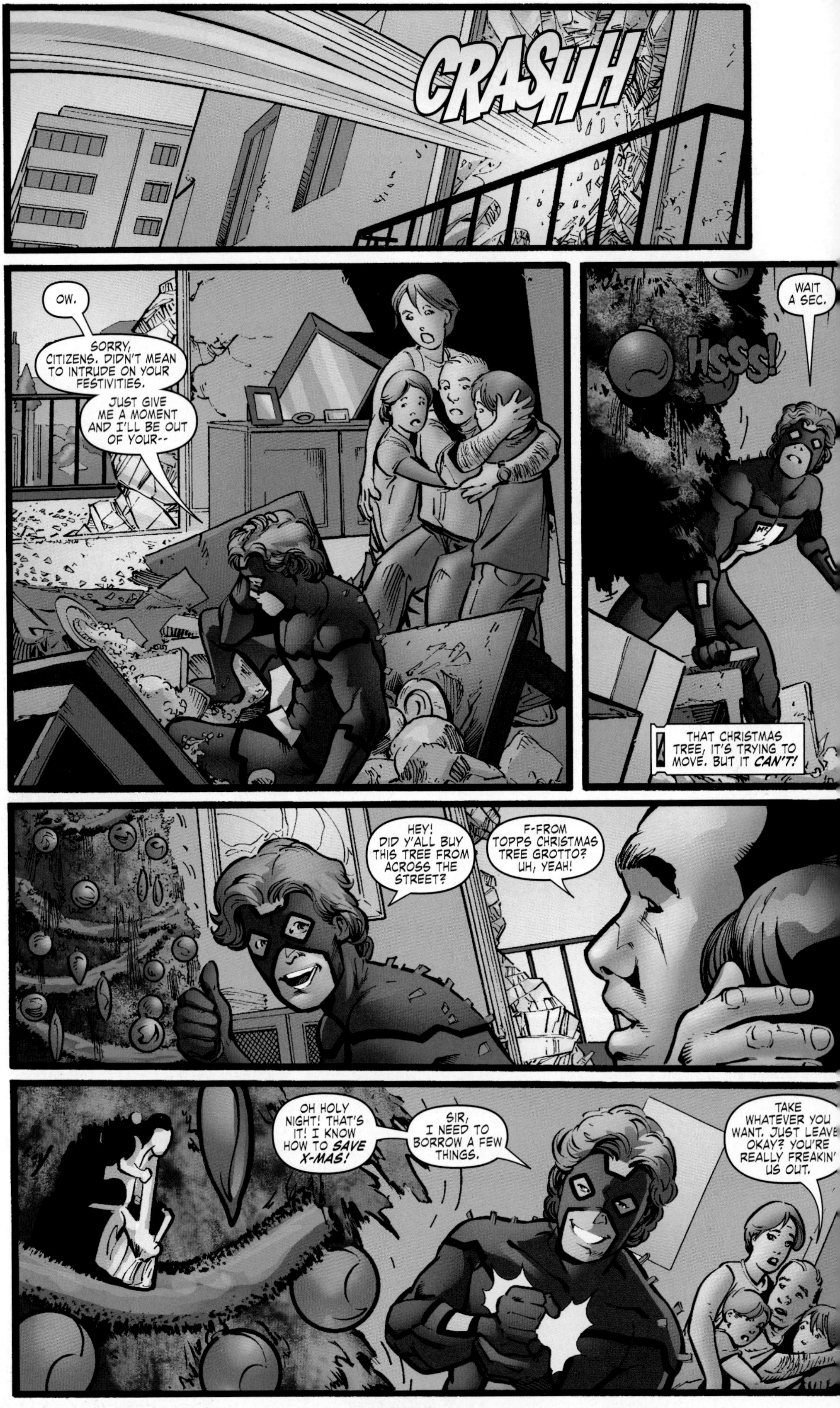
CRASHH
OW.
SORRY, CITIZENS. DIDN'T MEAN TO INTRUDE ON YOUR FESTIVITIES.
JUST GIVE ME A MOMENT AND I'LL BE OUT OF YOUR--
WAIT A SEC.
HSSS!
THAT CHRISTMAS TREE, IT'S TRYING TO MOVE. BUT IT CAN'T!
HEY! DID Y'ALL BUY THIS TREE FROM ACROSS THE STREET?
F-FROM TOPPS CHRISTMAS TREE GROTTO? UH, YEAH!
OH HOLY NIGHT! THAT'S IT! I KNOW HOW TO SAVE X-MAS!
SIR, I NEED TO BORROW A FEW THINGS.
TAKE WHATEVER YOU WANT. JUST LEAVE, OKAY? YOU'RE REALLY FREAKIN' US OUT.

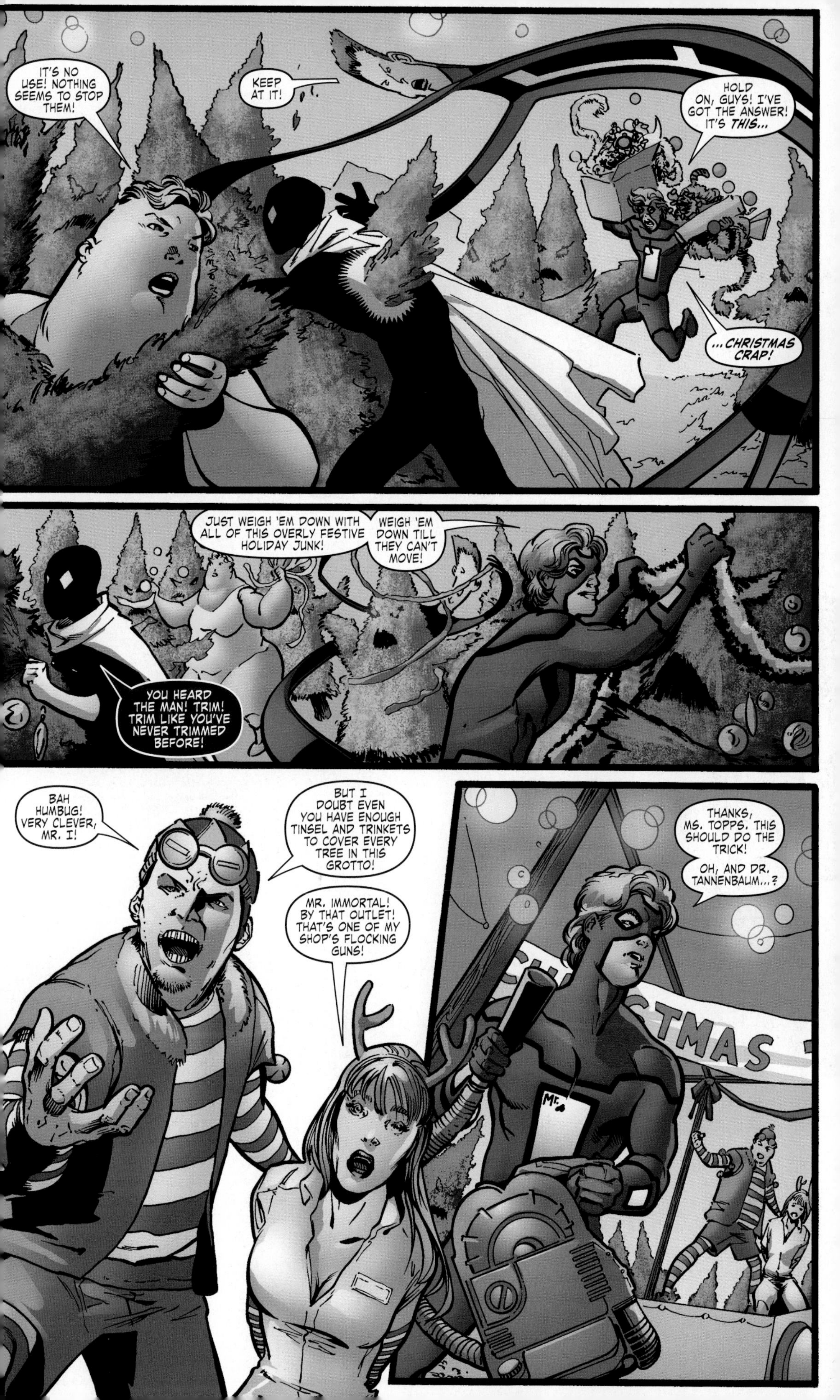
IT'S NO USE! NOTHING SEEMS TO STOP THEM!
KEEP AT IT!
HOLD ON, GUYS! I'VE GOT THE ANSWER! IT'S THIS...
...CHRISTMAS CRAP!
JUST WEIGH 'EM DOWN WITH ALL OF THIS OVERLY FESTIVE HOLIDAY JUNK!
WEIGH 'EM DOWN TILL THEY CAN'T MOVE!
YOU HEARD THE MAN! TRIM! TRIM LIKE YOU'VE NEVER TRIMMED BEFORE!
BAH HUMBUG! VERY CLEVER, MR. I!
BUT I DOUBT EVEN YOU HAVE ENOUGH TINSEL AND TRINKETS TO COVER EVERY TREE IN THIS GROTTO!
MR. IMMORTAL! BY THAT OUTLET! THAT'S ONE OF MY SHOP'S FLOCKING GUNS!
THANKS, MS. TOPPS. THIS SHOULD DO THE TRICK!
OH, AND DR. TANNENBAUM...?
CHRISTMAS

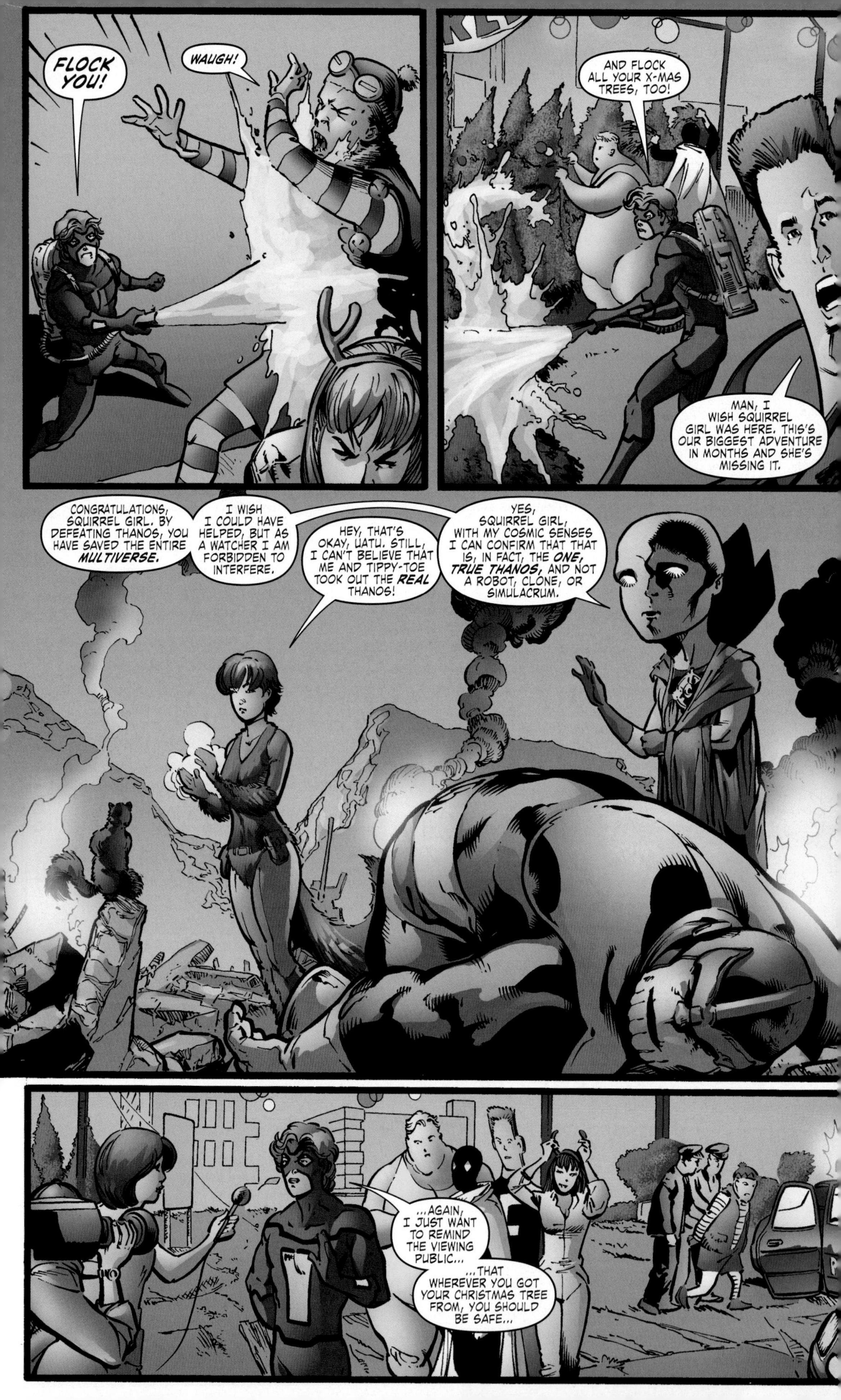
FLOCK YOU!
WAUGH!
AND FLOCK ALL YOUR X-MAS TREES, TOO!
MAN, I WISH SQUIRREL GIRL WAS HERE. THIS'S OUR BIGGEST ADVENTURE IN MONTHS AND SHE'S MISSING IT.
CONGRATULATIONS, SQUIRREL GIRL. BY DEFEATING THANOS, YOU HAVE SAVED THE ENTIRE MULTIVERSE.
I WISH I COULD HAVE HELPED, BUT AS A WATCHER I AM FORBIDDEN TO INTERFERE.
HEY, THAT'S OKAY, UATU. STILL, I CAN'T BELIEVE THAT ME AND TIPPY-TOE TOOK OUT THE REAL THANOS!
YES, SQUIRREL GIRL, WITH MY COSMIC SENSES I CAN CONFIRM THAT THAT IS, IN FACT, THE ONE, TRUE THANOS, AND NOT A ROBOT, CLONE, OR SIMULACRUM.
...AGAIN, I JUST WANT TO REMIND THE VIEWING PUBLIC...
...THAT WHEREVER YOU GOT YOUR CHRISTMAS TREE FROM, YOU SHOULD BE SAFE...

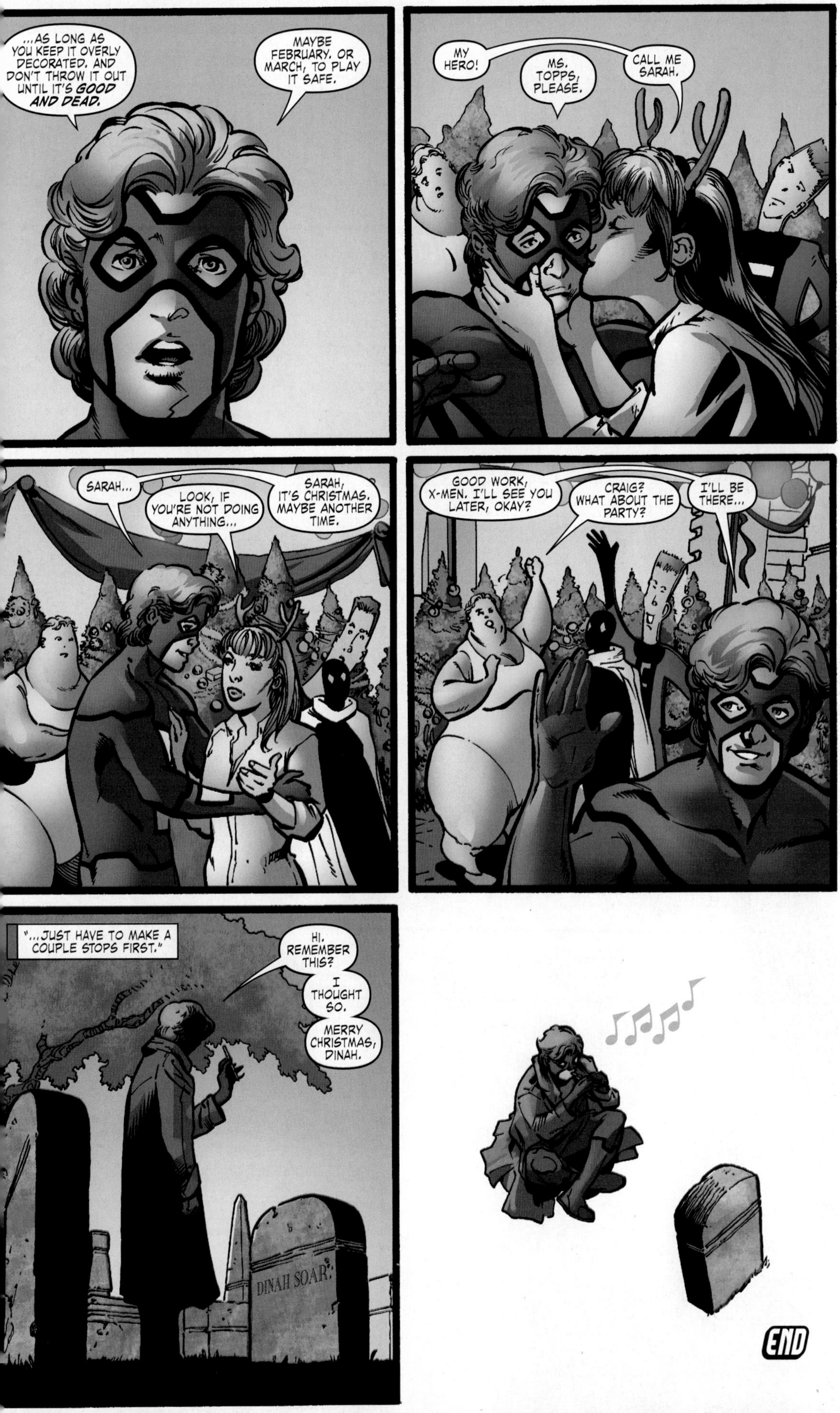

...AS LONG AS YOU KEEP IT OVERLY DECORATED. AND DON'T THROW IT OUT UNTIL IT'S GOOD AND DEAD.
MAYBE FEBRUARY. OR MARCH, TO PLAY IT SAFE.
MY HERO!
MS. TOPPS, PLEASE.
CALL ME SARAH.
SARAH...
LOOK, IF YOU'RE NOT DOING ANYTHING...
SARAH, IT'S CHRISTMAS. MAYBE ANOTHER TIME.
GOOD WORK, X-MEN. I'LL SEE YOU LATER, OKAY?
CRAIG? WHAT ABOUT THE PARTY?
I'LL BE THERE...
"...JUST HAVE TO MAKE A COUPLE STOPS FIRST."
HI. REMEMBER THIS?
I THOUGHT SO.
MERRY CHRISTMAS, DINAH.
DINAH SOAR
END

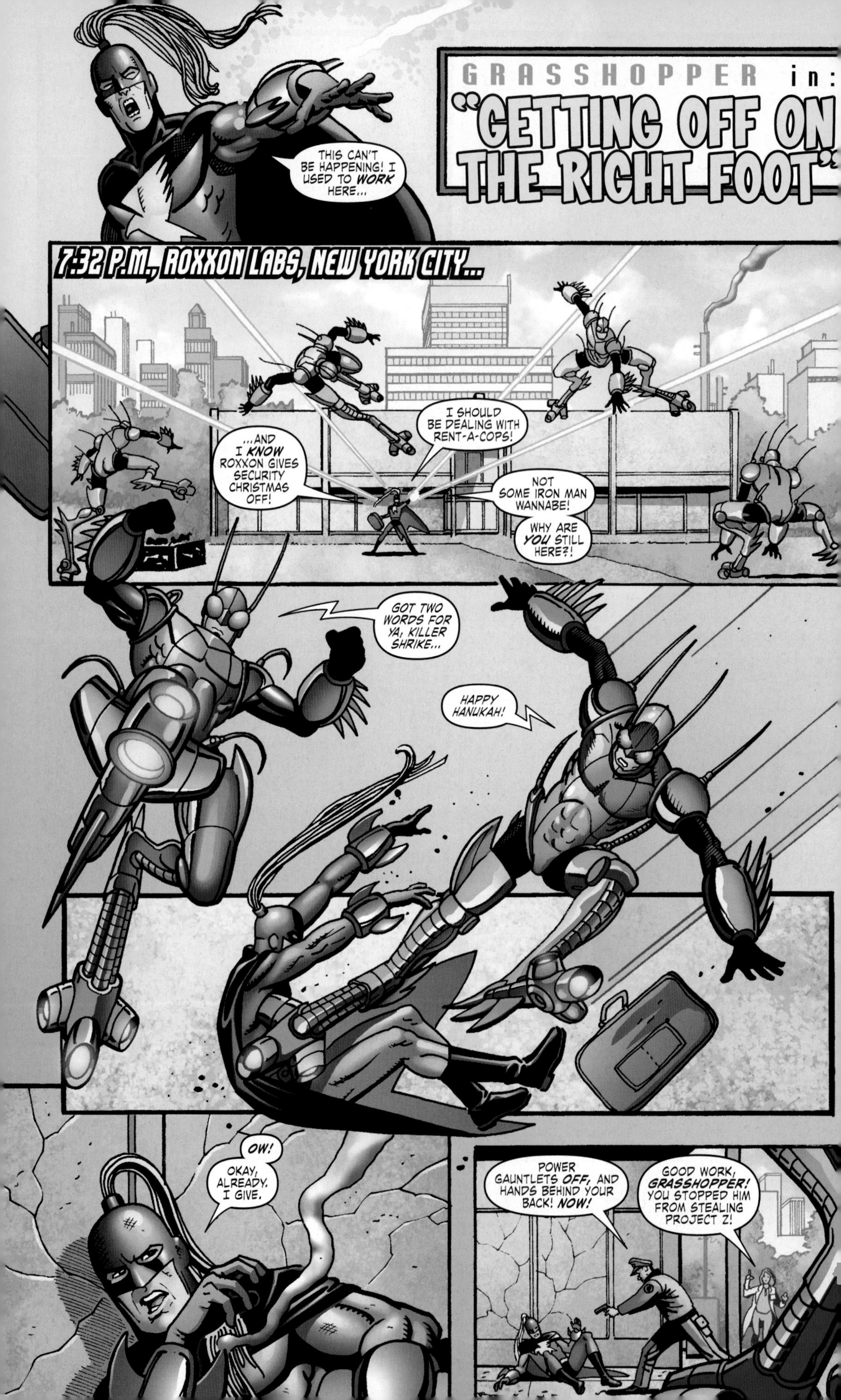
GRASSHOPPER in:
"GETTING OFF ON THE RIGHT FOOT"
THIS CAN'T BE HAPPENING! I USED TO WORK HERE...
7:32 P.M., ROXXON LABS, NEW YORK CITY...
...AND I KNOW ROXXON GIVES SECURITY CHRISTMAS OFF!
I SHOULD BE DEALING WITH RENT-A-COPS!
NOT SOME IRON MAN WANNABE!
WHY ARE YOU STILL HERE?!
GOT TWO WORDS FOR YA, KILLER SHRIKE...
HAPPY HANUKAH!
OW!
OKAY, ALREADY. I GIVE.
POWER GAUNTLETS OFF, AND HANDS BEHIND YOUR BACK! NOW!
GOOD WORK, GRASSHOPPER! YOU STOPPED HIM FROM STEALING PROJECT Z!

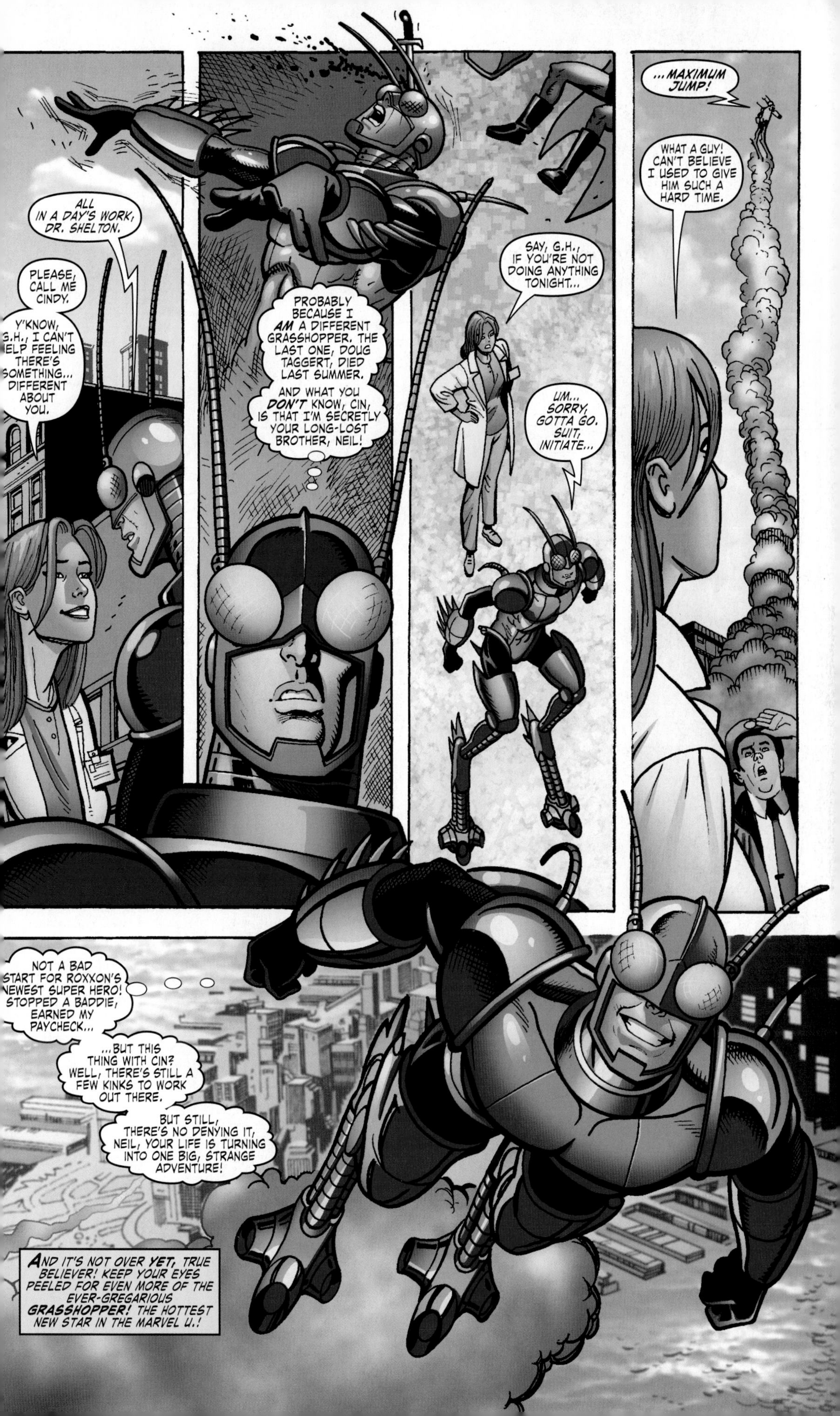

ALL IN A DAY'S WORK, DR. SHELTON.
PLEASE, CALL ME CINDY.
Y'KNOW, G.H., I CAN'T HELP FEELING THERE'S SOMETHING... DIFFERENT ABOUT YOU.
PROBABLY BECAUSE I AM A DIFFERENT GRASSHOPPER. THE LAST ONE, DOUG TAGGERT, DIED LAST SUMMER.
AND WHAT YOU DON'T KNOW, CIN, IS THAT I'M SECRETLY YOUR LONG-LOST BROTHER, NEIL!
SAY, G.H., IF YOU'RE NOT DOING ANYTHING TONIGHT...
UM... SORRY, GOTTA GO. SUIT, INITIATE...
...MAXIMUM JUMP!
WHAT A GUY! CAN'T BELIEVE I USED TO GIVE HIM SUCH A HARD TIME.
NOT A BAD START FOR ROXXON'S NEWEST SUPER HERO! STOPPED A BADDIE, EARNED MY PAYCHECK...
...BUT THIS THING WITH CIN? WELL, THERE'S STILL A FEW KINKS TO WORK OUT THERE.
BUT STILL, THERE'S NO DENYING IT, NEIL, YOUR LIFE IS TURNING INTO ONE BIG, STRANGE ADVENTURE!
AND IT'S NOT OVER YET, TRUE BELIEVER! KEEP YOUR EYES PEELED FOR EVEN MORE OF THE EVER-GREGARIOUS GRASSHOPPER! THE HOTTEST NEW STAR IN THE MARVEL U.!

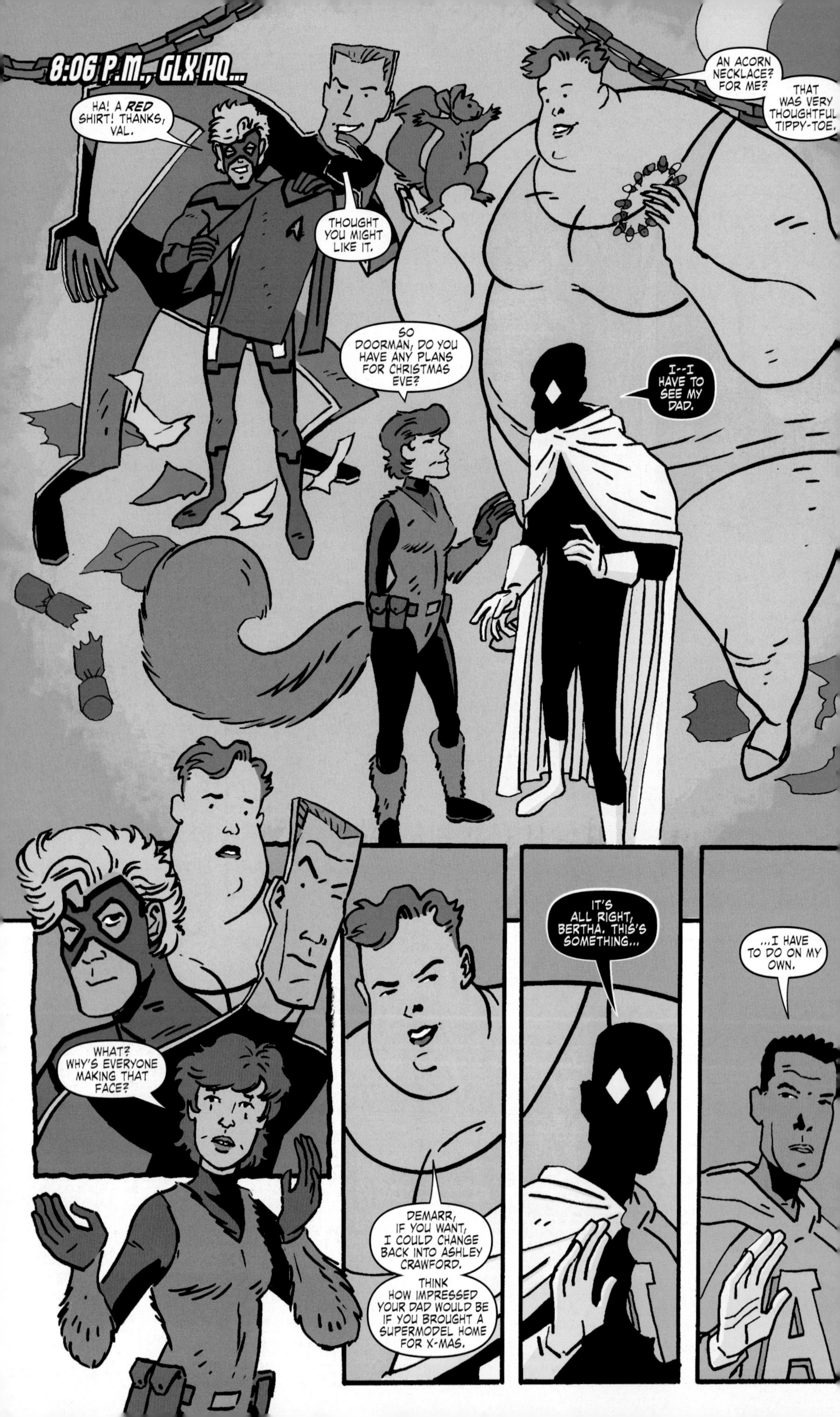
8:06 P.M., GLX HQ...
HA! A RED SHIRT! THANKS, VAL.
THOUGHT YOU MIGHT LIKE IT.
AN ACORN NECKLACE? FOR ME?
THAT WAS VERY THOUGHTFUL TIPPY-TOE.
SO DOORMAN, DO YOU HAVE ANY PLANS FOR CHRISTMAS EVE?
I--I HAVE TO SEE MY DAD.
WHAT? WHY'S EVERYONE MAKING THAT FACE?
DEMARR, IF YOU WANT, I COULD CHANGE BACK INTO ASHLEY CRAWFORD.
THINK HOW IMPRESSED YOUR DAD WOULD BE IF YOU BROUGHT A SUPERMODEL HOME FOR X-MAS.
IT'S ALL RIGHT, BERTHA. THIS'S SOMETHING...
...I HAVE TO DO ON MY OWN.

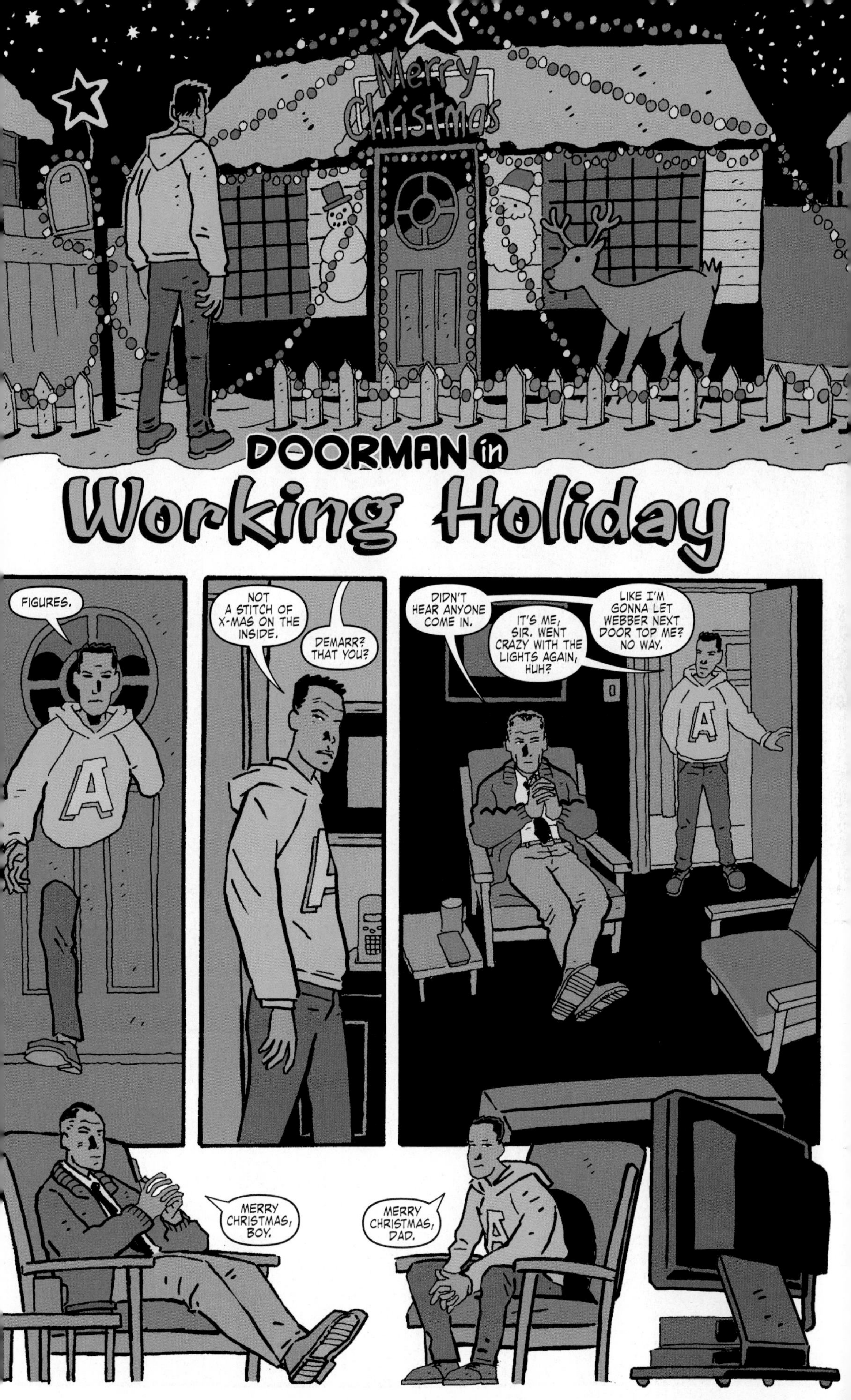
Merry Christmas
DOORMAN in
Working Holiday
FIGURES.
NOT A STITCH OF X-MAS ON THE INSIDE.
DEMARR? THAT YOU?
DIDN'T HEAR ANYONE COME IN.
IT'S ME, SIR. WENT CRAZY WITH THE LIGHTS AGAIN, HUH?
LIKE I'M GONNA LET WEBBER NEXT DOOR TOP ME? NO WAY.
MERRY CHRISTMAS, BOY.
MERRY CHRISTMAS, DAD.

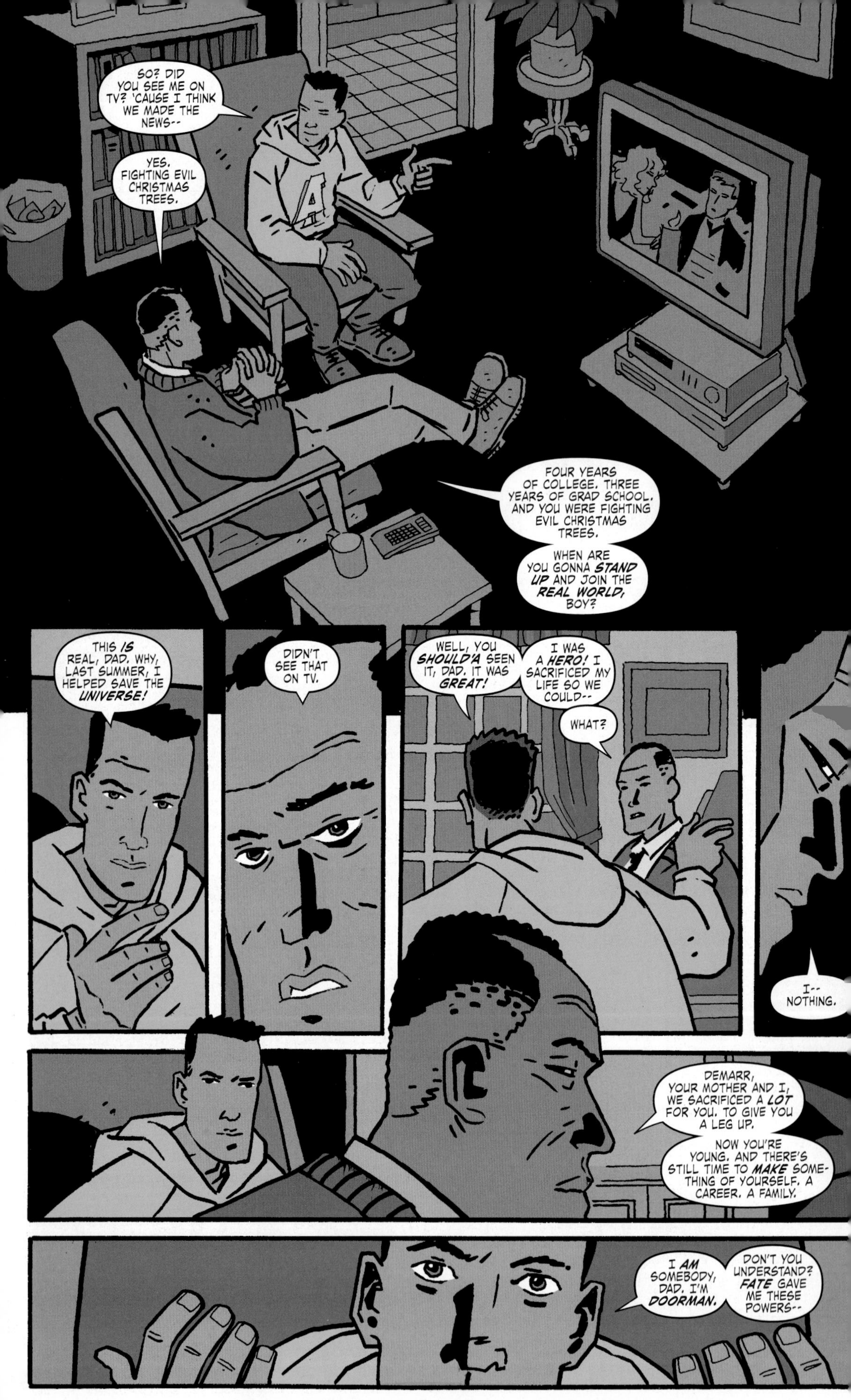
SO? DID YOU SEE ME ON TV? 'CAUSE I THINK WE MADE THE NEWS--
YES. FIGHTING EVIL CHRISTMAS TREES.
FOUR YEARS OF COLLEGE. THREE YEARS OF GRAD SCHOOL. AND YOU WERE FIGHTING EVIL CHRISTMAS TREES.
WHEN ARE YOU GONNA STAND UP AND JOIN THE REAL WORLD, BOY?
THIS IS REAL, DAD. WHY, LAST SUMMER, I HELPED SAVE THE UNIVERSE!
DIDN'T SEE THAT ON TV.
WELL, YOU SHOULD'A SEEN IT, DAD. IT WAS GREAT!
I WAS A HERO! I SACRIFICED MY LIFE SO WE COULD--
WHAT?
I-- NOTHING.
DEMARR, YOUR MOTHER AND I, WE SACRIFICED A LOT FOR YOU. TO GIVE YOU A LEG UP.
NOW YOU'RE YOUNG. AND THERE'S STILL TIME TO MAKE SOMETHING OF YOURSELF. A CAREER. A FAMILY.
I AM SOMEBODY, DAD. I'M DOORMAN.
DON'T YOU UNDERSTAND? FATE GAVE ME THESE POWERS--

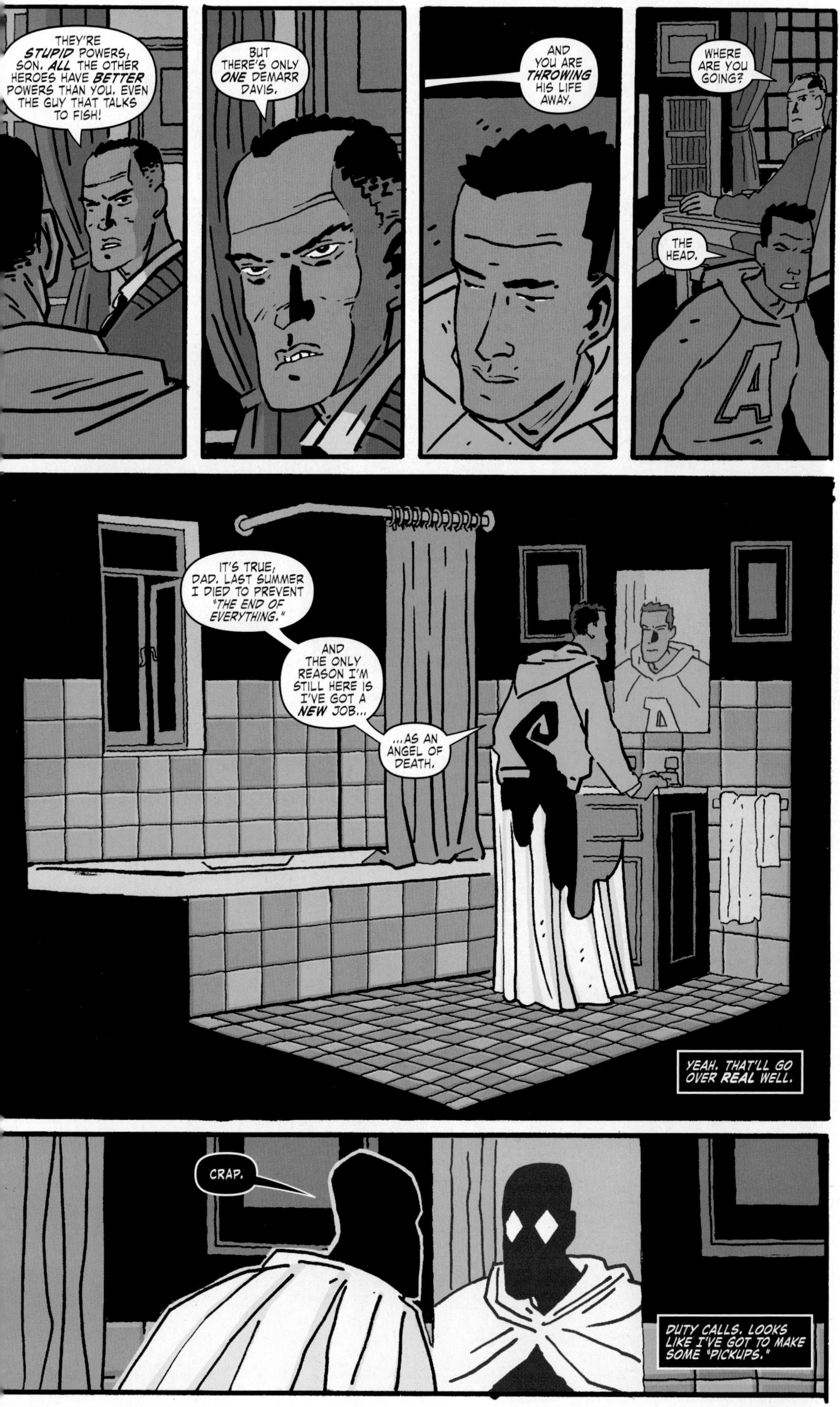
THEY'RE STUPID POWERS, SON. ALL THE OTHER HEROES HAVE BETTER POWERS THAN YOU. EVEN THE GUY THAT TALKS TO FISH!
BUT THERE'S ONLY ONE DEMARR DAVIS.
AND YOU ARE THROWING HIS LIFE AWAY.
WHERE ARE YOU GOING?
THE HEAD.
IT'S TRUE, DAD. LAST SUMMER I DIED TO PREVENT "THE END OF EVERYTHING."
AND THE ONLY REASON I'M STILL HERE IS I'VE GOT A NEW JOB...
...AS AN ANGEL OF DEATH.
YEAH. THAT'LL GO OVER REAL WELL.
CRAP.
DUTY CALLS. LOOKS LIKE I'VE GOT TO MAKE SOME "PICKUPS."

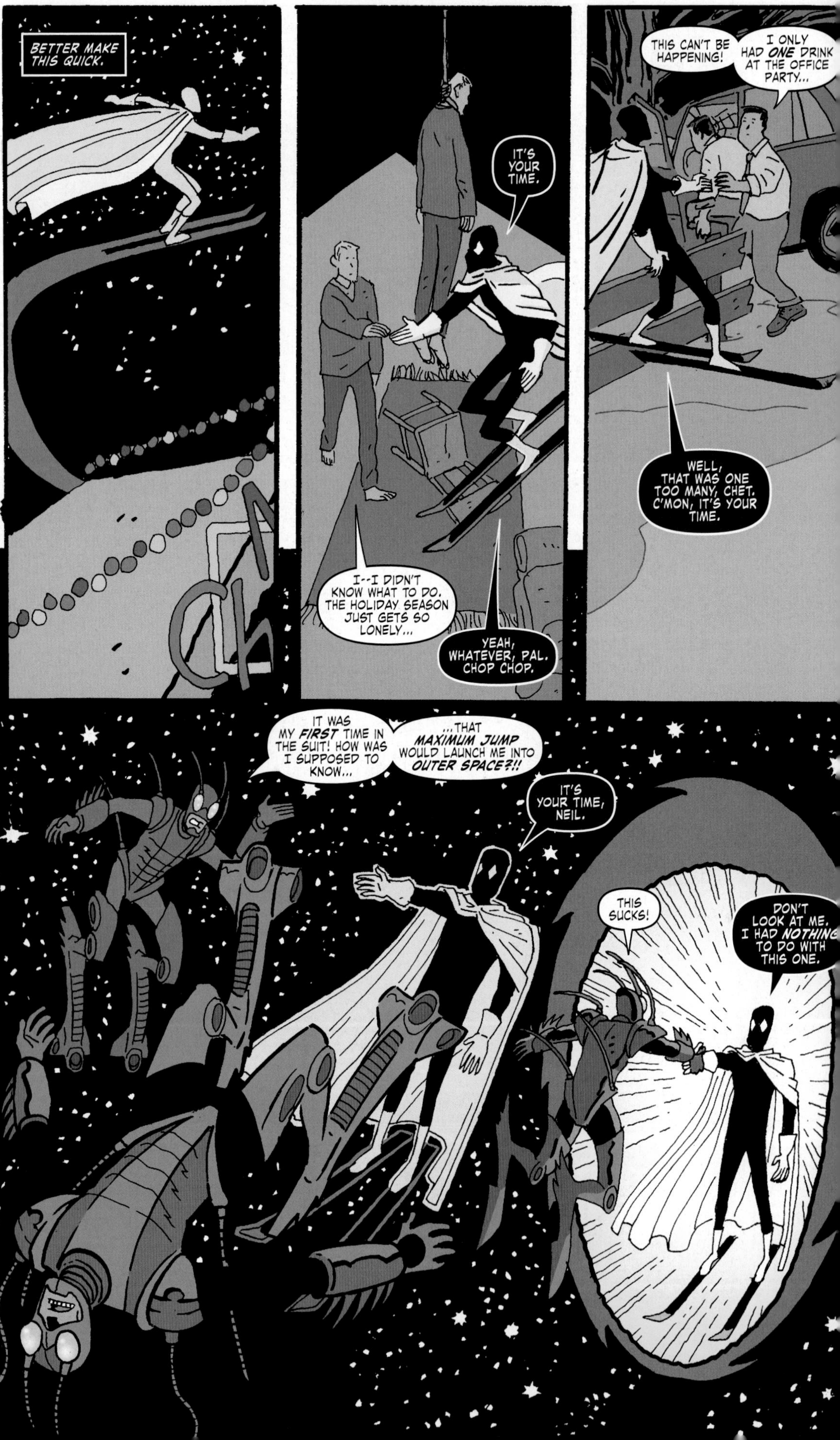

BETTER MAKE THIS QUICK.
IT'S YOUR TIME.
I--I DIDN'T KNOW WHAT TO DO. THE HOLIDAY SEASON JUST GETS SO LONELY...
YEAH, WHATEVER, PAL. CHOP CHOP.
THIS CAN'T BE HAPPENING!
I ONLY HAD *ONE* DRINK AT THE OFFICE PARTY...
WELL, THAT WAS ONE TOO MANY, CHET. C'MON, IT'S YOUR TIME.
IT WAS MY *FIRST* TIME IN THE SUIT! HOW WAS I SUPPOSED TO KNOW...
...THAT *MAXIMUM JUMP* WOULD LAUNCH ME INTO *OUTER SPACE?!!*
IT'S YOUR TIME, NEIL.
THIS SUCKS!
DON'T LOOK AT ME. I HAD *NOTHING* TO DO WITH THIS ONE.

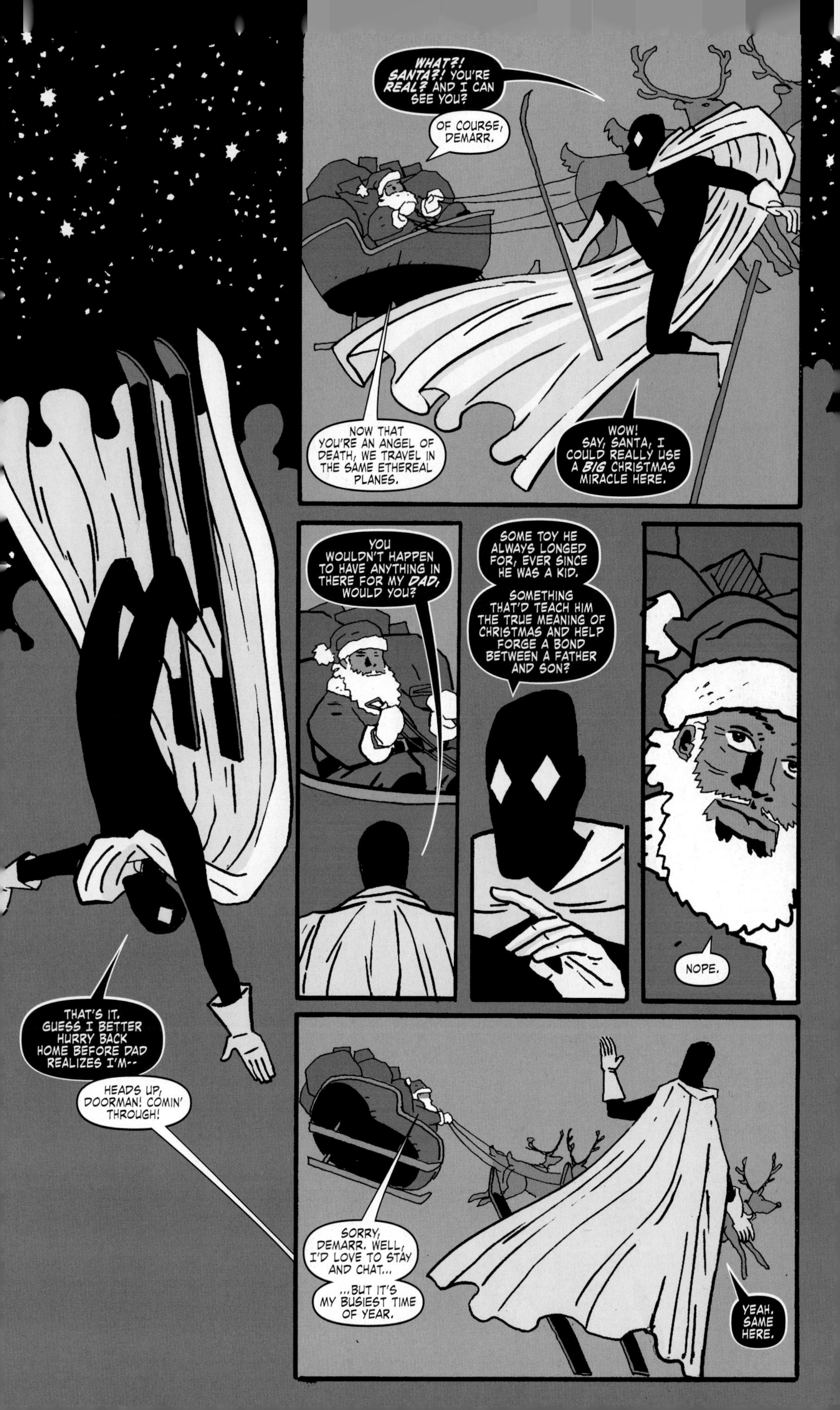
WHAT?! SANTA?! YOU'RE REAL? AND I CAN SEE YOU?
OF COURSE, DEMARR.
NOW THAT YOU'RE AN ANGEL OF DEATH, WE TRAVEL IN THE SAME ETHEREAL PLANES.
WOW! SAY, SANTA, I COULD REALLY USE A BIG CHRISTMAS MIRACLE HERE.
YOU WOULDN'T HAPPEN TO HAVE ANYTHING IN THERE FOR MY DAD, WOULD YOU?
SOME TOY HE ALWAYS LONGED FOR, EVER SINCE HE WAS A KID.
SOMETHING THAT'D TEACH HIM THE TRUE MEANING OF CHRISTMAS AND HELP FORGE A BOND BETWEEN A FATHER AND SON?
NOPE.
SORRY, DEMARR. WELL, I'D LOVE TO STAY AND CHAT...
...BUT IT'S MY BUSIEST TIME OF YEAR.
YEAH. SAME HERE.
THAT'S IT. GUESS I BETTER HURRY BACK HOME BEFORE DAD REALIZES I'M--
HEADS UP, DOORMAN! COMIN' THROUGH!

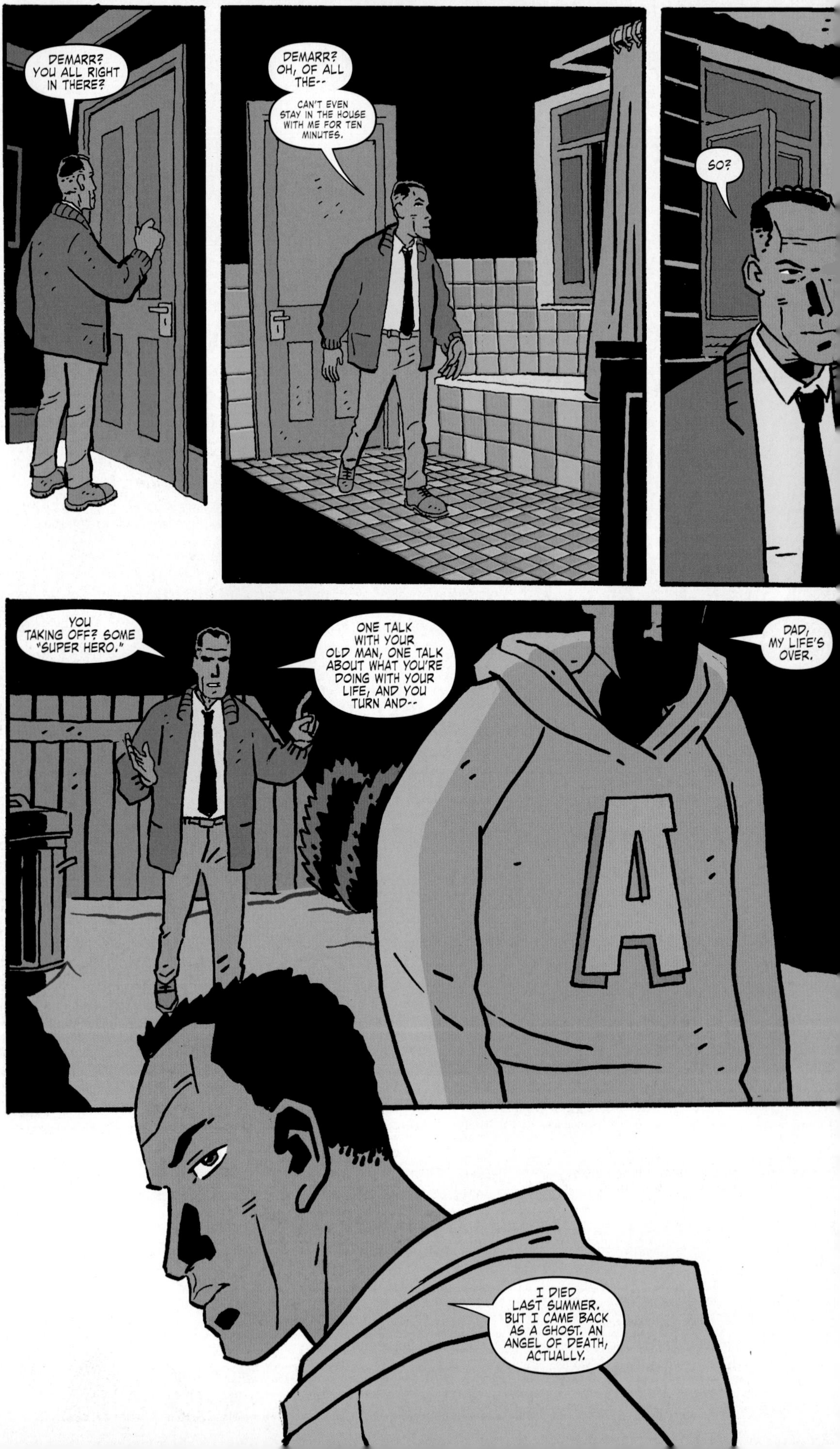
DEMARR? YOU ALL RIGHT IN THERE?
DEMARR? OH, OF ALL THE--
CAN'T EVEN STAY IN THE HOUSE WITH ME FOR TEN MINUTES.
SO?
YOU TAKING OFF? SOME "SUPER HERO."
ONE TALK WITH YOUR OLD MAN, ONE TALK ABOUT WHAT YOU'RE DOING WITH YOUR LIFE, AND YOU TURN AND--
DAD, MY LIFE'S OVER.
I DIED LAST SUMMER. BUT I CAME BACK AS A GHOST. AN ANGEL OF DEATH, ACTUALLY.

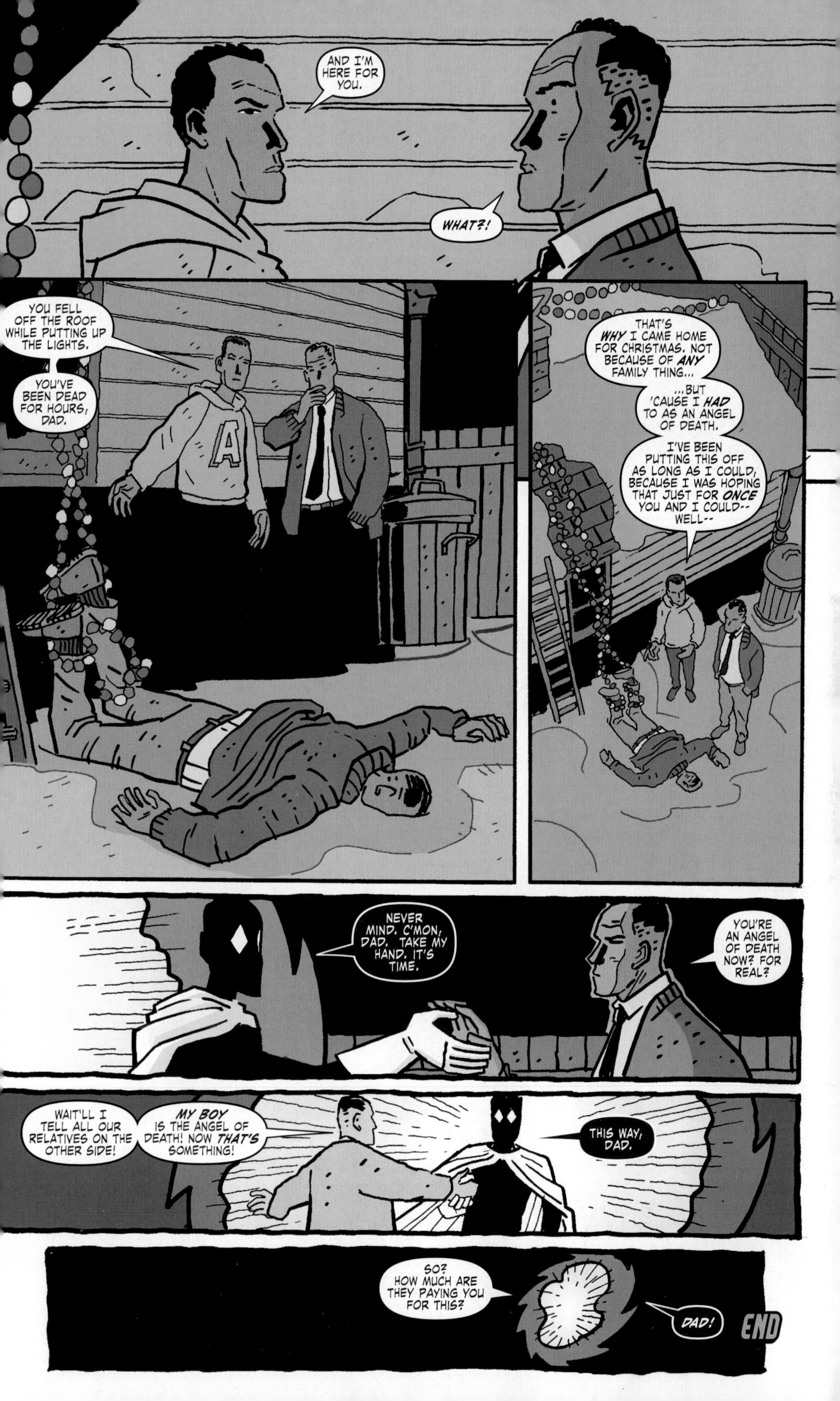
AND I'M HERE FOR YOU.
WHAT?!
YOU FELL OFF THE ROOF WHILE PUTTING UP THE LIGHTS.
YOU'VE BEEN DEAD FOR HOURS, DAD.
THAT'S WHY I CAME HOME FOR CHRISTMAS. NOT BECAUSE OF ANY FAMILY THING...
...BUT 'CAUSE I HAD TO AS AN ANGEL OF DEATH.
I'VE BEEN PUTTING THIS OFF AS LONG AS I COULD, BECAUSE I WAS HOPING THAT JUST FOR ONCE YOU AND I COULD-- WELL--
NEVER MIND. C'MON, DAD. TAKE MY HAND. IT'S TIME.
YOU'RE AN ANGEL OF DEATH NOW? FOR REAL?
WAIT'LL I TELL ALL OUR RELATIVES ON THE OTHER SIDE!
MY BOY IS THE ANGEL OF DEATH! NOW THAT'S SOMETHING!
THIS WAY, DAD.
SO? HOW MUCH ARE THEY PAYING YOU FOR THIS?
DAD!
END

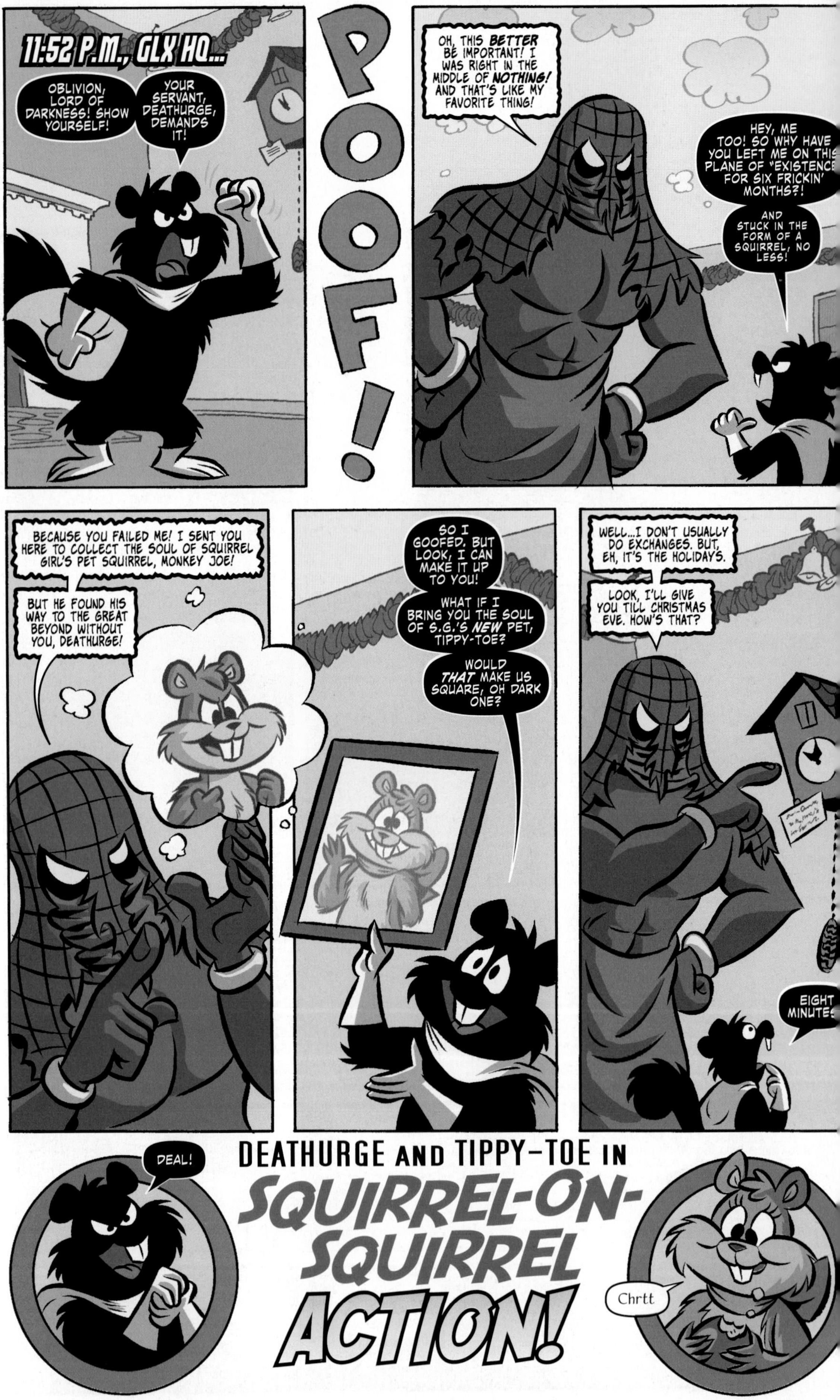
11:52 P.M., GLX HQ...
OBLIVION, LORD OF DARKNESS! SHOW YOURSELF!
YOUR SERVANT, DEATHURGE, DEMANDS IT!
POOF!
OH, THIS BETTER BE IMPORTANT! I WAS RIGHT IN THE MIDDLE OF NOTHING! AND THAT'S LIKE MY FAVORITE THING!
HEY, ME TOO! SO WHY HAVE YOU LEFT ME ON THIS PLANE OF "EXISTENCE" FOR SIX FRICKIN' MONTHS?!
AND STUCK IN THE FORM OF A SQUIRREL, NO LESS!
BECAUSE YOU FAILED ME! I SENT YOU HERE TO COLLECT THE SOUL OF SQUIRREL GIRL'S PET SQUIRREL, MONKEY JOE!
BUT HE FOUND HIS WAY TO THE GREAT BEYOND WITHOUT YOU, DEATHURGE!
SO I GOOFED. BUT LOOK, I CAN MAKE IT UP TO YOU!
WHAT IF I BRING YOU THE SOUL OF S.G.'S NEW PET, TIPPY-TOE?
WOULD THAT MAKE US SQUARE, OH DARK ONE?
WELL...I DON'T USUALLY DO EXCHANGES. BUT, EH, IT'S THE HOLIDAYS.
LOOK, I'LL GIVE YOU TILL CHRISTMAS EVE. HOW'S THAT?
EIGHT MINUTES
DEAL!
DEATHURGE AND TIPPY-TOE IN
SQUIRREL-ON-SQUIRREL ACTION!
Chrtt

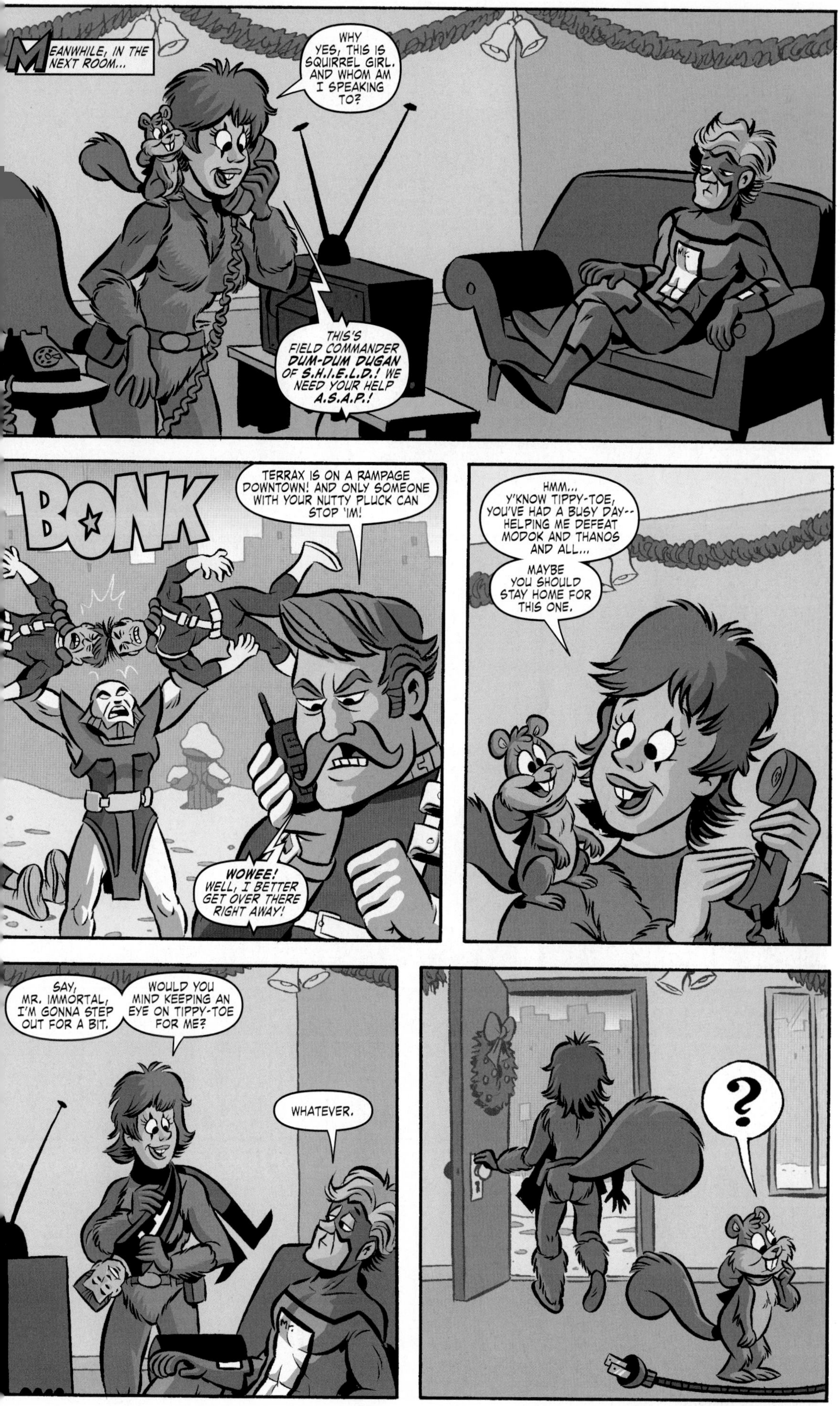
MEANWHILE, IN THE NEXT ROOM...
WHY YES, THIS IS SQUIRREL GIRL. AND WHOM AM I SPEAKING TO?
THIS'S FIELD COMMANDER DUM-DUM DUGAN OF S.H.I.E.L.D.! WE NEED YOUR HELP A.S.A.P.!
BONK
TERRAX IS ON A RAMPAGE DOWNTOWN! AND ONLY SOMEONE WITH YOUR NUTTY PLUCK CAN STOP 'IM!
WOWEE! WELL, I BETTER GET OVER THERE RIGHT AWAY!
HMM... Y'KNOW TIPPY-TOE, YOU'VE HAD A BUSY DAY-- HELPING ME DEFEAT MODOK AND THANOS AND ALL...
MAYBE YOU SHOULD STAY HOME FOR THIS ONE.
SAY, MR. IMMORTAL, I'M GONNA STEP OUT FOR A BIT.
WOULD YOU MIND KEEPING AN EYE ON TIPPY-TOE FOR ME?
WHATEVER.
?

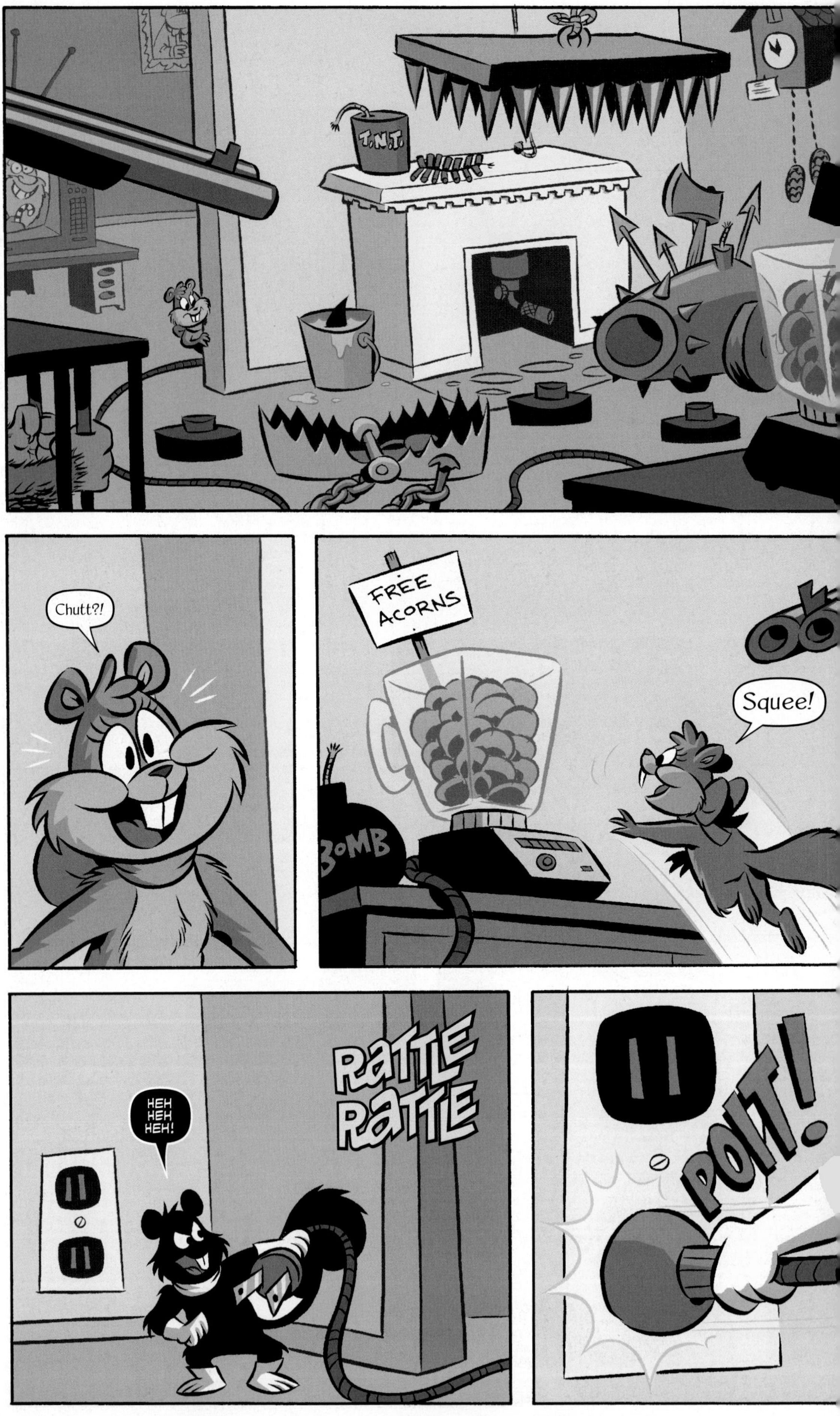
T.N.T.
Chutt?!
FREE ACORNS
BOMB
Squee!
HEH HEH HEH!
RATTLE RATTLE
POIT!

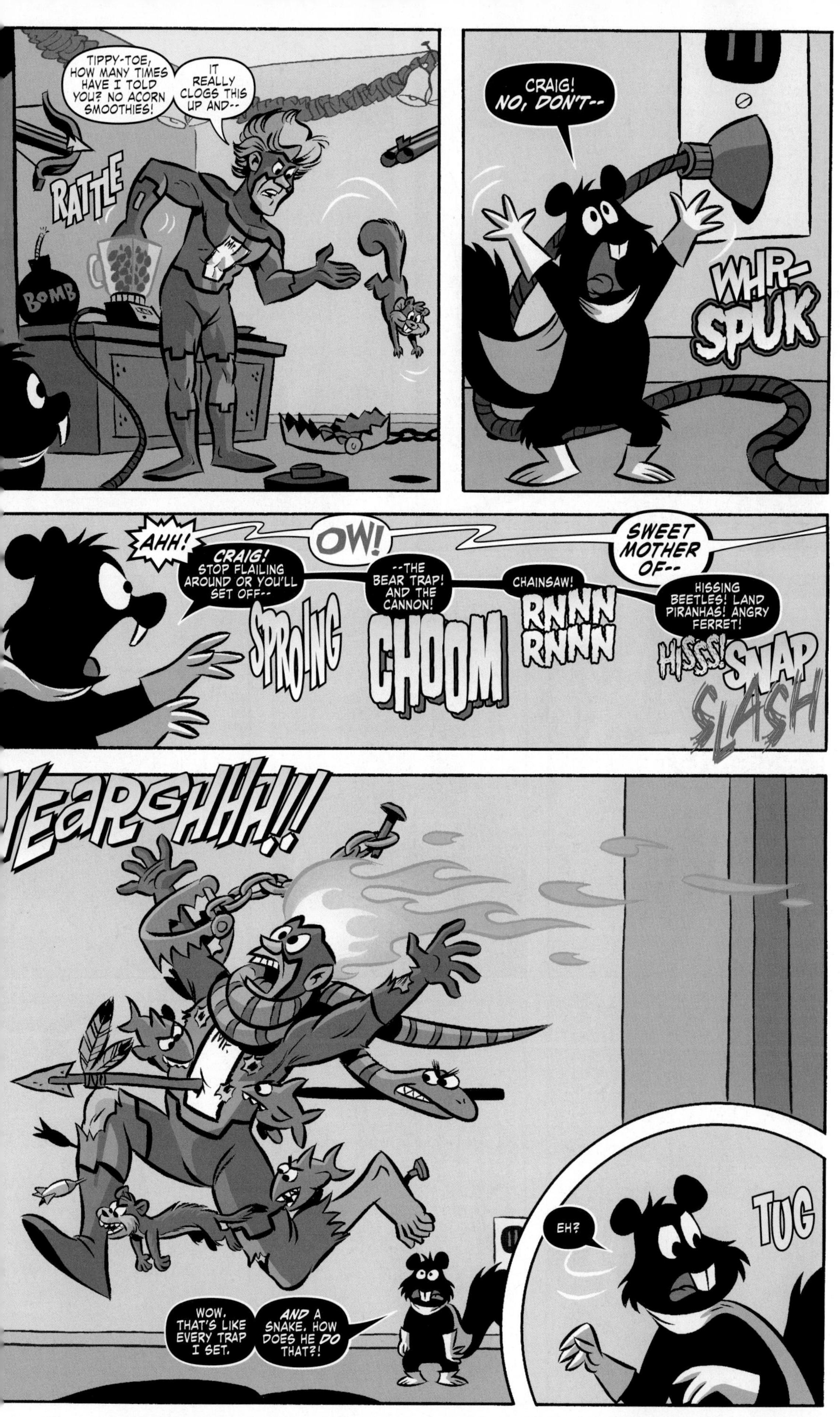
TIPPY-TOE, HOW MANY TIMES HAVE I TOLD YOU? NO ACORN SMOOTHIES!
IT REALLY CLOGS THIS UP AND--
RATTLE
BOMB
CRAIG! NO, DON'T--
WHR-SPUK
AHH!
OW!
SWEET MOTHER OF--
CRAIG! STOP FLAILING AROUND OR YOU'LL SET OFF--
SPROING
--THE BEAR TRAP! AND THE CANNON!
CHOOM
CHAINSAW!
RNNN RNNN
HISSING BEETLES! LAND PIRANHAS! ANGRY FERRET!
HISSS! SNAP
SLASH
YEARGHHH!!
WOW, THAT'S LIKE EVERY TRAP I SET.
AND A SNAKE. HOW DOES HE DO THAT?!
EH?
TUG

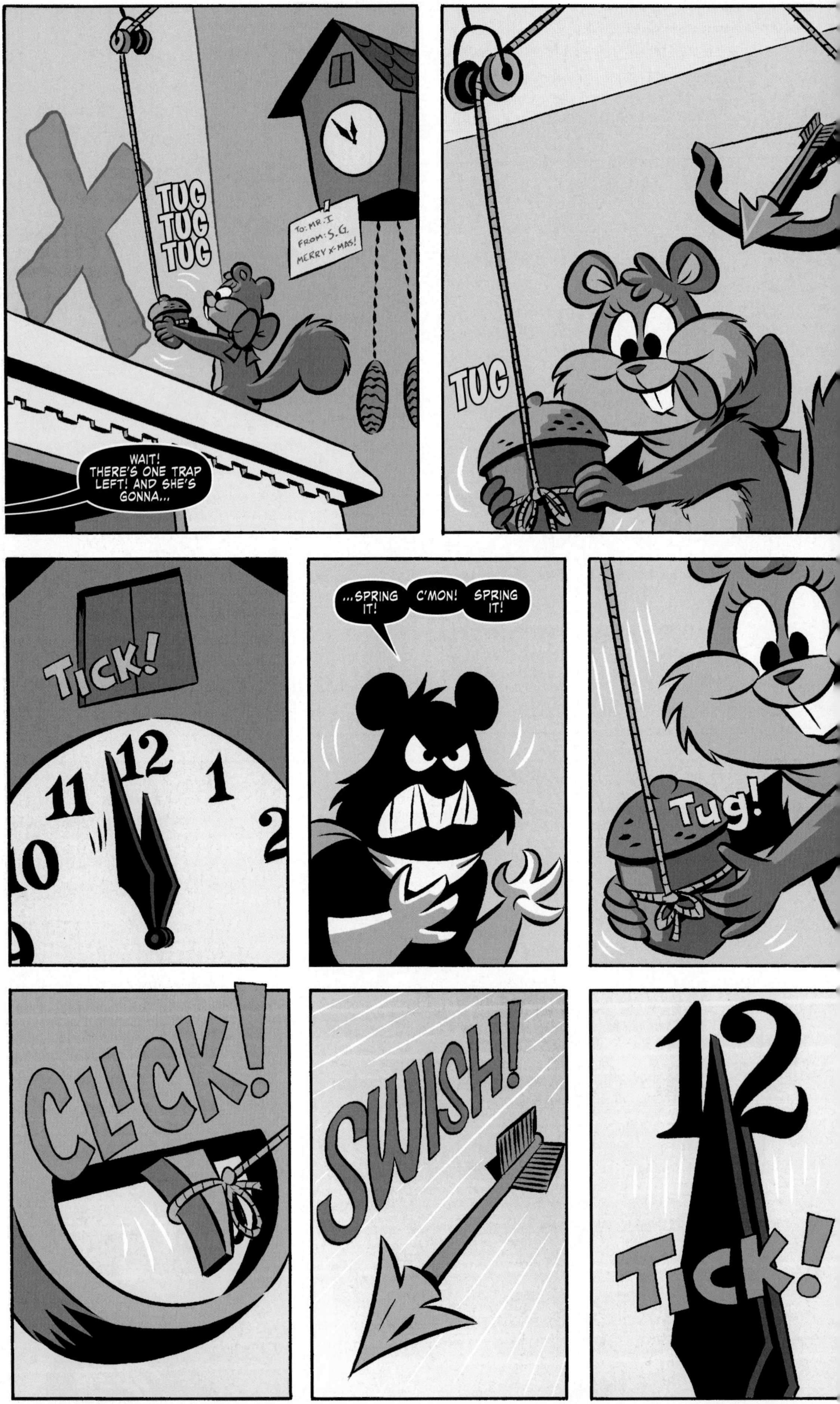
TUG
TUG
TUG
TO: MR. I
FROM: S.G.
MERRY X-MAS!
WAIT! THERE'S ONE TRAP LEFT! AND SHE'S GONNA...
TUG
TICK!
...SPRING IT!
C'MON!
SPRING IT!
Tug!
CLICK!
SWISH!
12
TICK!

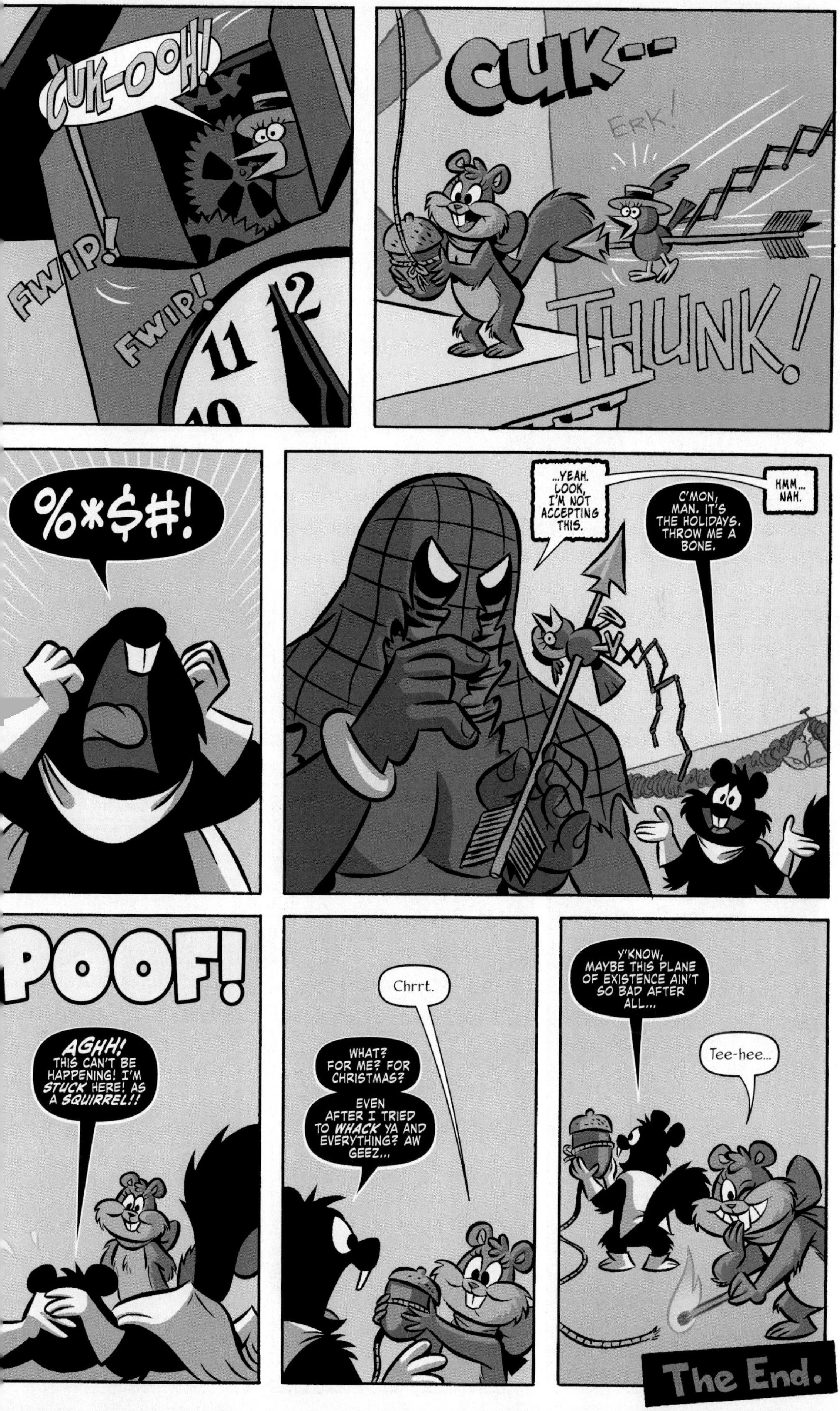
CUK-OOH!
FWIP!
FWIP!
12
11
CUK--
ERK!
THUNK!
%*$#!
...YEAH. LOOK, I'M NOT ACCEPTING THIS.
HMM... NAH.
C'MON, MAN. IT'S THE HOLIDAYS. THROW ME A BONE.
POOF!
AGHH! THIS CAN'T BE HAPPENING! I'M STUCK HERE! AS A SQUIRREL!!
Chrrt.
WHAT? FOR ME? FOR CHRISTMAS?
EVEN AFTER I TRIED TO WHACK YA AND EVERYTHING? AW GEEZ...
Y'KNOW, MAYBE THIS PLANE OF EXISTENCE AIN'T SO BAD AFTER ALL...
Tee-hee...
The End.

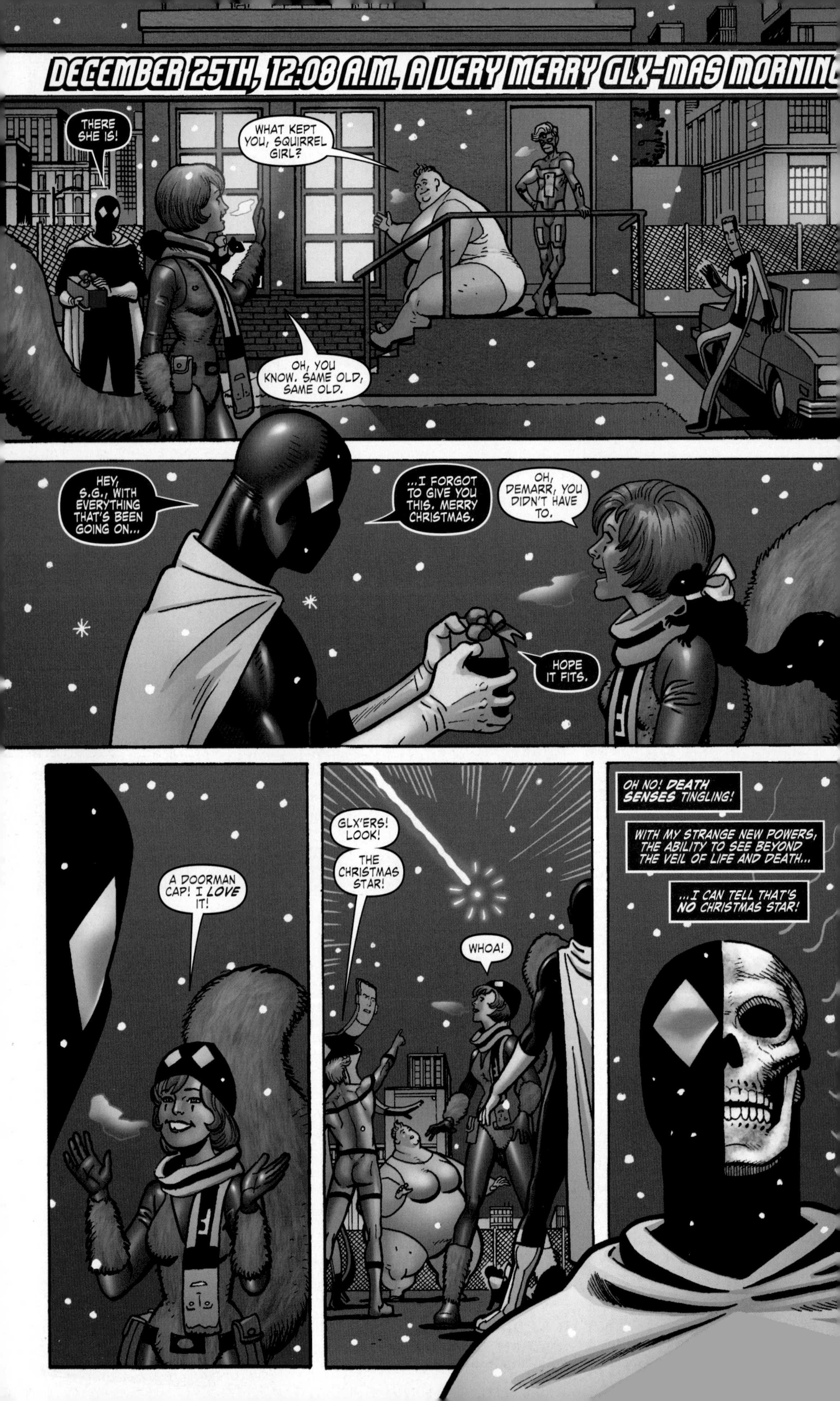
DECEMBER 25TH, 12:08 A.M. A VERY MERRY GLX-MAS MORNING
THERE SHE IS!
WHAT KEPT YOU, SQUIRREL GIRL?
OH, YOU KNOW. SAME OLD, SAME OLD.
HEY, S.G., WITH EVERYTHING THAT'S BEEN GOING ON...
...I FORGOT TO GIVE YOU THIS. MERRY CHRISTMAS.
OH, DEMARR, YOU DIDN'T HAVE TO.
HOPE IT FITS.
A DOORMAN CAP! I LOVE IT!
GLX'ERS! LOOK!
THE CHRISTMAS STAR!
WHOA!
OH NO! DEATH SENSES TINGLING!
WITH MY STRANGE NEW POWERS, THE ABILITY TO SEE BEYOND THE VEIL OF LIFE AND DEATH...
...I CAN TELL THAT'S NO CHRISTMAS STAR!

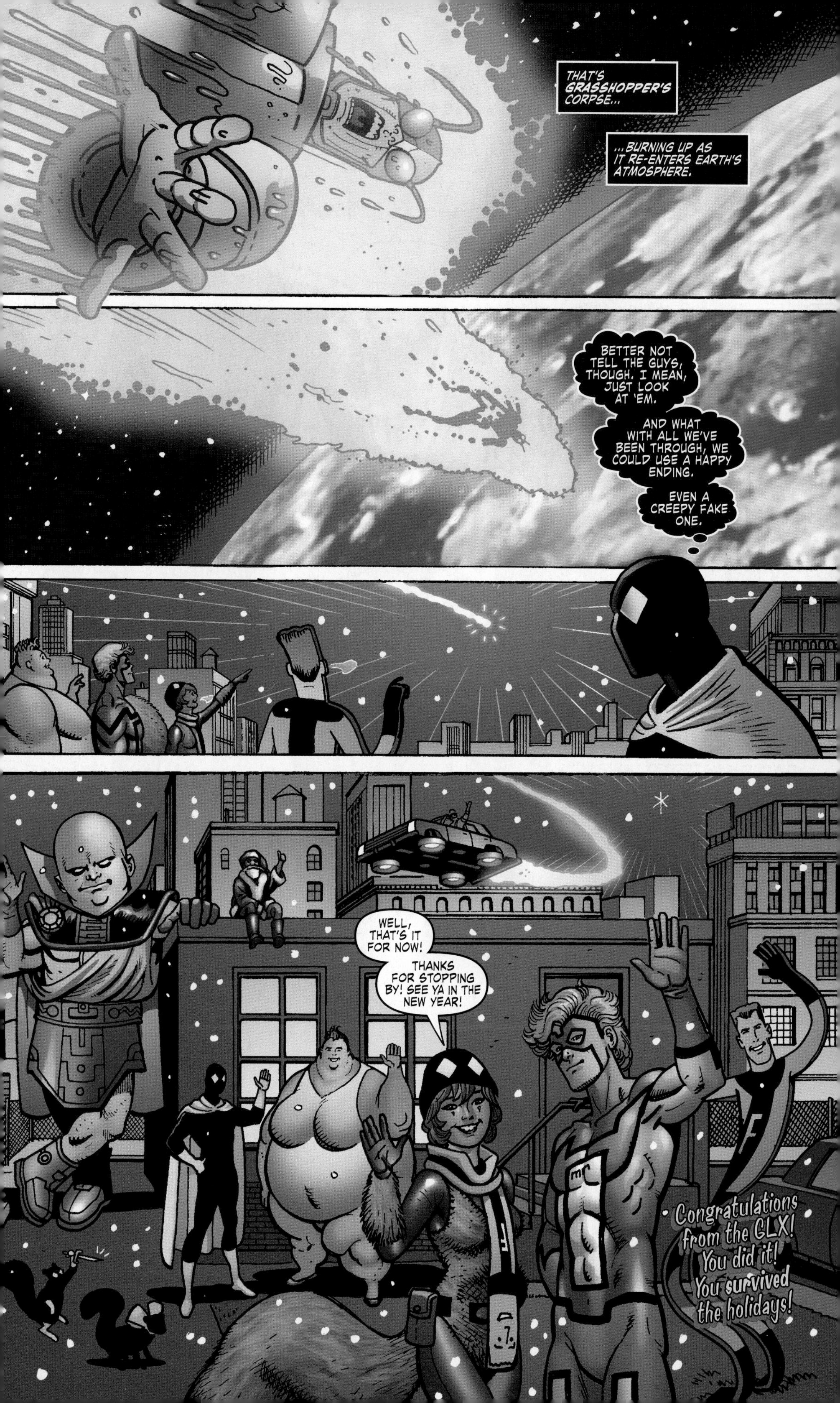
THAT'S GRASSHOPPER'S CORPSE...
...BURNING UP AS IT RE-ENTERS EARTH'S ATMOSPHERE.
BETTER NOT TELL THE GUYS, THOUGH. I MEAN, JUST LOOK AT 'EM.
AND WHAT WITH ALL WE'VE BEEN THROUGH, WE COULD USE A HAPPY ENDING.
EVEN A CREEPY FAKE ONE.
WELL, THAT'S IT FOR NOW!
THANKS FOR STOPPING BY! SEE YA IN THE NEW YEAR!
Congratulations from the GLX! You did it! You survived the holidays!

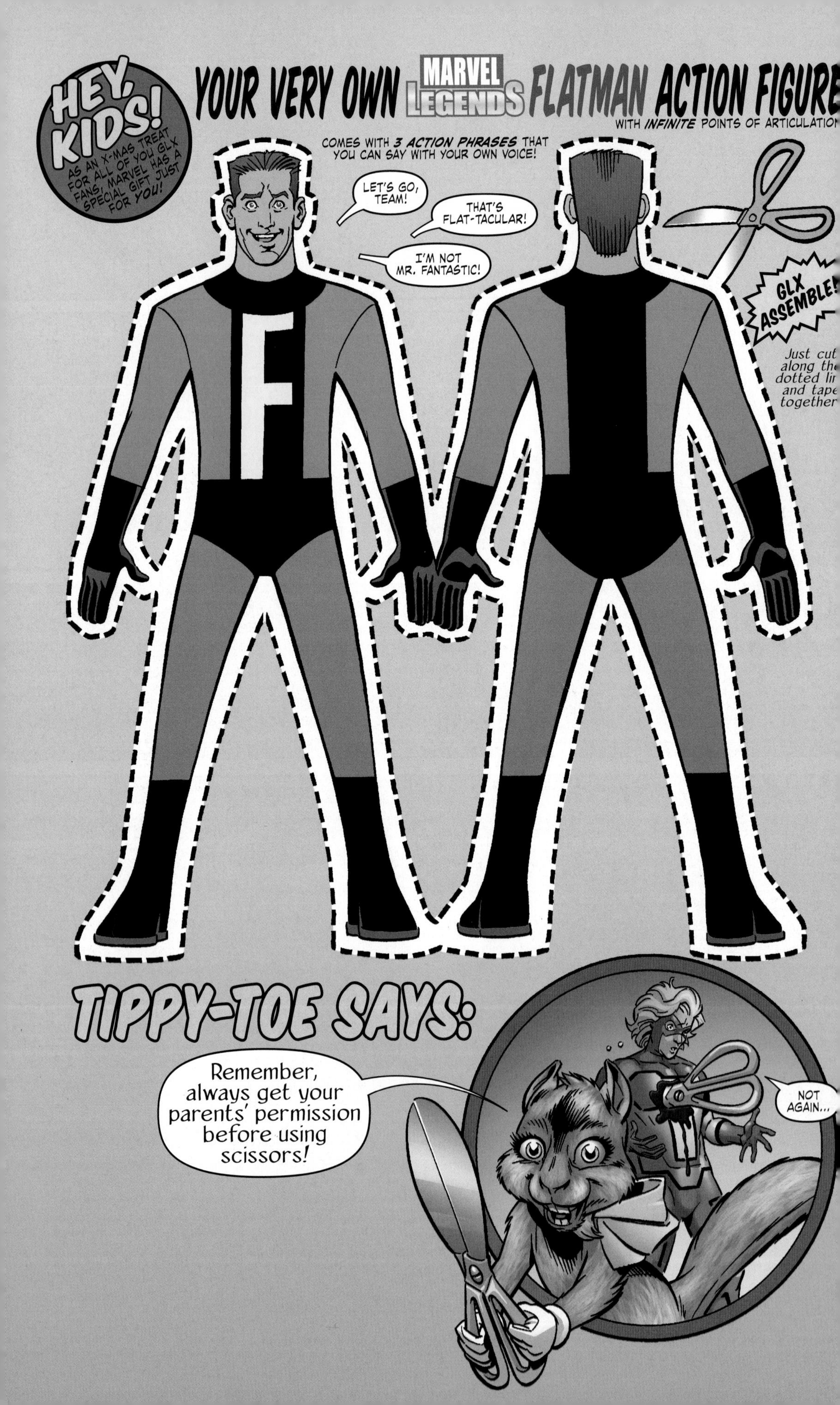
HEY, KIDS!
AS AN X-MAS TREAT FOR ALL OF YOU GLX FANS, MARVEL HAS A SPECIAL GIFT JUST FOR YOU!
YOUR VERY OWN MARVEL LEGENDS FLATMAN ACTION FIGURE
WITH INFINITE POINTS OF ARTICULATION
COMES WITH 3 ACTION PHRASES THAT YOU CAN SAY WITH YOUR OWN VOICE!
LET'S GO, TEAM!
THAT'S FLAT-TACULAR!
I'M NOT MR. FANTASTIC!
GLX ASSEMBLE!
F
TIPPY-TOE SAYS:
Remember, always get your parents' permission before using scissors!
NOT AGAIN...

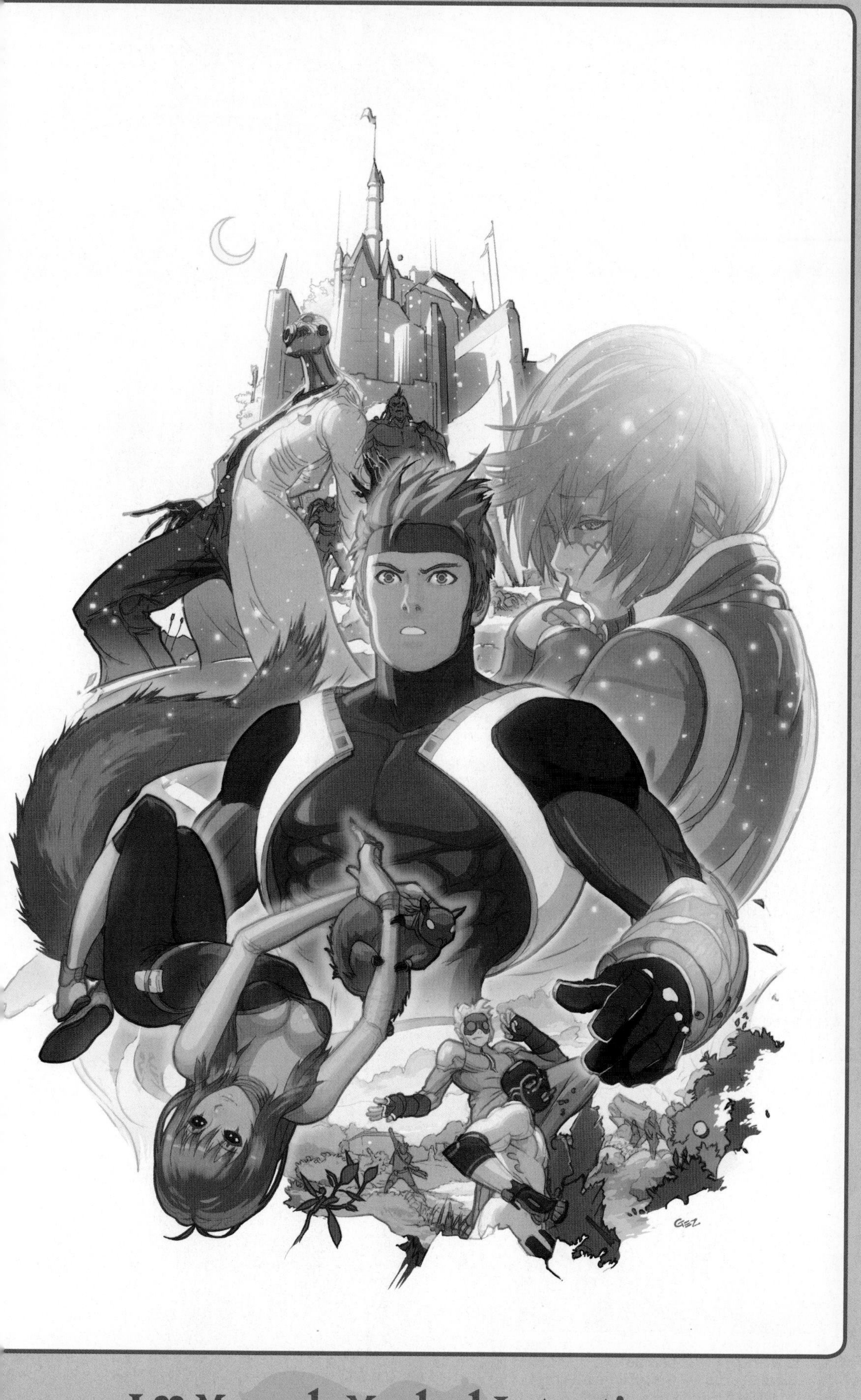
GEZ

I ♥ Marvel: Masked Intentions

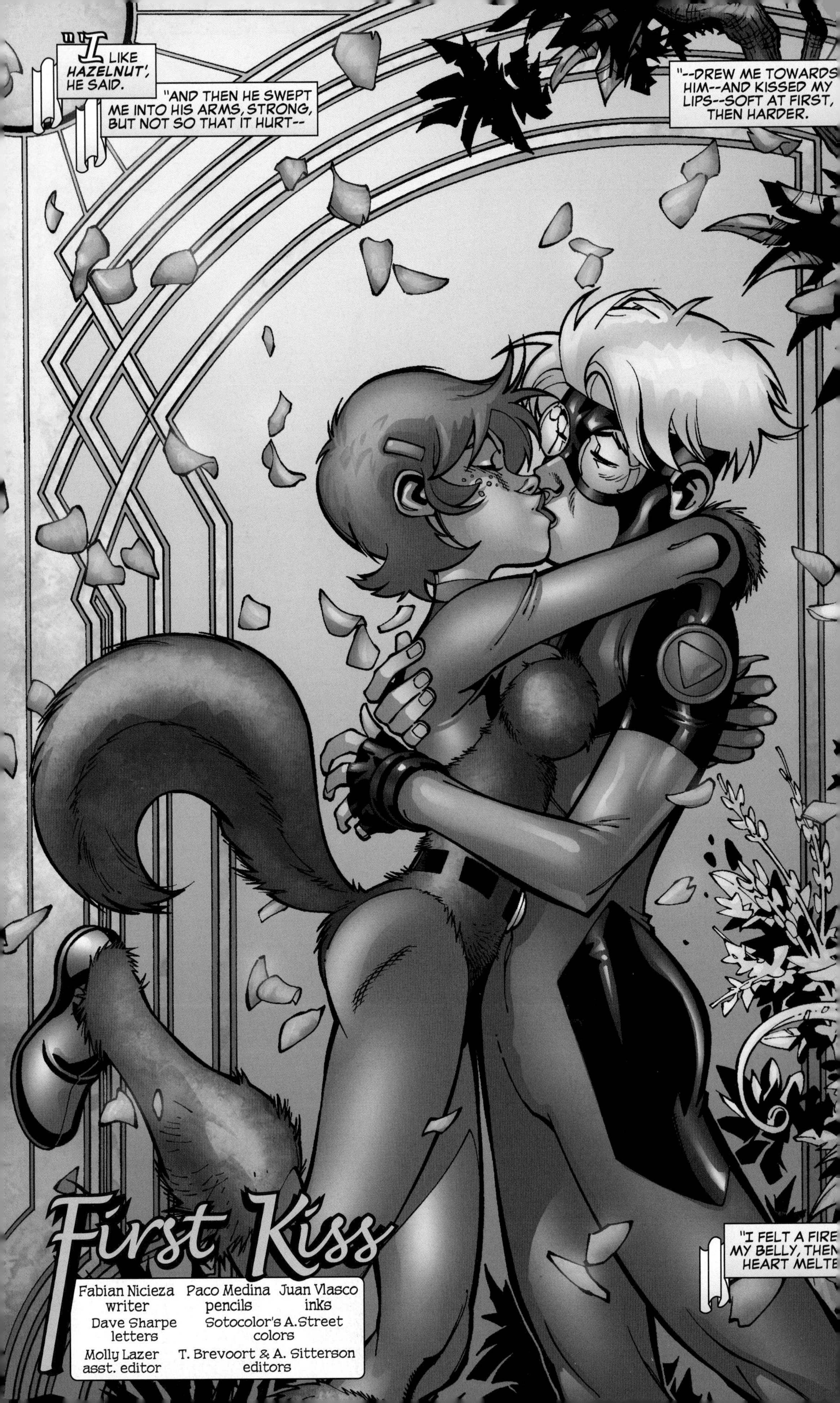

"I LIKE HAZELNUT', HE SAID.
"AND THEN HE SWEPT ME INTO HIS ARMS, STRONG, BUT NOT SO THAT IT HURT--
"--DREW ME TOWARDS HIM--AND KISSED MY LIPS--SOFT AT FIRST, THEN HARDER.
"I FELT A FIRE MY BELLY, THEN HEART MELTE
First Kiss
Fabian Nicieza writer
Paco Medina pencils
Juan Vlasco inks
Dave Sharpe letters
Sotocolor's A. Street colors
Molly Lazer asst. editor
T. Brevoort & A. Sitterson editors

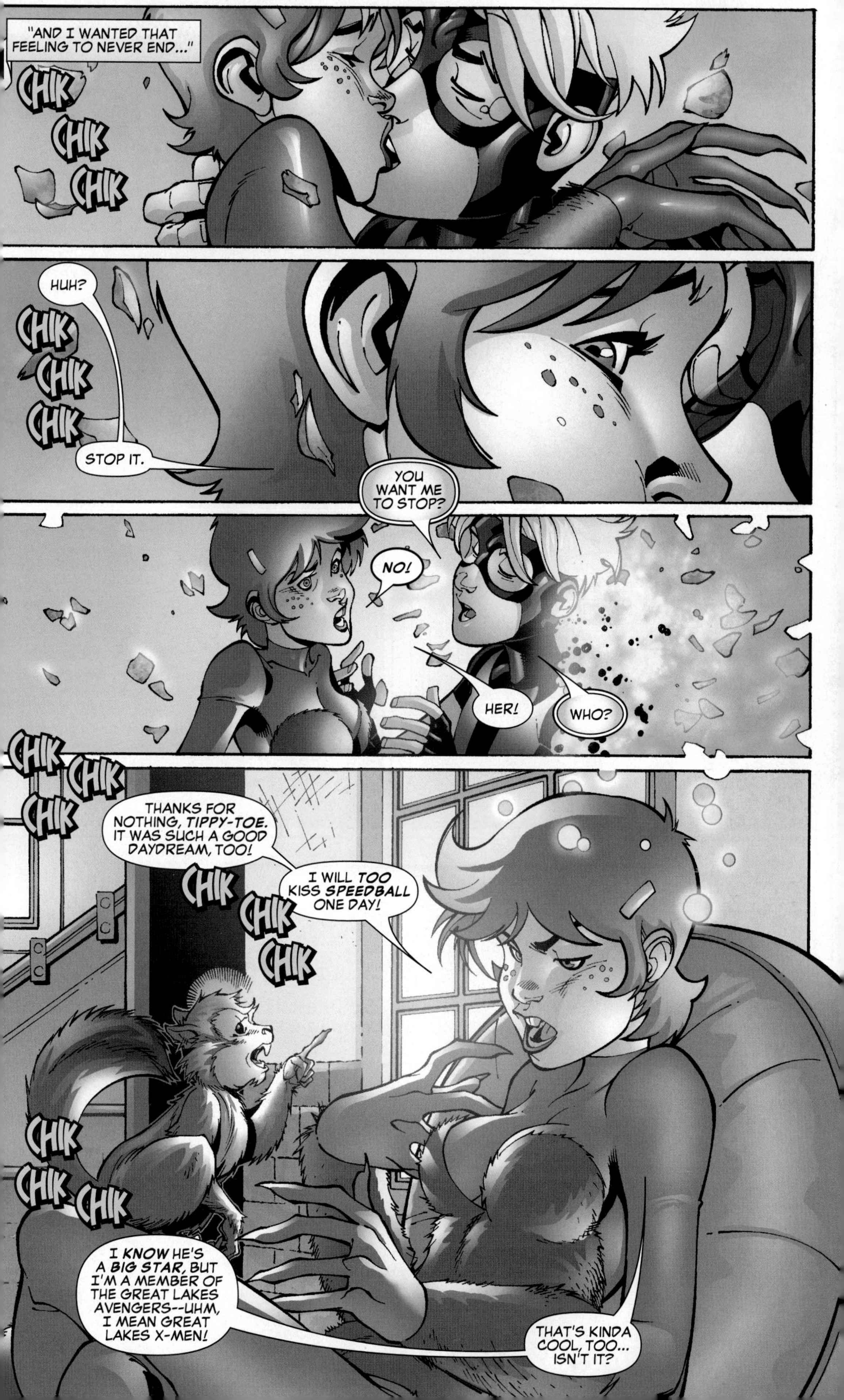

"AND I WANTED THAT FEELING TO NEVER END..."
CHIK CHIK CHIK
HUH?
CHIK CHIK CHIK
STOP IT.
YOU WANT ME TO STOP?
NO!
HER!
WHO?
CHIK CHIK CHIK
THANKS FOR NOTHING, TIPPY-TOE. IT WAS SUCH A GOOD DAYDREAM, TOO!
I WILL TOO KISS SPEEDBALL ONE DAY!
CHIK CHIK CHIK
CHIK CHIK CHIK
I KNOW HE'S A BIG STAR, BUT I'M A MEMBER OF THE GREAT LAKES AVENGERS--UHM, I MEAN GREAT LAKES X-MEN!
THAT'S KINDA COOL, TOO... ISN'T IT?

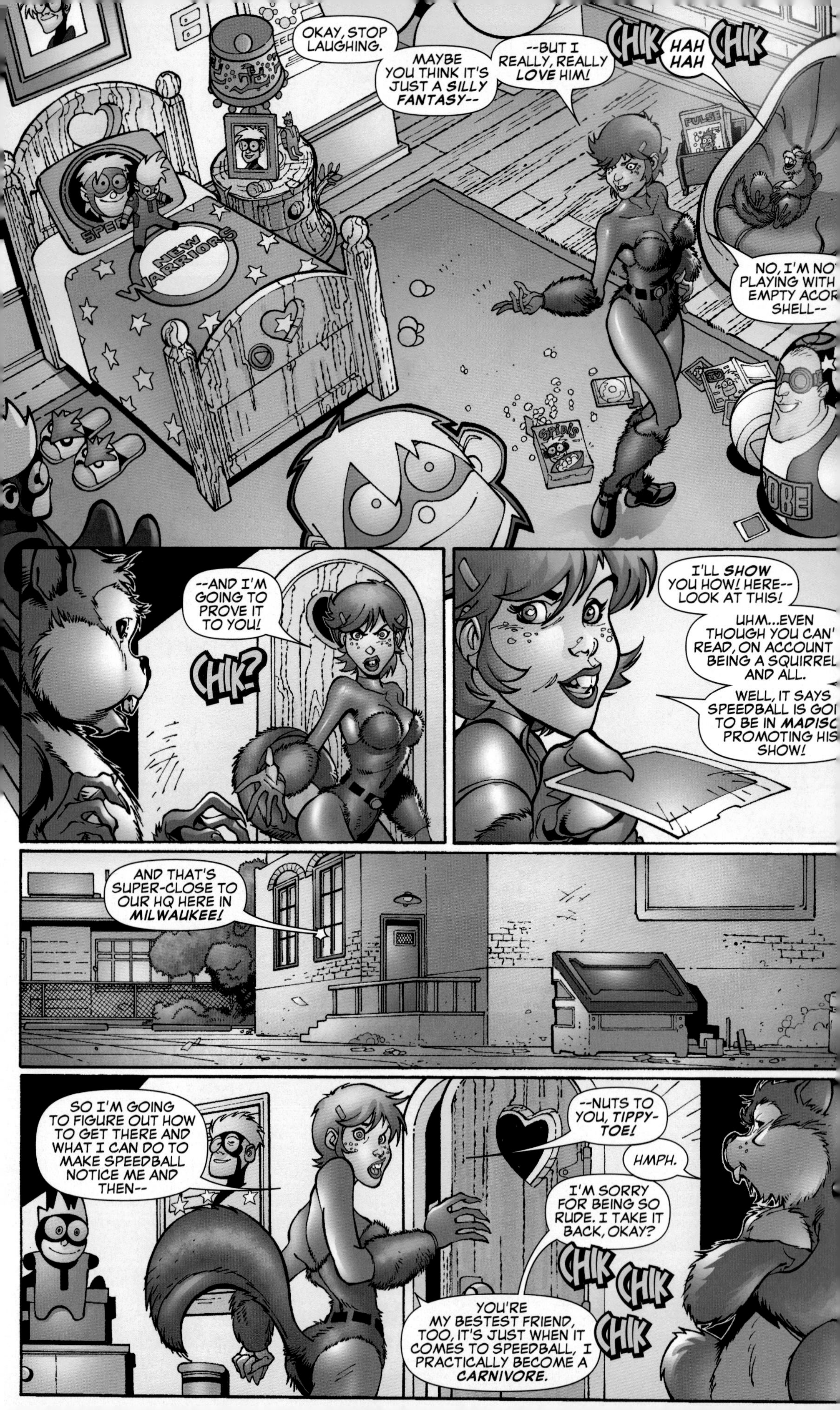

OKAY, STOP LAUGHING.
MAYBE YOU THINK IT'S JUST A *SILLY FANTASY*--
--BUT I REALLY, REALLY *LOVE* HIM!
CHIK
HAH HAH
CHIK
PULSE
NEW WARRIORS
NO, I'M NO PLAYING WITH EMPTY ACOR SHELL--
SPIDIS
--AND I'M GOING TO PROVE IT TO YOU!
CHIK?
I'LL *SHOW* YOU HOW! HERE-- LOOK AT THIS!
UHM...EVEN THOUGH YOU CAN' READ, ON ACCOUNT BEING A SQUIRREL AND ALL.
WELL, IT SAYS SPEEDBALL IS GOI TO BE IN *MADISC* PROMOTING HIS SHOW!
AND THAT'S SUPER-CLOSE TO OUR HQ HERE IN *MILWAUKEE!*
SO I'M GOING TO FIGURE OUT HOW TO GET THERE AND WHAT I CAN DO TO MAKE SPEEDBALL NOTICE ME AND THEN--
--NUTS TO YOU, *TIPPY-TOE!*
HMPH.
I'M SORRY FOR BEING SO RUDE. I TAKE IT BACK, OKAY?
CHIK
CHIK
CHIK
YOU'RE MY BESTEST FRIEND, TOO, IT'S JUST WHEN IT COMES TO SPEEDBALL, I PRACTICALLY BECOME A *CARNIVORE.*

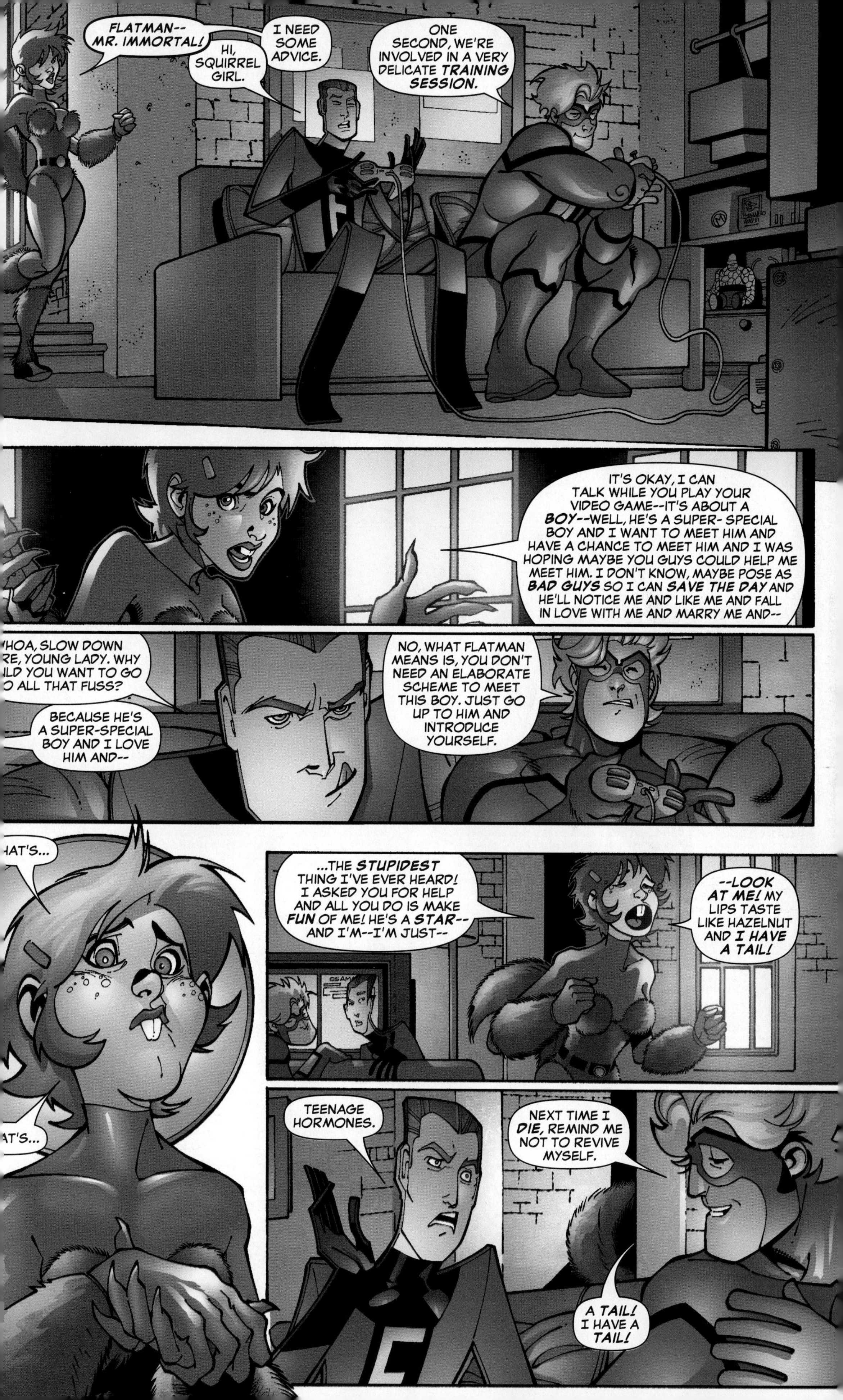
FLATMAN-- MR. IMMORTAL!
HI, SQUIRREL GIRL.
I NEED SOME ADVICE.
ONE SECOND, WE'RE INVOLVED IN A VERY DELICATE TRAINING SESSION.
IT'S OKAY, I CAN TALK WHILE YOU PLAY YOUR VIDEO GAME--IT'S ABOUT A BOY--WELL, HE'S A SUPER- SPECIAL BOY AND I WANT TO MEET HIM AND HAVE A CHANCE TO MEET HIM AND I WAS HOPING MAYBE YOU GUYS COULD HELP ME MEET HIM. I DON'T KNOW, MAYBE POSE AS BAD GUYS SO I CAN SAVE THE DAY AND HE'LL NOTICE ME AND LIKE ME AND FALL IN LOVE WITH ME AND MARRY ME AND--
HOA, SLOW DOWN RE, YOUNG LADY. WHY LD YOU WANT TO GO ALL THAT FUSS?
BECAUSE HE'S A SUPER-SPECIAL BOY AND I LOVE HIM AND--
NO, WHAT FLATMAN MEANS IS, YOU DON'T NEED AN ELABORATE SCHEME TO MEET THIS BOY. JUST GO UP TO HIM AND INTRODUCE YOURSELF.
HAT'S...
AT'S...
...THE STUPIDEST THING I'VE EVER HEARD! I ASKED YOU FOR HELP AND ALL YOU DO IS MAKE FUN OF ME! HE'S A STAR-- AND I'M--I'M JUST--
--LOOK AT ME! MY LIPS TASTE LIKE HAZELNUT AND I HAVE A TAIL!
TEENAGE HORMONES.
NEXT TIME I DIE, REMIND ME NOT TO REVIVE MYSELF.
A TAIL! I HAVE A TAIL!

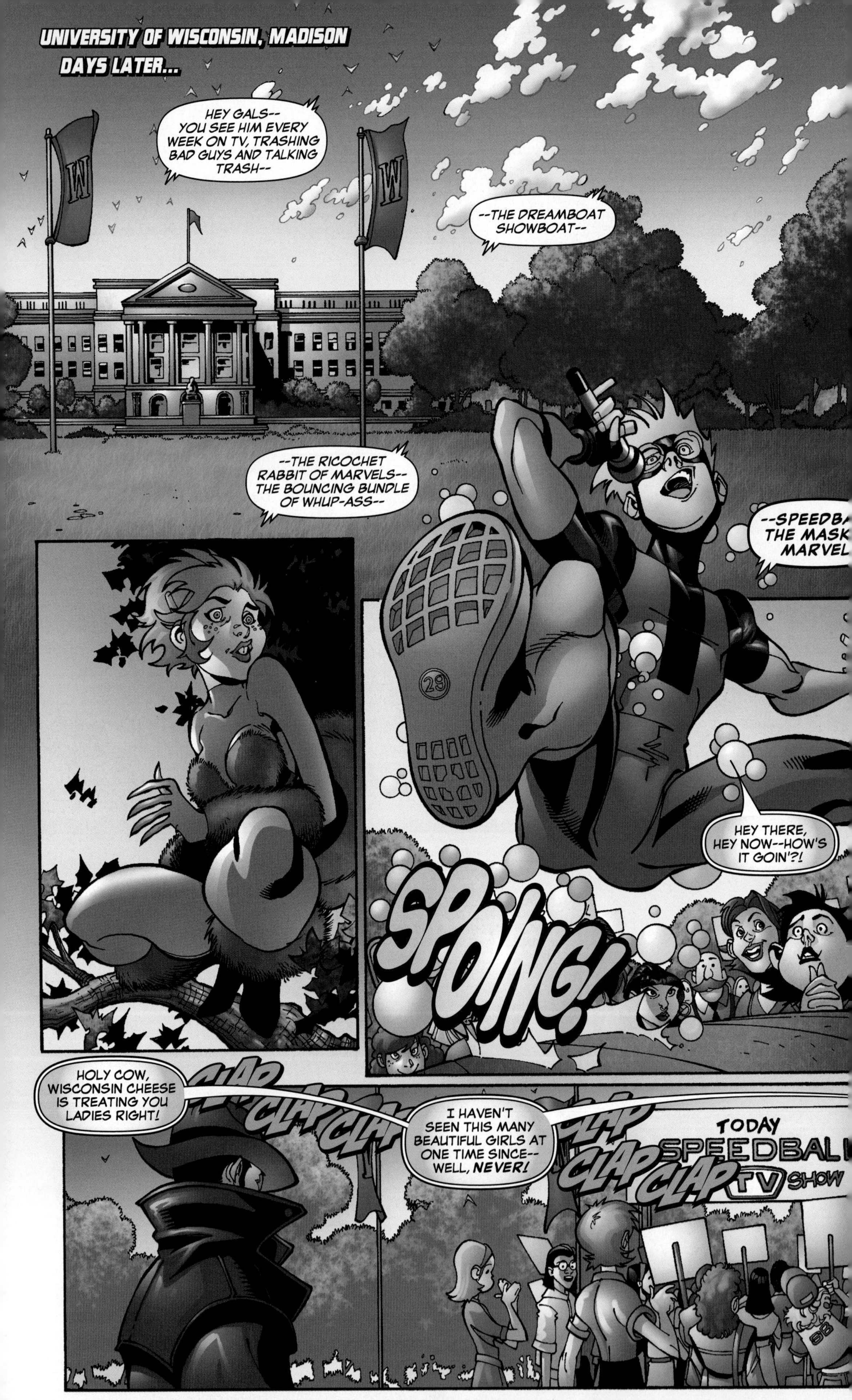
UNIVERSITY OF WISCONSIN, MADISON
DAYS LATER...
HEY GALS-- YOU SEE HIM EVERY WEEK ON TV, TRASHING BAD GUYS AND TALKING TRASH--
--THE DREAMBOAT SHOWBOAT--
--THE RICOCHET RABBIT OF MARVELS-- THE BOUNCING BUNDLE OF WHUP-ASS--
--SPEEDBA THE MASK MARVEL
HEY THERE, HEY NOW--HOW'S IT GOIN'?!
SPOING!
HOLY COW, WISCONSIN CHEESE IS TREATING YOU LADIES RIGHT!
CLAP CLAP CLAP CLAP CLAP CLAP CLAP
I HAVEN'T SEEN THIS MANY BEAUTIFUL GIRLS AT ONE TIME SINCE-- WELL, NEVER!
TODAY SPEEDBALL TV SHOW

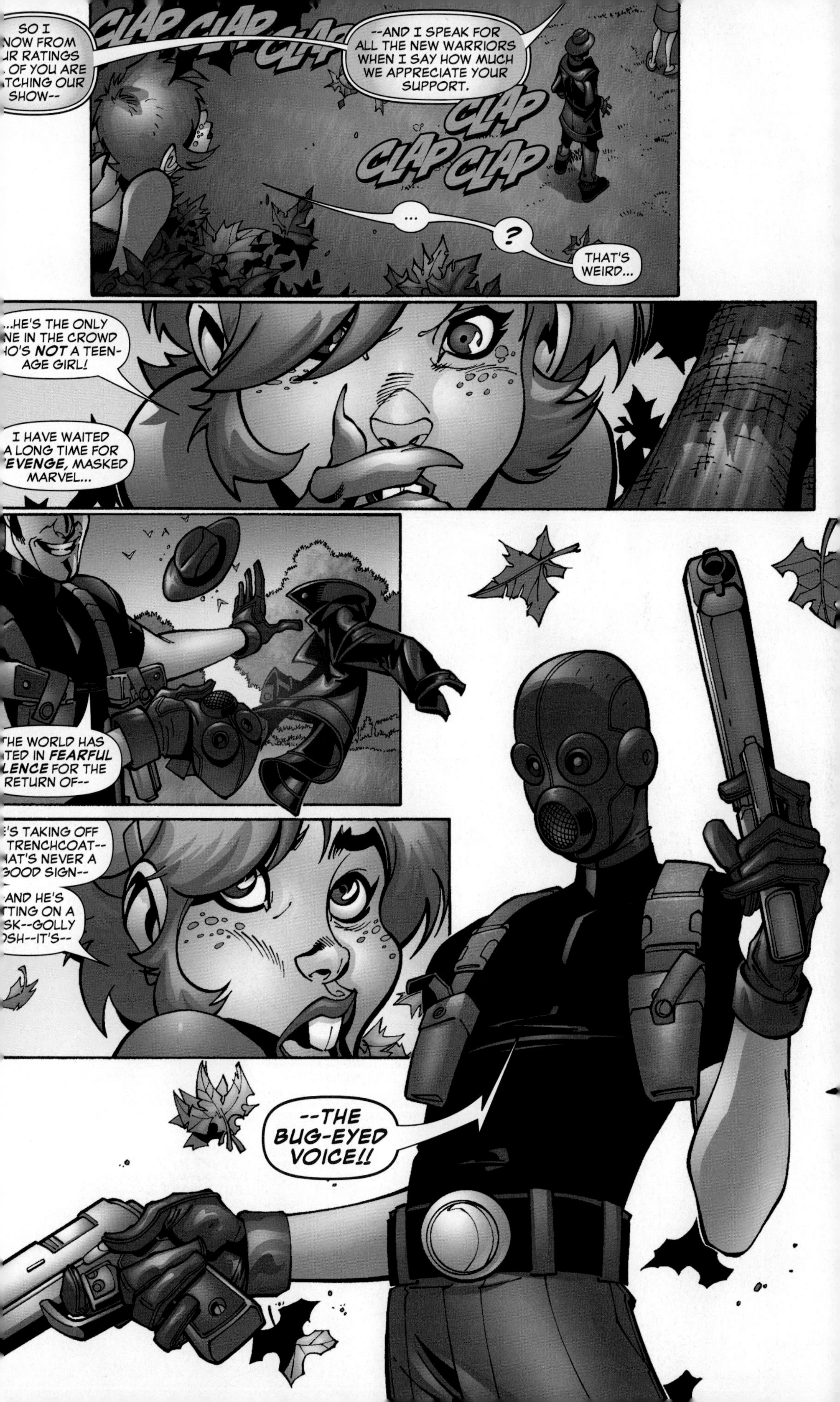

CLAP CLAP CLAP
SO I
NOW FROM
UR RATINGS
. OF YOU ARE
TCHING OUR
SHOW--
--AND I SPEAK FOR ALL THE NEW WARRIORS WHEN I SAY HOW MUCH WE APPRECIATE YOUR SUPPORT.
CLAP
CLAP CLAP
...
?
THAT'S WEIRD...
...HE'S THE ONLY
NE IN THE CROWD
HO'S NOT A TEEN-
AGE GIRL!
I HAVE WAITED
A LONG TIME FOR
EVENGE, MASKED
MARVEL...
THE WORLD HAS
TED IN FEARFUL
LENCE FOR THE
RETURN OF--
'S TAKING OFF
TRENCHCOAT--
IAT'S NEVER A
GOOD SIGN--
AND HE'S
TING ON A
SK--GOLLY
SH--IT'S--
--THE BUG-EYED VOICE!!

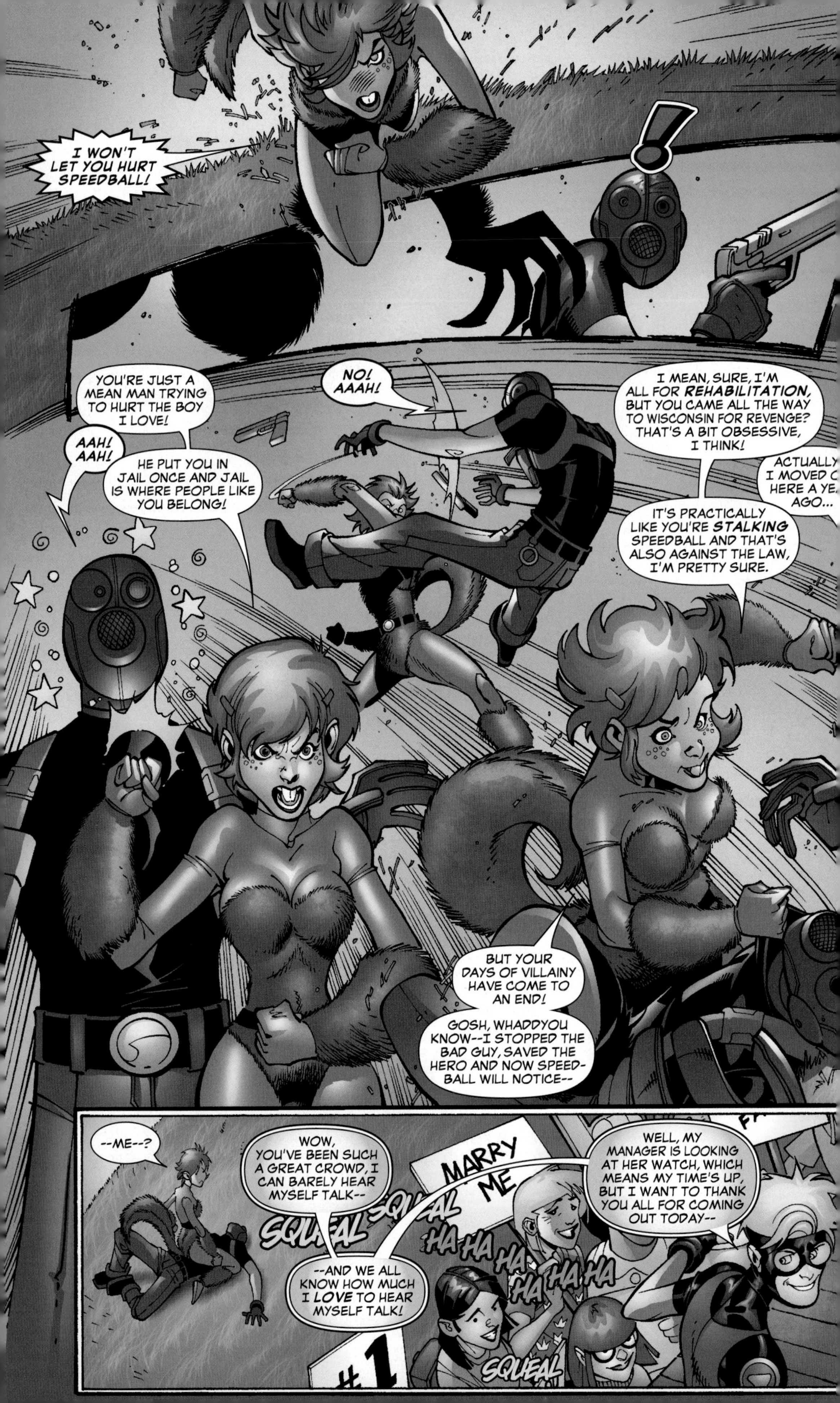
I WON'T LET YOU HURT SPEEDBALL!
!
YOU'RE JUST A MEAN MAN TRYING TO HURT THE BOY I LOVE!
NO! AAAH!
AAH! AAH!
HE PUT YOU IN JAIL ONCE AND JAIL IS WHERE PEOPLE LIKE YOU BELONG!
I MEAN, SURE, I'M ALL FOR REHABILITATION, BUT YOU CAME ALL THE WAY TO WISCONSIN FOR REVENGE? THAT'S A BIT OBSESSIVE, I THINK!
IT'S PRACTICALLY LIKE YOU'RE STALKING SPEEDBALL AND THAT'S ALSO AGAINST THE LAW, I'M PRETTY SURE.
BUT YOUR DAYS OF VILLAINY HAVE COME TO AN END!
GOSH, WHADDYOU KNOW--I STOPPED THE BAD GUY, SAVED THE HERO AND NOW SPEEDBALL WILL NOTICE--
--ME--?
WOW, YOU'VE BEEN SUCH A GREAT CROWD, I CAN BARELY HEAR MYSELF TALK--
--AND WE ALL KNOW HOW MUCH I LOVE TO HEAR MYSELF TALK!
WELL, MY MANAGER IS LOOKING AT HER WATCH, WHICH MEANS MY TIME'S UP, BUT I WANT TO THANK YOU ALL FOR COMING OUT TODAY--
MARRY ME
SQUEAL SQUEAL
HA HA HA HA HA HA HA
SQUEAL
#1

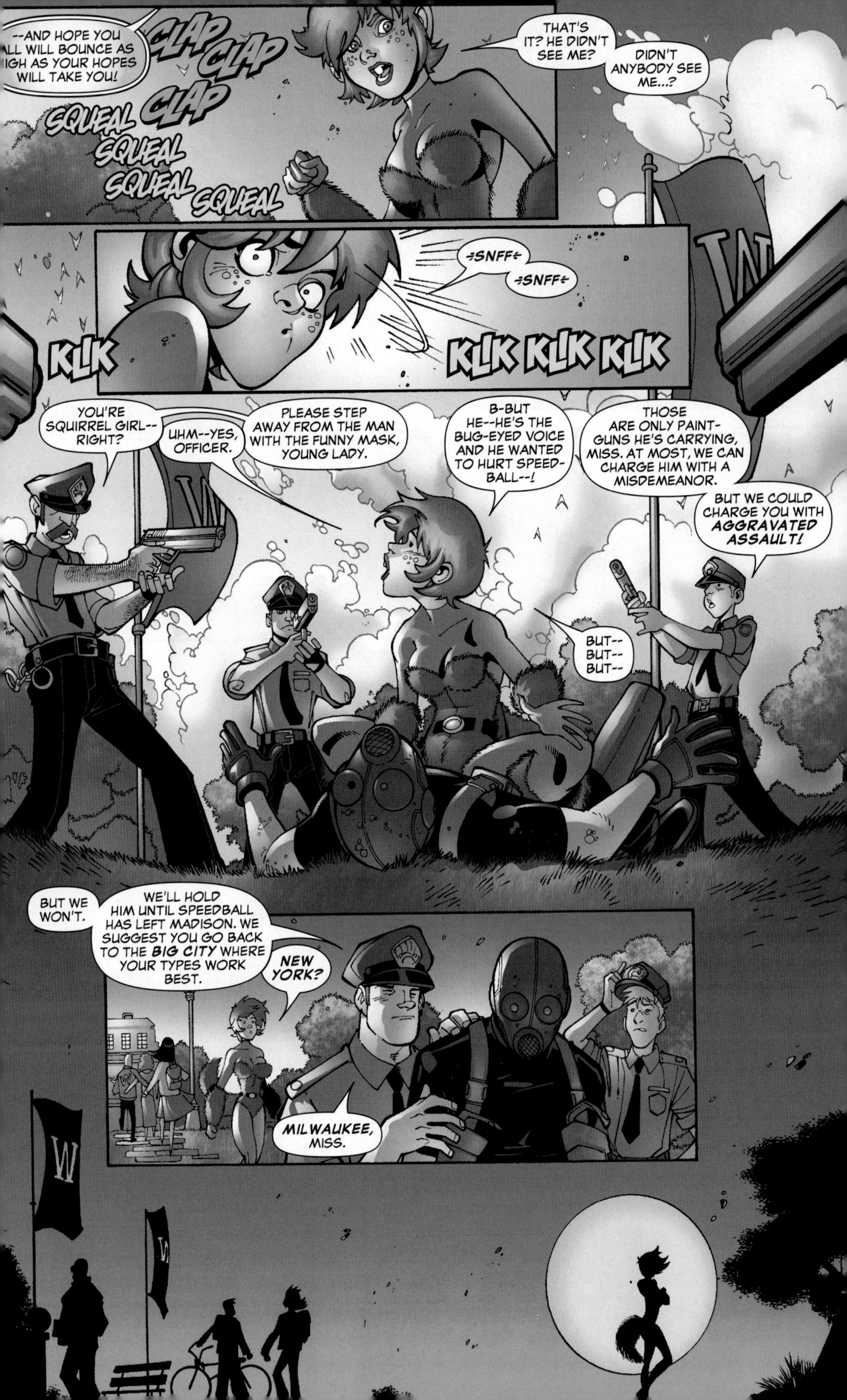
--AND HOPE YOU ALL WILL BOUNCE AS HIGH AS YOUR HOPES WILL TAKE YOU!
CLAP CLAP CLAP CLAP
SQUEAL SQUEAL SQUEAL SQUEAL
THAT'S IT? HE DIDN'T SEE ME?
DIDN'T ANYBODY SEE ME...?
SNFF
SNFF
KLIK
KLIK KLIK KLIK
YOU'RE SQUIRREL GIRL--RIGHT?
UHM--YES, OFFICER.
PLEASE STEP AWAY FROM THE MAN WITH THE FUNNY MASK, YOUNG LADY.
B-BUT HE--HE'S THE BUG-EYED VOICE AND HE WANTED TO HURT SPEED-BALL--!
THOSE ARE ONLY PAINT-GUNS HE'S CARRYING, MISS. AT MOST, WE CAN CHARGE HIM WITH A MISDEMEANOR.
BUT WE COULD CHARGE YOU WITH AGGRAVATED ASSAULT!
BUT--BUT--BUT--
BUT WE WON'T.
WE'LL HOLD HIM UNTIL SPEEDBALL HAS LEFT MADISON. WE SUGGEST YOU GO BACK TO THE BIG CITY WHERE YOUR TYPES WORK BEST.
NEW YORK?
MILWAUKEE, MISS.

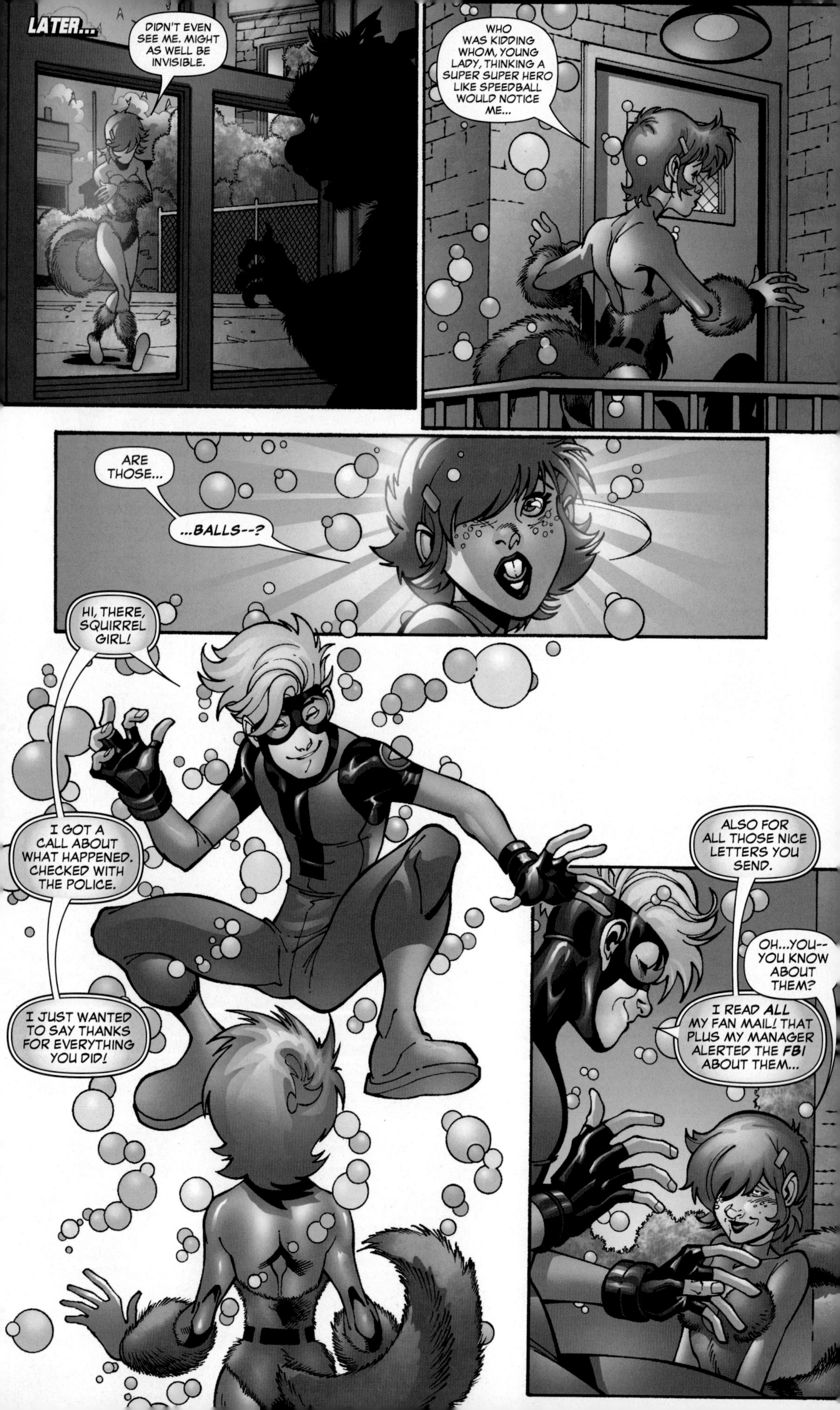
LATER...
DIDN'T EVEN SEE ME. MIGHT AS WELL BE INVISIBLE.
WHO WAS KIDDING WHOM, YOUNG LADY, THINKING A SUPER SUPER HERO LIKE SPEEDBALL WOULD NOTICE ME...
ARE THOSE...
...BALLS--?
HI, THERE, SQUIRREL GIRL!
I GOT A CALL ABOUT WHAT HAPPENED. CHECKED WITH THE POLICE.
I JUST WANTED TO SAY THANKS FOR EVERYTHING YOU DID!
ALSO FOR ALL THOSE NICE LETTERS YOU SEND.
OH...YOU--YOU KNOW ABOUT THEM?
I READ ALL MY FAN MAIL! THAT PLUS MY MANAGER ALERTED THE FBI ABOUT THEM...

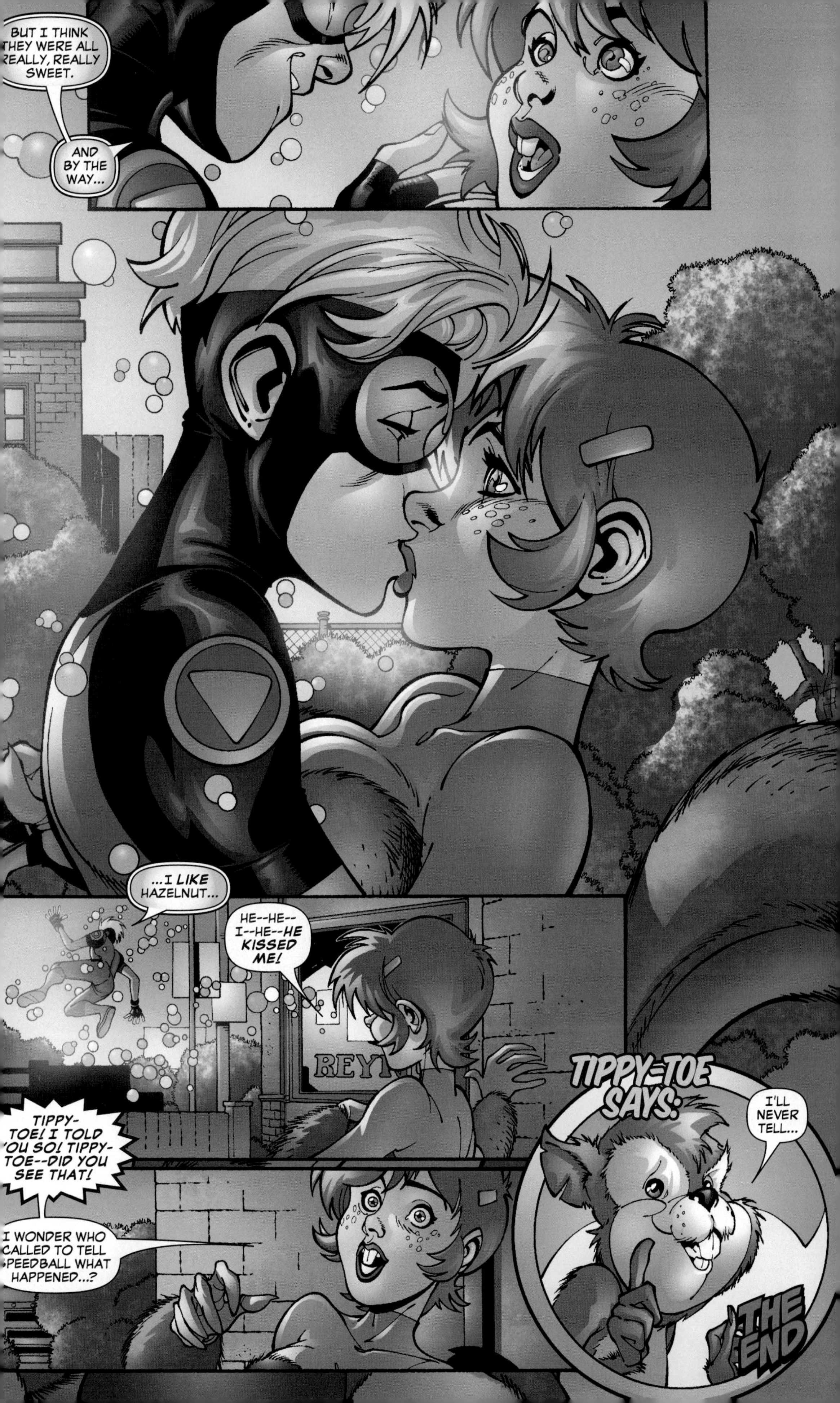
BUT I THINK THEY WERE ALL REALLY, REALLY SWEET.
AND BY THE WAY...
...I LIKE HAZELNUT...
HE--HE-- I--HE--HE KISSED ME!
TIPPY-TOE! I TOLD YOU SO! TIPPY-TOE--DID YOU SEE THAT!
I WONDER WHO CALLED TO TELL SPEEDBALL WHAT HAPPENED...?
TIPPY-TOE SAYS:
I'LL NEVER TELL...
THE END

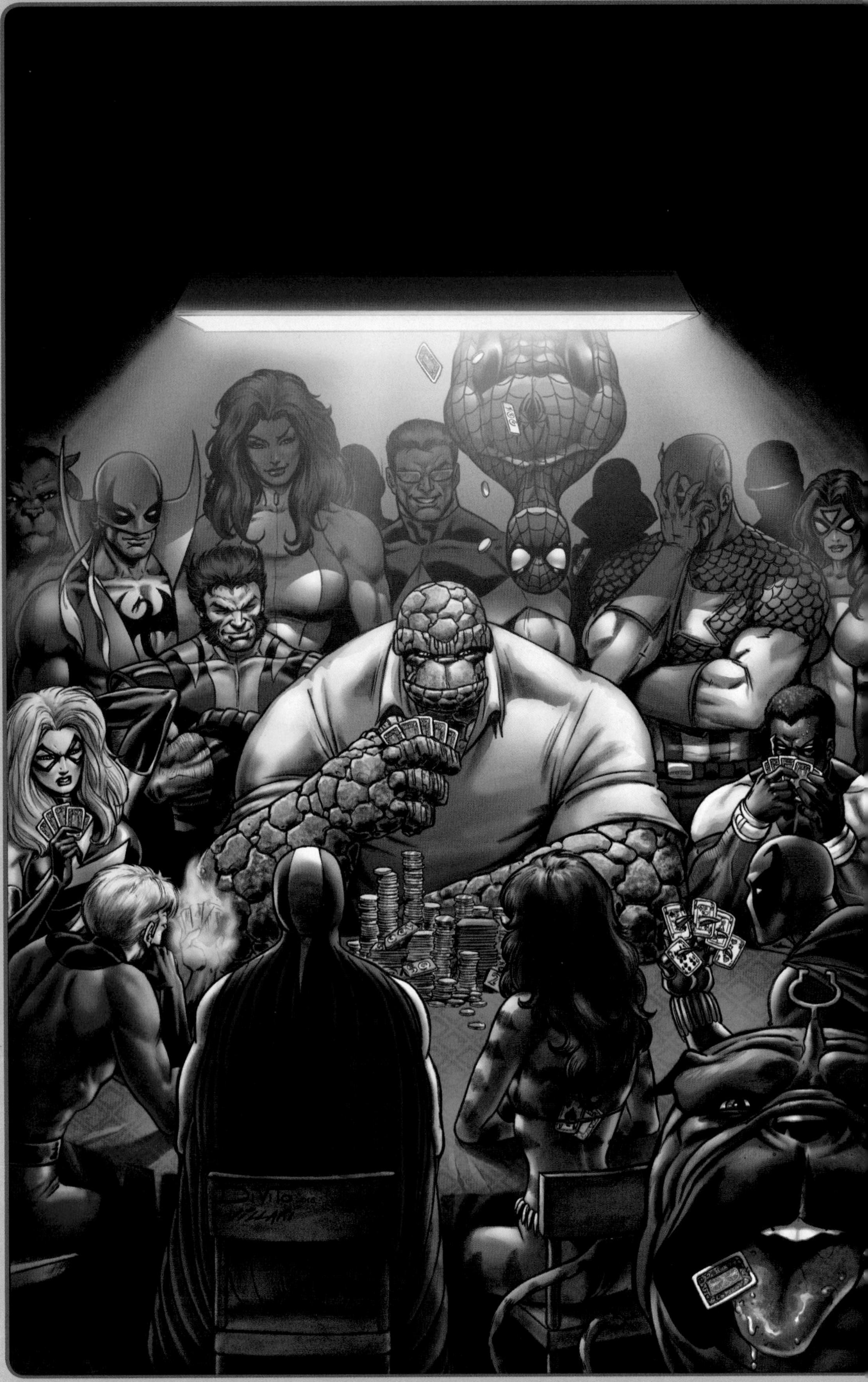

Thing #8

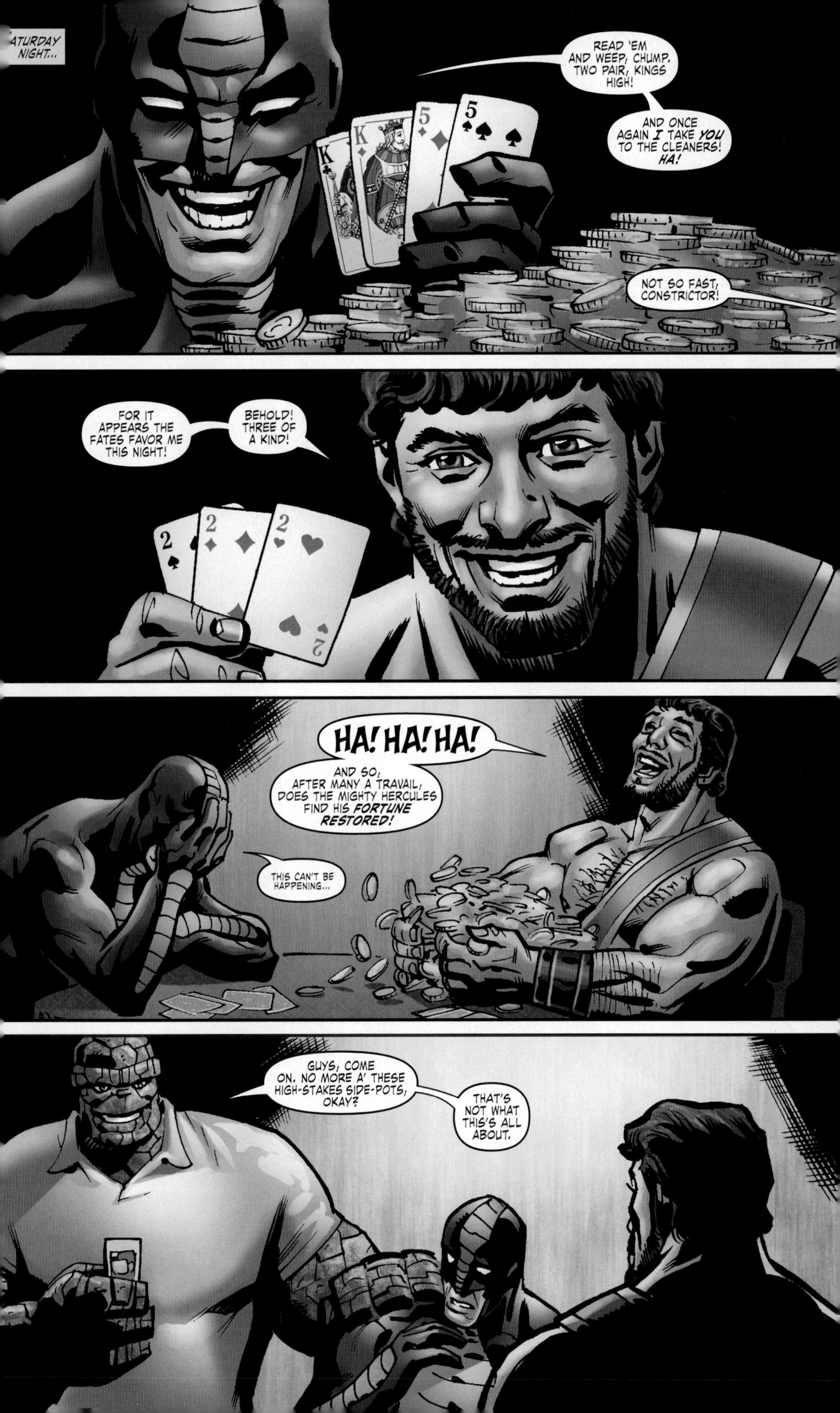
SATURDAY NIGHT...
READ 'EM AND WEEP, CHUMP. TWO PAIR, KINGS HIGH!
AND ONCE AGAIN I TAKE YOU TO THE CLEANERS! HA!
NOT SO FAST, CONSTRICTOR!
FOR IT APPEARS THE FATES FAVOR ME THIS NIGHT!
BEHOLD! THREE OF A KIND!
HA! HA! HA!
AND SO, AFTER MANY A TRAVAIL, DOES THE MIGHTY HERCULES FIND HIS FORTUNE RESTORED!
THIS CAN'T BE HAPPENING...
GUYS, COME ON. NO MORE A' THESE HIGH-STAKES SIDE-POTS, OKAY?
THAT'S NOT WHAT THIS'S ALL ABOUT.

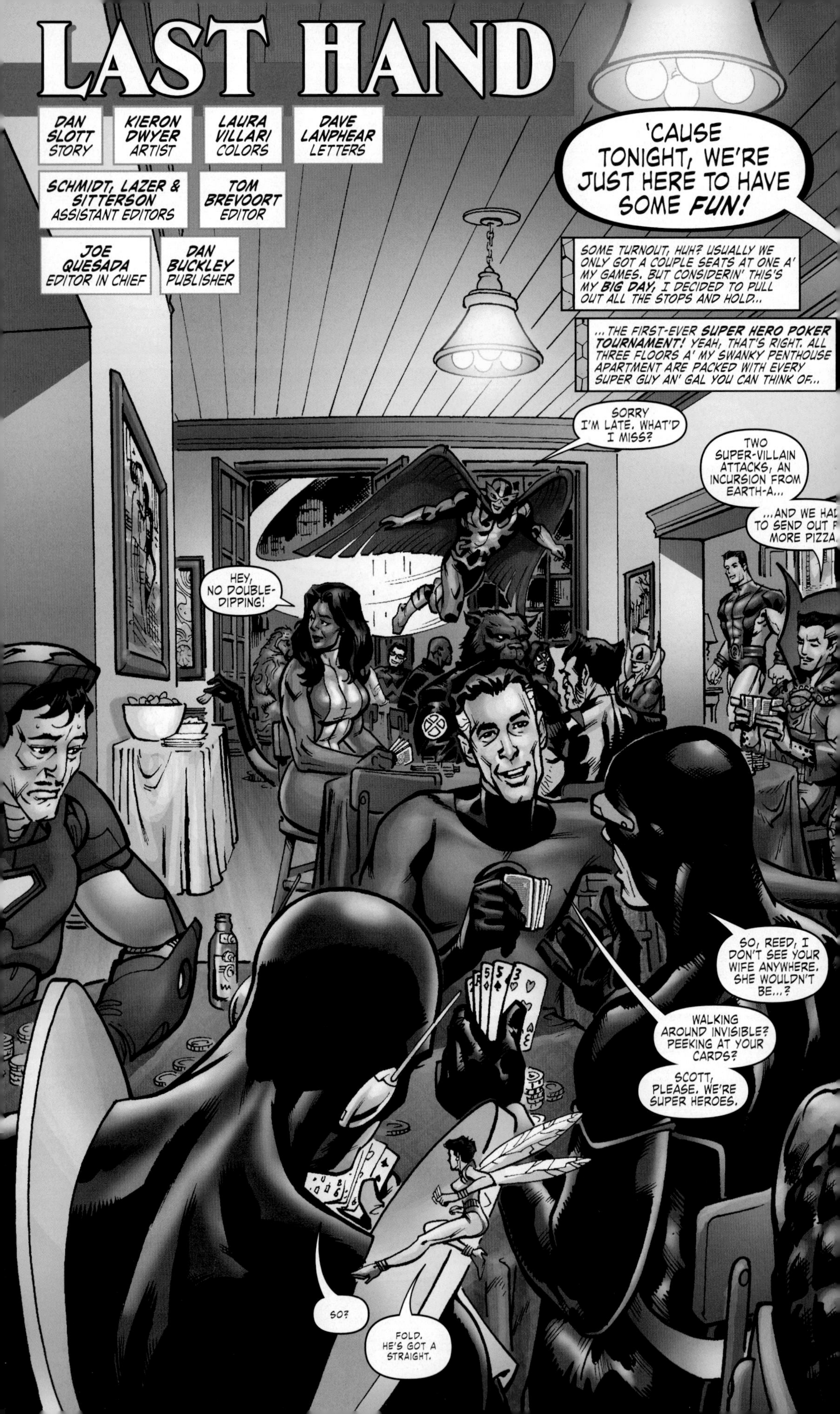
LAST HAND
DAN SLOTT STORY
KIERON DWYER ARTIST
LAURA VILLARI COLORS
DAVE LANPHEAR LETTERS
SCHMIDT, LAZER & SITTERSON ASSISTANT EDITORS
TOM BREVOORT EDITOR
JOE QUESADA EDITOR IN CHIEF
DAN BUCKLEY PUBLISHER
'CAUSE TONIGHT, WE'RE JUST HERE TO HAVE SOME FUN!
SOME TURNOUT, HUH? USUALLY WE ONLY GOT A COUPLE SEATS AT ONE A' MY GAMES. BUT CONSIDERIN' THIS'S MY BIG DAY, I DECIDED TO PULL OUT ALL THE STOPS AND HOLD...
...THE FIRST-EVER SUPER HERO POKER TOURNAMENT! YEAH, THAT'S RIGHT. ALL THREE FLOORS A' MY SWANKY PENTHOUSE APARTMENT ARE PACKED WITH EVERY SUPER GUY AN' GAL YOU CAN THINK OF...
SORRY I'M LATE. WHAT'D I MISS?
TWO SUPER-VILLAIN ATTACKS, AN INCURSION FROM EARTH-A...
...AND WE HA
TO SEND OUT
MORE PIZZA
HEY, NO DOUBLE-DIPPING!
SO, REED, I DON'T SEE YOUR WIFE ANYWHERE. SHE WOULDN'T BE...?
WALKING AROUND INVISIBLE? PEEKING AT YOUR CARDS?
SCOTT, PLEASE. WE'RE SUPER HEROES.
SO?
FOLD. HE'S GOT A STRAIGHT.

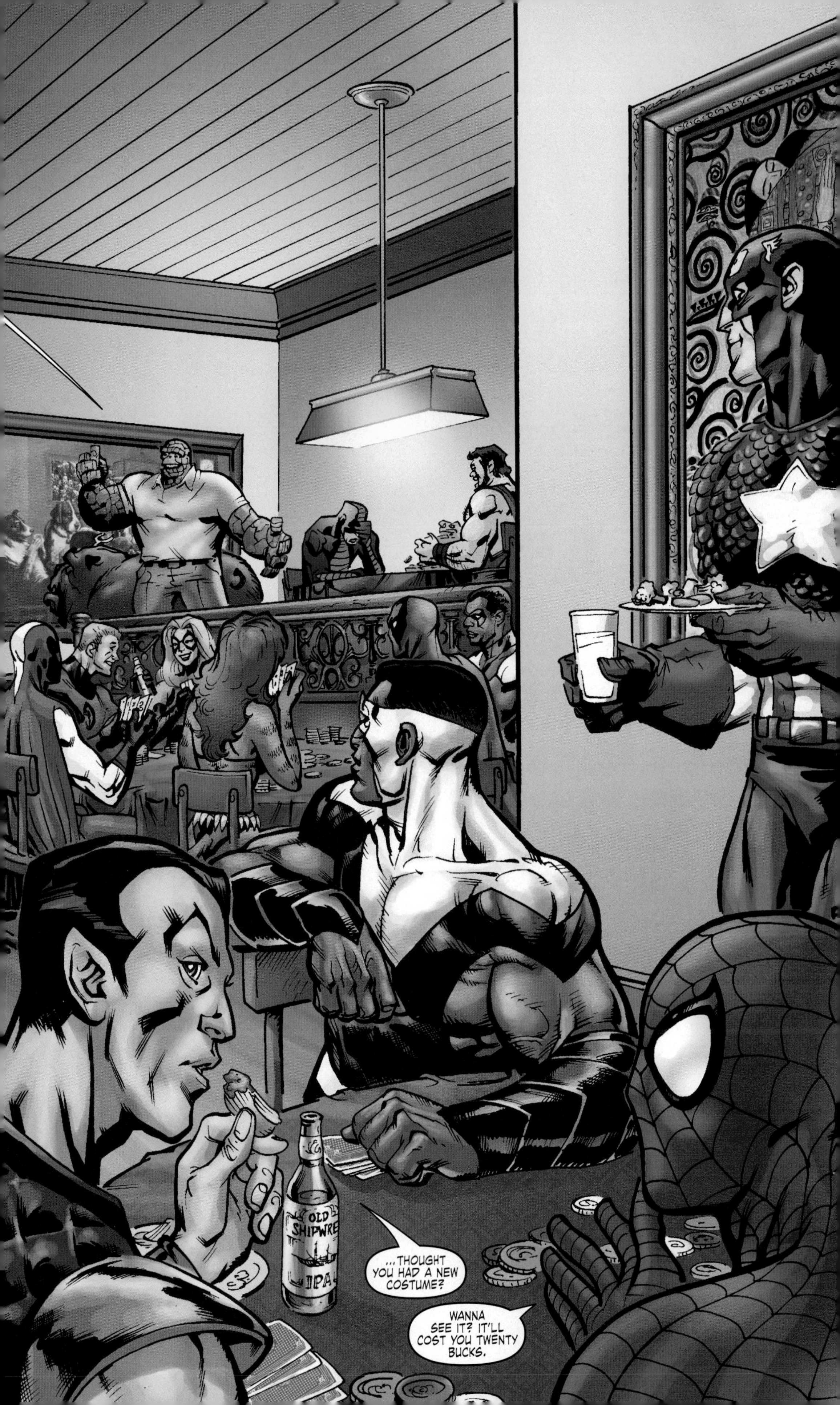

OLD SHIPWRE
IPA
...THOUGHT YOU HAD A NEW COSTUME?
WANNA SEE IT? IT'LL COST YOU TWENTY BUCKS.

GREAT LAKES AVENGERS

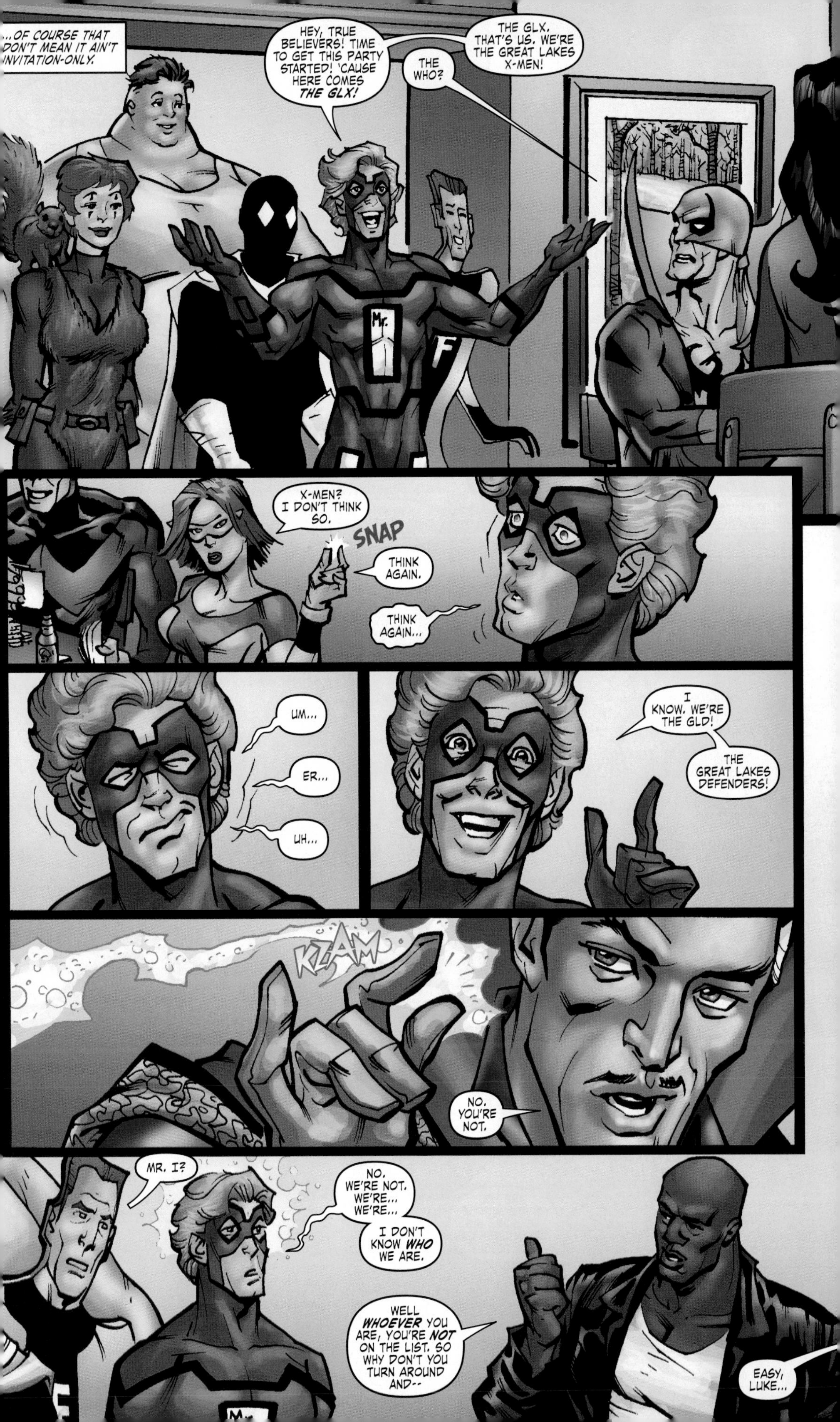
...OF COURSE THAT DON'T MEAN IT AIN'T INVITATION-ONLY.
HEY, TRUE BELIEVERS! TIME TO GET THIS PARTY STARTED! 'CAUSE HERE COMES THE GLX!
THE WHO?
THE GLX. THAT'S US. WE'RE THE GREAT LAKES X-MEN!
X-MEN? I DON'T THINK SO.
SNAP
THINK AGAIN.
THINK AGAIN...
UM...
ER...
UH...
I KNOW. WE'RE THE GLD!
THE GREAT LAKES DEFENDERS!
KLAM
NO. YOU'RE NOT.
MR. I?
NO. WE'RE NOT. WE'RE... WE'RE...
I DON'T KNOW WHO WE ARE.
WELL WHOEVER YOU ARE, YOU'RE NOT ON THE LIST. SO WHY DON'T YOU TURN AROUND AND--
EASY, LUKE...

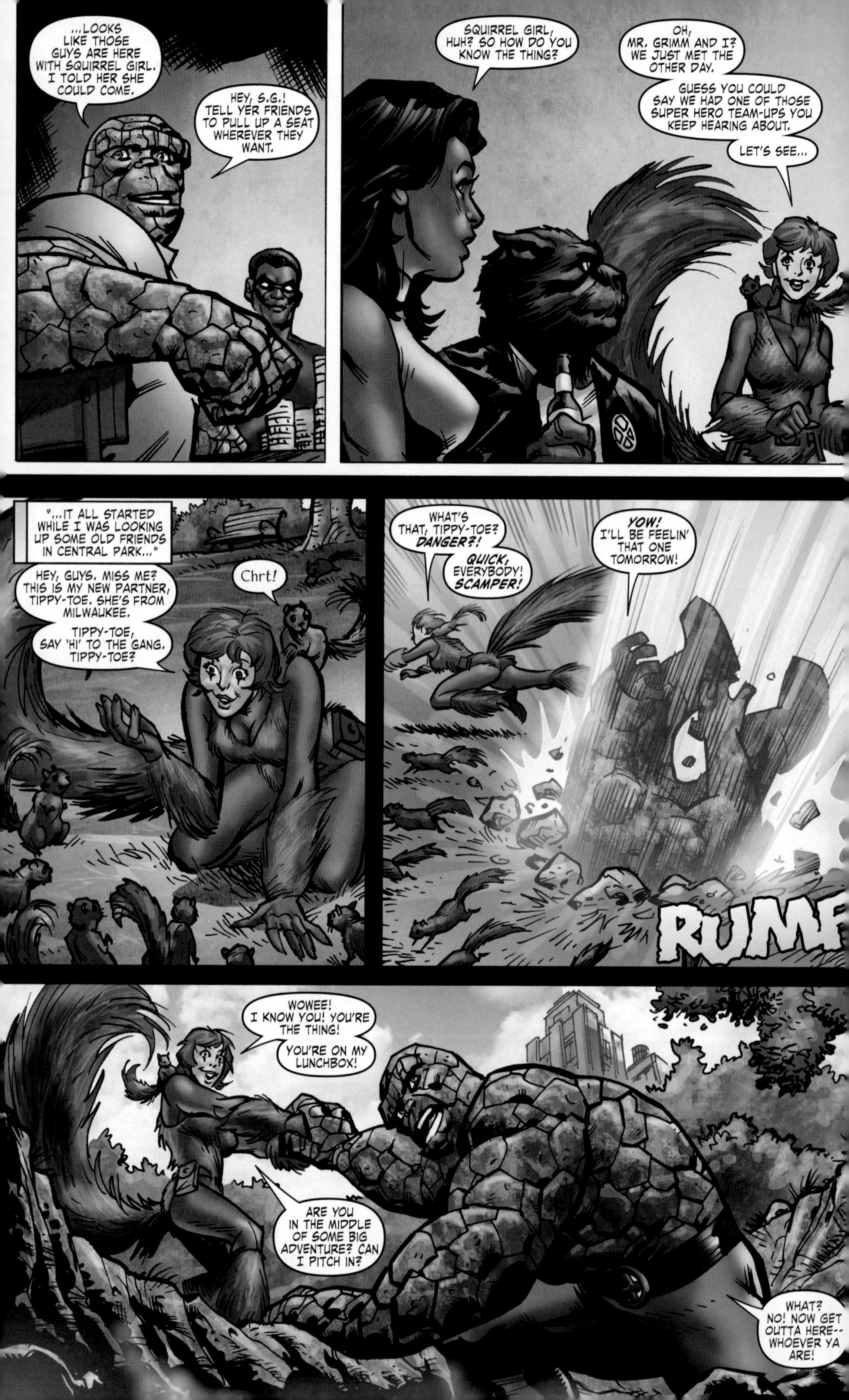
...LOOKS LIKE THOSE GUYS ARE HERE WITH SQUIRREL GIRL. I TOLD HER SHE COULD COME.
HEY, S.G.! TELL YER FRIENDS TO PULL UP A SEAT WHEREVER THEY WANT.
SQUIRREL GIRL, HUH? SO HOW DO YOU KNOW THE THING?
OH, MR. GRIMM AND I? WE JUST MET THE OTHER DAY.
GUESS YOU COULD SAY WE HAD ONE OF THOSE SUPER HERO TEAM-UPS YOU KEEP HEARING ABOUT.
LET'S SEE...
"...IT ALL STARTED WHILE I WAS LOOKING UP SOME OLD FRIENDS IN CENTRAL PARK..."
HEY, GUYS. MISS ME? THIS IS MY NEW PARTNER, TIPPY-TOE. SHE'S FROM MILWAUKEE.
TIPPY-TOE, SAY 'HI' TO THE GANG. TIPPY-TOE?
Chrt!
WHAT'S THAT, TIPPY-TOE? DANGER?!
QUICK, EVERYBODY! SCAMPER!
YOW! I'LL BE FEELIN' THAT ONE TOMORROW!
RUMF
WOWEE! I KNOW YOU! YOU'RE THE THING!
YOU'RE ON MY LUNCHBOX!
ARE YOU IN THE MIDDLE OF SOME BIG ADVENTURE? CAN I PITCH IN?
WHAT? NO! NOW GET OUTTA HERE-- WHOEVER YA ARE!

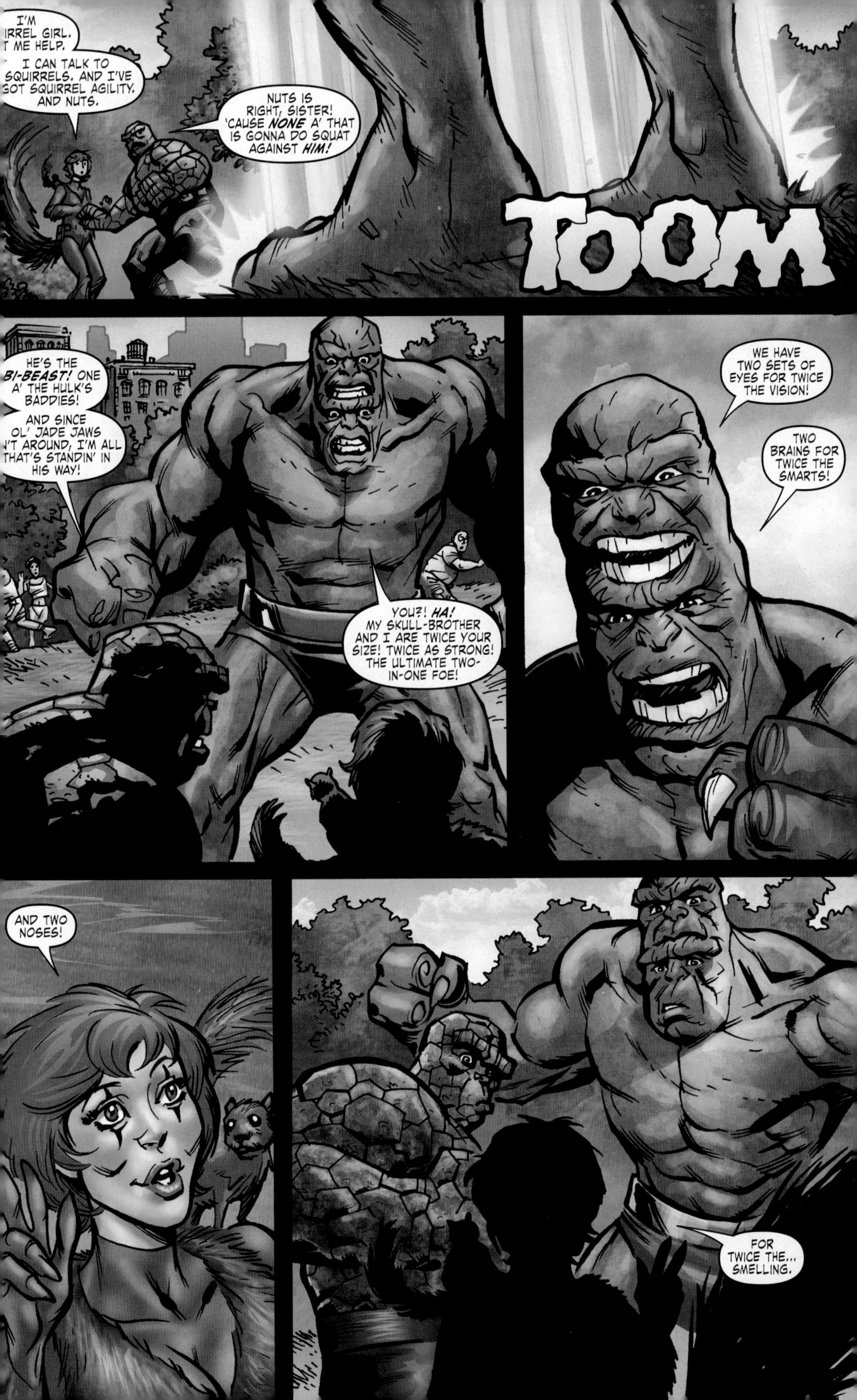

I'M IRREL GIRL. T ME HELP.
I CAN TALK TO SQUIRRELS. AND I'VE GOT SQUIRREL AGILITY. AND NUTS.
NUTS IS RIGHT, SISTER! 'CAUSE NONE A' THAT IS GONNA DO SQUAT AGAINST HIM!
TOOM
HE'S THE BI-BEAST! ONE A' THE HULK'S BADDIES!
AND SINCE OL' JADE JAWS N'T AROUND, I'M ALL THAT'S STANDIN' IN HIS WAY!
YOU?! HA! MY SKULL-BROTHER AND I ARE TWICE YOUR SIZE! TWICE AS STRONG! THE ULTIMATE TWO-IN-ONE FOE!
WE HAVE TWO SETS OF EYES FOR TWICE THE VISION!
TWO BRAINS FOR TWICE THE SMARTS!
AND TWO NOSES!
FOR TWICE THE... SMELLING.

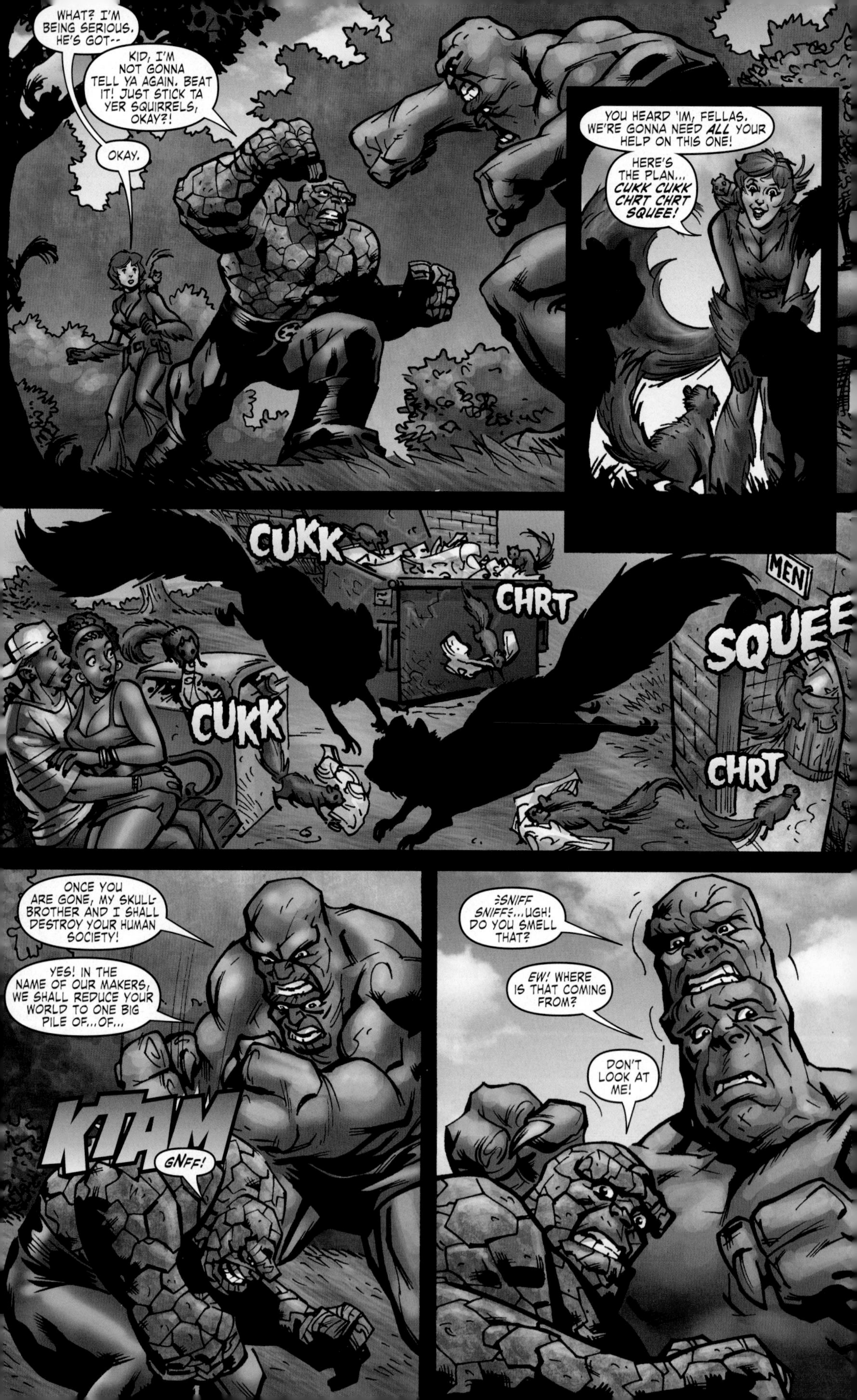
WHAT? I'M BEING SERIOUS. HE'S GOT--
KID, I'M NOT GONNA TELL YA AGAIN. BEAT IT! JUST STICK TA YER SQUIRRELS, OKAY?!
OKAY.
YOU HEARD 'IM, FELLAS. WE'RE GONNA NEED ALL YOUR HELP ON THIS ONE!
HERE'S THE PLAN... CUKK CUKK CHRT CHRT SQUEE!
CUKK
CHRT
MEN
SQUEE
CUKK
CHRT
ONCE YOU ARE GONE, MY SKULL-BROTHER AND I SHALL DESTROY YOUR HUMAN SOCIETY!
YES! IN THE NAME OF OUR MAKERS, WE SHALL REDUCE YOUR WORLD TO ONE BIG PILE OF...OF...
KTAM
GNFF!
=SNIFF SNIFF=...UGH! DO YOU SMELL THAT?
EW! WHERE IS THAT COMING FROM?
DON'T LOOK AT ME!

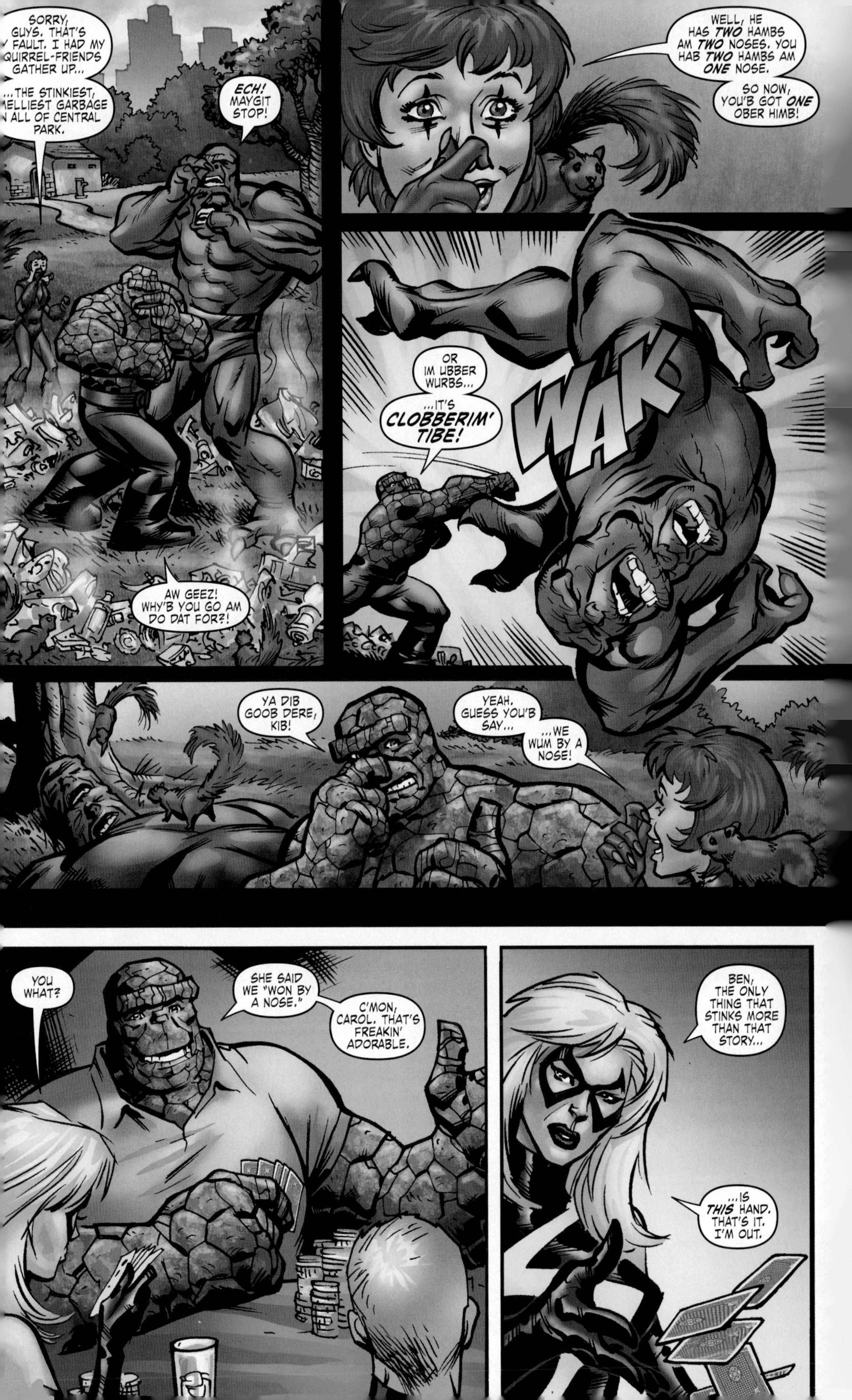

SORRY, GUYS. THAT'S MY FAULT. I HAD MY SQUIRREL-FRIENDS GATHER UP...
...THE STINKIEST, SMELLIEST GARBAGE IN ALL OF CENTRAL PARK.
ECH! MAYGIT STOP!
AW GEEZ! WHY'B YOU GO AM DO DAT FOR?!
WELL, HE HAS TWO HAMBS AM TWO NOSES. YOU HAB TWO HAMBS AM ONE NOSE.
SO NOW, YOU'B GOT ONE OBER HIMB!
OR IM UBBER WURBS...
...IT'S CLOBBERIM' TIBE!
WAK
YA DIB GOOB DERE, KIB!
YEAH. GUESS YOU'B SAY...
...WE WUM BY A NOSE!
YOU WHAT?
SHE SAID WE "WON BY A NOSE."
C'MON, CAROL. THAT'S FREAKIN' ADORABLE.
BEN, THE ONLY THING THAT STINKS MORE THAN THAT STORY...
...IS THIS HAND. THAT'S IT. I'M OUT.

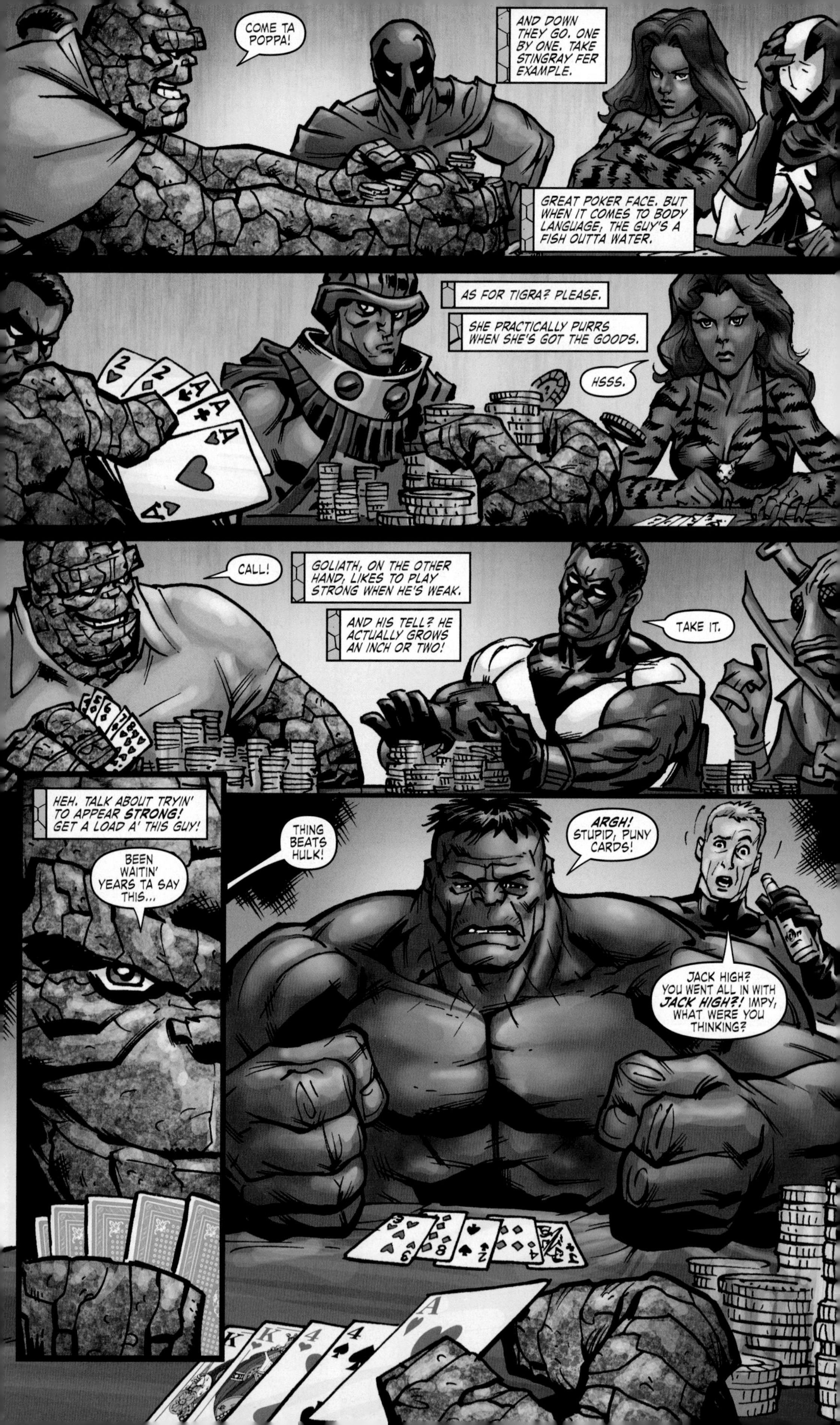
COME TA POPPA!
AND DOWN THEY GO. ONE BY ONE. TAKE STINGRAY FER EXAMPLE.
GREAT POKER FACE. BUT WHEN IT COMES TO BODY LANGUAGE, THE GUY'S A FISH OUTTA WATER.
AS FOR TIGRA? PLEASE.
SHE PRACTICALLY PURRS WHEN SHE'S GOT THE GOODS.
HSSS.
CALL!
GOLIATH, ON THE OTHER HAND, LIKES TO PLAY STRONG WHEN HE'S WEAK.
AND HIS TELL? HE ACTUALLY GROWS AN INCH OR TWO!
TAKE IT.
HEH. TALK ABOUT TRYIN' TO APPEAR STRONG! GET A LOAD A' THIS GUY!
BEEN WAITIN' YEARS TA SAY THIS...
THING BEATS HULK!
ARGH! STUPID, PUNY CARDS!
JACK HIGH? YOU WENT ALL IN WITH JACK HIGH?! IMPY, WHAT WERE YOU THINKING?

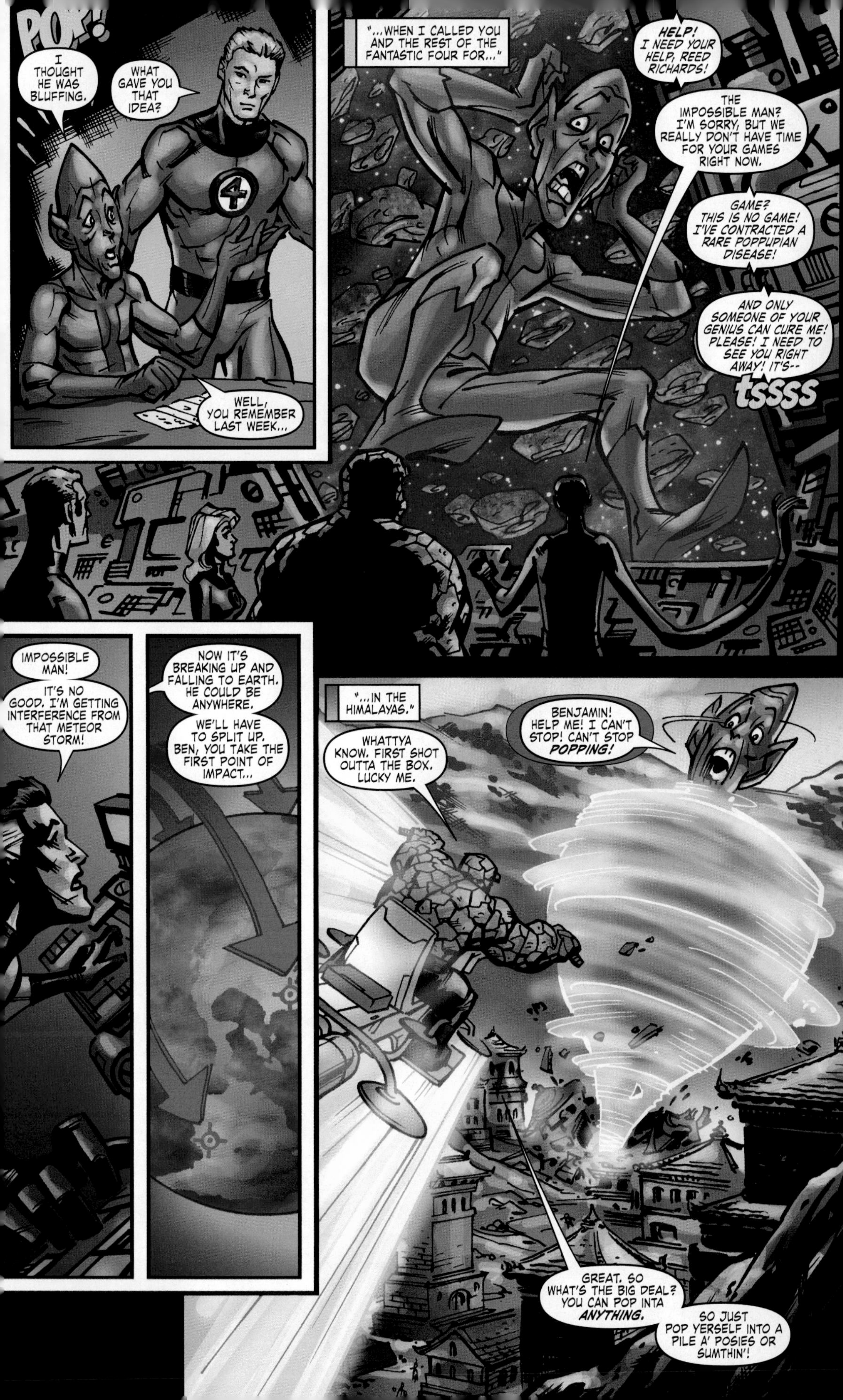
POP!
I THOUGHT HE WAS BLUFFING.
WHAT GAVE YOU THAT IDEA?
WELL, YOU REMEMBER LAST WEEK...
"...WHEN I CALLED YOU AND THE REST OF THE FANTASTIC FOUR FOR..."
HELP! I NEED YOUR HELP, REED RICHARDS!
THE IMPOSSIBLE MAN? I'M SORRY, BUT WE REALLY DON'T HAVE TIME FOR YOUR GAMES RIGHT NOW.
GAME? THIS IS NO GAME! I'VE CONTRACTED A RARE POPPUPIAN DISEASE!
AND ONLY SOMEONE OF YOUR GENIUS CAN CURE ME! PLEASE! I NEED TO SEE YOU RIGHT AWAY! IT'S--
tssss
IMPOSSIBLE MAN!
IT'S NO GOOD. I'M GETTING INTERFERENCE FROM THAT METEOR STORM!
NOW IT'S BREAKING UP AND FALLING TO EARTH. HE COULD BE ANYWHERE.
WE'LL HAVE TO SPLIT UP. BEN, YOU TAKE THE FIRST POINT OF IMPACT...
"...IN THE HIMALAYAS."
WHATTYA KNOW. FIRST SHOT OUTTA THE BOX. LUCKY ME.
BENJAMIN! HELP ME! I CAN'T STOP! CAN'T STOP POPPING!
GREAT. SO WHAT'S THE BIG DEAL? YOU CAN POP INTA ANYTHING.
SO JUST POP YOURSELF INTO A PILE A' POSIES OR SUMTHIN'!

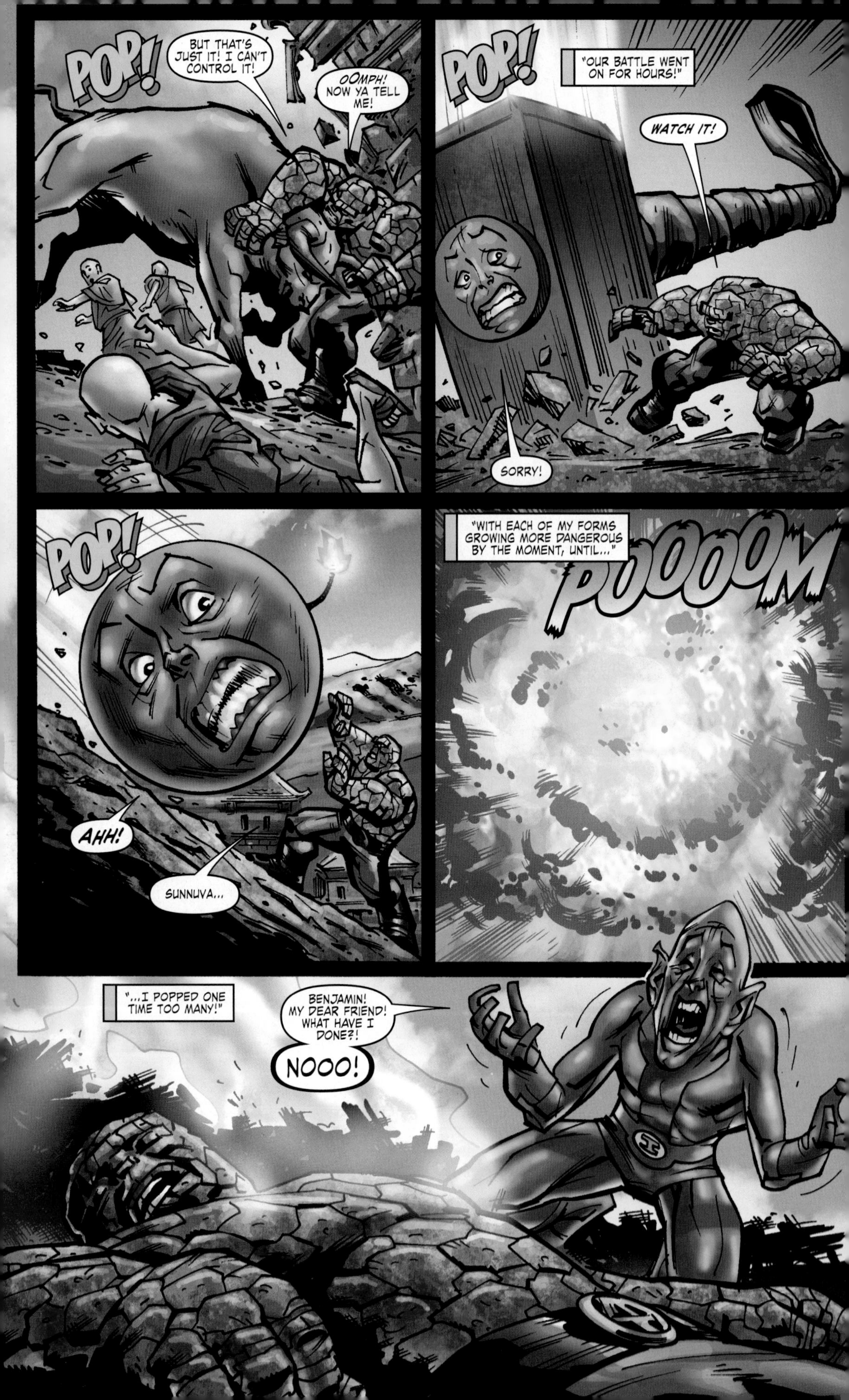
POP!
BUT THAT'S JUST IT! I CAN'T CONTROL IT!
OOMPH! NOW YA TELL ME!
POP!
"OUR BATTLE WENT ON FOR HOURS!"
WATCH IT!
SORRY!
POP!
AHH!
SUNNUVA...
"WITH EACH OF MY FORMS GROWING MORE DANGEROUS BY THE MOMENT, UNTIL..."
POOOOM
"...I POPPED ONE TIME TOO MANY!"
BENJAMIN! MY DEAR FRIEND! WHAT HAVE I DONE?!
NOOO!

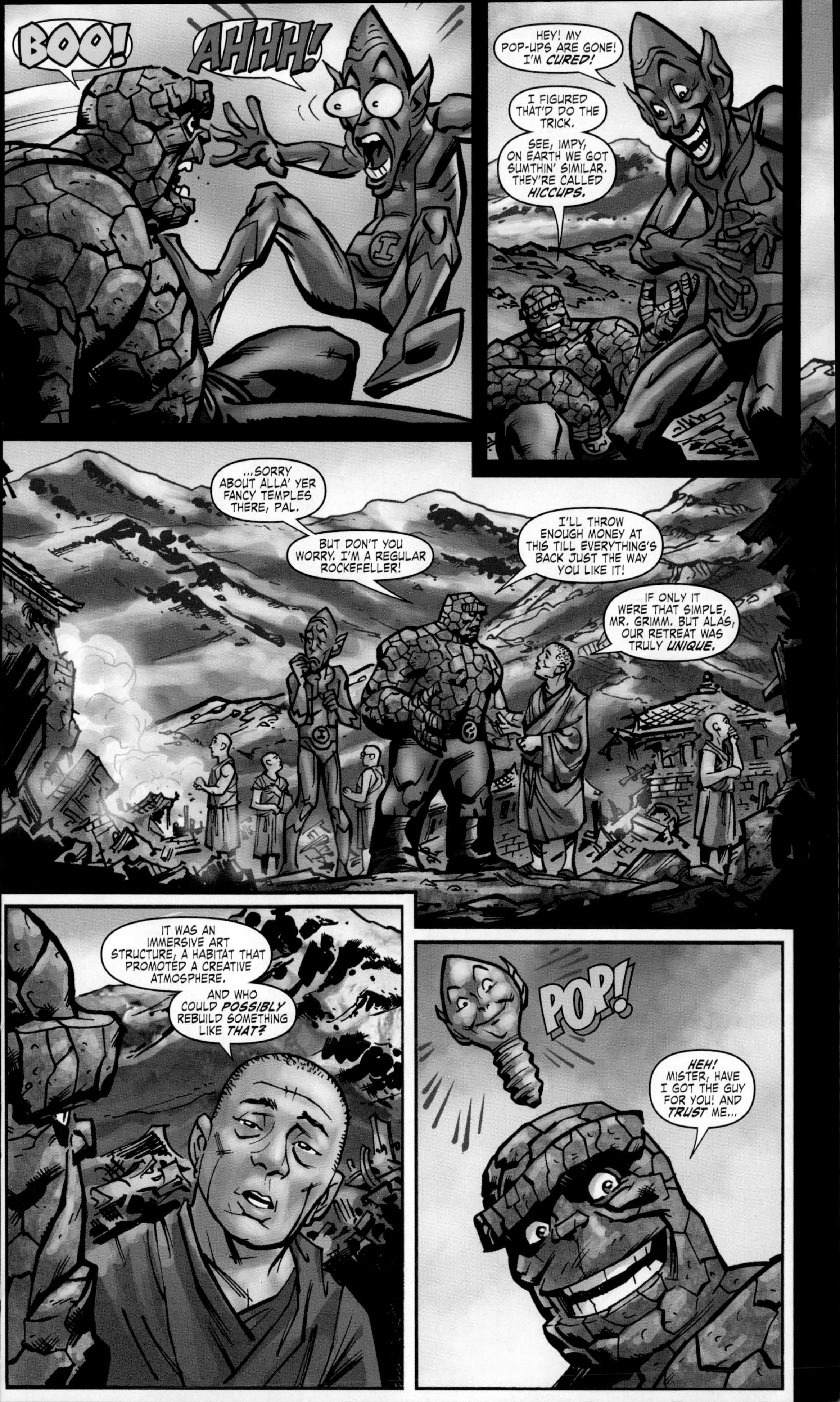
BOO!
AHHH!
HEY! MY POP-UPS ARE GONE! I'M *CURED!*
I FIGURED THAT'D DO THE TRICK.
SEE, IMPY, ON EARTH WE GOT SUMTHIN' SIMILAR. THEY'RE CALLED *HICCUPS.*
...SORRY ABOUT ALLA' YER FANCY TEMPLES THERE, PAL.
BUT DON'T YOU WORRY. I'M A REGULAR ROCKEFELLER!
I'LL THROW ENOUGH MONEY AT THIS TILL EVERYTHING'S BACK JUST THE WAY YOU LIKE IT!
IF ONLY IT WERE THAT SIMPLE, MR. GRIMM. BUT ALAS, OUR RETREAT WAS TRULY *UNIQUE.*
IT WAS AN IMMERSIVE ART STRUCTURE, A HABITAT THAT PROMOTED A CREATIVE ATMOSPHERE.
AND WHO COULD *POSSIBLY* REBUILD SOMETHING LIKE *THAT?*
POP!
HEH! MISTER, HAVE I GOT THE GUY FOR YOU! AND *TRUST* ME...

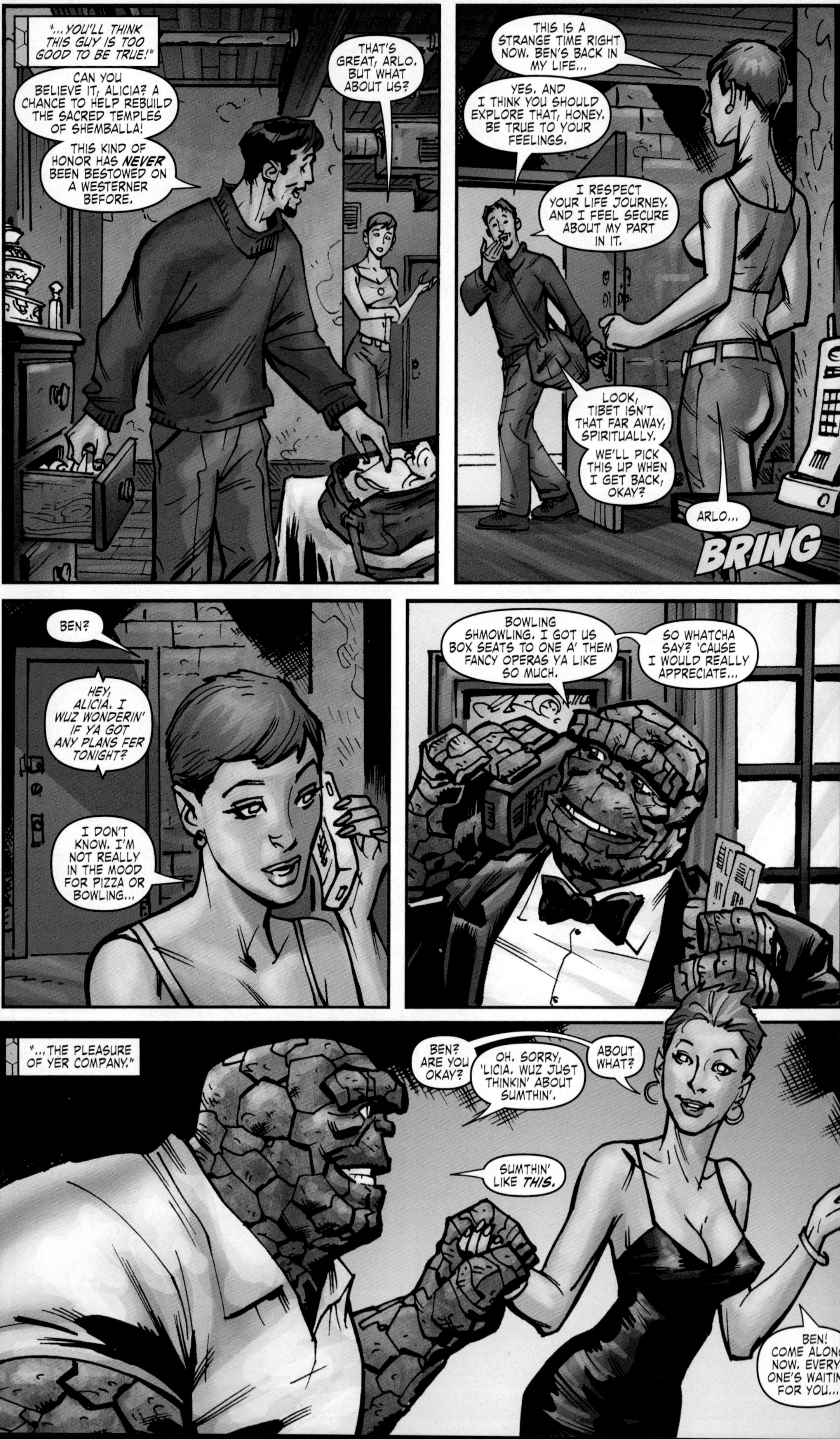
"...YOU'LL THINK THIS GUY IS TOO GOOD TO BE TRUE!"
CAN YOU BELIEVE IT, ALICIA? A CHANCE TO HELP REBUILD THE SACRED TEMPLES OF SHEMBALLA!
THIS KIND OF HONOR HAS *NEVER* BEEN BESTOWED ON A WESTERNER BEFORE.
THAT'S GREAT, ARLO. BUT WHAT ABOUT US?
THIS IS A STRANGE TIME RIGHT NOW. BEN'S BACK IN MY LIFE...
YES. AND I THINK YOU SHOULD EXPLORE THAT, HONEY. BE TRUE TO YOUR FEELINGS.
I RESPECT YOUR LIFE JOURNEY. AND I FEEL SECURE ABOUT MY PART IN IT.
LOOK, TIBET ISN'T THAT FAR AWAY, SPIRITUALLY.
WE'LL PICK THIS UP WHEN I GET BACK, OKAY?
ARLO...
BRING
BEN?
HEY, ALICIA. I WUZ WONDERIN' IF YA GOT ANY PLANS FER TONIGHT?
I DON'T KNOW. I'M NOT REALLY IN THE MOOD FOR PIZZA OR BOWLING...
BOWLING SHMOWLING. I GOT US BOX SEATS TO ONE A' THEM FANCY OPERAS YA LIKE SO MUCH.
SO WHATCHA SAY? 'CAUSE I WOULD REALLY APPRECIATE...
"...THE PLEASURE OF YER COMPANY."
BEN? ARE YOU OKAY?
OH. SORRY, 'LICIA. WUZ JUST THINKIN' ABOUT SUMTHIN'.
ABOUT WHAT?
SUMTHIN' LIKE *THIS*.
BEN! COME ALONG NOW. EVERY ONE'S WAITIN FOR YOU...

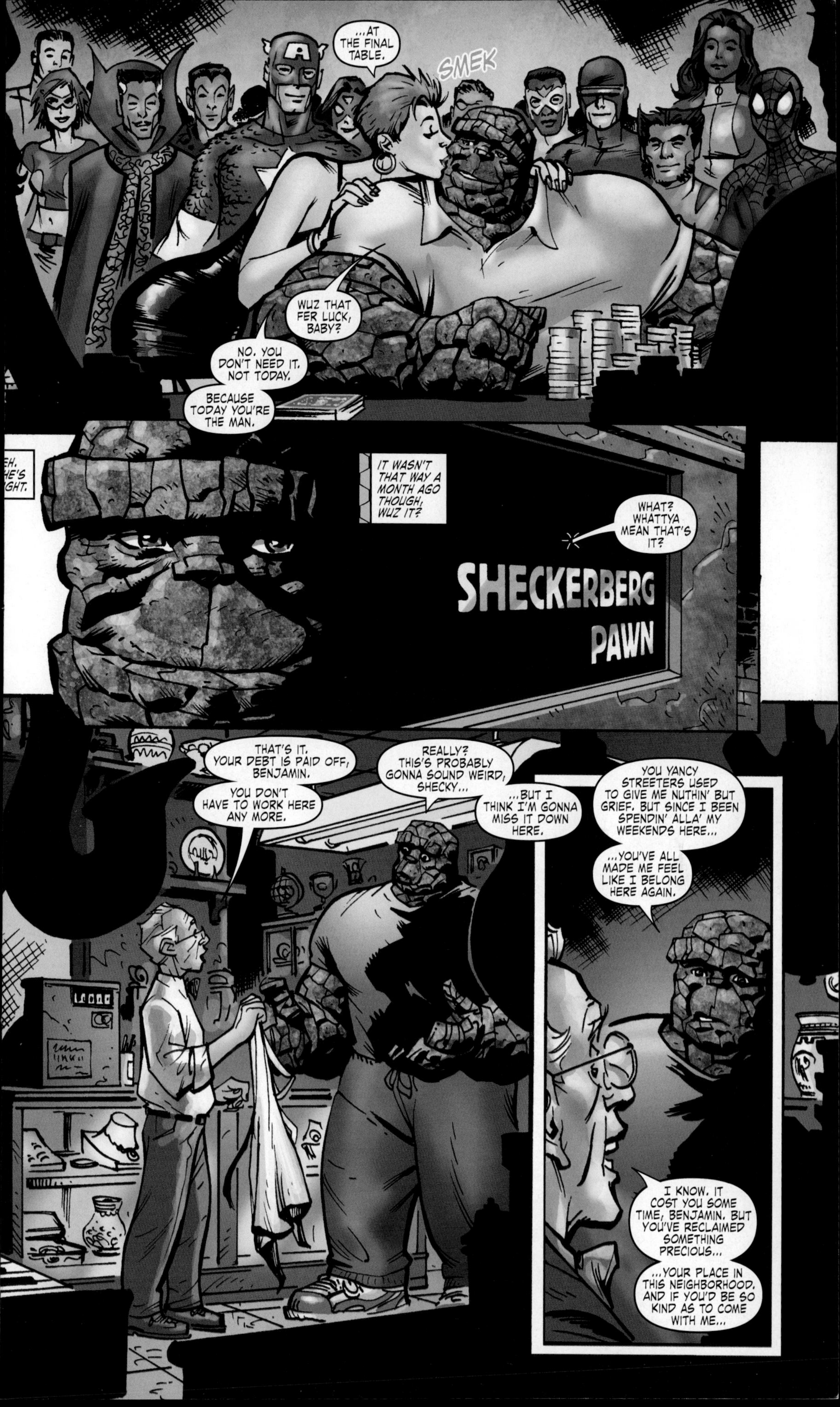

...AT THE FINAL TABLE.
SMEK
WUZ THAT FER LUCK, BABY?
NO. YOU DON'T NEED IT. NOT TODAY.
BECAUSE TODAY YOU'RE THE MAN.
EH. SHE'S RIGHT.
IT WASN'T THAT WAY A MONTH AGO THOUGH, WUZ IT?
WHAT? WHATTYA MEAN THAT'S IT?
SHECKERBERG PAWN
THAT'S IT. YOUR DEBT IS PAID OFF, BENJAMIN.
YOU DON'T HAVE TO WORK HERE ANY MORE.
REALLY? THIS'S PROBABLY GONNA SOUND WEIRD, SHECKY...
...BUT I THINK I'M GONNA MISS IT DOWN HERE.
YOU YANCY STREETERS USED TO GIVE ME NUTHIN' BUT GRIEF. BUT SINCE I BEEN SPENDIN' ALLA' MY WEEKENDS HERE...
...YOU'VE ALL MADE ME FEEL LIKE I BELONG HERE AGAIN.
I KNOW. IT COST YOU SOME TIME, BENJAMIN. BUT YOU'VE RECLAIMED SOMETHING PRECIOUS...
...YOUR PLACE IN THIS NEIGHBORHOOD. AND IF YOU'D BE SO KIND AS TO COME WITH ME...

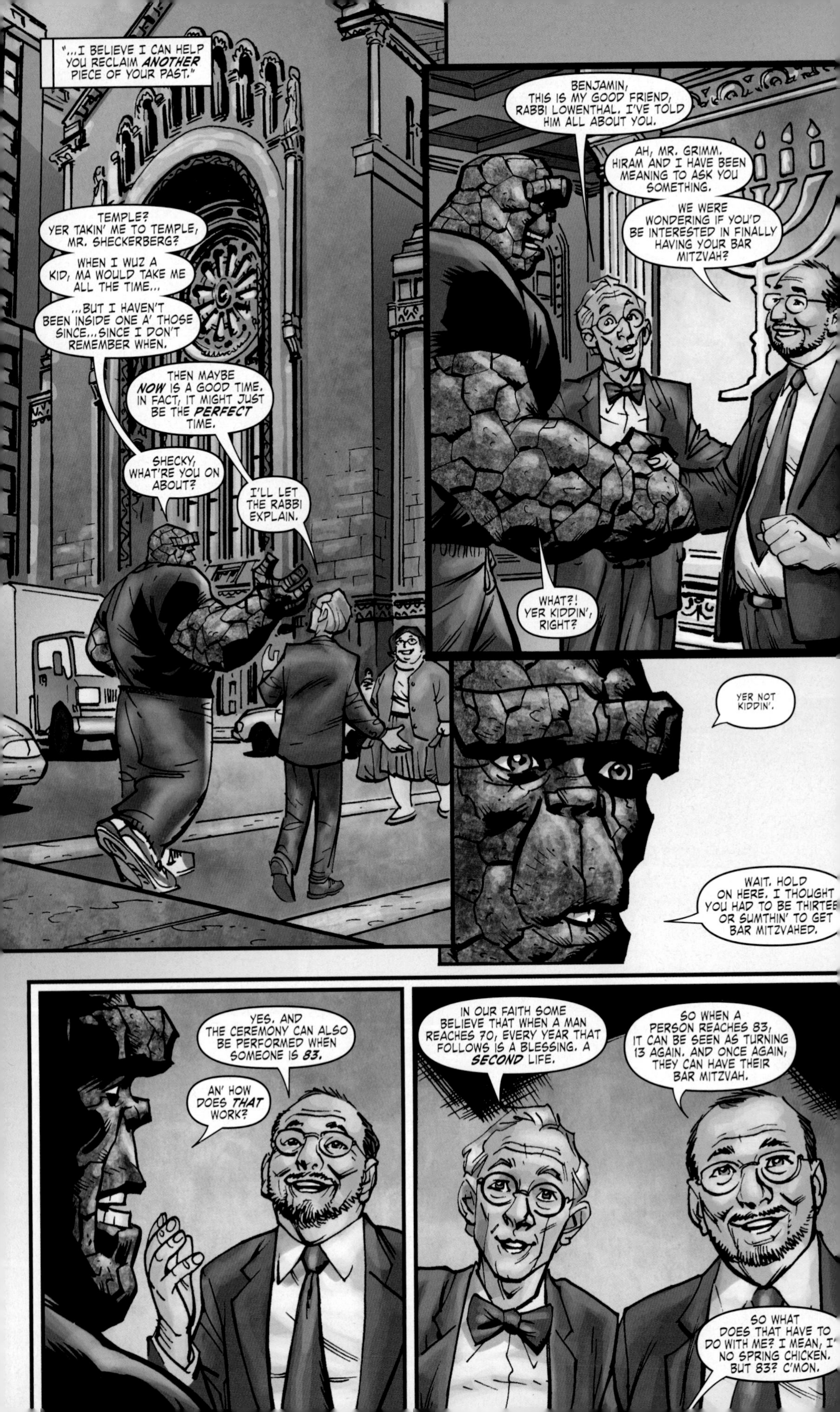
"...I BELIEVE I CAN HELP YOU RECLAIM ANOTHER PIECE OF YOUR PAST."
TEMPLE? YER TAKIN' ME TO TEMPLE, MR. SHECKERBERG?
WHEN I WUZ A KID, MA WOULD TAKE ME ALL THE TIME...
...BUT I HAVEN'T BEEN INSIDE ONE A' THOSE SINCE...SINCE I DON'T REMEMBER WHEN.
THEN MAYBE NOW IS A GOOD TIME. IN FACT, IT MIGHT JUST BE THE PERFECT TIME.
SHECKY, WHAT'RE YOU ON ABOUT?
I'LL LET THE RABBI EXPLAIN.
BENJAMIN, THIS IS MY GOOD FRIEND, RABBI LOWENTHAL. I'VE TOLD HIM ALL ABOUT YOU.
AH, MR. GRIMM. HIRAM AND I HAVE BEEN MEANING TO ASK YOU SOMETHING.
WE WERE WONDERING IF YOU'D BE INTERESTED IN FINALLY HAVING YOUR BAR MITZVAH?
WHAT?! YER KIDDIN', RIGHT?
YER NOT KIDDIN'.
WAIT. HOLD ON HERE. I THOUGHT YOU HAD TO BE THIRTEE OR SUMTHIN' TO GET BAR MITZVAHED.
YES. AND THE CEREMONY CAN ALSO BE PERFORMED WHEN SOMEONE IS 83.
AN' HOW DOES THAT WORK?
IN OUR FAITH SOME BELIEVE THAT WHEN A MAN REACHES 70, EVERY YEAR THAT FOLLOWS IS A BLESSING. A SECOND LIFE.
SO WHEN A PERSON REACHES 83, IT CAN BE SEEN AS TURNING 13 AGAIN. AND ONCE AGAIN, THEY CAN HAVE THEIR BAR MITZVAH.
SO WHAT DOES THAT HAVE TO DO WITH ME? I MEAN, I' NO SPRING CHICKEN. BUT 83? C'MON.

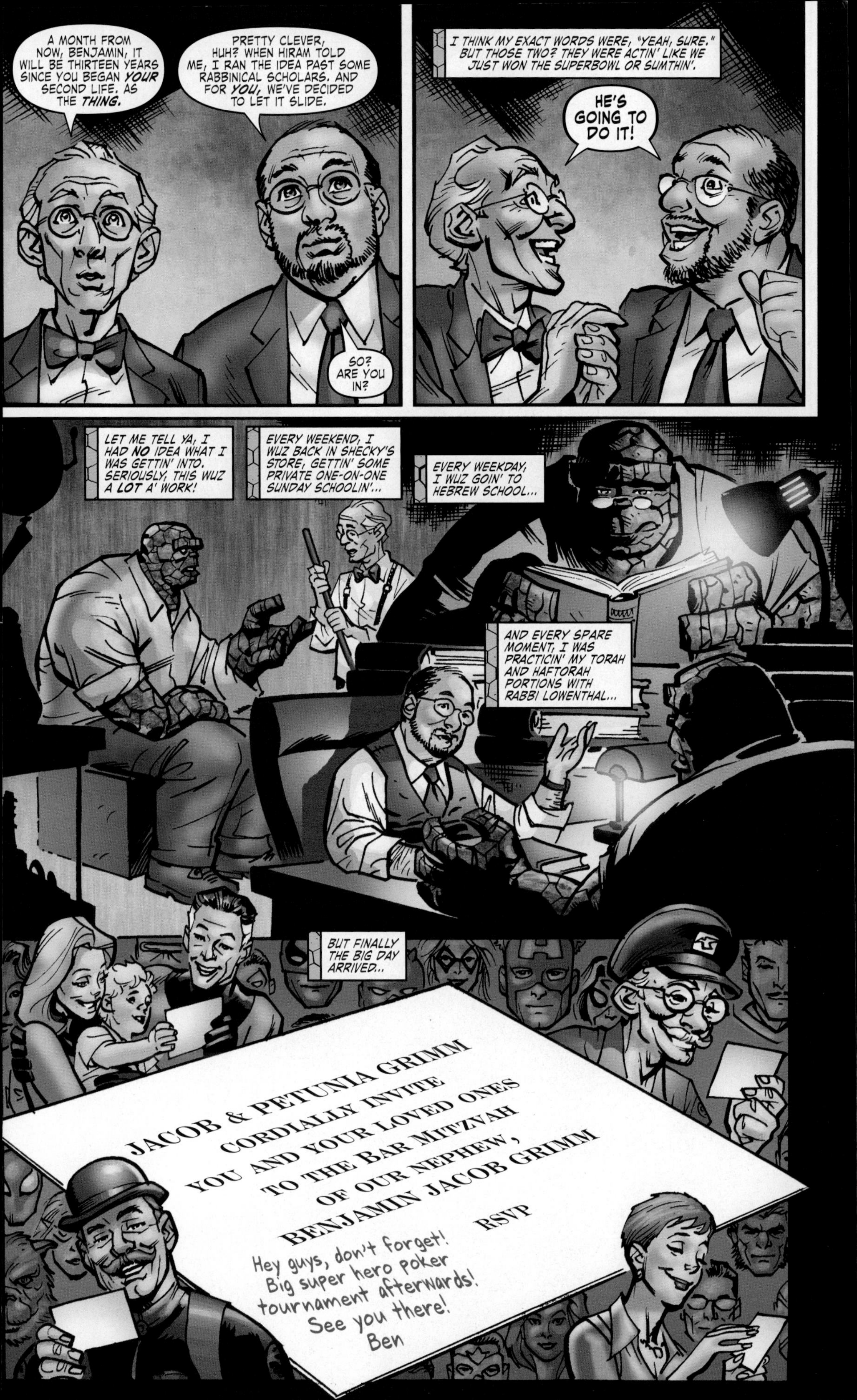

A MONTH FROM NOW, BENJAMIN, IT WILL BE THIRTEEN YEARS SINCE YOU BEGAN YOUR SECOND LIFE. AS THE THING.
PRETTY CLEVER, HUH? WHEN HIRAM TOLD ME, I RAN THE IDEA PAST SOME RABBINICAL SCHOLARS. AND FOR YOU, WE'VE DECIDED TO LET IT SLIDE.
SO? ARE YOU IN?
I THINK MY EXACT WORDS WERE, "YEAH, SURE." BUT THOSE TWO? THEY WERE ACTIN' LIKE WE JUST WON THE SUPERBOWL OR SUMTHIN'.
HE'S GOING TO DO IT!
LET ME TELL YA, I HAD NO IDEA WHAT I WAS GETTIN' INTO. SERIOUSLY, THIS WUZ A LOT A' WORK!
EVERY WEEKEND, I WUZ BACK IN SHECKY'S STORE, GETTIN' SOME PRIVATE ONE-ON-ONE SUNDAY SCHOOLIN'...
EVERY WEEKDAY, I WUZ GOIN' TO HEBREW SCHOOL...
AND EVERY SPARE MOMENT, I WAS PRACTICIN' MY TORAH AND HAFTORAH PORTIONS WITH RABBI LOWENTHAL...
BUT FINALLY THE BIG DAY ARRIVED...
JACOB & PETUNIA GRIMM
CORDIALLY INVITE
YOU AND YOUR LOVED ONES
TO THE BAR MITZVAH
OF OUR NEPHEW,
BENJAMIN JACOB GRIMM
RSVP
Hey guys, don't forget! Big super hero poker tournament afterwards! See you there! Ben

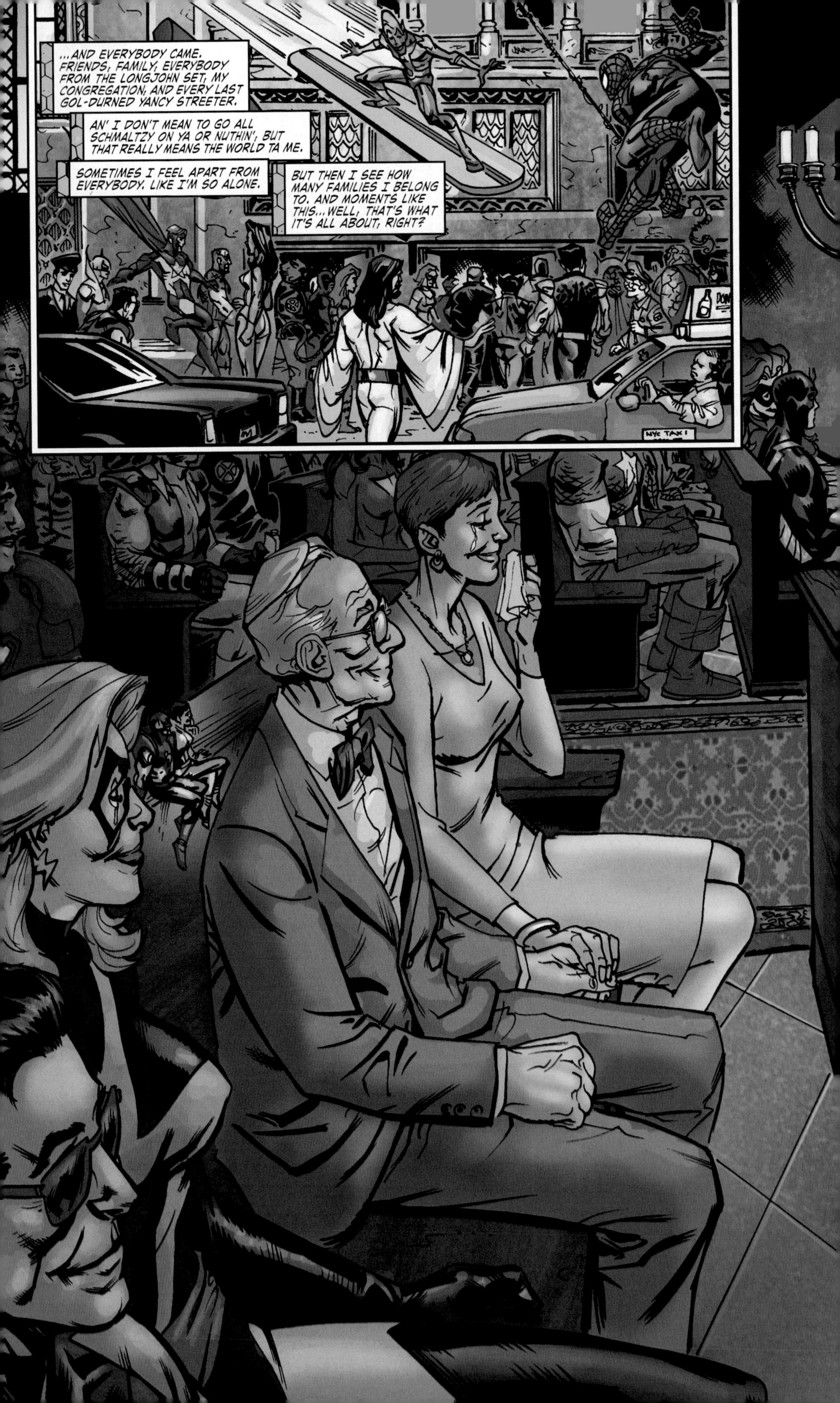
...AND EVERYBODY CAME. FRIENDS, FAMILY, EVERYBODY FROM THE LONGJOHN SET, MY CONGREGATION, AND EVERY LAST GOL-DURNED YANCY STREETER.
AN' I DON'T MEAN TO GO ALL SCHMALTZY ON YA OR NUTHIN', BUT THAT REALLY MEANS THE WORLD TA ME.
SOMETIMES I FEEL APART FROM EVERYBODY. LIKE I'M SO ALONE.
BUT THEN I SEE HOW MANY FAMILIES I BELONG TO. AND MOMENTS LIKE THIS...WELL, THAT'S WHAT IT'S ALL ABOUT, RIGHT?
NYC TAXI

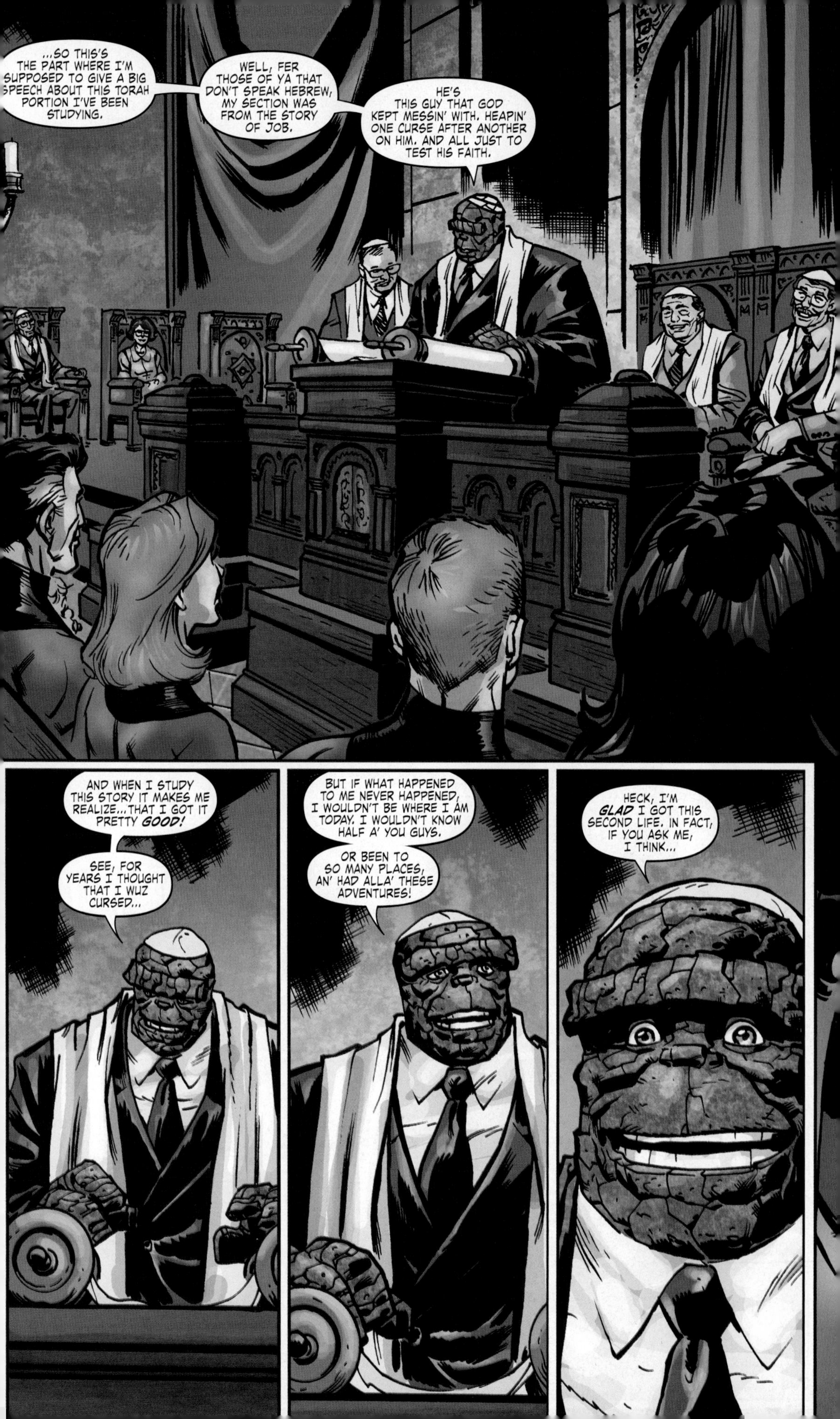
...SO THIS'S THE PART WHERE I'M SUPPOSED TO GIVE A BIG SPEECH ABOUT THIS TORAH PORTION I'VE BEEN STUDYING.
WELL, FER THOSE OF YA THAT DON'T SPEAK HEBREW, MY SECTION WAS FROM THE STORY OF JOB.
HE'S THIS GUY THAT GOD KEPT MESSIN' WITH. HEAPIN' ONE CURSE AFTER ANOTHER ON HIM. AND ALL JUST TO TEST HIS FAITH.
AND WHEN I STUDY THIS STORY IT MAKES ME REALIZE...THAT I GOT IT PRETTY ***GOOD!***
SEE, FOR YEARS I THOUGHT THAT I WUZ CURSED...
BUT IF WHAT HAPPENED TO ME NEVER HAPPENED, I WOULDN'T BE WHERE I AM TODAY. I WOULDN'T KNOW HALF A' YOU GUYS.
OR BEEN TO SO MANY PLACES, AN' HAD ALLA' THESE ADVENTURES!
HECK, I'M ***GLAD*** I GOT THIS SECOND LIFE. IN FACT, IF YOU ASK ME, I THINK...

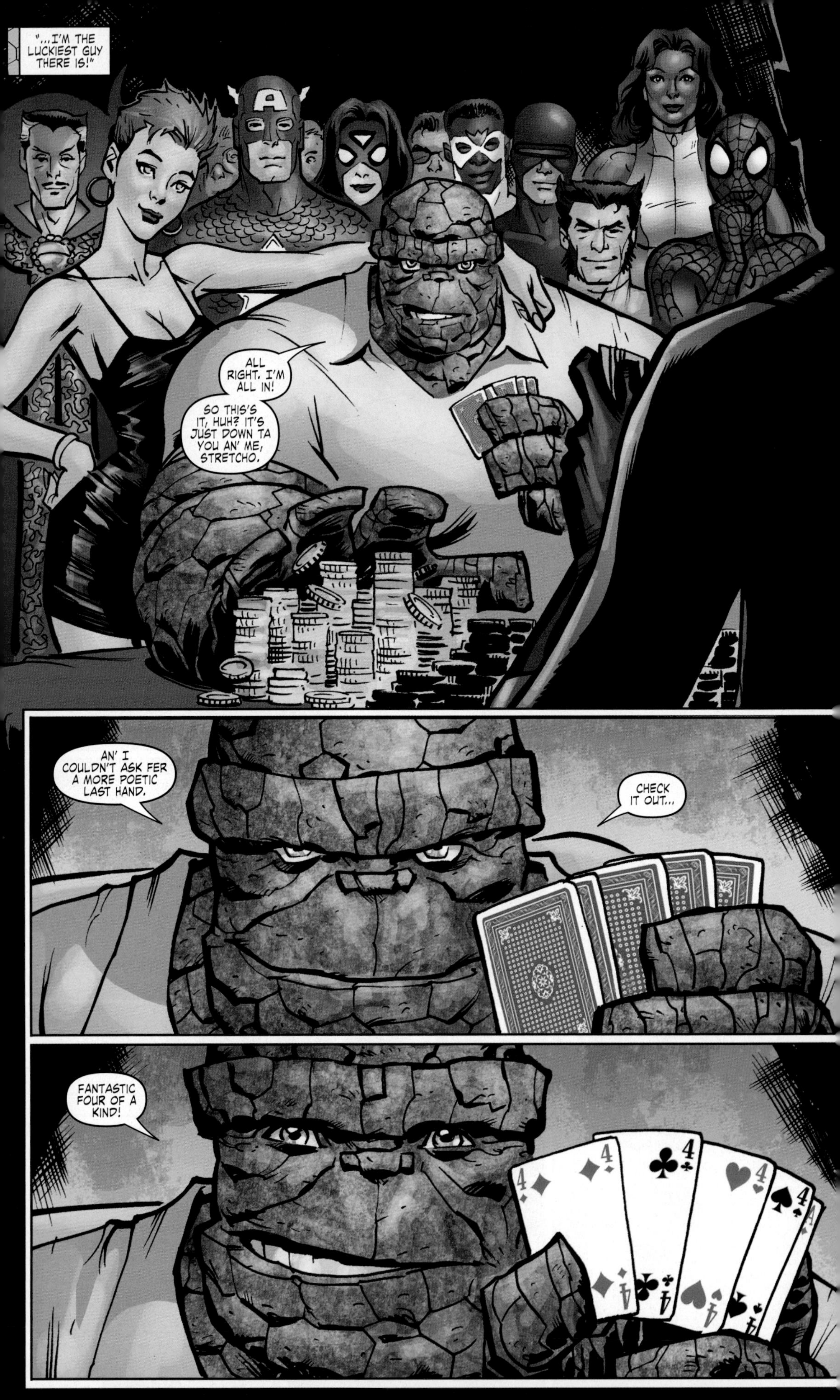
"...I'M THE LUCKIEST GUY THERE IS!"
ALL RIGHT. I'M ALL IN!
SO THIS'S IT, HUH? IT'S JUST DOWN TA YOU AN' ME, STRETCHO.
AN' I COULDN'T ASK FER A MORE POETIC LAST HAND.
CHECK IT OUT...
FANTASTIC FOUR OF A KIND!

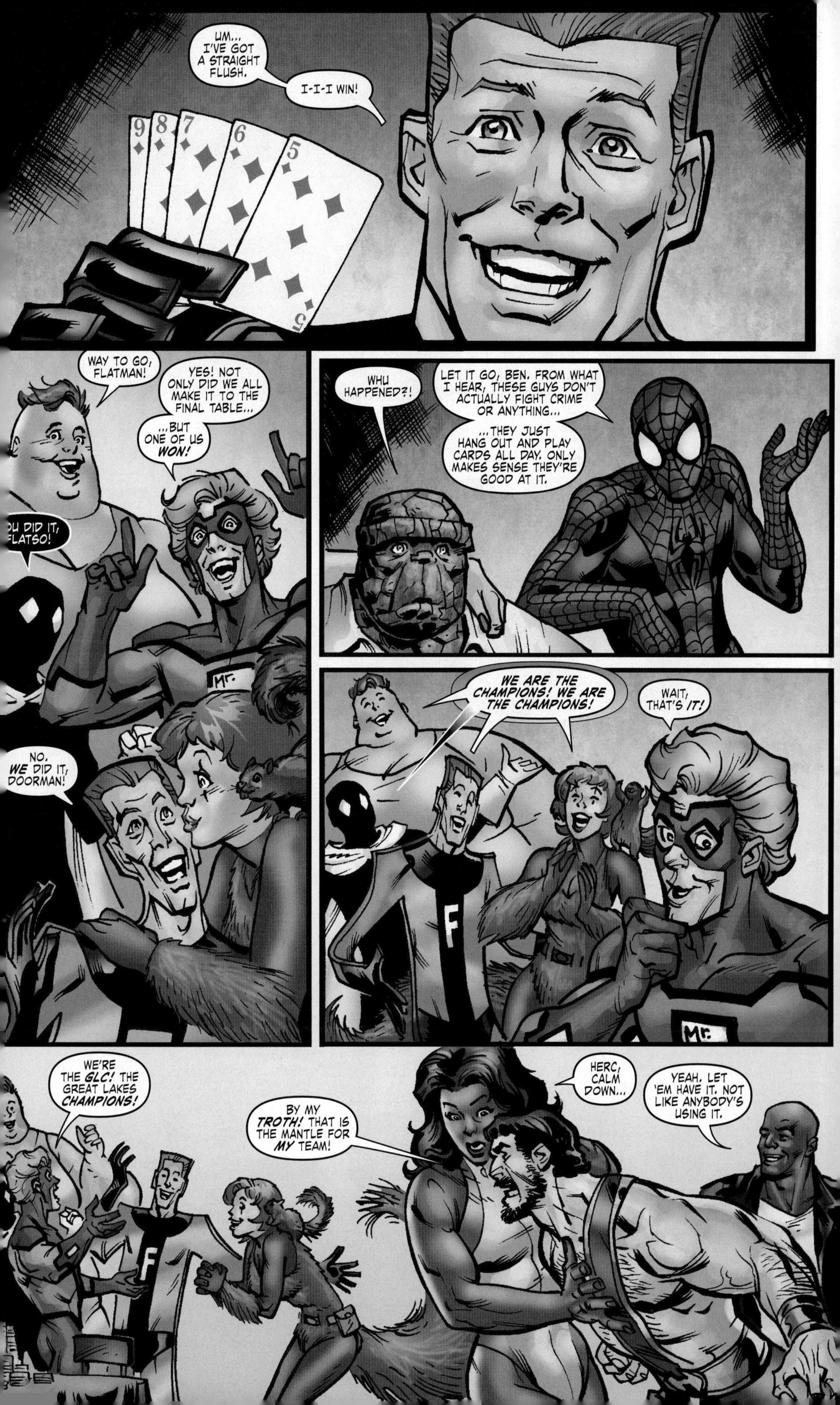
UM... I'VE GOT A STRAIGHT FLUSH.
I-I-I WIN!
WAY TO GO, FLATMAN!
YES! NOT ONLY DID WE ALL MAKE IT TO THE FINAL TABLE...
...BUT ONE OF US WON!
U DID IT, FLATSO!
NO. WE DID IT, DOORMAN!
WHU HAPPENED?!
LET IT GO, BEN. FROM WHAT I HEAR, THESE GUYS DON'T ACTUALLY FIGHT CRIME OR ANYTHING...
...THEY JUST HANG OUT AND PLAY CARDS ALL DAY. ONLY MAKES SENSE THEY'RE GOOD AT IT.
WE ARE THE CHAMPIONS! WE ARE THE CHAMPIONS!
WAIT, THAT'S IT!
WE'RE THE GLC! THE GREAT LAKES CHAMPIONS!
BY MY TROTH! THAT IS THE MANTLE FOR MY TEAM!
HERC, CALM DOWN...
YEAH. LET 'EM HAVE IT. NOT LIKE ANYBODY'S USING IT.

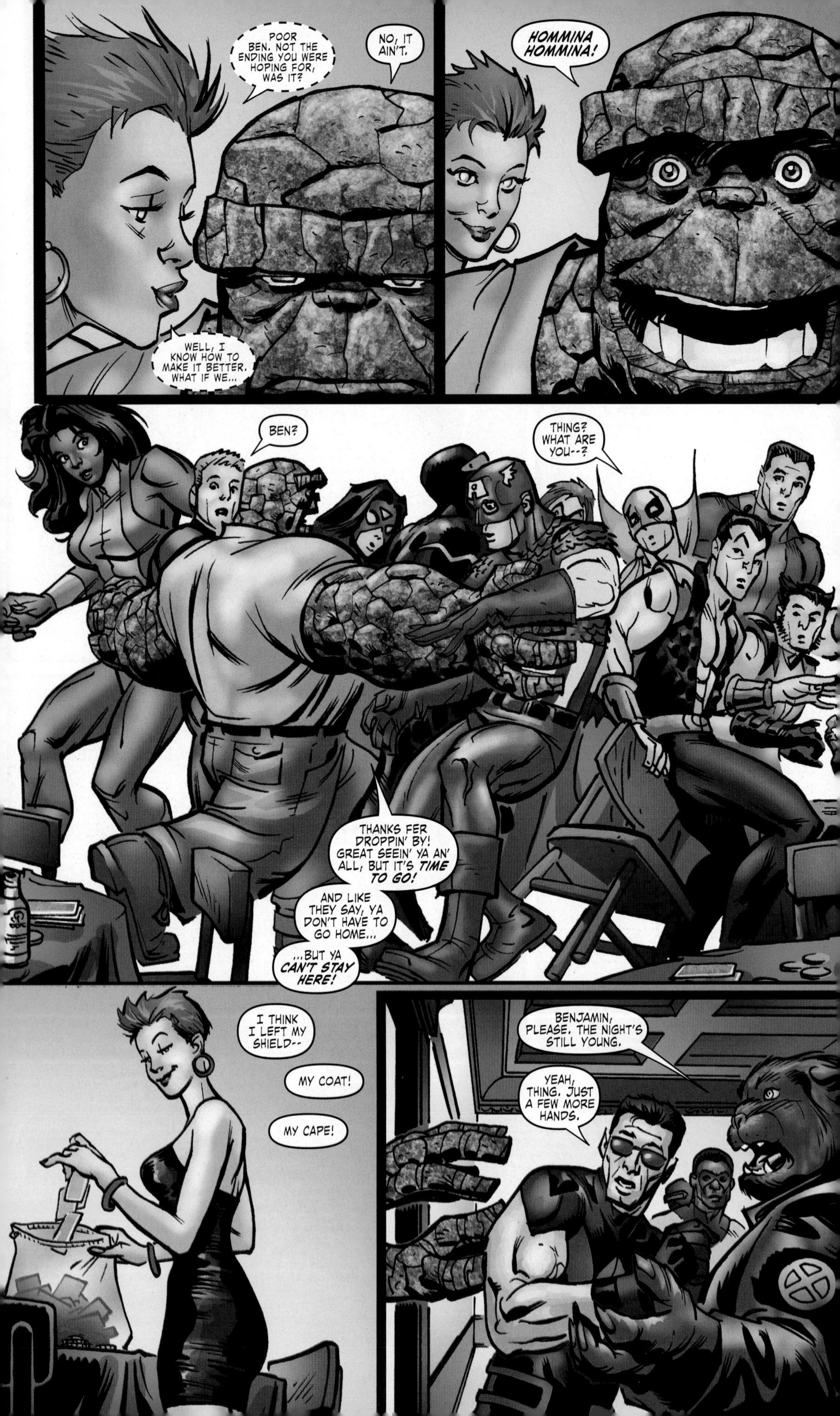
POOR BEN. NOT THE ENDING YOU WERE HOPING FOR, WAS IT?
NO, IT AIN'T.
WELL, I KNOW HOW TO MAKE IT BETTER. WHAT IF WE...
HOMMINA HOMMINA!
BEN?
THING? WHAT ARE YOU--?
THANKS FER DROPPIN' BY! GREAT SEEIN' YA AN' ALL, BUT IT'S TIME TO GO!
AND LIKE THEY SAY, YA DON'T HAVE TO GO HOME...
...BUT YA CAN'T STAY HERE!
I THINK I LEFT MY SHIELD--
MY COAT!
MY CAPE!
BENJAMIN, PLEASE. THE NIGHT'S STILL YOUNG.
YEAH, THING. JUST A FEW MORE HANDS.

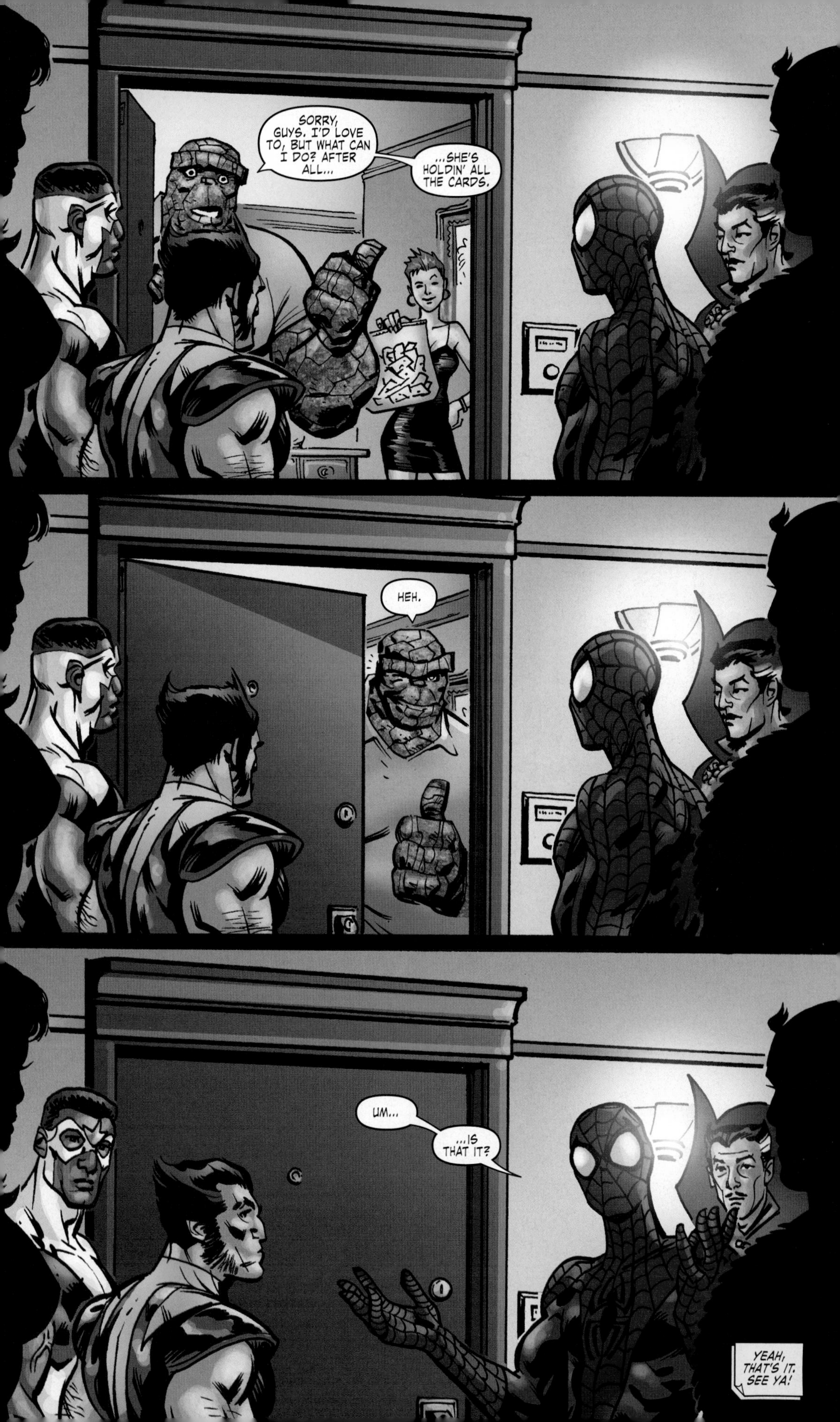
SORRY, GUYS. I'D LOVE TO, BUT WHAT CAN I DO? AFTER ALL...
...SHE'S HOLDIN' ALL THE CARDS.
HEH.
UM...
...IS THAT IT?
YEAH, THAT'S IT. SEE YA!

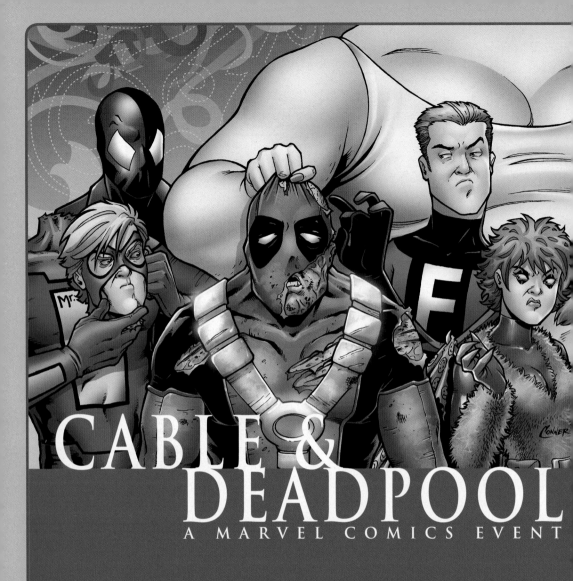

CABLE & DEADPOOL

A MARVEL COMICS EVENT

CIVIL WAR

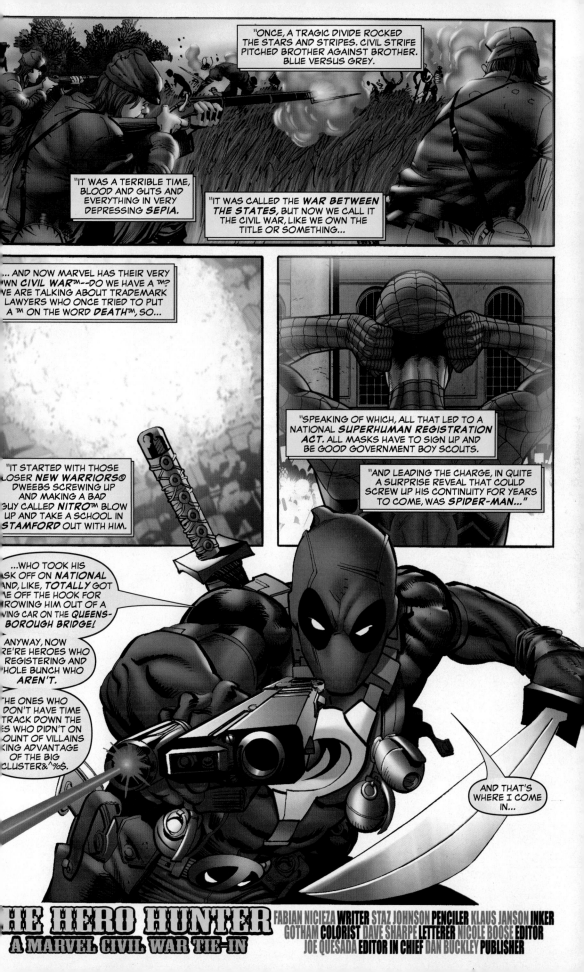

"ONCE, A TRAGIC DIVIDE ROCKED THE STARS AND STRIPES. CIVIL STRIFE PITCHED BROTHER AGAINST BROTHER. BLUE VERSUS GREY.

"IT WAS A TERRIBLE TIME, BLOOD AND GUTS AND EVERYTHING IN VERY DEPRESSING *SEPIA.*

"IT WAS CALLED THE *WAR BETWEEN THE STATES,* BUT NOW WE CALL IT THE CIVIL WAR, LIKE WE OWN THE TITLE OR SOMETHING...

... AND NOW MARVEL HAS THEIR VERY OWN *CIVIL WAR*™--DO WE HAVE A ™? WE ARE TALKING ABOUT TRADEMARK LAWYERS WHO ONCE TRIED TO PUT A ™ ON THE WORD *DEATH*™, SO...

"IT STARTED WITH THOSE LOSER *NEW WARRIORS*® DWEEBS SCREWING UP AND MAKING A BAD GUY CALLED *NITRO*™ BLOW UP AND TAKE A SCHOOL IN *STAMFORD* OUT WITH HIM.

"SPEAKING OF WHICH, ALL THAT LED TO A NATIONAL *SUPERHUMAN REGISTRATION ACT.* ALL MASKS HAVE TO SIGN UP AND BE GOOD GOVERNMENT BOY SCOUTS.

"AND LEADING THE CHARGE, IN QUITE A SURPRISE REVEAL THAT COULD SCREW UP HIS CONTINUITY FOR YEARS TO COME, WAS *SPIDER-MAN...*"

...WHO TOOK HIS MASK OFF ON *NATIONAL* TV AND, LIKE, *TOTALLY* GOT ME OFF THE HOOK FOR THROWING HIM OUT OF A MOVING CAR ON THE *QUEENS-BOROUGH BRIDGE!*

ANYWAY, NOW WE'RE HEROES WHO ARE REGISTERING AND A WHOLE BUNCH WHO *AREN'T.*

THE ONES WHO DON'T HAVE TIME TRACK DOWN THE ONES WHO DIDN'T ON ACCOUNT OF VILLAINS TAKING ADVANTAGE OF THE BIG CLUSTER&^%$.

AND THAT'S WHERE I COME IN...

HE HERO HUNTER
A MARVEL CIVIL WAR TIE-IN

FABIAN NICIEZA **WRITER** STAZ JOHNSON **PENCILER** KLAUS JANSON **INKER** GOTHAM **COLORIST** DAVE SHARPE **LETTERER** NICOLE BOOSE **EDITOR** JOE QUESADA **EDITOR IN CHIEF** DAN BUCKLEY **PUBLISHER**

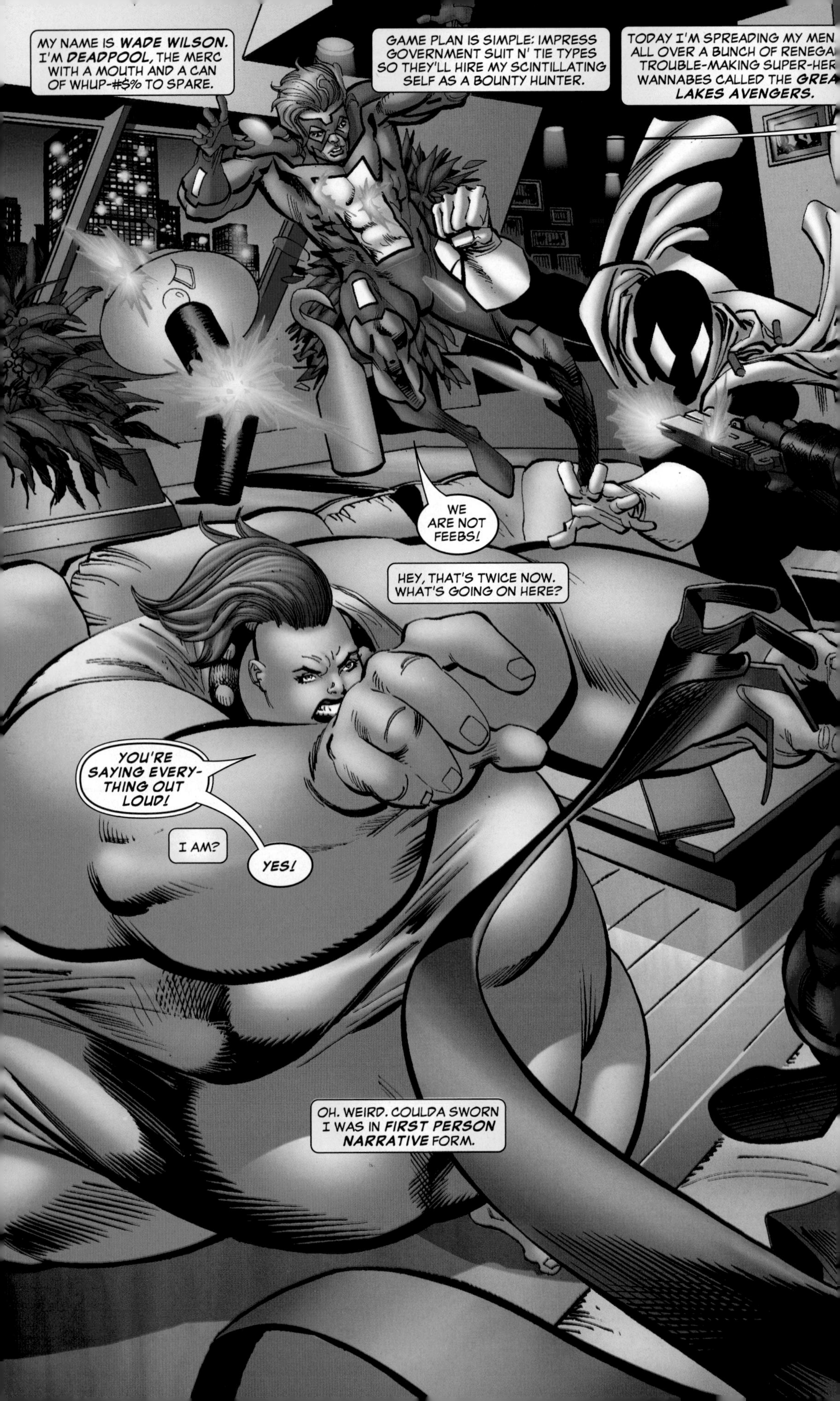

MY NAME IS WADE WILSON. I'M DEADPOOL, THE MERC WITH A MOUTH AND A CAN OF WHUP-#$% TO SPARE.
GAME PLAN IS SIMPLE: IMPRESS GOVERNMENT SUIT N' TIE TYPES SO THEY'LL HIRE MY SCINTILLATING SELF AS A BOUNTY HUNTER.
TODAY I'M SPREADING MY MEN ALL OVER A BUNCH OF RENEGA TROUBLE-MAKING SUPER-HER WANNABES CALLED THE GREA LAKES AVENGERS.
WE ARE NOT FEEBS!
HEY, THAT'S TWICE NOW. WHAT'S GOING ON HERE?
YOU'RE SAYING EVERY-THING OUT LOUD!
I AM?
YES!
OH. WEIRD. COULDA SWORN I WAS IN FIRST PERSON NARRATIVE FORM.

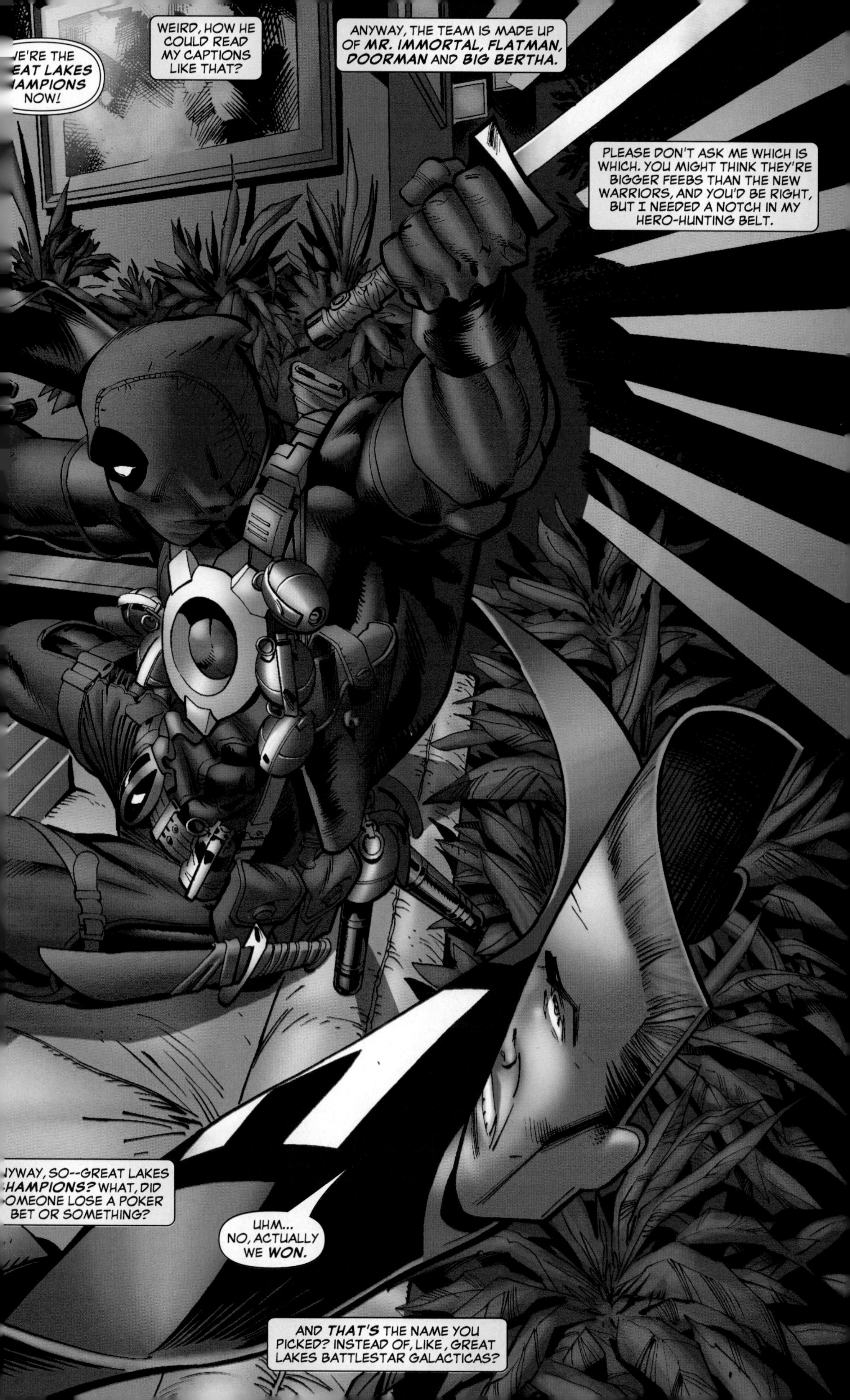
E'RE THE EAT LAKES AMPIONS NOW!
WEIRD, HOW HE COULD READ MY CAPTIONS LIKE THAT?
ANYWAY, THE TEAM IS MADE UP OF MR. IMMORTAL, FLATMAN, DOORMAN AND BIG BERTHA.
PLEASE DON'T ASK ME WHICH IS WHICH. YOU MIGHT THINK THEY'RE BIGGER FEEBS THAN THE NEW WARRIORS, AND YOU'D BE RIGHT, BUT I NEEDED A NOTCH IN MY HERO-HUNTING BELT.
NYWAY, SO--GREAT LAKES HAMPIONS? WHAT, DID OMEONE LOSE A POKER BET OR SOMETHING?
UHM... NO, ACTUALLY WE WON.
AND THAT'S THE NAME YOU PICKED? INSTEAD OF, LIKE, GREAT LAKES BATTLESTAR GALACTICAS?

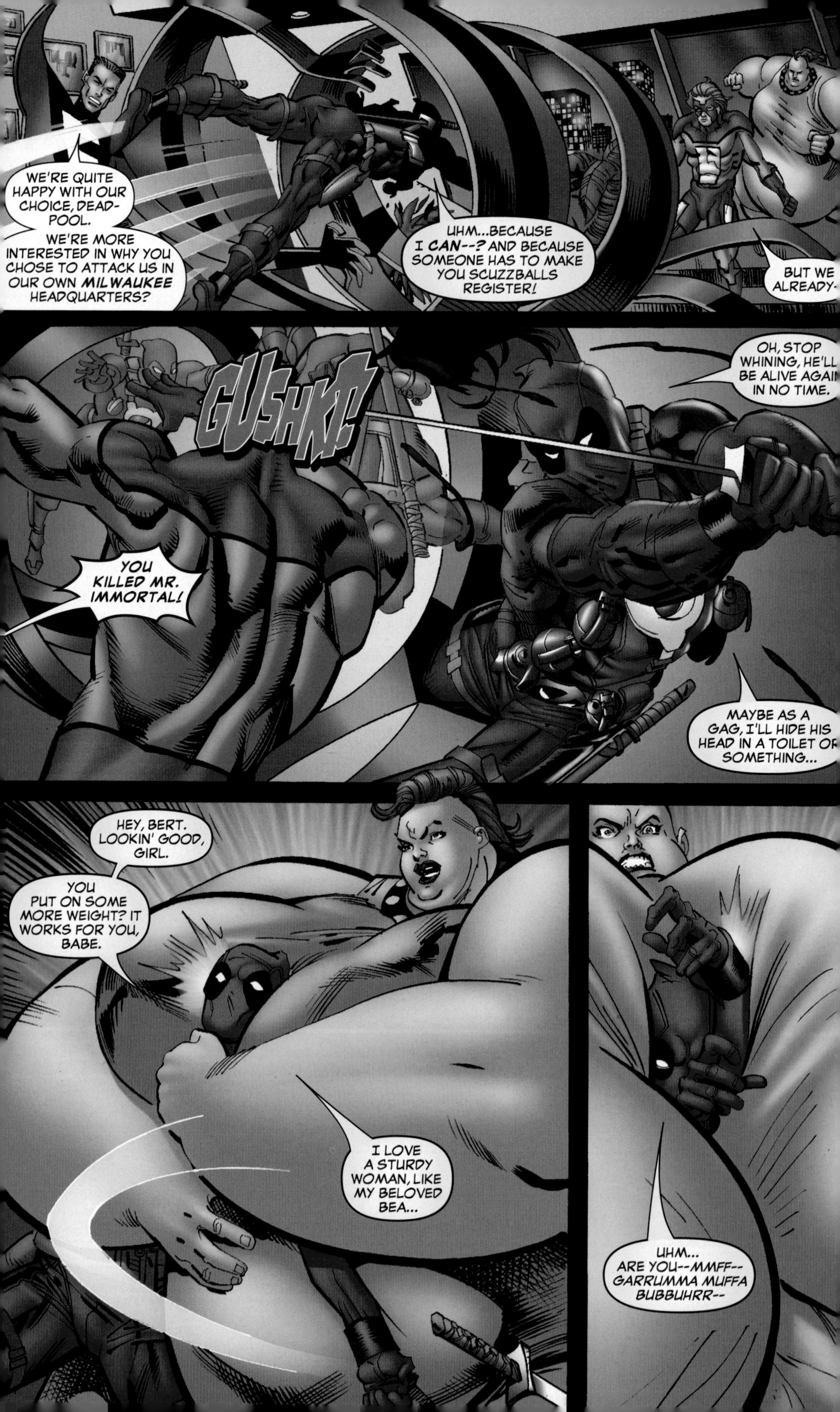
WE'RE QUITE HAPPY WITH OUR CHOICE, DEAD-POOL.
WE'RE MORE INTERESTED IN WHY YOU CHOSE TO ATTACK US IN OUR OWN MILWAUKEE HEADQUARTERS?
UHM...BECAUSE I CAN--? AND BECAUSE SOMEONE HAS TO MAKE YOU SCUZZBALLS REGISTER!
BUT WE ALREADY-
GUSHK!
YOU KILLED MR. IMMORTAL!
OH, STOP WHINING, HE'LL BE ALIVE AGAI IN NO TIME.
MAYBE AS A GAG, I'LL HIDE HIS HEAD IN A TOILET OR SOMETHING...
HEY, BERT. LOOKIN' GOOD, GIRL.
YOU PUT ON SOME MORE WEIGHT? IT WORKS FOR YOU, BABE.
I LOVE A STURDY WOMAN, LIKE MY BELOVED BEA...
UHM... ARE YOU--MMFF-- GARRUMMA MUFFA BUBBUHRR--

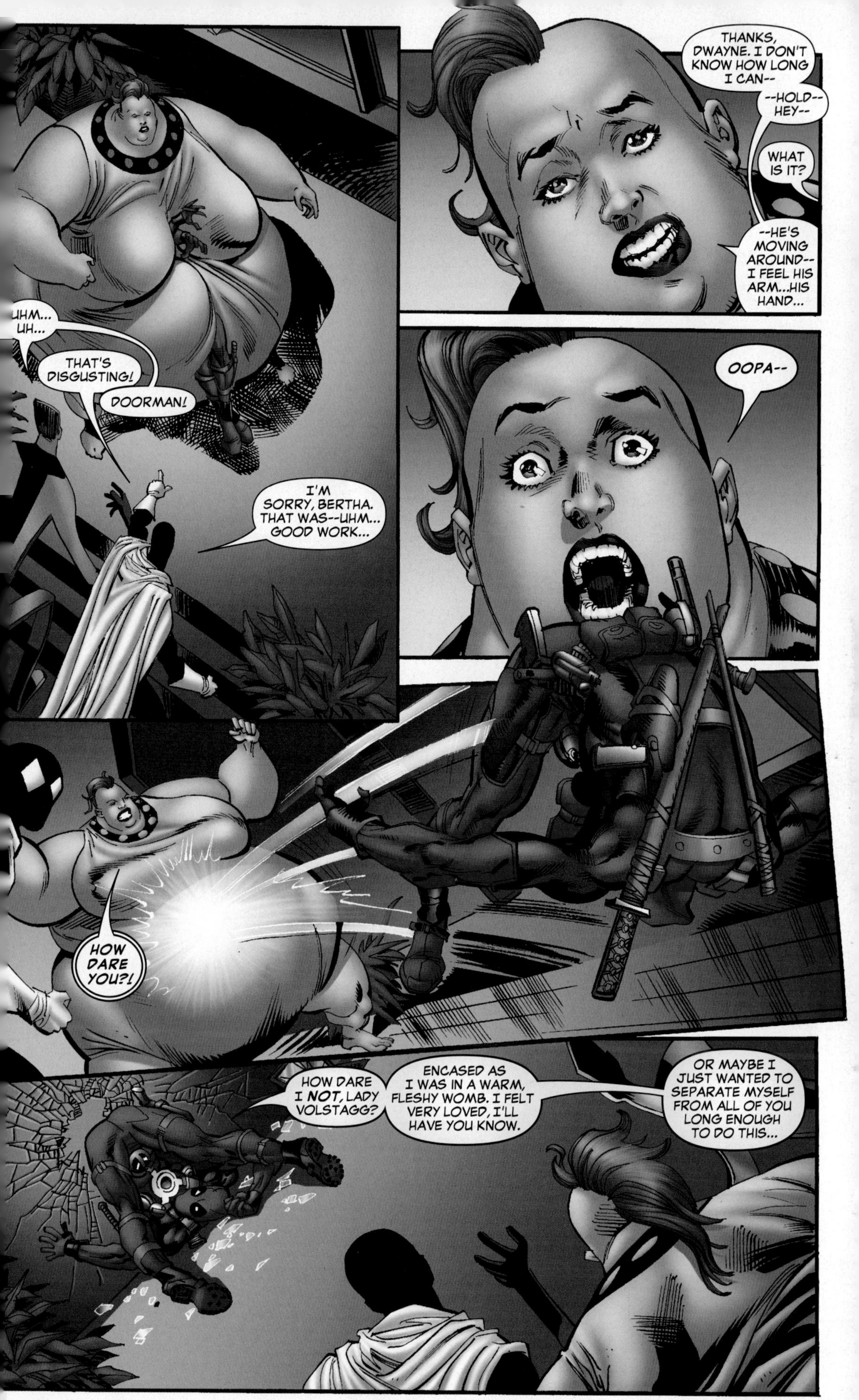
THANKS, DWAYNE. I DON'T KNOW HOW LONG I CAN--
--HOLD--
HEY--
WHAT IS IT?
--HE'S MOVING AROUND--I FEEL HIS ARM...HIS HAND...
UHM... UH...
THAT'S DISGUSTING!
DOORMAN!
I'M SORRY, BERTHA. THAT WAS--UHM... GOOD WORK...
OOPA--
HOW DARE YOU?!
HOW DARE I NOT, LADY VOLSTAGG?
ENCASED AS I WAS IN A WARM, FLESHY WOMB. I FELT VERY LOVED, I'LL HAVE YOU KNOW.
OR MAYBE I JUST WANTED TO SEPARATE MYSELF FROM ALL OF YOU LONG ENOUGH TO DO THIS...

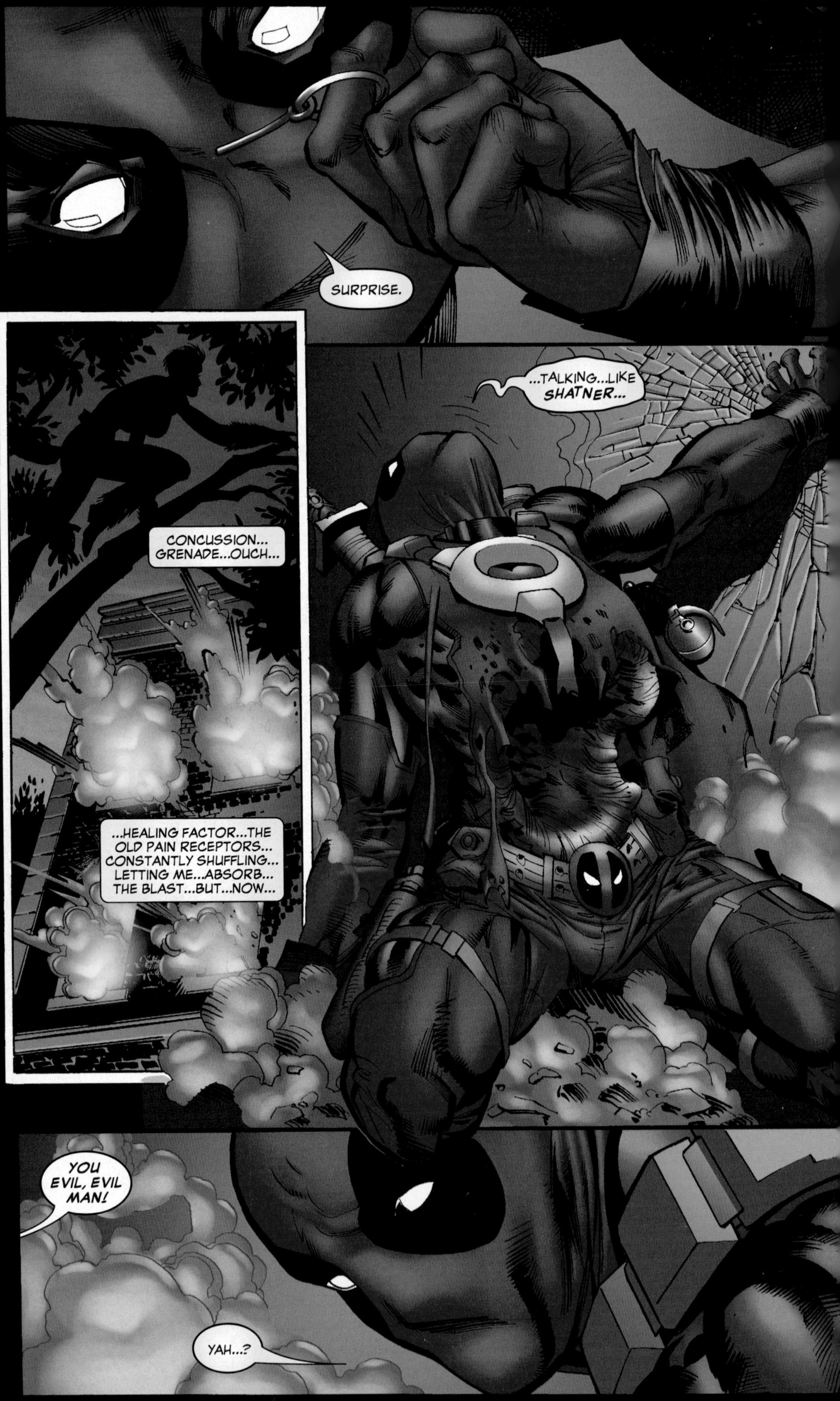
SURPRISE.
...TALKING...LIKE SHATNER...
CONCUSSION... GRENADE...OUCH...
...HEALING FACTOR...THE OLD PAIN RECEPTORS... CONSTANTLY SHUFFLING... LETTING ME...ABSORB... THE BLAST...BUT...NOW...
YOU EVIL, EVIL MAN!
YAH...?

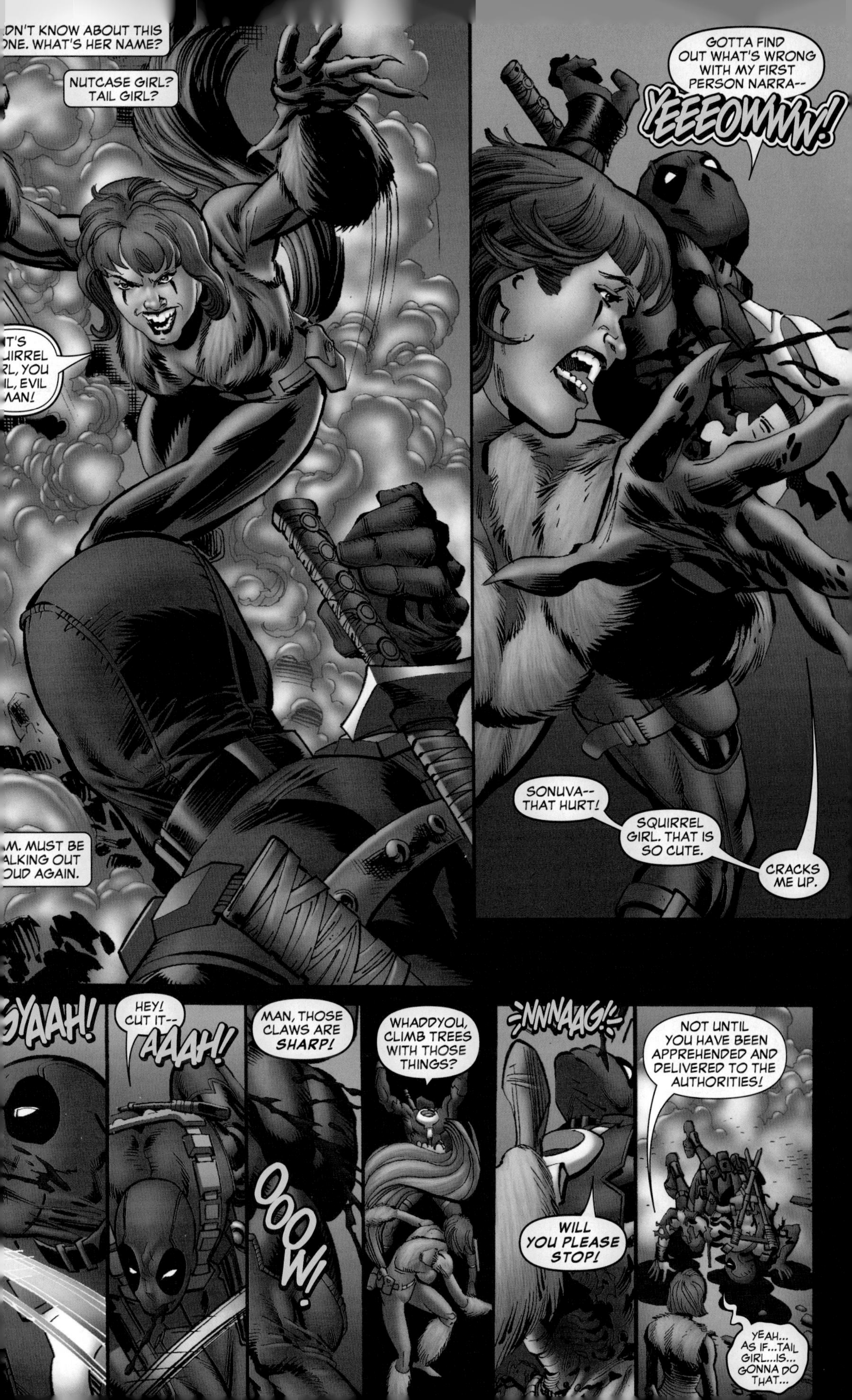

DN'T KNOW ABOUT THIS
ONE. WHAT'S HER NAME?
NUTCASE GIRL? TAIL GIRL?
T'S
UIRREL
RL, YOU
IL, EVIL
MAN!
M. MUST BE
ALKING OUT
OUD AGAIN.
GOTTA FIND OUT WHAT'S WRONG WITH MY FIRST PERSON NARRA--
YEEEOWWW!
SONUVA-- THAT HURT!
SQUIRREL GIRL. THAT IS SO CUTE.
CRACKS ME UP.
GYAAH!
HEY! CUT IT--
AAAH!
MAN, THOSE CLAWS ARE SHARP!
OOOW!
WHADDYOU, CLIMB TREES WITH THOSE THINGS?
NNNAAG!
WILL YOU PLEASE STOP!
NOT UNTIL YOU HAVE BEEN APPREHENDED AND DELIVERED TO THE AUTHORITIES!
YEAH... AS IF...TAIL GIRL...IS... GONNA DO THAT...

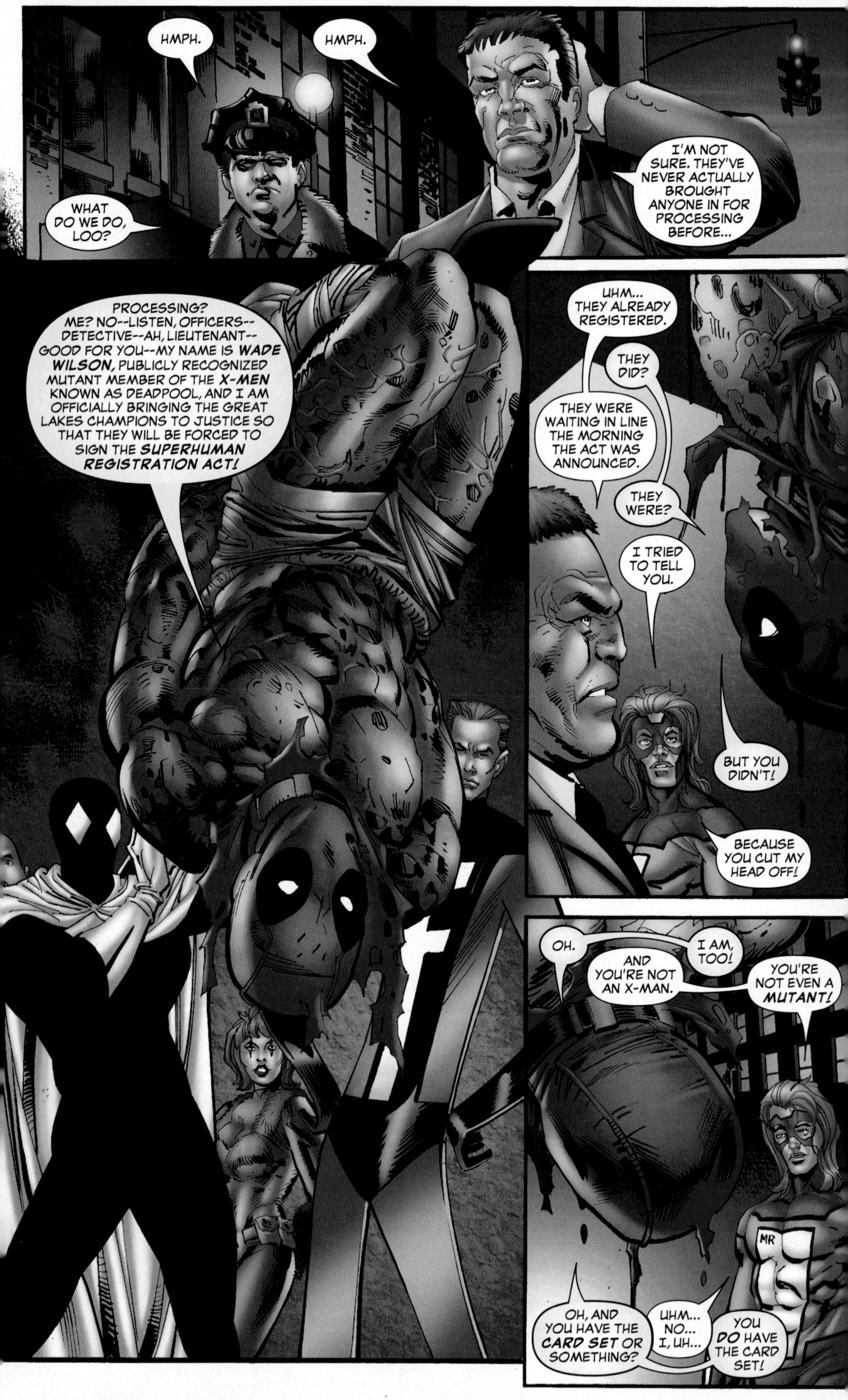
HMPH.
HMPH.
WHAT DO WE DO, LOO?
I'M NOT SURE. THEY'VE NEVER ACTUALLY BROUGHT ANYONE IN FOR PROCESSING BEFORE...
PROCESSING? ME? NO--LISTEN, OFFICERS--DETECTIVE--AH, LIEUTENANT--GOOD FOR YOU--MY NAME IS WADE WILSON, PUBLICLY RECOGNIZED MUTANT MEMBER OF THE X-MEN KNOWN AS DEADPOOL, AND I AM OFFICIALLY BRINGING THE GREAT LAKES CHAMPIONS TO JUSTICE SO THAT THEY WILL BE FORCED TO SIGN THE SUPERHUMAN REGISTRATION ACT!
UHM... THEY ALREADY REGISTERED.
THEY DID?
THEY WERE WAITING IN LINE THE MORNING THE ACT WAS ANNOUNCED.
THEY WERE?
I TRIED TO TELL YOU.
BUT YOU DIDN'T!
BECAUSE YOU CUT MY HEAD OFF!
OH.
I AM, TOO!
AND YOU'RE NOT AN X-MAN.
YOU'RE NOT EVEN A MUTANT!
MR
OH, AND YOU HAVE THE CARD SET OR SOMETHING?
UHM... NO... I, UH...
YOU DO HAVE THE CARD SET!

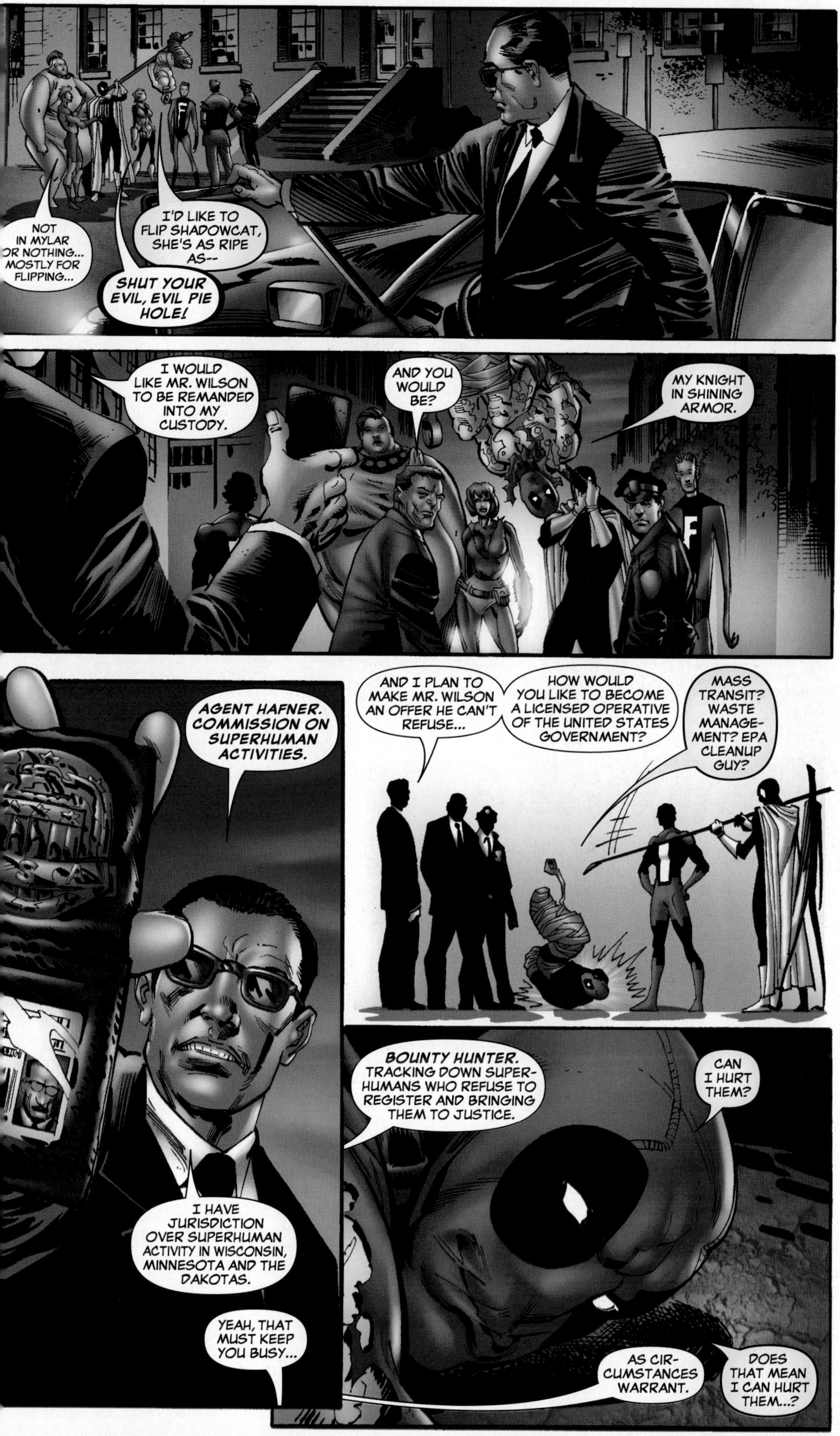
NOT IN MYLAR OR NOTHING... MOSTLY FOR FLIPPING...
I'D LIKE TO FLIP SHADOWCAT, SHE'S AS RIPE AS--
SHUT YOUR EVIL, EVIL PIE HOLE!
I WOULD LIKE MR. WILSON TO BE REMANDED INTO MY CUSTODY.
AND YOU WOULD BE?
MY KNIGHT IN SHINING ARMOR.
AGENT HAFNER. COMMISSION ON SUPERHUMAN ACTIVITIES.
I HAVE JURISDICTION OVER SUPERHUMAN ACTIVITY IN WISCONSIN, MINNESOTA AND THE DAKOTAS.
YEAH, THAT MUST KEEP YOU BUSY...
AND I PLAN TO MAKE MR. WILSON AN OFFER HE CAN'T REFUSE...
HOW WOULD YOU LIKE TO BECOME A LICENSED OPERATIVE OF THE UNITED STATES GOVERNMENT?
MASS TRANSIT? WASTE MANAGEMENT? EPA CLEANUP GUY?
BOUNTY HUNTER. TRACKING DOWN SUPERHUMANS WHO REFUSE TO REGISTER AND BRINGING THEM TO JUSTICE.
CAN I HURT THEM?
AS CIRCUMSTANCES WARRANT.
DOES THAT MEAN I CAN HURT THEM...?

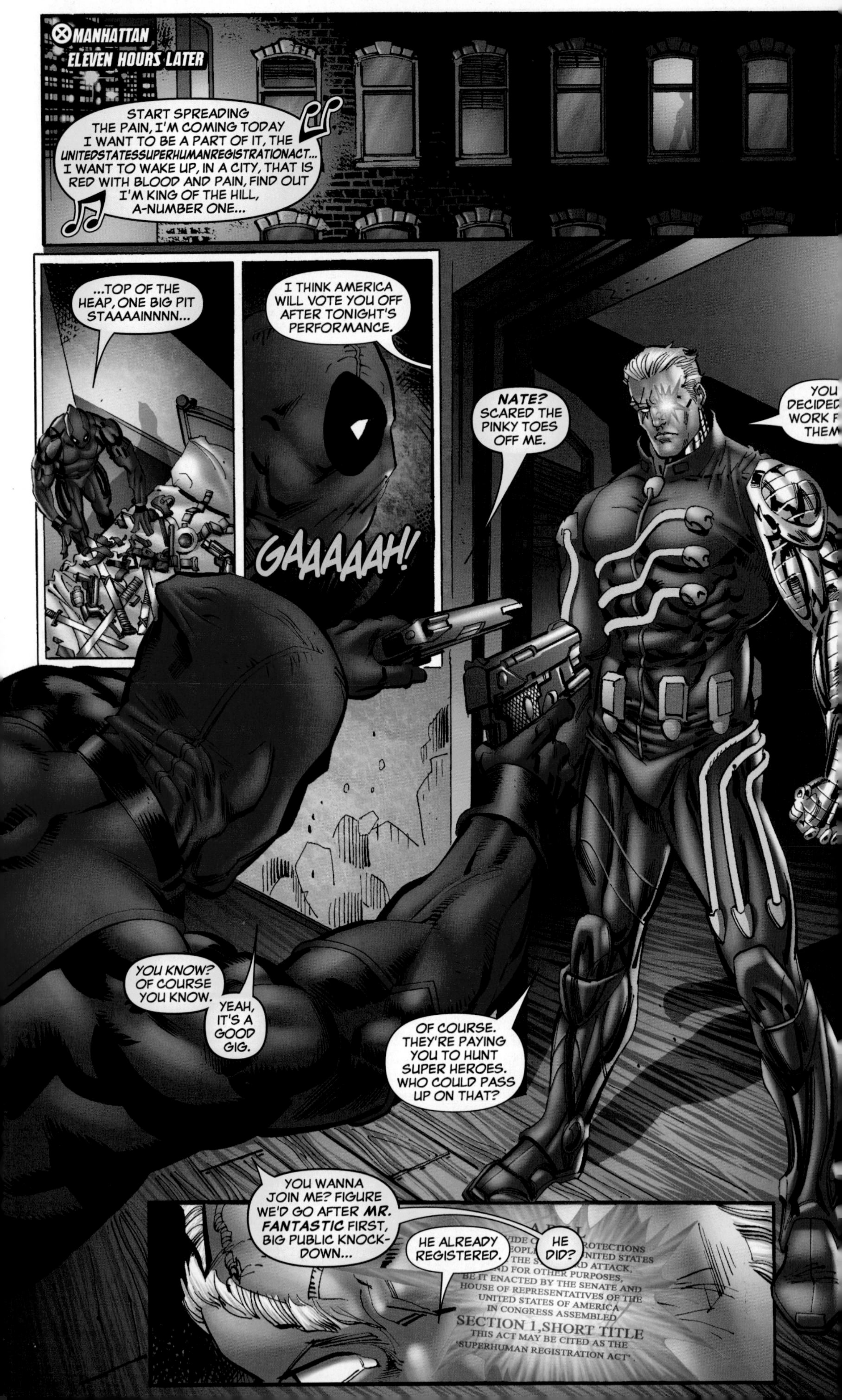
MANHATTAN
ELEVEN HOURS LATER
START SPREADING THE PAIN, I'M COMING TODAY I WANT TO BE A PART OF IT, THE UNITEDSTATESSUPERHUMANREGISTRATIONACT... I WANT TO WAKE UP, IN A CITY, THAT IS RED WITH BLOOD AND PAIN, FIND OUT I'M KING OF THE HILL, A-NUMBER ONE...
...TOP OF THE HEAP, ONE BIG PIT STAAAAINNNN...
I THINK AMERICA WILL VOTE YOU OFF AFTER TONIGHT'S PERFORMANCE.
GAAAAAH!
NATE? SCARED THE PINKY TOES OFF ME.
YOU DECIDED WORK F THEM
YOU KNOW? OF COURSE YOU KNOW.
YEAH, IT'S A GOOD GIG.
OF COURSE. THEY'RE PAYING YOU TO HUNT SUPER HEROES. WHO COULD PASS UP ON THAT?
YOU WANNA JOIN ME? FIGURE WE'D GO AFTER MR. FANTASTIC FIRST, BIG PUBLIC KNOCK-DOWN...
HE ALREADY REGISTERED.
HE DID?
BE IT ENACTED BY THE SENATE AND HOUSE OF REPRESENTATIVES OF THE UNITED STATES OF AMERICA IN CONGRESS ASSEMBLED
SECTION 1, SHORT TITLE
THIS ACT MAY BE CITED AS THE 'SUPERHUMAN REGISTRATION ACT'.

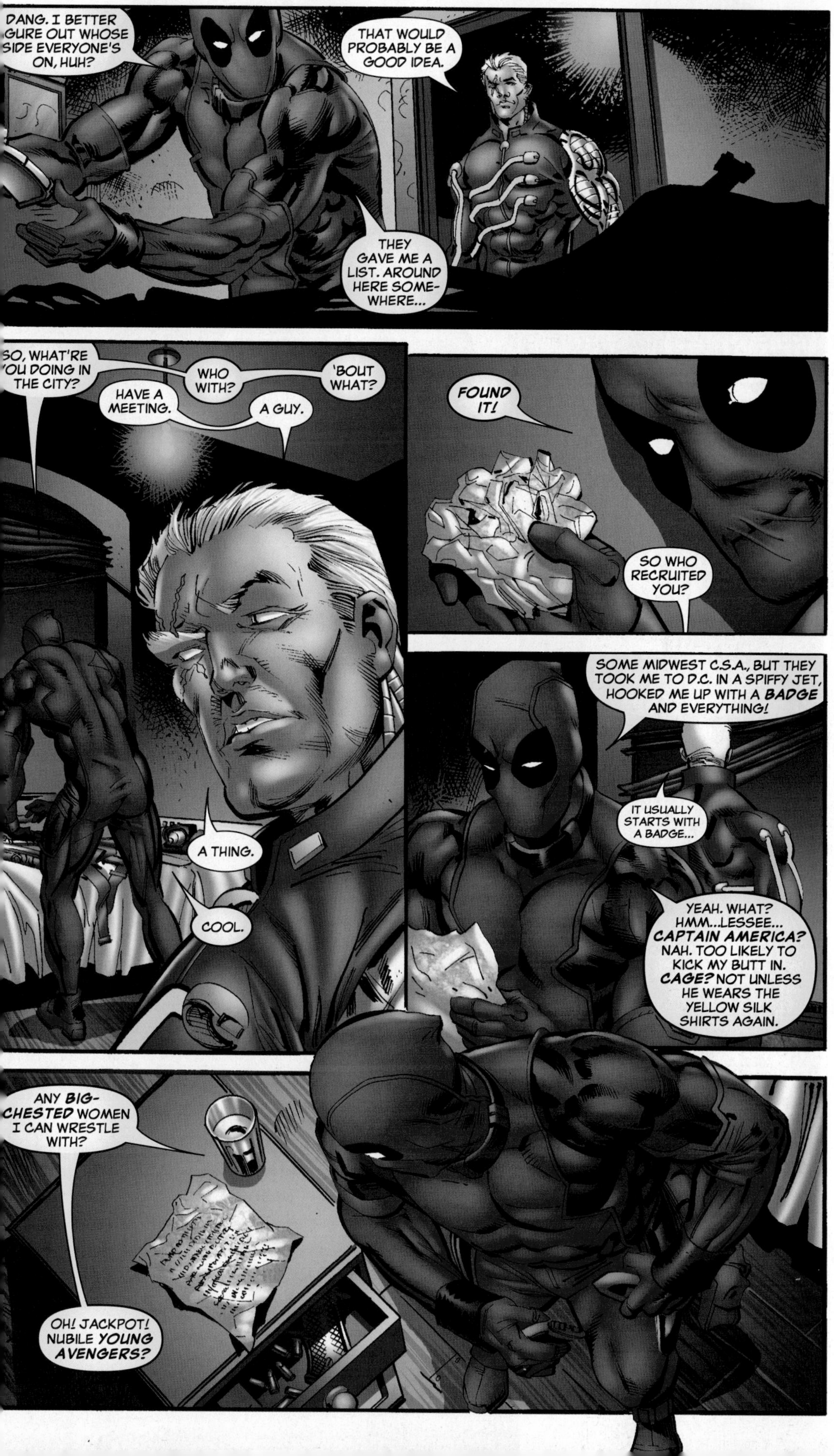
DANG. I BETTER GURE OUT WHOSE SIDE EVERYONE'S ON, HUH?
THAT WOULD PROBABLY BE A GOOD IDEA.
THEY GAVE ME A LIST. AROUND HERE SOME-WHERE...
SO, WHAT'RE YOU DOING IN THE CITY?
HAVE A MEETING.
WHO WITH?
A GUY.
'BOUT WHAT?
A THING.
COOL.
FOUND IT!
SO WHO RECRUITED YOU?
SOME MIDWEST C.S.A., BUT THEY TOOK ME TO D.C. IN A SPIFFY JET, HOOKED ME UP WITH A BADGE AND EVERYTHING!
IT USUALLY STARTS WITH A BADGE...
YEAH. WHAT? HMM...LESSEE... CAPTAIN AMERICA? NAH. TOO LIKELY TO KICK MY BUTT IN. CAGE? NOT UNLESS HE WEARS THE YELLOW SILK SHIRTS AGAIN.
ANY BIG-CHESTED WOMEN I CAN WRESTLE WITH?
OH! JACKPOT! NUBILE YOUNG AVENGERS?

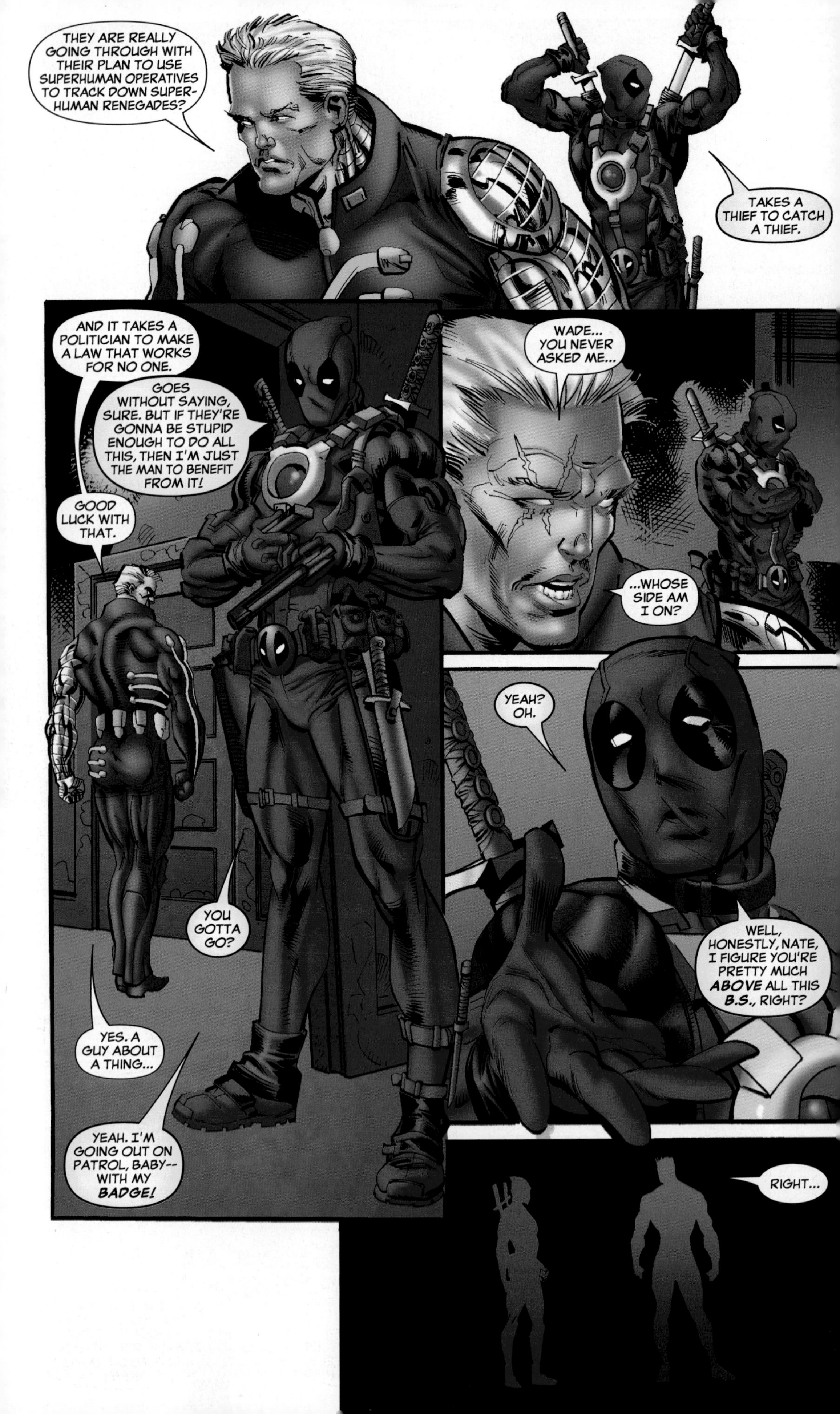
THEY ARE REALLY GOING THROUGH WITH THEIR PLAN TO USE SUPERHUMAN OPERATIVES TO TRACK DOWN SUPER-HUMAN RENEGADES?
TAKES A THIEF TO CATCH A THIEF.
AND IT TAKES A POLITICIAN TO MAKE A LAW THAT WORKS FOR NO ONE.
GOES WITHOUT SAYING, SURE. BUT IF THEY'RE GONNA BE STUPID ENOUGH TO DO ALL THIS, THEN I'M JUST THE MAN TO BENEFIT FROM IT!
GOOD LUCK WITH THAT.
YOU GOTTA GO?
YES. A GUY ABOUT A THING...
YEAH. I'M GOING OUT ON PATROL, BABY-- WITH MY **BADGE!**
WADE... YOU NEVER ASKED ME...
...WHOSE SIDE AM I ON?
YEAH? OH.
WELL, HONESTLY, NATE, I FIGURE YOU'RE PRETTY MUCH ***ABOVE*** ALL THIS ***B.S.***, RIGHT?
RIGHT...

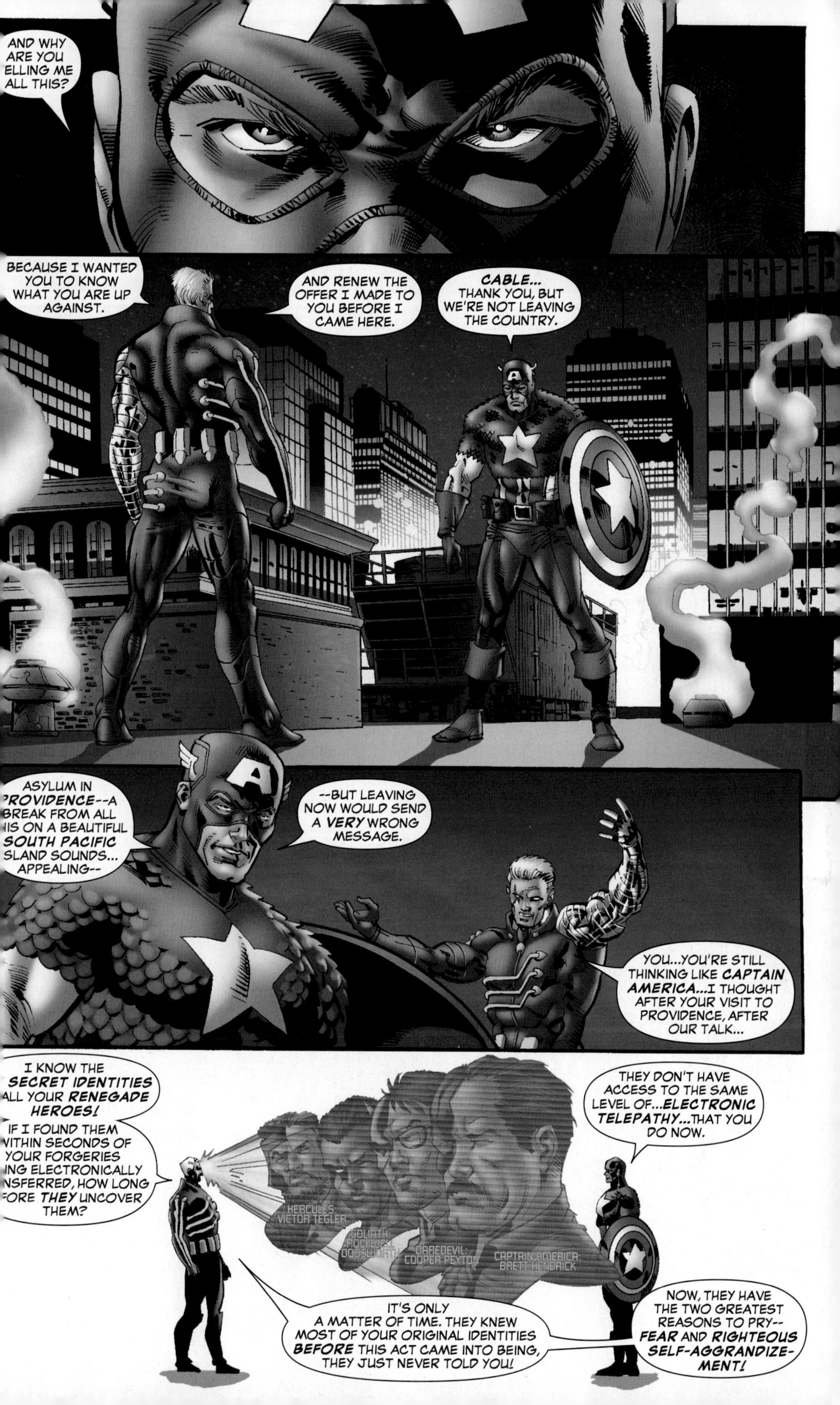
AND WHY ARE YOU ELLING ME ALL THIS?
BECAUSE I WANTED YOU TO KNOW WHAT YOU ARE UP AGAINST.
AND RENEW THE OFFER I MADE TO YOU BEFORE I CAME HERE.
CABLE... THANK YOU, BUT WE'RE NOT LEAVING THE COUNTRY.
ASYLUM IN PROVIDENCE--A BREAK FROM ALL IS ON A BEAUTIFUL SOUTH PACIFIC SLAND SOUNDS... APPEALING--
--BUT LEAVING NOW WOULD SEND A VERY WRONG MESSAGE.
YOU...YOU'RE STILL THINKING LIKE CAPTAIN AMERICA...I THOUGHT AFTER YOUR VISIT TO PROVIDENCE, AFTER OUR TALK...
I KNOW THE SECRET IDENTITIES ALL YOUR RENEGADE HEROES! IF I FOUND THEM WITHIN SECONDS OF YOUR FORGERIES ING ELECTRONICALLY NSFERRED, HOW LONG FORE THEY UNCOVER THEM?
THEY DON'T HAVE ACCESS TO THE SAME LEVEL OF...ELECTRONIC TELEPATHY...THAT YOU DO NOW.
HERCULES: VICTOR TEGLER
DAREDEVIL: COOPER PEYTON
CAPTAIN AMERICA: BRETT HENDRICK
IT'S ONLY A MATTER OF TIME. THEY KNEW MOST OF YOUR ORIGINAL IDENTITIES BEFORE THIS ACT CAME INTO BEING, THEY JUST NEVER TOLD YOU!
NOW, THEY HAVE THE TWO GREATEST REASONS TO PRY-- FEAR AND RIGHTEOUS SELF-AGGRANDIZE-MENT!

YOU'RE SAYING WE'RE GOING TO LOSE?

I'M SAYING YOU'VE *ALREADY* LOST!

YOU KNOW THIS BECAUSE YOU'RE FROM THE *FUTURE* AND KNOW EVERY-THING, RIGHT?

NO...I'M SAYING THIS BECAUSE I'VE SEEN WHAT THEY HAVE PLANNED.

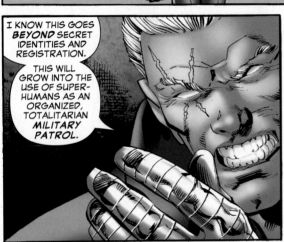

I KNOW THIS GOES *BEYOND* SECRET IDENTITIES AND REGISTRATION.

THIS WILL GROW INTO THE USE OF SUPER-HUMANS AS AN ORGANIZED, TOTALITARIAN *MILITARY PATROL.*

I KNOW *IRON MAN.* TONY STARK WOULD *NEVER* AGREE TO SOMETHING LIKE THAT.

AND WE'RE BACK TO SQUARE ONE. YOU'RE THINKING IN TERMS OF *MONTHS* AND *YEARS,* I'M TALKING ABOUT *DECADES* AND *CENTURIES.*

NATHAN...I'VE THOUGHT ABOUT OUR TALK A LOT...YOU CAN'T FIGHT TIME, YOU CAN'T CHANGE THE BIG PICTURE IN A *DAILY* STRUGGLE...

NO, BUT THROUGHOUT THE COURSE OF HISTORY, THE ACTIONS AND DECISIONS OF INDIVIDUALS--OR THEIR *NON-ACTIONS*--HAVE AFFECTED THE "BIG PICTURE."

MY OFFER OF ASYLUM IS IN CONSIDERATION OF THE BIG PICTURE-- THE *WORLD* PICTURE.

I AM PRESIDENT PRO TEM OF *RUMEKISTAN* NOW. EUROPEAN AND FORMER SOVIET BLOC COUNTRIES HAVE ALWAYS CONSIDERED SUPER-HUMANS A DANGEROUSLY "AMERICAN THING."

AND YOU CAN HELP MAKE IT A "DANGEROUSLY *GLOBAL* THING"--?

CYNICAL HUMOR DOESN'T WORK FOR YOU. GIVE UP THIS FIGHT TO WIN A MUCH, MUCH *BIGGER* ONE. THE FIGHT FOR THE *FUTURE!*

I CAN'T DO THAT.

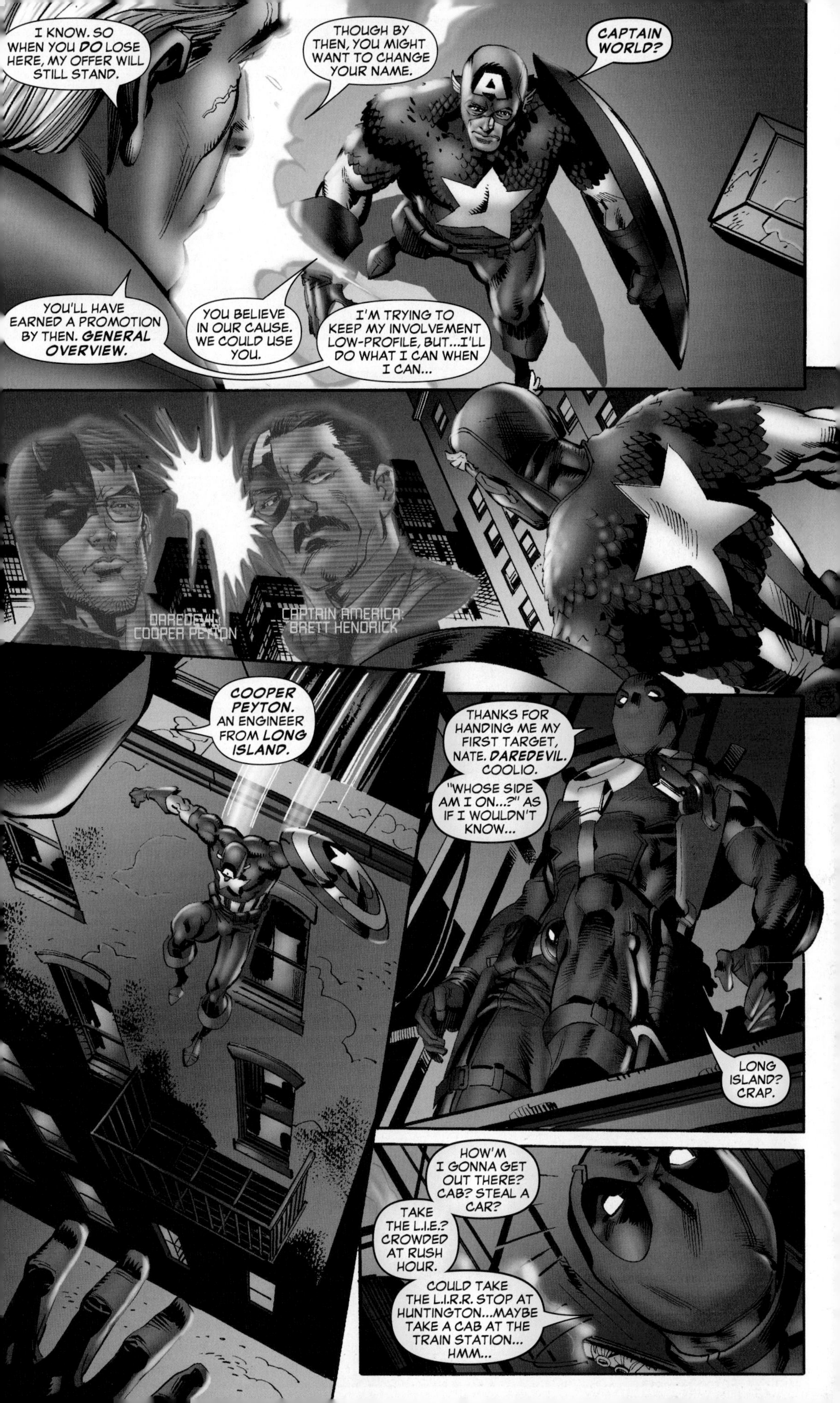

I KNOW. SO WHEN YOU DO LOSE HERE, MY OFFER WILL STILL STAND.
THOUGH BY THEN, YOU MIGHT WANT TO CHANGE YOUR NAME.
CAPTAIN WORLD?
YOU'LL HAVE EARNED A PROMOTION BY THEN. GENERAL OVERVIEW.
YOU BELIEVE IN OUR CAUSE. WE COULD USE YOU.
I'M TRYING TO KEEP MY INVOLVEMENT LOW-PROFILE, BUT...I'LL DO WHAT I CAN WHEN I CAN...
DAREDEVIL: COOPER PEYTON
CAPTAIN AMERICA: BRETT HENDRICK
COOPER PEYTON. AN ENGINEER FROM LONG ISLAND.
THANKS FOR HANDING ME MY FIRST TARGET, NATE. DAREDEVIL. COOLIO.
"WHOSE SIDE AM I ON...?" AS IF I WOULDN'T KNOW...
LONG ISLAND? CRAP.
HOW'M I GONNA GET OUT THERE? CAB? STEAL A CAR?
TAKE THE L.I.E.? CROWDED AT RUSH HOUR.
COULD TAKE THE L.I.R.R. STOP AT HUNTINGTON...MAYBE TAKE A CAB AT THE TRAIN STATION... HMM...

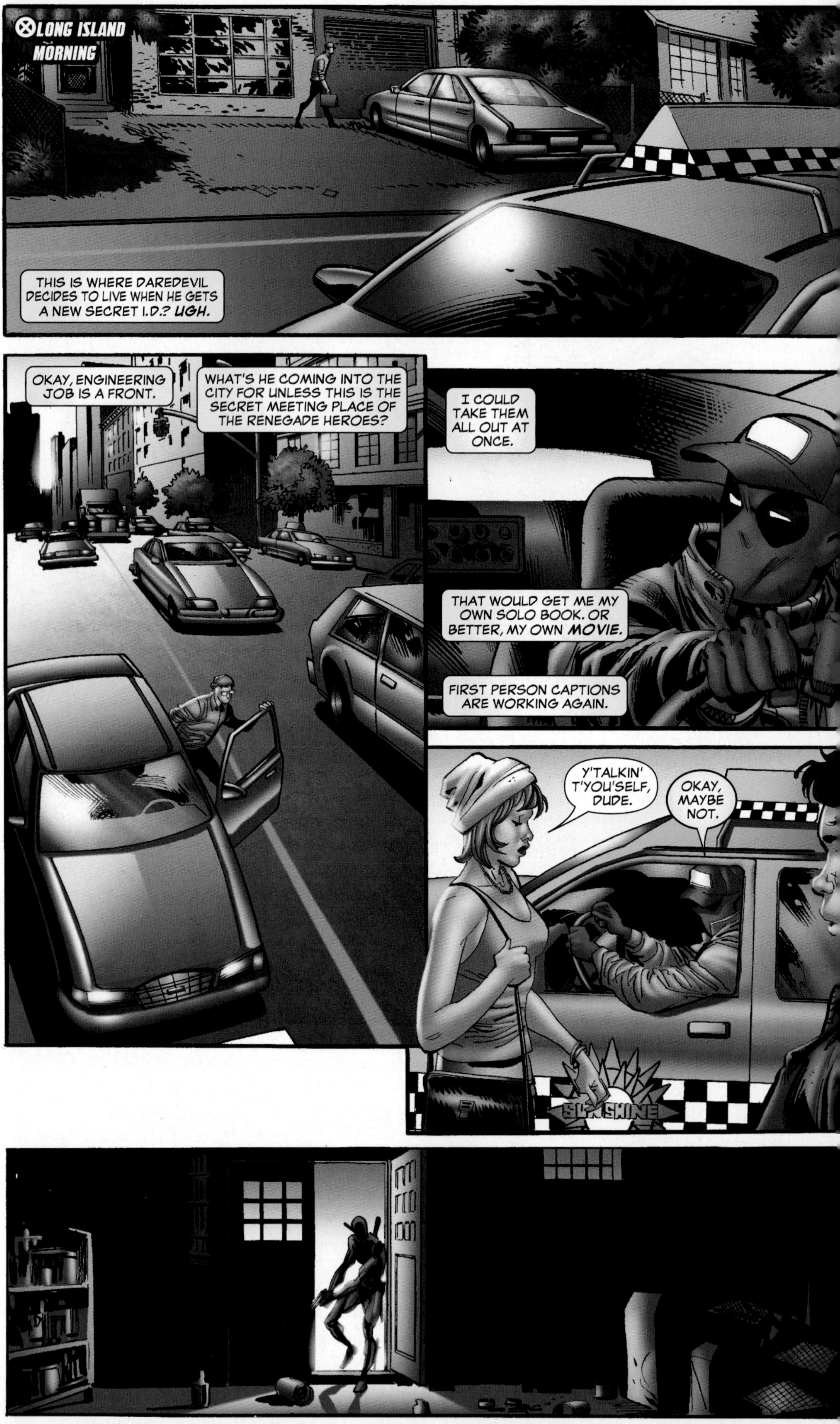

LONG ISLAND
MORNING
THIS IS WHERE DAREDEVIL DECIDES TO LIVE WHEN HE GETS A NEW SECRET I.D.? UGH.
OKAY, ENGINEERING JOB IS A FRONT.
WHAT'S HE COMING INTO THE CITY FOR UNLESS THIS IS THE SECRET MEETING PLACE OF THE RENEGADE HEROES?
I COULD TAKE THEM ALL OUT AT ONCE.
THAT WOULD GET ME MY OWN SOLO BOOK. OR BETTER, MY OWN MOVIE.
FIRST PERSON CAPTIONS ARE WORKING AGAIN.
Y'TALKIN' T'YOU'SELF, DUDE.
OKAY, MAYBE NOT.

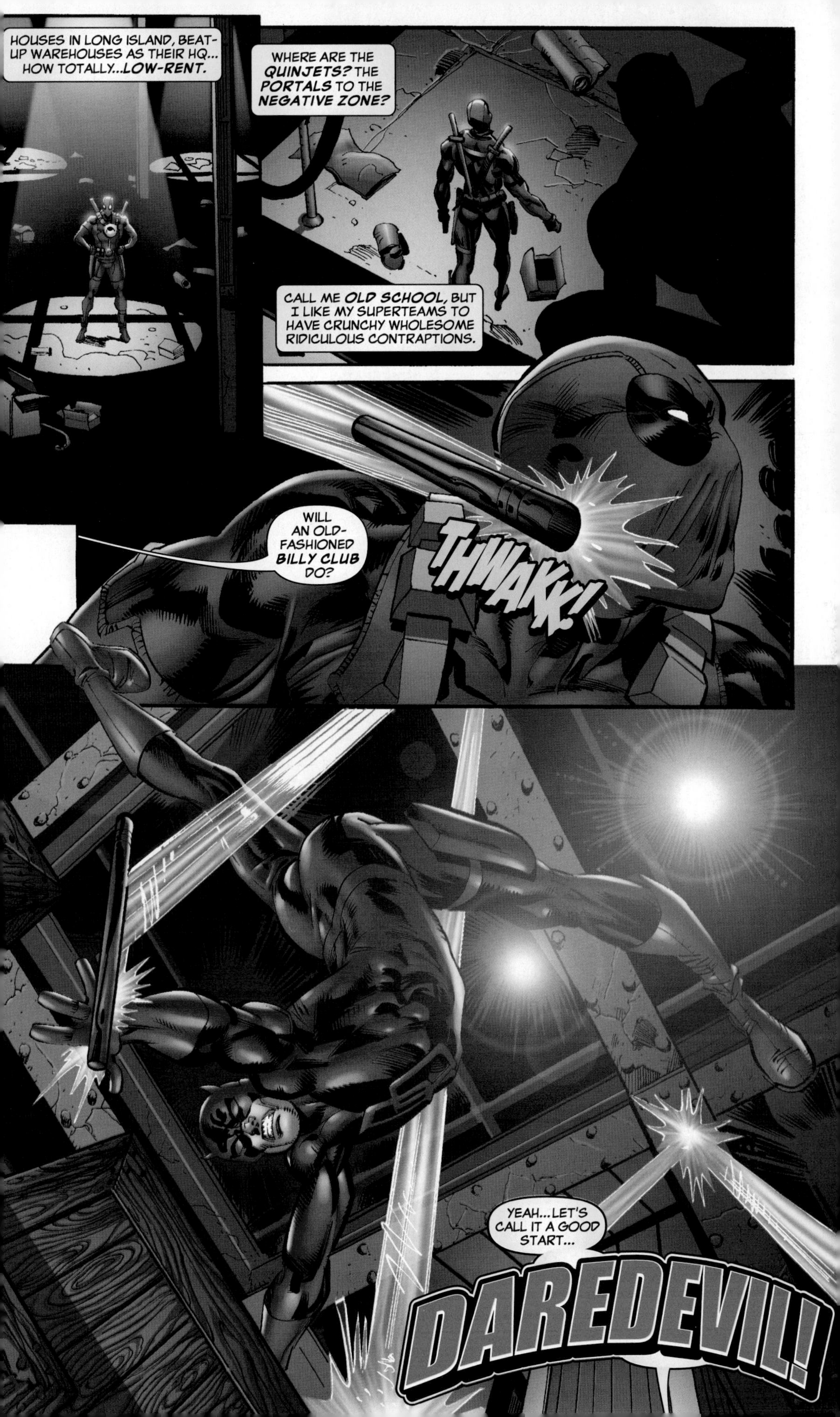
HOUSES IN LONG ISLAND, BEAT-UP WAREHOUSES AS THEIR HQ... HOW TOTALLY...LOW-RENT.
WHERE ARE THE QUINJETS? THE PORTALS TO THE NEGATIVE ZONE?
CALL ME OLD SCHOOL, BUT I LIKE MY SUPERTEAMS TO HAVE CRUNCHY WHOLESOME RIDICULOUS CONTRAPTIONS.
WILL AN OLD-FASHIONED BILLY CLUB DO?
THWAKK!
YEAH...LET'S CALL IT A GOOD START...
DAREDEVIL!

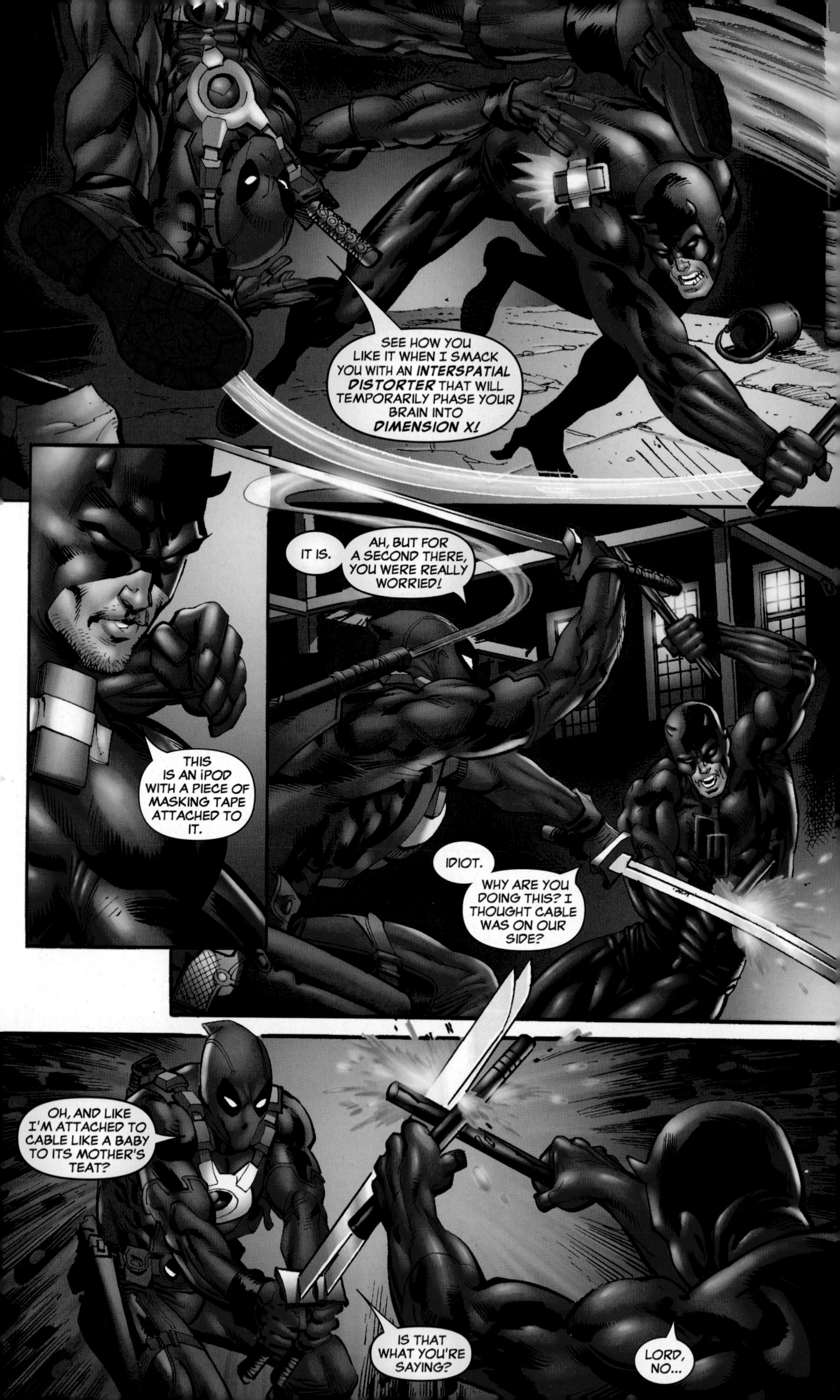
SEE HOW YOU LIKE IT WHEN I SMACK YOU WITH AN INTERSPATIAL DISTORTER THAT WILL TEMPORARILY PHASE YOUR BRAIN INTO DIMENSION X!
THIS IS AN iPOD WITH A PIECE OF MASKING TAPE ATTACHED TO IT.
IT IS.
AH, BUT FOR A SECOND THERE, YOU WERE REALLY WORRIED!
IDIOT.
WHY ARE YOU DOING THIS? I THOUGHT CABLE WAS ON OUR SIDE?
OH, AND LIKE I'M ATTACHED TO CABLE LIKE A BABY TO ITS MOTHER'S TEAT?
IS THAT WHAT YOU'RE SAYING?
LORD, NO...

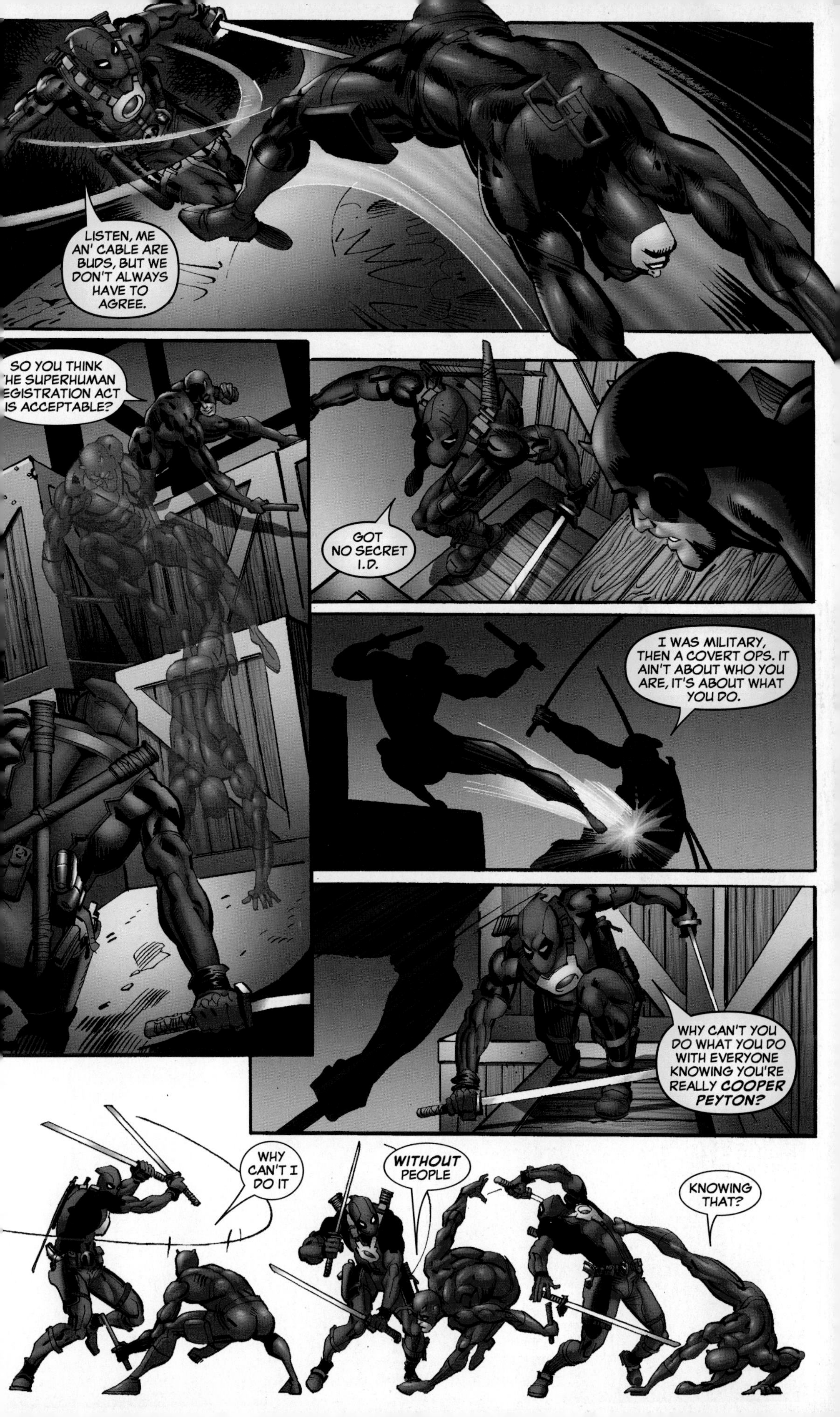
LISTEN, ME AN' CABLE ARE BUDS, BUT WE DON'T ALWAYS HAVE TO AGREE.
SO YOU THINK HE SUPERHUMAN EGISTRATION ACT IS ACCEPTABLE?
GOT NO SECRET I.D.
I WAS MILITARY, THEN A COVERT OPS. IT AIN'T ABOUT WHO YOU ARE, IT'S ABOUT WHAT YOU DO.
WHY CAN'T YOU DO WHAT YOU DO WITH EVERYONE KNOWING YOU'RE REALLY *COOPER PEYTON?*
WHY CAN'T I DO IT
WITHOUT PEOPLE
KNOWING THAT?

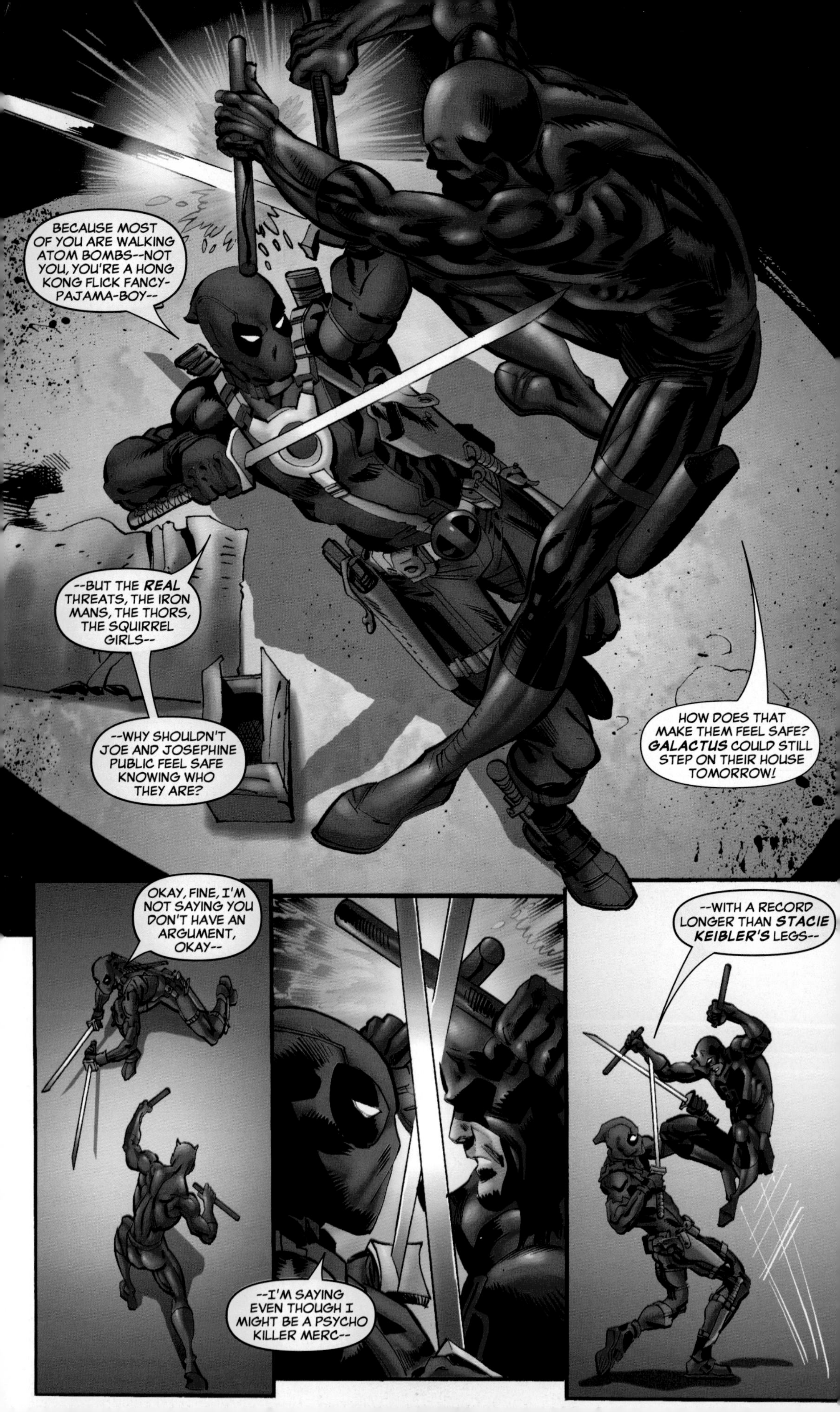
BECAUSE MOST OF YOU ARE WALKING ATOM BOMBS--NOT YOU, YOU'RE A HONG KONG FLICK FANCY-PAJAMA-BOY--
--BUT THE REAL THREATS, THE IRON MANS, THE THORS, THE SQUIRREL GIRLS--
--WHY SHOULDN'T JOE AND JOSEPHINE PUBLIC FEEL SAFE KNOWING WHO THEY ARE?
HOW DOES THAT MAKE THEM FEEL SAFE? GALACTUS COULD STILL STEP ON THEIR HOUSE TOMORROW!
OKAY, FINE, I'M NOT SAYING YOU DON'T HAVE AN ARGUMENT, OKAY--
--I'M SAYING EVEN THOUGH I MIGHT BE A PSYCHO KILLER MERC--
--WITH A RECORD LONGER THAN STACIE KEIBLER'S LEGS--

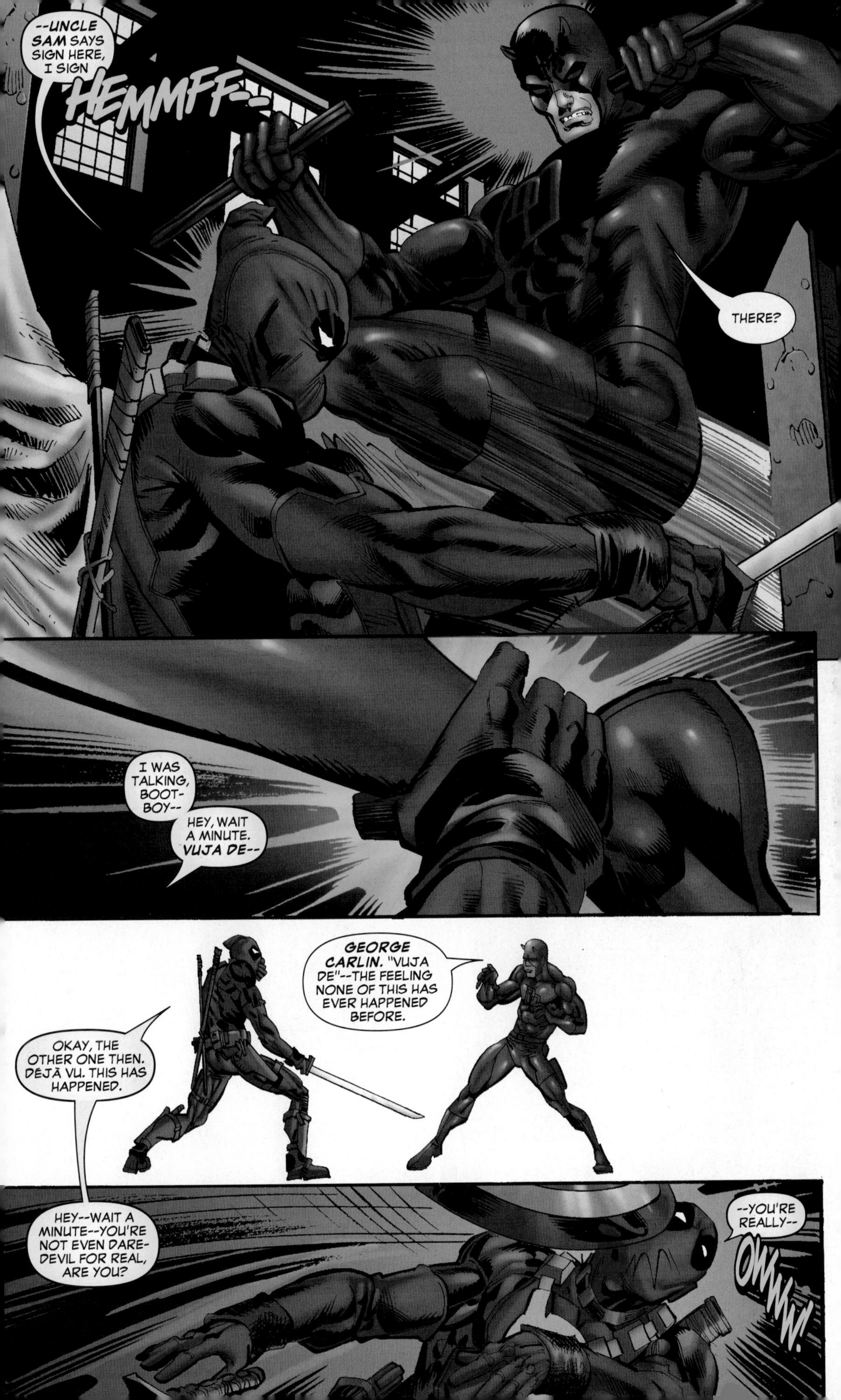
--UNCLE SAM SAYS SIGN HERE, I SIGN
HEMMFF--
THERE?
I WAS TALKING, BOOT-BOY--
HEY, WAIT A MINUTE. VUJA DE--
GEORGE CARLIN. "VUJA DE"--THE FEELING NONE OF THIS HAS EVER HAPPENED BEFORE.
OKAY, THE OTHER ONE THEN. DÉJÀ VU. THIS HAS HAPPENED.
HEY--WAIT A MINUTE--YOU'RE NOT EVEN DARE-DEVIL FOR REAL, ARE YOU?
--YOU'RE REALLY--
OWWW!

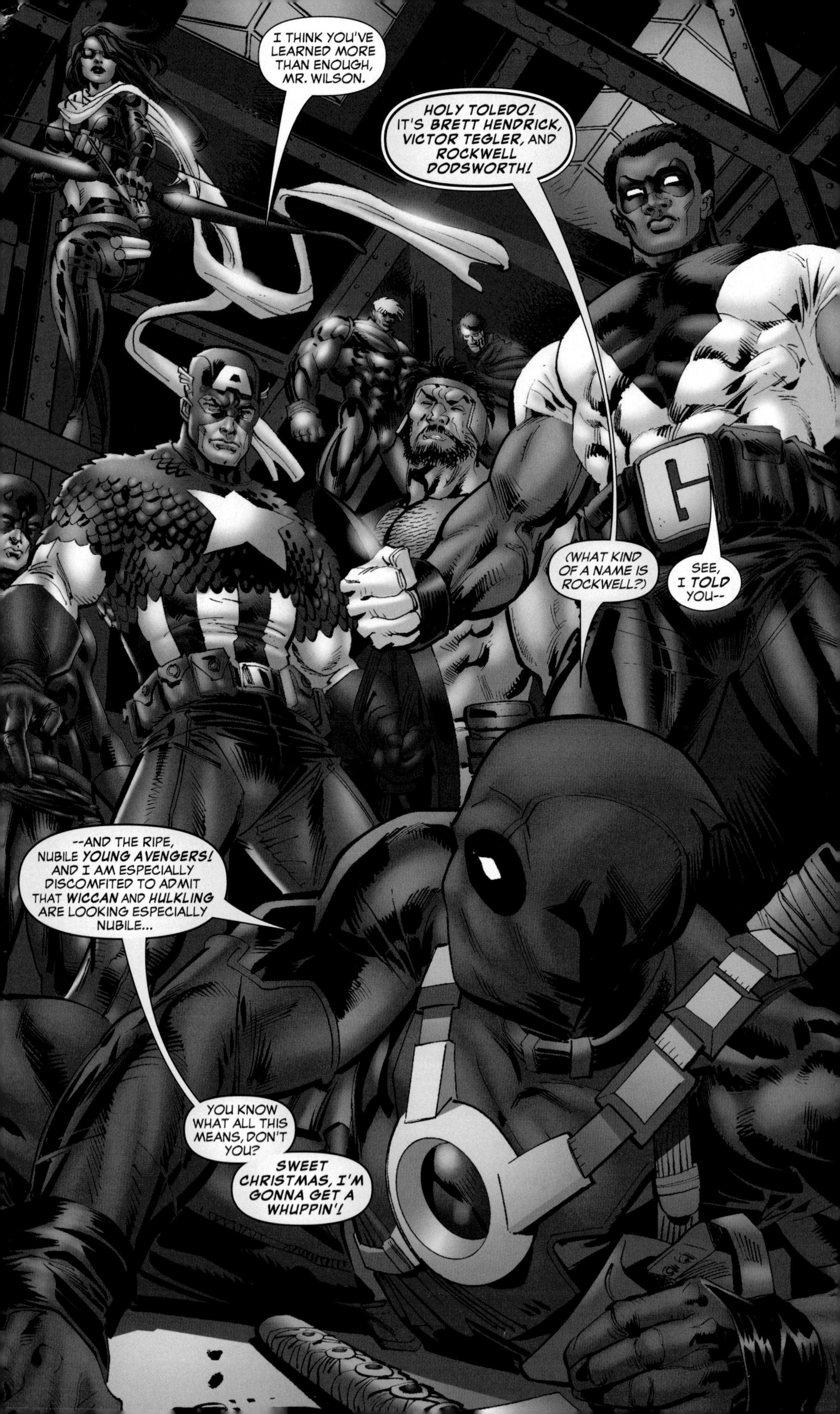
I THINK YOU'VE LEARNED MORE THAN ENOUGH, MR. WILSON.
HOLY TOLEDO! IT'S BRETT HENDRICK, VICTOR TEGLER, AND ROCKWELL DODSWORTH!
(WHAT KIND OF A NAME IS ROCKWELL?)
SEE, I TOLD YOU--
--AND THE RIPE, NUBILE YOUNG AVENGERS! AND I AM ESPECIALLY DISCOMFITED TO ADMIT THAT WICCAN AND HULKLING ARE LOOKING ESPECIALLY NUBILE...
YOU KNOW WHAT ALL THIS MEANS, DON'T YOU?
SWEET CHRISTMAS, I'M GONNA GET A WHUPPIN'!

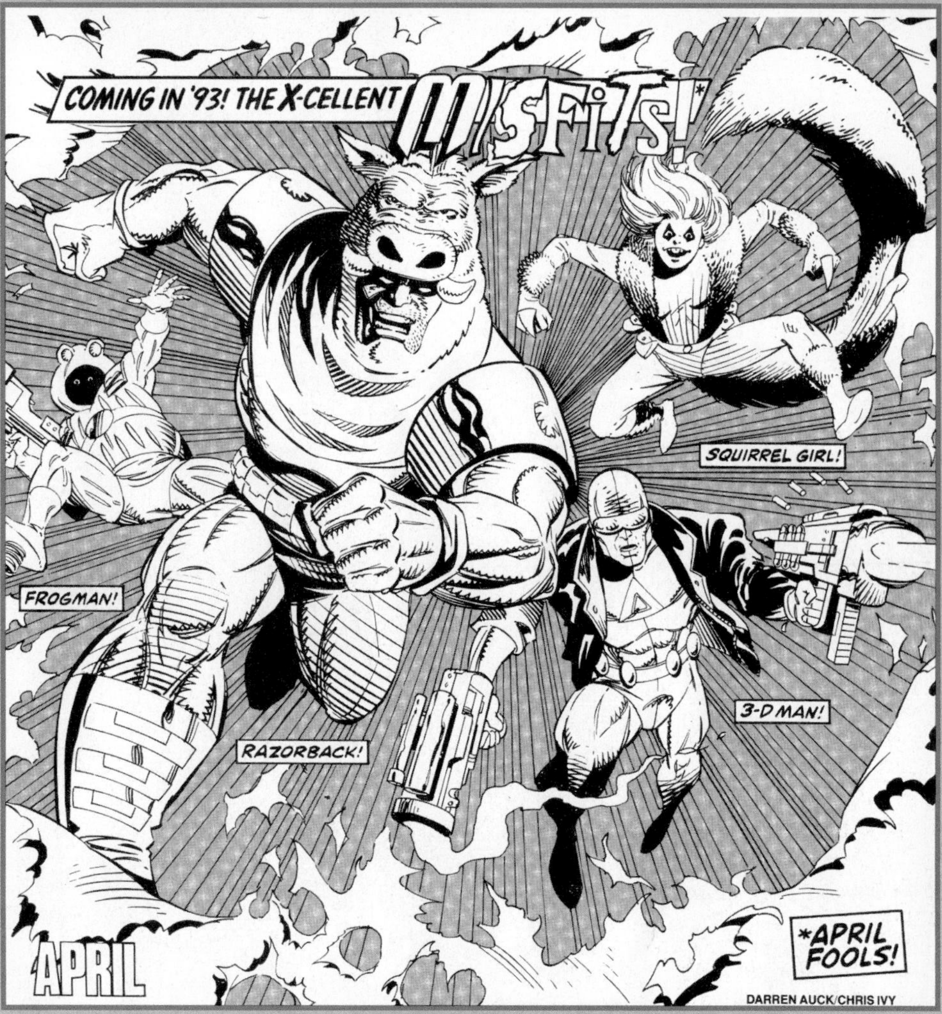
COMING IN '93! THE X-CELLENT MISFITS!*
SQUIRREL GIRL!
FROGMAN!
3-D MAN!
RAZORBACK!
APRIL
*APRIL FOOLS!
DARREN AUCK/CHRIS IVY

Marvel Age #124 parody pinup by **Darren Auck** & **Chris Ivy**

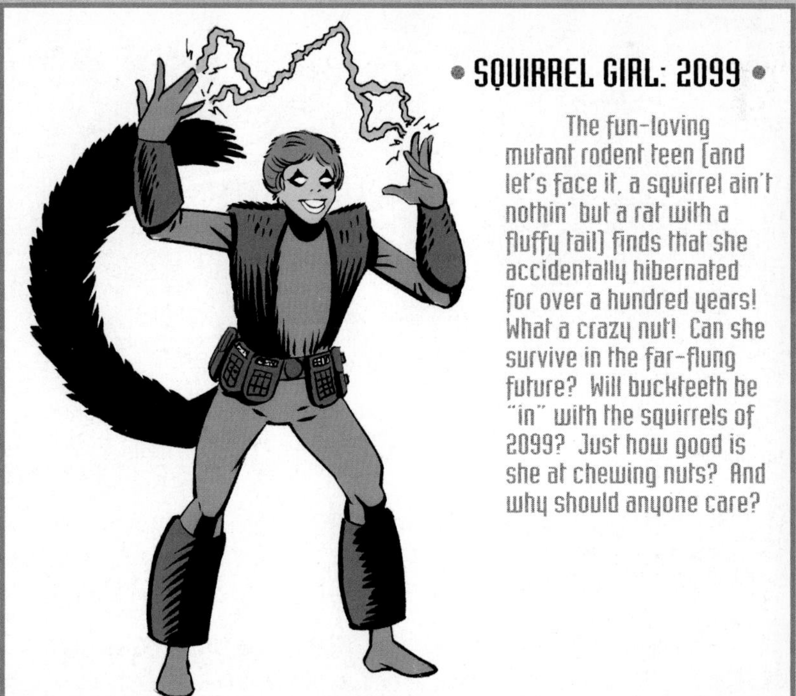
• SQUIRREL GIRL: 2099 •
The fun-loving mutant rodent teen (and let's face it, a squirrel ain't nothin' but a rat with a fluffy tail) finds that she accidentally hibernated for over a hundred years! What a crazy nut! Can she survive in the far-flung future? Will buckteeth be "in" with the squirrels of 2099? Just how good is she at chewing nuts? And why should anyone care?

"Marvel 2099: A Look At What You WON'T Be Seeing in the Future"
Marvel Year-In-Review '92 parody-article excerpt by **Fabian Nicieza**

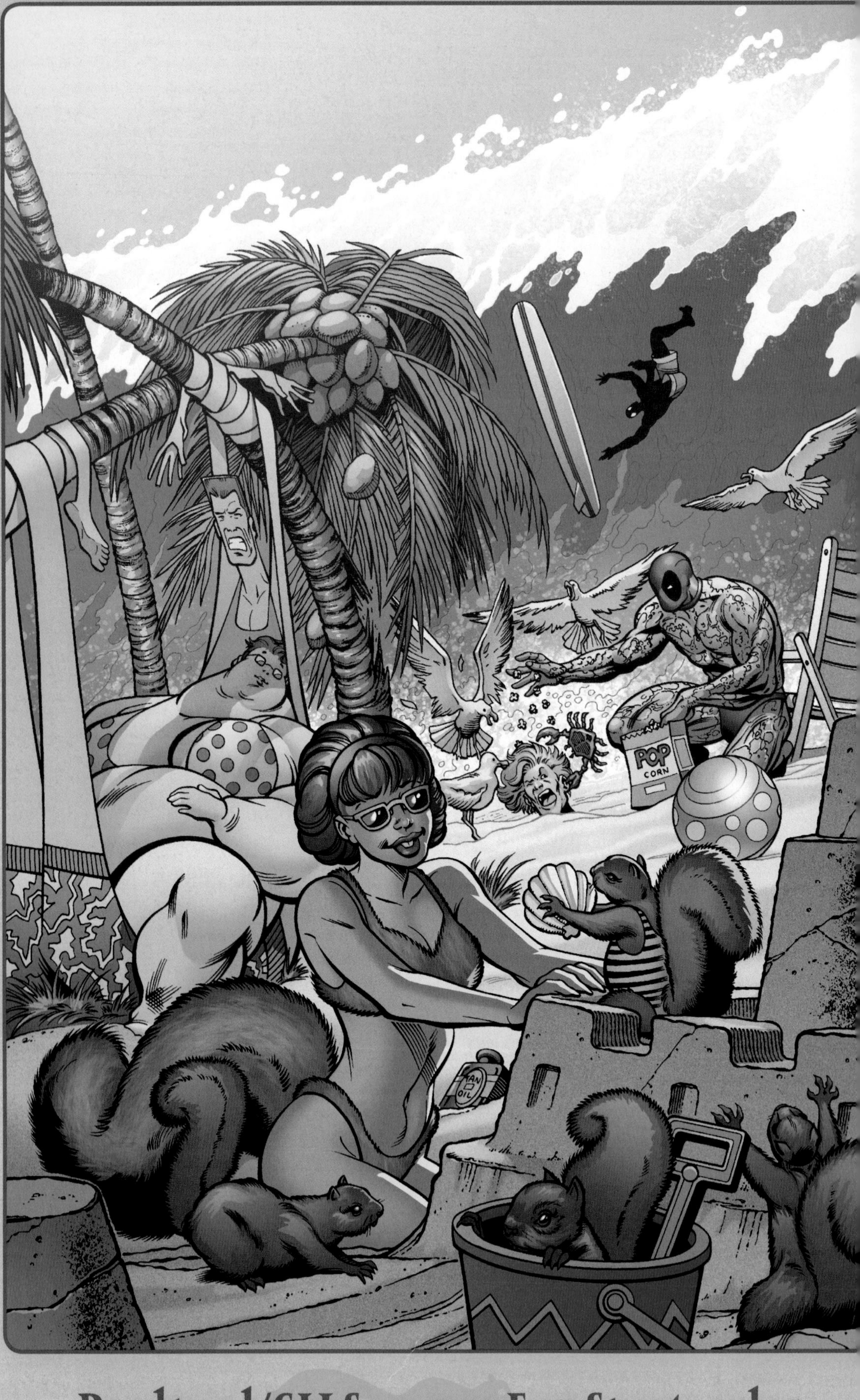
POP
CORN
TAN
OIL

Deadpool/GLI Summer Fun Spectacular

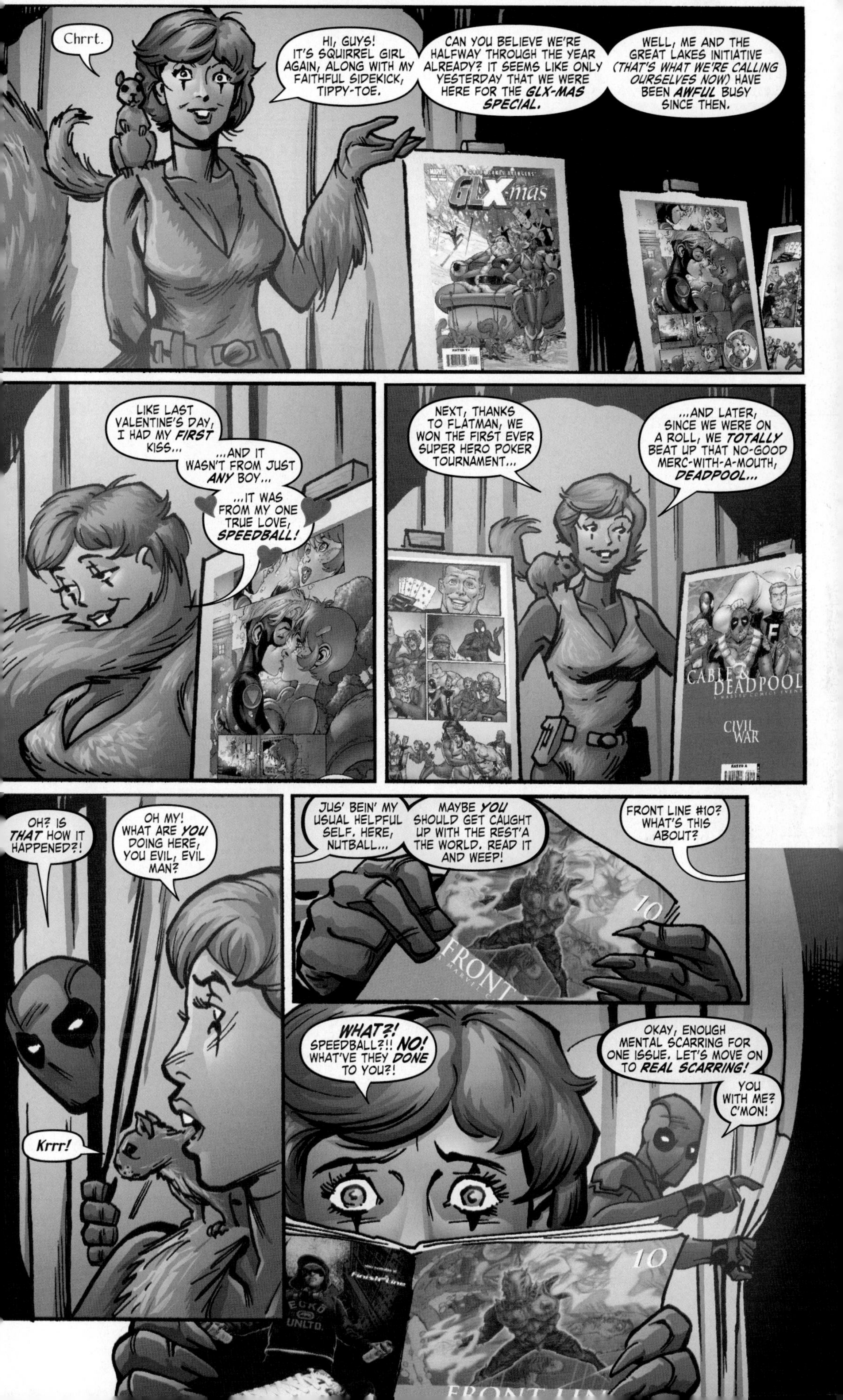
Chrrt.
HI, GUYS! IT'S SQUIRREL GIRL AGAIN, ALONG WITH MY FAITHFUL SIDEKICK, TIPPY-TOE.
CAN YOU BELIEVE WE'RE HALFWAY THROUGH THE YEAR ALREADY? IT SEEMS LIKE ONLY YESTERDAY THAT WE WERE HERE FOR THE GLX-MAS SPECIAL.
WELL, ME AND THE GREAT LAKES INITIATIVE (THAT'S WHAT WE'RE CALLING OURSELVES NOW) HAVE BEEN AWFUL BUSY SINCE THEN.
GLX-mas
LIKE LAST VALENTINE'S DAY, I HAD MY FIRST KISS...
...AND IT WASN'T FROM JUST ANY BOY...
...IT WAS FROM MY ONE TRUE LOVE, SPEEDBALL!
NEXT, THANKS TO FLATMAN, WE WON THE FIRST EVER SUPER HERO POKER TOURNAMENT...
...AND LATER, SINCE WE WERE ON A ROLL, WE TOTALLY BEAT UP THAT NO-GOOD MERC-WITH-A-MOUTH, DEADPOOL...
CABLE & DEADPOOL
CIVIL WAR
OH? IS THAT HOW IT HAPPENED?!
OH MY! WHAT ARE YOU DOING HERE, YOU EVIL, EVIL MAN?
Krrr!
JUS' BEIN' MY USUAL HELPFUL SELF. HERE, NUTBALL...
MAYBE YOU SHOULD GET CAUGHT UP WITH THE REST'A THE WORLD. READ IT AND WEEP!
FRONT LINE #10? WHAT'S THIS ABOUT?
10
FRONT
WHAT?! SPEEDBALL?!! NO! WHAT'VE THEY DONE TO YOU?!
OKAY, ENOUGH MENTAL SCARRING FOR ONE ISSUE. LET'S MOVE ON TO REAL SCARRING!
YOU WITH ME? C'MON!
ECKŌ UNLTD.
10

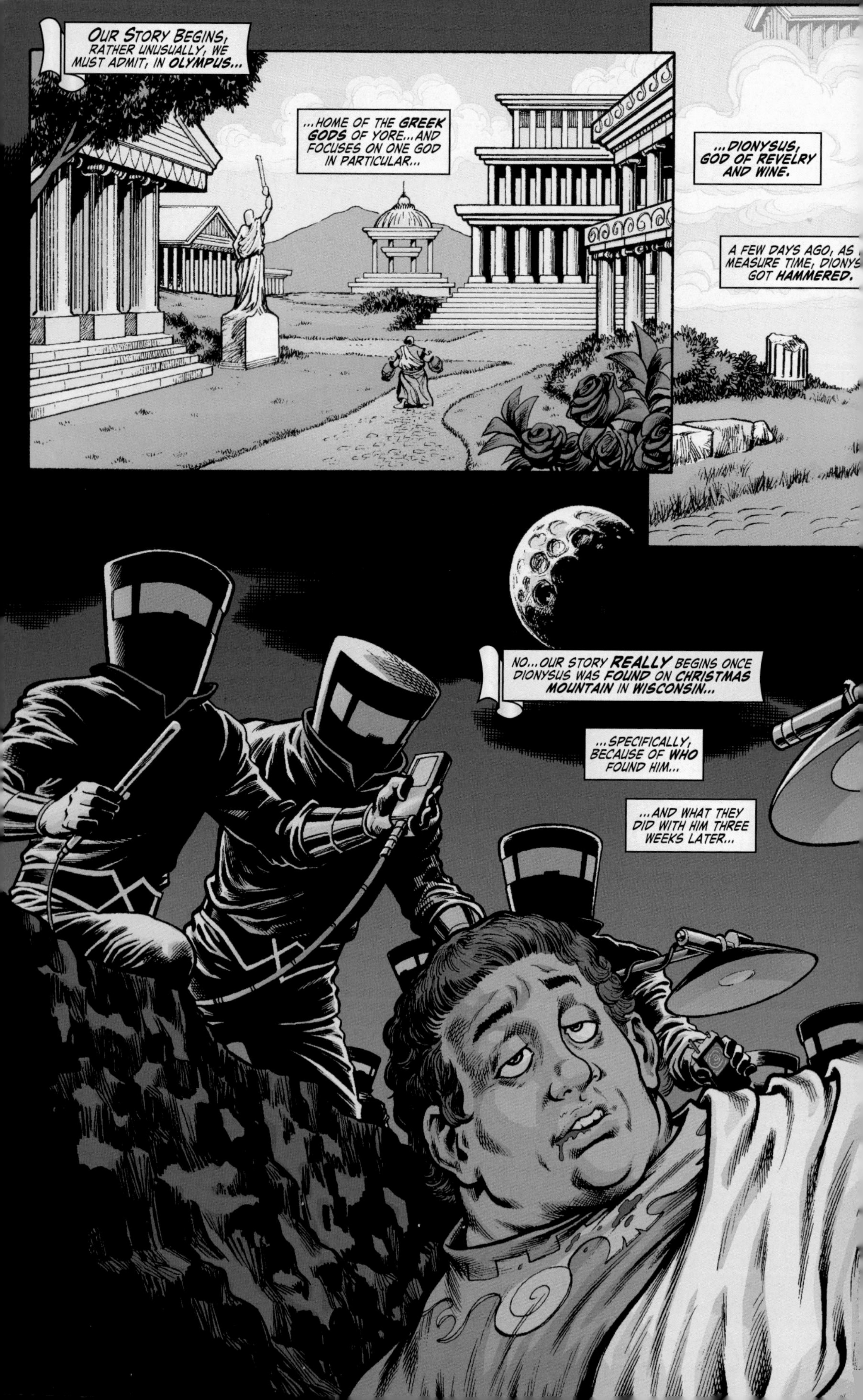
OUR STORY BEGINS, RATHER UNUSUALLY, WE MUST ADMIT, IN OLYMPUS...
...HOME OF THE GREEK GODS OF YORE...AND FOCUSES ON ONE GOD IN PARTICULAR...
...DIONYSUS, GOD OF REVELRY AND WINE.
A FEW DAYS AGO, AS MEASURE TIME, DIONYS GOT HAMMERED.
NO...OUR STORY REALLY BEGINS ONCE DIONYSUS WAS FOUND ON CHRISTMAS MOUNTAIN IN WISCONSIN...
...SPECIFICALLY, BECAUSE OF WHO FOUND HIM...
...AND WHAT THEY DID WITH HIM THREE WEEKS LATER...

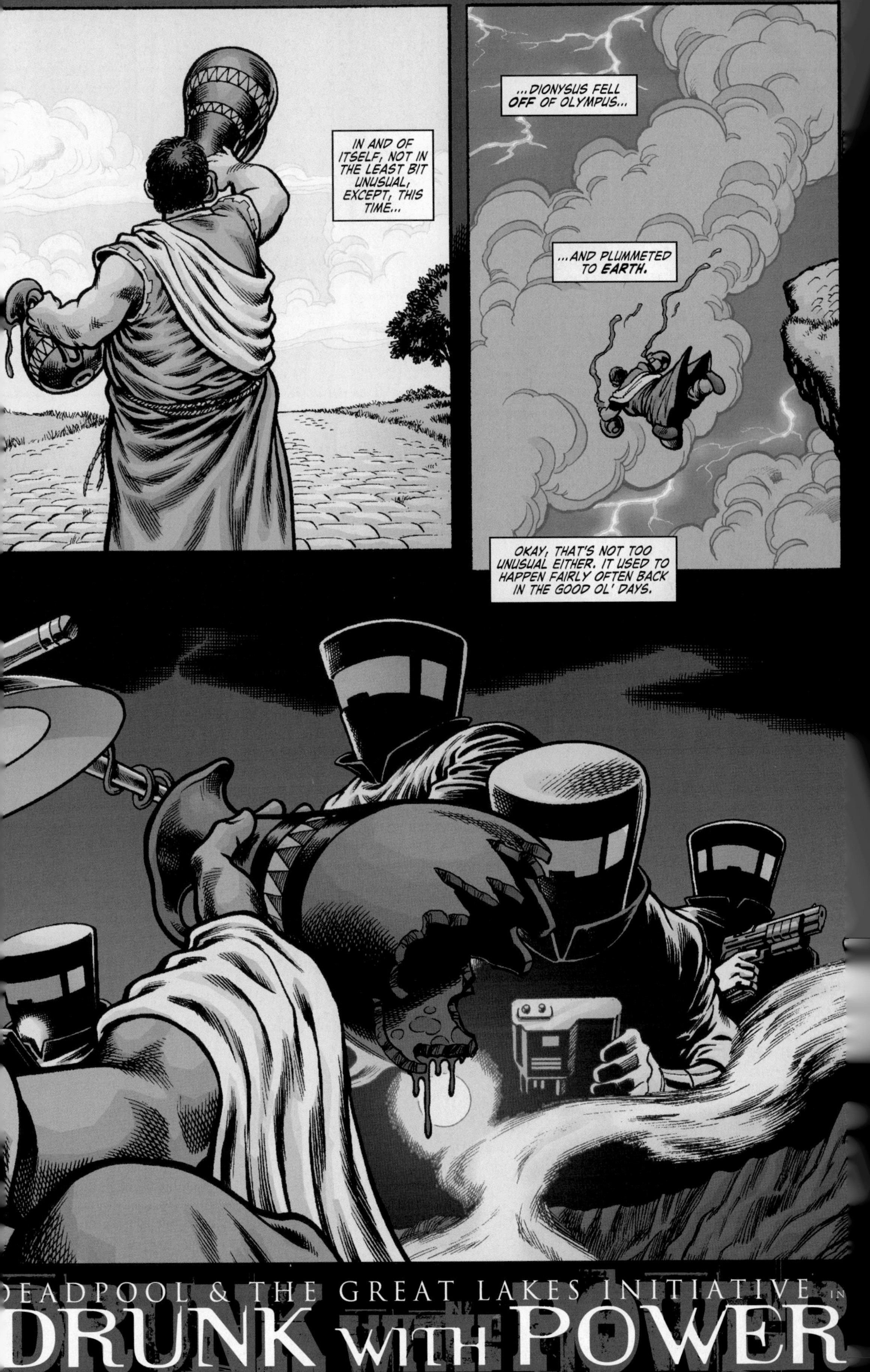
IN AND OF ITSELF; NOT IN THE LEAST BIT UNUSUAL, EXCEPT, THIS TIME...
...DIONYSUS FELL OFF OF OLYMPUS...
...AND PLUMMETED TO EARTH.
OKAY; THAT'S NOT TOO UNUSUAL EITHER. IT USED TO HAPPEN FAIRLY OFTEN BACK IN THE GOOD OL' DAYS.
DEADPOOL & THE GREAT LAKES INITIATIVE IN
DRUNK WITH POWER

THIS IS A BIT OUT OF THE NORM EVEN FOR *MANHATTAN*...

IT'S NOT LIKE THE *HUMAN TORCH* TO BE SO DRUNK. IN THE MORNING. ON A *MONDAY*.

LOOKS LIKE HE'S FLYING TO *THE BAXTER BUILDING*, LEGENDARY *HEADQUARTERS* OF THE *SCIENTIFIC EXPLORERS*, THE *FANTASTIC FOUR*.

OKAY... HE FLEW *INTO* THE BUILDING. HMN I SHOULDN'T CARE REALLY. BUT...WHATEV HE'S BEEN DRINKING I GOTS TO GET ME SOME...

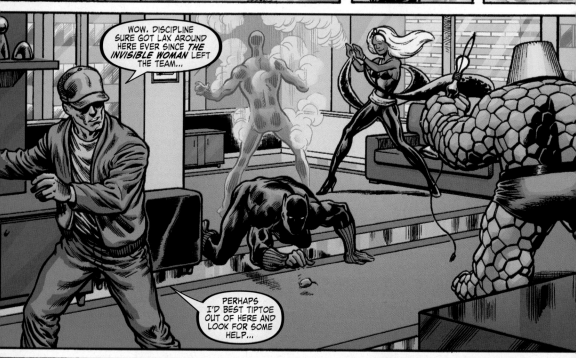

WOW. DISCIPLINE SURE GOT LAX AROUND HERE EVER SINCE *THE INVISIBLE WOMAN* LEFT THE TEAM...

PERHAPS I'D BEST TIPTOE OUT OF HERE AND LOOK FOR SOME HELP...

STOP!

KAZZAAK

NORMALLY, THIS WOULD MEAN WAR, BUT...

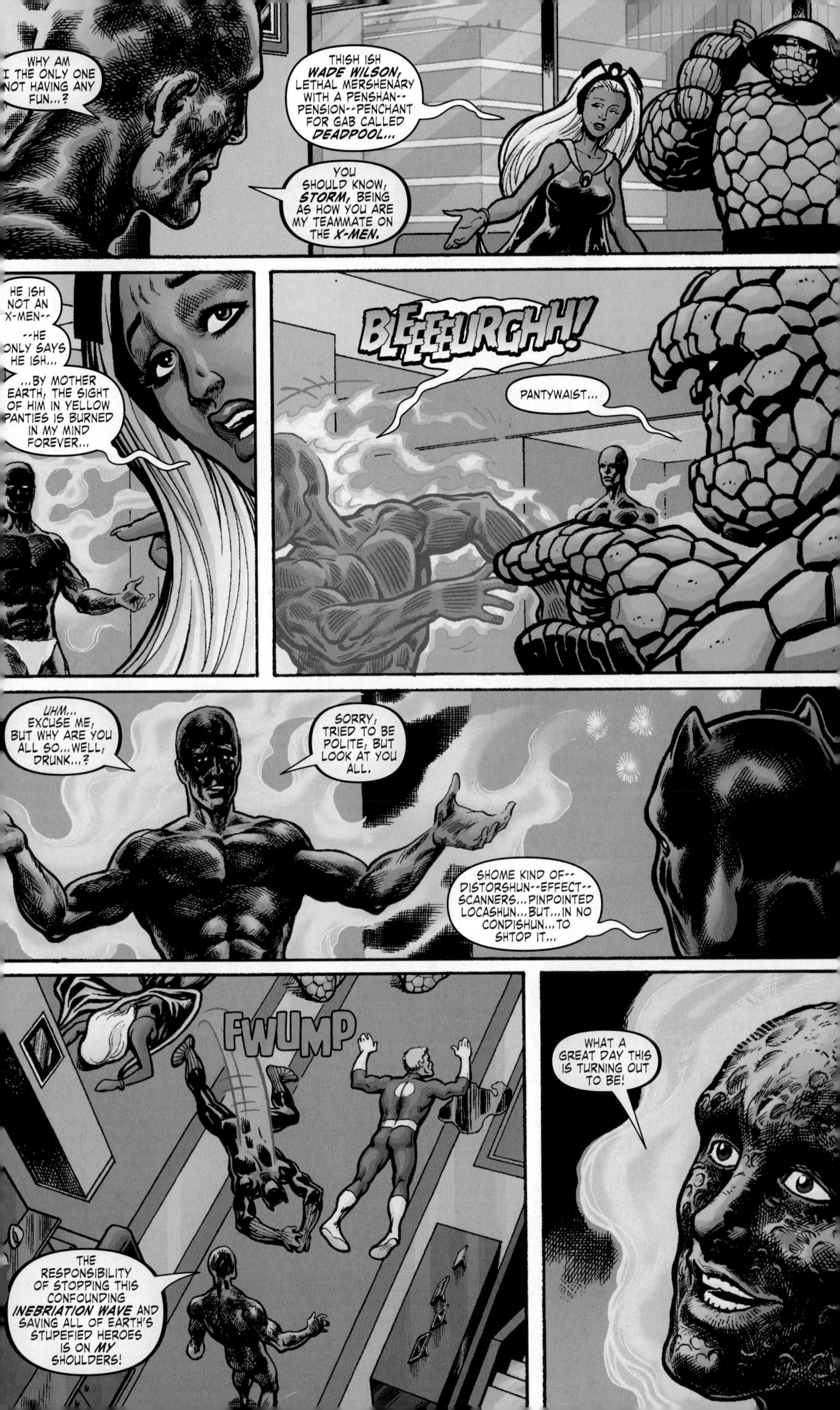
WHY AM I THE ONLY ONE NOT HAVING ANY FUN...?
THISH ISH WADE WILSON, LETHAL MERSHENARY WITH A PENSHAN--PENSION--PENCHANT FOR GAB CALLED DEADPOOL...
YOU SHOULD KNOW, STORM, BEING AS HOW YOU ARE MY TEAMMATE ON THE X-MEN.
HE ISH NOT AN X-MEN--
--HE ONLY SAYS HE ISH...
...BY MOTHER EARTH, THE SIGHT OF HIM IN YELLOW PANTIES IS BURNED IN MY MIND FOREVER...
BLEEEEURGHH!
PANTYWAIST...
UHM... EXCUSE ME, BUT WHY ARE YOU ALL SO...WELL, DRUNK...?
SORRY, TRIED TO BE POLITE, BUT LOOK AT YOU ALL.
SHOME KIND OF--DISTORSHUN--EFFECT--SCANNERS...PINPOINTED LOCASHUN...BUT...IN NO CONDISHUN...TO SHTOP IT...
FWUMP
THE RESPONSIBILITY OF STOPPING THIS CONFOUNDING INEBRIATION WAVE AND SAVING ALL OF EARTH'S STUPEFIED HEROES IS ON MY SHOULDERS!
WHAT A GREAT DAY THIS IS TURNING OUT TO BE!

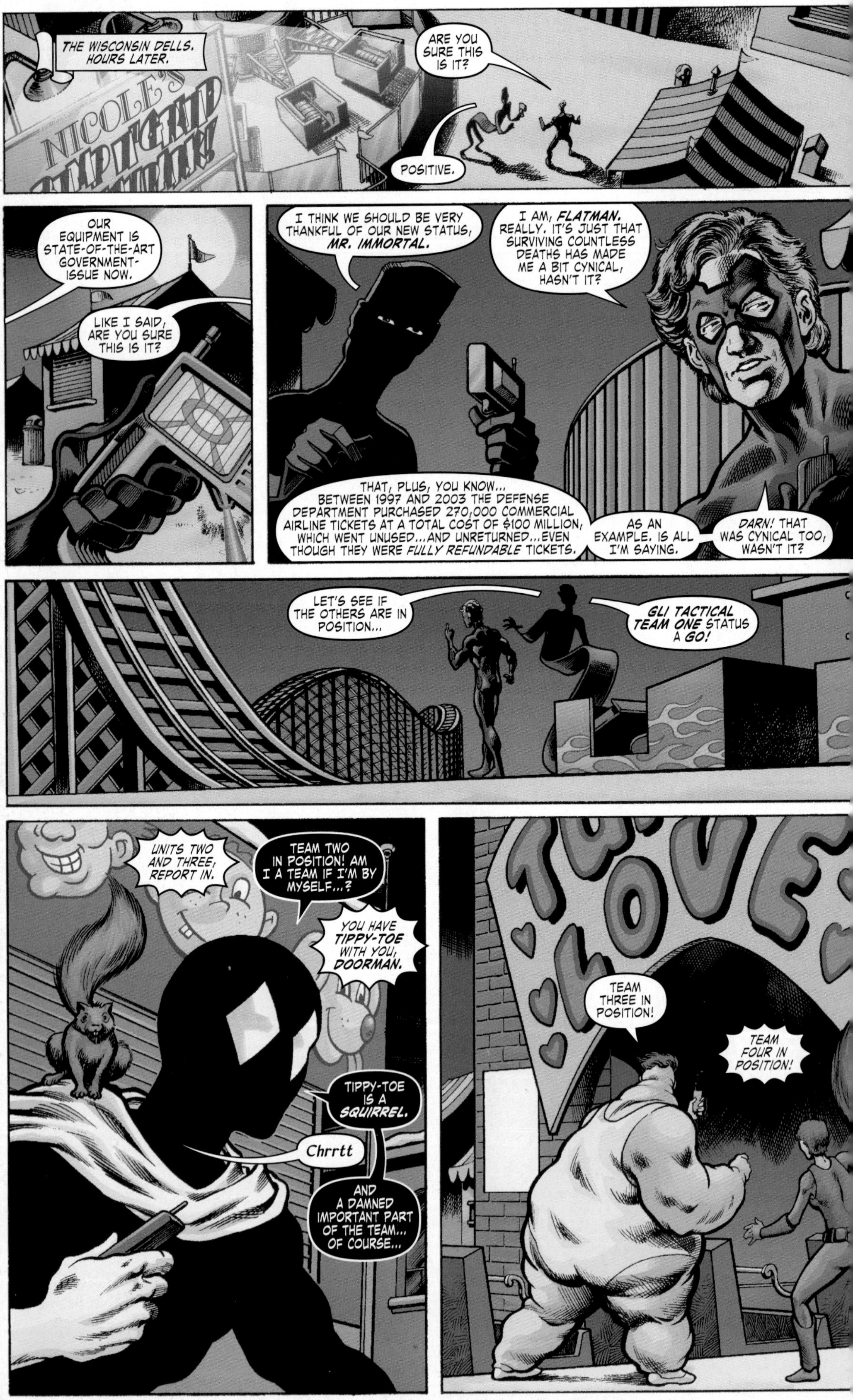
THE WISCONSIN DELLS. HOURS LATER.
NICOLE'S
ARE YOU SURE THIS IS IT?
POSITIVE.
OUR EQUIPMENT IS STATE-OF-THE-ART GOVERNMENT-ISSUE NOW.
LIKE I SAID, ARE YOU SURE THIS IS IT?
I THINK WE SHOULD BE VERY THANKFUL OF OUR NEW STATUS, MR. IMMORTAL.
I AM, FLATMAN. REALLY. IT'S JUST THAT SURVIVING COUNTLESS DEATHS HAS MADE ME A BIT CYNICAL, HASN'T IT?
THAT, PLUS, YOU KNOW... BETWEEN 1997 AND 2003 THE DEFENSE DEPARTMENT PURCHASED 270,000 COMMERCIAL AIRLINE TICKETS AT A TOTAL COST OF $100 MILLION, WHICH WENT UNUSED...AND UNRETURNED...EVEN THOUGH THEY WERE FULLY REFUNDABLE TICKETS.
AS AN EXAMPLE. IS ALL I'M SAYING.
DARN! THAT WAS CYNICAL TOO, WASN'T IT?
LET'S SEE IF THE OTHERS ARE IN POSITION...
GLI TACTICAL TEAM ONE STATUS A GO!
UNITS TWO AND THREE, REPORT IN.
TEAM TWO IN POSITION! AM I A TEAM IF I'M BY MYSELF...?
YOU HAVE TIPPY-TOE WITH YOU, DOORMAN.
TIPPY-TOE IS A SQUIRREL.
Chrrtt
AND A DAMNED IMPORTANT PART OF THE TEAM... OF COURSE...
LOVE
TEAM THREE IN POSITION!
TEAM FOUR IN POSITION!

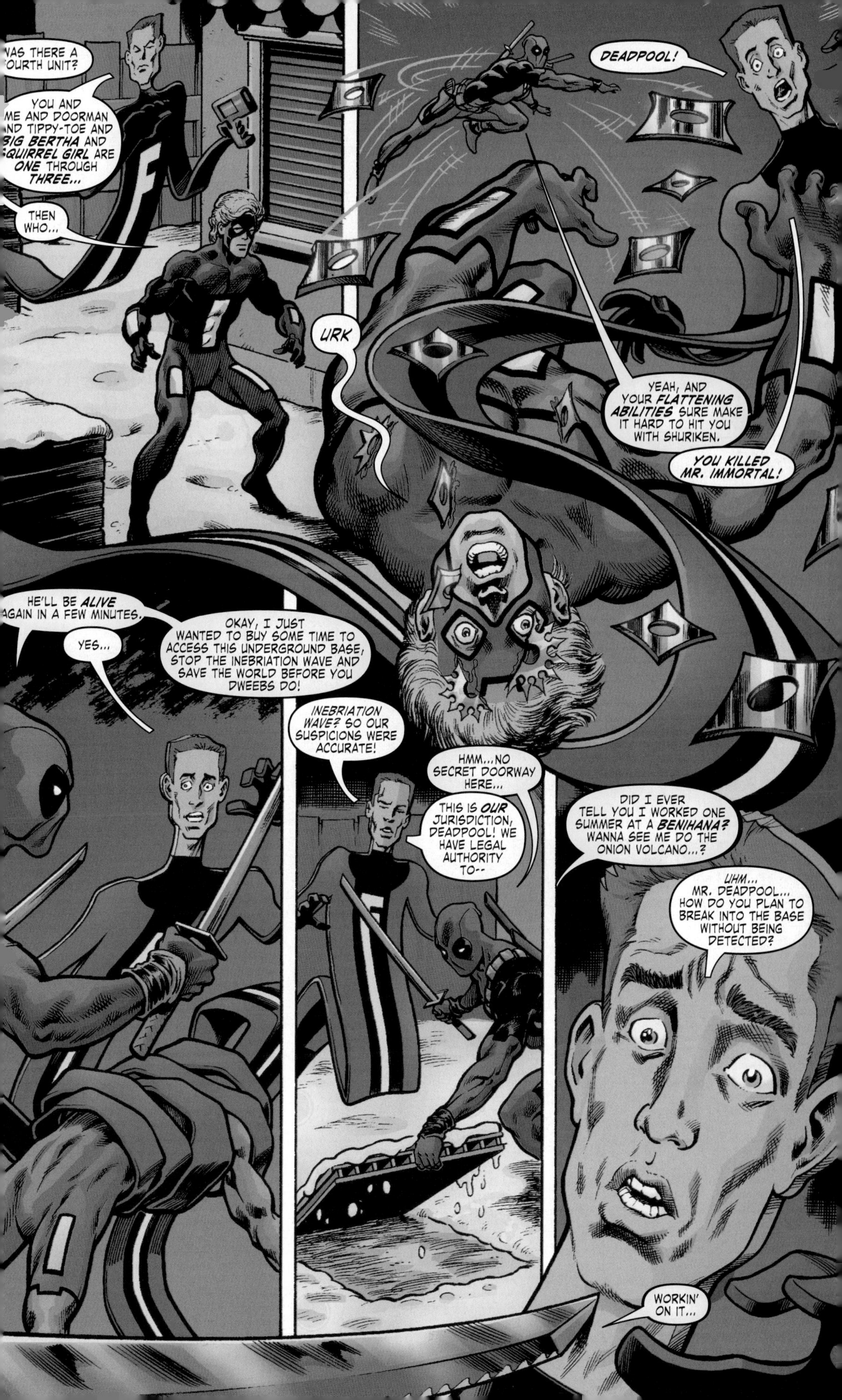

WAS THERE A FOURTH UNIT?
YOU AND ME AND DOORMAN AND TIPPY-TOE AND BIG BERTHA AND SQUIRREL GIRL ARE ONE THROUGH THREE...
THEN WHO...
DEADPOOL!
URK
YEAH, AND YOUR FLATTENING ABILITIES SURE MAKE IT HARD TO HIT YOU WITH SHURIKEN.
YOU KILLED MR. IMMORTAL!
HE'LL BE ALIVE AGAIN IN A FEW MINUTES.
YES...
OKAY, I JUST WANTED TO BUY SOME TIME TO ACCESS THIS UNDERGROUND BASE, STOP THE INEBRIATION WAVE AND SAVE THE WORLD BEFORE YOU DWEEBS DO!
INEBRIATION WAVE? SO OUR SUSPICIONS WERE ACCURATE!
HMM...NO SECRET DOORWAY HERE...
THIS IS OUR JURISDICTION, DEADPOOL! WE HAVE LEGAL AUTHORITY TO--
DID I EVER TELL YOU I WORKED ONE SUMMER AT A BENIHANA? WANNA SEE ME DO THE ONION VOLCANO...?
UHM... MR. DEADPOOL... HOW DO YOU PLAN TO BREAK INTO THE BASE WITHOUT BEING DETECTED?
WORKIN' ON IT...

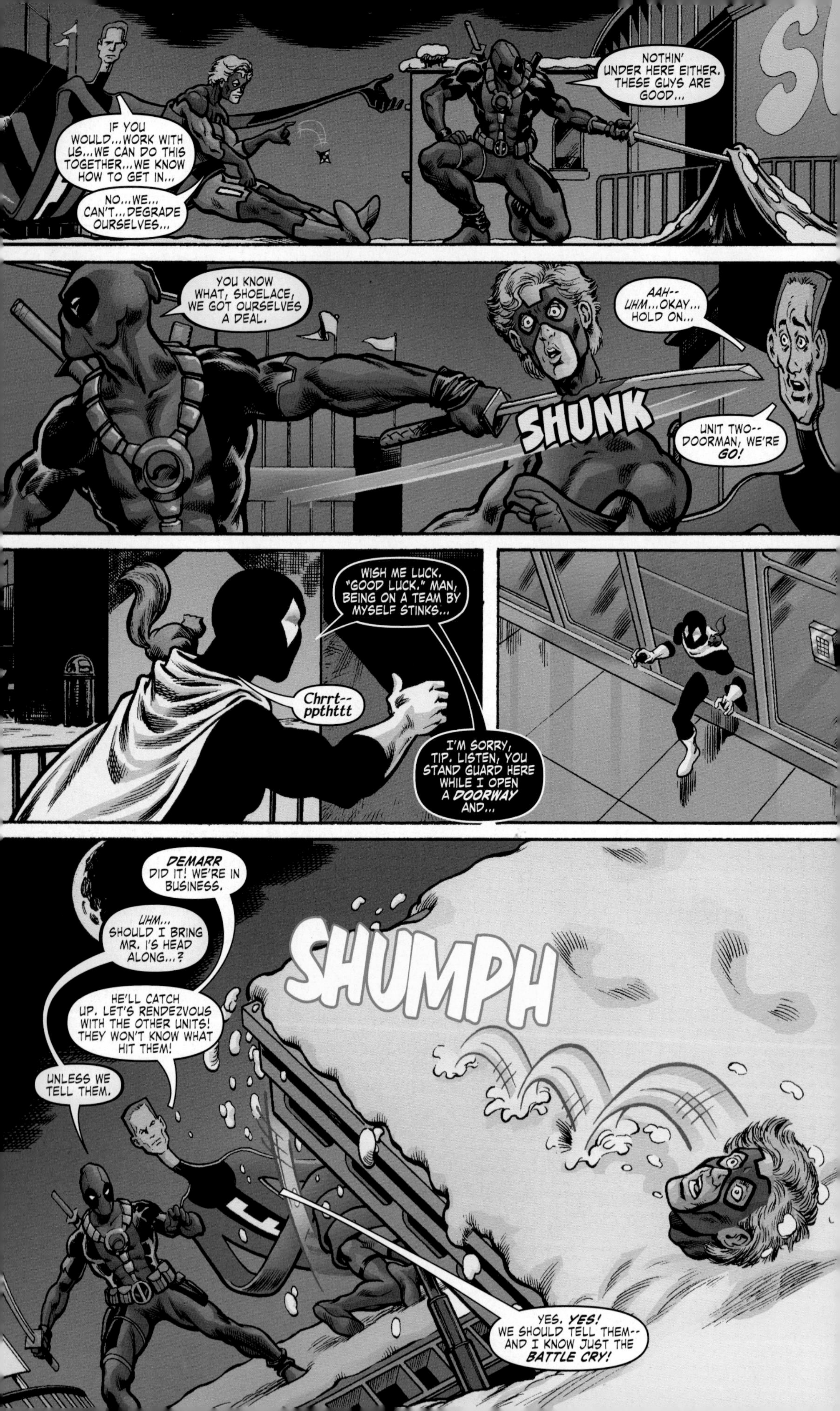
IF YOU WOULD...WORK WITH US...WE CAN DO THIS TOGETHER...WE KNOW HOW TO GET IN...
NO...WE... CAN'T...DEGRADE OURSELVES...
NOTHIN' UNDER HERE EITHER. THESE GUYS ARE GOOD...
YOU KNOW WHAT, SHOELACE, WE GOT OURSELVES A DEAL.
SHUNK
AAH-- UHM...OKAY... HOLD ON...
UNIT TWO-- DOORMAN, WE'RE GO!
WISH ME LUCK. "GOOD LUCK." MAN, BEING ON A TEAM BY MYSELF STINKS...
Chrrt-- ppthttt
I'M SORRY, TIP. LISTEN, YOU STAND GUARD HERE WHILE I OPEN A DOORWAY AND...
DEMARR DID IT! WE'RE IN BUSINESS.
UHM... SHOULD I BRING MR. I'S HEAD ALONG...?
SHUMPH
HE'LL CATCH UP. LET'S RENDEZVOUS WITH THE OTHER UNITS! THEY WON'T KNOW WHAT HIT THEM!
UNLESS WE TELL THEM.
YES. YES! WE SHOULD TELL THEM-- AND I KNOW JUST THE BATTLE CRY!

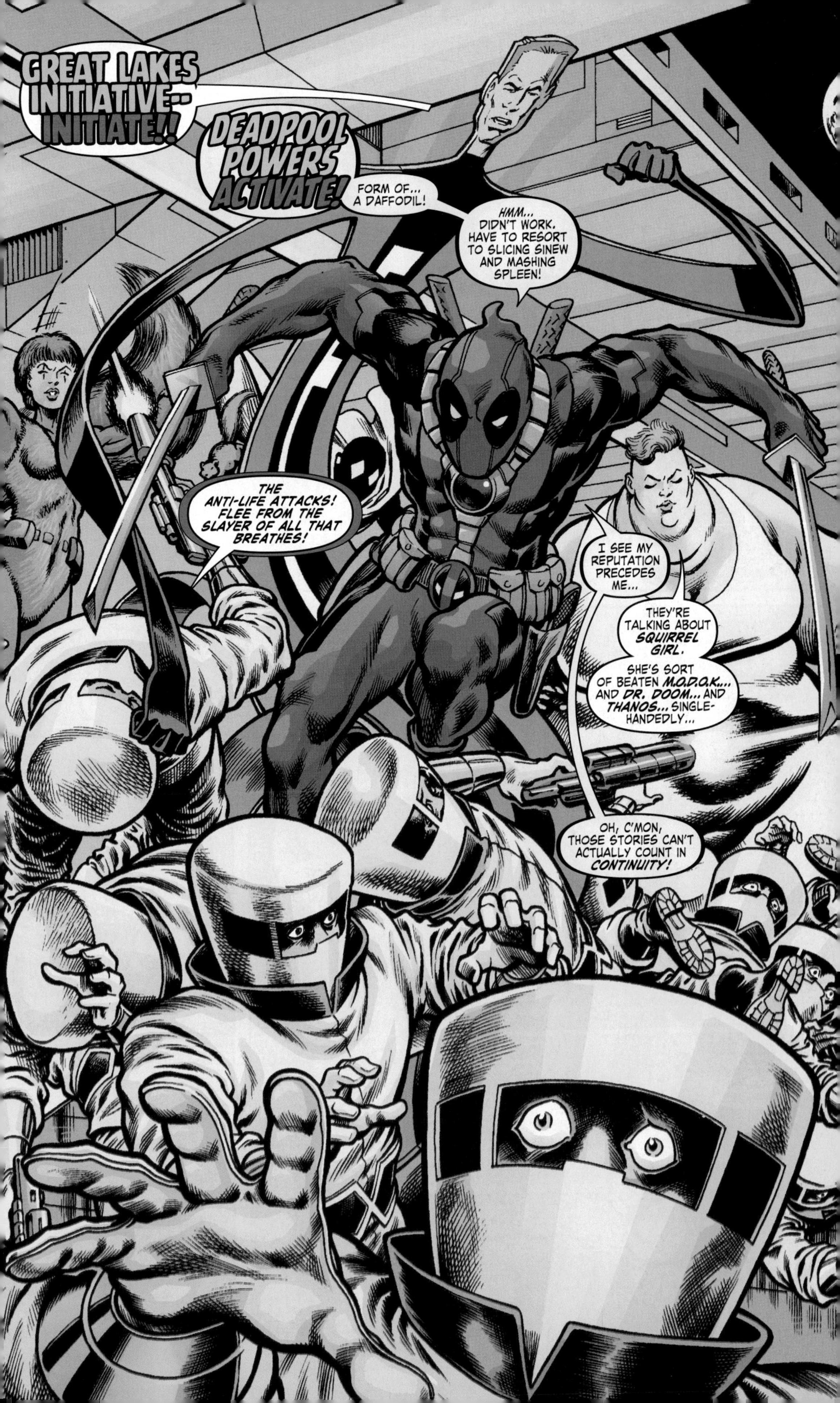
GREAT LAKES INITIATIVE-- INITIATE!!
DEADPOOL POWERS ACTIVATE!
FORM OF... A DAFFODIL!
HMM... DIDN'T WORK. HAVE TO RESORT TO SLICING SINEW AND MASHING SPLEEN!
THE ANTI-LIFE ATTACKS! FLEE FROM THE SLAYER OF ALL THAT BREATHES!
I SEE MY REPUTATION PRECEDES ME...
THEY'RE TALKING ABOUT SQUIRREL GIRL.
SHE'S SORT OF BEATEN M.O.D.O.K... AND DR. DOOM... AND THANOS... SINGLE-HANDEDLY...
OH, C'MON, THOSE STORIES CAN'T ACTUALLY COUNT IN CONTINUITY!

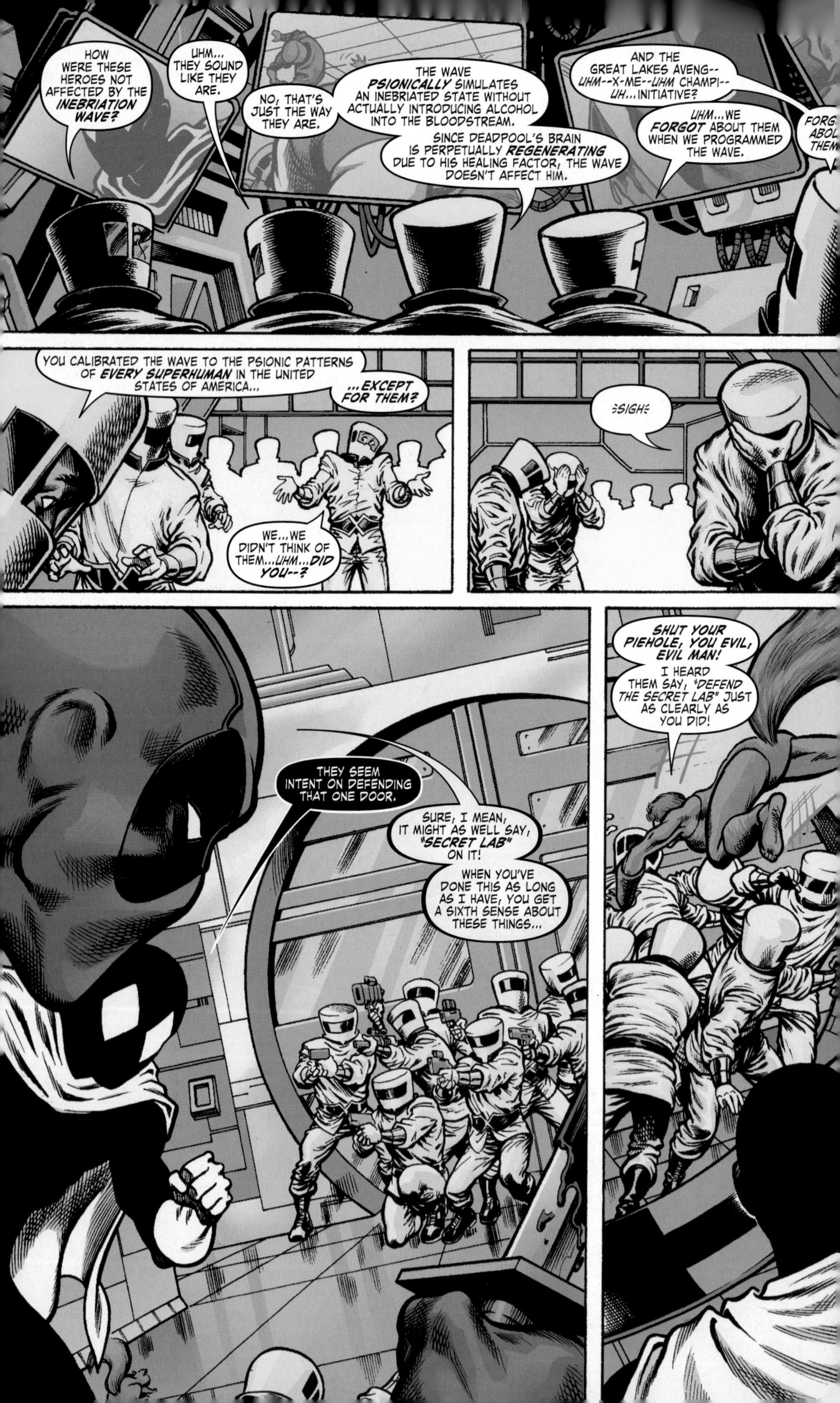

HOW WERE THESE HEROES NOT AFFECTED BY THE INEBRIATION WAVE?
UHM... THEY SOUND LIKE THEY ARE.
NO, THAT'S JUST THE WAY THEY ARE.
THE WAVE PSIONICALLY SIMULATES AN INEBRIATED STATE WITHOUT ACTUALLY INTRODUCING ALCOHOL INTO THE BLOODSTREAM.
SINCE DEADPOOL'S BRAIN IS PERPETUALLY REGENERATING DUE TO HIS HEALING FACTOR, THE WAVE DOESN'T AFFECT HIM.
AND THE GREAT LAKES AVENG--UHM--X-ME--UHM CHAMPI--UH...INITIATIVE?
UHM...WE FORGOT ABOUT THEM WHEN WE PROGRAMMED THE WAVE.
YOU CALIBRATED THE WAVE TO THE PSIONIC PATTERNS OF EVERY SUPERHUMAN IN THE UNITED STATES OF AMERICA...
...EXCEPT FOR THEM?
WE...WE DIDN'T THINK OF THEM...UHM...DID YOU--?
SIGH
THEY SEEM INTENT ON DEFENDING THAT ONE DOOR.
SURE, I MEAN, IT MIGHT AS WELL SAY, "SECRET LAB" ON IT!
WHEN YOU'VE DONE THIS AS LONG AS I HAVE, YOU GET A SIXTH SENSE ABOUT THESE THINGS...
SHUT YOUR PIEHOLE, YOU EVIL, EVIL MAN!
I HEARD THEM SAY, "DEFEND THE SECRET LAB" JUST AS CLEARLY AS YOU DID!

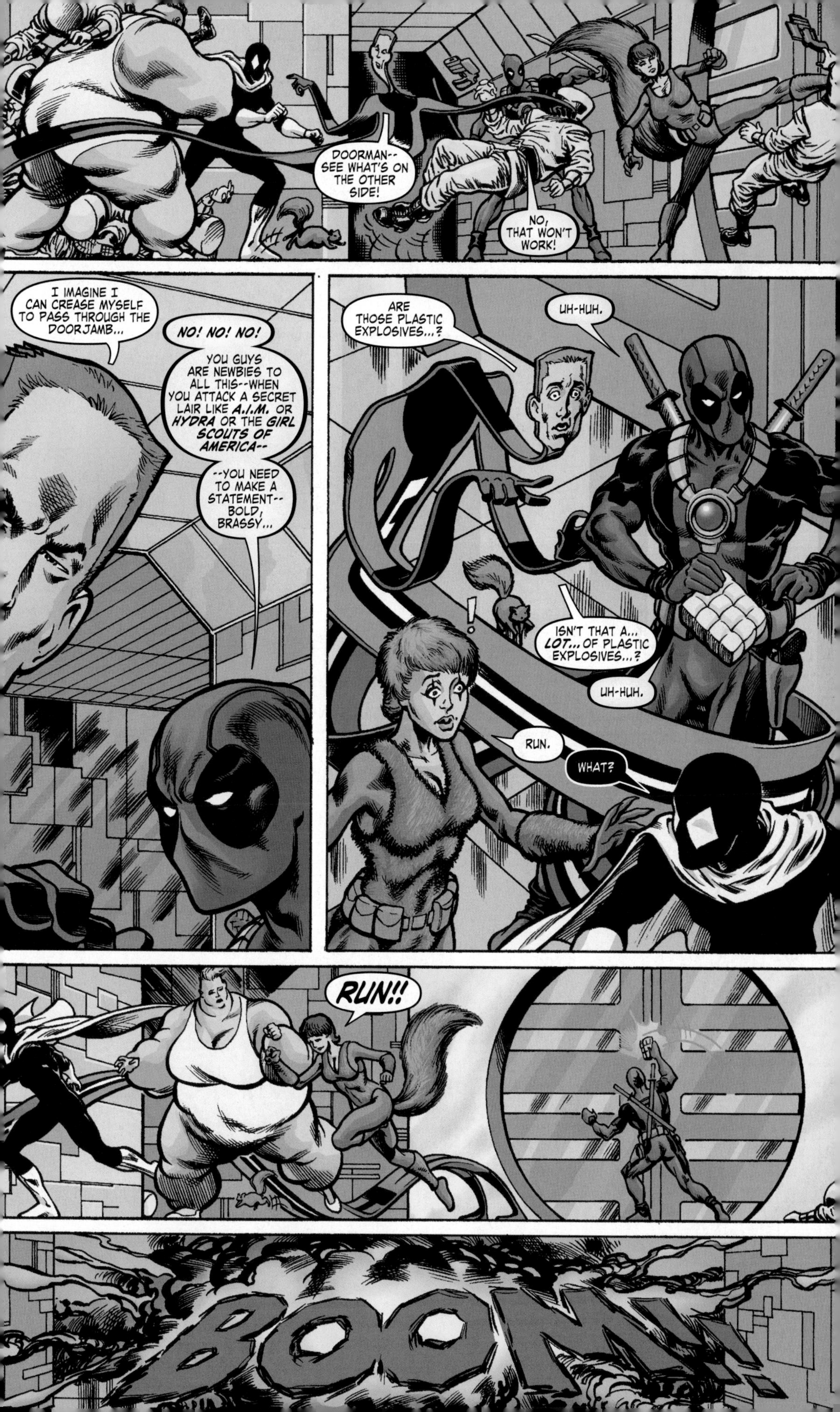
DOORMAN--
SEE WHAT'S ON THE OTHER SIDE!
NO, THAT WON'T WORK!
I IMAGINE I CAN CREASE MYSELF TO PASS THROUGH THE DOORJAMB...
NO! NO! NO!
YOU GUYS ARE NEWBIES TO ALL THIS--WHEN YOU ATTACK A SECRET LAIR LIKE A.I.M. OR HYDRA OR THE GIRL SCOUTS OF AMERICA--
--YOU NEED TO MAKE A STATEMENT--BOLD, BRASSY...
ARE THOSE PLASTIC EXPLOSIVES...?
UH-HUH.
!
ISN'T THAT A... LOT... OF PLASTIC EXPLOSIVES...?
UH-HUH.
RUN.
WHAT?
RUN!!
BOOM!!

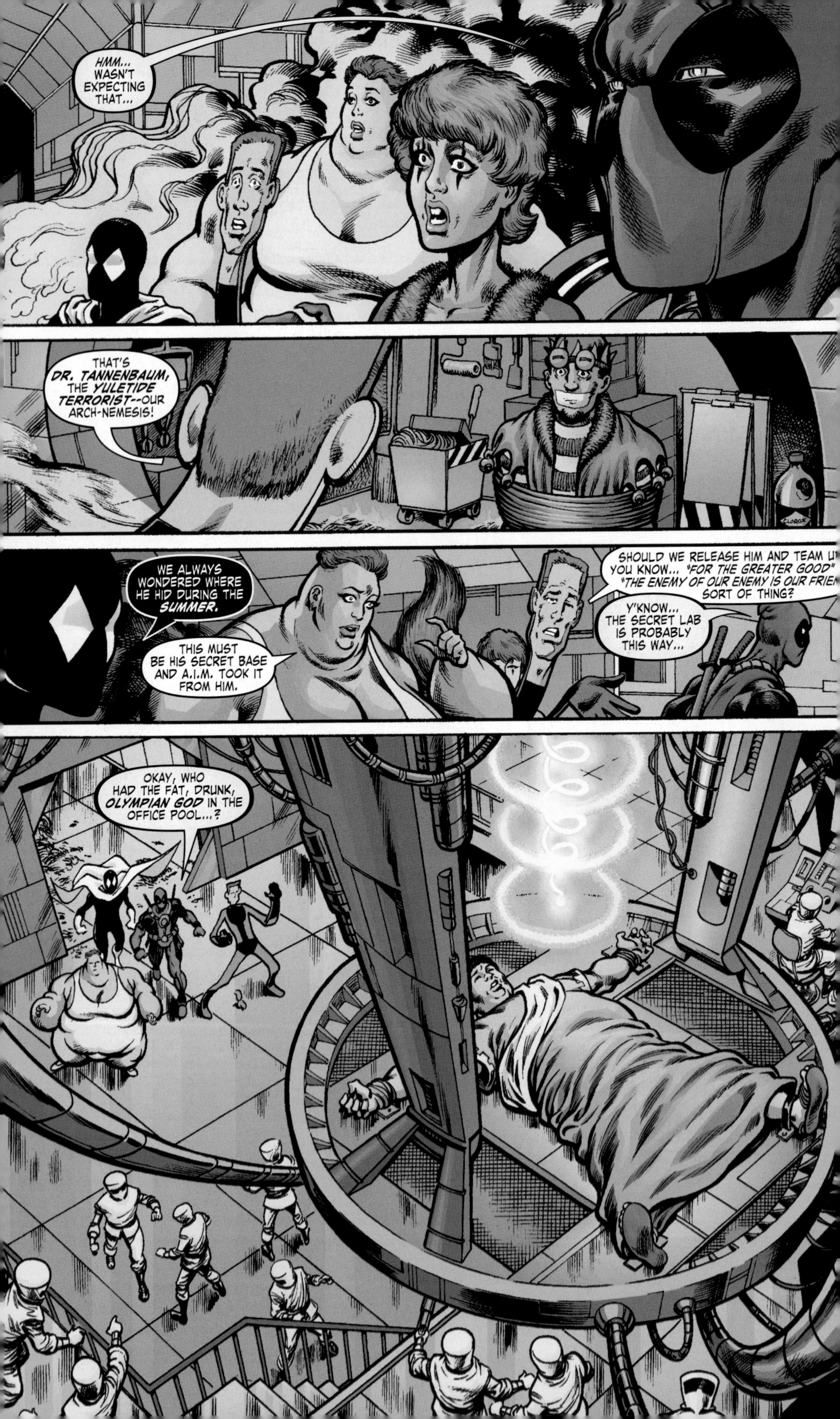

HMM... WASN'T EXPECTING THAT...
THAT'S *DR. TANNENBAUM,* THE *YULETIDE TERRORIST*--OUR ARCH-NEMESIS!
CLOROX
WE ALWAYS WONDERED WHERE HE HID DURING THE *SUMMER.*
THIS MUST BE HIS SECRET BASE AND A.I.M. TOOK IT FROM HIM.
SHOULD WE RELEASE HIM AND TEAM U
YOU KNOW... *"FOR THE GREATER GOOD"*
"THE ENEMY OF OUR ENEMY IS OUR FRIE
SORT OF THING?
Y'KNOW... THE SECRET LAB IS PROBABLY THIS WAY...
OKAY, WHO HAD THE FAT, DRUNK, *OLYMPIAN GOD* IN THE OFFICE POOL...?

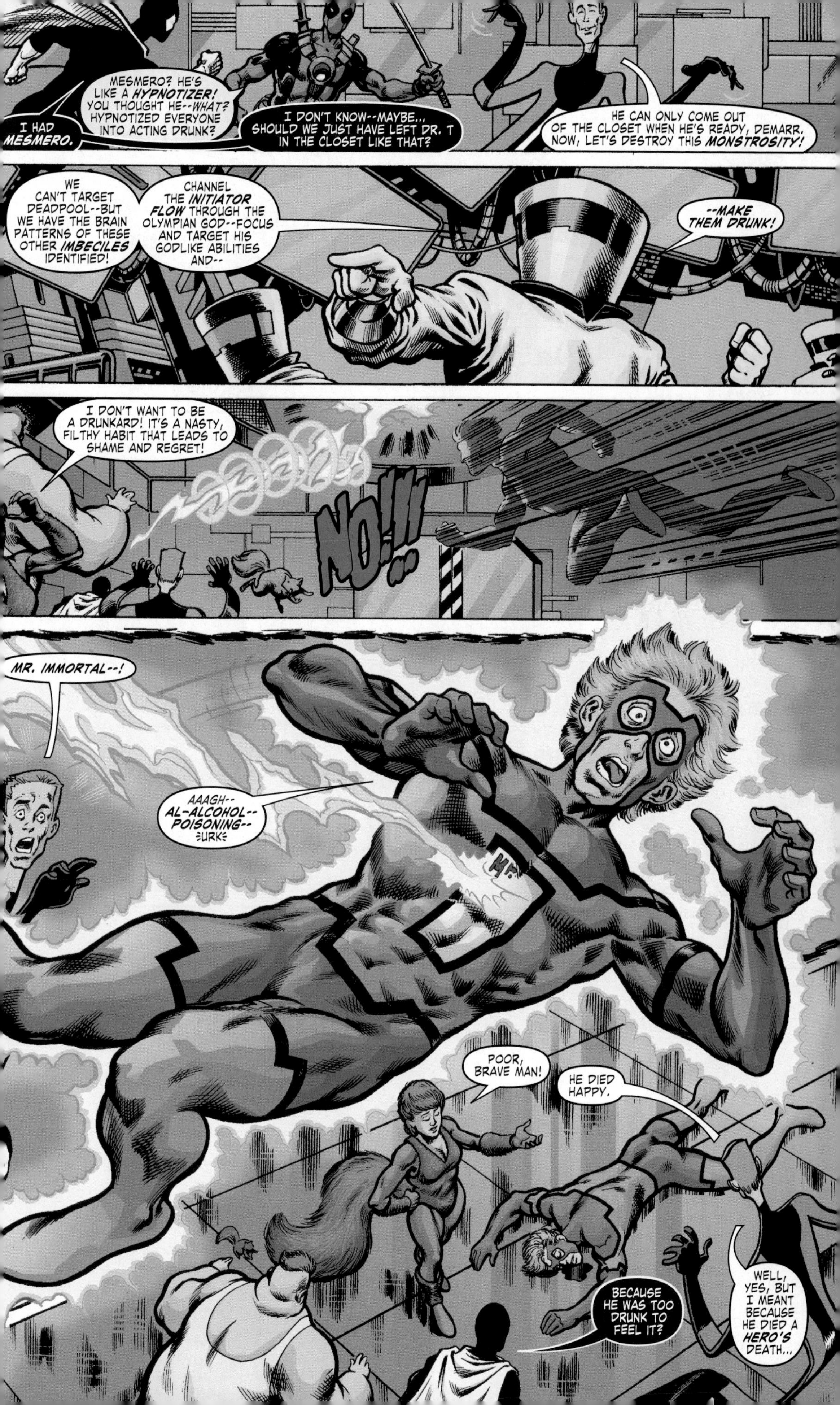

I HAD MESMERO.
MESMERO? HE'S LIKE A HYPNOTIZER! YOU THOUGHT HE--WHAT? HYPNOTIZED EVERYONE INTO ACTING DRUNK?
I DON'T KNOW--MAYBE... SHOULD WE JUST HAVE LEFT DR. T IN THE CLOSET LIKE THAT?
HE CAN ONLY COME OUT OF THE CLOSET WHEN HE'S READY, DEMARR. NOW, LET'S DESTROY THIS MONSTROSITY!
WE CAN'T TARGET DEADPOOL--BUT WE HAVE THE BRAIN PATTERNS OF THESE OTHER IMBECILES IDENTIFIED!
CHANNEL THE INITIATOR FLOW THROUGH THE OLYMPIAN GOD--FOCUS AND TARGET HIS GODLIKE ABILITIES AND--
--MAKE THEM DRUNK!
I DON'T WANT TO BE A DRUNKARD! IT'S A NASTY, FILTHY HABIT THAT LEADS TO SHAME AND REGRET!
NO!!!
MR. IMMORTAL--!
AAAGH-- AL-ALCOHOL-- POISONING-- URK
POOR, BRAVE MAN!
HE DIED HAPPY.
BECAUSE HE WAS TOO DRUNK TO FEEL IT?
WELL, YES, BUT I MEANT BECAUSE HE DIED A HERO'S DEATH...

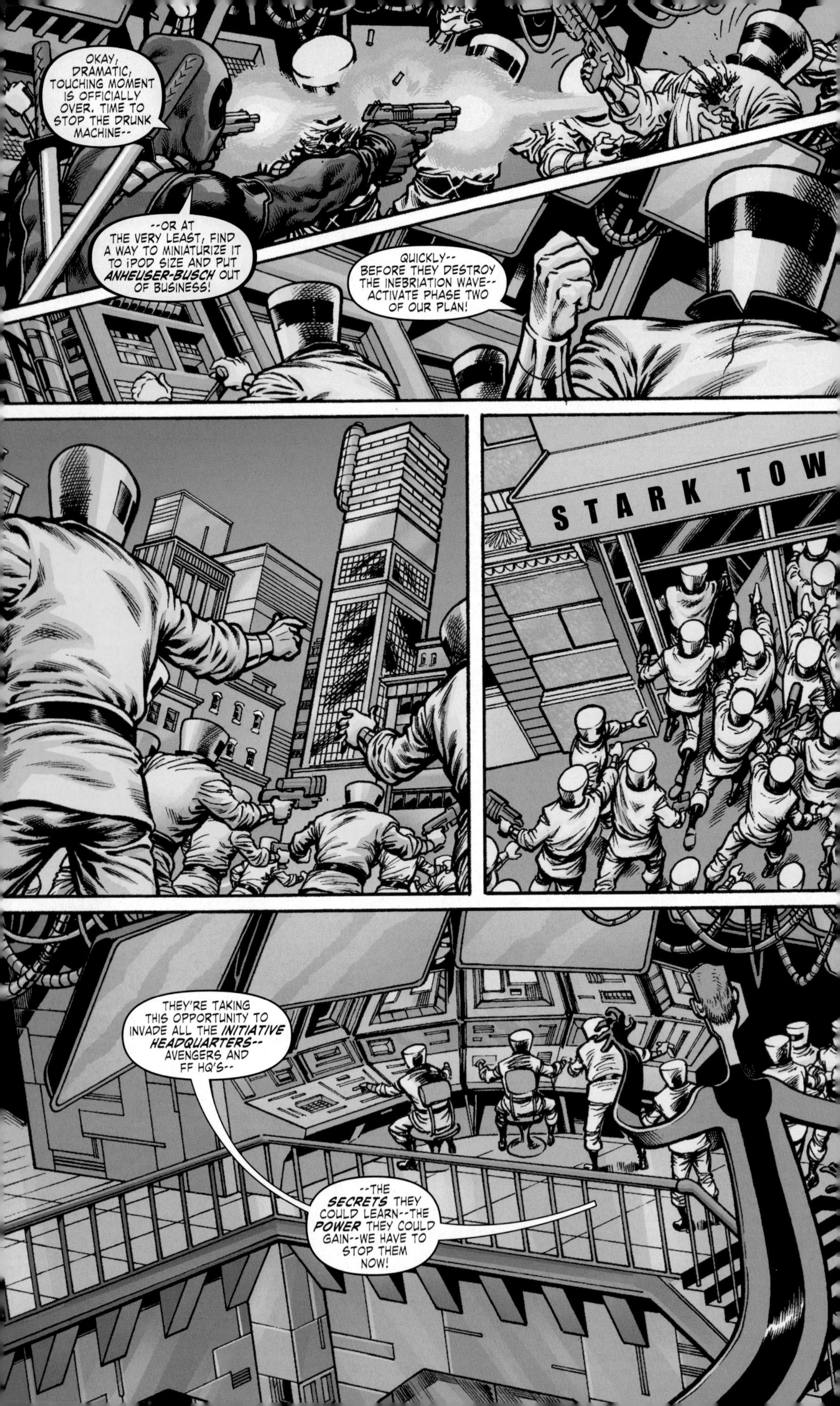

OKAY, DRAMATIC, TOUCHING MOMENT IS OFFICIALLY OVER. TIME TO STOP THE DRUNK MACHINE--
--OR AT THE VERY LEAST, FIND A WAY TO MINIATURIZE IT TO iPOD SIZE AND PUT ANHEUSER-BUSCH OUT OF BUSINESS!
QUICKLY-- BEFORE THEY DESTROY THE INEBRIATION WAVE-- ACTIVATE PHASE TWO OF OUR PLAN!
STARK TOW
THEY'RE TAKING THIS OPPORTUNITY TO INVADE ALL THE INITIATIVE HEADQUARTERS-- AVENGERS AND FF HQ'S--
--THE SECRETS THEY COULD LEARN--THE POWER THEY COULD GAIN--WE HAVE TO STOP THEM NOW!

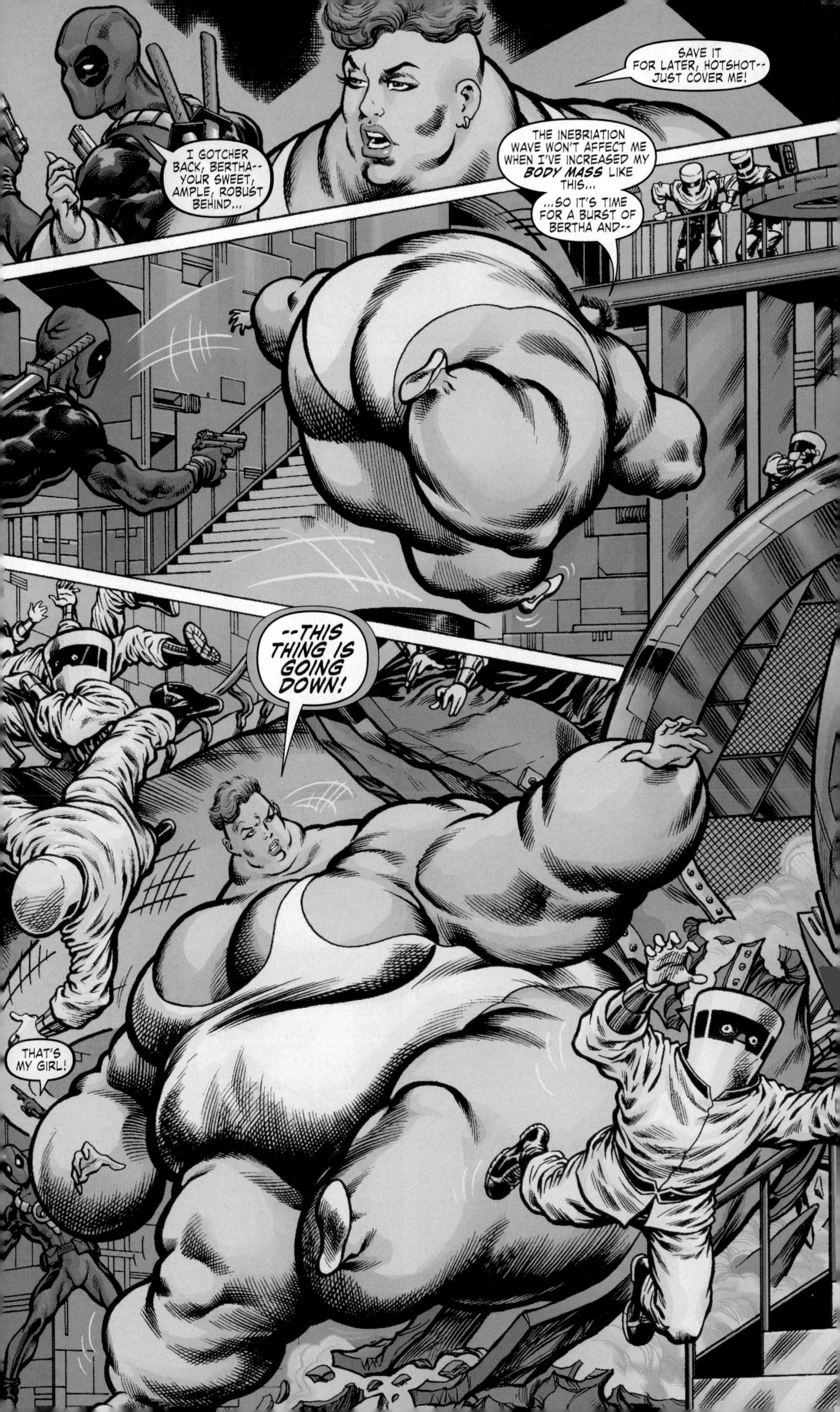
SAVE IT FOR LATER, HOTSHOT-- JUST COVER ME!
I GOTCHER BACK, BERTHA-- YOUR SWEET, AMPLE, ROBUST BEHIND...
THE INEBRIATION WAVE WON'T AFFECT ME WHEN I'VE INCREASED MY BODY MASS LIKE THIS...
...SO IT'S TIME FOR A BURST OF BERTHA AND--
--THIS THING IS GOING DOWN!
THAT'S MY GIRL!

SO... GOD-GUY, YOU'RE SAYING DRINKS ARE ALWAYS ON THE HOUSE WHEN YOU'RE AROUND...?

≈HIC≈-- INDEED... ≈HIC≈

WANNA BE MY PARTNER? OR MY SIDEKICK? YOU CAN BE MY WARD...

BUT WITH THE INEBRIATION W... DESTROYED, SUPERHUMANS EMERGE FRO THEIR DRUNK STUPOR...

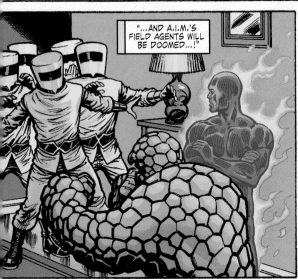

"...AND A.I.M.'S FIELD AGENTS WILL BE DOOMED...!"

UHM... WHAT DO WE DO NOW?

WHAT DO YOU MEAN?

WELL... WE'VE NEVER ACTUALLY...UHM... SUCCESSFULLY... DONE THIS.

UNTIL NOW.

WE *WON?*

YUP.

PLEASE DON'T KILL ME AGAIN.

LATER?

MAYBE LATER.

WOW. WE WON.

YEAH. WE SHOULD GO TO DISNEYWORLD OR SOMETHING.

WE CAN'T ABUSE VALUABLE TAXPAYER DOLLARS THAT WAY, MR. DEADPOOL. BUT WE HAVE THE NEXT BEST THING NOW...

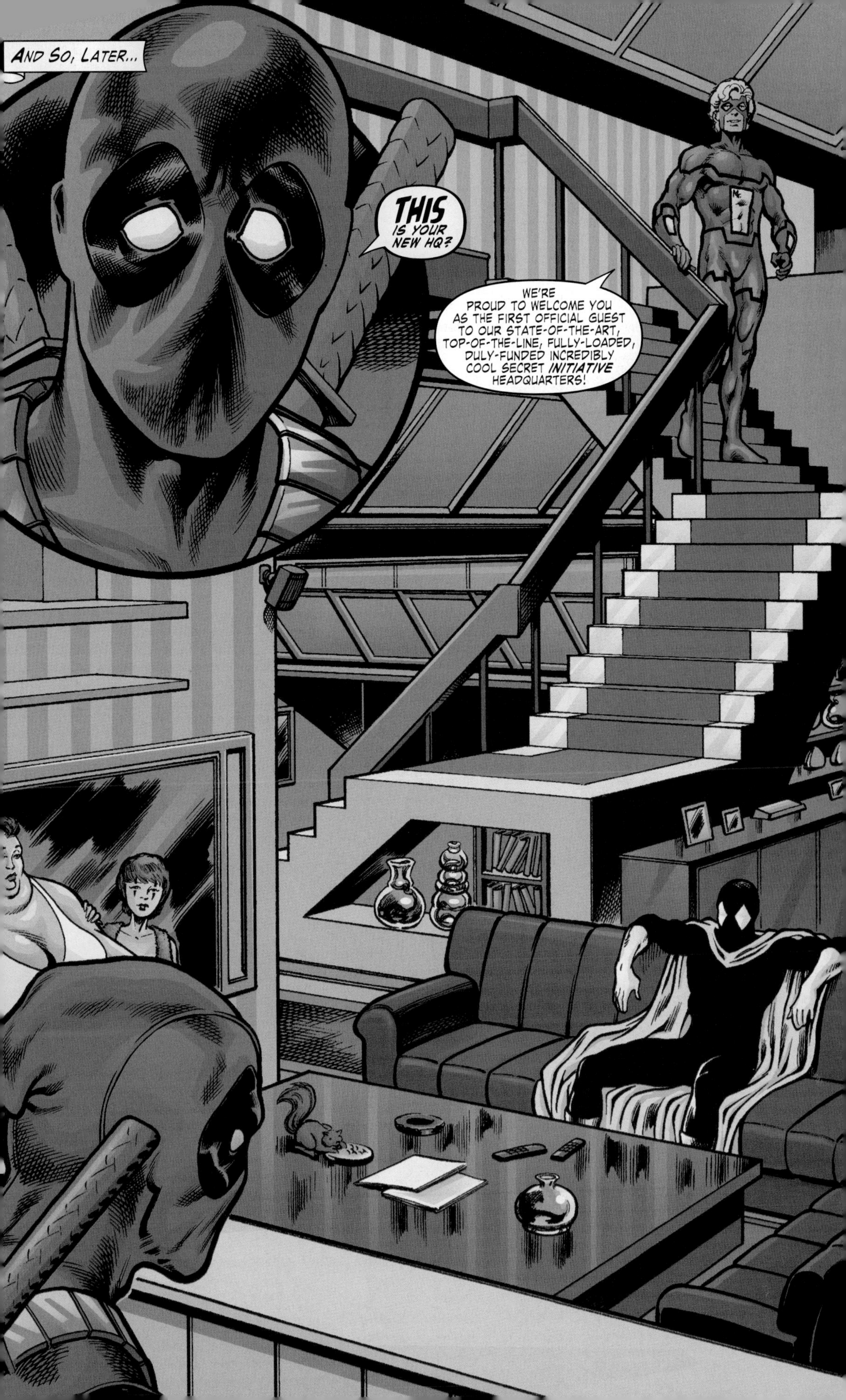
AND SO, LATER...
THIS IS YOUR NEW HQ?
WE'RE PROUD TO WELCOME YOU AS THE FIRST OFFICIAL GUEST TO OUR STATE-OF-THE-ART, TOP-OF-THE-LINE, FULLY-LOADED, DULY-FUNDED INCREDIBLY COOL SECRET *INITIATIVE* HEADQUARTERS!

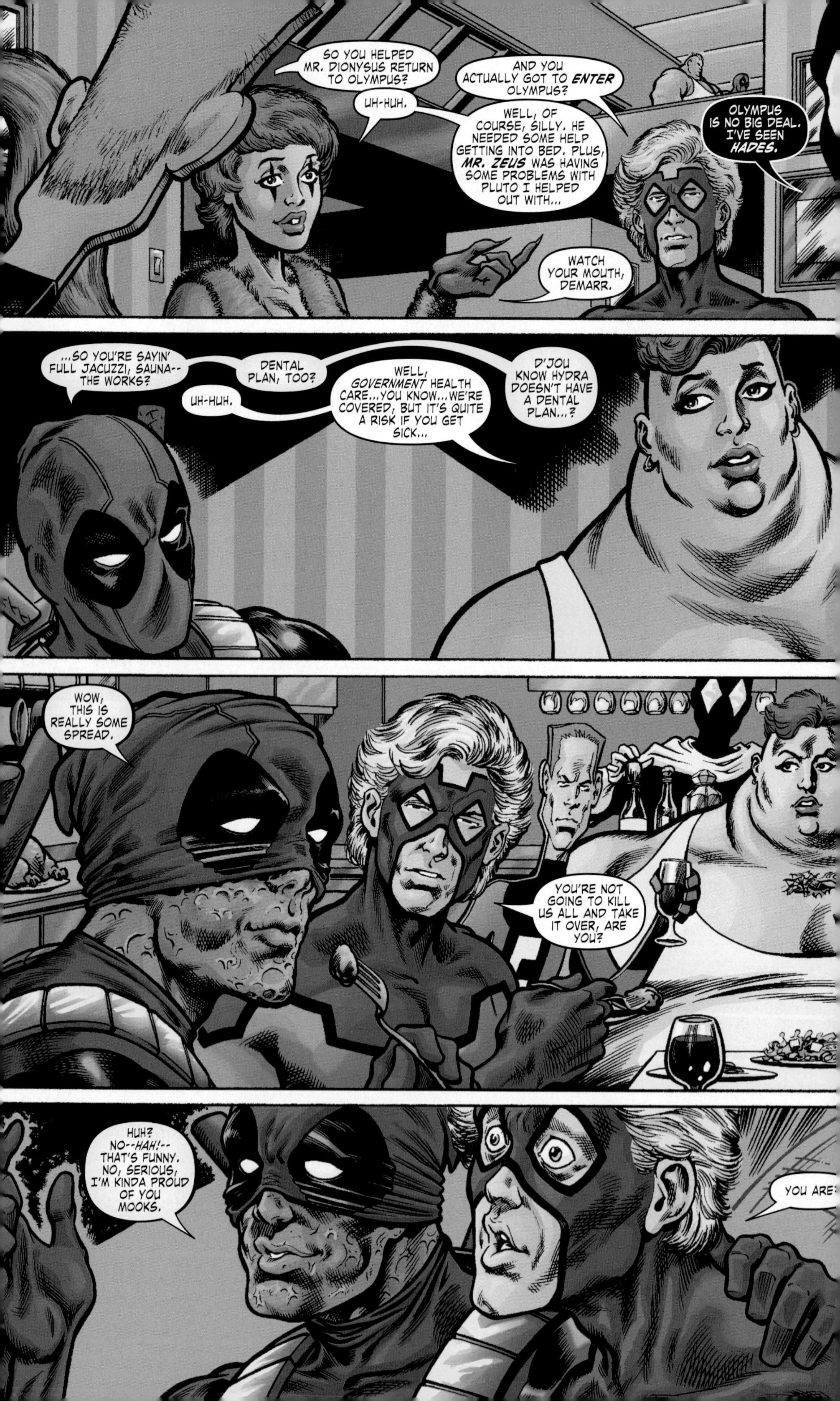
SO YOU HELPED MR. DIONYSUS RETURN TO OLYMPUS?
AND YOU ACTUALLY GOT TO *ENTER* OLYMPUS?
UH-HUH.
WELL, OF COURSE, SILLY. HE NEEDED SOME HELP GETTING INTO BED. PLUS, *MR. ZEUS* WAS HAVING SOME PROBLEMS WITH PLUTO I HELPED OUT WITH...
OLYMPUS IS NO BIG DEAL. I'VE SEEN *HADES.*
WATCH YOUR MOUTH, DEMARR.
...SO YOU'RE SAYIN' FULL JACUZZI, SAUNA-- THE WORKS?
UH-HUH.
DENTAL PLAN, TOO?
WELL, *GOVERNMENT* HEALTH CARE...YOU KNOW...WE'RE COVERED, BUT IT'S QUITE A RISK IF YOU GET SICK...
D'JOU KNOW HYDRA DOESN'T HAVE A DENTAL PLAN...?
WOW, THIS IS REALLY SOME SPREAD.
YOU'RE NOT GOING TO KILL US ALL AND TAKE IT OVER, ARE YOU?
HUH? NO--*HAH!*-- THAT'S FUNNY. NO, SERIOUS, I'M KINDA PROUD OF YOU MOOKS.
YOU ARE?

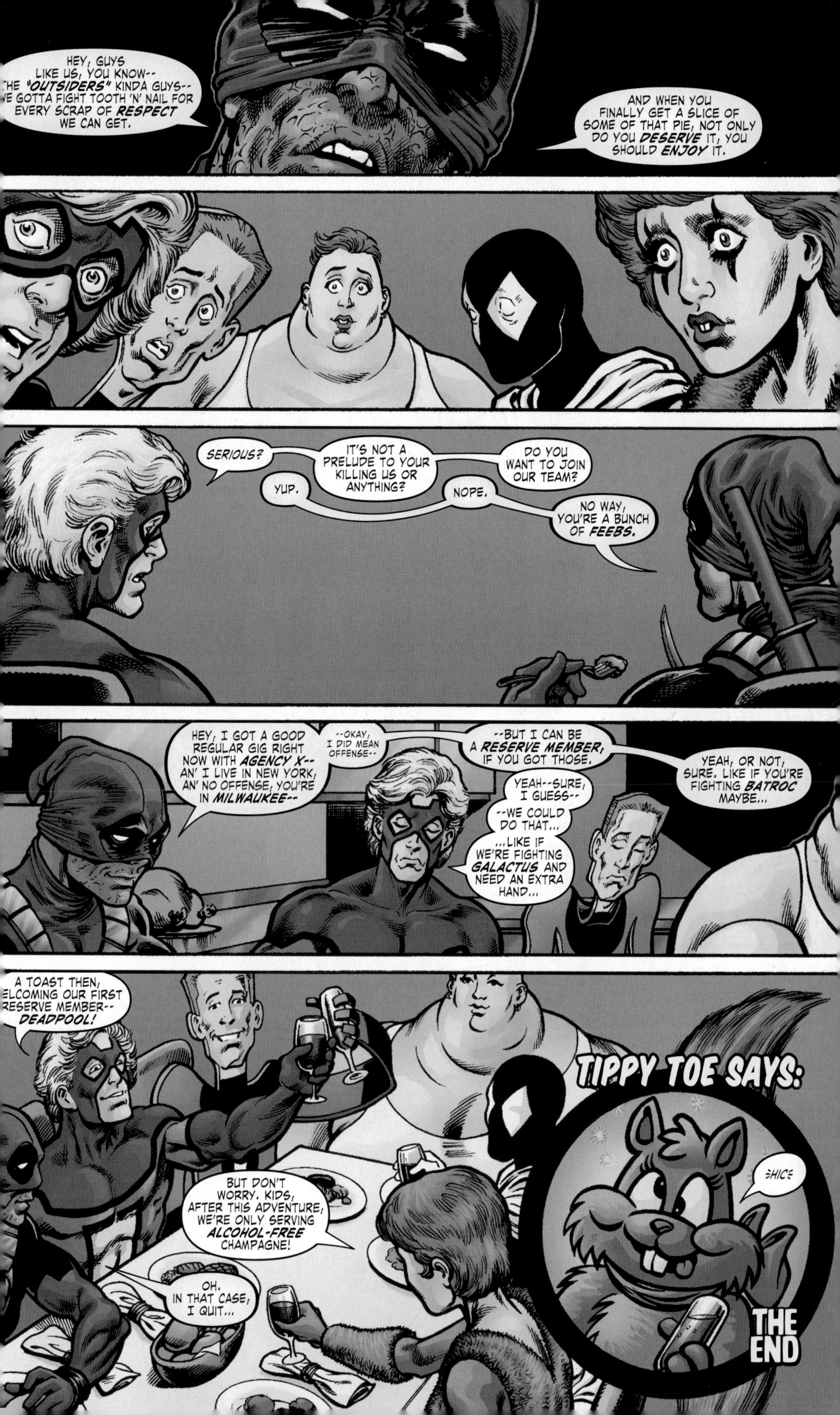

HEY, GUYS LIKE US, YOU KNOW-- THE "OUTSIDERS" KINDA GUYS-- WE GOTTA FIGHT TOOTH 'N' NAIL FOR EVERY SCRAP OF RESPECT WE CAN GET.
AND WHEN YOU FINALLY GET A SLICE OF SOME OF THAT PIE, NOT ONLY DO YOU DESERVE IT, YOU SHOULD ENJOY IT.
SERIOUS?
YUP.
IT'S NOT A PRELUDE TO YOUR KILLING US OR ANYTHING?
NOPE.
DO YOU WANT TO JOIN OUR TEAM?
NO WAY, YOU'RE A BUNCH OF FEEBS.
HEY, I GOT A GOOD REGULAR GIG RIGHT NOW WITH AGENCY X-- AN' I LIVE IN NEW YORK, AN' NO OFFENSE, YOU'RE IN MILWAUKEE--
--OKAY, I DID MEAN OFFENSE--
--BUT I CAN BE A RESERVE MEMBER, IF YOU GOT THOSE.
YEAH--SURE, I GUESS--
--WE COULD DO THAT...
...LIKE IF WE'RE FIGHTING GALACTUS AND NEED AN EXTRA HAND...
YEAH, OR NOT, SURE. LIKE IF YOU'RE FIGHTING BATROC MAYBE...
A TOAST THEN, WELCOMING OUR FIRST RESERVE MEMBER-- DEADPOOL!
BUT DON'T WORRY, KIDS, AFTER THIS ADVENTURE, WE'RE ONLY SERVING ALCOHOL-FREE CHAMPAGNE!
OH. IN THAT CASE, I QUIT...
TIPPY TOE SAYS:
HIC
THE END

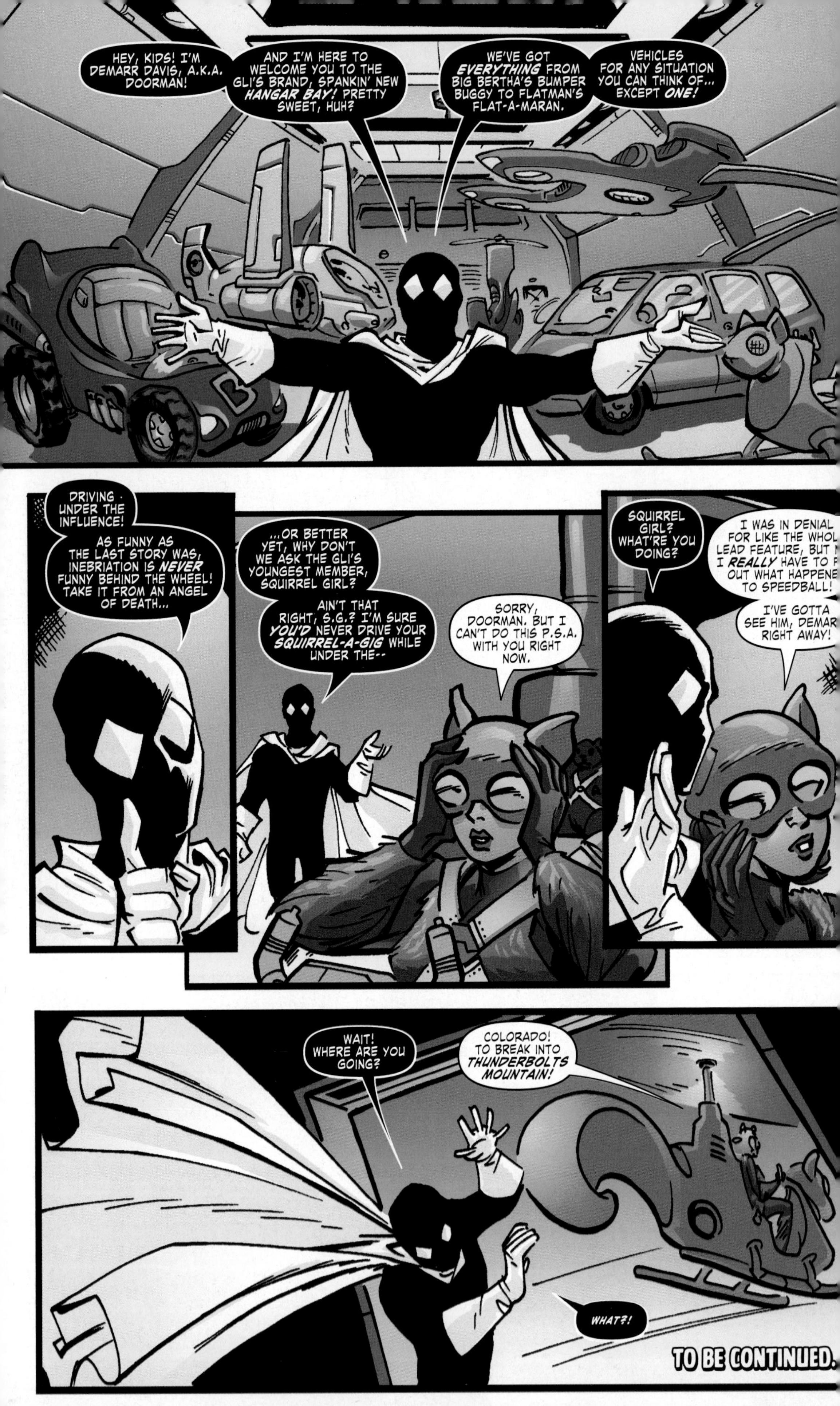
HEY, KIDS! I'M DEMARR DAVIS, A.K.A. DOORMAN!
AND I'M HERE TO WELCOME YOU TO THE GLI'S BRAND, SPANKIN' NEW HANGAR BAY! PRETTY SWEET, HUH?
WE'VE GOT EVERYTHING FROM BIG BERTHA'S BUMPER BUGGY TO FLATMAN'S FLAT-A-MARAN.
VEHICLES FOR ANY SITUATION YOU CAN THINK OF... EXCEPT ONE!
DRIVING UNDER THE INFLUENCE!
AS FUNNY AS THE LAST STORY WAS, INEBRIATION IS NEVER FUNNY BEHIND THE WHEEL! TAKE IT FROM AN ANGEL OF DEATH...
...OR BETTER YET, WHY DON'T WE ASK THE GLI'S YOUNGEST MEMBER, SQUIRREL GIRL?
AIN'T THAT RIGHT, S.G.? I'M SURE YOU'D NEVER DRIVE YOUR SQUIRREL-A-GIG WHILE UNDER THE--
SORRY, DOORMAN. BUT I CAN'T DO THIS P.S.A. WITH YOU RIGHT NOW.
SQUIRREL GIRL? WHAT'RE YOU DOING?
I WAS IN DENIAL FOR LIKE THE WHOL LEAD FEATURE, BUT I REALLY HAVE TO OUT WHAT HAPPENE TO SPEEDBALL!
I'VE GOTTA SEE HIM, DEMAR RIGHT AWAY!
WAIT! WHERE ARE YOU GOING?
COLORADO! TO BREAK INTO THUNDERBOLTS MOUNTAIN!
WHAT?!
TO BE CONTINUED.

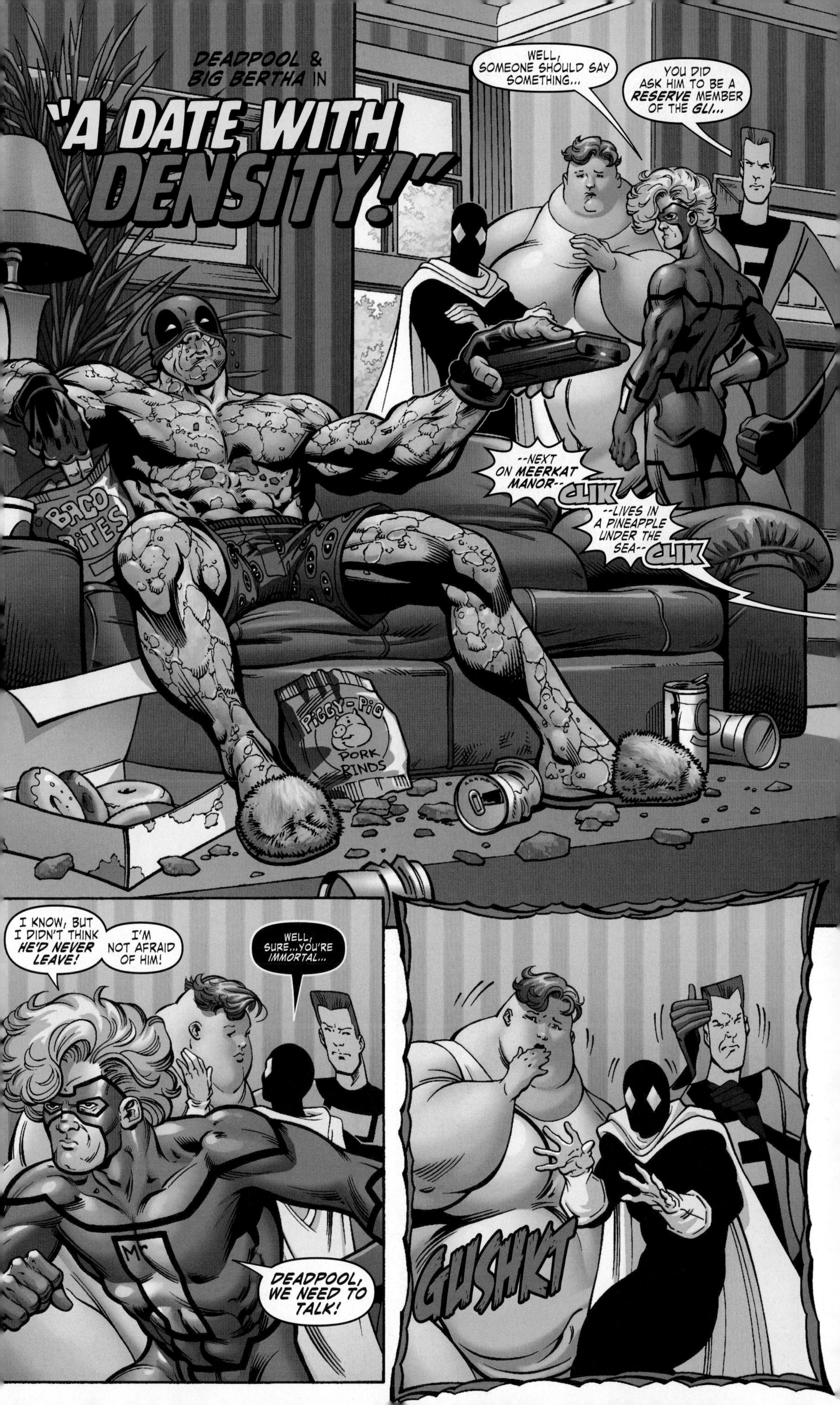

DEADPOOL & BIG BERTHA IN
"A DATE WITH DENSITY!"
WELL, SOMEONE SHOULD SAY SOMETHING...
YOU DID ASK HIM TO BE A RESERVE MEMBER OF THE GLI...
BACO BITES
--NEXT ON MEERKAT MANOR--
CLIK
--LIVES IN A PINEAPPLE UNDER THE SEA--
CLIK
PIGGY-PIG PORK RINDS
I KNOW, BUT I DIDN'T THINK HE'D NEVER LEAVE!
I'M NOT AFRAID OF HIM!
WELL, SURE...YOU'RE IMMORTAL...
DEADPOOL, WE NEED TO TALK!
GUSHKT

AAK

AAK

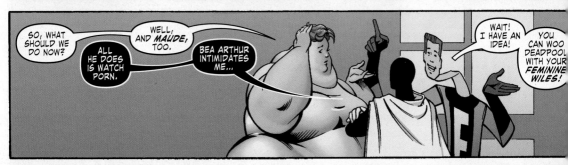

FWUMPH

WAS THAT THE UNIVERSAL REMOTE...?

YEAH.

SO, WHAT SHOULD WE DO NOW?

ALL HE DOES IS WATCH PORN.

WELL, AND MAUDE, TOO.

BEA ARTHUR INTIMIDATES ME...

WAIT! I HAVE AN IDEA! YOU CAN WOO DEADPOOL WITH YOUR FEMININE WILES!

YOU'RE SERIOUS ABOUT THIS?

THIS'LL WORK. HE'S TOTALLY GOT A THING FOR YOU. I CAN TELL.

GO ASK HIM OUT ON A DATE.

UHM... HI, WADE...

...I WAS WONDERING...

...IF YOU'RE NOT DOING ANYTHING TONIGHT...

WHY WOULD TONIGHT BE ANY DIFF'RENT THAN EVERY OTHER NIGHT, SWEETCHEEKS?

SO, MAYBE... YOU AND I... THE TWO OF US... COULD, Y'KNOW...?

WOOHOOOO!

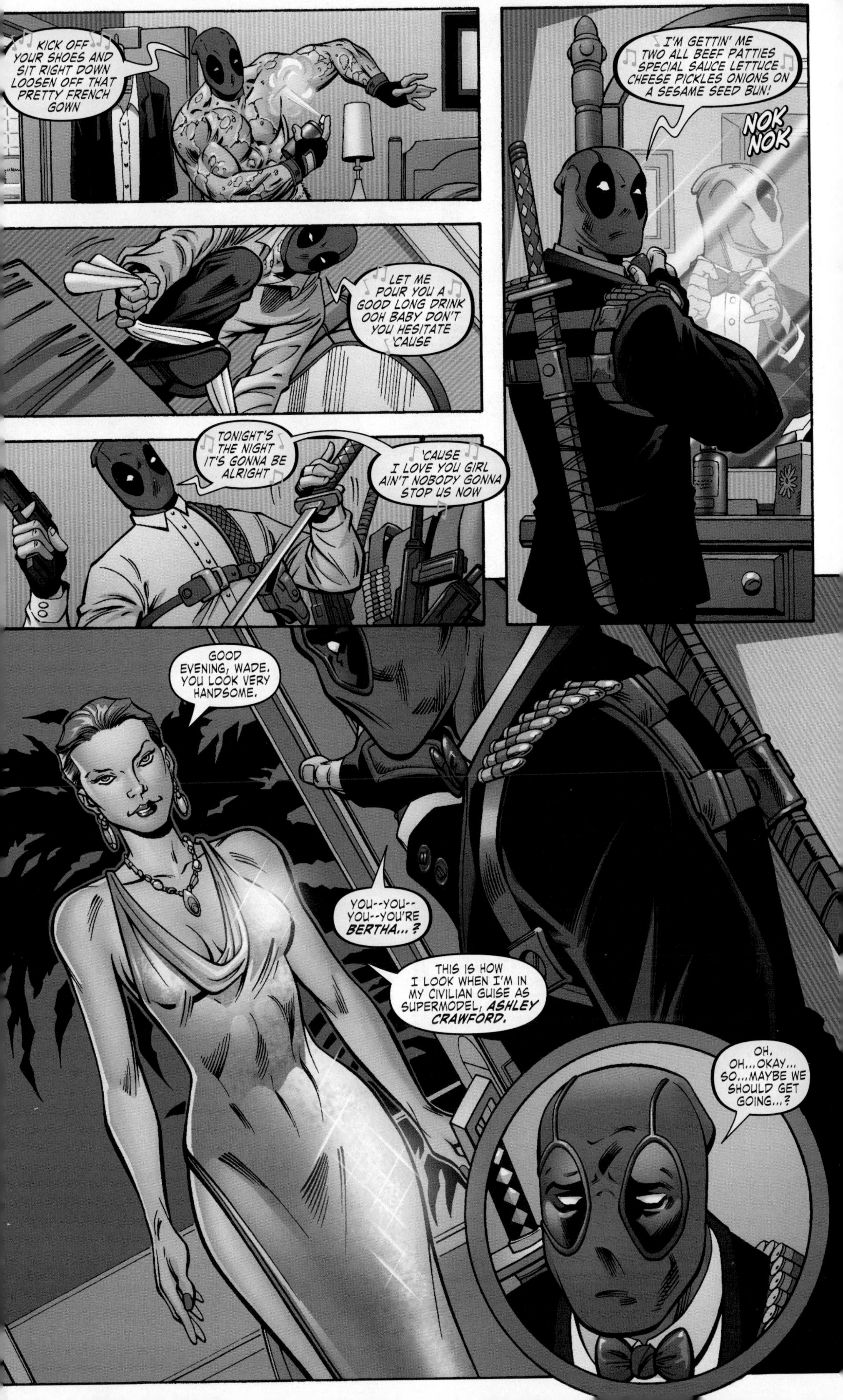
KICK OFF YOUR SHOES AND SIT RIGHT DOWN LOOSEN OFF THAT PRETTY FRENCH GOWN
LET ME POUR YOU A GOOD LONG DRINK OOH BABY DON'T YOU HESITATE 'CAUSE
TONIGHT'S THE NIGHT IT'S GONNA BE ALRIGHT
'CAUSE I LOVE YOU GIRL AIN'T NOBODY GONNA STOP US NOW
I'M GETTIN' ME TWO ALL BEEF PATTIES SPECIAL SAUCE LETTUCE CHEESE PICKLES ONIONS ON A SESAME SEED BUN!
NOK NOK
GOOD EVENING, WADE. YOU LOOK VERY HANDSOME.
YOU--YOU--YOU--YOU'RE BERTHA...?
THIS IS HOW I LOOK WHEN I'M IN MY CIVILIAN GUISE AS SUPERMODEL, ASHLEY CRAWFORD.
OH. OH...OKAY... SO...MAYBE WE SHOULD GET GOING...?

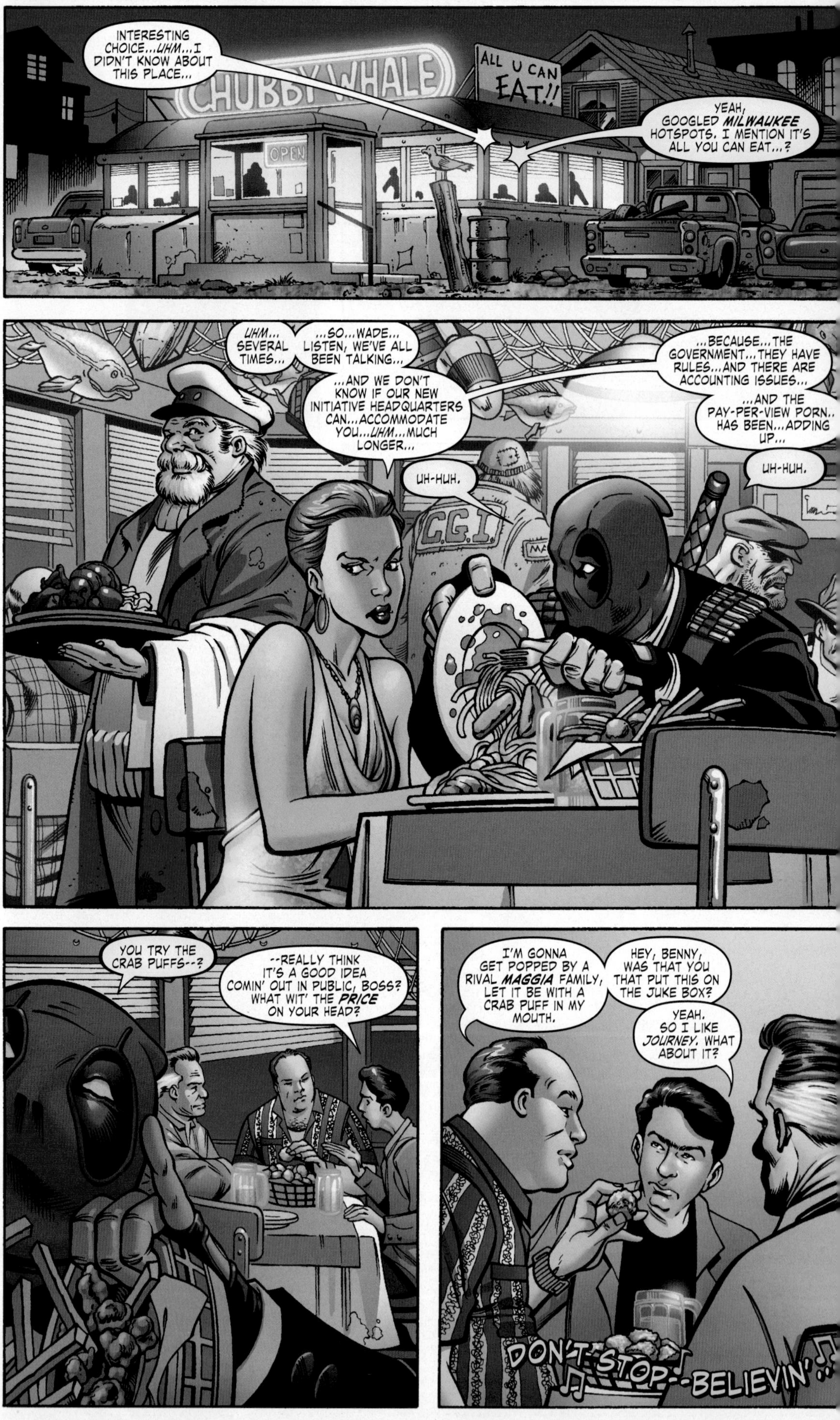
INTERESTING CHOICE...UHM...I DIDN'T KNOW ABOUT THIS PLACE...
CHUBBY WHALE
ALL U CAN EAT!!
OPEN
YEAH, GOOGLED MILWAUKEE HOTSPOTS. I MENTION IT'S ALL YOU CAN EAT...?
UHM... SEVERAL TIMES...
...SO...WADE... LISTEN, WE'VE ALL BEEN TALKING...
...AND WE DON'T KNOW IF OUR NEW INITIATIVE HEADQUARTERS CAN...ACCOMMODATE YOU...UHM...MUCH LONGER...
UH-HUH.
...BECAUSE...THE GOVERNMENT...THEY HAVE RULES...AND THERE ARE ACCOUNTING ISSUES...
...AND THE PAY-PER-VIEW PORN... HAS BEEN...ADDING UP...
UH-HUH.
C.G.I.
YOU TRY THE CRAB PUFFS--?
--REALLY THINK IT'S A GOOD IDEA COMIN' OUT IN PUBLIC, BOSS? WHAT WIT' THE PRICE ON YOUR HEAD?
I'M GONNA GET POPPED BY A RIVAL MAGGIA FAMILY, LET IT BE WITH A CRAB PUFF IN MY MOUTH.
HEY, BENNY, WAS THAT YOU THAT PUT THIS ON THE JUKE BOX?
YEAH. SO I LIKE JOURNEY. WHAT ABOUT IT?
DON'T STOP--BELIEVIN'

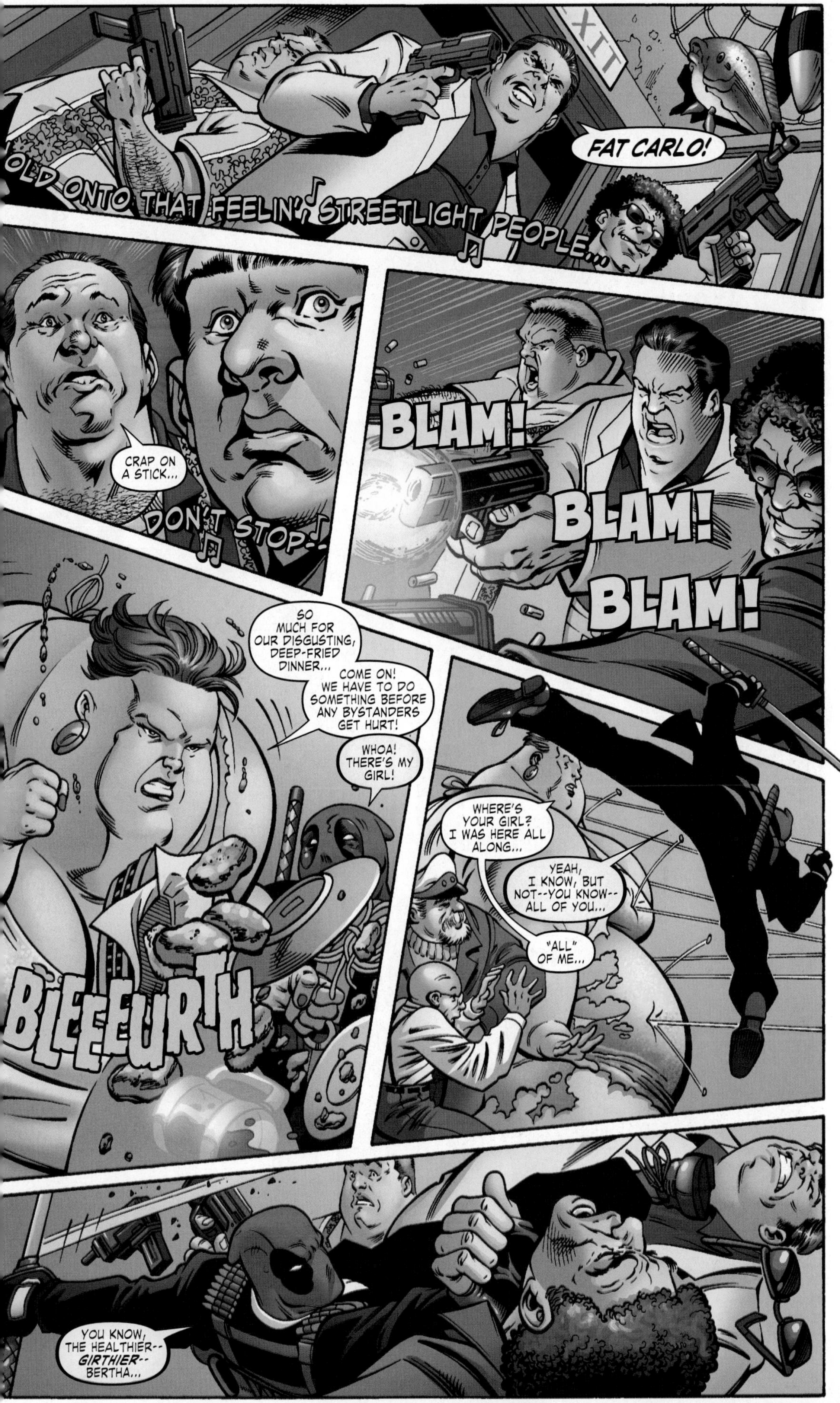
FAT CARLO!
OLD ONTO THAT FEELIN', STREETLIGHT PEOPLE...
CRAP ON A STICK...
DON'T STOP
BLAM!
BLAM!
BLAM!
SO MUCH FOR OUR DISGUSTING, DEEP-FRIED DINNER...
COME ON! WE HAVE TO DO SOMETHING BEFORE ANY BYSTANDERS GET HURT!
WHOA! THERE'S MY GIRL!
BLEEEURTH
WHERE'S YOUR GIRL? I WAS HERE ALL ALONG...
YEAH, I KNOW, BUT NOT--YOU KNOW--ALL OF YOU...
"ALL" OF ME...
YOU KNOW, THE HEALTHIER--*GIRTHIER*--BERTHA...

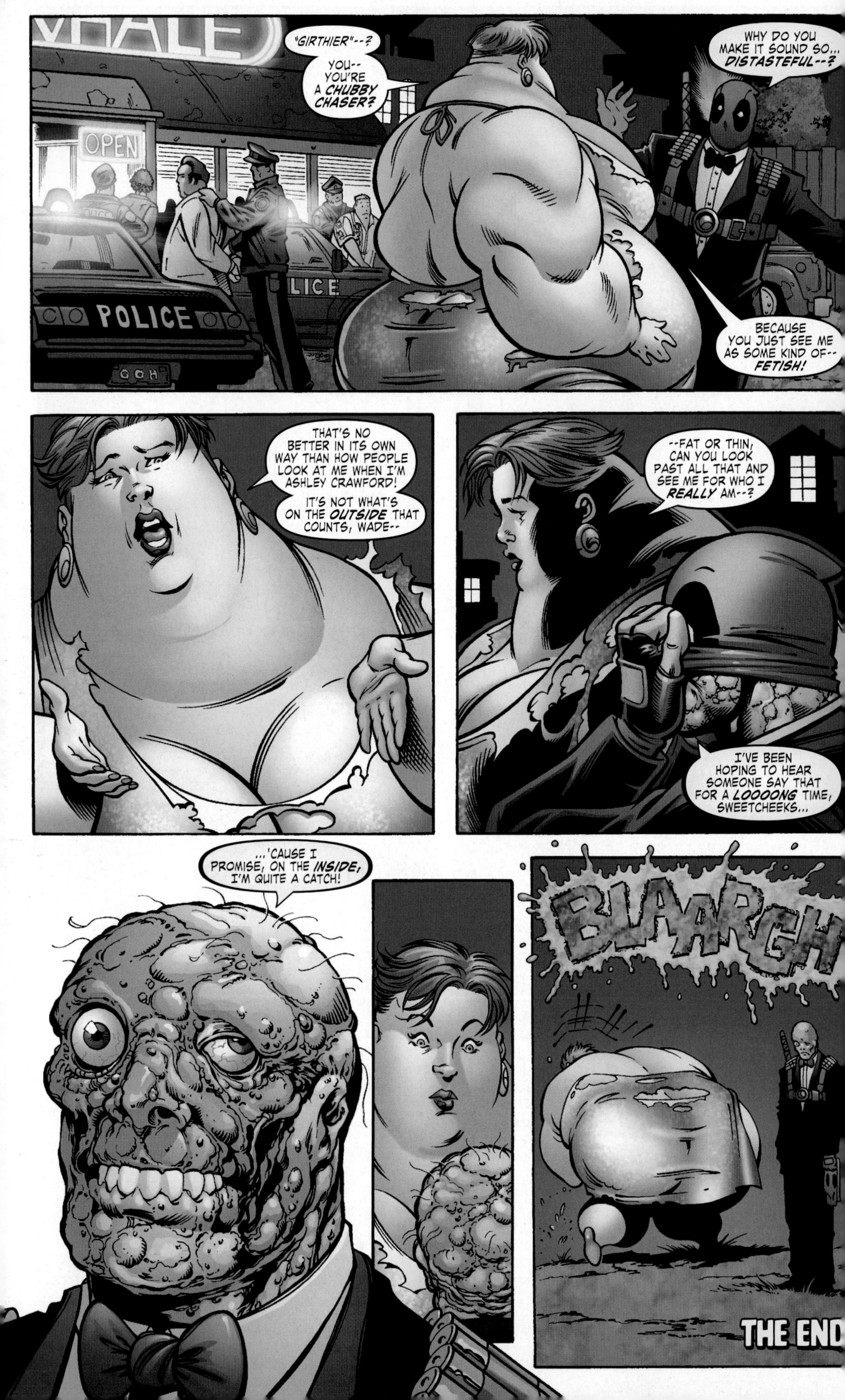

"GIRTHIER"--?
YOU-- YOU'RE A CHUBBY CHASER?
WHY DO YOU MAKE IT SOUND SO... DISTASTEFUL--?
BECAUSE YOU JUST SEE ME AS SOME KIND OF-- FETISH!
OPEN
POLICE
LICE
THAT'S NO BETTER IN ITS OWN WAY THAN HOW PEOPLE LOOK AT ME WHEN I'M ASHLEY CRAWFORD!
IT'S NOT WHAT'S ON THE OUTSIDE THAT COUNTS, WADE--
--FAT OR THIN, CAN YOU LOOK PAST ALL THAT AND SEE ME FOR WHO I REALLY AM--?
I'VE BEEN HOPING TO HEAR SOMEONE SAY THAT FOR A LOOOONG TIME, SWEETCHEEKS...
...'CAUSE I PROMISE, ON THE INSIDE, I'M QUITE A CATCH!
BLAARGH
THE END

THUNDERBOLTS
MOUNTAIN...

KTANG
TANG
TANG

POK!

HRMM?

squee
squee

SQUIRREL
GIRL?!

HI, ROBBIE.
LONG TIME NO SEE,
HUH?

WHAT--
WHAT ARE
YOU DOING
HERE?

I HEARD
WHAT HAPPENED
AND I THOUGHT, H
IF ANYONE CAN GE
THE BOUNCE BAC
INTO YOUR
STEP...

...THEN I'M
THE GAL FOR T
JOB! SERIOUSL
ROB, THIS WHO
EMO-THING? I
SO NOT YOU

STOP IT! THERE *IS* NO ROBBIE BALDWIN ANYMORE. SPEEDBALL IS GONE! NOW, THERE IS ONLY... *PENANCE!*

DON'T YOU UNDERSTAND? I'M RESPONSIBLE FOR DESTROYING AN ENTIRE TOWN!

OVER 600 PEOPLE ARE *DEAD* NOW--BECAUSE OF *ME!*

UM..., NO, THEY'RE NOT.

WAIT, I DON'T THINK I HEARD THAT RIGHT. LET ME TAKE THIS OFF...

COME AGAIN?

I DID SOME CHECKING, BROKE INTO THE S.H.I.E.L.D. HELICARRIER, AND GOT YOUR FILE.

YOU DIDN'T KILL ANYBODY.

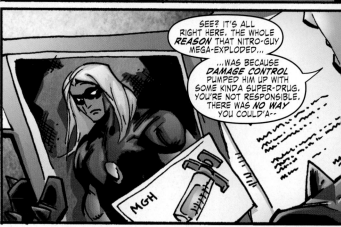

SEE? IT'S ALL RIGHT HERE. THE WHOLE *REASON* THAT NITRO-GUY MEGA-EXPLODED...

...WAS BECAUSE *DAMAGE CONTROL* PUMPED HIM UP WITH SOME KINDA SUPER-DRUG. YOU'RE NOT RESPONSIBLE. THERE WAS *NO WAY* YOU COULD'A--

MGH

NO! THAT *COULDN'T* HAVE HAPPENED! I *KNOW* DAMAGE CONTROL! I'VE WORKED FOR THEM!

THEY'RE FUNNY, SILLY, AND GOOFY! THEY'D *NEVER* DO ANYTHING THAT... *DARK!*

UH... ROB, *YOU* SHOULDN' BE DARK EITHE

YOU'RE *SPEEDBALL!* YOU BOUNCE! WITH BALLS!

YOU EVEN HAD A BOUNCING *CAT,* FOR PETE'S SAKE!

REMEMBER, NIELS?

STOP! THERE *IS* NO NIELS, THE BOUNCING CAT! HE'S GONE! NOW THERE IS ONLY...

...*P-CAT,* THE PENITENT PUSS!

OH MY...

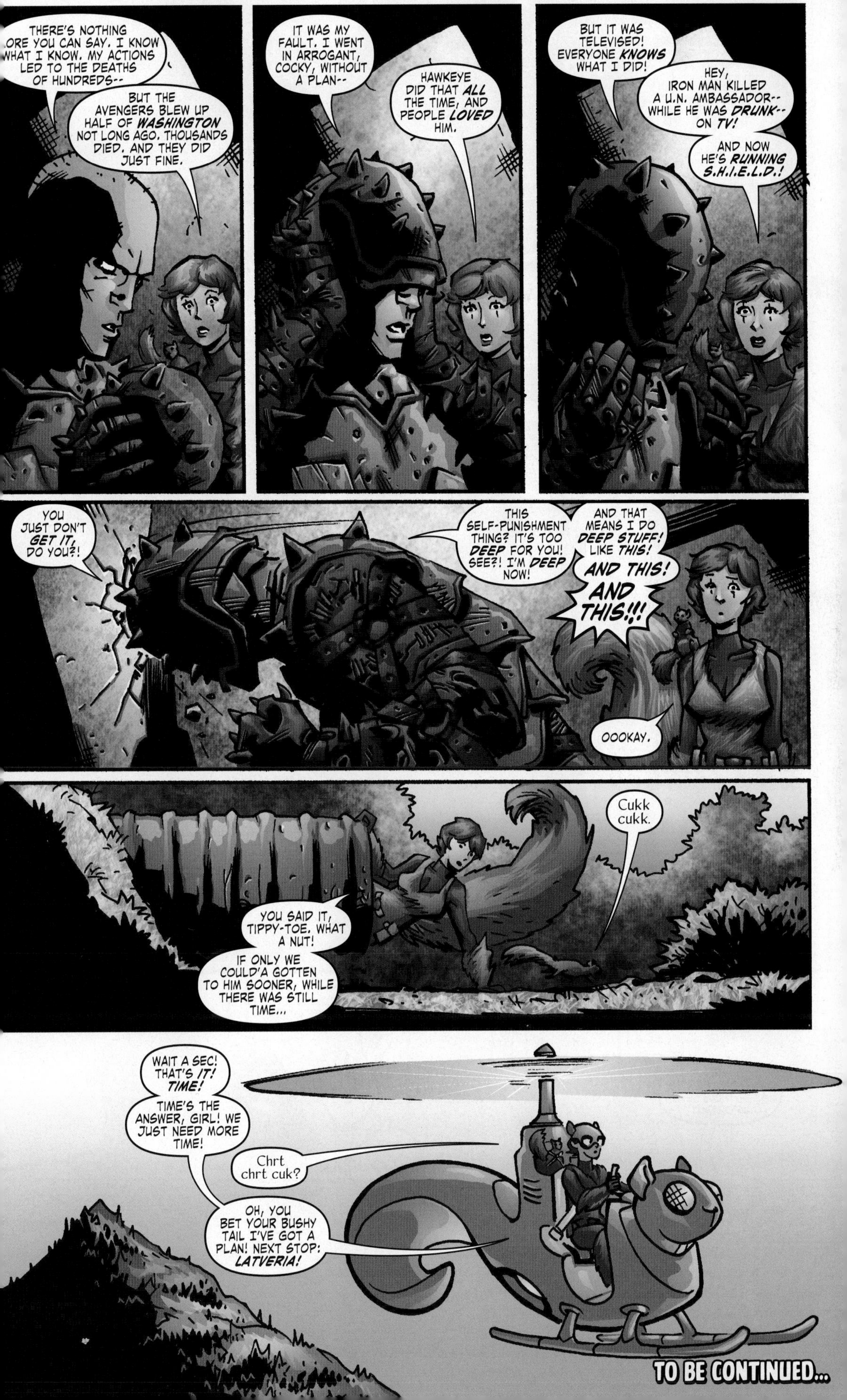

THERE'S NOTHING MORE YOU CAN SAY. I KNOW WHAT I KNOW. MY ACTIONS LED TO THE DEATHS OF HUNDREDS--
BUT THE AVENGERS BLEW UP HALF OF WASHINGTON NOT LONG AGO. THOUSANDS DIED. AND THEY DID JUST FINE.
IT WAS MY FAULT. I WENT IN ARROGANT, COCKY, WITHOUT A PLAN--
HAWKEYE DID THAT ALL THE TIME, AND PEOPLE LOVED HIM.
BUT IT WAS TELEVISED! EVERYONE KNOWS WHAT I DID!
HEY, IRON MAN KILLED A U.N. AMBASSADOR-- WHILE HE WAS DRUNK-- ON TV!
AND NOW HE'S RUNNING S.H.I.E.L.D.!
YOU JUST DON'T GET IT, DO YOU?!
THIS SELF-PUNISHMENT THING? IT'S TOO DEEP FOR YOU! SEE?! I'M DEEP NOW!
AND THAT MEANS I DO DEEP STUFF! LIKE THIS!
AND THIS!
AND THIS!!!
OOOKAY.
Cukk cukk.
YOU SAID IT, TIPPY-TOE. WHAT A NUT!
IF ONLY WE COULD'A GOTTEN TO HIM SOONER, WHILE THERE WAS STILL TIME...
WAIT A SEC! THAT'S IT! TIME!
TIME'S THE ANSWER, GIRL! WE JUST NEED MORE TIME!
Chrt chrt cuk?
OH, YOU BET YOUR BUSHY TAIL I'VE GOT A PLAN! NEXT STOP: LATVERIA!
TO BE CONTINUED...

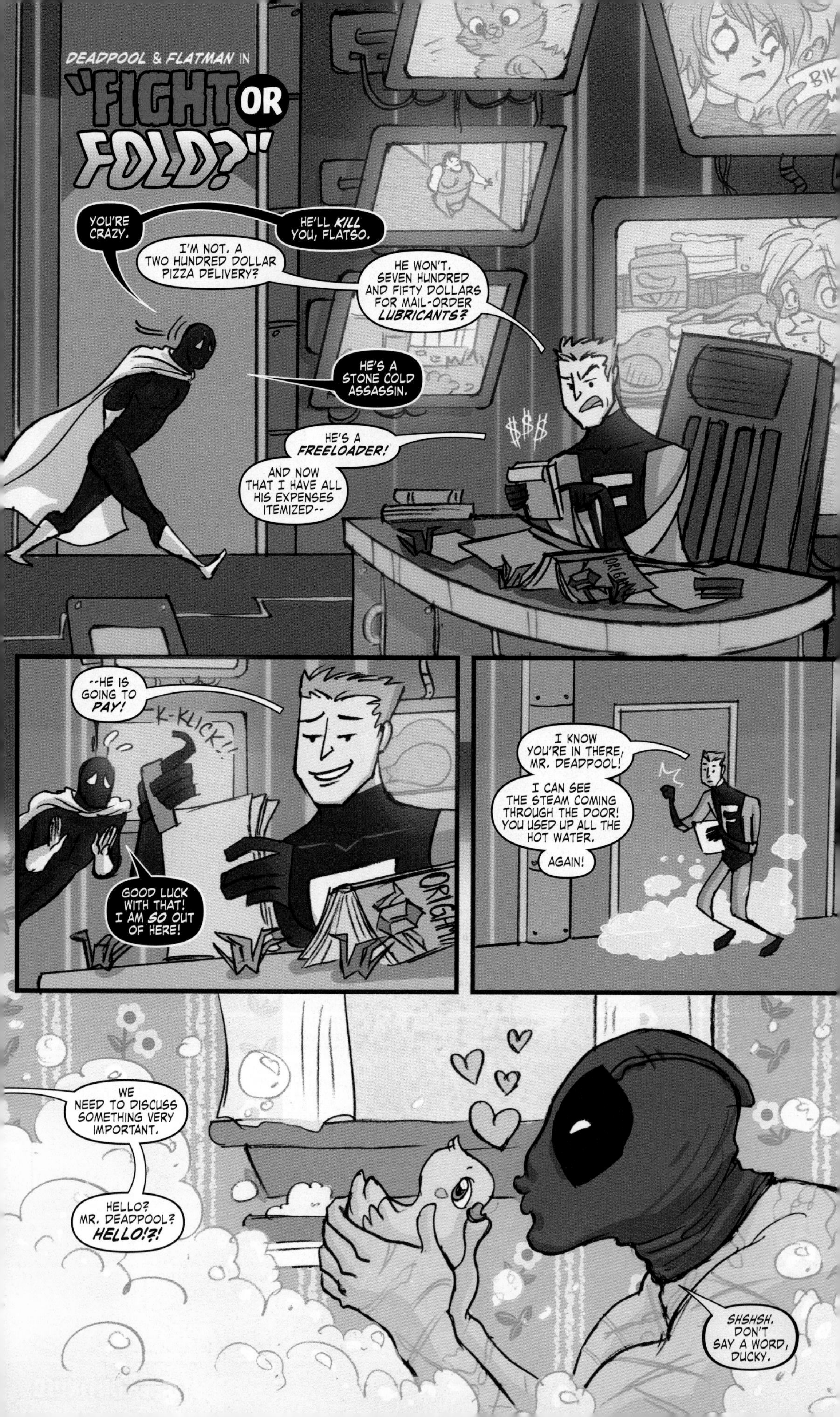
DEADPOOL & FLATMAN IN
"FIGHT OR FOLD?"
YOU'RE CRAZY.
HE'LL KILL YOU, FLATSO.
I'M NOT. A TWO HUNDRED DOLLAR PIZZA DELIVERY?
HE WON'T. SEVEN HUNDRED AND FIFTY DOLLARS FOR MAIL-ORDER LUBRICANTS?
HE'S A STONE COLD ASSASSIN.
HE'S A FREELOADER!
AND NOW THAT I HAVE ALL HIS EXPENSES ITEMIZED--
ORIGAMI
--HE IS GOING TO PAY!
K-KLICK!!
GOOD LUCK WITH THAT! I AM SO OUT OF HERE!
I KNOW YOU'RE IN THERE, MR. DEADPOOL!
I CAN SEE THE STEAM COMING THROUGH THE DOOR! YOU USED UP ALL THE HOT WATER.
AGAIN!
WE NEED TO DISCUSS SOMETHING VERY IMPORTANT.
HELLO? MR. DEADPOOL? HELLO!?!
SHSHSH. DON'T SAY A WORD, DUCKY.

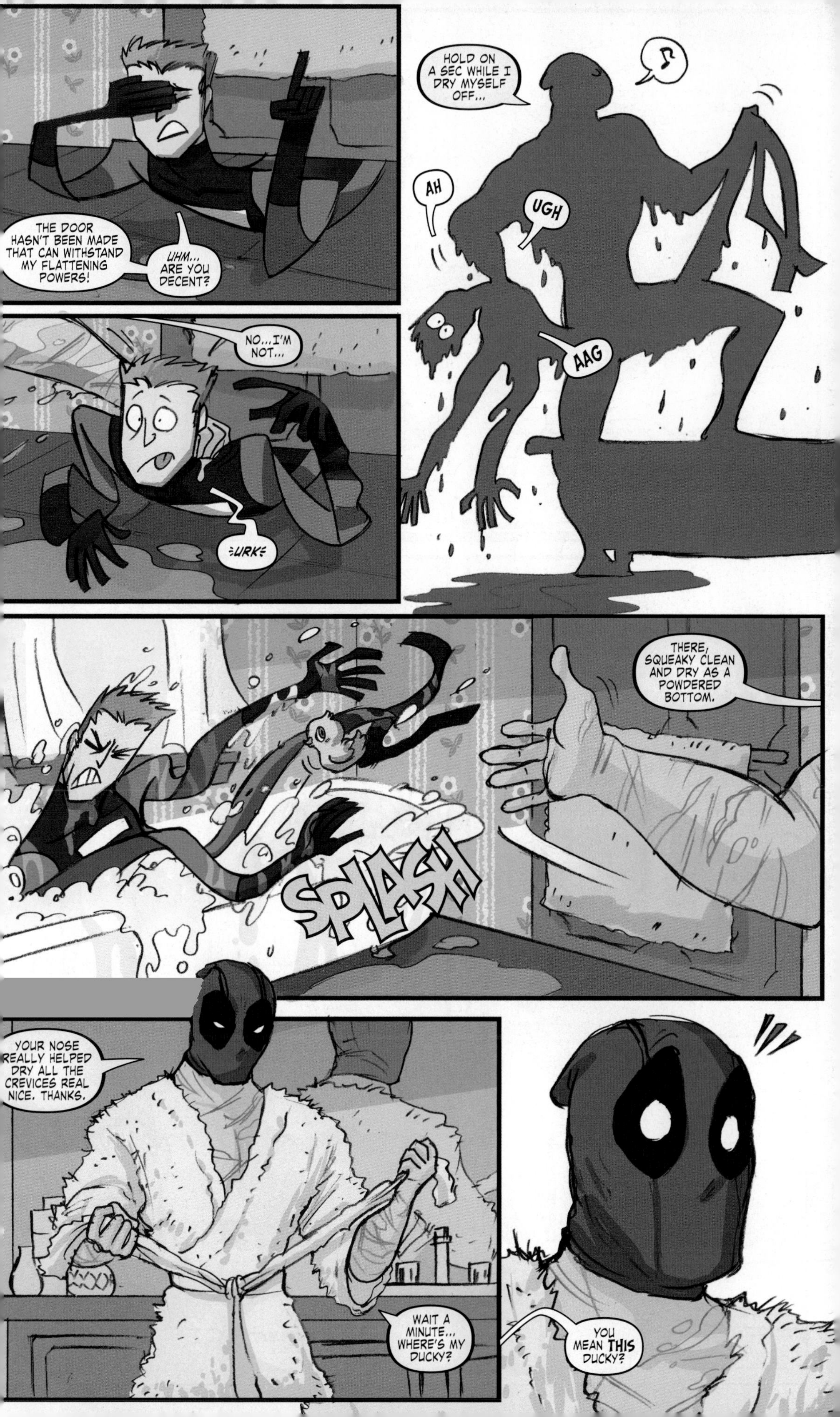
THE DOOR HASN'T BEEN MADE THAT CAN WITHSTAND MY FLATTENING POWERS!
UHM... ARE YOU DECENT?
NO...I'M NOT...
URK
HOLD ON A SEC WHILE I DRY MYSELF OFF...
AH
UGH
AAG
THERE, SQUEAKY CLEAN AND DRY AS A POWDERED BOTTOM.
SPLASH
YOUR NOSE REALLY HELPED DRY ALL THE CREVICES REAL NICE. THANKS.
WAIT A MINUTE... WHERE'S MY DUCKY?
YOU MEAN THIS DUCKY?

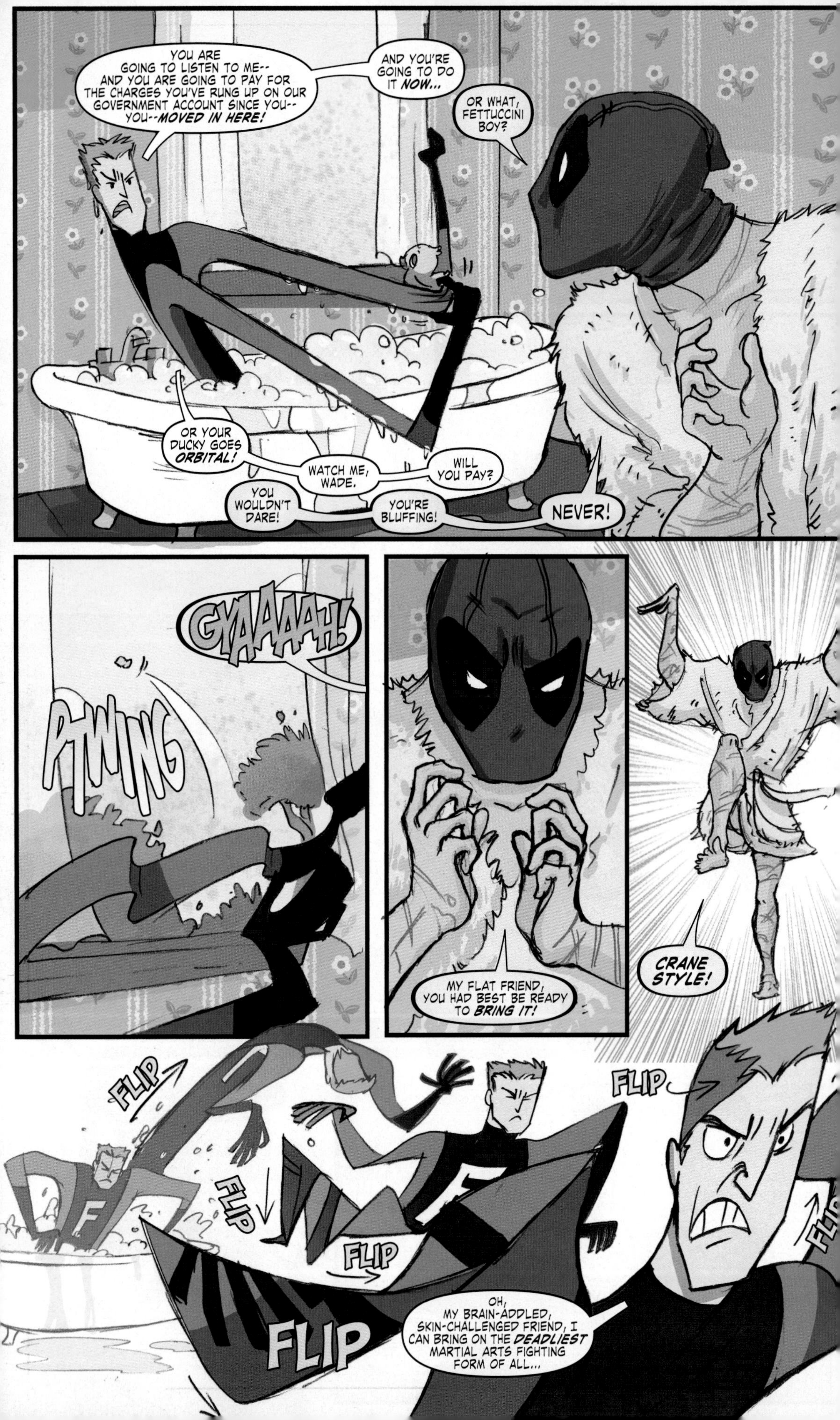

YOU ARE GOING TO LISTEN TO ME-- AND YOU ARE GOING TO PAY FOR THE CHARGES YOU'VE RUNG UP ON OUR GOVERNMENT ACCOUNT SINCE YOU-- YOU--MOVED IN HERE!
AND YOU'RE GOING TO DO IT NOW...
OR WHAT, FETTUCCINI BOY?
OR YOUR DUCKY GOES ORBITAL!
YOU WOULDN'T DARE!
WATCH ME, WADE.
YOU'RE BLUFFING!
WILL YOU PAY?
NEVER!
GYAAAAH!
PTWING
MY FLAT FRIEND, YOU HAD BEST BE READY TO BRING IT!
CRANE STYLE!
FLIP
FLIP
FLIP
FLIP
FLIP
OH, MY BRAIN-ADDLED, SKIN-CHALLENGED FRIEND, I CAN BRING ON THE DEADLIEST MARTIAL ARTS FIGHTING FORM OF ALL...

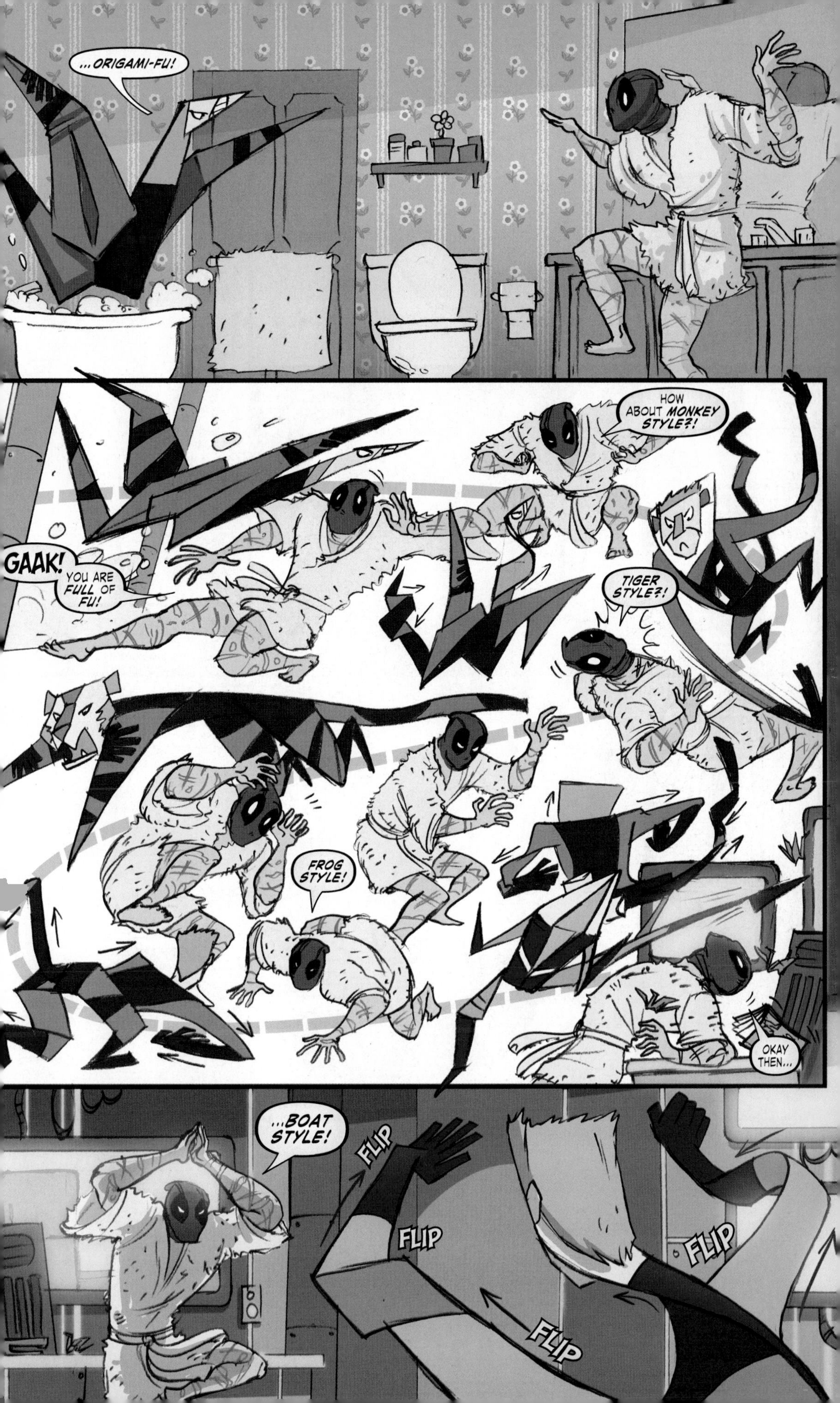
...ORIGAMI-FU!
HOW ABOUT MONKEY STYLE?!
GAAK!
YOU ARE FULL OF FU!
TIGER STYLE?!
FROG STYLE!
OKAY THEN...
...BOAT STYLE!
FLIP
FLIP
FLIP
FLIP

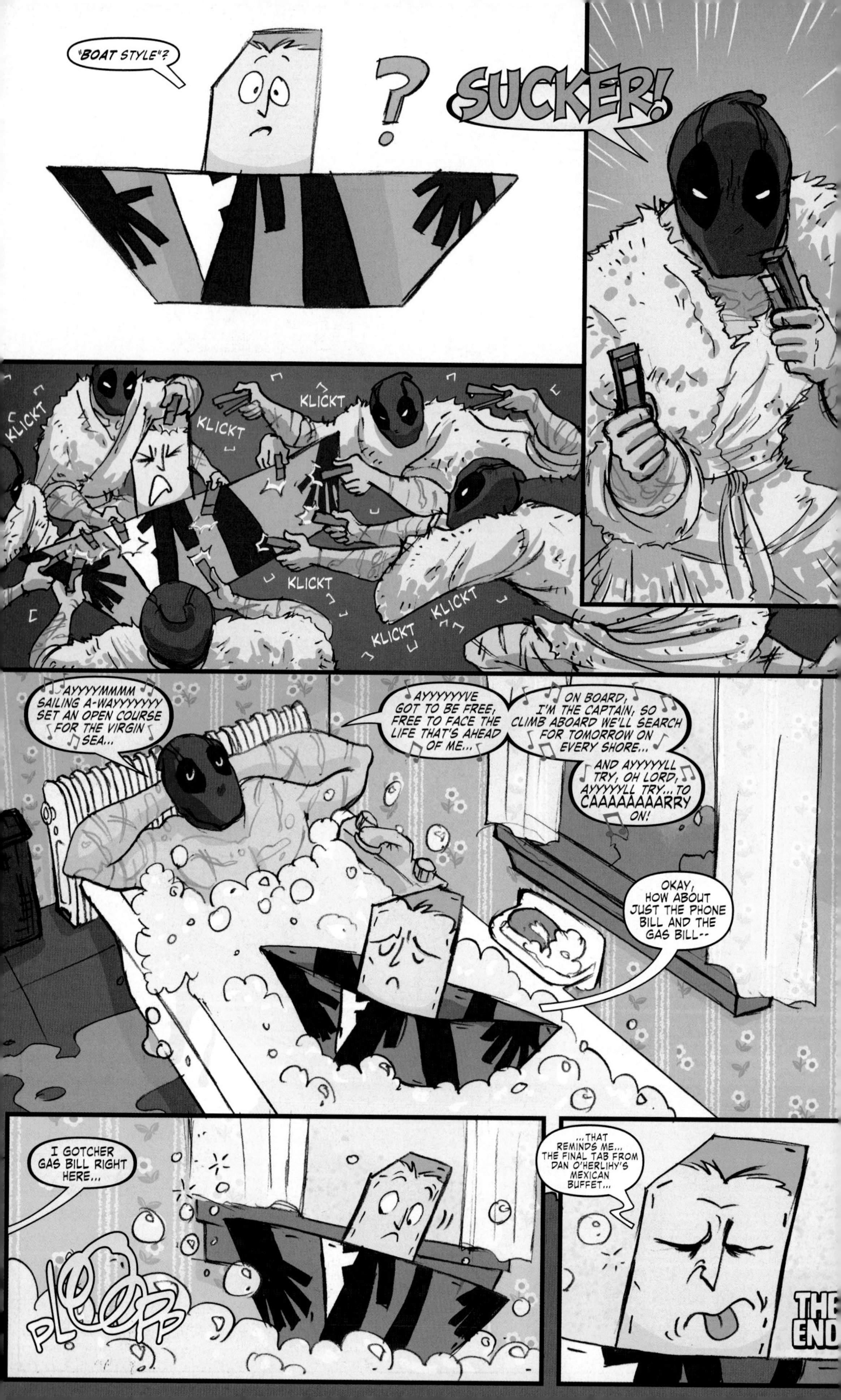
"BOAT STYLE"?
?
SUCKER!
KLICKT
KLICKT
KLICKT
KLICKT
KLICKT
KLICKT
AYYYYMMMM SAILING A-WAYYYYYYY SET AN OPEN COURSE FOR THE VIRGIN SEA...
AYYYYYYVE GOT TO BE FREE, FREE TO FACE THE LIFE THAT'S AHEAD OF ME...
ON BOARD, I'M THE CAPTAIN, SO CLIMB ABOARD WE'LL SEARCH FOR TOMORROW ON EVERY SHORE...
AND AYYYYYLL TRY, OH LORD, AYYYYYLL TRY... TO CAAAAAAAARRY ON!
OKAY, HOW ABOUT JUST THE PHONE BILL AND THE GAS BILL--
I GOTCHER GAS BILL RIGHT HERE...
PLOOP
...THAT REMINDS ME... THE FINAL TAB FROM DAN O'HERLIHY'S MEXICAN BUFFET...
THE END

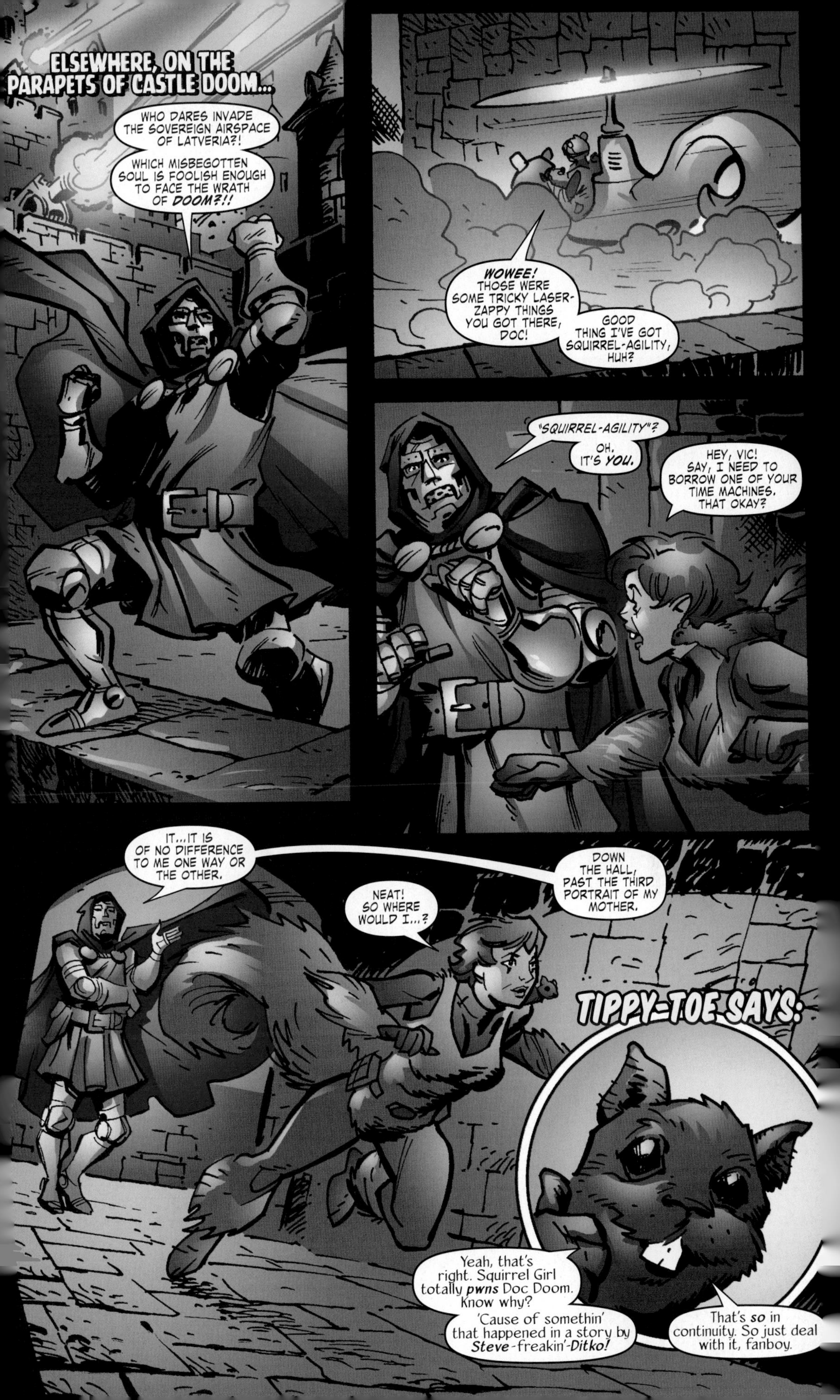
ELSEWHERE, ON THE PARAPETS OF CASTLE DOOM...
WHO DARES INVADE THE SOVEREIGN AIRSPACE OF LATVERIA?!
WHICH MISBEGOTTEN SOUL IS FOOLISH ENOUGH TO FACE THE WRATH OF DOOM?!!
WOWEE! THOSE WERE SOME TRICKY LASER-ZAPPY THINGS YOU GOT THERE, DOC!
GOOD THING I'VE GOT SQUIRREL-AGILITY, HUH?
"SQUIRREL-AGILITY"? OH. IT'S YOU.
HEY, VIC! SAY, I NEED TO BORROW ONE OF YOUR TIME MACHINES. THAT OKAY?
IT...IT IS OF NO DIFFERENCE TO ME ONE WAY OR THE OTHER.
NEAT! SO WHERE WOULD I...?
DOWN THE HALL, PAST THE THIRD PORTRAIT OF MY MOTHER.
TIPPY-TOE SAYS:
Yeah, that's right. Squirrel Girl totally pwns Doc Doom. Know why?
'Cause of somethin' that happened in a story by Steve-freakin'-Ditko!
That's so in continuity. So just deal with it, fanboy.

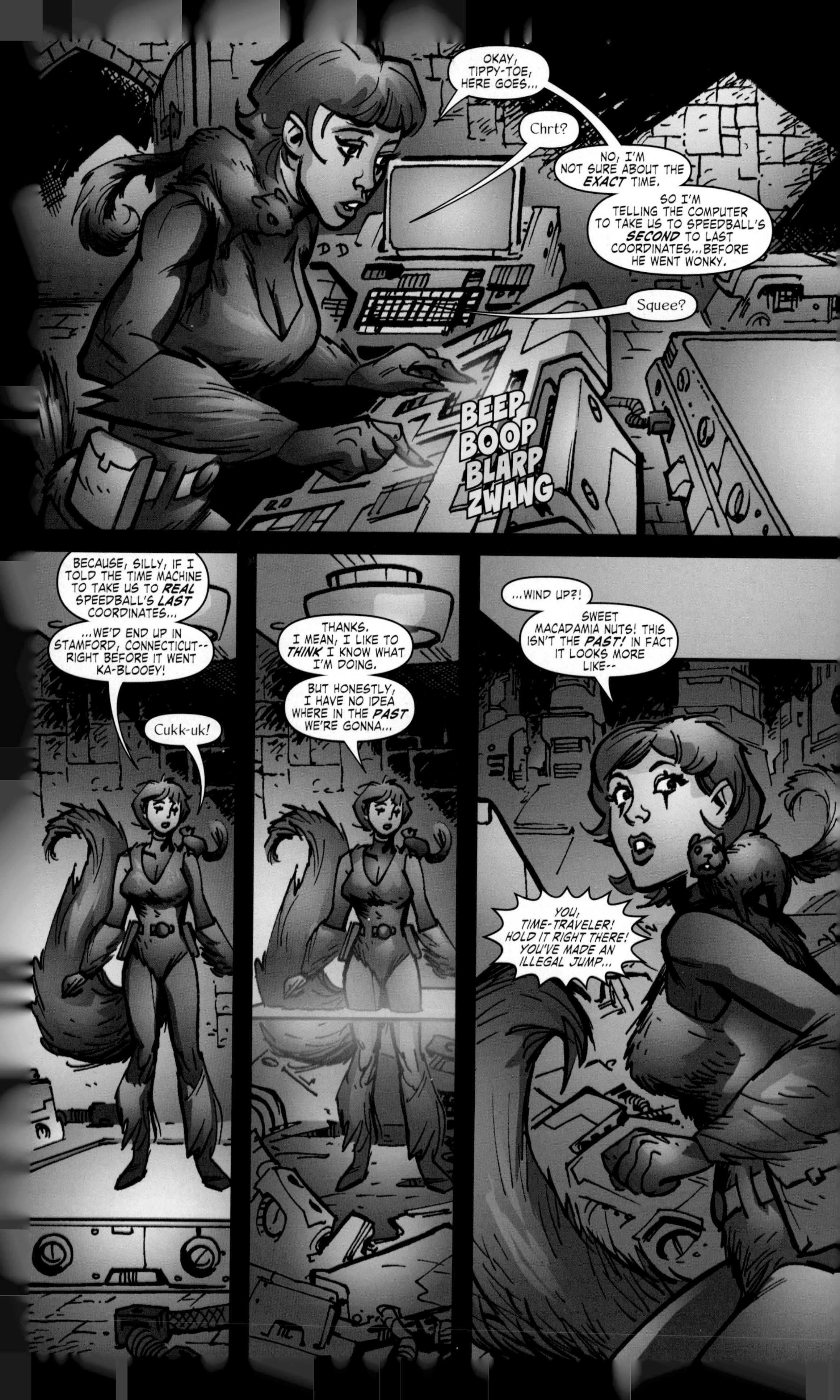
OKAY, TIPPY-TOE, HERE GOES...
Chrt?
NO, I'M NOT SURE ABOUT THE EXACT TIME.
SO I'M TELLING THE COMPUTER TO TAKE US TO SPEEDBALL'S SECOND TO LAST COORDINATES...BEFORE HE WENT WONKY.
Squee?
BEEP BOOP BLARP ZWANG
BECAUSE, SILLY, IF I TOLD THE TIME MACHINE TO TAKE US TO REAL SPEEDBALL'S LAST COORDINATES...
...WE'D END UP IN STAMFORD, CONNECTICUT--RIGHT BEFORE IT WENT KA-BLOOEY!
Cukk-uk!
THANKS. I MEAN, I LIKE TO THINK I KNOW WHAT I'M DOING.
BUT HONESTLY, I HAVE NO IDEA WHERE IN THE PAST WE'RE GONNA...
...WIND UP?!
SWEET MACADAMIA NUTS! THIS ISN'T THE PAST! IN FACT IT LOOKS MORE LIKE--
YOU, TIME-TRAVELER! HOLD IT RIGHT THERE! YOU'VE MADE AN ILLEGAL JUMP...

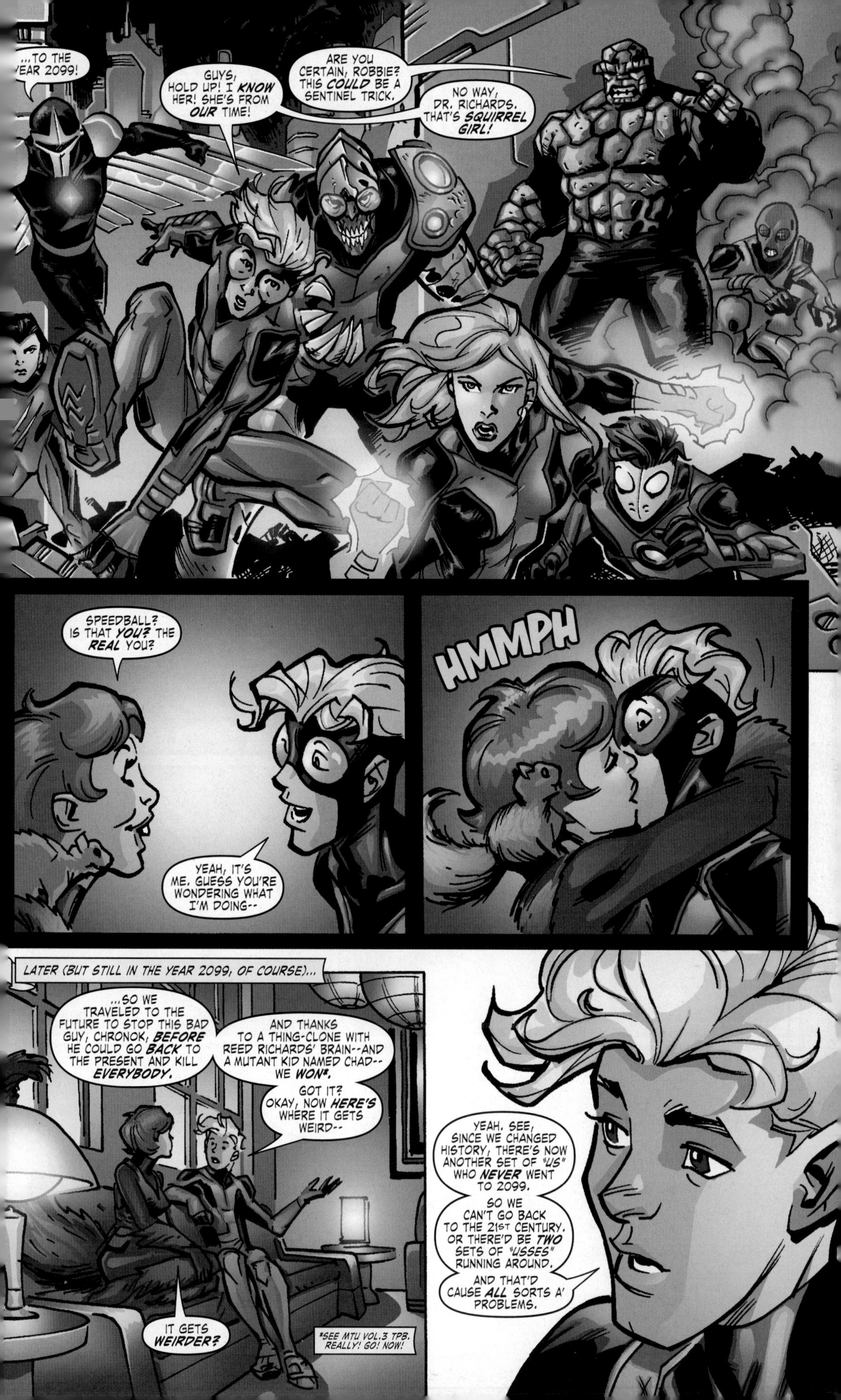

...TO THE YEAR 2099!
GUYS, HOLD UP! I KNOW HER! SHE'S FROM OUR TIME!
ARE YOU CERTAIN, ROBBIE? THIS COULD BE A SENTINEL TRICK.
NO WAY, DR. RICHARDS. THAT'S SQUIRREL GIRL!
SPEEDBALL? IS THAT YOU? THE REAL YOU?
YEAH, IT'S ME. GUESS YOU'RE WONDERING WHAT I'M DOING--
HMMPH
LATER (BUT STILL IN THE YEAR 2099, OF COURSE)...
...SO WE TRAVELED TO THE FUTURE TO STOP THIS BAD GUY, CHRONOK, BEFORE HE COULD GO BACK TO THE PRESENT AND KILL EVERYBODY.
AND THANKS TO A THING-CLONE WITH REED RICHARDS' BRAIN--AND A MUTANT KID NAMED CHAD--WE WON*.
GOT IT? OKAY, NOW HERE'S WHERE IT GETS WEIRD--
IT GETS WEIRDER?
*SEE MTU VOL.3 TPB. REALLY! GO! NOW!
YEAH. SEE, SINCE WE CHANGED HISTORY, THERE'S NOW ANOTHER SET OF "US" WHO NEVER WENT TO 2099.
SO WE CAN'T GO BACK TO THE 21ST CENTURY, OR THERE'D BE TWO SETS OF "USSES" RUNNING AROUND.
AND THAT'D CAUSE ALL SORTS A' PROBLEMS.

NO, IT WOULDN'T. NOT FOR YOU. TRUST ME. THE "YOU" THAT'S IN THE PAST...

...HE'S SO MESSED UP NOW, NO ONE WOULD EVER MIX YOU UP!

PLEASE, SPEEDBALL, COME BACK WITH ME.

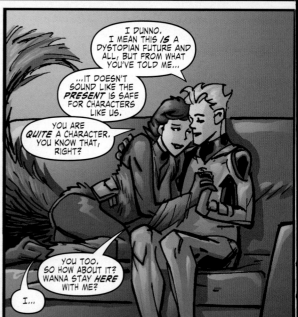

I DUNNO. I MEAN THIS IS A DYSTOPIAN FUTURE AND ALL, BUT FROM WHAT YOU'VE TOLD ME...

...IT DOESN'T SOUND LIKE THE PRESENT IS SAFE FOR CHARACTERS LIKE US.

YOU ARE QUITE A CHARACTER, YOU KNOW THAT, RIGHT?

YOU TOO. SO HOW ABOUT IT? WANNA STAY HERE WITH ME?

I...

SQUIRREL GIRL, STOP! DON'T DO IT!

SORRY TO INTERRUPT YOU TWO. BUT THERE'S SOMEONE HERE TO SEE YOU, SQUIRREL GIRL.

AND HE'S BEEN WAITING A LONNNNG TIME.

HI, KID. IT'S BEEN A WHILE.

MR. IMMORTAL?! CRAIG? WHAT ARE YOU DOING HERE? OH DEAR...

YOU DIDN'T TIME-TRAVEL, DID YOU? YOU JUST NEVER DIED!

Mr.

YES, AND I'VE WAITED OVER NINE DECADES TO TELL YOU THIS: COME HOME, PLEASE. THE GLI NEEDS YOU!

GOLLY! WHAT'S THE MATTER?

THERE'S A TASK FOR YOU. IT'S IN THE PAST. IT'S URGENT. AND IT'S SOMETHING ONLY YOU CAN DO.

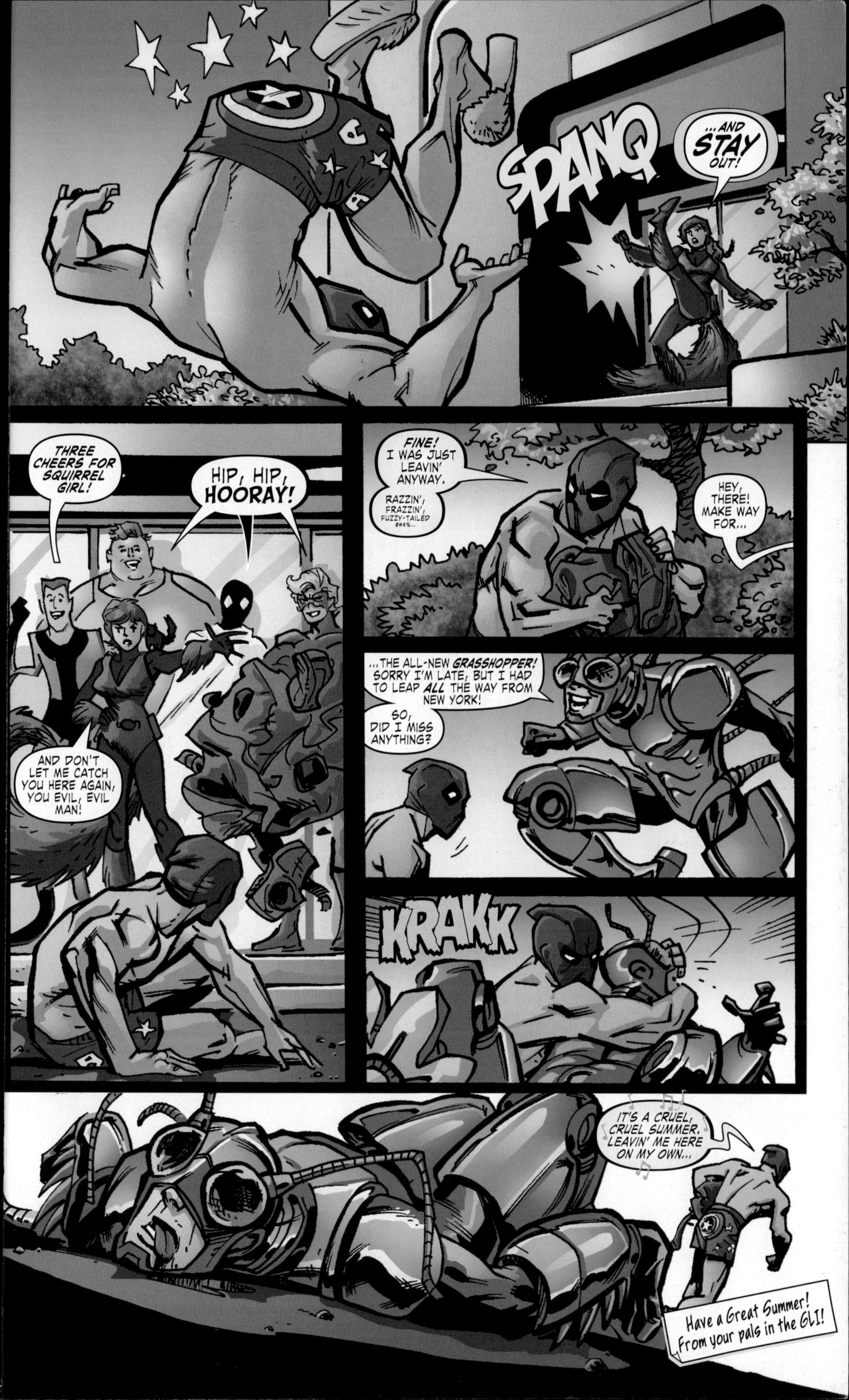
SPANQ
...AND STAY OUT!
THREE CHEERS FOR SQUIRREL GIRL!
HIP, HIP, HOORAY!
AND DON'T LET ME CATCH YOU HERE AGAIN, YOU EVIL, EVIL MAN!
FINE! I WAS JUST LEAVIN' ANYWAY.
RAZZIN', FRAZZIN', FUZZY-TAILED @#$%...
HEY, THERE! MAKE WAY FOR...
...THE ALL-NEW GRASSHOPPER! SORRY I'M LATE, BUT I HAD TO LEAP ALL THE WAY FROM NEW YORK!
SO, DID I MISS ANYTHING?
KRAKK
IT'S A CRUEL, CRUEL SUMMER. LEAVIN' ME HERE ON MY OWN...
Have a Great Summer! From your pals in the GLI!

DEADPOOL GLI
Summer Fun Spectacular

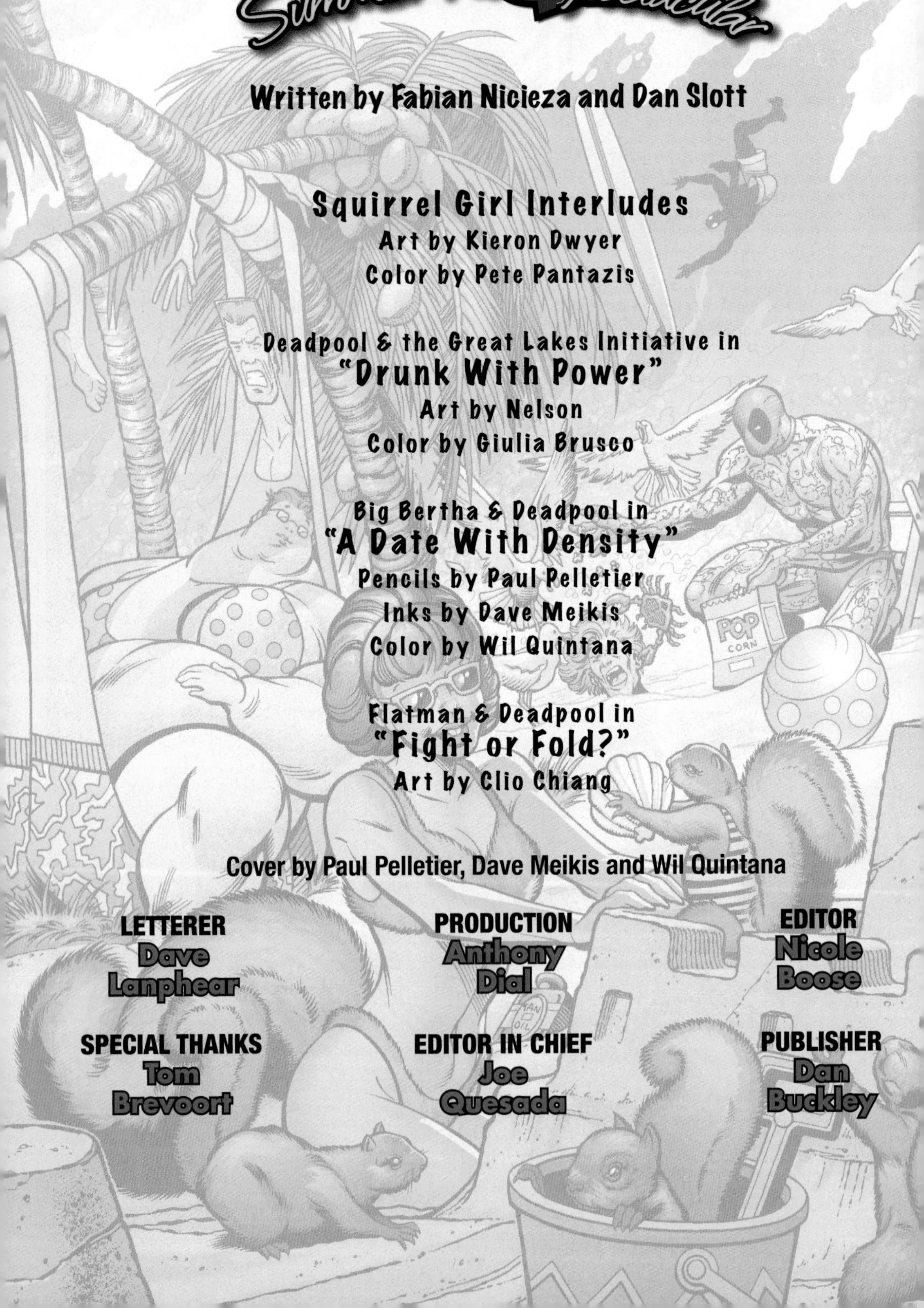

Written by Fabian Nicieza and Dan Slott

Squirrel Girl Interludes
Art by Kieron Dwyer
Color by Pete Pantazis

Deadpool & the Great Lakes Initiative in
"Drunk With Power"
Art by Nelson
Color by Giulia Brusco

Big Bertha & Deadpool in
"A Date With Density"
Pencils by Paul Pelletier
Inks by Dave Meikis
Color by Wil Quintana

Flatman & Deadpool in
"Fight or Fold?"
Art by Clio Chiang

Cover by Paul Pelletier, Dave Meikis and Wil Quintana

LETTERER
Dave Lanphear

PRODUCTION
Anthony Dial

EDITOR
Nicole Boose

SPECIAL THANKS
Tom Brevoort

EDITOR IN CHIEF
Joe Quesada

PUBLISHER
Dan Buckley

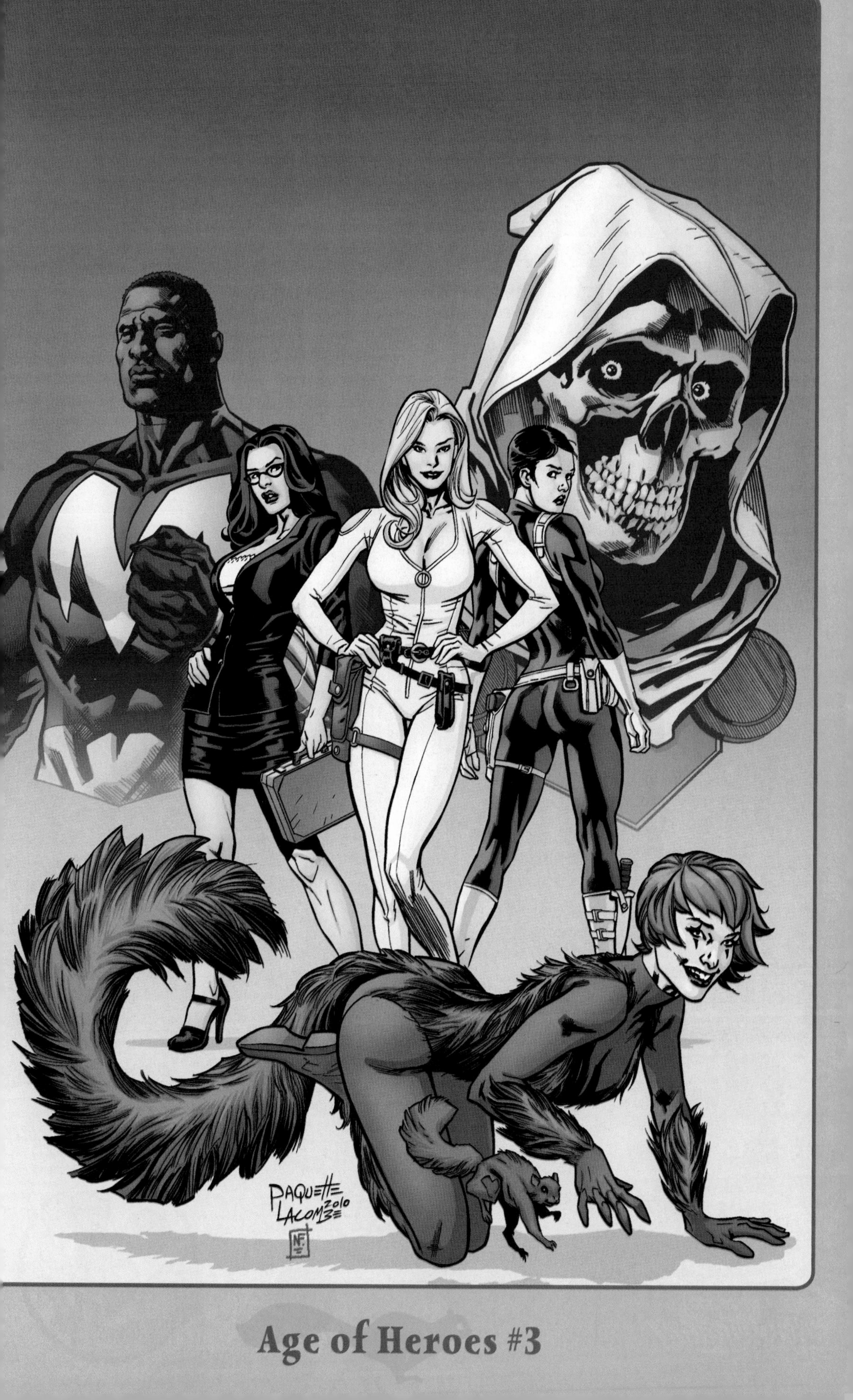
PAQUETTE
LACOMBE 2010

Age of Heroes #3

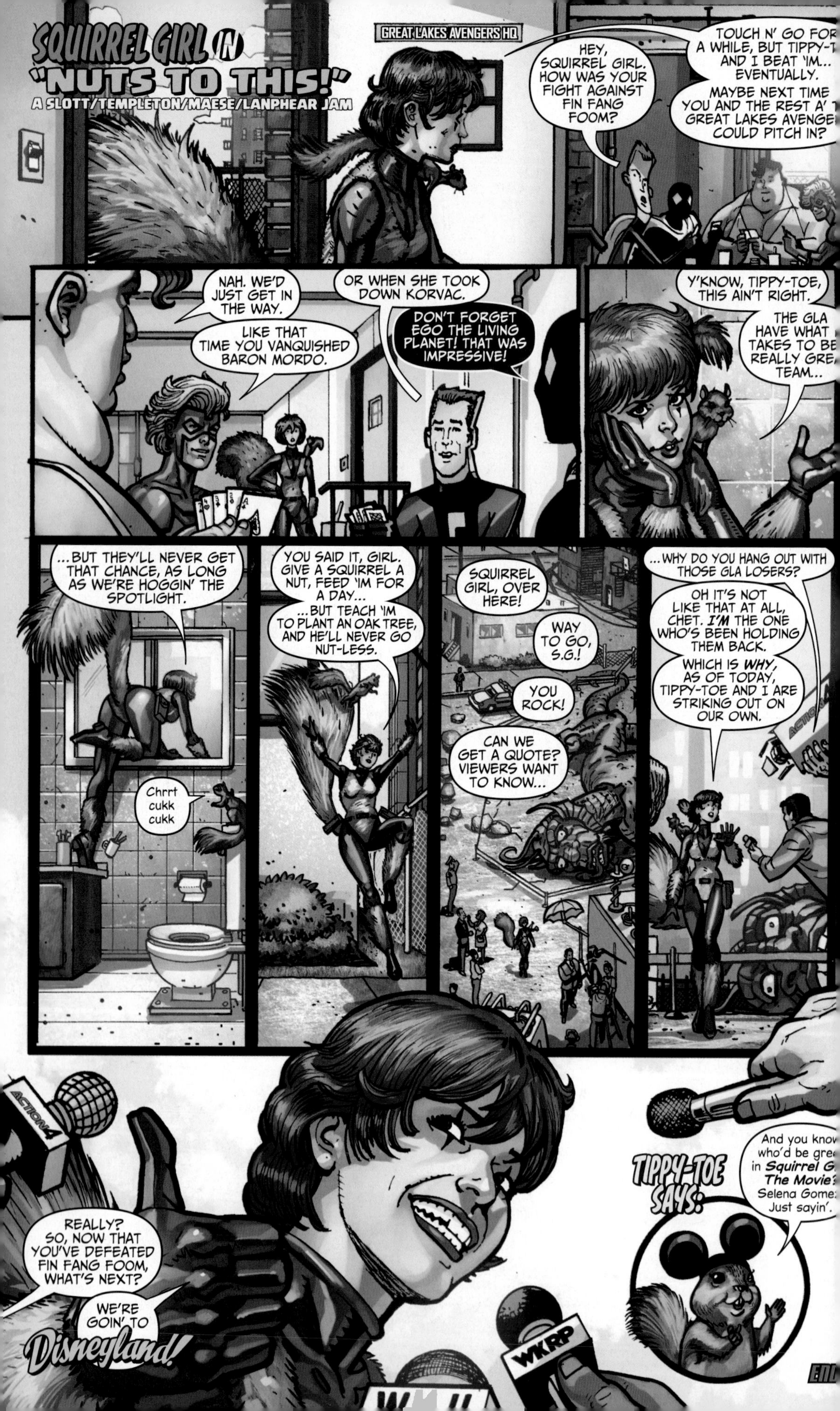
SQUIRREL GIRL IN
"NUTS TO THIS!"
A SLOTT/TEMPLETON/MAESE/LANPHEAR JAM
GREAT LAKES AVENGERS HQ
HEY, SQUIRREL GIRL. HOW WAS YOUR FIGHT AGAINST FIN FANG FOOM?
TOUCH N' GO FOR A WHILE, BUT TIPPY-T AND I BEAT 'IM... EVENTUALLY.
MAYBE NEXT TIME YOU AND THE REST A' T GREAT LAKES AVENGE COULD PITCH IN?
NAH. WE'D JUST GET IN THE WAY.
LIKE THAT TIME YOU VANQUISHED BARON MORDO.
OR WHEN SHE TOOK DOWN KORVAC.
DON'T FORGET EGO THE LIVING PLANET! THAT WAS IMPRESSIVE!
Y'KNOW, TIPPY-TOE, THIS AIN'T RIGHT.
THE GLA HAVE WHAT TAKES TO BE REALLY GRE TEAM...
...BUT THEY'LL NEVER GET THAT CHANCE, AS LONG AS WE'RE HOGGIN' THE SPOTLIGHT.
Chrrt cukk cukk
YOU SAID IT, GIRL. GIVE A SQUIRREL A NUT, FEED 'IM FOR A DAY...
...BUT TEACH 'IM TO PLANT AN OAK TREE, AND HE'LL NEVER GO NUT-LESS.
SQUIRREL GIRL, OVER HERE!
WAY TO GO, S.G.!
YOU ROCK!
CAN WE GET A QUOTE? VIEWERS WANT TO KNOW...
...WHY DO YOU HANG OUT WITH THOSE GLA LOSERS?
OH IT'S NOT LIKE THAT AT ALL, CHET. I'M THE ONE WHO'S BEEN HOLDING THEM BACK.
WHICH IS WHY, AS OF TODAY, TIPPY-TOE AND I ARE STRIKING OUT ON OUR OWN.
ACTION 4
REALLY? SO, NOW THAT YOU'VE DEFEATED FIN FANG FOOM, WHAT'S NEXT?
WE'RE GOIN' TO
Disneyland!
WKRP
TIPPY-TOE SAYS:
And you know who'd be gre in Squirrel G The Movie? Selena Gome Just sayin'.

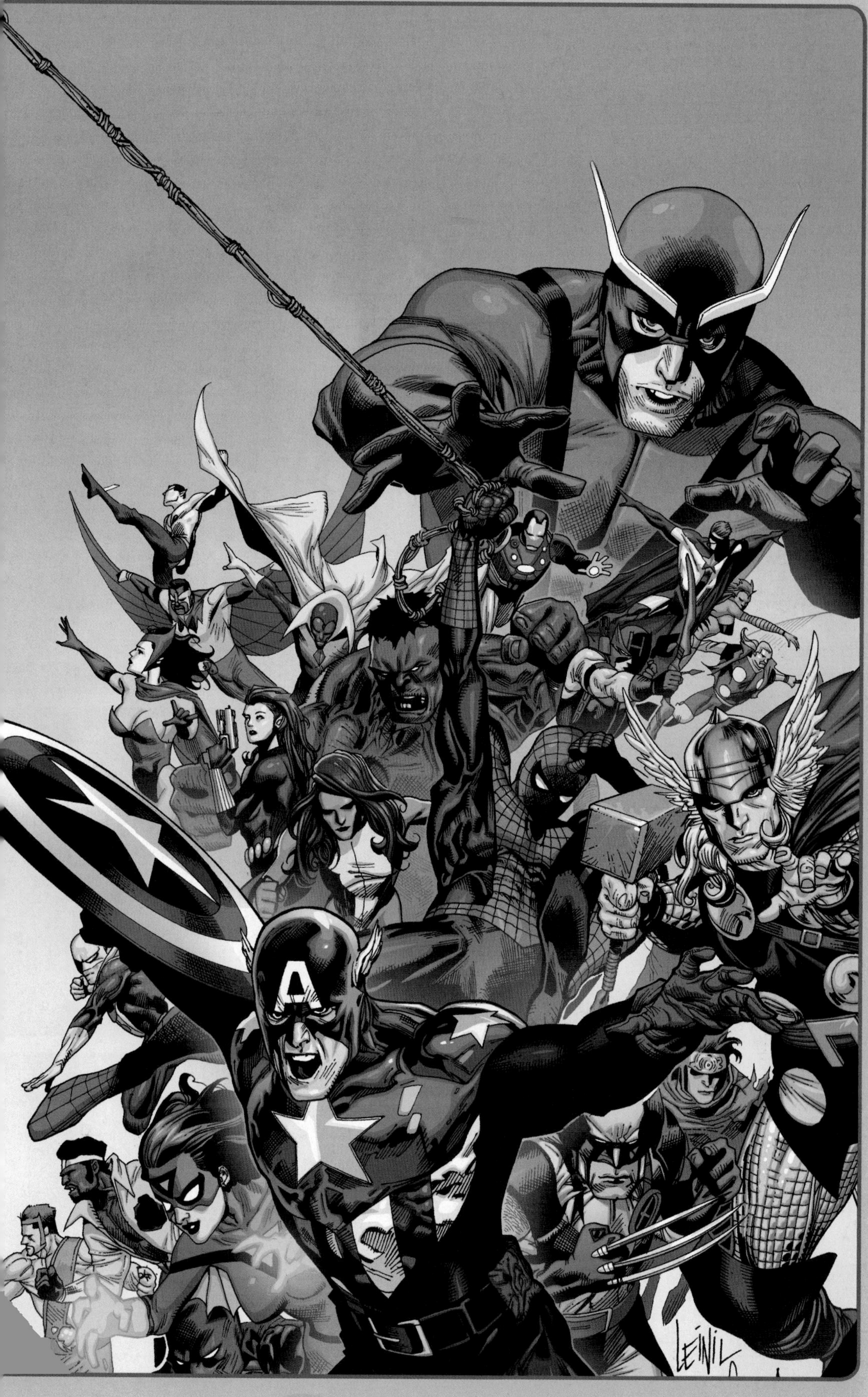
LEINIL

I Am an Avenger #1

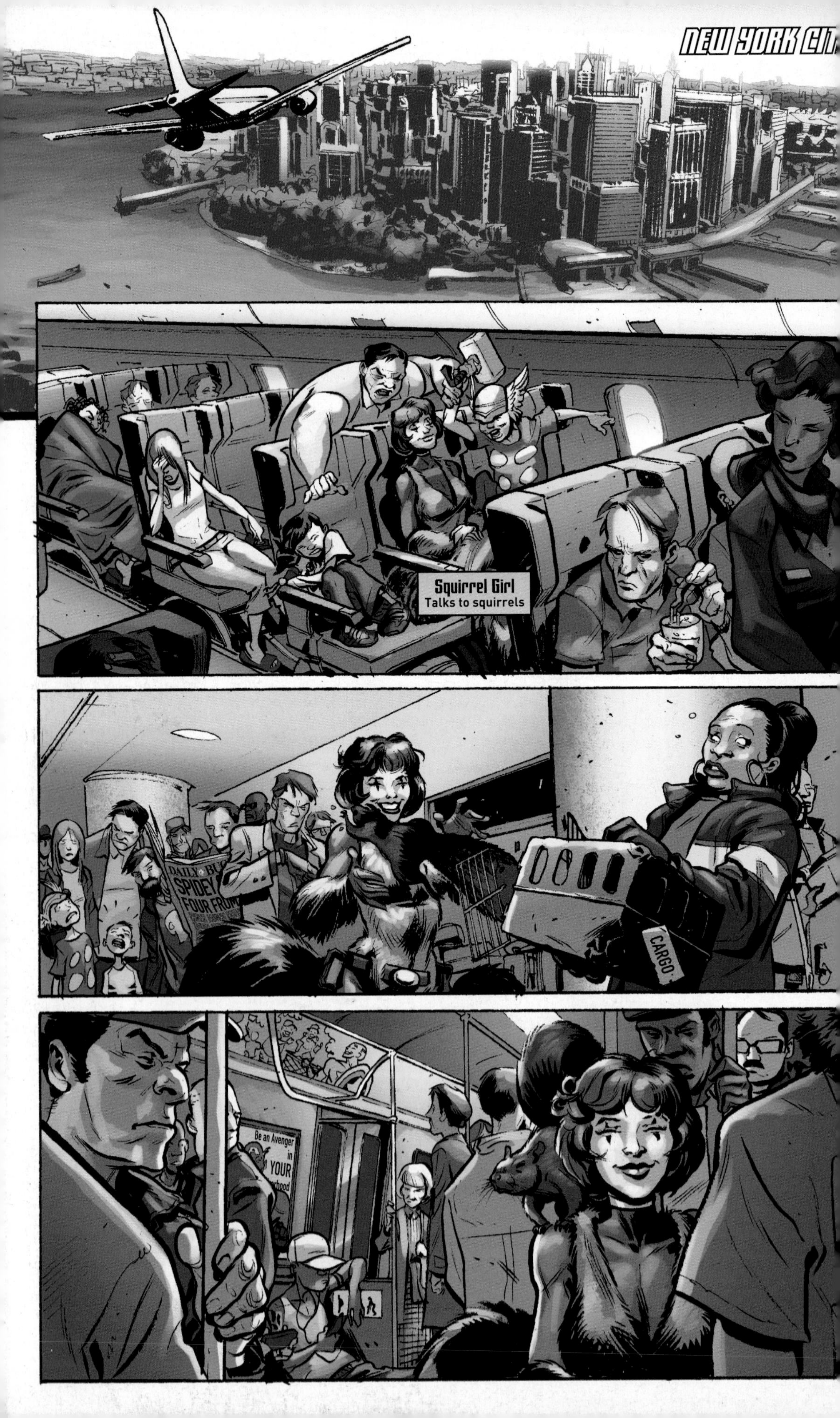
NEW YORK CIT
Squirrel Girl
Talks to squirrels
DAILY BU
SPIDEY
FOUR FROM
CARGO
Be an Avenger
in
YOUR

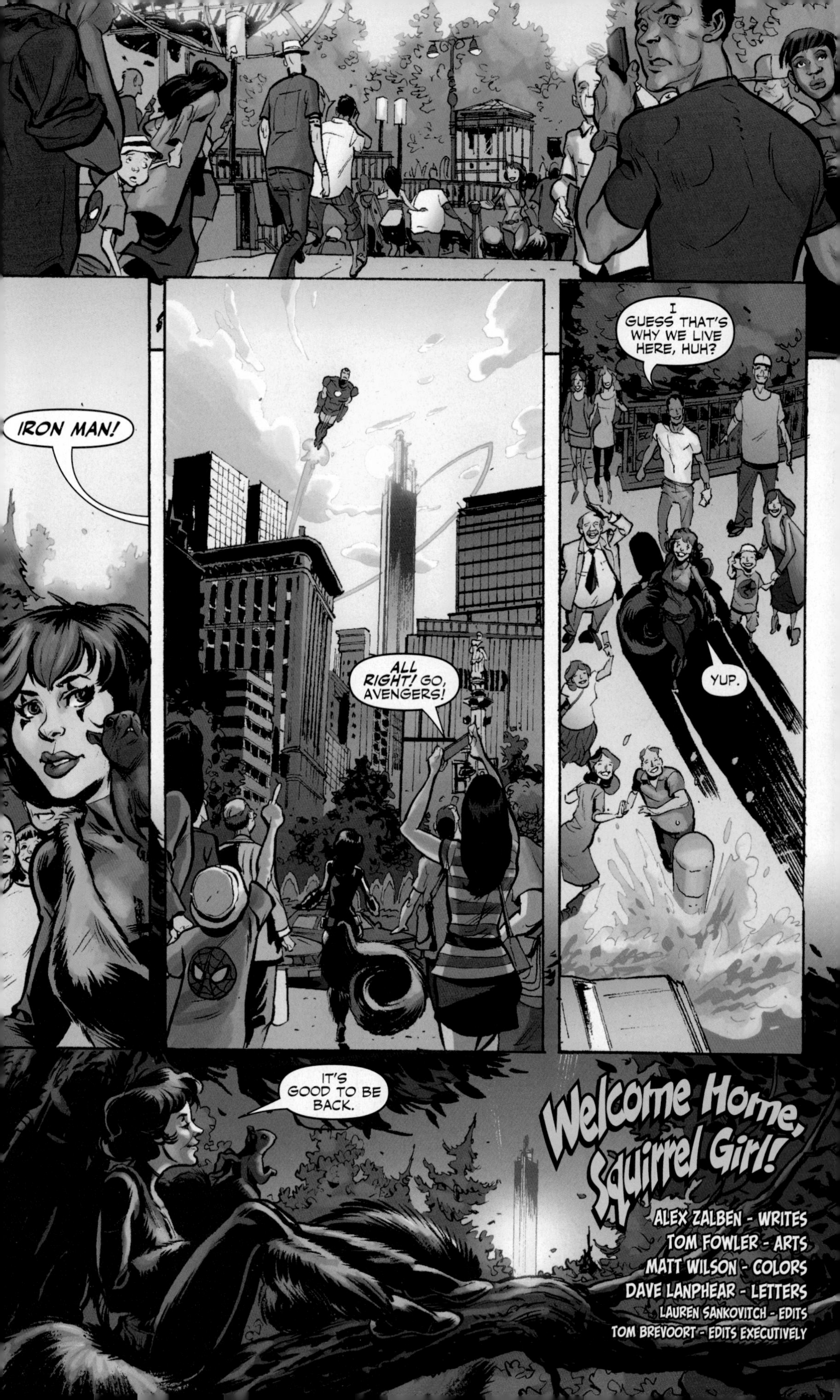
IRON MAN!
ALL RIGHT! GO, AVENGERS!
I GUESS THAT'S WHY WE LIVE HERE, HUH?
YUP.
IT'S GOOD TO BE BACK.
Welcome Home, Squirrel Girl!
ALEX ZALBEN - WRITES
TOM FOWLER - ARTS
MATT WILSON - COLORS
DAVE LANPHEAR - LETTERS
LAUREN SANKOVITCH - EDITS
TOM BREVOORT - EDITS EXECUTIVELY

MONKEY JOE
1992-2005

HE LIKED NUTS.
HE WILL BE MISSED.